Bankruptcy, Credit Risk, and High Yield Junk Bonds

Bankruptcy, Credit Risk, *and* High Yield Junk Bonds

Edward I. Altman

Stern School of Business, New York University

BLACKWELL *Publishers*

First published 2002

2 4 6 8 10 9 7 5 3 1

Blackwell Publishers Inc.
350 Main Street
Malden, Massachusetts 02148
USA

Blackwell Publishers Ltd
108 Cowley Road
Oxford OX4 1JF
UK

Library of Congress Cataloging-in-Publication Data
Altman, Edward I., 1941–
    Bankruptcy, credit risk, and high yield junk bonds / Edward I. Altman.
      p. cm.
    Collection of previously published and never before published articles written with others.
    Includes bibliographical references and index.
    ISBN 0–631–22563–3 (alk. paper)
    1. Bankruptcy—Forecasting. 2. Credit—Management. 3. Risk management. 4. Junk bonds. I. Title.
    HG3761 .A378 2002
    658.15—dc21
                      2001025266

British Library Cataloguing in Publication Data
A CIP catalogue record for this book is available from the British Library.

Typeset in Times 10/11½ pt
by Graphicraft Limited, Hong Kong
Printed in Great Britain by TJ International, Padstow, Cornwall

This book is printed on acid-free paper.

Contents*

*   Unless otherwise specified articles are authored solely by Edward I. Altman

Figures

Tables

Contributors

Edward I. Altman (editor) is the Max L. Heine Professor of Finance at the Leonard N. Stern School of Business, New York University. Since 1990, he has directed the research effort in Fixed Income and Credit Markets at the NYU Salomon Center and is currently the Vice-Director of the Center. Prior to serving in his present position, Professor Altman chaired the Stern School's MBA program for 12 years. He has been a visiting Professor at the Hautes Etudes Commerciales and Universite de Paris-Dauphine in France, at the Pontificia Catolica Universidade in Rio de Janeiro, at the Australian Graduate School of Management in Sydney and Luigi Bocconi University in Milan.

Dr. Altman has an international reputation as an expert on corporate bankruptcy, high yield bonds, distressed debt and credit risk analysis. He was named Laureate 1984 by the Hautes Etudes Commerciales Foundation in Paris for his accumulated works on corporate distress prediction models and procedures for firm financial rehabilitation, was awarded the Graham & Dodd Scroll for 1985 by the Financial Analysts Federation for his work on Default Rates on High Yield Corporate Debt and was named "Profesor Honorario" by the University of Buenos Aires in 1996. He is currently an advisor to the Centrale dei Bilanci in Italy and a member of its Scientific and Technical Committee and to several foreign central banks. Dr. Altman was named to the Max L. Heine endowed professorship at Stern in 1988. He received his MBA and Ph.D. in Finance from the University of California, Los Angeles.

Professor Altman is one of the founders and an Executive Editor of the international publication, the *Journal of Banking and Finance* and Advisory Editor of a publisher series, the *John Wiley Frontiers in Finance Series*. Professor Altman has published over a dozen books and over 100 articles in scholarly finance, accounting and economic journals. He is the current editor of the *Handbook of Corporate Finance* and the *Handbook of Financial Markets and Institutions* and the author of the recently published books on *Recent Advances in Corporate Finance*; *Investing in Junk Bonds*; *Default Risk,*

Mortality Rates and the Performance of Corporate Bonds; *Distressed Securities: Analyzing and Evaluating Market Potential and Investment Risk*; *Corporate Financial Distress and Bankruptcy* and his most recent work on *Managing Credit Risk: The Next Great Financial Challenge* (1998). His work has appeared in many languages including French, German, Italian, Japanese, Korean, Portuguese and Spanish.

Dr. Altman's primary areas of research include bankruptcy analysis and prediction, credit and lending policies, risk management in banking, corporate finance and capital markets. He has been a consultant to several government agencies, major financial and accounting institutions and industrial companies and has lectured to executives in North America, South America, Europe, Australia-New Zealand, Asia and Africa. He has testified before the US Congress, the New York State Senate and several other government and regulatory organizations and is a Director and a member of the Advisory Board of a number of corporate, publishing, academic and financial institutions. He is the current (2002–2003) President of the Financial Management Association.

Dr. Altman is Chairman of the Board of Trustees of the InterSchool Orchestras of New York and a member of the Board of Trustees of the Museum of American Financial History.

Joseph C. Bencivenga, in 1995, was a Managing Director at Salomon Brothers Inc., when he teamed up with Professor Altman to write the article which appears as chapter 18 in this volume. The model discussed in the article is still being used, in 2001, by high-yield bond analysts in today's environments.

John B. Caouette is Vice Chairman and Director of International Operations for MBIA Inc., a credit insurance firm.

Yehning Chen is a Professor of Economics and Finance at the National Taiwan University.

Keith Cyrus was an MBA student at the NYU Stern School of Business when he teamed up with Professor Altman to research the study presented as chapter 24 in this volume.

Allan C. Eberhart is a Professor of Finance at Georgetown University's School of Business.

Halina Frydman is a Professor of Statistics and Operations Research at the NYU Stern School of Business.

Laurie S. Goodman was an Assistant Professor of Finance at the NYU Stern School of Business when she co-wrote the article which appears as chapter 8 in this volume. She is now a senior practitioner in the securities industry.

John Hartzell is an investment banker in the Latin American Emerging Market Section of Salomon Smith Barney, Inc., and worked as an analyst with consultant Professor Altman in Salomon's Global Corporate Board Research Group.

Duen-Li Kao is a Managing Director in charge of Global Fixed Income Investments at General Motors Investment Management Corporation (New York).

Brenda Karlin is a Masters student at NYU and a Research Assistant at the NYU Stern School of Business.

Vellore M. Kishore was a Research Associate at the NYU Salomon Center, Stern School of Business when he teamed up with Professor Altman to write the paper which appears as chapter 13 in this volume. His untimely death in 2000 was mourned by those who knew of his loyal service at NYU for over ten years.

James K. La Fleur was CEO and Chairman of GTI Corporation when he teamed up with Professor Altman to write the article presented as chapter 6 in this volume.

Giancarlo Marco was an analyst with the Centrale dei Bilanci.

Scott A. Nammacher is a Managing Director at Empire Valuation Consultants (New York). He was an MBA student at the Stern School of Business when he teamed up with Professor Altman to research the article which appears as chapter 17 in this volume.

Paul Narayanan is a private financial consultant to financial institutions, specializing in credit risk and portfolio management.

Matthew Peck is a board security analyst in the Emerging Market Section of Salomon Smith Barney Inc. who worked with consultant Professor Altman in Salomon's Global Corporate Board Research Group.

Anthony Saunders is the John M. Schiff Professor of Finance at the NYU Stern School of Business.

Roy C. Smith is the Kenneth Langone Professor of Entrepreneurship and Finance at the NYU Stern School of Business. He was also a Limited Partner of Goldman Sachs when he teamed up with Professor Altman to write the article which appears as chapter 26 in this volume.

Heather, J. Suggitt was an MBA candidate at the NYU Stern School of Business when she teamed up with Professor Altman to write the paper which appears as chapter 12 in this volume. She is now a finance syndication officer at Credit Suisse First Boston (2001).

Franco Varetto is Managing Director of the Centrale dei Bilanci, based in Turin, Italy.

J. Fred Weston is Professor Emeritus Recalled, The Anderson School of the University of California, Los Angeles.

Foreword

In 1966, I put a note on Ed Altman's desk suggesting that he study the corporate bankruptcy phenomenon. His initial inquiries evolved into models to predict, from business financial statements and security valuations, the likelihood that a firm would encounter financial distress. This was a challenging endeavour, but Ed's outstanding work as a doctoral student suggested to me that he could handle it. Now some 35 years later, he has more than fulfilled his early promise. Dr. Altman's research has revolved around four related aspects of the corporate financial distress and bankruptcy phenomena. These involve

1 the assessment of firm performance, especially the prediction of corporate distress, and approaches to financial rehabilitation;
2 the measurement of bankruptcy costs and its relevance to capital structure issues;
3 the measurement and analysis of default rates on corporate fixed income securities; and
4 the more general, and currently critical, issue of measuring and managing credit risk.

His works are well known throughout the world and have been utilized by financial institutions, government regulators, global institutions, market practitioners and scholars in order to better understand and extend our understanding of credit risk. Related to these four areas, Dr. Altman has published a number of seminal works which are among the most quoted articles and books in the financial–economic literature. He has published about 20 books and well over 100 scholarly articles in these areas. His works have been translated into at least a half dozen languages.

Professor Altman is perhaps best known for his pioneering works in the construction of statistical models to classify and predict corporate distress and bankruptcy. His first seminal work developed the Z-Score model (Altman, 1968; chapter 1, this volume). The model utilizes financial statement and security market data in a multivariate context to give early warnings of impending firm financial problems. This work has spawned a larger number of similar studies in the USA and abroad. Indeed, the World Bank used this model to assess the financial vulnerability of a number of Asian and other countries by aggregating firm Z-Scores and assessing the average score for each country. Their conclusion was that countries like South Korea, Thailand and Indonesia displayed unmistakable early warning indications of distress prior to the start of problems in 1997. In 1984, for his works on predicting corporate distress and using such models to assist firms to restructure successfully (chapters 1 and 6, this volume), Altman was awarded the Laureate by the HEC Foundation in Paris.

A related topic is the question of whether a firm incurs significant expected bankruptcy and other distress costs as its failure probability increases; and if these costs eventually overwhelm the tax benefit of debt and impact firm valuation and cost of capital measures. His 1984 article discussed and measured (for the first time) the so-called indirect bankruptcy costs which are, by construction and definition, impossible to directly measure; proxies are necessary.

Professor Altman is widely acclaimed to be the leading academic analyzing default rates on corporate bonds, especially so-called high yield "junk" bonds (chapters 17–24, this volume). His seminal works in this area involved the now traditional default rate calculation and, later, the innovative mortality rate approach. The latter utilizes an actuarial approach to corporate bond analysis and default rate (chapter 11, this volume), and is now a standard technique used by practitioners.

Probably the most important aspect of risk management today revolves around credit risk. When J. P. Morgan unveiled, in April 1997, their much discussed CreditMetrics approach for analyzing portfolio management of credit assets, Altman's works were by far the most prominent source of scholarly and pragmatic articles and books. His co-authored book on *Managing Credit Risk: The Next Great Financial Challenge* (Caouette, Altman and Narayanan, John Wiley & Sons, NY, 1998) received favorable reviews.

The articles in this volume reflect a continued production of research studies for over three decades. They will make these materials more accessible to scholars and to a wide range of business firms and institutions. Ed Altman's research contributions will long inform and guide further research, business practices, and public policy.

J. Fred Weston
Professor Emeritus Recalled
The Anderson School of the
University of California, Los Angeles

Preface

How It All Started: The Z-Score Approach

For more than three decades, I have been fascinated by what one might observe as the "dark side" of Finance – bankruptcies, corporate distress, defaults, etc. It all started when my mentor, Professor J. Fred Weston, left a small piece of paper on my Ph.D. carrel-desk at UCLA suggesting that I look into some aspect of bankruptcy as a possible dissertation topic. During those times, the mid-1960s, there was absolutely no interest among finance academics for any topic with a negative sign before the growth rate. What little research on bankruptcy done at that time was in the Accounting area (e.g., William Beaver's work at roughly the same time as my bankruptcy prediction efforts) or from some classic but no longer used corporate finance texts, like Arthur Stone Dewing's wonderful volumes. The experiences and lessons from the great depression were fading fast from the literature and from the memories of scholars and practitioners. To be sure, there were some bankruptcy law and bank workout specialists, but little in the way of analytics was evident. The simple reason for this lack of attention to "dark" finance, was the almost total lack of medium or large firm distress situations. Without these problems and the resulting small number of data points, it was no wonder that few, if any, researchers were motivated to pursue serious efforts and demonstrate the "perverse enthusiasm" that I somehow have grown to possess.

After plowing through several case studies involving relatively small (under $25 million in assets) Chapter X and XI bankruptcies, I decided that another theme was more attractive and "exciting" – namely the potential to predict corporate distress by using a combination of published, traditional financial statement data and some rather sophisticated (at least at that time) multivariate statistical techniques to attempt to enhance the information content of the familiar accounting and stock market information. Hence, the birth of the Z-Score model, published first in the *Journal of Finance* in September 1968.

The construction of the Z-Score model and its tests, empirical results and extensions, as well as a description of the second-generation model[1] is included as the first chapter (written for this volume) of this book. Despite several dozen new approaches and proposed models to improve on the results and methodology of the original Z-Score model over the last three decades, the initial model remains very much alive and still in use in a wide variety of applications. Several of the attempts to test the efficiency of Z-Score vs. other types of models were actually performed by myself. For example, papers discussing recursive partitioning analysis (Chapter 2) or neural networks (chapter 3), railroads[2] and S&L's,[3] as well as those built in at least 20 countries outside the USA – summarized in a paper written in 1996 (chapter 4, this volume) – and for corporates in emerging markets (chapter 5), are described in this book.

Among the many applications of failing firm prediction models are three described in this volume. These deal with Managing a Financial Turnaround (chapter 6), investing in common stock as a part of a long–short investment strategy,[4] fixed income valuation techniques (chapter 7) and finance/legal dimensions (chapter 8), involving the Failing Company Doctrine, are also included. Application of the Z-Score model, not developed or written by myself, have been extended to the macro-economic arena by the World Bank[5] and the New York Federal Reserve Bank[6] in their efforts to estimate sovereign country financial health for Asian economics and the US economy, respectively.

CREDIT RISK AS A RELATED THEME

Almost from the beginning, the primary application of failure prediction models was thought to be as a credit risk tool for bank and other financial institution lenders. While always an important dimension of credit risk management, risk rating and credit scoring models have been catapulted into increased prominence in the last few years (1998–2001) as new recommended standards on bank capital adequacy from the Bank for International Settlement (BIS) have been presented, debated and will shortly be submitted in their final form.

Part II of this book on Credit Risk Management commences with an overview article I co-authored in 1998 (chapter 9). The last 20 or so years of credit risk modeling is also discussed in chapter 10, as well as some aspects of portfolio models for credit assets. Related to scoring models are the bond ratings provided by the rating agencies on corporate bond and bank loan issues. Two papers on mortality rates of bonds (chapter 11) and bank loans (chapter 12) are included in this section. In my opinion, the input as

---

[1] ZETA, "ZETA Analysis, A New Model for Bankruptcy Classification," *Journal of Banking and Finance*, June 1977 (with R. Huldeman and P. Narayanan).
[2] Altman, E. 1973, "Predicting Railroad Bankruptcies in America," *Bell Jounal of Economics and Management Science*, Spring, 184–211.
[3] Altman, E. 1977, "Predicting Performance in the Savings & Loans Association Industry," *Journal of Monetary Economics*, October, 443–66.
[4] Altman, E. and Brenner, M. 1981, "Information Effects and Stock Market Response to Signs of Firm Deterioration," *Journal of Financial and Qualitative Analysis*, 16 (1), 35–51.
[5] Pomerleano, M., "Corporate Finance Lessons from the East Asian Countries," *Viewpoint*, The World Bank Group, Washington DC, 155, October 1998.
[6] New York Federal Reserve Bank, "Risk in the Corporate Market," Unpublished report, 2000.

to the expected and unexpected default and loss rates on various quality corporate, bank, and sovereign debt is the most critical in any credit risk approach – whether it involves a stand-alone asset or portfolio framework. The loss rate statistics involve expected defaults as well as recovery rates on the defaulted security. A number of relevant seniority issues and recovery statistics are reported in our 1996 article (chapter 15) on recovery rates (at default) and in our 1994 article (chapter 14) on recoveries at the conclusion of the Chapter 11 process. Finally, an article (Altman, 1983) on macro-influences on default rates in included as chapter 15. Since that time, there have been several attempts to include macro conditions in predictive default rate models. Chapter 16 offers a co-authored commentary on the proposed BIS standards on capital allocation for credit assets. The foundation for these new standards is proposed to be external ratings of credit assets, so our loss statistics are extremely relevant in our critique and for our own recommendations.

TRANSITION TO "JUNK" BONDS

After 1970 and the Penn Central bankruptcy, larger, publicly owned firms found that they were not immune from corporate distress. Concurrent with larger firm vulnerability came the development of the high yield, "junk" bond market in the late 1970s and particularly in the mid-1980s. This non-investment grade market required independent, credible research on risk and return attributes in order to better understand its role as a possible new asset class. The major risk component of junk bonds is default risk. We set out to qualify this risk factor both with a traditional measurement tool (chapter 17) and a few years later using a new, mortality approach (chapter 11). Both articles are included in this book as well as ones which discussed the problems of increasing default rates of 1989–1991 and again in 1999 and 2000. The latter paper (chapter 20) shows the similarities and differences between the state of affairs in 1990, a year that many predicted would prove to be the downfall of the market, and the uneasy sense of *déjà-vu* felt a decade later, when defaulted bonds reached record levels and similar concerns, again, were manifest. I argued in 2001 (chapter 23), just as I did a decade earlier, that the "junk" bond market will persevere and, on the contrary, the current situation presents great investment opportunities once the default rate peaks.

In 1995, Bencivenga and I explored the relationship between yield spreads and expected default and loss rates (chapter 18). This relationship reveals a type of breakeven analytical method for bonds of any rating *vis-à-vis* Treasuries. Finally, the most recent data on defaults and returns in the high yield and also distressed securities markets (chapters 23 and 24) are provided in unpublished reports to update our analysis.

OTHER BANKRUPTCY RELATED PAPERS

Throughout my research career, the unifying theme of corporate bankruptcy has been evident. Starting with the classification and prediction models, articles on the failing company doctrine (an unpublished paper, chapter 8) argues that such prediction models could be used to test for whether a firm was failing and an otherwise illegal merger should be permitted to occur since one or more of the partner firms would have failed anyway.

In 1984, an article on the direct and indirect costs of bankruptcy showed that these costs, especially the latter, could be sizeable and that firms that leveraged up beyond their optimum debt level could expect decreasing values (chapter 25). In other words, I measured the expected costs of bankruptcy compared to the expected tax benefits of leverage and, for the first time, provided a more complete measurement of the impact of bankruptcy costs. Expected bankruptcy costs also play an important role in assessing the relationship between firm valuation and the leveraged restructurings which took place in ever-increasing frequency in the late 1980s. In 1993, an article (chapter 26) described and observed those highly leveraged transactions (e.g., LBOs) which were successful vs. those which ended in a bankruptcy or similar distressed outcomes.

Bankruptcy reorganizations are not always successful and many reorganized firms suffer continued problems and even file again for protection under the Bankruptcy Code (chapter 22). Indeed, many observers have criticized the Chapter 11 process. On balance, I have argued (chapter 27) that the process is fairly effective in preserving firm value. The majority of chapter 11 bankruptcies are successful and the old creditors and possibly, but not often, the old shareholders do well in the post-bankruptcy period. A 1999 article (not included in this volume) assesses the equity performance of firms emerging from bankruptcy and finds that the average performance in the post-emergence period is positive and significant – at least for the sample period examined.

The final article in this volume (chapter 28) reunites me with the man who first suggested that I study corporate bankruptcy – J. Fred Weston. Indeed, after almost 30 years since leaving UCLA, we finally wrote our first co-authored paper together (with Y. Chen) in 1995. The paper deals with financial distress and models of corporate restructuring.

Over the years, I have been very fortunate to work with talented co-authors on many occasions and to be blessed with a continuous stream of reliable and hard-working graduate research assistants. Many of the co-authors of articles in this book are practitioners: J. Bencivenga, J. Caouette, K. Cyrus, G. Franco, L. Goodman, R. Haldeman, J. Hartzell, D. L. Kao, B. Karlin, V. Kishore, J. LaFleur, S. Nammacher, P. Narayanan, M. Peck, H. Suggitt and F. Varetto. Many are academics: Y. Chen, A. Eberhart, H. Frydman, A. Saunders, J. F. Weston. And one is both a practitioner and an academic: R. Smith. I would also like to thank the staff at the New York University Salomon Center for their support over the years, especially M. Jaffier, R. Vanterpool and L. Tanglao, as well as Blackwell Publishers, especially Al Bruckner, for their interest in putting together this collection of my ideas and writings.

Edward I. Altman
Max L. Heine Professor of Finance
NYU Salomon Center
August 2000

Acknowledgments

The editor and publishers gratefully acknowledge the following for permission to reproduce copyright material.

From Association for Investment Managment and Research, Charlottesville, VA

Chapter 9 Edward I. Altman, John B. Caouette and Paul Narayanan, 1998, Credit-Risk Measurement and Management: The Ironic Challenge in the Next Decade. Reprinted with permission from *Financial Analysts Journal*, January–February 1998.

Chapter 13 Edward I. Altman and Vellore M. Kishore, 1996, Almost Everything You Wanted to Know About Recoveries on Defaulted Bonds. Reprinted with permission from *Financial Analysts Journal*, November–December 1996, 57–63.

Chapter 17 Edward I. Altman and Scott A. Nammacher, 1985, The Default Rate Experience on High-Yield Corporate Debt. Reprinted with permission from *Financial Analysts Journal*, July–August 1985, 25–41.

Chapter 18 Edward I. Altman and Joseph C. Bencivenga, 1995, A Yield Premium Model for the High-Yield Debt Market. Reprinted with permission from *Financial Analysts Journal*, September–October 1995.

Chapter 19 Edward I. Altman, 1989, Should We Regulate Junk Bonds? Reprinted with permission from *Financial Analysts Journal*, January–February 1989.

Chapter 21 Edward I. Altman and Duen-Li Kao, 1992, The Implications of Corporate Bond Ratings Drift. Reprinted with permission from *Financial Analysts Journal*, May–June 1992, 64–75.

From Blackwell Publishers

Chapter 1   Edward I. Altman, 1968, Predicting Financial Distress of Companies: Revisiting the Z-Score and Zeta® Models. Adapted from E. Altman, 1968, Financial Ratios, Discriminant Analysis and the Prediction of Corporate Bankruptcy, *The Journal of Finance*, September, 23, 189–209.

Chapter 2   Edward I. Altman, Halina Frydman and Duen-Li Kao, 1985, Introducing Recursive Partitioning for Financial Classification: The Case of Financial Distress, *The Journal of Finance*, 50 (1), 269–91.

Chapter 11   Edward I. Altman, 1989, Measuring Corporate Bond Mortality and Performance, *The Journal of Finance*, 54 (4), 909–22.

Chapter 25   Edward I. Altman, 1984, A Further Empirical Investigation of the Bankruptcy Cost Equation, *The Journal of Finance*, 34 (4), September, 1067–89.

From Columbia Business Law Review

Chapter 27   Edward I. Altman, 1993, Evaluating the Chapter 11 Bankruptcy-Reorganization Process, *Columbia Business Law Review*, 1, 1–21.

From Elsevier Science B.V.

Chapter 1   Edward I. Altman, 1968, Predicting Financial Distress of Companies: Revisiting the Z-Score and Zeta® Models. Adapted from E. Altman, 1968, Financial Ratios, Discriminant Analysis and the Prediction of Corporate Bankruptcy, *The Journal of Finance*, September, 23, 189–209; and E. Altman, R. Haldmann and P. Narayanan, 1977, Zeta Analysis: A New Model to Identify Bankruptcy Risk of Corporations, *Journal of Banking and Finance*, 1, 29–54.

Chapter 3   Edward I. Altman, Giancarlo Marco and Franco Varetto, 1994, Corporate Distress Diagnosis: Comparisons Using Linear Discriminant Analysis and Neural Networks (The Italian Experience), *Journal of Banking and Finance*, 18, 505–29

Chapter 10   Edward I. Altman and Anthony Saunders, 1998, Credit Risk Management: Developments Over the Last 20 Years, *Journal of Banking and Finance*, 21, 1721–42.

Chapter 12   Edward I. Altman and Heather J. Suggitt, 2000, Default Rates in the Syndicated Bank Loan Market: A Mortality Analysis, *Journal of Banking and Finance*, 24, 229–53.

Chapter 16   Edward I. Altman and Anthony Saunders, 2001, An Analysis and Critique of the BIS Proposal on Capital Adequacy and Ratings, *Journal of Banking and Finance*, 25, 25–46.

From Financial Management

Chapter 28   Edward I. Altman, Yehning Chen and J. Fred Weston, 1995, Financial Distress and Restructuring Models, *Financial Management*, 24 (2), 57–75.

From John Wiley & Sons

Chapter 15   Edward I. Altman, 1983, Aggregate Influences on Business Failure Rates, ch. 2 of *Corporate Financial Distress*, J. Wiley, NY.

From Journal of Business Strategy
Chapter 6   Edward I. Altman and James K. La Fleur, 1984, Managing a Return to Financial Health, *Journal of Business Strategy*, Summer, 31–8.

From Journal of Portfolio Management (Institutional Investor)
Chapter 14   Edward I. Altman and Allan C. Eberhart, 1994, Do Seniority Provisions Protect Bondholders' Investments?, *The Journal of Portfolio Management*, Summer, 67–75.

From NYU Salomon Center, Stern School of Business
Chapter 23   Edward I. Altman and Brenda Karlin, 2001, Defaults and Returns on High Yield Bonds: Analysis Through 2000 and Default Outlook, special report, January 2001.
Chapter 24   Edward I. Altman and Keith Cyrus, 2001, Market Size and Investment Performance of Defaulted Bonds and Bank Loans: 1987–2000, special report, January 2001.
Chapter 26   Edward I. Altman and Ray C. Smith, 1991, Firm Valuation and Corporate Leveraged Restructurings, 5, 91–26.

From Robert Morris Associates
Chapter 7   Edward I. Altman, 1993, Valuation, Loss Reserves, and Pricing of Commercial Loans, *Journal of Commercial Lending*, Robert Morris Associates, PA.

From Salomon Bros
Chapter 5   Edward I. Altman, John Hartzell and Matthew Peck, 1995, Emerging Market Corporate Bonds: A Scoring System, May 15.

The publishers apologize for any errors or omissions in the above list and would be grateful to be notified of any corrections that should be incorporated in the next edition or reprint of this book.

Introduction – Corporate Bankruptcy and Financial Markets: An Overview

Edward I. Altman

Financial distress of private and public entities throughout the world are frequent occurrences, with important implications to their many stakeholders. The most severe forms of corporate distress involve a number of similar conditions, including business failure, insolvency, default on creditor claims and filing for bankruptcy. The latter event can take two distinct forms: liquidation or reorganization. While the theory and role of corporate bankruptcy laws are clear – either to provide a legal framework that permits firms, which have temporary liquidity problems, to restructure and successfully emerge as continuing entities or, to provide an orderly procedure to liquidate assets for the benefit of creditors before asset values are dissipated – bankruptcy laws differ markedly from country to country. It is generally agreed that the US Chapter 11 provisions under the Bankruptcy Reform Act of 1978 provide the most protection for bankrupt firms' assets and result in a greater likelihood of successful reorganization than is found in other countries where liquidation and sale of the assets for the benefit of creditors is more likely the result. But, the US Code's process is usually lengthy (averaging close to two years, except where a sufficient number of creditors agree in advance via a "pre-packaged" Chapter 11) and expensive, and the reorganized entity is not always successful in avoiding subsequent distress. Since abuses in all bankruptcy systems exist, it is not clear that the US system is "best." What is clear, however, is that the debtor and its management have more power to influence the terms of the reorganization under Chapter 11 than under other systems. If the reorganization is not successful, then liquidation under Chapter 7 will usually ensue.

Bankruptcy processes in the industrialized world outside the USA strongly favor senior creditors who obtain control of the firm and seek to enforce greater adherence to debt contracts. The UK process, for example, is speedy and less costly, but the reduced costs can result in undesirable liquidations, unemployment and underinvestment. The new bankruptcy code in Germany attempts to reduce the considerable power of secured creditors, but it is still closer to the UK system in that creditors have control of the process. Another aspect of the US system is that creditors and owners can negotiate "violations" to the "absolute priority rule" – this "rule" holds that more senior creditors must be paid prior to any payments to more junior creditors or to owners. (However, the so-called "violations" have empirically been shown to be relatively small, e.g., under 10 percent of firm value). Finally, the US system gives the court the right to sanction post-petition debt financing, usually with super-priority status over existing claims, thereby facilitating the continuing operation of the firm. Recently, France and now Japan has had similar successful experience with such "debtor-in-possession" financing.

A measure of performance of the US bankruptcy system is the proportion of firms which emerge successfully. The results in the USA of late are somewhat mixed with close to 70 percent of large firms emerging but probably less than 20 percent of smaller entities. And, a not insignificant number of firms suffer subsequent distress and may file again (Chapter 22!).

Regardless of the location, one of the objectives of bankruptcy and other distressed workout arrangements is that creditors and other suppliers of capital clearly know their rights and expected recoveries in the event of a distressed situation. When these are not transparent and/or are based on outdated processes with arbitrary and possibly corrupt outcomes, then the entire economic system suffers and growth is inhibited. Such is the case in several emerging market countries. Revision of these outdated systems should be a priority.

In addition to the comparative benefits of different national restructuring systems, a number of intriguing theoretical and empirical issues are related to the distressed firm. Among these are corporate debt capacity and firm valuation, manager-creditor-owner incentives and behavior, ability to predict distress, data and computations for default rate estimation and credit-risk management, investment in securities of distressed firms and post-reorganization performance measurement.

Corporate distress has a major impact on creditor/debtor relationships and, combined with business risk and tax considerations, affects corporate capital structure. One key question is how costly are the *expected* distress costs compared to the *expected* tax benefits of using leverage – the so-called trade-off theory. The costs are categorized as direct and indirect, with the former representing tangible, out-of-pocket expenses (e.g., legal fees) while the latter are more difficult to measure and usually involve lost sales, profits, and investment opportunities as well as diversion of managerial efforts from cash flow generation to survival. Most analysts agree that the sum of these costs is in the range of 10–20 percent of firm value. Where analysts differ is in the interpretation of whether these costs are significant. This writer is firmly in the "relevant and significant" camp with respect to bankruptcy costs, leading to lower optimal debt ratios compared to prescriptions based on the conclusion that distress costs are trivial.

Managerial and owner incentives for risk taking and investment strategy can be in conflict with creditor desires when a firm is in financial distress. Whether the taking of excess risk and over-investment is an example of an agency conflict rests on one's view as to who are the true residual owners of a distressed firm – the existing equity holders or the creditors who will more than likely be the new owners of a reorganized entity. And, since existing management under Chapter 11 has the exclusive right to file the first plan of reorganization within 120 days of filing, with exclusivity extentions possible, their incentives and influence are obvious and not always in accord with other stakeholders, primarily creditors. Limiting this exclusivity would appear to be desirable to speed up the process and restrict managerial abuse.

Distress prediction models have intrigued researchers and practitioners for more than 50 years. Models have evolved from the use of univariate financial statement ratios to multivariate statistical classification, discriminant and regression models, to contingent claim, market value based approaches and, finally, to the most recent attempts using artificial intelligence techniques. Statistical and option pricing models directly search for profiles of failing firms to facilitate early warnings, while rating replication models seek to mimic systems used to estimate the probability, or not, of timely payment of interest and principal on outstanding claims.

Most large financial institutions today have one or more of the above types of models in place as more sophisticated credit-risk management frameworks are being introduced, sometimes combined with aggressive credit asset portfolio strategies. Increasingly, credit assets, loans for example, are being treated as securities with estimates of default and recovery on default the critical inputs. The linkage between credit-scoring systems and publicly available bond ratings are providing empirical data on historical default patterns.

Perhaps the most intriguing by-product of corporate distress is the development of a relatively new class of investors known as "vultures." These money managers specialize in securities of distressed and defaulted companies, with primary emphasis on public debt securities and privately placed loans. Defaulted bonds have had a small following ever since the Great Depression of the 1930s, but the last decade has witnessed the creation of perhaps 50–60 institutional "vulture" specialists, actively managing over $35 billion in 2001.

Typically, distressed debt investors have target annual rates of return of 20–25 percent. Although this has been attained, or surpassed, in almost half of the number of years in the last decade, the overall annual rate of return from 1978–97 has been about 12 percent per year – about the same as high yield bonds but below returns in the stock market. It remains to be seen if these historic patterns will continue to exist as distressed securities become more publicized and increasing numbers of investors compete for the limited supply of bonds and shares. The demand/supply situation has reversed in 2000/2001, with a huge supply of new distressed and defaulted securities, far outweighing the slightly increased amount of distressed money managed capital.

A related investment strategy centers on the equity securities of firms emerging from Chapter 11. There is evidence that these equities do extremely well, on average, in the first year after emergence, which could be caused by a systematic under-valuation of the firm during the reorganization process. (Managers have a vested interest in valuing the entity sufficiently high to justify its restructuring rather than liquidation, but not so high as to jeopardize their post-emergence performance evaluation. Senior creditors like values that result in their being paid in full, but not so high as to give significant value to subordinated debtholders and the old owners.)

All these issues, and more, are discussed in the following papers and reports authored by Dr. Edward I. Altman over the last three decades.

Part I: Distress Prediction Models and Some Applications

1 | Predicting Financial Distress of Companies: Revisiting the Z-Score and ZETA® Models*

Edward I. Altman

BACKGROUND

This paper discusses two of the venerable models for assessing the distress of industrial corporations. These are the so-called Z-Score model (Altman, 1968) and ZETA® (1977) credit-risk model. Both models are still being used by practitioners throughout the world. The latter is a proprietary model for subscribers to ZETA Services, Inc. (Hoboken, NJ).

The purpose of this summary is two-fold. First, those unique characteristics of business failures are examined in order to specify and quantify the variables which are effective indicators and predictors of corporate distress. By doing so, I hope to highlight the analytic as well as the practical value inherent in the use of financial ratios. Specifically, a set of financial and economic ratios will be analyzed in a corporate distress predication context using a multiple discriminant statistical methodology. Through this exercise, I will explore not only the quantifiable characteristics of potential bankrupts but also the utility of a much-maligned technique of financial analysis: ratio analysis. Although the models that we will discuss were developed in the late 1960s and mid-1970s, I will extend our tests and findings to include application to firms not traded publicly, to non-manufacturing entities, and also refer to a new bond-rating equivalent model for emerging markets corporate bonds. The latter utilizes a version of the Z-Score model called Z". This paper also updates the predictive tests on defaults and bankruptcies through the year 1999.

As I first wrote in 1968, and it seems even truer in the late 1990s, academicians seem to be moving toward the elimination of ratio analysis as an analytical technique in

* This paper is adapted and updated from E. Altman, "Financial Ratios, Discriminant Analysis and the Prediction of Corporate Bankruptcy," *Journal of Finance*, September 1968; and E. Altman, R. Haldeman and P. Narayanan, "Zeta Analysis: A New Model to Identify Bankruptcy Risk of Corporations," *Journal of Banking & Finance*, 1, 1977. R. Haldeman is President of ZETA® Services Inc. and Paul Narayanan is a private financial consultant.

assessing the performance of the business enterprise. Theorists downgrade arbitrary rules of thumb (such as company ratio comparisons) widely used by practitioners. Since attacks on the relevance on ratio analysis emanate from many esteemed members of the scholarly world, does this mean that ratio analysis is limited to the world of "nuts and bolts?" Or, has the significance of such an approach been unattractively garbed and therefore unfairly handicapped? Can we bridge the gap, rather than sever the link, between traditional ratio analysis and the more rigorous statistical techniques which have become popular among academicians in recent years? Along with our primary interest, corporate bankruptcy, I am also concerned with an assessment of ratio analysis as an analytical technique.

It should be pointed out that the basic research for much of the material in this paper was performed in 1967 and that several subsequent studies have commented on the Z-Score model and its effectiveness, including an adaptation in 1995 for credit analysis of emerging market corporates. And this author co-developed a "second generation" model, ZETA® (ZETA®, 1977).

TRADITIONAL RATIO ANALYSIS

The detection of company operating and financial difficulties is a subject which has been particularly amenable to analysis with financial ratios. Prior to the development of quantitative measures of company performance, agencies were established to supply a qualitative type of information assessing the creditworthiness of particular merchants. (For instance, the forerunner of the well-known Dun & Bradstreet, Inc. was organized in 1849 in Cincinnati, Ohio, to provide independent credit investigations). Formal aggregate studies concerned with portents of business failure were evident in the 1930s.

One of the classic works in the area of ratio analysis and bankruptcy classification was performed by Beaver (1967). In a real sense, his univariate analysis of a number of bankruptcy predictors set the stage for the multivariate attempts, by this author and others, which followed. Beaver found that a number of indicators could discriminate between matched samples of failed and nonfailed firms for as long as five years prior to failure. He questioned the use of multivariate analysis, although a discussant recommended attempting this procedure. The Z-Score model did just that. A subsequent study by Deakin (1972) utilized the same 14 variables that Beaver analyzed, but he applied them within a series of multivariate discriminant models.

The aforementioned studies imply a definite potential of ratios as predictors of bankruptcy. In general, ratios measuring profitability, liquidity, and solvency prevailed as the most significant indicators. The order of their importance is not clear since almost every study cited a different ratio as being the most effective indication of impending problems.

Although these works established certain important generalizations regarding the performance and trends of particular measurements, the adaptation of the results for assessing bankruptcy potential of firms, both theoretically and practically, is questionable. In almost every case, the methodology was essentially univariate in nature and emphasis was placed on individual signals of impending problems. Ratio analysis presented in this fashion is susceptible to faulty interpretation and is potentially confusing. For instance, a firm with a poor profitability and/or solvency record may be regarded as a potential bankrupt. However, because of its above average liquidity, the situation may not be considered serious. The potential ambiguity as to the relative performance of several firms is clearly evident. The crux of the shortcomings inherent in any univariate analysis lies therein. An appropriate extension of the previously cited studies, therefore, is to build on their findings and to combine several measures into a meaningful predictive model. In so doing, the highlights of ratio analysis as an analytical technique will be emphasized rather than downgraded. The questions are:

- Which ratios are most important in detecting bankruptcy potential?
- What weights should be attached to those selected ratios?
- How should the weights be objectively established?

DISCRIMINANT ANALYSIS

After careful consideration of the nature of the problem and of the purpose of this analysis, I chose multiple discriminant analysis (MDA) as the appropriate statistical technique. Although not as popular as regression analysis, MDA has been utilized in a variety of disciplines since its first application in the 1930s. During those earlier years, MDA was used mainly in the biological and behavioral sciences. In recent years, this technique has become increasingly popular in the practical business world as well as in academia. Altman et al. (1981) discusses discriminant analysis in-depth and reviews several financial application areas.

MDA is a statistical technique used to classify an observation into one of several *a priori* groupings dependent on the observation's individual characteristics. It is used primarily to classify and/or make predictions in problems where the dependent variable appears in qualitative form, for example, male or female, bankrupt or non-bankrupt. Therefore, the first step is to establish explicit group classifications. The number of original groups can be two or more. Some analysts refer to discriminant analysis as "multiple" only when the number of groups exceeds two. We prefer that the multiple concepts refer to the multivariate nature of the analysis.

After the groups are established, data are collected for the objects in the groups; MDA in its most simple form attempts to derive a linear combination of these characteristics which "best" discriminates between the groups. If a particular object, for instance, a corporation, has characteristics (financial ratios) which can be quantified for all of the companies in the analysis, the MDA determines a set of discriminant coefficients. When these coefficients are applied to the actual ratios, a basis for classification into one of the mutually exclusive groupings exists. The MDA technique has the advantage of considering an entire profile of characteristics common to the relevant firms, as well as the interaction of these properties. A univariate study, on the other hand, can only consider the measurements used for group assignments one at a time.

Another advantage of MDA is the reduction of the analyst's space dimensionally, that is, from the number of different independent variables to G-1 dimension(s), where G equals the number of original *a priori* groups. This analysis is concerned with two groups, consisting of bankrupt and non-bankrupt firms. Therefore, the analysis is transformed into its simplest form: one dimension. The discriminant function, of the form

$$Z = V_1 X_1 + V_2 X_2 + \cdots + V_n X_n$$

transforms the individual variable values to a single discriminant score, or z value, which is then used to classify the object where

$V_1, V_2, \ldots, V_n$ = discriminant coefficients, and
$X_1, X_2, \ldots, X_n$ = independent variables

The MDA computes the discriminant coefficient; V_i while the independent variables X_i are the actual values.

When utilizing a comprehensive list of financial ratios in assessing a firm's bankruptcy potential, there is reason to believe that some of the measurements will have a high degree of correlation or collinearity with each other. While this aspect is not serious in discriminant analysis, it usually motivates careful selection of the predictive variables (ratios). It also has the advantage of potentially yielding a model with a relatively small number of selected measurements which convey a great deal of information. This information might very well indicate differences among groups, but whether or not these differences are significant and meaningful is a more important aspect of the analysis.

Perhaps the primary advantage of MDA in dealing with classification problems is the potential of analyzing the entire variable profile of the object simultaneously rather than sequentially examining its individual characteristics. Just as linear and integer programming have improved on traditional techniques in capital budgeting, the MDA approach to traditional ratio analysis has the potential to reformulate the problem correctly. Specifically, combinations of ratios can be analyzed together so as to remove possible ambiguities and misclassifications observed in earlier traditional ratio studies.

As we will see, the Z-Score model is a linear analysis in that five measures are objectively weighted and summed to arrive at an overall score that then becomes the basis for classification of firms into one of the *a priori* groupings (distressed and nondistressed).

DEVELOPMENT OF THE Z-SCORE MODEL

The initial sample is composed of 66 corporations with 33 firms in each of the two groups. The bankrupt (distressed) group (Group 1) are manufacturers that filed a bankruptcy petition under Chapter X of the National Bankruptcy Act from 1946 through 1965. A 20-year period is not the best choice since average ratios do shift over time. Ideally, we would prefer to examine a list of ratios in time period t and to make predictions about other firms in the following period $(t + 1)$. Unfortunately, it was not possible to do this because of data limitations. Recognizing that this group is not completely homogeneous (due to industry and size differences), I attempted to make a careful selection of non-bankrupt (nondistressed) firms. Group 2 consists of a paired sample of manufacturing firms chosen on a stratified random basis. The firms are stratified by industry and by size, with the asset size range restricted to between $1 million and $25 million. The mean asset size of the firms in Group 2 ($9.6 million) was slightly greater than that of Group 1, but matching exact asset size of the two groups seemed unnecessary. Firms in Group 2 were still in existence at the time of the analysis. Also, the data collected are from the same years as those compiled for the bankrupt firms. For the initial sample test, the data are derived from financial statements dated one annual reporting period prior to bankruptcy. The data were derived from *Moody's Industrial Manuals* and also from selected annual reports. The average lead-time of the financial statements was approximately seven and one-half months.

An important issue is to determine the asset-size group to be sampled. The decision to eliminate both the small firms (under $1 million in total assets) and the very large companies from the initial sample essentially is due to the asset range of the firms in Group 1. In addition, the incidence of bankruptcy in the large-asset-size firm was quite rare prior to 1966. This changed, starting in 1970, with the appearance of several very large bankruptcies, e.g., Penn-Central R.R. Large industrial bankruptcies also increased in appearance, since 1978. In all, there have been at least 100 Chapter 11 bankruptcies with over $1 billion in liabilities since 1978 (the year of the existing Bankruptcy Code's enactment).

A frequent argument is that financial ratios, by their very nature, have the effect of deflating statistics by size, and that therefore a good deal of the size effect is eliminated. The Z-Score model, discussed below, appears to be sufficiently robust to accommodate large firms. The ZETA model did include larger-sized distressed firms and is unquestionably relevant to both small and large firms.

Variable Selection

After the initial groups are defined and firms selected, balance sheet and income statement data are collected. Because of the large number of variables found to be significant indicators of corporate problems in past studies, a list of 22 potentially helpful variables (ratios) was complied for evaluation. The variables are classified into five standard ratio categories: liquidity, profitability, leverage, solvency, and activity. The ratios are chosen on the basis of their popularity in the literature and their potential relevancy to the study, and there are a few "new" ratios in this analysis. The Beaver study (1967) concluded that the cash flow to debt ratio was the best single ratio predictor. This ratio was not considered in my 1968 study because of the lack of consistent and precise depreciation and cash flow data. The results obtained, however, were still superior to the results Beaver attained with his single best ratio. Cash flow measures were included in the ZETA® model tests (see later discussion).

From the original list of 22 variables, five are selected as doing the best overall job together in the prediction of corporate bankruptcy. This profile did not contain all of the most significant variable measured independently. This would not necessarily improve on the univariate, traditional analysis described earlier. The contribution of the entire profile is evaluated and, since this process is essentially iterative, there is no claim regarding the optimality of the resulting discriminant function. The function, however, does the best job among the alternatives which include numerous computer runs analyzing different ratio profiles.

To arrive at a final profile of variables, the following procedures are utilized:

1 Observation of the statistical significance of various alternative functions, including determination of the relative contributions of each independent variable
2 Evaluation of intercorrelations among the relevant variables
3 Observation of the predictive accuracy of the various profiles
4 Judgment of the analyst

The final discriminant function is as follows:

$$Z = 0.012X_1 + 0.014X_2 + 0.033X_3 + 0.006X_4 + 0.999X_5$$

where

    X_1 = working capital/total assets
    X_2 = retained earnings/total assets
    X_3 = earnings before interest and taxes/total assets
    X_4 = market value of equity/book value of total liabilities
    X_5 = sales/total assets
    Z = overall index

Note that the model does not contain a constant (y-intercept) term. This is due to the particular software utilized and, as a result, the relevant cut-off score between the two groups is not zero. Other software programs, like SAS and SPSS, have a constant term, which standardizes the cut-off score at zero if the sample sizes of the two groups are equal.

X_1, WORKING CAPITAL/TOTAL ASSETS (WC/TA)

The working capital/total assets ratio, frequently found in studies of corporate problems, is a measure of the net liquid assets of the firm relative to the total capitalization. Working capital is defined as the difference between current assets and current liabilities. Liquidity and size characteristics are explicitly considered. Ordinarily, a firm experiencing consistent operating losses will have shrinking current assets in relation to total assets. Of the three liquidity ratios evaluated, this one proved to be the most valuable. Two other liquidity ratios tested were the current ratio and the quick ratio. There were found to be less helpful and subject to perverse trends for some failing firms.

X_2, RETAINED EARNINGS/TOTAL ASSETS (RE/TA)

Retained earnings is the account which reports the total amount of reinvested earnings and/or losses of a firm over its entire life. The account is also referred to as earned surplus. It should be noted that the retained earnings account is subject to "manipulation" via corporate quasi-reorganizations and stock dividend declarations. While these occurrences are not evident in this study, it is conceivable that a bias would be created by a substantial reorganization or stock dividend, and appropriate readjustments should be made to the accounts.

This measure of cumulative profitability over time is what I referred to earlier as a "new" ratio. The age of a firm is implicitly considered in this ratio. For example, a relatively young firm will probably show a low RE/TA ratio because it has not had time to build up its cumulative profits. Therefore, it may be argued that the young firm is somewhat discriminated against in this analysis, and its chance of being classified as bankrupt is relatively higher than that of another older firm, *ceteris paribus*. But, this is precisely the situation in the real world. The incidence of failure is much higher in a firm's earlier years. In 1993, approximately 50 percent of all firms that failed did so in the first five years of their existence (Dun & Bradstreet, 1994).

In addition, the RE/TA ratio measures the leverage of a firm. Those firms with high RE, relative to TA, have financed their assets through retention of profits and have not utilized as much debt.

X_3, EARNINGS BEFORE INTEREST AND TAXES / TOTAL ASSETS (EBIT/TA)

This ratio is a measure of the true productivity of the firm's assets, independent of any tax or leverage factors. Since a firm's ultimate existence is based on the earning power of its assets, this ratio appears to be particularly appropriate for studies dealing with corporate failure. Furthermore, insolvency in a bankrupt sense occurs when the total liabilities exceed a fair valuation of the firm's assets with value determined by the earning power of the assets. As we will show, this ratio continually outperforms other profitability measures, including cash flow.

X_4, MARKET VALUE OF EQUITY/BOOK VALUE OF TOTAL LIABILITIES (MVE/TL)

Equity is measured by the combined market value of all shares of stock, preferred and common, while liabilities include both current and long term. The measure shows how much the firm's assets can decline in value (measured by market value of equity plus debt) before the liabilities exceed the assets and the firm becomes insolvent. For example, a company with a market value of its equity of $1,000 and debt of $500 could experience a two-thirds drop in asset value before insolvency. However, the same firm with $250 equity will be insolvent if assets drop only one-third in value. This ratio adds a market value dimension which most other failure studies did not consider. The reciprocal of X_4 is a slightly modified version of one of the variables used effectively by Fisher (1959) in a study of corporate bond yield–spread differentials. It also appears to be a more effective predictor of bankruptcy than a similar, more commonly used ratio: net worth/total debt (book values). At a later point, we will substitute the book value of net worth for the market value to derive a discriminant function for privately held firms (Z') and for non-manufacturers (Z'').

More recent models, such as the KMV[1] approach, are essentially based on the market value of equity and its volatility. The equity market value serves as a proxy for the firm's asset values.

X_5, SALES / TOTAL ASSETS (S/TA)

The capital–turnover ratio is a standard financial ratio illustrating the sales generating ability of the firm's assets. It is one measure of management's capacity in dealing with competitive conditions. This final ratio is quite important because it is the least significant ratio on an individual basis. In fact, based on the univariate statistical significance test, it would not have appeared at all. However, because of its unique relationship to other variables in the model, the sales/total assets ratio ranks second in its contribution to the overall discriminating ability of the model. Still, there is a wide variation among industries in asset turnover, and we will specify an alternative model (Z''), without X_5 at a later point.

---

[1]   KMV is a San Francisco based credit risk modeling company.

A Clarification

The reader is cautioned to utilize the model in the appropriate manner. Due to the original computer format arrangement, variables X_1 through X_4 must be calculated as absolute percentage values. For instance, the firm whose net working capital to total assets (X_1) is 10 percent should be included as 10.0 percent and not 0.10. Only variable X_5 (sales to total assets) should be expressed in a different manner: that is, a S/TA ratio of 200 percent should be included as 2.0. The practical analyst may have been concerned by the extremely high relative discriminant coefficient of X_5. This seeming irregularity is due to the format of the different variables. Table 1.1 illustrates the proper specification and form for each of the five independent variables.

Over the years, many individuals have found that a more convenient specification of the model is of the form:

$$Z = 1.2X_1 + 1.4X_2 + 3.3X_3 + 0.6X_4 + 1.0X_5$$

Using this formula, one inserts the more commonly written percentage, for example, 0.10 for 10 percent, for the first four variables (X_1–X_4) and rounds the last coefficient off to equal 1.0 (from 0.99). The last variable continues to be written in terms of number of times. The scores for individual firms and related group classification and cutoff scores remain identical. We merely point this out and note that we have utilized this format in some practical application, for example, Altman and LaFleur (1981).

Table 1.1   Variable means and test significance

Variable	Bankrupt group mean[a]	Non-bankrupt group mean[a]	F ratio[a]
X_1	−6.1%	41.4%	32.50*
X_2	−62.6%	35.5%	58.86*
X_3	−31.8%	15.4%	26.56*
X_4	40.1%	247.7%	33.26*
X_5	1.5X	1.9X	2.84

[a] N = 33.
$F_{1.60}(0.001) = 12.00$; $F_{1.60}(0.01) = 7.00$; $F_{1.60}(0.05) = 4.00$.
* Significant at the 0.001 level.

Variable Tests

A test to determine the overall discriminating power of the model is the F-value which is the ratio of the sums-of-squares between-groups to the within-groups sums-of-squares. When this ratio is maximized, it has the effect of spreading the means (centroids) of the groups apart and, simultaneously, reducing dispersion of the individual points (firm Z-values) about their respective group means. Logically, this test (commonly called the F-test) is appropriate because the objective of the MDA is to identify and utilize those variables which best discriminate between groups and which are most similar within groups.

The group means of the original two-group sample are:

- For Group 1: -0.29, F = 20.7
- For Group 2: $+5.02$, $F_{4n}(0.01) = 3.84$

The significance test therefore rejects the null hypothesis that the observations come from the same population.

Variable means measured at one financial statement prior to bankruptcy and the resulting F-statistics a shown in table 1.1. Variables X_1 through X_4 are all significant at the 0.001 level, indicating extremely significant differences in these variables among groups. Variable X_5 does not show a significant difference among groups and the reason for its inclusion in the variable profile is not apparent as yet. On a strictly univariate level, all of the ratios indicate higher values for the non-bankrupt firms. Also, all of the discriminant coefficients display positive signs, which is what one would expect. Therefore, the greater a firm's distress potential, the lower its discriminant score. It is clear that four of the five variables display significant differences between groups, but the importance of MDA is its ability to separate groups using multivariate measures.

Once the values of the discriminant coefficients are estimated, it is possible to calculate discriminant scores for each observation in the samples, or any firm, and to assign the observations to one of the groups based on this score. The essence of the procedure is to compare the profile of an individual firm with that of the alternative groupings. The comparisons are measured by a χ^2 value and assignments are made based on the relative proximity of the firms' score to the various group centroids.

Initial Sample (Group 1)

The initial sample of 33 firms in each of the two groups is examined using data compiled one financial statement prior to distress. Since the discriminant coefficients and the group distributions are derived from this sample, a high degree of successful classification is expected. This should occur because the firms are classified using a discriminant function which, in fact, is based upon the individual measurements of these same firms. The classification matrix for the original sample is shown in table 1.2.

The model is extremely accurate in classifying 95 percent of the total sample correctly. The Type I error proved to be only 6 percent while the Type II error was even

Table 1.2 Classification results, original sample

	Number correct	% correct	% error	n	Actual	Predicted	
						Group 1	Group 2
					Group 1	31	2
					Group 2	1	32
Type I	31	94	6	33			
Type II	32	97	3	33			
Total	63	95	5	66			

lower at 3 percent. The results, therefore, are encouraging, but the obvious upward bias should be kept in mind, and further validation techniques are appropriate.

Results Two Statements Prior to Bankruptcy

The second test observes the discriminating ability of the model for firms using data compiled two statements prior to distress. The two-year period is an exaggeration since the average lead time for the correctly classified firms is approximately 20 months, with two firms having a 13-month lead. The results are shown in table 1.3. The reduction in accuracy is understandable because impending bankruptcy is more remote and the indications are less clear. Nevertheless, 72 percent correct assignment is evidence that bankruptcy can be predicted two years prior to the event. The Type II error is slightly larger (6 percent vs. 3 percent) in this test, but still it is extremely accurate. Further tests are applied below to determine the accuracy of predicting bankruptcy as much as five years prior to the actual event.

Table 1.3 Classification results, two statements prior to bankruptcy

	Number correct	% correct	% error	n	Actual	Predicted Group 1 (Bankrupt)	Group 2 (Non-bankrupt)
					Group 1	23	9
					Group 2	2	31
Type I	23	72	28	32			
Type II	31	94	6	33			
Total	54	83	17	65			

Potential Bias and Validation Techniques

When the firms used to determine the discriminant coefficients are reclassified, the resulting accuracy is biased upward by

1 sampling errors in the original sample; and
2 search bias.

The latter bias is inherent in the process of reducing the original set of variables (22) to the best variable profile (5). The possibility of bias due to intensive searching is inherent in any empirical study. While a subset of variables is effective in the initial sample, there is no guarantee that it will be effective for the population in general.

The importance of secondary sample testing cannot be overemphasized. One type of secondary sample testing is to estimate parameters for the model using only a subset of the original sample, and then to classify the remainder of the sample based on the parameters established. A simple t-test is then applied to test the significance of the results. Five different replications of the suggested method of choosing subsets (16 firms) of the original sample are tested.

The test results reject the hypothesis that there is no difference between the groups and substantiate that the model does, in fact, possess discriminating power on observations other than those used to establish the parameters of the model. Therefore, any search bias does not appear significant.

Secondary Sample of Bankrupt Firms

To test the model rigorously for both bankrupt and non-bankrupt firms, two new samples are introduced. The first contains a new sample of 25 bankrupt firms whose asset size range is similar to that of the initial bankrupt group. On the basis of the parameters established in the discriminant model to classify firms in this secondary sample, the predictive accuracy for this sample as of one statement prior to bankruptcy is described in table 1.4.

The results here are surprising in that one would not usually expect a secondary sample's results to be superior to the initial discriminant sample (96 percent vs. 94 percent). Two possible reasons are that the upward bias normally present in the initial sample tests is not manifested in this investigation and/or that the model, as stated before, is not optimal.

Table 1.4 Classification results, secondary sample of bankrupt firms

Bankrupt	Group	(Actual)	Predicted	
Number correct	% correct	% error	Bankrupt	Non-bankrupt
			24	1
Type I (Total) 24	96	4	N = 25	

Testing the Model on Subsequent Distressed Firm's Samples

In three subsequent tests, I examined 86 distressed companies from 1969–75, 110 bankrupts from 1976–95 and 120 from 1997–99. I found that the Z-Score model, using a cutoff score of 2.675, was between 82 percent and 94 percent accurate. For an in-depth discussion of these studies, see below. In repeated tests up to the present (1999), the accuracy of the Z-Score model on samples of distressed firms has been in the vicinity of 80–90 percent, based on data from one financial reporting period prior to bankruptcy.

The Type II error (classifying the firm as distressed when it does not go bankrupt), however, has increased substantially with as much as 15–20 percent of all firms and 10 percent of the largest firms having Z-Scores below 1.81. Recent tests, however, show the average Z-Score increasing significantly with the average rising from the 4–5 level in 1970–95 period to almost 10 (ten) in 1999; see Osler and Hong (2000) for these results, shown also in figure 1.1. But, the median level has not increased much. The majority of increase in average Z-Scores was due to the dramatic climb in stock prices and its impact on X_4.

I advocate using the lower bond of the zone-of-ignorance (1.81) as a more realistic cutoff Z-Score than the score 2.675. The latter resulted in the lowest overall error in the

Figure 1.1   Average Z-Scores: US industrial firms 1975–99

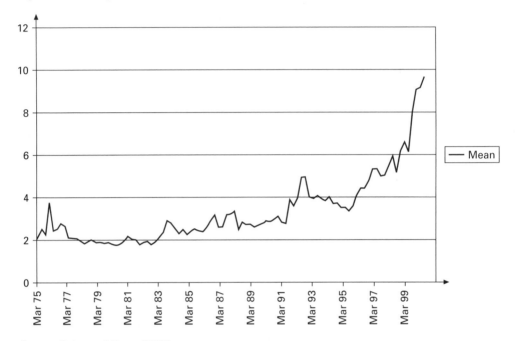

Source: Osler and Hong (2000).

original tests. In 1999, the proportion of US industrial firms, comprised in the *Compustat* data tapes, that had Z-Scores below 1.81 was over 20 percent.

Secondary Sample of Non-Bankrupt Firms

Up to this point, the sample companies were chosen either by their bankruptcy status (Group I) or by their similarity to Group I in all aspects except their economic well-being. But what of the many firms which suffer temporary profitability difficulties, but actually do not become bankrupt? A bankruptcy classification of a firm from this group is an example of a Type II error. An exceptionally rigorous test of the discriminant model's effectiveness would be to search out a large sample of firms that have encountered earning problems and then to observe the Z-Score's classification results.

To perform the above test, a sample of 66 firms is selected on the basis of net income (deficit) reports in the years 1958 and 1961, with 33 from each year. Over 65 percent of these firms had suffered two or three years of negative profits in the previous three years. The firms are selected regardless of their asset size, with the only two criteria being that they were manufacturing firms which suffered losses in the year 1958 or 1961. The companies are then evaluated by the discriminant model to determine their bankruptcy potential.

The results show that 14 of the 66 firms are classified as bankrupt, with the remaining 52 correctly classified. Therefore, the discriminant model correctly classified 79 percent of the sample firms. This percentage is all the more impressive when one considers that these firms constitute a secondary sample of admittedly below-average performance. The t-test for the significance of the result is $t = 4.8$; significant at the 0.001 level. Another interesting facet of this test is the relationship of these "temporarily" sick firms' Z-Scores and the "zone of ignorance." The zone of ignorance is that range of Z-Scores where misclassification can be observed.

Of the 14 misclassified firms in this secondary sample, 10 have Z-Scores between 1.81 and 2.67, which indicates that although they are classified as bankrupt, the prediction of their bankruptcy is not as definite as it is for the vast majority in the initial sample of bankrupt firms. In fact, just under one-third of the 66 firms in this last sample have Z-Scores within the entire overlap area, which emphasizes that the selection process is successful in choosing firms which showed signs (profitability) of deterioration. Although these tests are based on data from over 40 years ago, they do indicate the robustness of the model which is still in use in the year 2000.

Long-Range Accuracy

The previous results give important evidence of the reliability of the conclusions derived from the initial and holdout samples of firms. An appropriate extension would be to examine the overall effectiveness of the discriminant model for a longer period of time prior to bankruptcy.

To answer this question, data are gathered for the 33 original firms from the third, fourth, and fifth years prior to bankruptcy. One would expect on an *a priori* basis that, as the lead time increases, the relative predictive ability of any model would decrease. This was true in the univariate studies cited earlier, and it is also quite true for the multiple discriminant model. We will shortly see, however, that the more recent model (e.g., ZETA®) has demonstrated higher accuracy over a longer period of time.

Based on the above results, it is suggested that the Z-Score model is an accurate forecaster of failure up to two years prior to distress and that accuracy diminishes substantially as the lead time increases. We also performed a trend analysis on the individual ratios in the model. The two most important conclusions of this trend analysis are that

1 all of the observed ratios show a deteriorating trend as bankruptcy approaches; and
2 the most serious change in the majority of these ratios occurred between the third and the second years prior to bankruptcy.

The degree of seriousness is measured by the yearly change in the ratio values. The latter observation is extremely significant as it provides evidence consistent with conclusions derived from the discriminant model. Therefore, the important information inherent in the individual ratio measurement trends takes on deserved significance only when integrated with the more analytical discriminant analysis findings.

Average Z-Scores Over Time

As table 1.5 shows, we have tested the Z-Score model for various sample periods over the last 30 years. In each test, the Type I accuracy using a cutoff score of 2.67 had a

Table 1.5   Classification and prediction accuracy Z-Score (1968) failure model*

Year prior to failure	Original sample (33)	Holdout sample (25)	1969–75 Predictive sample (86)	1976–95 Predictive sample (110)	1997–99 Predictive sample (120)
1	94% (88%)	96% (92%)	82% (75%)	85% (78%)	94% (84%)
2	72%	80%	68%	75%	74%
3	48%	–	–	–	–
4	29%	–	–	–	–
5	36%	–	–	–	–

* Using 2.67 as cutoff score (1.81 cutoff accuracy in parenthesis).

range of 82–94 percent, based on data from one financial statement prior to bankruptcy or default on outstanding bonds. Indeed, in the most recent test, based on 120 firms which defaulted on their publicly held debt during 1997–99, the default prediction accuracy rate was 94 percent (113 out of 120). Using the more conservative 1.81 cutoff, the accuracy rate was still an impressive 84 percent. The 94 percent, 2.67 cutoff accuracy is comparable to the original sample's accuracy which was based on data used to construct the model itself.

We can, therefore, conclude that the Z-Score model has retained its reported high accuracy and is still robust despite its development over 30 years ago. In the last decade, however, the Type II accuracy has increased to about 15–20 percent of those manufacturing firms listed on *Compustat*.

Adaptation for Private Firms' Application

Perhaps the most frequent inquiry that I have received from those interested in using the Z-Score model is, "What should we do to apply the model to firms in the private sector?" Credit analysts, private placement dealers, accounting auditors, and firms themselves are concerned that the original model is only applicable to publicly traded entities (since X_1 requires stock price data). And, to be perfectly correct, the Z-Score model is a publicly traded firm model and *ad hoc* adjustments are not scientifically valid. For example, the most obvious modification is to substitute the book value of equity for the market value and then recalculate V_4X_4. Prior to this writing, analysts had little choice but to do this procedure since valid alternatives were not available.

A REVISED Z-SCORE MODEL

Rather than simply insert a proxy variable into an existing model to calculate z-scores, I advocate a complete reestimation of the model, substituting the book values of equity for the market value in X_4. One expects that all of the coefficients will change (not only the new variable's parameter) and that the classification criterion and related cutoff scores would also change. That is exactly what happens.

The results of our revised Z-Score model with a new X_4 variable is:

$$Z' = 0.717X_1 + 0.847X_2 + 3.107X_3 + 0.420X_4 + 0.998X_5$$

The equation now looks different than the earlier model (page 14); note, for instance, the coefficient for X_1 went from 1.2 to 0.7. But, the model looks quite similar to the one using market values. The actual variable that was modified, X_4, showed a coefficient change to 0.42 from 0.60; that is, it now has less of an impact on the Z-Score. X_3 and X_5 are virtually unchanged. The univariate F-test for the book value of X_4 (25.8) is lower than the 33.3 level for the market value but the scaled vector results show that the revised book value measure is still the third most important contributor.

Table 1.6 lists the classification accuracy, group means, and revised cutoff scores for the Z'-Score model. The Type I accuracy is only slightly less impressive than the model utilizing market value of equity (91 percent vs. 94 percent) but the Type II accuracy is identical (97 percent). The non-bankrupt group's mean Z'-Score is lower than that of the original model (4.14 vs. 5.02). Therefore, the distribution of scores is now tighter with larger group overlap. The gray area (or ignorance zone) is wider, however, since the lower boundary is now 1.23 as opposed to 1.81 for the original Z-Score model. All of this indicates that the revised model is probably somewhat less reliable than the original, but only slightly less. Due to lack of a private firm data base, we have not tested this model extensively on secondary sample distressed and nondistressed entities. A recent model from Moody's (2000) utilizing data on middle market firms and over 1600 defaults, concentrates on private firms.

Table 1.6 Revised Z'-Score model: Classification results, group means, and cutoff boundaries

Actual	Classified		Total
	Bankrupt	Non-bankrupt	
Bankrupt	30 (90.9%)	3 (9.1%)	33
Non-bankrupt	1 (3.0%)	32 (97.0%)	33

Note: Bankrupt group mean = 0.15; non-bankrupt group mean = 4.14.
  Z' < 1.23 = Zone I (no errors in bankruptcy classification):
  Z' > 2.90 = Zone II (no errors in non-bankruptcy classification):
  gray area = 1.23 to 2.90.

A FURTHER REVISION – ADAPTING THE MODEL FOR NON-MANUFACTURERS

The next modification of the Z-Score model analyzed the characteristics and accuracy of a model without X_1 – sales/total assets. We do this to minimize the potential industry effect which is more likely to take place when such an industry-sensitive variable as asset turnover is included. In addition, I have used this model to assess the financial health of non-US corporates. In particular, Altman et al. (1995; ch. 5, this volume) have applied this enhanced Z"-Score model to emerging markets corporates, specifically Mexican firms that had issued Eurobonds denominated in US dollars. The book value of equity was used for X_4 in this case.

The classification results are identical to the revised five-variable model (Z'-Score). The new Z''-Score model is:

$$Z'' = 6.56X_1 + 3.26X_2 + 6.72X_3 + 1.05X_4$$

All of the coefficients for variables X_1–X_4 are changed as are the group means and cutoff scores. This particular model is also useful within an industry where the type of financing of assets differs greatly among firms and important adjustments, like lease capitalization, are not made. In the emerging market model, we added a constant term of +3.25 so as to standardize the scores with a score of Zero (0) equated to a D (default) rated bond.

EMERGING MARKET SCORING (EMS) MODEL AND PROCESS

Emerging markets credits may initially be analyzed in a manner similar to that used for traditional analysis of US corporates. Once a quantitative risk assessment has emerged, an analyst can then use a qualitative assessment to modify it for such factors as currency and industry risk, industry characteristics, and the firm's competitive position in that industry. It is not often possible to build a model specific to an emerging market country based on a sample from that country because of the lack of credit experience there. To deal with this problem, Altman et al. (1995; ch. 5, this volume) have modified the original Altman Z-Score model to create the EMS model.

The process of deriving the rating for a Mexican corporate credit is as follows:

1   The EMS score is calculated, and equivalent rating is obtained based on the calibration of the EMS scores with US bond-rating equivalents (table 1.7).
2   The company's bond is then analyzed for the issuing firm's vulnerability concerning the servicing of its foreign currency-denominated debt. This vulnerability is based on the relationship between the nonlocal currency revenues minus costs, compared with nonlocal currency expense. Then the level of nonlocal currency cash flow is compared with the debt coming due in the next year. The analyst adjusts the rating downward depending on the degree of vulnerability seen.
3   The rating is further adjusted downward (or upward) if the company is in an industry considered to be relatively riskier (or less risky) than the bond-rating equivalent from the first EMS result.
4   The rating is further adjusted up or down depending on the dominance of the firm's position in its industry.
5   If the debt has special features, such as collateral or a bona fide guarantor, the rating is adjusted accordingly.
6   Finally, the market value of equity is substituted for the book value in variable X_4, and the resulting bond-rating equivalents are compared. If there are significant differences in the bond-rating equivalents, the final rating is modified, up or down.

For relative value analysis, the corresponding US corporates' credit spread is added to the sovereign bond's option-adjusted spread. Only a handful of the Mexican companies were rated by the rating agencies. Thus, risk assessments such as those provided by EMS are often the only reliable indicators of credit risk to overseas investors in Mexico. Altman et al. (1995) report that the modified ratings have proven accurate in

Table 1.7   US bond rating equivalent based on EM score

US equivalent rating	Average EM score
AAA	8.15
AA+	7.60
AA	7.30
AA−	7.00
A+	6.85
A	6.65
A−	6.40
BBB+	6.25
BBB	5.85
BBB−	5.65
BB+	5.25
BB	4.95
BB−	4.75
B+	4.50
B	4.15
B−	3.75
CCC+	3.20
CCC	2.50
CCC−	1.75
D	0

Source: In-depth Data Corp. Average based on over 750 US corporates with rated debt outstanding: 1994 data.

anticipating both downgrades and defaults – Group Synkro (10/95), Situr (3/96), GMD (8/97), Tribasa (3/99), etc. – and upgrades (Aeromexico in July 1995).

THE ZETA® CREDIT-RISK MODEL

In 1977, Altman et al. (1977) constructed a second generation model with several enhancements to the original Z-Score approach. The purpose of this study was to construct, analyze and test a new bankruptcy classification model which considers explicitly recent developments with respect to business failures. The new study also incorporated refinements in the utilization of discriminant statistical techniques. Several reasons for building a new model, despite the availability of several fairly impressive "old" models, are presented below and the empirical results seem to substantiate the effort. The new model, which we call ZETA®, was effective in classifying bankrupt companies up to five years prior to failure on a sample of corporations consisting of manufacturers and retailers. Since the ZETA® model is a proprietary effort, I cannot fully disclose the parameters of the market.

Reasons for Attempting to Construct a New Model

There are at least five valid reasons why a revised Z-Score bankruptcy classification model can improve on and extend those statistical models which had been published in the literature in the prior decade:

1 One such reason is the change in the size, and perhaps the financial profile, of business failures. The average size of bankrupt firms had increased dramatically with the consequent greater visibility and concern from financial institutions, regulatory agencies and the public at large. Most of the past studies used relatively small firms in their samples with the exception of Altman's (1973) railroad study and the commercial bank studies. Any new model should be as relevant as possible to the population to which it will eventually be applied. This present study utilizes a bankrupt firm sample where the average asset size two annual reporting periods prior to failure was approximately $100 million. No firm had less than $20 million in assets.

2 Following (1) above, a new model should be as current as possible with respect to the temporal nature of the data.

3 Past failure models concentrated either on the broad classification of manufacturers or on specific industries. I feel that with the appropriate analytical adjustments, retailing companies, a particularly vulnerable group, could be analyzed on an equal basis with manufacturers.

4 An important feature of this study is that the data and footnotes to financial statements have been scrupulously analyzed to include the most recent changes in financial reporting standards and accepted accounting practices. Indeed, in at least one instance, a change which was scheduled to be implemented in a very short time was applied. The purpose of these modifications was to make the model not only relevant to past failures, but to the data that will appear in the future. The predictive as well as the classification accuracy of the ZETA® model is implicit in our efforts.

5 It is also important to test and assess several of the then recent advances and still controversial aspects of discriminant analysis.

Principal Findings

We concluded that the new ZETA® model for bankruptcy classification appeared to be accurate for up to five years prior to failure with successful classification of well over 90 percent of our sample one year prior and 70 percent accuracy up to five years. We also observed that the inclusion of retailing firms in the same model as manufacturers does not seem to affect our results negatively. This is probably true due to the adjustments to our data based on recent and anticipated financial reporting changes – primarily the capitalization of leases.

We also find that the ZETA® model outperformed alternative bankruptcy classification strategies in terms of expected cost criteria utilizing prior probabilities and explicit cost of error estimates. In our investigation, we were surprised to observe that, despite the statistical properties of the data which indicate that a quadratic structure is appropriate, the linear structure of the same model outperformed the quadratic in tests of model validity. This was especially evident regarding the long-term accuracy of the model and in holdout sample testing.

Sample and Data Characteristics, and Statistical Methodology

Our two samples of firms consist of 53 bankrupt firms and a matched sample of 58 non-bankrupt entities. The latter are matched to the failed group by industry and year of data. Our sample is almost equally divided into manufacturers and retailer groups, and 94 percent of the firms failed during the period 1969–75. The average asset size of our failed group is almost $100 million indicative of the increasing size of failures. The bankrupt firms represent all publicly held industrial failures which had at least $20 million in assets, with no known fraud involved and where sufficient data was available. Five non-bankruptcy petition companies were included due to either substantial government support, or a forced merger, or, the banks taking over the business or accepting a distressed restructuring rather than forcing the Chapter 11 petition.

VARIABLES ANALYZED

In other studies, a number of financial ratios and other measures have been found to be helpful in providing statistical evidence of impending failures. We have assembled data to calculate these variables and, in addition, have included several "new" measures that were thought to be potentially helpful as well. The 27 variables are listed in table 1.8, along with certain relevant statistics which will be discussed shortly. Note that in a few cases – e.g., nos. 7 and 9, tangible assets and interest coverage – the variables are expressed in logarithmic form so as to reduce outlier possibilities and to adhere to statistical assumptions. The variables can be classified as profitability (1–6), coverage and other earnings relative to leverage measures (8–14), liquidity (15–18), capitalization ratios (19–23), earnings variability (24–26) and a few miscellaneous measures (7 and 27).

REPORTING ADJUSTMENTS

As noted earlier, we have adjusted the basic data of our sample to consider explicitly several of the most recent and, in our opinion, the most important accounting modifications:

1 *Capitalization of leases*
   Without doubt, the most important and pervasive adjustment made was to capitalize all noncancelable operating and finance leases. The resulting capitalized lease amount was added to the firms' assets and liabilities and also we imputed an interest cost to the "new" liability. The procedure involved preparation of schedules of current and expected lease payment obligations from information found in footnotes to the financial statements. The discount rate used to capitalize leases was the average interest rate for new issue, high grade corporate bonds in the year being analyzed plus a risk premium of 10 percent of the interest rate. An amount equal to the interest rate used in the capitalization process times the capitalized lease amount was added to interest costs. Subsequent to our analysis, the Financial Accounting Standards Board (FASB 13, 1980) stipulated that the appropriate discount rate to use is the lessee's cost of debt capital (before taxes) or the internal rate of return on the lease to the lessor, whichever is lower.
2 *Reserves*
   If the firms' reserves were of a contingency nature, they were included in equity, and income was adjusted for the net change in the reserve for the year. If the reserve was related to the valuation of certain assets, it was netted against those assets. If the reserve was for contingent liabilities, e.g., law-suits, then it was added to the liabilities. This was the case for Johns Manville (bankruptcy filed in 1982) and A. H. Robins (in 1985) and several other healthcare lawsuits.

Table 1.8 Listing of all variables, group mean, and F-tests based on one period prior to bankruptcy data (ZETA model sample)

Variable		Population means		Univariate
No.	Name	Failed	Non-failed	F-test
(1)	EBIT/TA	−0.0055	0.1117	54.3
(2)	NATC/TC	−0.0297	0.0742	36.6
(3)	Sales/TA	1.3120	1.6200	3.3
(4)	Sales/TC	2.1070	2.1600	0.0
(5)	EBIT/Sales	0.0020	0.0070	30.2
(6)	NATC/Sales	−0.0153	0.0400	33.1
(7)	Log tang. Assets	1.9854	2.2220	5.5
(8)	Interest coverage	−0.5995	5.3410	26.1
(9)	Log no. (8)	0.9625	1.1620	26.1
(10)	Fixed charge coverage	0.2992	2.1839	15.7
(11)	Earnings/debt	−0.0792	0.1806	32.8
(12)	Earnings 5 yr Maturities	−0.1491	0.6976	8.8
(13)	Cash/flow fixed charges	0.1513	2.9512	20.9
(14)	Cash flow/TD	−0.0173	0.3136	31.4
(15)	WC/LTD	0.3532	2.4433	6.0
(16)	Current ratio	1.5757	2.6040	38.2
(17)	WC/total assets	0.1498	0.3086	40.6
(18)	WC/cash expenses	0.1640	0.2467	5.2
(19)	Ret. earn/total assets	−0.0006	0.2935	114.6
(20)	Book equity/TC	0.2020	0.5260	64.5
(21)	MV equity/TC	0.3423	0.6022	32.1
(22)	5 yr MV equity/TC	0.4063	0.6210	31.0
(23)	MV equity/total liabilities	0.6113	1.8449	11.6
(24)	S. e. of estimate of EBIT/TA (norm)	1.6870	5.784	33.8
(25)	BEIT drop	−3.2272	3.179	9.9
(26)	Margin drop	−0.2173	0.179	15.6
(27)	Capital lease/assets	0.2514	0.178	4.2
(28)	Sales/fixed assets	3.1723	4.179	3.5

Notation:
  EBIT = earnings before interest and taxes
  NATC = net available for total capital
  TA = total tangible assets
  LTD = long term debt
  MV = market value of equity
  TC = total capital
  TD = total debt
  WC = working capital
  CF = cash flow (before interest #13, after interest #14)

3 *Minority interests and other liabilities on the balance sheet*
These items were netted against other assets. This allowed for a truer comparison of earnings with the assets generating the earning.

4 *Captive finance companies and other nonconsolidated subsidiaries*
These were consolidated with the parent company accounts as well as the information would allow. The pooling of interest method was used. This was made mandatory by the FASF in 1987.

5 *Goodwill and intangibles*
   These were deducted from assets and equity because of the difficulty in assigning economic value to them.
6 *Capitalized R&D costs, capitalized interest and certain other deferred charges*
   These costs were expensed rather than capitalized. This was done to improve comparability and to give a better picture of actual funds flows.

STATISTICAL METHODOLOGY

Distress classification is again attempted via the use of a multivariate statistical technique known as discriminant analysis. In this study, the results using both linear and quadratic structure are analyzed. The test for assessing whether a linear or quadratic structure is appropriate – sometimes referred to as the H_1 test, provides the proper guidance when analyzing a particular sample's classification characteristics. Essentially, if it is assessed that the variance–covariance matrices of the G groups are statistically identical, then the linear format which pools all observations is appropriate. If, however, the dispersion matrices are not identical, then the quadratic structure will provide the more efficient model since each group's characteristics can be assessed independently as well as between groups. Efficiency will result in more significant multivariate measures of group differences and greater classification accuracy of that particular sample. What has not been assessed up to this point, is the relative efficiency of the linear vs. quadratic structures when the sample data are not the same as that used to construct the model, i.e., holdout or secondary samples. This point is analyzed in the next section.

Empirical Results: The 7-variable Model

After an iterative process of reducing the number of variables, we selected a 7-variable model which not only classified our test sample well, but also proved the most reliable in various validation procedures. That is, we could not significantly improve on our results by adding more variables, and no model with fewer variables performed as well.

- X_1, return on assets, measured by the earnings before interest and taxes/total assets
  This variable has proven to be extremely helpful in assessing firm performance in several past multivariate studies.
- X_2, stability of earnings, measured by a normalized measure of the standard error of estimate around a 5–10-year trend in X_1
  Business risk is often expressed in terms of earnings fluctuations and this measure proved to be particularly effective. We did assess the information content of several similar variables which attempted to measure the potential susceptibility of a firm's earnings level to decline which could jeopardize its ability to meet its financial commitments. These variables were quite significant on a univariate level but did not enter into our final multivariate model.
- X_3, debt service, measured by the familiar interest coverage ratio, i.e., earnings before interest and taxes/total interest payments (including that amount imputed from the capitalized lease liability)

We have transposed this measure by taking the log to the base 10 so as to improve the normality and homoscedasticity of this measure.

- X_4, cumulative profitability, measured by the firm's retained earnings (balance sheet)/total assets

  This ratio, which imputes such factors as the age of the firm, debt and dividend policy as well as its profitability record over time, was found to be quite helpful in the Z-Score model, discussed earlier. As our results show, this cumulative profitability measure is unquestionably the most important variable-measured univariately and multivariately.

- X_5, liquidity, measured by the familiar current ratio

  Despite previous findings that the current ratio was not as effective in identifying failures as some other liquidity measures, we now find it slightly more informative than others, such as the working capital/total assets ratio.

- X_6, capitalization, measured by common equity/total capital

  In both the numerator and the denominator, the common equity is measured by a five-year average of the total market value, rather than book value. The denominator also includes preferred stock at liquidating value, long-term debt and capitalized leases. We have utilized a 5-year average to smooth out possible severe, temporary market fluctuations and to add a trend component (along with X_2 above) to the study.

- X_7, size, measured by the firms' total assets

  This variable, as is the case with the others, was adjusted for financial reporting changes. No doubt, the capitalization of leasehold rights has added to the average asset size of both the bankrupt and non-bankrupt groups. We have also transformed the size variable to help to normalize the distribution of the variable due to outlier observations. Again, a logarithmic transformation was applied.

RELATIVE IMPORTANCE OF DISCRIMINANT VARIABLES

The procedure of reducing a variable set to an acceptable number is closely related to an attempt to determine the relative importance within a given variable set. Several of the prescribed procedures for attaining the "best" set of variables, e.g., stepwise analysis, can also be used as a criterion for ranking importance. Unfortunately, there is no one best method for establishing a relative ranking of variable importance. Hence, we have assessed this characteristic by analyzing the ranks suggested by five different tests:

1 forward stepwise
2 backward stepwise
3 scaled vector (multiplication of the discriminant coefficient by the appropriate variance–covariance matrix item)
4 separation of means test
5 the conditional deletion test, which measures the additional contribution of the variable to the multivariate F-test given that the other variables have already been included.

In several studies that we have observed, the rankings across these tests are inconsistent and the researcher is left with a somewhat ambiguous answer. This was definitely not the case in our study.

Regardless of which test statistic is observed, the most important variable is the cumulative profitability ratio, X_4. In fact, our scaled vector analysis indicates that this single ratio contributes 25 percent of the total discrimination. Second in importance is the stability of earnings ratio (X_2) and, except for the univariate test of significance, it too has a consistent across tests.

LINEAR VS. QUADRATIC ANALYSIS

The H_1 test of the original sample characteristics clearly rejects the hypothesis that the group dispersion matrices are equal. Therefore, the linear structure classification rule (excluding error costs), is not appropriate and the quadratic structure appears to be the more efficient one.

As can be observed in table 1.9, the quadratic and linear models yield essentially equal total sample accuracy results for the original sample classifications, but the holdout sample tests indicate a clear superiority for the linear framework. This creates a dilemma and we have chosen to concentrate on the linear test due to

1   the possible high sensitivity to individual sample observaions of the quadratic parameters (that is, we observe 35 different parameters in the quadratic model compared with only 7 in the linear case, not including the intercept), and

2   the fact that all of the relative tests of importance are based on the linear model.

Table 1.9   Overall classification accuracy

Years prior to bankrupcy	Bankrupt firms		Non-bankrupt firms		Total	
	% Linear	% Quadratic	% Linear	% Quadratic	% Linear	% Quadratic
1 Original sample	96.2	94.3	89.7	91.4	92.8	92.8
1 (Lachenbruch validation test)	(92.5)	(85.0)	(89.7)	(87.9)	(91.0)	(86.5)
2 Holdout	84.9	77.4	93.1	91.9	89.0	84.7
3 Holdout	74.5	62.7	91.4	92.1	83.5	78.9
4 Holdout	68.1	57.4	89.5	87.8	79.8	74.0
5 Holdout	69.8	46.5	82.1	87.5	76.8	69.7

CLASSIFICATION ACCURACY – ORIGINAL AND HOLDOUT SAMPLES

Table 1.10 presents classification and holdout sample accuracy of the original sample based on data from one year prior to bankruptcy. Lachenbruch (1967) suggests an almost unbiased validation test of original sample results by means of a type of jack-knife, or one isolated observation at a time approach. The individual observations' classification accuracy is then cumulated over the entire sample. Years 2–5 "holdout" sample results are also presented. These results are listed for both the linear and quadratic structures of the 7-variable model.

The linear model's accuracy, based on one year prior data, is 96.2 percent for the bankrupt group and 89.7 percent for the non-bankrupt. The upward bias in these results appears to be slight since the Lachenbruch results are only 3 percent less for the

Table 1.10 Classification accuracy between the ZETA® model and various forms of the Z-Score model

Years prior to bankruptcy (1)	ZETA model		Altman's 1968 model		1968 model, ZETA sample		1968 variables, ZETA parameters	
	Bankrupt (2)	Non-bankrupt (3)	Bankrupt (4)	Non-bankrupt (5)	Bankrupt (6)	Non-bankrupt (7)	Bankrupt (8)	Non-bankrupt (9)
1	96.2	89.7	93.9	97.0	86.8	82.4	92.5	84.5
2	84.9	93.1	71.9	93.9	83.0	89.3	83.0	86.2
3	74.5	91.4	48.3	n.a.	70.6	91.4	72.7	89.7
4	68.1	89.5	28.6	n.a.	61.7	86.0	57.5	83.0
5	69.8	82.1	36.0	n.a.	55.8	86.2	44.2	82.1

Note: All figures given as percentages.

failed group and identical for the nonfailed group. As expected, the failed group's classification accuracy is lower as the data become more remote from bankruptcy, but still quite high. In fact, we observe 70 percent accuracy as far back as five years prior to failure. This compares very favorably to the results recorded by the Z-Score model, where the accuracy dropped precipitously after two years prior.

An interesting result was observed by comparing the quadratic structure's results for that of the linear (table 1.9). As noted earlier, the total samples' classification accuracy is identical for the two structures in period 1, with the linear showing a slight edge in the bankrupt group and the quadratic in the non-bankrupt group. The most obvious and important differences, however, are in the validation and "holdout" tests of the bankrupt group. Here, the linear model is clearly superior, with the quadratic mis-classifying over 50 percent of the future bankrupts five years prior. The Lachenbruch validation test also shows a large bankrupt classification accuracy difference (over 7 percent favoring the linear model). Subsequent analysis will report only the linear results.

COMPARISON WITH THE Z-SCORE MODEL

Table 1.10 compares the original sample classification accuracy and also the accuracy for up to five years prior to financial distress of the Z-Score and ZETA® models. Note that the one-year prior classification accuracy of bankrupt firms is quite similar for both models (96.2 percent for ZETA® and 93.9 percent for Z-Score) but that the accuracy is consistently higher for the ZETA® model in years 2–5 prior to the distress date. Indeed, by the fifth year, the ZETA® model is still about 70 percent accurate but the Z-Score's accuracy falls to 36 percent. Note also that the Z-Score's accuracy on the ZETA® sample (columns 6 and 7) is actually considerably higher in years 2–5 than on the original sample. Finally, when we recalibrate the Z-Score model's coefficients based on the ZETA® sample, the classification results (column 8) are much better than the originals (column 4) in all but the first year prior.

Group Prior Probabilities, Error Costs and Model Efficiency

Earlier, we showed the classification rules for both linear and quadratic analyses. If one assumes equal prior probabilities of group membership, the linear model will result in a cutoff or critical score of zero. This is due to the constant term in the ZETA® model. All firms scoring above zero are classified as having characteristics similar to the non-bankrupt group and those with negative scores similar to bankrupts. The same zero cutoff score will result if one desired to minimize the total cost of misclassification. That is, assuming multi-normal populations and a common convariance matrix, the optimal cutoff score ZETA, is equal to

$$ZETA_c = \ln \frac{q_1 c_I}{q_2 c_{II}}$$

where q_1, q_2 is the prior probability of bankrupt (q_1) or non-bankrupt (q_2), and c_I, c_{II} are the costs of Type I and Type II errors, respectively.

Further, if one wanted to compare the efficiency of the ZETA® bankruptcy classification model with alternative strategies, the following cost function is appropriate for the expected cost of ZETA (EC_{ZETA}).

$$EC_{ZETA} = q_1 \frac{M_{12}}{N_1} c_I + q_2 \frac{M_{21}}{N_2} c_{II}$$

where M_{12}, M_{21} are the observed Type I and Type II errors (misses) respectively, and N_1, N_2 are the number of observations in the bankrupt (N_1) and non-bankrupt (N_2) groups.

In our tests, we have implicitly assumed equal prior probabilities and equal costs of errors, resulting in a zero cutoff score. We are actually aware, however, of the potential bias involved in doing so. Instead of attempting earlier to integrate probability priors and error costs, we have assumed equal estimates for each parameter, because to a great extent the two parameters neutralize each other, and it was much easier than attempting to state them precisely. The following is our reasoning.

The "correct" estimate of q_1 is probably in the range 0.01–0.05. That is, the prior probability that a firm will go bankrupt within a year or two is probably in this 0.01–0.05 range. Although the ZETA® model's parameters are based on data from one year prior to bankruptcy, it is not specifically a one-year prediction model. The procedure, in this sense, is attemporal. It is, in our opinion, incorrect to base one's prior probability estimates on a single year's reported statistics. In addition, there are many definitions of financial distress which economically approximate bankruptcy. These include non-judicial arrangements, extreme liquidity problems which require the firm's creditors or other external forces to take over the business or agree to a distressed restructuring (composition or extension of claims), bond default, etc. In the final analysis, we simply do not know the precise estimate of bankruptcy priors, but at the same time assert that one must assume the estimate is greater than a single year's reported data. Hence, we believe the prior probability estimate is in the 1–5 percent range. In the subsequent analysis, we utilize 2 percent.

COST OF CLASSIFICATION ERRORS

Another input that is imperative to the specification of an alternative to the zero cutoff score is the cost of error in classification. No prior study to the ZETA® analysis (Altman et al., 1977) had explicitly included this element analysis. To attempt to precise the cost component into an analysis of model efficiency, it is necessary to specify the decision maker's role. In this study, we utilize the commercial bank loan function as the framework of analysis. The Type I bankruptcy classification is analogous to that of an accepted loan that defaults and the Type II error to a rejected loan that would have resulted in a successful payoff. Many of the commercial factors involved in assessing these error costs were first noted in an excellent discussion [following Beaver's, (1967) paper] by Neter. It should be noted that even in 1999, commercial bankers are still struggling with a credible assumption of the total cost of lending errors.

An empirical study was performed to assess the costs of these lending errors with the following specification for the equivalent Type I (c_I) and Type II (c_{II}) error costs.

$$c_I = 1 - \frac{LLR}{GLL} \qquad c_{II} = r - i$$

where

> LLR = amount of loan losses recovered
> GLL = gross loan losses (charged-off)
>   r = effective interest rate on the loan
>   i = effective opportunity cost for the bank.

The commercial bank takes the risk of losing all or a portion of the loan should the applicant eventually default. The exact amount is a function of the success the bank has in recovering the loan principal. We are quite aware that there are additional costs involved in the recovery process, including legal, transaction, and loan charge-off officer opportunity costs. These costs are not reported but obviously increase the Type I error cost. In addition, if the Type II error (c_{II}) is positive, i.e., $r > 1$, then there will be an added cost element in c_I. This added element involves the lost interest on that remaining part of the loan which is not recovered (GLL – LLR) for the duration of the defaulted loan. We will examine c_{II} below, but will not include this added element in our calculation of c_I. Again, however, it is clear that we are underestimating c_I somewhat.

Recoveries in the Public Bond Market

While there has been almost no rigorous studies published which quantify the effective costs of lending errors for loans and other private placements, a number of recent studies have documented losses in the public bond markets (Altman and Eberhart, 1994; Moody's, 1995; Standard & Poor's, 1995). The former documents recoveries at default and also upon emergence from Chapter 11. These public bond market studies observe recoveries stratified by bond seniority. For commercial loans, the most likely equivalents to the public bond market are the straight (non-convertible) senior secured and senior unsecured classes. Table 1.11 lists these recoveries at the time of default and upon emergence from Chapter 11.

We have measured c_I based on annual report data from 26 of the largest US commercial banks and questionnaire returns from a sample of smaller, regional banks in the Southeast USA. A questionnaire was sent to approximately 100 Southeast banks

Table 1.11   Bond recoveries (% of par value), by seniority, at default and upon emergence from Chapter 11

Bond priority	N	Recovery at default (%)	Recovery upon emergence (%)
Senior secured	24	60.51	100.91
Senior unsecured	71	52.28	81.05
Senior subordinated	35	30.70	23.38
Subordinated	54	27.96	32.41

Source: Altman and Eberhart (1994), Altman (1993).

with 33 usable responses. The range of commercial bank asset sizes in this small-bank sample was between $12 million and $3 billion, with the average equal to $311 million and the median equal to $110 million. The large-bank sample's asset size averaged $13.4 billion with a $10 billion median.

Both the data sources encompass a five-year period, 1971–75 inclusive, and we measure the average loan loss recovery statistics for senior unsecured loans on a contemporary and a one-year lag (recoveries lagging charge-offs) basis. The results of this investigation show that the average c_1 on a contemporary basis is in the 76.7–83.0 percent range; when measured on a one-year lag basis, the averages are lower (68.6–72.2 percent). The year 1975 was an abnormally high loan charge-off year in the US banking system and since this data is included in the contemporary statistics but not in the one-year lag data, we believe the more representative result for c_1 is in the vicinity of 70 percent. We use this statistic for c_1.

The simple formula for c_{II} specifies that the decision not to lend to an account that would have repaid successfully forgoes the return on that loan, but the loss is mitigated by the alternative use of loanable funds. In its strictest sense, the bank's opportunity cost implies another loan at the same risk which is assumed to pay off. In this case, c_{II} is probably zero or extremely small. Conservatively speaking, however, an account is rejected due to its high risk characteristics and alternative uses probably will carry lower risk attributes. Hence, $r - i$ will be positive but still quite low. Carried to the other extreme, the alternative use would be an investment in a riskless asset, i.e., government securities of the same maturity as the loan, and $r - i$ will be somewhat higher – perhaps 2–4 percent. The relationship between r and i will vary over time and is particularly sensitive to the demand and supply equilibrium relationship for loanable funds. As an approximation, we specify c_{II} as 2 percent; hence c_1/c_{II} is equal to 35 times (0.70/0.20).

Revised Cutoff Score and Model Efficiency Tests

With respect now to the calculation of the critical or cutoff score ZETA_c, we have,

$$\text{ZETA}_c = \ln \frac{q_1 c_1}{q_2 c_{II}} = \ln \frac{0.02 \cdot 0.70}{0.98 \cdot 0.02} = \ln 0.714$$

$$\text{ZETA}_c = -0.337.$$

Before comparing the efficiency of the various alternative bankruptcy classification strategies, it should be noted that the observed classification accuracy of a model such as ZETA will change with the new cutoff score. For example, with the cutoff score of −0.337, the number of Type I errors increases from two (3.8 percent) to four (7.6 percent), while the Type II errors decreases from 6 (10.3 percent) to 4 (7.0 percent).

Adjustments to the Cutoff Score and Practical Applications

In addition to the utilization of prior probabilities of group membership and cost estimates of classification errors for comparative model efficiency assessment, these inputs could prove valuable for practical application purposes. For instance, the bank lending-officer or loan-review analyst may wish to be able to logically adjust the critical cutoff score to consider his own estimates of group priors and error costs and/or to reflect current economic conditions in the analysis. One could imagine the cutoff score falling (thereby lowering the acceptance criterion) as business conditions improve and the banker's prior probability of bankruptcy estimate falls from say 0.02 to 0.015. Or, a rise in cutoff scores could result from a change (rise) in the estimate of the Type I error cost *vis-à-vis* the Type II error cost. The latter condition possibly will occur for different decision makers. For instance, the cost to a portfolio manager of not selling a security destined for failure is likely to be extremely high relative to his cost of not investing in a stock (which does not fail) due to its relatively low $ZETA_c$. The portfolio manager may indeed want to raise the cutoff or threshold level to reduce the possibility of intangible (law suit costs) as well as tangible (lower prices) costs involved with holding a failed company's stock.

Another example of a practical application of cutoff score adjustment is the case of an accounting auditor. He might wish to use the model to decide whether a "going concern" qualified opinion should be applied. His expected cost for doing so is likely to be quite high (loss of client) relative to the expected cost of a stockholder law suit. This might lead to a fairly low cutoff score. On the other hand, the environment may be such that the law suit expected cost is prohibitive.

Conclusions

The ZETA® model for assessing bankruptcy risk of corporations demonstrates improved accuracy over existing failure classification model (Z-Score) and, perhaps more importantly, is based on data more relevant to current conditions and to a larger number of industrial firms. Recall, however, our use of the Z″ model for non-manufacturers. We are concerned with refining existing distress classification techniques by the use of the most relevant data, combined with developments in the application of discriminant analysis to finance. The ZETA® model's bankruptcy classification accuracy ranges from over 96 percent (93 percent holdout) one period prior to bankruptcy to 70 percent five annual reporting periods prior. We have assessed the effect of several elements involved with the application of discriminant analysis to financial problems. These include linear vs. quadratic analysis for the original and holdout samples, introduction of prior probabilities of group membership and costs of error estimates into the classification rule, and comparison of the model's results with naïve bankruptcy classification strategies.

The potential applications of the ZETA® bankruptcy identification model are in the same spirit as previously developed models. These include creditworthiness analysis of firms for financial and non-financial institutions, identification of undesirable investment risk for portfolio managers and individual investors, and to aid in more effective internal and external audits of firms with respect to going-concern considerations, among others.

REFERENCES

Altman, E., "Financial Ratios, Discriminant Analysis and the Prediction of Corporate Bankruptcy," *Journal of Finance* 23, September 1968, 589–609.
Altman, E., "Predicting Railroad Bankruptcies in America," *Bell Journal of Economics and Management Service*, Spring 1973.

Altman, E., *Corporate Financial Distress and Bankruptcy*, 2nd ed., John Wiley & Sons, New York, 1993.

Altman, E., and A. C. Eberhart, "Do Seniority Provisions Protect Bondholders' Investments?" *Journal of Portfolio Management*, Summer 1994.

Altman, E., and J. LaFleur, "Managing a Return to Financial Health," *Journal of Business Strategy*, Summer 1981.

Altman, E., R. Eisenbeis, and J. Sinkey, *Applications of Classification Procedures in Business, Banking and Finance*, JAI Press, Greenwich, CT, 1981.

Altman, E., R. Haldeman, and P. Narayanan, "ZETA Analysis: A New Model to Identify Bankruptcy Risk of Corporations," *Journal of Banking and Finance*, June 1977.

Altman, E., J. Hartzell, and M. Peck, *"Emerging Markets Corporate Bonds: A Scoring System,"* Salomon Brothers Inc, New York, 1995.

Beaver, W., "Financial Ratios as Predictors of Failures," in *Empirical Research in Accounting*, selected studies, 1966 in supplement to the *Journal of Accounting Research*, January 1967.

Deakin, E. B., "A Discriminant Analysis of Predictors of Business Failure," *Journal of Accounting Research*, March 1972.

Dun & Bradstreet, "The Failure Record," 1994, and annually.

Fisher, L., "Determinants of Risk Premiums on Corporate Bonds," *Journal of Political Economy*, June 1959.

Lachenbruch, P. A., "An Almost Unbiased Method of Obtaining Confidence Intervals for the Probability of Misclassification in Discriminant analysis," *Biometrics*, 23, 1967.

Moody's, "Corporate Bond Defaults and Default Rates," L. Carty, D. Lieberman, and J. Fons, January 1995.

Moody's, E. Falkensten, A. Boral and L. Carty, "RiskCalc™ Private Model: Moody's Default Model for Private Firms," Global Credit Research, May 2000.

Osler, C. and G. Hong, "Rapidly Rising Corporate Debt: Are Firms Now Vulnerable to an Economic Slowdown?" *Current Issues in Economics & Finance*, Federal Reserve Bank of New York, June 2000.

Standard & Poor's, "Corporate Defaults Level Off in 1994," L. Brand, T. K. Ho, and R. Bahar, *CreditWeek*, May 1, 1995.

ZETA®, "ZETA Analysis, A New Model for Bankruptcy Classification," *Journal of Banking and Finance*, June 1977.

2 | Introducing Recursive Partitioning for Financial Classification: The Case of Financial Distress

Halina Frydman, Edward I. Altman, and Duen-Li Kao

In the last decade and a half, numerous statistical classification models have been constructed for finance-related purposes. These models typically link a set of "independent" variables to a "dependent" variable; the latter can take on two or more discrete values. Classification problems in finance are usually based on two groups whereby observations are assigned to one of the groups after data analysis (e.g., commercial loans classified into default vs. nondefault groups, convertible bonds into conversion–nonconversion groups, public vs. private ownership of firms, and bankrupt vs. non-bankrupt groups). Studies involved with a dependent variable which can take on more than two values, i.e., multigroup models, are less common, e.g., bond or common stock ratings. The relationship of the dependent variable can be ordered or not, although in finance there is usually some implicit, if not explicit, hierarchy of groupings, e.g., bond ratings. Even if there is an implicit ranking, the intervals between the rankings are not specified.

With respect to the explanatory variables, multivariate techniques have replaced univariate approaches as data sources, and computer programs to manipulate and examine data have become available and more powerful. Researchers have found that greater information content and accuracy can be derived from more complex model specifications. The most commonly used multivariate classification technique has been discriminant analysis with a number of other parametric techniques suggested to overcome some of the perceived shortcomings in the discriminant methodology. For example, multigroup logit models have been used to provide a more realistic and explicit interval measure between adjacent groups (e.g., Kaplan and Urwitz [17]) in bond rating studies. Probit models attempt to provide explicit probabilities of group membership. Two-group regression analysis can provide a more accepted method for evaluating an individual variable's relative contribution.

One thing that all of these models have in common is the parametric quality of the linkage between the explanatory variables and the groupings. While this enables explicit

linkages, a host of statistical problems have been cited as rendering the results somewhat problematic. The potential problems can be categorized as

1 violations of the underlying normality and independence assumptions of the
   classical linear regression or discriminant approaches
2 reduction of dimensionality issues
3 interpretation of the relative importance of individual variables
4 specification of the appropriate classification algorithm, and
5 time-series prediction test interpretation.[1]

Several of these issues will be explored later in section II.

Despite these problems and the perceived lack of a formal theoretical underpinning
of most of the models, multivariate procedures have flourished in a number of areas
with increased acceptance by both academics and financial practitioners. Perhaps the
best illustration of this flourishing, distinguished by a number of attempts over time to
improve classification, is the area of financial distress prediction. The emphasis put on
models of bankruptcy classification and prediction is partly the result of the dramatic
increase in business failures all over the world but also of the relative success that these
models have enjoyed since the original multivariate Z-Score approach (Altman [1])
which followed the more traditional univariate method of Beaver [6]. The specter of
statistical validity questions as well as attempts to improve classification and prediction
accuracy have motivated a steady stream of "new models." Scott [21] reviews many of
these empirical models and finds that some of the more well-known ones conform to his
notion of a theoretical distress scenario.

The purpose of this paper is to present a new classification procedure called Recursive Partitioning Algorithm (RPA) for financial analysis and to compare it to discriminant analysis (DA). The essence of RPA was originally presented by Friedman [13]. A
more general treatment of RPA was given in Breiman and Stone [8] and its statistical
properties were discussed in Gordon and Olshen [15]. An excellent and comprehensive
exposition of RPA methodology can be found in the recent book by Breiman et al. [9].
RPA is a computerized, nonparametric classification technique, based on pattern recognition. It has attributes of both the classical univariate approach to classification and
multivariate procedures. The model which results from RPA is in the form of a binary
classification tree which assigns objects into selected *a priori* groups.

RPA has been applied in the area of medical decision making (Goldman et al. [14],
Levy et al. [18]), in mass spectra classification (Breiman [7]), and in a recent paper by
Marais et al. [19] to commercial loan classification for public and privately held firms.
The latter compare RPA results with a polytomous probit function in order to replicate
a commercial bank loan review department's classifications into four problem loan
rating classes. Some of the interesting features of this study are the use of both financial
statement ratios and nonratio indicators, public and private firm data comparison, an
examination of the results using uniform vs. bank-specific loss functions, and use of a
bootstrap procedure to estimate the expected cost of misclassification.[2]

---

[1] See Altman et al. [3] for a detailed discussion of these points.
[2] We were made aware of this working paper by the *Journal*'s referee and, to our knowledge, our study and
the Marais et al. paper [19] are the only applications of the RPA methodology in finance.

Our vehicle for illustrating RPA is the classification of financial distress of firms. We will show that, while both RPA and the classical discriminant analysis techniques lead to rather accurate classification results on a data set of bankrupt and non-bankrupt firms, the RPA usually dominates the DA. The magnitude of dominance, which depends on the specification of costs of misclassification and prior probabilities, varies from slight to large. At the same time, RPA's simple, unambiguous binary classification scheme does not have a precise scoring system that is associated with discriminant analysis. It should be made clear at the outset that the purpose of our paper is not to produce the most efficient financial distress prediction model to date. We are more concerned with the qualities of an alternative classification technique and its potential for future applications in finance.

This paper concentrates mainly on RPA and its unique qualities. Although a number of techniques have been put forth to tackle the bankruptcy issue, the standard for comparison is still the DA structure. Since the discriminant analysis format is well known, little time will be spent on its description except when we contrast it with RPA. Sections I and II present RPA and these contrasts. Sections III and IV present the sample properties and empirical results of our comparison tests. Section V discusses the implications of these results, including an analysis of the information benefits derived from utilizing both RPA and DA models for evaluating the performance of firms. Section VI concludes with a summary.

I   THE RECURSIVE PARTITIONING ALGORITHM

The purpose of this section is to provide a brief but self-contained description of the essential features of RPA. To facilitate the exposition we restrict the analysis to a two-group case and use classification of financial distress of firms as an illustrative context. We find it instructive to describe first the nature of the RPA classification model and next the steps in the construction of the model.

A   *The RPA Classification Tree*

The inputs to RPA include an original sample consisting of observed data of N objects, together with their actual group classification as well as specification of prior probabilities and costs of misclassifications. We will denote the prior probability of the object belonging to group i by π_i and the cost of misclassifying a group i object to group j by c_{ij}.

The model is in the form of a binary classification tree. As an illustration, in figure 2.1 we present an actual tree, constructed by RPA from financial data of 200 bankrupt (group 1) and non-bankrupt (group 2) firms, based on the stated prior probabilities and misclassification costs. This tree has five terminal nodes, which are the circled nodes in figure 2.1. These represent the final classification of all firms. The 200 firms are distributed among terminal nodes according to their financial characteristics, e.g., the firms with Cash Flow/Total Debt ≤ .1309 and Retained Earnings/Total Assets ≤ .1453 fall into the leftmost terminal node.

In essence, the RPA model partitions variable space into several rectangular regions defined by the characteristics of terminal nodes. All objects falling into a given terminal node, that is, a given region of variable space, are assigned to the same group, e.g., the

Figure 2.1   Tree (1)

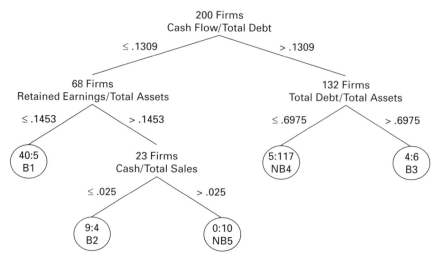

Classification tree based on financial data on 200 firms, prior probabilites of bankrupt and non-bankrupt groups $(\pi_1, \pi_2) = (0.02, 0.98)$, and misclassification costs $c_{12} = 50$, $c_{21} = 1$. The firms with the value of the partitioning variable higher than the cutoff value go right. The terminal nodes are circled. The leftmost terminal node has 45 firms of which 40 are group 1 and five are group 2 firms. This is a group 1 (bankrupt) node which is denoted by letter B in the circle. The group 2 terminal nodes are denoted by letters NB. The numbers following the letters B and NB can be ignored in this section. This tree misclassifies five bankrupt and 15 non-bankrupt firms. Its resubstitution risk $R(T) = 0.19$.

leftmost node of Tree (1) in figure 2.1 is a group 1, distressed firm classification, node. A new object to be classified descends down the tree and is assigned to the group identified with the terminal node into which it falls.

B   Resubstitution Risk of RPA Classification Tree

The terminal nodes of a classification tree are assigned to groups in such a way as to minimize the observed expected cost of misclassification of each assignment. Another term for the observed expected cost of misclassification, which we will use in what follows, is resubstitution risk.[3] Consider a terminal node t which has $n_i(t)$ objects from group i and let N_i be the size of the entire original sample for the ith group, $i = 1, 2$. The risk of assigning node t to group 1 is defined as

$$R_1(t) = c_{21}p(2, t) = c_{21}\pi_2 p(t \mid 2) = c_{21}\pi_2 n_2(t)/N_2$$

---

[3]   Risk is another term for expected cost of misclassification, and "resubstitution" refers to the fact that risk is evaluated with the original sample's data. When the term risk is used alone, it should be understood as resubstitution risk. Similarly, when the term probability is used, it should be understood as the probability estimated from the original sample's data.

Here $p(2, t)$ is the probability that an object is from group 2 and falls into node t and $p(t \mid 2) = n_2(t)/N_2$ is the conditional probability of a group 2 object falling into node t. Similarly,

$$R_2(t) = c_{12}\pi_1 n_1(t)/N_1$$

The terminal node t is assigned to a group corresponding to the minimum risk; thus the assignment rule is a Bayesian rule. The resulting Bayes risk of node t is

$$R(t) = \min(R_1(t), R_2(t))$$

The risk of the entire tree T, denoted $R(T)$, is the sum of risks of its terminal nodes. Note that if $c_{12} = c_{21} = 1$ and $\pi_i = N_i/N$, $i = 1, 2$, i.e., the prior probabilities are the original sample proportions of group 1 and group 2 objects, then $R_i(t) = n_i(t)/N$ is a sample proportion of group i objects falling into node t. In this case, the assignment rule is particularly simple: each terminal node is assigned to a group which has majority representation in this node, and the risk of the tree is simply the overall misclassification rate of the tree.

C   RPA Model Construction

STEP 1: CONSTRUCTING SMALL RESUBSTITUTION RISK TREES

The objective in Step 1 is to construct a classification tree with a small resubstitution risk. The following procedure for tree construction used in RPA usually achieves this objective. First, the original sample, thought of as located at the root (top) of the tree, is split into two subsamples according to the "best" splitting rule defined below. The two subsamples "land" in the left and right subnodes of the root node. Next, the process is repeated for each subsample, i.e., each subsample is split further according to the best splitting rule for the subsample. The process continues until the termination criterion, described below, is satisfied.

The best splitting rule for a subsample is selected from the class of univariate splitting rules, i.e., rules which involve splitting an axis of one variable at one point.[4] The criterion for selecting the best splitting rule is based on the measure of sample impurity. The general measure of sample impurity used in RPA is described in Appendix A.

The best splitting rule for the given sample is defined as the one which maximizes the decrease in the sum of the impurities of the two resulting subsamples compared with the impurity of the parent sample (see Appendix A). In order to find the best splitting rule, the algorithm first searches for the best splitting point for each explanatory variable and then the best of these splits is selected.[5]

---

[4]   For this study, we restrict the class of splitting rules to univariate rules. It is possible to utilize RPA with the class of rules which involve linear combinations of variables, but the resulting model can be extremely cumbersome and difficult to interpret.

[5]   For each ordered variable X, the original sample contains at most N distinct values $X_1 < X_2 < X_3 < \cdots < X_N$. The candidate splits are of the form "Is $X \le c?$," where c is the midpoint between consecutive distinct values of variable X. Thus, for each ordered variable there are at most $N - 1$ candidate splits. For a categorical variable taking on L distinct values, there are 2^{L-1} candidate splits.

The impurity measure has a simple definition when misclassification costs are equal to unit costs and prior probabilities are given by sample proportions of group 1 and group 2 objects. Suppose that group 1 objects in the sample are assigned numerical value 1 and group 2 objects the value 0. The measure of impurity is then given by the sample variance of the numerical values. The sample impurity is equal to zero if and only if all objects in the sample belong to the same group and attains its maximum value when the sample contains the same number of group 1 and group 2 objects.

The splitting procedure terminates when it is impossible, by further splitting, to decrease the impurity of a current tree (defined as the sum of the impurities of all the terminal nodes). The obtained tree will be referred to as T_{max}.

STEP 2: SELECTING THE CORRECT COMPLEXITY FOR A TREE BY CROSS-VALIDATION TESTS

T_{max} trees are usually complex trees which overfit the data. That is, their resubstitution risks usually underestimate, often by much, their true risks. To put it differently, T_{max} trees involve splits specific to the original sample characteristics but not necessarily representative of the population structure. The objective of Step 2 is to select a tree of correct complexity, from the subtrees of the T_{max} tree, according to the following procedure. Consider all possible trees obtained by arbitrarily terminating the splitting procedure described in Step 1. For each tree T in this set compute,

$$R(T) + K \times \text{Number of terminal nodes of } T \qquad (1)$$

where K is a nonnegative constant interpreted as a penalty for complex trees. For a given K, choose tree T which minimizes the function in (1). Clearly, when $K = 0$, the optimal tree, i.e., the one which minimizes (1), is T_{max}. For any positive value of K, the optimal tree is a subtree of T_{max}. As K increases, the optimal tree becomes less complex but has a larger resubstitution risk. For a sufficiently large value of K, the optimal tree is a no-split tree. For example, Tree (1), in Figure 2.1, is optimal for small values of penalty K. When K is increased, the split on Total Debt/Total Assets is eliminated. In this case, there is no value of the penalty parameter for which the tree with two splits is optimal; that is, further increase in K results in a no-split tree.

Thus, criterion (1) gives rise to a nested sequence of classification trees of decreasing complexity and increasing resubstitution risk. The final classification tree is selected from this sequence as the one with the smallest cross-validated risk. The cross-validated risk of tree T is computed using a V-fold cross-validation procedure. In this procedure, all observations in the sample are randomly divided into V groups of approximately equal sizes. Observations in $V - 1$ groups are used to construct the tree corresponding to the penalty K chosen from the range of values of penalty parameters for which tree T was optimal, based on all of the observations. The observations in the group left out are classified by the newly constructed tree. The procedure is repeated V times, each time with a different group being left out. The cross-validated error rates and risk of tree T are obtained by averaging the resubstitution error rates and risks from all cross-validation trials. Typically, the minimum cross-validated risk tree is less complex than T_{max}.

In addition to the V-fold procedure, other criteria can be used to choose the final tree. These include bootstrap analysis, expert judgment concerning the appropriate complexity of the model, holdout samples, etc. Our rationale for adopting the minimum

V-fold cross-validation approach is that it yields reliable estimates of the true risk of classification trees when the sample size is large, as it is in our study.[6]

II COMPARISON OF THE RECURSIVE PARTITIONING ALGORITHM AND DISCRIMINANT ANALYSIS

RPA and DA are both Bayesian procedures with their classification rules derived in such a way as to minimize the expected cost of misclassification. To be more specific, recall that the general Bayes rule in the two-group case is of the form:

Assign an observation with a vector of attribute variables x to group 1 if

$$\frac{f_1(x)}{f_2(x)} \geq \frac{\pi_2 c_{21}}{\pi_1 c_{12}}$$

otherwise assign it to group 2. Here f_1 and f_2 represent the multivariate probability density functions of variables for groups 1 and 2.

DA makes the Bayes rule operational by assuming that densities f_1 and f_2 are multivariate normal. If we also assume that covariance matrices of the two densities are equal, Bayes rule reduces to the:

Linear discriminant rule: Assign observation x to groups 1 if

$$x'\gamma - a \geq \ln\left[\frac{c_{21}\pi_2}{c_{12}\pi_1}\right]$$

otherwise assign it to group 2, where $\gamma = \Sigma^{-1}(\pi_1 - \pi_2)$, $\alpha = (\mu_1 + \mu_2)'$. $\gamma/2$, μ_1, μ_2 are group means, and Σ is a common covariance matrix.

RPA is a nonparametric technique which minimizes the expected cost of misclassification by the univariate splitting procedure described in section I.

One of the primary differences in the two classification techniques is the manner in which they partition the variable space into classification regions. In order to illustrate this difference, suppose that variable space is two-dimensional and consider a hypothetical

---

[6] Simulation studies have shown (Breiman et al. [9]) that estimates resulting from V-fold cross-validation, with $V = 5$ or $V = 10$, are satisfactorily close to the true risk of classification trees. V-fold cross-validation is preferred to the holdout sample method of estimating risk if the sample size is not large. It is also preferred to the bootstrap method of estimating true risk (see footnote 11 for a brief description of the bootstrap method) because theoretical considerations and simulation studies show that bootstrap estimates of the true risks of classification trees are substantially downwardly biased for some data structures. This downward bias is especially serious for complex trees. Cross-validated estimates are only slightly biased but have larger variances than bootstrap estimates. Thus, unless variances of cross-validated estimates are unacceptably large, which is likely to happen when the sample size is small, these estimates are preferred to bootstrap estimates and are used in Breiman et al. [9] in all of the empirical examples. But Marais et al. [19] use the bootstrap procedure to estimate true risks of their models because the effective size of their samples is very small (less than 10). For a recent analysis of these issues in the context of general classification techniques and an introduction to modified bootstrap procedures, see Efron [11].

RPA model (figure 2.2a) constructed from a sample consisting of objects from two groups. This model partitions the variable space (A, B) into four rectangular regions as shown in figure 2.2b. Objects falling into regions 1 and 2 are classified as group 1 and those falling into regions 3 and 4 as group 2. Now consider a hypothetical discriminant function $f(x) = x'\gamma - \alpha$, where $x = (A, B)$, constructed from the same data, and a cutoff point c. The line $f(x) = c$ divides variable space into two half-plane regions with the region $\{x: f(x) \geq c\}$ assigned to group 2 and the region $\{x: f(x) < c\}$ to group 1 (figure 2.2b). The essence of the space partitioning by the two models for higher dimensional problems is the same.

The RPA classification rule partitions variable space, in general, into a number of rectangular regions. The two-group DA classification rule, on the other hand, partitions the variable space into only two half-plane regions. Again referring to figure 2.2b, one can observe that differences in the final classification of RPA and DA are denoted by observations falling into the shaded areas.

Another important difference in the two classification techniques is the manner in which prior probabilities and costs of misclassification impact the resulting model. DA models are established first by group separation criteria, i.e., by maximizing the between-group to within-group variance, and only then is the classification rule established for assigning observations into the specified groups based on specified error costs and prior probabilities. RPA, on the other hand, simultaneously determines the variables selection and group assignments with the costs and priors helping to determine the specific variables and splitting score. Changing the costs and priors might very well change the variable selected for splitting; this is not so for DA. Hence, RPA models appear to be more sensitive to costs and priors than DA models.

Figure 2.2 (a) "Hypothetical" tree for two-group classification. (B) Partitioning of the variable space (A, B) corresponding to tree in (a) and to the discriminant function constructed from the same hypothetical data

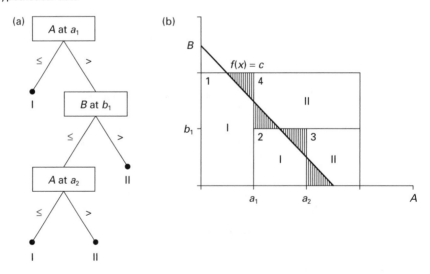

The numbering of the regions is indicated in the upper left corner of the region.

We have also noted that RPA is a nonparametric technique which eliminates many of the statistical problems attributed to DA (Eisenbeis [12]). Three key assumptions of the linear DA model are that

1   variables describing the members of the group observations are multivariate normally distributed within each group
2   group covariances are equal across all groups, and
3   groups are discrete, nonoverlapping, and identifiable.

Only the latter assumption is also necessary for RPA.

In fact, deviations from the normality assumption in studies dealing with financial and economic variables are usually the rule. For example, many common ratios are lower bounded by zero but possess no theoretical upper bound and can get quite large, e.g., Sales/Total Assets. Nonnormal distributions can bias the classification results by impacting the assignment rule away from the optimal value. While results may be suboptimal, accuracies still can be acceptable despite the lack of normality (Altman et al. [5]). RPA is not limited by any distributional assumptions and, in this respect, represents an attractive alternative to DA. RPA is also particularly suited for analyzing discrete variables.

The assumption of equal group covariance matrices is also often violated. Relaxation of this assumption in the linear case affects the significance tests for differences in group means and also the appropriate form of classification rules. Tests of covariance are now quite readily available. When covariances are found not to be equal, the theoretical prescription is to apply a quadratic structure which does not rely on the equal covariances between group assumption. Quadratic models, however, while quite accurate on original samples, are uniformly disappointing *vis-à-vis* linear models in holdout sample tests (Altman et al. [5] and Martin [20]). Tests have also shown that violations of the equality of group covariances are a function of the number of variables and the relative sizes of the groups. Smaller number of variables and equal group sizes seem to lead to less biased results. Again, RPA is completely unaffected by group covariance attributes since the splitting point is not influenced by outliers.

With respect to the interpretation of the relative importance of individual variables, both the DA and RPA models present some unique aspects which could lead to interpretation problems. It is fair to say that there is a distinct lack of agreement as to which test is most appropriate in determining the relative importance of discriminant variables. Indeed, we are aware of as many as six different tests as discussed in Joy and Tollefson [16] and Altman and Eisenbeis [4]. While we are not concerned with the individual variable significance compared to the overall profile of variables, it is instructive to assess the univariate contribution.

RPA has a similar quality that is found in most forward stepwise approaches to variable selection. Once a variable is selected as the first splitting variable, the tree is constrained to include that measure first. But, as illustrated in figure 2.2a, in RPA the same variable may be used more than once as the partitioning variable. Similar constraints are manifest as additional variables are chosen. Since the RPA is not looking forward beyond the splitting it is currently performing, the resulting model is not an optimal one. Therefore, in both DA and RPA models, individual variable contributions are not completely unambiguous.

In section V we will compare a different aspect of the two techniques, namely, their scoring systems.

III   SAMPLE CHARACTERISTICS AND CHOICE OF VARIABLES

Our sample has 58 bankrupt industrial companies which failed during 1971–81.[7] We randomly selected 142 non-bankrupt manufacturing and retailing companies from the COMPUSTAT universe. The financial years investigated were also randomly chosen from the period 1971–81 and not matched to the exact years of the bankrupt group. This 200-firm sample is available from the authors.

We used 20 financial variables which had been found significant in predicting business failure by three relevant studies (Altman [1], Deakin [10]; Altman et al. [5]) as our variable set. An adjustment for the capitalization of leases was applied to all the variables. Firms have been required to capitalize financial leases since 1980, so models which purport to have applicability in the post-1980 period should adjust past data based on the latest reporting standards (Altman et al. [5]). The variable set is described in appendix B.

IV   DEVELOPMENT OF MODELS AND CLASSIFICATION RESULTS

A   Prior Probabilities and Misclassification Costs

In this section we empirically compare recursive partitioning with discriminant analysis models. The comparison is based on a sample of 200 firms and carried out for misclassification cost c_{12} ranging from 1 to 70, in the way indicated in table 2.1, while $c_{21} = 1$. The prior probabilities of the bankrupt and non-bankrupt groups were fixed at $(\pi_1, \pi_2) = (0.02, 0.98)$.

B   Recursive Partitioning Models (RPA)

For each cost specified in table 2.1, we chose two classification trees, from the sequence of trees resulting from RPA, as RPA models for comparison with DA models. For the first RPA model (RPA1), we chose a relatively complex tree. For the second RPA model (RPA2), we chose the tree with the smallest fivefold cross-validated risk. The smallest cross-validated risk tree was always less complex than the first model tree and, with one exception, it never had more than three splits.

We next illustrate the sensitivity of the obtained RPA models to change in misclassification costs. The classification trees in figure 2.1 and 2.3 are based on $c_{12} = 50$ and $c_{12} = 20$, respectively. These trees were chosen from the more complex RPA models. We observe that the first split in both trees involves the variable Cash Flow/Total Debt, but the actual splitting point on the axis of this variable is different for the two trees. In fact, the inspection of all the models, including those not presented here, shows that Cash Flow/Total Debt is the most important discriminator between bankrupt and

---

[7]   The bankrupt group includes 16 companies that filed for bankruptcy under Chapter 11 but still were listed on the regular COMPUSTAT tape. The *Wall Street Journal Index* was used to find the date that the companies filed for bankruptcy.

Table 2.1 Misclassification of firms in the original sample by the models for different misclassification costs*

| | c_{12} | | | | | | | | | | | | | | | | | | | | | | | |
| | 1 | | | 10 | | | 20 | | | 30 | | | 40 | | | 50 | | | 60 | | | 70 | | |
Model	I	II	T	I	II	T	I	II	T	I	II	T	I	II	T	I	II	T	I	II	T	I	II	T
RPA1	18	0	(18)	14	3	(17)	9	2	(11)	6	11	(17)	6	11	(17)	5	15	(20)	5	12	(17)	2	18	(20)
RPA2	58	0	(58)	19	3	(22)	14	2	(16)	9	19	(28)	9	19	(28)	9	19	(28)	9	9	(18)	4	25	(29)
DA1	48	0	(48)	25	5	(30)	17	11	(28)	13	14	(27)	11	15	(26)	9	17	(26)	8	18	(26)	7	22	(29)
DA2	54	1	(55)	33	6	(39)	18	12	(30)	12	16	(28)	11	21	(32)	8	27	(35)	6	29	(35)	6	30	(36)

* For each model and cost, we list the number of Type I misclassifications (a bankrupt firm classified as non-bankrupt), Type II misclassifications (a non-bankrupt firm classified as bankrupt), and a total number of misclassifications (in parentheses).

non-bankrupt groups for the cost c_{12} ranging from 10 to 70.[8] While the trees are stable in terms of the first split, further splits result in somewhat different variables, number of variables, sequencing, and split points.

We next observe, for costs 20 and 50, the trees with the smallest cross-validated risk. For $c_{12} = 20$, the smallest cross-validated risk tree is obtained from Tree (2), shown in

Table 2.2 Resubstitution risks of the model*

Model				c_{12}				
	1	10	20	30	40	50	60	70
RPA1	0.006	0.069	0.076	0.138	0.159	0.190	0.186	0.173
RPA2	0.020	0.086	0.111	0.224	0.255	0.286	0.248	0.269
DA1	0.017	0.121	0.193	0.231	0.255	0.272	0.290	0.321
DA2	0.022	0.155	0.207	0.235	0.297	0.324	0.324	0.352

* *Resubstitution risk* $= \pi_1 c_{12} n_1/N_1 + \pi_2 c_{21} n_2/N_2$ *where* n_i = *total number of Type i misclassifications,* N_i = *sample size of the ith group, i = 1, 2.*

Figure 2.3 Tree (2)

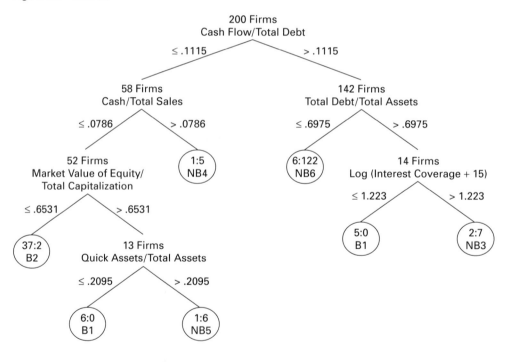

Classification tree based on financial data on 200 firms, prior probabilities $(\pi_1, \pi_2) = (0.02, 0.98)$, and misclassification costs $c_{12} = 20, c_{21} = 1$.

---

[8] Cash Flow/Total Debt was also Beaver's [6] best univariate measure. For equal misclassification costs $(c_{12} = 1)$, however, the first split involves the variable Cash/Total Sales.

figure 2.3, by eliminating splits on variables Total Debt/Total Assets and Log (Interest Coverage + 15). For $c_{12} = 50$, it is a one-split subtree of Tree (1).

Table 2.1 illustrates the dependence of classification results on the cost structure. Typically, specification of costs would depend on the context in which bankruptcy prediction is made and may involve subjective judgment.[9] Table 2.1 allows assessment of the consequences in terms of error rates and risks of different specifications of misclassification costs and may lead to a re-evaluation of any particular specification.

C Discriminant Analysis Models (DA)

We constructed two discriminant functions. The first (DA1) was obtained by a forward stepwise method. It included 10 of the 20 variables considered. The variables and their coefficients are presented in table 2.3. We also constructed a second discriminant function (DA2 model) using only the four most important variables according to the forward stepwise method. The coefficients of the 4-variable discriminant function are also presented in table 2.3.

D Comparing RPA and DA Models

The resubstitution classification results of the RPA1 models dominate the results of both DA1 and DA2 models for all costs. Recall from section I that, for every cost,

Table 2.3 Discriminant analysis models

Variable	Unstandardized coefficient	Standardized coefficient
DA1 Model: Stepwise Forward Discriminant Function		
Net Income/Total Assets	5.452	0.527
Current Assets/Current Liabilities	1.758	1.419
Log (Total Assets)	0.505	0.348
Market Value of Equity/Total Capitalization	1.850	0.409
Current Assets/Total Assets	−6.292	−1.068
Cash Flow/Total Debt	−1.021	−0.331
Quick Assets/Total Assets	8.970	1.062
Quick Assets/Current Liabilities	−1.995	−1.112
Earnings Before Interest and Taxes/Total Assets	3.482	0.350
Log (Interest Coverage + 15)	−1.033	−0.165
Constant term = −1.761		
DA2 Model: 4-Variable Discriminant Function		
Net Income/Total Assets	5.322	0.514
Current Assets/Current Liabilities	0.622	0.528
Log (Total Assets)	0.712	0.491
Market Value of Equity/Total Capitalization	1.149	0.328
Constant term = −4.041		

[9] Many studies have implicitly assumed that the costs of misclassifications are equal. However, Altman [2] estimated that, for commercial bank lending officers, classification of a bankrupt firm in the non-bankrupt group is 32 to 62 times more costly than the reverse misclassification.

RPA2 tree is a subtree of RPA1 tree, hence RPA2 has a larger resubstitution risk. This can be seen clearly in figure 2.4.

The RPA2 model outperforms the DA2 model in terms of fewer number of misclassifications for all costs except $c_{12} = 1$ and is tied for $c_{12} = 30$. For this cost, the RPA2 model coincides with the "naive" model, which classifies all firms to the non-bankrupt group.

The comparison of RPA2 with DA1 for costs ranging from 10 to 70 shows that either RPA2 dominates DA1 substantially (by at least eight correct classifications) or DA1 slightly dominates RPA2 (by at most two correct classifications). For the cost $c_{12} = 50$, the number of type I misclassifications is the same for both models. Finally, the comparison of the results of DA1 and DA2 shows the DA1 dominates DA2 in terms of the total number of correct classifications for all costs, but for costs 30 and above, DA2 classifies correctly more bankrupt firms than DA1.

In table 2.2, we compute the risks for all models and all costs. RPA1 models dominate the other models for all costs. RPA2 models are second best for all costs except costs 1 and 50; for these costs, DA1 models have slightly lower risks than RPA2 models. For cost 40, the risks of RPA2 and DA1 models are identical, but note (in table 2.1) that classification results are not. In general, RPA2 and DA1 models have very similar risks in the middle range of costs, ($c_{12} = 30$–60) while the risk of RPA2 is smaller for the low and high costs (except for $c_{12} = 1$). As expected, risks of DA2 models are somewhat larger than those of DA1 models.

Figure 2.4 Resubstitution risks

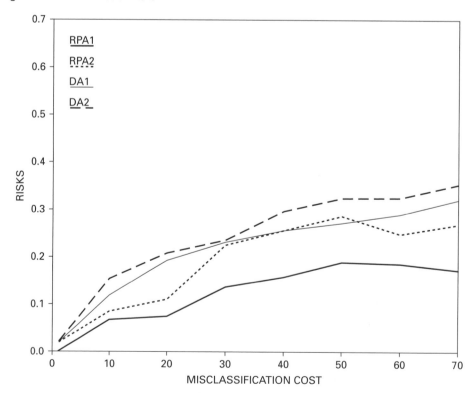

The performance of the models can also be evaluated in the following way. For each model and cost, compute the ratio of the model's risk to the "naive" risk, i.e., the Bayes risk of assigning all objects in the original sample to one group (tables 2.4 and 2.5). The resulting ratio indicates what proportion of "naive" risk is saved by the construction of the model. It is interesting to observe that for all types of models, except RPA1 models, the saving in risk increases monotonically as a function of c_{12}, until $c_{12} = 50$ or $c_{12} = 60$, after which it monotonically decreases.[10]

Up to this point, we have compared the models based on their resubstitution error rates and risks. In table 2.6 we report the cross-validated risks of the models based on the fivefold cross-validation procedure. The DA1 model, constructed on each cross-validation trial by the forward stepwise method, was neither constrained to include the variables chosen by the original model nor to be a 10-variable model. The set of variables was chosen based on negligible increased explanatory power beyond a derived set of variables. DA2 cross-validation models were constrained to be 4-variable

Table 2.4 The ratios of the model's risk to the risk of the "naive" classification rule*

	Model			
c_{12}	RPA1	RPA2	DA1	DA2
10	0.34	0.43	0.60	0.78
20	0.19	0.28	0.48	0.52
30	0.23	0.37	0.38	0.39
40	0.20	0.32	0.32	0.37
50	0.19	0.29	0.28	0.33
60	0.19	0.25	0.29	0.33
70	0.18	0.27	0.33	0.36

Table 2.5 The ratios of the model's cross-validated risk to the risk of the "naive" classification rule*

	Model			
c_{12}	RPA1	RPA2	DA1	DA2
10	0.62	0.62	0.89	0.77
20	0.59	0.55	0.74	0.62
30	0.63	0.45	0.45	0.52
40	0.55	0.41	0.41	0.46
50	0.51	0.39	0.39	0.41
60	0.51	0.39	0.44	0.40
70	0.54	0.46	0.53	0.38

* The naive classification rule assigns all firms to the non-bankrupt group for cost $c_{12} < 49$, to the bankrupt group for cost $c_{12} > 49$, and is indifferent with respect to the assignment for cost $c_{12} = 49$. Thus, for costs 10 through 40 "naive" risk is computed as $\pi_1 c_{12} = 0.02 c_{12}$ and for costs 50 through 70 as $\pi_2 c_{21} = 0.98 c_{21} = 0.98$. We exclude the results for $c_{12} = 1$ because for this cost either the actual or the cross-validated risk of each model is lower than the risk of the "naive" classification rule.

[10] The last part of this statement is based on the results obtained for costs $c_{12} > 70$, not reported in table 2.4.

models, but not constrained to include the same variables as the original 4-variable model.

We observe, in table 2.6, that cross-validated risks of RPA2 models are smaller than those of DA models for all costs except 50 for which risk of DA1 is the same as that of RPA2 and cost 70 for which the DA2 model has a smaller risk. The RPA1 models, which were by far the best in terms of resubstitution risks, are the worst of all models in terms of cross-validated risks for all costs except 10 and 20. These relations can be seen clearly in figure 2.5.

The DA2 models, which had larger resubstitution risks than DA1 models, have smaller cross-validated risks than DA1 models for low and high costs. Thus, for low and high costs, the comparison between DA1 and DA2 is somewhat analogous to that between RPA1 and RPA2. Both DA1 and RPA1 are complex models which do better in terms of resubstitution results and, in most cases, worse in terms of cross-validated results than less complex RPA2 and DA2 models.

In table 2.5 we illustrate, estimate by cross-validation, the potential of RPA and DA models to reduce the risk of the "naive" classification rule. The ratios in table 2.5 behave similarly, as a function of c_{12}, to the ratios in table 2.4. For cost $c_{12} = 50$, the estimated saving in risk for RPA2, DA1, and DA2 models is about 60 percent, which is about 10 percent less than the saving in risk estimated by resubstitution. For RPA1, the cross-validated saving in risk is about 50 percent, which is 30 percent less than the saving in risk estimated by resubstitution.

Table 2.6 Cross-validated risks of the models*

	c_{12}			
Model	1	10	20	30
RPA1	0.091 (0.020)	0.124 (0.025)	0.235 (0.036)	0.376 (0.049)
RPA2	0.020 (0.000)	0.124 (0.021)	0.221 (0.035)	0.269 (0.043)
DA1	0.056 (0.022)	0.179 (0.016)	0.296 (0.019)	0.272 (0.042)
DA2	0.035 (0.016)	0.155 (0.010)	0.249 (0.021)	0.307 (0.075)
Model	40	50	60	70
RPA1	0.442 (0.058)	0.497 (0.069)	0.497 (0.077)	0.531 (0.087)
RPA2	0.324 (0.053)	0.386 (0.063)	0.386 (0.069)	0.455 (0.080)
DA1	0.329 (0.036)	0.386 (0.080)	0.427 (0.079)	0.518 (0.097)
DA2	0.365 (0.036)	0.402 (0.058)	0.397 (0.090)	0.369 (0.064)

* Standard deviations of the estimated risks are in parentheses.

E Cross-Validation and Bootstrap Procedure Comparisons

Finally, we have also estimated the risks of our models using a bootstrap procedure.[11] As discussed in section I and footnote 6, for classification trees the V-fold cross-validation

[11] The bootstrap estimate of the "true" risk of tree T corresponding to the penalty parameter K is $R(T) +$ bias correction, where the bias correction is obtained as follows: Choose a sample, with replacement, from the original sample of the same size as the original sample and refer to it as a bootstrap sample. Using the

Figure 2.5 Cross-validated risks

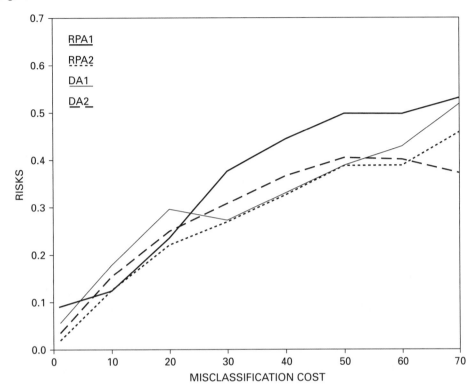

procedure is preferred to the bootstrap procedure, especially when, as is the case in our study, the effective size of the sample is relatively large. Still it is of interest to compare the two procedures' results. The estimates in table 2.7 were obtained using five bootstrap samples. The bootstrap results confirm the cross-validated results in terms of the comparisons between RPA and DA models. However, the striking feature of the results in table 2.7 is that bootstrapped risks of RPA1 models are much lower than cross-validated risks of these models and usually lower than bootstrapped risks of RPA2 models, making them "better" models, as judged by bootstrap estimates, than RPA2 models. Most likely these results are due (see footnote 6) to the large downward bias of bootstrapped risks for complex trees. Note that, for less complex RPA2 trees, the cross-

bootstrap sample, construct a tree corresponding to penalty K and call it the bootstrap tree. Then classify the bootstrap sample by the bootstrap tree and the original sample also by the bootstrap tree. Typically the risk resulting from the first classification is smaller than that of the second. The difference between these risks is one iteration on bias correction. Now obtain a new bootstrap sample, repeat the process and average the differences in risks. This average is the estimated bias correction. The number of iterations required to obtain stable estimates of the bias correction depends on the sample size and the number of variables. For a more extensive description of the bootstrap procedure in the context of risk estimation of tree classifiers, see Marais et al. [19] and for a general introduction to the bootstrap method of estimating the bias of a variety of statistics and their standard errors, see Efron [11].

Table 2.7   Bootstrapped risks of the models*

Model	c_{12}			
	1	10	20	30
RPA1	0.041 (0.003)	0.114 (0.009)	0.154 (0.016)	0.236 (0.020)
RPA2	0.023 (0.008)	0.132 (0.011)	0.190 (0.008)	0.267 (0.023)
DA1	0.037 (0.002)	0.172 (0.008)	0.222 (0.031)	0.286 (0.009)
DA2	0.020 (0.002)	0.165 (0.012)	0.207 (0.018)	0.274 (0.022)
Model	40	50	60	70
RPA1	0.269 (0.031)	0.333 (0.037)	0.355 (0.035)	0.353 (0.042)
RPA2	0.328 (0.025)	0.310 (0.052)	0.374 (0.045)	0.381 (0.045)
DA1	0.318 (0.018)	0.393 (0.017)	0.458 (0.029)	0.409 (0.021)
DA2	0.323 (0.029)	0.374 (0.025)	0.376 (0.041)	0.426 (0.025)

* Standard deviations of the estimated risks are in parentheses.

validated and bootstrapped risks are generally similar. We also observe, as expected, that cross-validated risks have somewhat higher variances than bootstrapped risks.

In summary, our empirical results show that, in most cases, RPA2 models do better than DA models both in terms of actual, cross-validated, and bootstrapped results. RPA1 models, which are most accurate on resubstitution, are worse than DA models on cross-validation. The noteworthy feature of RPA2 models is their lack of complexity, especially *vis-à-vis* a 10-variable DA model. RPA models are usually 1-, 2-, or 3-variable models, and in only one case, for cost 20, is RPA2 a 4-variable model.

V   COMPARISON OF THE SCORING SYSTEMS OF RPA AND DA

In this section we briefly discuss RPA's and DA's ability to assess the performance of a firm, relative to its prior condition or relative to other firms. While accuracy is the most important attribute of a classification technique, the information from a relative comparison is valuable from a practical viewpoint. The DA scoring system is well known. It is very precise in that it allows for relative ranking between firms and within a firm over time.

As discussed in section II, the RPA models usually partition the variable space into several "bankrupt" and "non-bankrupt" regions. With each region, there is associated a probability of bankruptcy given by $p(1 \mid t)$ as defined in Appendix A, i.e., the probability that a firm with the observation vector corresponding to this region will go bankrupt. We propose that this probability (or the probability of non-bankruptcy) be considered as a "score" of this region. All firms with the observation vectors in a given region have the same score. Thus, the RPA scoring system is discrete with the number of scores equal to the number of regions and therefore cannot be used to compare firms classified within the same region. In this respect, it appears to be less sensitive than DA's continuous scoring system. However, it may be argued that all that one may want is a grouping of firms into different "risk" categories, which RPA provides.

In order to illustrate RPA vs. DA scoring systems, we consider four recently bankrupt firms with the DA and RPA classifications and scores for five years prior to bankruptcy[12] (figure 2.6). To arrive at the classifications and scores, we used the RPA1 and DA1 models for cost $c_{12} = 50$ (see section IV).[13] For this cost, the RPA1 model has five terminal regions which can be ordered according to their scores. The ordering is indicated in figure 2.1 by the number following "group designation." The region corresponding to B1 is the most "risky," i.e., the firms in this region have the highest probability (0.29) of going bankrupt. Region B2 is the second most "risky," with bankruptcy probability equal to 0.11, etc. The remaining regions correspond to B3, NB4, and NB5.

Inspection of the trend in "scores" in figure 2.6 shows that RPA1 usually picks up the deteriorating condition of the firm by "moving" it from a less "risky" to a more "risky" category as the number of years to bankruptcy decreases. For example, we can observe that AM International was classified as bankrupt by RPA and DA for three years prior to its April 1982 bankruptcy filing date. The DA score for AM International graphically shows its deterioration. RPA classified AM International in the second risk category (B2) three and two years prior to its bankruptcy and, in the most risky category (B1), one year prior to its bankruptcy, thus also showing the deterioration trend.

The relative performance of firms is more clearly demonstrated using DA since a population of companies can be partitioned into percentiles or other categorizations. The RPA technique's partition of firms into "risk" categories does not allow for comparisons among the firms in the same risk category. For example, one year prior to their bankruptcies, RPA and DA models classify all four firms in figure 2.6 in the bankrupt group. At that time, the DA score for AM International is –1.6, for KDT Industries –2.7, for White Motor –1.1, and for HRT Industries, –0.6. RPA classified HRT Industries in the second risk category (B2) and the remaining three firms in the first risk category (B1), thus not allowing for relative comparisons among the firms classified as B1. However, the fact that categorization according to "risk" is objectively determined by RPA and not a decision variable for a user may be an appealing feature in some application contexts.

VI SUMMARY OF RESULTS

We have explored the qualities of a new statistical classification methodology applied to the corporate distress issue. RPA was found to possess the joint positive attributes of multivariate information content and univariate simplicity. Since this methodology is nonparametric, RPA is not vulnerable to the criticisms ascribed to parametric techniques and, in our example, the classification accuracy actually is superior to the

---

[12] Only one of these four companies, namely White Motor Corp., was used in the construction of the DA and RPA models. The DA and RPA scores for years 1–5 prior to bankruptcy are based on the models constructed from data one year to failure. We prefer this methodology to the alternative of using a completely different model for each year prior to bankruptcy.

[13] For the purpose of illustration, we have chosen RPA1 and DA1 models rather than less risky (as estimated by cross-validation) RPA2 and DA2 models because the RPA2 model for cost $c_{12} = 50$ is a one-split model and as such does not provide an interesting illustration of the scoring system of recursive partitioning models.

Figure 2.6 Four recent bankrupt firms with their DA and RPA classifications and scores for five years prior to bankruptcy (cutoff score = −0.41)

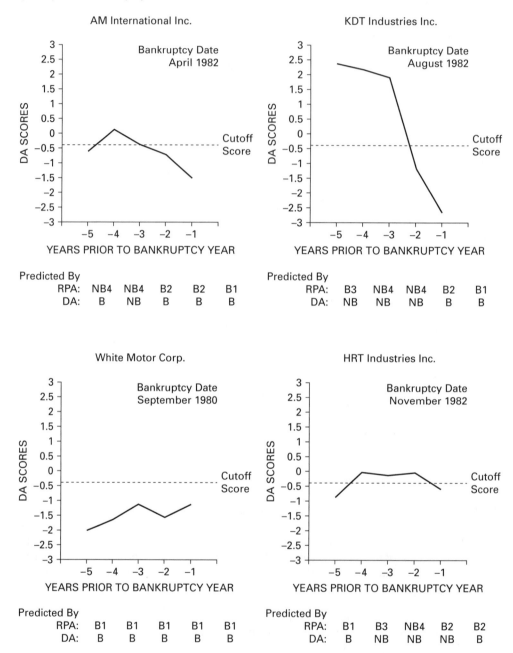

Predicted By					
RPA:	NB4	NB4	B2	B2	B1
DA:	B	NB	B	B	B

Predicted By					
RPA:	B3	NB4	NB4	B2	B1
DA:	NB	NB	NB	B	B

Predicted By					
RPA:	B1	B1	B1	B1	B1
DA:	B	B	B	B	B

Predicted By					
RPA:	B1	B3	NB4	B2	B2
DA:	B	NB	NB	NB	B

more traditional discriminant framework. We are not claiming that RPA will always outperform the numerous other statistical classification techniques, nor does it have the continuous scoring system qualities of discriminant analysis. From a rigorous statistical standpoint, as well as its likely appeal to practitioners, RPA does present several very attractive features.

Classification techniques applied to financial issues continue to be refined and improved. We feel that the attributes of new techniques like RPA can be presented and evaluated in a rigorous framework without the necessity of proving its absolute superiority over existing procedures. Indeed, as we have shown, a technique like RPA can be utilized as a practical decision tool in tandem with another procedure. In our future research, we plan to examine the possibilities and benefits of utilizing the combination of RPA and DA techniques for classification and prediction in other areas of finance. For example, an extension of distressed firm classification is to classify those firms, already in bankruptcy, according to their potential for successful reorganization.

Appendix A: Criterion for Selection of the Optimal Splitting Rules in RPA

In RPA a measure of impurity of node t, $I(t)$, is defined as

$$I(t) = R_1(t)p(1 \mid t) + R_2(t)p(2 \mid t) = 2(c_{12} + c_{21})p(1 \mid t)p(2 \mid t)p(t)$$

where

$$p(i \mid t) = (\pi_i n_i(t)/N_i)/(\textstyle\sum_{k=1}^{2} \pi_k n_k(t)/N_k)$$

is the conditional probability that an object in node t belongs to group i, and

$$p(t) = \textstyle\sum_{k=1}^{2} p(k, t) = \textstyle\sum_{k=1}^{2} \pi_k n_k(t)/N_k$$

is the probability of an object falling into node t.

$I(t)$ can be interpreted as the expected cost of misclassification when objects in node t are randomly assigned to two groups with the probability of assigning an object to group i being equal to $p(i \mid t)$. $I(t) = 0$ if and only if t is a pure node, i.e., all objects in node t belong to the same group. It attains maximum value at $p(1 \mid t) = p(2 \mid t) = 0.5$ and is symmetric in $p(1 \mid t)$ and $p(2 \mid t)$. The impurity of tree T, denoted $I(T)$, is defined as the sum of impurities of its terminal nodes. Consider a tree T and tree T' obtained from it by splitting a sample in a terminal node t of T into two subsamples which land in left and right subnodes, t_L and t_R, of node t. Then

$$\Delta I(t) = I(T) - I(T') = I(t) - I(t_L) - I(t_R)$$

is the decrease in the impurity of tree T' over tree T. $\Delta I(t)$ is nonnegative and its magnitude depends on the choice of the split. The best split for the current terminal node t is defined as the allowable split which maximizes $\Delta I(t)$.

APPENDIX B: LIST OF VARIABLES

Cash/Total Assets
Cash/Total Sales
Cash Flow/Total Debt
Current Assets/Current Liabilities
Current Assets/Total Assets
Current Assets/Total Sales
Earnings Before Interest and Taxes/Total Assets
Log (Interest Coverage + 15)
Log (Total Assets)
Market Value of Equity/Total Capitalization
Net Income/Total Assets
Quick Assets/Current Liabilities
Quick Assets/Total Assets
Quick Assets/Total Sales
Retained Earnings/Total Assets
Standard Deviation of (Earnings Before Interest and Taxes/Total Assets)
Total Debt/Total Assets
Total Sales/Total Assets
Working Capital/Total Assets
Working Capital/Total Sales

REFERENCES

1. E. I. Altman. "Financial Ratios, Discriminant Analysis and the Prediction of Corporate Bankruptcy." *Journal of Finance* 23 (September 1968), 589–609.
2. ——. "Commercial Bank Lending: Process, Credit Scoring, and Costs of Errors in Lending." *Journal of Financial and Quantitative Analysis* 15 (November 1980), 813–32.
3. ——, R. B. Avery, R. A. Eisenbeis, and J. F. Sinkey, Jr. *Application of Classification Techniques in Business, Banking and Finance.* Greenwich, CT: Jai Press, 1981.
4. —— and R. A. Eisenbeis. "Financial Applications of Discriminant Analysis: A Clarification." *Journal of Financial and Quantitative Analysis* 13 (March 1978), 185–95.
5. ——, R. G. Haldeman, and R. Narayanan. "ZETA Analysis: A New Model to Identify Bankruptcy Risk of Corporations." *Journal of Banking and Finance* 1 (June 1977), 29–54.
6. W. H. Beaver. "Financial Ratios as Predictors of Failure." *Empirical Research in Accounting: Selected Studies 1996, Journal of Accounting Research*, Supplement to Volume 4 (January 1967), 71–111.
7. L. Breiman. *Automatic Identification of Chemical Spectra: Technical Report.* Santa Monica, CA: Technology Service Corporation, 1981.
8. —— and C. J. Stone. *Parsimonious Binary Classification Trees: Technical Report.* Santa Monica, CA: Technology Service Corporation, 1978.
9. ——, J. H. Friedman, R. A. Olshen, and C. J. Stone. *Classification and Regression Trees.* Belmont, CA: Wadsworth, 1984.
10. E. B. Deakin. "A Discriminant Analysis of Predictors of Business Failure." *Journal of Accounting Research* 10 (March 1972), 167–79.
11. B. Efron. "Estimating the Error Rate of a Prediction Rule: Improvement on Cross-Validation." *Journal of the American Statistical Association* 78 (June 1983), 316–31.

12. R. A. Eisenbeis. "Pitfalls in the Application of Discriminant Analysis in Business, Finance, and Economics." *Journal of Finance* 32 (June 1977), 875–900.

13. J. H. Friedman. "A Recursive Partitioning Decision Rule for Nonparametric Classification." *IEEE Transactions on Computers* (April 1977), 404–09.

14. L. Goldman, M. Weinberg, M. Weisberg, R. Olshen, F. Cook, R. K. Sargent, G. A. Lamas, C. Dennis, L. Deckelbaum, H. Fineberg, R. Stiratelli, and the Medical Housestaffs at Yale-New Haven Hospital and Brigham and Women's Hospital. "A Computer-derived Protocol to Aid in the Diagnosis of Emergency Room Patients with Acute Chest Pain." *New England Journal of Medicine* 307 (1982), 588–96.

15. L. Gordon and R. A. Olshen. "Asymptotically Efficient Solutions to the Classification Problem." *Annals of Statistics* 6 (May 1978), 515–33.

16. O. M. Joy and J. O. Tollefson. "On the Financial Applications of Discriminant Analysis." *Journal of Financial and Quantitative Analysis* 101 (December 1975), 723–39.

17. R. Kaplan and G. Urwitz. "Statistical Models of Bond Ratings: A Methodological Inquiry." *Journal of Business* 52 (April 1979), 231–61.

18. D. E. Levy, J. J. Caronna, B. H. Singer, R. G. Lapinski, H. Frydman, and F. Plum. "Prognosis in Hypoxic-Ischemic Coma Based on Early Neurologic Findings." Working Paper, Cornell Medical Center, 1983.

19. M. L. Marais, J. M. Patell, and M. A. Wolfson. "The Experimental Design of Classification Tests: The Case of Commercial Bank Loan Classifications." *Journal of Accounting Research* 22 (1984), Supplement, March-April 1985.

20. D. Martin. "Logit Analysis and Early Warning Systems for Bank Supervision." *Journal of Banking and Finance* 1 (November 1977), 249–76.

21. J. Scott. "The Probability of Bankruptcy: A Comparison of Empirical Predictions and Theoretical Models." *Journal of Banking and Finance* 5 (September 1981), 317–44.

3 Corporate Distress Diagnosis: Comparisons Using Linear Discriminant Analysis and Neural Networks (The Italian Experience)

with Giancarlo Marco and Franco Varetto

1 INTRODUCTION

The Centrale dei Bilanci (CB) is an organization established in 1983 by the Banca d'Italia, the Associazione Bancaria Italiana and over forty leading banks and special credit institutions in Italy. In 1993, the 'Sistema Informativo Economico e Finanziario' (the Economic and Financial Information System of the CB which monitors Italian businesses) included approximately seventy members.[1]

One of the 'products' of the CB is a system designed to provide banks with a tool to quickly identify companies that are in financial trouble. The development of this system commenced in 1988 with the creation of an initial version based on a pair of linear discriminant functions, working parallel to one another and adapted to the industrial sector. The functions were estimated from a sample of 213 unsound (distressed) companies compared to a sample group of the same number of healthy companies; the estimation was made on the second year prior to the time that the state of distress was recognized.[2] This system correctly classified, in the year immediately prior to distress, 87.6 percent of healthy companies and 92.6 percent cases of unsound companies. For a description of the features of this initial system, see Varetto (1990). In 1989, the

---

[1] In addition to the management of data bases with information on the financial statements of over 37,000 companies collected every year, the CB is actively engaged in several lines of operation: the development of financial analysis methodology, production of user software, management education and financial and industrial economic research.

[2] At the time that the distressed state is recognized, there is a break in the historical series of the annual reports in the data base. For companies subject to the law governing bankruptcy and failure, a period of time passes between the suspension of the availability of balance sheets and the moment of the final declaration of bankruptcy or composition.

system was distributed to half of the banks belonging to CB for actual application in credit analysis at their head offices. The result of the experiment confirmed the system's soundness. In practical terms, automatic diagnosis systems can be used to preselect businesses to examine more thoroughly, quickly and inexpensively, thereby managing the financial analyst's time efficiently. These systems can also be used to check and monitor the uniformity of the judgements made about businesses by the various branches of the bank, without replacing credit analyst personnel.

On the basis of the experiments performed and making use of an extended data base, the CB created a second version of the Diagnostic System that was completed and distributed to the banks belonging to Centrale's information system during 1991. In the same year, initial tests were conducted into the use of neural networks (NNs) for the identification of businesses showing economic and financial distress.

The aim of this paper is to illustrate the results achieved with NNs, comparing them with discriminant analysis results and its applications. The next section gives a brief description of the existing version of the Diagnostic System obtained using what is now recognized as traditional statistical discriminant analysis methodology. The third section examines the essential aspects of the NN approach. The main conclusions that can be drawn from the experiments in the use of the NNs may be summed up as follows:

a) NNs are able to approximate the *numeric* values of the scores generated by the discriminant functions even with a different set of business indicators from the set used by the discriminant functions.

b) NNs are able to accurately classify groups of businesses as to their financial and operating health, with results that are very close to or, in some cases, even better than those of the discriminant analysis.

c) The use of integrated families of simple networks and networks with a 'memory' has shown considerable power and flexibility. Their performance has almost always been superior to the performance of single networks with complex architecture.

d) The long processing time for completing the NN training phase, the need to carry out a large number of tests to identify the NN structure, as well as the trap of 'overfitting' can considerably limit the use of NNs. The resulting weights inherent in the system are not transparent and are sensitive to structural changes.

e) The possibility of deriving an illogical network behavior, in response to different variations of the input values, constitutes an important problem from a financial analysis point of view.

f) In the comparison with NNs, discriminant analysis proves to be a very effective tool that has the significant advantage for the financial analyst of making the underlying economic and financial model transparent and easy to interpret.

g) We recommend that the two systems be used in tandem.

Perhaps the main conclusion of this study is that NNs are *not* a clearly dominant mathematical technique compared to traditional statistical techniques, such as discriminant analysis. The tendency for recently published articles on the use of NN approaches in financial distress classification (a number of references to these studies follows shortly) is that this 'new' technique is clearly superior. We find that a more balanced conclusion is appropriate, indicating advantages and disadvantages of the 'black-box' NN technique.

In addition, our study is one that is being applied and tested within an operation that has the potential for being implemented in an actual business and financial context by concerned practitioners. Finally, our samples, consisting of over 1,000 Italian firms, is by far the largest of any distressed prediction study to date – including those using discriminant analysis or NN approaches.

2   CENTRALE DEI BILANCI'S SYSTEM OF DIAGNOSTIC RISK OF DISTRESS

Distressed firm risk analysis is one of the CB's permanent projects aimed at developing analytical methodologies concerning business credit. This project allows for the periodic updating of the discriminant functions to maintain or enhance their diagnostic capabilities. The integral parts of the project are the construction and maintenance of a specific data base of unsound companies and the development of research on the companies' dynamics of economic decline leading to distress and bankruptcy.

The System is based on the application of the traditional linear discriminant analysis methodology on the basis of two samples of businesses representative of healthy and unsound companies.[3] A numerical score is obtained from the discriminant function that expresses the 'risk profile' of the business.

Unlike the first version of the System, the new release includes special models each for trading and construction companies as well as the industrial model developed earlier.[4] Work discussed in this study only refers to the existing model for industrial companies.

The essential points are as follows:

a)   The Diagnostic System has been designed and set up to be applied to the medium and small sized businesses in Italy. For this reason, companies with sales of more than 100 billion liras (i.e. 60 million US dollars) have been excluded from the sample. Our tests involve data covering the period 1985–92.

b)   We have utilized a balanced sample of healthy and unsound companies, rather than to consider all the collected companies in the files of the CB (around 37,000 companies a year) since our sample is quite large in and of itself. This methodological line is common to other models of discriminant analysis.

c)   The discriminant models had only modest *ex-post* accuracies while using large samples of 'healthy' (non-bankrupt) businesses due to the fact that these companies are broken down into at least three large subsets: 'outstanding', 'normal' and 'vulnerable' companies. And, the breadth of these categories, just as their features, varies over time. The discriminant analysis model seems limited in its ability to differentiate between unsound companies and companies that are 'live' but belong to the vulnerable subset. Certainly, it is far more difficult to discriminate between two 'sick' firm samples (unsound and vulnerable) than between the clearly healthy vs. unsound firms. Consequently, with the increase in the size and industrial scope of the sample, rates of recognition decrease because of the

---

[3]   For a description of the methodological aspects of discriminant analysis and the main models available in different countries, see Altman (1993).

[4]   The trading and building sector models are still being tested and will be reported on in a subsequent publication.

increase in the variability of possible situations. The accuracy does not improve even if use is made of more sophisticated Bayesian-type statistical methodologies.

d) To tackle this problem, it was decided to take another path in the revised version of the System. The Diagnostic System was broken down into two sub-models working in sequence. The first model (F1) was estimated on samples of 404 unsound companies and 404 healthy companies: the former were identified from the entire population of companies collected in the files of Centrale dei Bilanci which underwent (1) some form of bankruptcy proceeding, (2) were wound up in temporary receivership, or (3) had stated they were in dire straits with regard to their payments to the banks. The sound-firm sample was obtained from the 'live' company file excluding 'vulnerable' businesses identified through the use of tests on a restricted number of business ratios over the span of a few years. These ratios are not part of those included in the discriminant functions. The sample of businesses 'running normally' was obtained by matching with similar distressed companies by size (in terms of net assets), industry and location. The first model consisted of a nine ratio linear function (F1) that distinguished between 'healthy' businesses and 'unsound' or 'vulnerable' businesses (figure 3.1).

e) The second phase of the model (F2) comes into play after F1 has diagnosed the business to be 'unsound'. The second discriminant function was estimated from two balanced samples, again each of 404 businesses, of unsound (the same ones used for the F1 estimation) and 'vulnerable' companies. The latter were extracted from among the 'live' sample but found to be diagnostically 'unsound' by F1. Both functions have been estimated based on ratio values from the annual report of the third year prior to the distress date.

f) All variables of the F1 and F2 models which contained coefficients with counter-intuitive signs were eliminated (even if they were statistically significant). Also, variables with unstable behavior were eliminated and only those that increased the capacity to classify the unsound companies as the time prior to distress approached and maintained (or increased) the capacity to classify healthy businesses were retained.

Figure 3.1 Diagnostic system flow

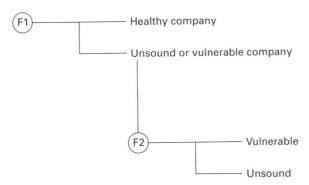

This chart indicates the basic progression of discriminant analysis models performed within the corporate monitoring system at the Centrale dei Bilanci, Torino, Italy.

g) Estimations were made using logit as well as discriminant analysis but no significant progress was made on *ex-post* classification. Therefore, we retained the discriminant functions.

h) The discriminatory capacity of the principal function (F1), on which most of the experiments with NNs are compared, is shown in table 3.1.

The percentage of correct *ex-post* classification improves as distress approaches; for the unsound companies it goes from 86.4 percent in T − 3 (estimation period) to 96.5 percent in period T − 1. The accuracy of the classification was checked with a holdout sample of 150 unsound businesses and 150 healthy ones, obtaining results that were similar to the estimation sample (90 percent and 95 percent in period T − 1).

The second function, as expected, has a lower discriminant capacity, especially for the unsound firms. Table 3.2 lists the F2 function results showing 82.7 percent correct classification of the unsound firms in the control period (T − 1) and 81.0 percent in the holdout sample for that group (vs. about 95 percent in the F1 Function).

To make it easier to interpret the results, the scores of the functions are represented on graphs where the business under examination is positioned on the two different reference systems: Figure 3.2a is an example of an unsound business monitored over the last five years of its life (1985–89). From F1, the firm is identified as a distressed company in the fifth year prior to failure. At this stage, the system does not yet distinguish if the unsound business is simply vulnerable (with a greater or lesser degree of vulnerability) or if it belongs to the set of unsound companies. Figure 3.2b shows the diagnosis of the same firm made by F2 and places the business in the uncertain area between vulnerability and risk of bankruptcy in the first two years of the series and then signals a rapid decline into the higher risk bankruptcy zone. As can be seen, the diagnosis of the company is carried out on the basis of a joint analysis of the two functions with additional reference points supplied by quartile comparisons with the entire CB data base of comparable companies.

The classificatory space described by F1 has been divided into five zones on the basis of the distribution of healthy, vulnerable and unsound companies. These include: (a1)

Table 3.1 Rate of successful recognition (F1 discriminant function)

		Healthy firms (%)	Unsound firms (%)
Estimation sample (404 companies in each group)			
Estimation period	T–3	90.3	86.4
Control period	T–1	92.8	96.5
Holdout sample (150 companies in each group)	T–1	90.3	95.1

Table 3.2 Rate of successful recognition (F2 discriminant function)

Estimation sample (404 cos.)		Vulnerable firms (%)	Unsound firms (%)
Estimation period	T–3	99.0	60.1
Control period	T–1	97.8	82.7
Holdout sample (150 cos.)	T–1	96.8	81.0

Figure 3.2 (a) Function F1 – example of unsound company. (b) Function F2 – example of unsound company

(a)

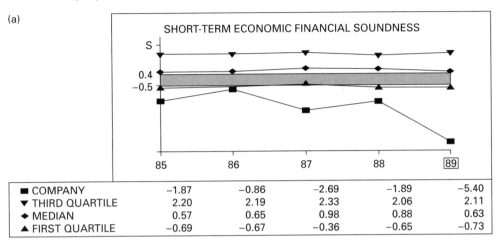

	85	86	87	88	89
■ COMPANY	−1.87	−0.86	−2.69	−1.89	−5.40
▼ THIRD QUARTILE	2.20	2.19	2.33	2.06	2.11
◆ MEDIAN	0.57	0.65	0.98	0.88	0.63
▲ FIRST QUARTILE	−0.69	−0.67	−0.36	−0.65	−0.73

(b)

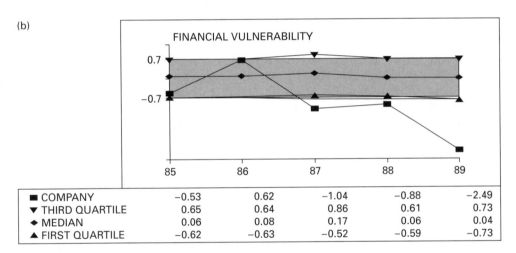

	85	86	87	88	89
■ COMPANY	−0.53	0.62	−1.04	−0.88	−2.49
▼ THIRD QUARTILE	0.65	0.64	0.86	0.61	0.73
◆ MEDIAN	0.06	0.08	0.17	0.06	0.04
▲ FIRST QUARTILE	−0.62	−0.63	−0.52	−0.59	−0.73

high security; (b1) security; (c1) uncertainly between security and vulnerability; (d1) vulnerability; and (e1) intense vulnerability. Function F2 is calculated as soon as F1's score falls in one of the zones (c1), (d1) or (e1). F2 has been split into zones of: (a2) high vulnerability; (b2) vulnerability; (c2) uncertainty between vulnerability and risk; (d2) risk; and (e2) high risk of bankruptcy.

Score values separating the different zones constitute the ordinates of the fixed classification system shown on the graphs.[5]

[5] The coefficients of all the functions are protected by secrecy for the purpose of safeguarding the investments of the CB's owners made in research, testing and data base creation. This latest version of the two-function system has been inserted in a procedure on the PC and distributed to around thirty of the member banks. Actual application in the field is underway and has already given significant, favorable signs.

3 NEURAL NETWORKS

For many years, NN models have been analyzed both by academics and practitioners, including those efforts outside the circle of artificial intelligence experts.[6] It is too early to say whether the use of experimental NN is simply a fad or it will result into something more permanent. Some aspects of the NNs, however, do seem promising in the area of business and finance applications.[7]

The application of the NN approach to company distress prediction, although relatively new, has seen a number of researchers attempt to improve upon the traditional discriminant analysis technique. An interesting procedure by Coats and Fant (1993), used a limited number of financial ratios to duplicate the 'going-concern' determination by accounting auditors. They utilize the cascade-correlation NN approach (Fahlman and Lebiere, 1992) to duplicate the auditor-expert conclusion on a sample of 94 manufacturing and non-manufacturing failed firms and conclude that it clearly dominates the LDA method in this application.[8] In addition, studies by Karels and Prakash (1987), Odom and Sharda (1990), Ragupathi et al. (1991) and Rahimian et al. (1992) have all assessed NNs for bankruptcy prediction. Interestingly, at least three of the above studies utilized the same five financial variables found in Altman's (1968) study.

This paper will explore the basic theory of NNs but we do not plan to discuss in detail the reasons that inspired the connectionist approach. Connectionist processing models (neural networks) consist of a potentially large number of elementary processing units; every unit is interconnected with other units and each is able to perform relatively simple calculations. The network's processing result derives from their collective behavior rather than from the specific behavior of a single unit. The links are not rigid but can be modified through learning processes generated by the network's interaction with the outside world or with a set of symbolic signals.

The individual units and the connections linking them can be shown as in figure 3.3: each unit (i) receives an input (x_i) from the outside, or from other neurons with which it is linked, with an intensity (weight) equal to w_{ji}. The overall input that the ith neuron receives equals an assumed potential (P_i) equal to:

---

[6] For an introduction to the theory of neural networks and the operating mechanisms, see Rumelhart and McClelland (1986), Cammarata (1990), Freeman and Skapura (1991) and Hertz et al. (1991).

[7] In the area of finance, there have been a number of recent attempts to apply NNs. Cadden (1991) has applied NNs to insolvency analysis by adopting a Boolean transformation of the financial ratios divided into quartiles; Chung and Tam (1993) have compared the performance of the NNs with that of other inductive learning algorithms for bankruptcy forecasting in the banking industry; Bell et al. (1990) have compared NNs with logistic regression for the prediction of bank failures. The networks have also been assigned to the rating of bonds (Dutta and Shelber, 1992), to the prediction of the progress of historical series of company data to the selection of investments and to operations on the financial market (Swales and Yoon, 1992; Wong et al., 1993; Trippi and de Sieno, 1992), and the recognition of accounting data patterns (Liang et al., 1993). Kryzanowski (1989) applied NN for positive vs. negative common stock return prediction and Kryzanowski and Galler (1994) have analyzed the financial statements of small businesses using neural nets. For a partial list of applications in the financial field, see Pau and Gianotti (1990) and Trippi and Turban (1993).

[8] While the Coats and Fant (1993) analysis is of relevance, we must point out that the auditors' qualification is itself an inexact and subjective process, and, as we have shown in an earlier study (Altman and McGough, 1974), that the discriminant analysis Z-score approach was far more accurate in predicting the actual bankruptcy of a sample of failed firms than was the so-called accountant-expert. Still, the auditing disclaimer report is an unambiguous, although possibly incorrect, indicator of distress. And, the Coats and Fant sample of distressed firms were those that discontinued operations after receiving a going-concern qualification.

Figure 3.3 General scheme of neural unit

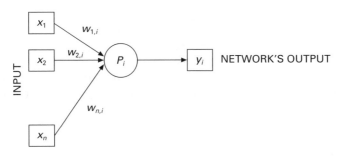

$$P_i = \sum_j nw_{ji}^* x_i - S_i$$

where S_i represents an excitation threshold value that limits the neuron's degree of response to the stimuli received: for example the neurons give a response signal in the 'jump-type' response function only if the total input arriving from outside and/or other neurons is greater than S_i. It is possible to eliminate the S_i threshold and replace it with a dummy input (k) of a value equal to 1 ($x_k = 1$) and by setting $w_{ki} = -S_i$, obtaining the general expression

$$P_i = \sum_j w_{ji} \cdot x_j$$

where k is included in x_j

The neuron's response (y_i) depends on the transfer of potential (P_i) to the output function. One of the most widely used functions is the literature and used in our tests is the logistic function, according to which

$$y_i = \frac{1}{1 + e^{-P_i}}$$

Generally, the response function determines values between a minimum and a maximum; in our case y_i is included between 0 and 1. Output (y_i) of the neuron can be either a total response value of the network (if it is the final output value) or an input for further neuron units. The network, made up of many elementary units of the ith type, can have different degrees of complexity. The simpler networks consist of a single neuron layer (in extreme cases by a single neuron) each of which is in direct contact with the outside stimuli i and generates output from the network directly. A slightly more complicated network has two layers: an intermediate, hidden layer, that receives stimuli from outside the network, and an output layer that generates the network's responses. Networks can be constructed with circuits for feedback between neurons from one layer to those of previous levels, just like self-connecting links.

Considerable limitations of a single-layer network have been shown. Networks with one layer, in addition to the input layer, can only perform linear separations of the input space. Two-layer networks can generate convex geometrical shapes, while networks with at least three layers enable the input space to be separated into shapes of any configuration (the complexity of the regions is determined by the number of neurons). There are no general rules to establish the optimal degree of network complexity.

The crucial aspect of NNs lies in the fact that the weightings of the connections are not fixed but can be modified on the basis of a learning procedure derived from the comparison of the network responses with those required by actual results. The network, in other words, behaves as an adaptive dynamic system that reacts to response differences.

The network is given a set of inputs generating a response that is compared with the response required; the weightings are not changed if the response obtained corresponds with the response required. If the difference exceeds a certain tolerance level, revisions are introduced into the weightings and learning starts again; then a new case is input. The analysis of all the cases supplied constitutes the maximum extension learning cycle. After the interaction of a large number of cycles, the error is reduced to acceptable levels and, once the holdout set accuracy has been exceeded, the learning ends and the weightings are locked. The network has achieved a stable equilibrium configuration that represents 'its capacity to solve a problem'.

The learning mechanism involves a number of problems; however:

a)   The learning stage can be very long (slow learning).
b)   The system might not achieve a stable absolute minimum configuration (optimal error reduction) but might lock on local minimums without being able to move to the optimum.
c)   The system might give rise to oscillating behavior in the learning phase, i.e., when the minimum point is reached and then exceeded. Hence, it then returns to the previous point.
d)   When the actual situation is significantly different, or changes, compared to the situation implicit in the training examples; it is then necessary to repeat the learning phase. The same applies when the set of examples is not representative of the reality of the problem or concept to be learned.
e)   The analysis of the weightings is complex and difficult to interpret. There is, in other words, little network transparency as far as the examination of the system's logic is concerned. This makes it difficult to identify the causes of the errors or defective responses.

The algorithm determining the network's learning is of fundamental importance for the final performance of the network itself.[9]

NNs do not require the pre-specification of a functional form, nor the adoption of restrictive assumptions about the characteristics of statistical distributions of the variables and errors of the model. Moreover, by their nature, NNs make it possible to work with imprecise variables and with changes of the models over time, thus being able to adapt gradually to the appearance of new cases representing changes in the situation. As noted earlier, the price to be paid using networks of neurons is their lack of transparency in the use of the variables within the network connections. While one is able to

---

[9]   The method considered here is the well-known Error Back Propagation Algorithm by Rumelhart et al. (1986).

identify the explanatory importance of each variable with the usual estimation techniques, signs of influence on the endogenous variables and the degree of their mutual correlation with each neuron remains unclear.

We know many things about how companies can fall into economic distress, about crisis processes and company decline, but we do not have a complete theory. One of the ways of tackling this problem in operative terms is that of using company classification techniques making use of the tools that statistical methodology supplies. Multiple discriminant analysis is one of the tools most often used and was described earlier in our F1 and F2 functions.

Results obtained appear to be very promising. Linear discriminant analysis can be considered equivalent to a network made up of a single neuron that receives signals from the set of indicators and generates an output with a linear transfer function without transformation, $y_i = P_i$. To exploit the advantages offered by the network of neurons, we have used a three-layer network based on a combination of simple (two-layer) elementary networks in a 'cascade' fashion. Figure 3.4 illustrates the differences between discriminant analysis and a multi-layer NN system.

The experimental program is subdivided into four parts:

- *Part 1*: Check the capacity of a neural network to reproduce the numeric values of the scores obtained using linear discriminant analysis, receiving, as input, the signals of ratios *different* from those employed in discriminant analysis. Note that in this first experiment, the multi-layer network has been forced to behave linearly, not exploiting its wealth of descriptive potential. Nonetheless, within this constraint, we can verify the network's capacity to approximate the discriminant analysis' linear functions using a different set of ratios.

Figure 3.4 Discriminant analysis and multilayer neural network (NN)

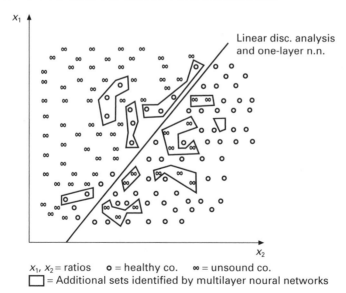

x_1, x_2 = ratios   o = healthy co.   ∞ = unsound co.
☐ = Additional sets identified by multilayer noural networks

- *Part 2*: Check the capacity of the neural network to separate the samples between bankrupt and healthy companies. The network's output unit is not the value of a score as in the previous section, but simply the binary values 0 (= healthy) and 1 (= unsound). The network's training stage was carried out in period T − 3 while the test of its correct recognition was done in either period T − 1 of the training sample or on an independent sample.
- *Part 3*: This section considers the change in company performance over time. One of the problems involved in identifying distressed companies is that of making the classificatory functions sensitive to the passing of time, and the changes of the companies' business patterns. See the work of Theodossiou (1993) for an analysis of the time series properties of distressed prediction. An attempt was made to capture these aspects by constructing complex networks divided into three segments.

   The output of the first sub-network summarizes the conclusions about the economic and financial profile observed in period T − 3; these are linked to the conclusions relating to period T − 2. If, during this period, the profile follows a trend that is consistent (inconsistent) with the trend in the prior period, then the conclusions come out reinforced (weakened). The same applies to the pattern of period T − 1. An alternative way of tackling the problem of time pattern analysis lies in using networks with 'memories'; the simplest network of this type is that of including among the input data the change in value of the variables. Figure 3.5 illustrates an example of such a network 'with memory'.

Figure 3.5   Networks with memory of input

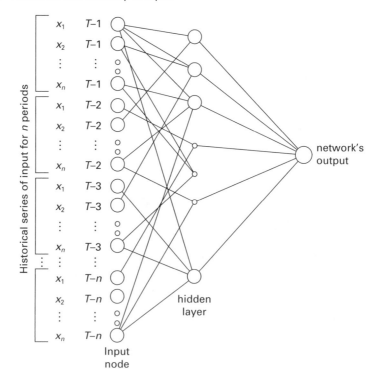

From an economic-logic point of view, it is as if there has been an attempt to reproduce the reasoning of the financial analyst when he examines a historical series of business data. The analyst forms an opinion on the state of business by observing how it has evolved over the entire time span available.

- *Part 4*: The aim of this section is to check the capacity of networks to separate the three categories of company: healthy, vulnerable and unsound. The networks used for this section have an output level comprising two output neurons: the first distinguishes healthy businesses from the unsound ones while the second separates the unsound businesses from the vulnerable and unsound businesses. The two neurons have the same role as the two functions F1 and F2.

Two types of experiment were carried out for this purpose: in the first case, network training was carried out over period T − 3 while the check of the capacity for generalization was conducted on period T − 1 and on an independent sample. In the second case, networks with memories were used over the whole three-year monitoring period, while the control sample was limited to healthy and vulnerable companies extracted from the continuing company data base.

All the experiments were carried out on the same samples used to fine tune the discriminant functions: an initial sample involved 1,212 businesses: 404 each of healthy, unsound and vulnerable firms. A second independent sample of 453 companies was used, 151 of each type, with data limited to the last year prior to bankruptcy. A final sample, independent of the other two, was analyzed comprising 900 healthy and 900 vulnerable companies for three years of historical series. These were taken from the files of 'live' companies.

4 RESULTS

4.1 Healthy vs. Unsound Firms

The first tests were conducted to estimate the accuracy of the numeric values of the linear discriminant function. We limited the analysis to approximating the function that separates the healthy from unsound companies (F1) for period T − 3. If these approximations can be obtained with a smaller set of indicators (input signals) than what was used for the estimation of the discriminant function, it will be a direct check of the NN's capacity for adaptation and simplification. The experiments were conducted using networks of varying complexity in terms of the number of input indicators, number of layers and the number of connections.

The best results were obtained with a three-layer network: one initial hidden layer of ten neurons, a second hidden layer with four neurons and an output layer consisting of a single neuron. The input comprised ten financial ratios: four relative to the firm's financial structure and indebtedness, two to liquidity, and four representative of company profitability and internal-financing.

The network neurons are totally interconnected. This means that each neuron on a layer is connected to all the others on the next level, including the input signals which are connected to all of the neurons on the first layer. Training was interrupted after 1000 learning cycles, each of which examined 808 companies, adjusting the weighting after each cycle. The resulting profile was extremely close to the desired level.

Another measure of the network results is summarized in table 3.3. This shows the distribution of the categorization of company creditworthiness by score intervals. The classification differences based on the scores and the actual categories seem small and concentrated mainly towards positive values near 1 (best credits).

Results obtained after 1,000 learning cycles are quite encouraging and lead one to believe that if the learning phase lasted longer the error could be reduced still further. It should be noted that the network built to replicate the discriminant function is comprised of completely different indicators from those included in the functions. The latter's selection required a significant number of man-hours. In the case of the NN, machine-hours were used more, while the selection of indicators, albeit careful and well thought out, required a tiny fraction of the total time. This is a clear indication of the network's capacity for adaptation.

4.2   Multi-Layer Networks

Networks with varying degrees of complexity were trained using ratios from period $T - 3$ followed by testing in period $T - 1$ from the same sample and also an independent sample. The most satisfactory results were obtained with a three-layer network, comprising fifteen neurons in the first hidden layer, six neurons in the second hidden layer and one neuron in the output layer. The fully interconnected network is fed with the numeric values of fifteen business ratios; these are a broader set than the one in the ten-ratio network described in the previous section. Not having observed substantial benefits with using a random selection of the cases, we used a sequential ordering of the observations.

Although the network training used slightly greater than 2,000 cycles, the analysis of the error sequence indicated a typical oscillating phenomenon.[10] At the end of the training period, the network was able to recognize correctly 97.7 percent of healthy and 97.0 percent of unsound companies. All the other networks which used a lower degree of complexity, even if trained with a higher number of cycles, did not achieve the same recognition capability as obtained using the 15, 4, 1 network.[11] This compares favorably with the recognition rates obtained by the linear discriminant function F1 in period $T - 3$: 90.3 percent of healthy companies and 86.4 percent of unsound ones.

Table 3.3   Distribution of companies by score intervals

	Score required (%)	Score calculated (%)
High security	15.2	10.2
Security	34.5	37.2
Uncertainty	11.3	12.0
Vulnerability	23.8	25.4
High level of vulnerability	15.2	15.2
Total	100.0	100.0

[10]   Training was conducted with a 0.75 learning rate and null momentum: these values were obtained on the basis of the results of experiments with alternative learning and momentum rates.

[11]   Experiments were also conducted, among others, using Cascade-Correlation but we did not obtain superior results; for the methodological aspects relating to Cascade-Correlation see Fahlman and Lebiere (1992).

The network's identification capability is clearly greater than the discriminant function's although it is obtained with a higher number of indicators: fifteen as opposed to nine. This aspect is important since the network is more complicated and uses a large number of learning cycles. The results of the learning, however, behave erratically. There are great and rapid improvements in the capacity to identify the two groups with the first cycles; nevertheless, as the cycle procedure continues the convergence becomes slower with frequent oscillations and jumps backward, and with deterioration in the recognition rates that are sometimes significant. As can be seen, the network had already achieved recognition levels that were not far off the final results, especially in the healthy group, in the earlier cycles. The unsound firm errors were reduced considerably as the number of cycles increased until the last 560 cycles, when the classification accuracy became erratic.

This network, trained in period T − 3, showed a lower recognition capacity than the one in the training period using period T − 1; period T − 1's identification error was 10.6 percent for healthy businesses and 5.2 percent for unsound firms. Compare these rates of error with those obtained with the discriminant functions: 7.2 percent for healthy and 3.5 percent for unsound companies (table 3.1).

This neural network shows a *lower* capacity for generalization than the traditional discriminant function's. This conclusion is reinforced by the results obtained on the independent samples of 302 companies for period T − 1: rates of error are 15.9 percent for the healthy and 9.5 percent for the unsound companies as opposed to the 9.7 percent and 4.9 percent respectively, obtained with the discriminant functions.[12]

The simpler network's results are more modest than the ones obtained from traditional discriminant analysis, but show a greater capacity for generalization than the more complex networks. This confirms what others have shown, i.e., the network judged to be most effective at the end of the learning cycle might not be as suitable with other sets of independent cases. The network is the victim of a phenomenon known as 'overfitting'. We encountered a similar phenomenon when we observed the holdout sample accuracy of quadratic discriminant functions vs. the less complex linear function (Altman et al., 1977).

4.3 Multi-Layer Networks with Discriminant Function Ratios

The results obtained in the previous section use networks fed with ratios different from the ones used in discriminant functions. The reason for this choice is the need to estimate the classification capacity of the networks using a standard information base (ratios) such as are normally available in financial analysis reports published by the CB. In a related test, nine of the 11 F1 discriminant function's indicators are utilized with networks of differing complexity. The intention was to check the networks' capacity to reproduce the 'knowledge' built into the discriminant functions and convert it into knowledge distributed over the neural connections.

[12] Increased generalization was achieved with the simpler, 10, 4, 1 type networks, fed with the ten ratios used in the first section of experiments. After 2,000 learning cycles, this network showed a recognition capacity of 93.3 percent for healthy companies and 84.7 percent for unsound companies in period T − 3, far lower than results obtained with the more complex 15, 6, 1 network. Nonetheless, the simpler network was able to limit the errors on the T − 1 sample to 8.2 percent and 3.7 percent, respectively, and, on the independent sample, to 14.6 percent and 6.8 percent for the two samples of firms.

The best result was obtained with a 9, 5, 1 network after 4,030 learning cycles with a 0.75 learning rate and 0.30 momentum.[13] Table 3.4 shows the rates of recognition of businesses in the T − 3 period (network estimation) and period T − 1 (control period). The results are not dissimilar, although slightly lower, from those obtained using the discriminant function. It is not, however, certain that the formalization of the knowledge built into the network is totally equivalent to the knowledge of the linear function since companies that the network recognized incorrectly were, in part, different from those incorrectly recognized by the discriminant function. Moreover, while the discriminant function always behaves in the same way when the values of the exogenous variables vary, with the use of the network we have seen behavior that is not always consistent when the input changes. We will postpone this discussion until the next section where it can be treated more thoroughly.

4.4   Simple Network Connections

NNs can have difficulty when tackling particularly complex problems. In our case, the complexity derives from the nature of the problem and from the wide range of observations. While the wealth of data makes it possible to construct a model that is general and robust, it also tends to make the training of the network more difficult. Complex networks with numerous inputs and neurons are perhaps better able to classify a more heterogeneous sample of firms but has the disadvantage of making the time required (and the expense) for training sometimes prohibitive. Moreover, these networks tend to adopt oscillating or non-convergent behavior as well as often being the victim of the overfitting trap.

One methodology for tackling these problems might be breaking down the total network into simpler networks connected to each other. We carried out experiments along these lines starting with the generation of elementary networks which were then connected to each other in a second level network. . . . [and illustrated] this with three of the eight simple structure networks (with one hidden and one output layer apiece). Every elementary network (e.g., leverage) is fed with a number of ratios that are representative of that characteristic.

The second level network coordinates the results of the eight elementary networks in order to generate the system's final response. That is, it is 'trained' to combine the conclusions reached by the elementary networks. This is equivalent to a multivariate discriminant or logit analysis with the same potential benefits over a univariate structure.

Table 3.4 Comparison of recognition rates: NN vs. LDA

Sample size = 404 in each group		Neural network		Linear discriminant function (F1)	
		Healthy (%)	Unsound (%)	Healthy (%)	Unsound (%)
Estimation period	T–3	89.4	86.2	90.3	86.4
Control period	T–1	91.8	95.3	92.8	96.5

---

[13] These values were obtained from the results using alternative parameter experiments.

The results obtained are shown in table 3.5. As expected, the classification accuracy of the elementary networks differs greatly from network to network and generally it is not very high. Furthermore, it does not always increase when passing from the estimation period (T − 3) to the control period (T − 1). The second level network, however, which generates the system's overall responses, performs very well, with correct classification of healthy companies of 98.3 percent and unsound companies of 92.5 percent in the estimation period (T − 3). This result is considerably better than that achieved through discriminant analysis (cf. table 3.1). In addition, the system of networks applied to the control period (T − 1) gives outstanding results in this case, too, with 92.8 percent of healthy companies and 94.5 percent of unsound companies classified correctly.

On the whole, the test of the simple network system's capacity for generalization on the independent sample of 302 companies in period T − 1 is also good. In the face of significant reduction in first level elementary rates of identification, second level networks generate correct classification rates of 93.6 percent for the healthy companies and 89.1 percent for unsound companies. Compared with results obtained with discriminant functions, there is a significant drop in the number of unsound companies identified correctly (−6 percent) but not enough to cancel out the effectiveness of the system.

These results are encouraging for the use of NNs. Note that the system's classification was obtained with a small effort on the part of the analyst and by using annual report ratios that are not particularly complex.

4.5   Analysis of Simple Network Systems − Some Concerns

As mentioned earlier, a problem that arises in the use of NNs concerns the low level of intelligibility of the knowledge base spread over the network and built into the weighting of the connections. We carried out an analysis of elementary and second level networks to try to better understand how they work. Distributed knowledge mapping, see Hinton, et al. (1986), implicit in the weighting values of the network, can be studied from various points of view including the identification of the significance assumed by the various neurons and the analysis of the network's behavior when input conditions change.

The significance of the neurons can be identified either by examining the weightings matrix, in the simplest cases, or by studying the role that individual neurons play in determining the output.[14] By modifying the initial weightings and repeating the learning process, the weightings matrix is modified which might also change the role of the various neurons.

Generally speaking, the behavior of a network can be studied on the basis of the derivatives (or elasticities) of the output compared with the individual inputs. For the analysis in the case where more than one input is changed at the same time, it is possible to refer to the total differential of the output compared with the inputs.

From a mathematical point of view, the neural network is a nonlinear system. Its input/output derivatives depend on the input value configuration vector. Therefore, the network's capacity to react to input changes is not always the same but strictly depends

---

[14]   The activation patterns that the hidden-layer neurons assume in response to different input value configurations can be observed to try to understand how the network has formed responses. An alternative method consists of causing voluntary 'damages' inside the network by deactivating certain of its connections or removing entire groups or by altering the size of its values.

Table 3.5 Connection of simple neural networks with one output

		% Correct classification					
		Sample of 808 companies Period T-3 Estimate		Period T-1 Control		Holdout sample of 302 companies Period T-1	
Variable types analyzed	Number of learning cycles	Healthy	Unsound	Healthy	Unsound	Healthy	Unsound
Specialized elementary NN							
1) Leverage; asset/liab. struc.	4,640	76.98	82.21	73.76	91.04	76.80	90.48
2) Ability to bear fin. debt	3,800	74.50	79.20	69.06	92.04	35.20	97.28
3) Liquidity	4,950	69.31	84.96	71.29	90.80	36.00	97.96
4) Profitability, internal fin.	4,770	87.87	85.71	84.90	92.29	56.80	96.60
5) Profit accumulation	4,050	81.44	75.94	88.61	71.14	59.20	85.03
6) Ability to bear cost of debt	5,000	75.25	87.97	76.73	95.77	7.20	99.32
7) General efficiency	1,260	62.38	60.40	65.10	69.65	63.20	57.82
8) Trade indebtedness	900	59.90	69.92	60.15	79.60	73.60	66.67
Second-level NN	2,850	98.27	92.48	92.82	94.53	93.60	89.12

NN trained at T–3 with learning rate = 0.75 and momentum = 0.25. The revision of the weight is done for each company; in each cycle there are 808 revisions.

on the starting position. This factor makes the identification of the individual contributions of the inputs to the formation of the output complex and uncertain.

Even in its simplicity, the second-level network shows peculiar behavior patterns. We examined the values of the partial derivatives between the output and the individual inputs in the case of different starting configurations. The calculation of the partial derivatives showed significant dependence on the base conditions, with sudden changes of sign. This feature of the networks is particularly awkward for the financial analyst because the behavior of the network may be unpredictable and contrary to business logic. For example, for a business to be considered unsound by the network, it only needs to have a very modest general efficiency, a relatively high leverage and an uncertain ability to bear financial indebtedness while having outstanding ratings in the other inputs. If the level of liquidity is worsened under this profile, the network shows an improvement in the output and, under some conditions, the company goes from being unsound to healthy, thus altering the initial conclusions! Such behavior does not occur if the profitability is worsened but it reappears in the case of increased commercial indebtedness.

4.6 Interconnection of Simple Networks with Memories

The next experiment made use of the logic of networks with memories on the inputs (see figure 3.5 for a general description of such a structure). The inputs of this type of network include the entire three-year historical series of the indicators used. The network is trained to consider all the data available about the company at the same time. This is like a financial analyst examining the historical time series of financial statements.

The correct recognition rates of healthy and unsound companies is high, even in several elementary networks, rising to over 99 percent in the second-level network. The overall accuracy of the interconnected system of elementary networks with memories commits errors of 4 healthy companies (out of 404) and 1 unsound company (out of 404).[15]

We did analyze the overall functioning of the system on simple, interconnected networks with memories. We found, in the second-level network, the same non-acceptable behavioral problems already identified above with a frequent inversion of the output value when the inputs are uniformly modified either individually or in limited subsets.

4.7 Multi-Group Analysis

The last set of experiments is aimed at the generation of a two-output network for the simultaneous, not sequential, separation of healthy, vulnerable and unsound companies. This test was very severe because of the difficulty in identifying in a single solution the characteristics separating the three groups of business. The best results were achieved with a network using families of simple NNs with memory consisting of three layers: one hidden layer with fifteen neurons, a second hidden layer with twelve neurons and one output layer with two neurons. This is somewhat analogous to the three group

---

[15]   The price paid for these performance levels has been the high number of elementary first-level network learning cycles. Consider that with 5000 cycles there are over four million changes made to the weightings via the backward propagation algorithm.

simultaneous distress S&L analysis of Altman (1977). Since these results are still experimental and not germane to our overall conclusions, we refer the reader to a lengthier working paper, Varetto and Marco (1993).

5 CONCLUSION

In the light of the experiments carried out, neural networks are a very interesting tool and have great potential capacities that undoubtedly make them attractive for application to the field of business classification. The networks assessed on our samples have shown significant capacities for recognizing the health of companies, with results that are, in many cases, near or superior to the results obtained through discriminant analysis. The results of the two-output networks trained to simultaneously recognize the three types of company performance: healthy, vulnerable and unsound, also proved to be very interesting. Nonetheless, taking into account the results obtained in the control periods and in the holdout samples, discriminant analysis was deemed to be better, on the whole, than the networks trained in our experiments.

The greatest problem concerns the existence of non-acceptable types of behavior in the network. These are intrinsic to the nonlinear nature of the mathematical model underlying the network, combining a large number of variables several times over in a complex fashion. These behavior patterns are characteristic of networks of any complexity that have at least two inputs.

The extent and frequency of illogical types of behavior (in the judgment of the financial analyst) grow with the increase in the complexity of the network architecture. Only extremely simple networks limit the probability of meeting these unacceptable results. The construction of ultra simplified networks cannot be a solution, however, because the problem is only delayed. It does in fact crop up again as a result of the need to coordinate simple networks with others of higher level.

The problem of understanding these types of behavior and how to remedy them is not an easy one to solve. As well as using real examples, it would be possible, for example, to train the network with artificial cases constructed to represent other possible combinations. Given the high number of artificial cases required, the network's capacity for analyzing real cases could be totally distorted if errors are committed at this stage.

On the whole, linear discriminant analysis compares rather well when compared to neural networks. The fine-tuning of the discriminant function does take longer, but the greater estimation speed makes it possible to carry out careful tuning at relatively low cost. Furthermore, the linear form, albeit with the limitations of its ability to perform well, ensures consistent behavior for any type of variable. This makes it possible to interpret the model's operating logic on the basis of the coefficients.

In the neural network, it is not possible to ascertain whether a particular variable comes into the interpretative model with the wrong sign and to eliminate or replace it, as can be accomplished with traditional econometric and statistical tools. With discriminant analysis, it is possible to learn what the most important variables are for explaining the differences between the companies in the sample. In the network fine-tuning process, the length of the training process, the rate of mean error decline, and the results on the recognition rates are the keys for estimating the soundness of the variables, ex-post.

Our conclusions on the use of neural networks are not straightforward and they recognize the undoubted advantages such networks have. A path we intend to adopt in the future is to integrate networks and discriminant functions, applying the former to less clear and more complex problems of classification in which the flexibility of networks and their capacity for structuring into simple, integrated families could prove to be very useful. The key determinant as to whether neural networks, in conjunction or not with traditional classification procedures, will be integrated into practitioner decisions is the accuracy, logic, and understandability of the process and its components. It must be emphasized again, however, that we have found illogical behavior patterns in all of the many NN systems tried in our research. These results have not been emphasized in previous applications of NN systems to business related problems.

Neural networks have shown enough promising features to provide an incentive for more thorough and creative testing. Analysts' fascination with artificial intelligence models will, no doubt, motivate continued firm related investigations.

REFERENCES

Altman, E., 1968, Financial ratios, discriminant analysis and the prediction of corporate bankruptcy, *Journal of Finance* (Sept.), 589–609.

Altman, E., 1977, Predicting performance in the S&L industry, *Journal of Monetary Economics*, October.

Altman, E., 1993, *Corporate financial distress and bankruptcy*, 2nd ed. (John Wiley and Sons, New York).

Altman, E. and T. McGough, 1974, Evaluation of a company as a going concern, *The Journal of Accountancy* (Dec.), 50–7.

Altman, E., R. Haldeman and P. Narayanan, 1977, ZETA analysis, a new model to identify bankruptcy risk of corporations, *Journal of Banking and Finance* 1, 29–54.

Bell, T., G. Ribar and J. Verchio, 1990, Neural networks vs. logistic regression in predicting bank failures, in: P. Srivastava, ed., *Auditing Symposium X* (University of Kansas).

Cadden, D., 1991, *Neural networks and the mathematics of chaos – an investigation of the methodologies as accurate predictors of corporate bankruptcy* (IEEE).

Cammarata, S., 1990, *Reti neuronali* (Etas Kompass).

Chung, H. and K. Y. Tam, 1993, A comparative analysis of inductive learning algorithms, *Intelligence Systems in Accounting, Finance and Management*.

Coats, P. and L. Fant, 1993, Recognizing financial distress patterns using a neural network tool, *Financial Management* (Nov.), 142–55.

Dutta, S. and S. Shekhar, 1992, Generalization with neural networks: an application to the financial domain, Working Paper 92/30 (INSEAD, Fontainebleau, France).

Fahlman, S. and C. Lebiere, 1992, *The cascade-correlation learning architecture technical report: CMU-90-100* (Carnegie Mellon University) February.

Freeman, J. and D. Skapura, 1991, *Neural networks* (Addison Wesley).

Hertz, J., A. Krogh and R. Palmer, 1991, *Introduction to the theory of neural computing* (Addison Wesley).

Hinton, G., J. McClelland and D. Rumelhart, 1986, Distributed representations, in: D. Rumelhart and J. McClelland, *Parallel distributed processing: exploration in the cognition* (MIT Press, Cambridge, MA).

Karels, G. V. and A. Prakash, 1987, Multivariate normality and forecasting of business bankruptcy, *Journal of Business, Finance and Accounting* (Winter), 573–93.

Kryzanowski, L., 1989, Using artificial neural networks to pick stocks, *Financial Analysis Journal* (July/Aug.), 21–7.

Kryzanowski, L. and M. Galler, 1994, Analysis of small business financial statements using neural nets, *Journal of Accounting, Auditing and Finance*, Forthcoming.

Liang, T., J. Chandler, I. Han and J. Roan, 1992, An empirical investigation of some data effects on the classification accuracy of probit, ID3 and neural networks, in: *Cont. Acc. Res.*, Fall.

Odom, M. and R. Sharda, 1990. A neural network model for bankruptcy prediction, *Proceedings of the IEEE International Conference on Neural Networks* (San Diego, CA) 163–8.

Pau, L. and C. Gianotti, 1990, *Economic and financial knowledge-based processing* (Springer, Berlin).

Raghupathi, W., L. Schleade and B. Raju, 1991, A neural network approach to bankruptcy prediction, *Proceedings of the IEEE 24th International Conference on System Sciences* (Hawaii); Reprinted in Trippi and Turban (1992).

Rahimian, E., S. Singh, T. Thammachofe and R. Virmani, 1992, Bankruptcy prediction by neural network, in: Trippi and Turban (1996).

Rumelhart, D. and J. McClelland, 1986, *Parallel distributed processing: exploration in the cognition* (MIT Press, Cambridge, MA).

Rumelhart, D., G. Hinton and R. Williams, 1986, *Learning internal representations by error propagation, in parallel distributed processing* (Cambridge, MA) 318–62.

Swales, G. and Y. Yoon, 1992, Applying artificial networks to investment analysis, *Financial Analysts Journal* (Sept./Oct.).

Theodossiou, P., 1993, Predicting shifts in the mean of a multivariate time series process: an application in predicting business failures, *Journal of the American Statistical Association* 88(422), 441–9.

Trippi, R. and D. De Sieno, 1992, Trading equity index futures with a neural network, *Journal of Portfolio Management* (Fall).

Trippi, R. and E. Turban, eds. 1996, *Neural networks in finance and investing* (Probus).

Varetto, F., 1990, Il sistema di diagnosi dei rischi di insolvenza della Centrale dei Bilanci, Bancaria edn (Rome). (The Diagnostic System of Risk of Insolvency in the Centrale dei Bilanci.)

Varetto, F. and G. Marco, 1993, Diagnosi delle insolvenze e reti neurali: esperimenti e confronti con l'Analisi discriminante lineare, *W. P. Centrale dei Bilanci*, Sept. 1993.

Wong, F., P. Wang, T. Goh and B. Quek, 1992, Fuzzy neural systems for stock selection, *Financial Analysts Journal* (Jan./Feb.), 47–52.

4 | Business Failure Classification Models: An International Survey

with Paul Narayanan

INTRODUCTION

Business failure identification and early warnings of impending financial crisis are important not only to analysts and practitioners in the USA. Indeed, countries throughout the world, even non-capitalist nations, have been concerned with individual entity performance assessment. Developing countries and smaller economies, as well as the larger industrialized nations of the world, are vitally concerned with avoiding financial crises in the private and public sectors. Some policy makers in smaller nations are particularly concerned with financial panics resulting from failures of individual entities.

From the late 1960s to the present day, numerous studies in the USA were devoted to assessing one's ability to combine publicly available data with statistical classification techniques in order to predict business failure. Studies by Beaver (1967) and Altman (1968) provided the stimulus for numerous other papers. One of the first attempts at modern statistical failure analysis was performed by Tamari (1964). We will not discuss his work here, but we point out its pioneering status. A steady stream of failure prediction papers have appeared in the English literature, and numerous textbooks and monographs include a section or chapter on these models; for example, see Brigham and Ehrhardt (2001) and Ross et al. (1999). What has gone relatively unnoticed is the considerable effort made to replicate and extend these models to environments outside the USA. With the exception of two special issues of the *Journal of Banking and Finance* (1984 and 1988), edited by one of the authors of this article, there is no work with which we are familiar that attempts to survey these studies and to comment on their similarities and differences. The purpose of this paper is to do just that.

We survey the works by academics and practitioners in 22 countries and give references to several other studies. This survey will bring together these myriad studies and highlight study designs, innovations and outcomes that will be of practical value to researchers and practitioners. While the economic forces shaping the outcomes in various countries may diverge, the researchers share a striking similarity in their approach to distress prediction. For example, nearly every study contrasts the profile of failed firms with that of healthier firms to draw conclusions about the coincident factors of failure. Causal studies of failure appear to be comparatively rare.

In several of the countries studied, notably Brazil, France, Canada, Australia, Korea, Mexico and Italy, the authors of this article have participated directly in the construction of a failure classification model. In many cases, we can present an in-depth discussion of the models including individual variable weights. In others, we present the models in more general terms due to the lack of precise documentation in the original article. In general, to make this survey useful to researchers and practitioners alike, we attempt to summarize the contents of the models under the following headings:

1   *Modeling techniques used*
    While multiple discriminant analysis (MDA) continues to be the most popular technique, researchers have tried other techniques such as multi-nomial logit analysis, probit analysis, recursive partitioning (decision tree analysis), Bayesian discriminant analysis, survival analysis and neural networks. For a variety of reasons, MDA appears to be a *de facto* standard for comparison of distress prediction models. Where the authors have used a technique other than MDA, they usually have compared its results with those from MDA. It is interesting to note that MDA results continue to compare favorably with the other techniques.

2   *Data issues*
    The size of the sample used and the sources of data are oftentimes critical in assessing the statistical validity of results as well as in the planning of replication or extension type studies. As in many areas of empirical research, the sophistication of the techniques is often not matched by the availability of good data, especially data on failed firms. This problem tends to be more pronounced in the smaller economies of some of the developed countries and in the case of most developing countries. As is common in all empirical research, the randomness and the size of the sample used are mentioned because they are generally indicative of the degree of confidence that may be placed in the conclusions being drawn.

3   *Definition of "failure" and "non-failure"*
    Most models employ a sample of two *a priori* groups consisting of "failed" and "non-failed" firms. Depending on the inclination of the researcher or on the local conditions, the definition of a failure may vary. Some examples are, bankruptcy filing by a company, bond default, bank loan default, delisting of a company, government intervention via special financing, and liquidation. Closely tied to the failure event is the date of the event. The quality of almost all conclusions drawn about how "early" the distress prediction was depends upon where the analyst placed the date of failure. The healthy firms data is, by definition, "censored" data because all that can be said of the healthy firms is that they were healthy at the time the sample was taken. It has been found, for example, that some firms that appear to be Type II errors by a model (healthy firms classified as failures) turned out to have failed at a later time.

4   *Test results*
    It is customary to expect test statistics (such as the t and F statistics) to indicate the statistical significance of the findings. While this is done to establish a baseline for measurement, it is important to note that useful conclusions may be

drawn from even small sample studies. In-sample and out-of-sample or hold-out results, Type I and Type II results, and analyst-modified results are also reported where available.

Developing and Developed Country Models

The failure prediction models reviewed in this chapter may be broadly grouped into two homogeneous categories: developed country models and developing country models. The classification of a country as a "developing" or a "developed" country in this survey is in the context of failure prediction and may deviate somewhat from the traditional grouping of the country.

The main characteristics of developed country models are:

1 failure prediction studies have a long history
2 corporate financial data are more readily available
3 failure is easier to identify because of the existence of bankruptcy laws and banking infrastructures
4 government intervention is somewhat less, but not nonexistent, and
5 there is a more sophisticated regulation of companies to protect investors.

The developing country models are characterized by the relative absence of the above factors. In developing countries, where free market economies have not taken hold, a company's failure is harder to see because of the degree of protection provided by the government. However, one may also point to similar practices in developed countries, notably the UK, Germany, Japan, to a lesser extent, and even the USA on some rare occasions, e.g., Chrysler in 1980.

Table 4.1 summarizes the 43 studies from 22 countries included in this survey.

While we believe this international treatment of failure prediction models is the most comprehensive effort to date, we recognize that some relevant works will possibly be overlooked in this survey and apologize for any omission.

Emerging Markets Application

One of the models presented in this chapter was developed by Altman, Hartzell and Peck (1995) to rate the credit quality of emerging markets corporate debt. We discuss it below in the context of Mexico – one of the prime countries whose companies have tapped the international bond markets in recent years. This application has particular relevance since the vast majority of Mexican, Latin American, and emerging market countries' corporate debt in general is as yet still unrated by the major rating agencies. The model is a variation on the original Z-Score model developed by Altman (1968).

AUSTRALIA

Australia has certain unique characteristics, with huge development potential (like Brazil) but with an already established industrial base. While the influence of multinational firms is quite important, the local corporate structure is large enough to support a fairly substantial capital market.

Table 4.1   List of international studies surveyed

Developed countries	
Australia	Castagna and Matolcsy (1982)
	Altman and Izan (1981) and Izan (1984)
	Lincoln (1984)
Canada	Knight (1979)
	Altman and Lavallee (1981)
England	Taffler and Tisshaw (1977)
	Marais (1979)
	Earl and Marais (1982)
	Argenti (1983)
France	Altman et al. (1973)
	Mader (1975, 1979)
	Collongues (1977)
	Bontemps (1981)
Germany	von Stein (1968)
	Beermann (1976)
	Weinrich (1978)
	Gebhardt (1980)
	Fischer (1981)
	von Stein and Ziegler (1984)
	Baetge et al. (1988)
Greece	Gloubos and Grammatikos (1988)
	Theodossiou and Papoulias (1988)
Italy	Cifarelli et al. (1988)
	Altman et al. (1994)
Japan	Takahashi et al. (1979)
	Ko (1982)
The Netherlands	Bilderbeek (1979)
	van Frederikslust (1978)
	Fire Scoring System (de Breed and Pantners 1996)
Spain	Briones et al. (1988)
	Fernandez (1988)
Switzerland	Weibel (1973)
Developing countries	
Argentina	Swanson and Tybout in Altman (1988)
Brazil	Altman et al. (1979)
Finland	Suominen (1988)
India	Bhatia (1988)
Ireland	Cahill (1981)
Korea	Altman, Kim and Eom (1995)
Malaysia	Bidin (1988)
Mexico	Altman, Hartzell and Peck (1995)
Singapore	Ta and Seah (1981)
Turkey	Unal (1988)
Uruguay	Pascale (1988)

Castagna and Matolcsy (1982)

The active financial environment in Australia is a motivation for rigorous individual firm analysis. A series of studies by Castagna and Matolcsy culminating in their published work (1982) have analyzed corporate failures in Australia and have concluded that there is a strong potential for models like those developed in the USA to assist analysts and managers.

RESEARCH DESIGN

One of the difficult requirements for failure analysis found in just about every country in the world outside the USA is assembling a data base of failed companies large enough to perform a reliable discriminant analysis model. Despite a relatively large number of liquidations, Australian data on failed firms are quite restricted. Castagna and Matolcsy were able to assemble a sample of only 21 industrial companies (the number of firms would have been much larger if mining companies were included). The failure dates spanned the years from 1963 through 1977, with the date determined by the appointment of a liquidator or receiver. An alternative criterion date might have been the time of delisting from the stock exchange or the liquidation/receiver date, whichever comes first. For every failed company in the sample, there is a randomly selected surviving quoted industrial firm from the same period. Industries represented include retailers, manufacturers, builders, and service firms.

EMPIRICAL RESULTS

Prior studies by Castagna and Matolcsy reduced the number of potential discriminating variables to ten, which were then analyzed in a linear and quadratic discriminant structure. Castagna and Matolcsy also attempted to test their results for various *a priori* group membership probabilities. The results suggest that it is difficult to identify a unique model to predict corporate failures and that some specification of user preferences is desirable. Still, they do indicate a 10-variable linear and 5-variable quadratic classification models.

As noted, the results of their work are not definitive. For example, if one is concerned with minimizing the misclassification of failed companies, then the linear model using equal priors outperforms all other models tried. This model also had the best overall results, except in the fourth year prior to failure. However, the linear model does not perform better than other models in the classification of surviving companies. A stepwise procedure indicated that a 5-variable model did not perform as well as the models based on the 10-ratio set in the overall classification tests. All of their comparisons are based on the Lachenbruch validation tests.

The Castagna and Matolcsy study does not address prediction accuracy *per se*. All of the tests are on the original sample of 21 firms. For the tests to be predictive in nature, their model(s) should be applied to subsequent firm performance in Australia. Castagna and Matolcsy do note that they expect to monitor their findings on samples of continuing companies listed on the Australian Stock Exchange.

Altman and Izan (1981) and Izan (1984)

Altman and Izan (1981) and Izan (1984) in an attempt to address the failure classification problem in Australia, analyzed a larger sample (50 failed firms and an industry-failure-year-matched sample of 50 non-failed firms). Perhaps the most distinctive aspect of this model is the attempt to standardize the ratios by the respective firms' industry medians. The argument to use industry-relatives is to point to the significant differences that exist among industries of the key financial ratios. As for the counter-argument that some industries are indeed riskier than others, Altman and Izan respond by stating that a near-bankrupt situation of any of the industries represented in the study is extremely remote. Having made the argument for using the industry-relatives, Izan proceeds to derive the value of this variable by dividing the failed and the non-failed firm's raw ratio by the industry median.

The ten candidate ratios chosen for analysis were the following:

- Ordinary earnings/Shareholder funds
- Earnings before interest and taxes/Total assets
- Earnings after interest and taxes/Total assets
- Cash flow/Borrowings
- EBIT/Interest
- Current assets/Current liabilities
- Current assets stocks/Current liabilities – overdrafts
- Funded debt/Shareholder funds
- Market value of equity/Total liabilities
- Book value of equity/Market value of equity

The final model was quite similar to the Altman (1968) model. The ratios in the model and their relative contributions are as shown in table 4.2. The classification accuracy of the models on the development sample one year prior to failure is presented in table 4.3.

The industry relative ratios model showed a Type I accuracy of 94.1 percent, 75 percent and 63.5 percent respectively on data one, two and three years prior to failure. Type II accuracy for the same periods was 89.6 percent, 89.6 percent and 85.4 percent

Table 4.2 Relative contribution tests and ranks of variables in the distress model

Variable	Univariate F		Standardized coefficient		Wilk's Lambda		Forward stepwise
	Amount	Rank	Amount	Rank	Amount	Rank	
EBIT/TA	26.4	3	0.79	3	0.23	5	3
EBIT/Interest	49.2	1	0.66	1	0.53	1	1
CA/CL	4.3	5	0.96	5	0.24	4	5
FD/SF	21.6	4	0.82	4	−0.25	3	4
MV/TL	36.9	2	0.72	2	0.44	2	2

Table 4.3 Classification accuracy of the industry relative and the raw ratio models

Actual Group	No of Cases	Industry relative ratios Classified		Raw ratios Classified	
		Failed	Non-failed	Failed	Non-failed
Failed	51	48 (94.1%)	3 (7.8%)	46 (90.2)	5 (9.8%)
Non-failed	48	5 (10.4%)	43 (89.6%)	5 (10.4%)	43 (89.6%)

respectively. The prediction accuracy on a small secondary sample (holdout) of ten failed firms was 100 percent one year prior to failure, 70 percent two years prior and 40 percent three years prior. In the absence of the corresponding Type II accuracy, this result is difficult to interpret, however. Izan believes that the model is sufficiently robust as to be applicable to a cross-section of firms and industries and appropriate for analyzing firms.

Lincoln (1984) also analyzed Australian business failures and started a type of rating service firm, based on his discriminant analysis models.

CANADA

Canada, like Australia, is a relatively small country in terms of business population, yet it too is concerned with the performance assessment of individual entities. The economy is very much tied to the fortunes of the USA and its financial reporting standards are often derived from the same accounting principles. Like many other environments, the key constraint in Canada is the availability of a large and reliable data base of failed companies. This requires both a sufficient number of failures and publicly available data on those firms. Both attributes do exist in Canada, but just barely.

Knight (1979)

Knight (1979) analyzed the records of a large number of small business failures as well as conducting interviews with the key persons involved. Knight contends that his study supplies information "to answer the question, why do small businesses fail in Canada and also generates certain guidelines as to how the failure rate in Canada may be decreased from its recent increasing level." Not surprisingly, Knight finds that a firm usually fails early in its life (50 percent of all failed firms do so within four years and 70 percent within six) and that some type of managerial incompetence accounts for almost all failures.

Knight also attempted to classify failure using a discriminant analysis model. He amassed a fairly large sample of 72 failed small firms with average sales and assets of about $100,000. A five-variable discriminant function realized disappointing results, however. Only 64 percent of the original sample of 36 failed and 36 non-failed firms and 54 percent of the test sample of a like number of firms were correctly classified. He concluded that the discriminant analysis procedure was not successful. Knight did combine firms in many different industries, including manufacturing, service, retail, and construction and this will contribute to estimation problems, especially if the data are not adjusted to take into consideration industry differences and/or accounting differences, for instance, lease capitalization. We discuss this industry effect at length in the Australian situation.

Altman and Lavallee (1981)

The results of Altman and Lavallee (1981) were more accurate when manufacturing and retailing firms were combined but they do not advocate a single model for both sectors. Indeed, the holdout tests of this study indicate that non-manufacturers cannot be confidently measured when the model contains variables which are industry sensitive.

The Altman and Lavallee study was based on a sample of 54 publicly traded firms, half failed and half continuing entities. The failures took place during the ten years 1970–79 and the average tangible asset size of these 27 failures was $12.6 million at one statement date prior to failure (average lag was 16 months). Manufacturers and retailer-wholesalers were combined although the data did not enable them to adjust assets and liabilities for lease capitalization. The continuing firms were stratified by industry, size, and data period, and had average assets of $15.6 million. One can observe, therefore, that the Canadian model for the 1970s consisted of firms with asset sizes similar to those of the previously reported US models (e.g. Altman, 1968) constructed from the 1950s and 1960s data period.

Altman and Lavallee examined just 11 ratios, and their resulting model contained five based on a forward stepwise selection procedure. The model for Canada (Z_C) is

$$Z_C = -1.626 + 0.234(X_1) - 0.531(X_2) + 1.002(X_3) + 0.972(X_4) + 0.612(X_5)$$

where

Z_C = Canadian Z-score
X_1 = Sales/Total assets
X_2 = total debt/total assets
X_3 = current assets/current liabilities
X_4 = net profits after tax/total debt, and
X_5 = rate of growth of equity – rate of asset growth.

CLASSIFICATION RESULTS

The overall classification accuracy of the Z_C model on the original 54-firm sample was 83.3 percent, which is quite high, although not as impressive as that reported in some of the other economic environments. Practically speaking, classification criteria are based on a zero cutoff score with positive scores indicating a non-failed classification and negative scores a failed assignment. Reliability, or holdout tests, included Lachenbruch (1967) test replications, the original sample broken into randomly chosen classification and test samples, and testing the model on prior years' data, for example years 2 through 4 before failure. The Lachenbruch and replication holdout results showed accuracies very similar to those of the original sample results and the prior year accuracies were 73 percent (year 2), 53 percent (year 3), and only 30 percent (year 4). Therefore, the model appears reasonably accurate for up to two statements prior to failure but not accurate for earlier periods. These findings are quite similar to those of Altman's (1968) model and we can suggest that the similarities in accuracies are partially related to the similarities of the data quality and the somewhat diverse industries represented in the sample.

Altman and Lavallee also simulated their results for various assumptions of prior probabilities of group membership and costs of error. Their findings were that Type I errors could be reduced, even eliminated, but that the resulting Type II error was unacceptably high and vice versa for eliminating the Type II error. The Z model's results were also compared to a naive classification strategy of assigning all observations to the non-bankrupt category or assuming that the resulting errors would be realized in proportion to the actual experience of bankrupts and non-bankrupts [proportional chance model; see Joy and Tollefson (1975)]. They concluded that, in every case, the Canadian Z model was more efficient; that is, it had a lower expected cost than a naive model.

Finally, Altman and Lavallee observe that the industry affiliations of the misclassified firms were predominantly retailers among the failed group and manufacturers among the non-failed. It appeared that one of the variables, sales/assets (X_1), was particularly sensitive to industry effects, with the misclassified failed retailers all having high asset turnovers and the misclassified manufacturers all with low turnovers.

IMPLICATIONS

Altman and Lavallee attempted to re-estimate the model without the sales/assets variable, but the results actually were worse. One can conclude that the Canadian investigations are at an early stage and follow-up work is needed in subdividing a larger sample into manufacturers and retailers-wholesalers and/or improving the information on critical industry differences, such as lease usage and capitalization. Only additional time will permit analysts to construct models with sufficiently large samples or to witness an improvement in the quality of reported data. We are aware of a move with the Canadian government to set up an early warning system to identify potential large publicly traded firm crisis situations, for instance, Massey-Ferguson. (The Canadian Import–Export Agency has been analyzing such models in the late 1990s.)

ENGLAND

Taffler and Tisshaw (1977)

Taffler and Tisshaw (1977) have approached the corporate distress problem primarily from the viewpoint of security analysis and adaptations of their work, and that of Taffler and Houston (1980) and Taffler (1976). They indicate that their model is also relevant for accounting firms to assess the going concern capability of clients and in their work as receivers and liquidators of firms that have already failed.

RESEARCH DESIGN

To construct their solvency model, Taffler and Tisshaw utilized linear discriminant analysis on a sample of 46 failed firms and 46 financially sound manufacturing companies. The latter sample was matched to the failed sample by size and industry (no information on these characteristics available), from period 1969 through 1975. Failed firms were those entering into receivership, creditors' voluntary liquidation, compulsory winding up by order of the court, or government action (bailouts) undertaken as an alternative to the other unfortunate fates. Eighty different ratios were examined for the two samples with a resulting model utilizing only four measures:

- X_1 = Profit before tax/Current liabilities
- X_2 = Current assets/Total liabilities
- X_3 = Current liabilities/Total assets
- X_4 = No-credit interval

The first three ratios are taken from the balance sheet and measure profitability, liquidity, and a type of leverage, respectively. The no-credit interval is the time for which the company can finance its continuing operations from its immediate assets if all other sources of short-term finance are cut-off. More directly, it is defined as Immediate assets – Current liabilities/Operating costs excluding depreciation. Taffler and Tisshaw state that the no-credit interval is "something akin to the acid-test ratio" (p. 52).

EMPIRICAL RESULTS

Both the model described above and an "unquoted model" (for non-listed companies) appeared to be quite accurate in classifying correctly over 97 percent of all observations. Another model by Taffler (1976), supposedly the one being used by practitioners in the UK investment community, had accuracies of 96 percent, 70 percent, 61 percent, and 35 percent for the four years prior to failure.

The nearly perfect one-year-prior accuracy that Taffler and Tisshaw observe utilizing their model contrasts sharply with the relatively small percentage of quoted and unquoted firms that were assessed to have a going concern problem by their auditors. In fact, Taffler and Tisshaw report that just 22 percent of the 46 quoted firms (and none of the 31 unquoted manufacturing bankrupt firms) had been qualified on going concern grounds prior to failure.

IMPLICATIONS

The drop-off in accuracy is quite noticeable as earlier year data are applied, although, for investment purposes, one needs less of a lead time before failure in order to disinvest without losing a major amount of his investment. It is fair to say, however, that as failure approaches, stock prices tend to move downward in a rather continuous manner. Taffler and Houston (1980) indicated that 12 percent of large quoted industrial firms had Z scores indicating high failure risk. This is a comparable figure to results we observed utilizing our own ZETA® model (Altman et al., 1977) in the USA.

Taffler and Tisshaw also point out that about 15–20 percent of those firms which display a profile similar to failed companies will actually fail. In addition, the British government appeared to them to be keeping many ailing firms alive. Although this type of paternalism is less common in the USA, examples like Lockheed and Chrysler Corp. periodically crop up. Finally, Taffler and Tisshaw conclude that accountants are too defensive when it comes to considering the value of conventional published historic statements. When several measures of a firm, described from a set of accounts, are considered together, the value of the information derived is enhanced dramatically. Essentially, Taffler and Tisshaw advocate a multivariate approach to financial analysis, and I certainly agree. It is unfortunate that they did not share with readers a more complete description of their findings and the data used in their analysis. Their results are certainly provocative and appear to be of some practical use in England.

In his latest attempt to revise the company failure discriminant model (Taffler, 1982), a smaller sample of 23 failed companies (1968–73) and 45 non-failed entities displaying financially healthy profiles were examined first within a principal component analysis framework. A large list of almost 150 potential variables was reduced to just five:

- Earnings before interest and taxes/Total assets
- Total liabilities/Net capital employed
- Quick assets/Total assets
- Working capital/Net worth
- Stock inventory turnover

The variables were discussed in terms of their discriminant standardized coefficients and other relative measures of contribution, but no function weights were provided. Taffler did utilize prior probability and cost-of-error estimates in his classification procedures. He concludes that such an approach is best used in an operational context as a means of identifying a short list of firms which might experience financial distress (p. 15). Another conclusion is that the actual bankruptcy event is essentially determined by the actions of the financial institutions and other creditors, and cannot strictly be predicted by using a model approach.

Other UK Studies

Marais (1979), while on a short-term assignment for the Industrial Finance Unit of the Bank of England, also utilized discriminant analysis to quantify relative firm performance. He too concentrated on UK industrials and incorporated flow of funds variables with conventional balance sheet and income statement measures. Using a sample of 38 failed and 53 non-failed companies (1974–1977), he tested several previously published models from the USA and the UK using both univariate and multivariate techniques.

He then went on to develop his own model, of which space does not permit a full discussion. His model included the following variables:

- X_1 = Current assets/Gross total assets
- X_2 = 1/Gross total assets
- X_3 = Cash flow/Current liabilities
- X_4 = Funds generated from operations – Net change in working capital to total debt

His results were considered "satisfactory" and his conclusions modest. He mainly advocated that firms whose scores fell below a certain cutoff point should be regarded as possible future problems; "that all Z scores can hope to do is act as a sophisticated screening device to those firms most urgently in need of analysis" (p. 29).

A later work, by Earl and Marais (1982), expanded upon this work with more enthusiastically reported results and implications. Classification results of 93 percent, 87 percent, and 84 percent respectively for the three years prior to failure were reported. The authors felt that funds flow data improved their classification accuracy. The single ratio of Cash flow/Current liabilities was a successful discriminator. Subsequent tests on failures and non-failures in 1978 revealed a very low Type I error but an unacceptably high Type II error assessment.

Argenti (1983) postulated a scoring system that included both quantitative and qualitative variables but his weights were not based on statistical analysis.

FRANCE

In France, the business failure rate increased dramatically in the early 1980s, prompting Altman et al. (1973) to attempt to apply credit scoring techniques to problem firms, many of which filed for bankruptcy (*faillite*). Working with a sample of textile firms and data provided by Banque de France, this study applied principal component analysis to a large number of financial indicators and proceeded to utilize the most important ones in a linear discriminant model. Their results were at best mediocre on test samples and, while the model did provide insights into that troublesome sector, it was not implemented on a practical basis.

A more recent study by Bontemps (1981), using a large sample of industrial companies and data from the Centrale de bilans of Credit National (supplier of long-term debt capital to French firms), achieved high accuracy on original and holdout tests. Bontemps' results are quite interesting in that as little as three variables were found to be useful indicators. He combined both the univariate technique developed by Beaver (1967) with arbitrary, qualitative weightings of the three most effective measures to classify correctly as much as 87 percent of his holdout sample of 34 failed and 34 non-failed firms. The original function was built based on a matched (by industry, size, and year) sample of 50 failed and non-failed entities from 1974 through 1979.

Collongues (1977), Mader (1975, 1979) also have attempted to combine financial ratios with data from failed and non-failed French firms. Mader's studies were descriptive of firms in difficulty and the utility of ratios as risk measures. These have led to several multivariate studies performed by the Banque de France in their Centrale de bilans group. Collongues did utilize discriminant analysis in his analysis of small and medium-size firms with some success.

The application of statistical credit scoring techniques in the French environment appears to be problematic, but the potential remains. One problem usually is the quality of data and the representativeness of them. But this is a problem in all countries and is not unique to France. The government has gone on record on several occasions as intending not to keep hopelessly insolvent firms alive artificially but to try to assist those ailing firms prior to total collapse. An accurate performance predictor model could very well help in this endeavor.

GERMANY

Many studies in Germany have investigated the causes and problems of insolvencies, especially for financial organizations, e.g., von Stein (1968).

Beerman (1976)

Beerman (1976) published one of the first German statistical classification models for insolvency analysis. He examined matched groups of 21 firms which operated or failed in 1966 through 1971. Applying dichotomous and linear discriminant tests, he analyzed 10 ratios encompassing profitability, cash flow, fixed asset growth, leverage, and turnover. His results, using the difference in means dichotomous test, were mixed, with one ratio type (profitability) yielding quite respectable results. The other ratios were far less impressive on a univariate basis.

Beerman advocates using discriminant analysis, and his 10-ratio model yielded classification error rates of 9.5 percent, 19.0 percent, 28.6 percent, and 38.1 percent for the four years prior to failure. He does not indicate which model to use, and the coefficients of each measure were quite unstable in the four different year models. Also, we are given no indication of holdout test results or predictive accuracy and, due to the small sample, we do not have confirming evidence of the model(s) reliability.

Weinrich (1978)

Weinrich's (1978) book, from his dissertation, attempted to construct risk classes in order to predict insolvency. His sample of failed firms was considerably larger (44) than Beermann's, concentrating on small and intermediate-size firms, with average sales of DM 4 million (less than $2 million), that failed from 1969 through 1975. Weinrich considered three consecutive annual financial statements (years 2 through 4 prior to failure) but did not utilize the one statement closest to insolvency. This is a marked difference from most of the other models we have studied.

Weinrich abandoned the use of parametric classification techniques because of his feeling that many assumptions were violated (normality, variance homogeneity of groups, and high correlation among the variables). His linear discriminant models were quite good in terms of classification accuracy (11 percent error for year 2, 15.7 percent and 21.9 percent for years 3 and 4, respectively).

Weinrich did use factor analysis and found the technique useful, indicating at least six different factors that explained 80 percent of the variance of the ratios. He then devised a model of credit-worthiness that contained eight relatively independent ratios and utilized both univariate and multivariate methods. A point evaluation system was devised based on quartile values of good and bad firms. For example, a net worth/debt ratio over 43.3 percent receives the best (lowest) point value. A firm with significant insolvency potential is one with 24 points or more (an average of three for each of the eight ratios). This arbitrary point system correctly classified over 90 percent of the failed firms two years prior to failure, but was only 60 percent accurate three years prior. The Type II error rate was quite high, averaging well over 20 percent in each year. Weinrich advocated the use of trend analysis of the point system as well as the point estimate.

Gebhardt (1980)

Gebhardt (1980) compared dichotomous and multivariate classification tests of samples of failed and non-failed firms based on models constructed before and after the 1965 Financial Statement Reform Law. The earlier model contained 13 matched pairs of industrial firms and the post-1965 model contained 28 pairs. He utilized a very large number of possible financial indicators which were reduced to 41 ratios for the dichotomous tests. He also incorporated crude measures of misclassification costs and tested his results with the Lachenbruch (1967) holdout test procedure. Gebhardt, like others, felt that the non-normality of some ratios implied the use of non-parametric procedures but found those results unsatisfactory. The multivariate results were far superior. Gebhardt concluded that the pre-1965 models' results were actually better than the ones following the reform law.

Fischer (1981)

Fischer's work concentrates on non-numerical data for forecasting failure. He is particularly interested in methods of credit evaluation for suppliers who do not have the ability or the data to perform comprehensive conventional analysis on their existing and potential customers. He advocates an electronic data processing system which can retrieve and analyze such non-numerical information as reports from newspapers, magazines, inquiry agencies, and credit information from other sellers. Unfortunately, according to Fischer, commercial rating agencies and banks are constrained as to how honest and revealing they choose to be with regard to their reports. In addition, the information provided may be outdated and certainly contains subjective elements. More than one source of credit information is therefore desirable.

Fischer advocates combining the permanent and transitory information on enterprises with microeconomic and sociopolitical data. Five arbitrary rating categories are devised based on non-numerical data and the delphi technique (numerous experts in various areas) is also recommended. Each characteristic is rated over time into the five categories. The sum of development patterns from varying sources of information builds the basis for a final classification. Clustering techniques are also used by Fischer to clarify information types.

von Stein and Ziegler (1984)

This is an ambitious attempt to identify bankruptcy risk from three separate, yet inter-related, perspectives:

1   balance sheet analysis using financial ratios
2   analysis of the bank accounts of firms, and
3   analysis of the behavioral characteristics of company management.

The study thus addresses criticism leveled at relying exclusively on one of the three approaches in assessing failure risk.

The balance sheet analysis considers medium-sized firms in Germany. The failure dates for the "bads" covered the years from 1971 to 1978. The date for all the "goods" was fixed (1977). There were 119 failed companies; the failure date was defined as the date of the first value adjustment or write-off, or only in a few cases, the date of the bankruptcy or composition petition. The "goods" consisted of 327 companies. The companies in the "bad" sample were from the following industries: manufacturing and processing (54.5 percent), building (17.7 percent), trade (22.7 percent), others (5.1). The companies in the "goods" sample were comparably distributed across industries.

Thirteen financial ratios were identified as the most discriminating of the 140 ratios initially considered:

1 Capital borrowed/Total capital
2 (Short-term borrowed capital × 360)/Total output)
3 (Accounts payable for purchases and deliveries × 360)/Material costs
4 (Bill of exchange liabilities + Accounts payable for purchases and deliveries × 360)/Total output
5 (Current assets – Short-term borrowed capital)/Total output
6 Equity/(Total assets – Liquid assets – Real estates and buildings)
7 Equity/(Tangible property – Real estates and buildings)
8 Short-term borrowed capital/Current assets
9 (Working expenditure – Depreciation on tangible property)/(Liquid assets + Accounts receivable for sales and services – Short-term borrowed capital)
10 Operational result/Total capital
11 (Operational result + Depreciation on tangible property)/Net turnover
12 (Operational result + Depreciation on tangible property)/Short-term borrowed capital
13 (Operational result + Depreciation on tangible property)/Capital borrowed

Three non-parametric methods (Nearest~Neighbor Classifications: Fix–Hodges, Loftsgaarden–Quiesenberry and Parzen) and two parametric methods (linear and quadratic multiple discriminant analysis) were tested. The method of Fix and Hodges was found to be the most discriminating. The results of the tests on the development sample are given in table 4.4.

Table 4.4 Classification results – Fix/Hodges non-parametric model

Group	Year before fixed date	Correct Classification (%)
Bad cases	5	71.4
	4	78.2
	3	86.6
	2	89.9
	1	95.0
Good cases	1977	83.7

In the second phase of the analysis, 45 bad and 37 good cases were examined using the following account characteristic variables:

1 Average balance with regard to value dates
2 Most favorable balance for the borrower
3 Most unfavorable balance for the borrower
4 Credit turnover
5 Debit turnover
6 Bill of exchange credits
7 Cheque credits
8 Transfer credits
9 Cash deposits
10 Bill of exchange debits

11   Cheque debits
12   Transfer debits
13   Cash payouts
14   Limit

Profile analysis, dichotomous classification and linear discriminant analysis were the three techniques applied on the data. All three methods revealed important differences between the bad and the good companies. Linear discriminant analysis provided the best results. The function contained the following variables:

1   (Most favorable balance for the borrower)/Limit
2   (Most favorable balance for the borrower)/Debit turnover
3   Cheque debits/Debit turnover
4   Debit turnover/Limit
5   Bill of exchange debits/Debit turnover
6   Transfer credits/Credit turnover

The classification results on the development sample are shown in table 4.5.

Table 4.5   Classification results on the development sample

Semi-annual period before fixed date	Correct classification (%)	Correct classification of good cases (%)
8	73.3	89.2
7	66.7	83.8
6	75.6	81.1
5	80.0	89.2
4	82.2	78.4
3	91.1	78.4
2	88.9	83.8
1	88.9	83.8

The third phase of the study attempted to identify the characteristics and concrete behavioral indications that distinguish the failed firms from the solvent ones. von Stein and Ziegler used a psychological technique named "nomethetical assessment" and the "principle of simultaneous vision." The later term is taken to mean that the authors looked for factors consistently found in the failed group that are consistently absent in the non-failed groups. The investigation was based on 135 bad companies and 25 good companies and consisted of

a)   an examination of the functional areas of the companies leading to their weak points and
b)   partly standardized interviews of bank lending personnel most familiar with the history and behavioral characteristics of the owner/managers.

The qualities found to set the failed company management apart were the following:

1 Being out of touch with reality
2 Large technical knowledge but poor commercial control
3 Great talents in salesmanship
4 Strong-willed
5 Sumptuous living and unreasonable withdrawals
6 Excessive risk-taking

The management of the solvent companies were found to be more homogeneous than the failed companies and seldom showed a lack of consciousness of reality. The authors recommend all three components of analysis (balance sheet, account behavior and management) be pursued to assess a company.

Baetge, Muss and Niehaus (1988)

Baetge et al.'s study reports the results of a multiple discriminant analysis model whose aim is to identify at least 80 percent of the endangered corporate borrowers three years before they become distressed.

The bad borrowers were defined as those that resulted in a final credit loss to the bank or wherever a temporal delay occurred or was feared in the payment of the obligations of the borrower as stipulated by contract. Good borrowers were those that did not possess the above characteristics. Samples were drawn from both bad and good enterprises representative of the line of business, legal form and size. Principal component analysis was used to reduce the initial universe of 42 financial ratios to seven factors. These factors in turn led to a three-variable MDA model consisting of the following ratios:

- *Capital structure*: Net worth/(Total assets – Quick assets – Property and plant [without equipment])
- *Profitability*: (Operating income + Ordinary depreciation + Addition to pension reserves)/Total assets
- *Financial strength*: (Cash income including extraordinary income – Cash expense including extraordinary expense)/Short-term liabilities.

Rather than using the cutoff point as the basis for separating the firms into good and bad groups, Baetge et al. created a gray area around the cutoff point where the probability of assigning to either group was low. By doing so, they were able to put the predictive accuracy of the model in a clearer perspective. The discriminant function was subsequently tested with about 40,000 financial statements of all corporate customers of the bank. The results of the tests were quite similar to that found on the analysis sample. The model proved very stable when tested using a simulation model developed at Gottingen University.

GREECE

Gloubos and Grammatikos (1988)

Companies in regulated economies are often sustained in operation long after they have become economically bankrupt. These cause taxonomic problems for the researcher because to treat such companies as healthy is clearly wrong, while including them in the bankrupt group causes biases because of the difficulties in identifying the date of the bankruptcy. Gloubos and Grammatikos suggest that estimated models in such economies as Greece may be expected to have a higher degree of misclassification than similar models estimated in market-driven economies. In this study, Gloubos and Grammatikos compare four techniques on a "new" sample of healthy and bankrupt firms:

- Linear Probability Model (LPM)
- Probit Analysis (PROBIT)
- Logit Analysis (LOGIT)
- Multiple Discriminant Analysis (MDA)

The LPM model is a multiple linear regression model where the dependent variable is a 0–1 variable which is regressed against a set of independent variables. The problems with this approach are that the error terms are heteroscedastic and their distribution is not normal. Also, when the predicted value lies outside the 0–1 range, it is difficult to interpret the result. This difficulty is overcome by applying suitable transformations that would restrict the probability predictions to the 0–1 interval. This is done in the PROBIT model where P the conditional probability of failure is expressed in terms of a cumulative standard normal distribution function. As to be expected, the introduction of the standard normal distribution involved nonlinear estimation. The LOGIT model uses a computationally simpler function based on the cumulative logistic probability function. In multiple discriminant analysis, the function is linear or quadratic in the variables.

The sample consisted of 30 Greek industrial firms that went bankrupt during the period 1977–81. Each failed firm was paired with a healthy firm of similar size in the same year and from the same industry. Data was gathered for one year prior to bankruptcy and was obtained from various issues of the *Government Gazette*. Seventeen accounting ratios were used in the analysis and the final models with all four techniques had the same variables. The group statistics for these ratios along with the T-statistics are presented in table 4.6.

The model results on the development sample are as reproduced in table 4.7. It was found that the MDA and LPM have the greater accuracy overall and also in the Type I and Type II categories. Gloubos and Grammatikos note that the MDA model's coefficients for two of the variables had counter-intuitive signs but go on to suggest that because of the interdependencies inherent in a multivariate model, this may be acceptable. The models were tested on 24 new paired samples of bankrupt and healthy firms for the period 1982–85. As to be expected, the classification performance of the models drops off somewhat in the holdout sample as shown in table 4.8.

Table 4.6 Group statistics

Variable	Group mean bankrupt	Group mean non-bankrupt	T-value
Current assets/Current liabilities	0.932	1.579	−3.95
Net working capital/Total assets	−0.092	0.196	−5.20
Total debt/Total assets	0.813	0.595	5.69
Gross income/Total assets	0.077	0.253	−4.51
Gross income/Current liabilities	0.106	0.607	6.16

Table 4.7   Correct classifications on the original sample

One year prior to bankruptcy	Overall (%)	Bankrupt (%)	Non-bankrupt (%)
MDA	91.7	96.7	86.7
LPM	91.7	93.3	90.0
PROBIT	85.0	83.3	86.7
LOGIT	86.7	83.3	90.0

Table 4.8   Correct classifications on a new sample

	Overall (%)	Bankrupt (%)	Non-bankrupt (%)
One year prior to bankruptcy			
MDA	66.7	66.7	66.7
LPM	72.9	70.8	75.0
PROBIT	72.9	70.8	75.0
LOGIT	77.1	66.7	87.5
Two years prior to bankruptcy			
MDA	71.7	60.9	82.6
LPM	71.7	60.9	82.6
PROBIT	71.7	60.9	82.6
LOGIT	71.7	60.9	82.6
Three years prior to bankruptcy			
MDA	75.0	64.3	85.7
LPM	71.4	64.3	78.6
PROBIT	60.7	42.9	78.6
LOGIT	64.3	50.0	78.6

The performance differences among the four models are marginal. Gloubos and Grammatikos recommend using probability models because they are more successful slightly before bankruptcy and their dependent variables can be interpreted directly as probabilities. The fact that the Type I accuracy of these models, which is more critical, is less than Type II accuracy is of some concern, however.

Theodossiou and Papoulias (1988)

The problematic firms in Greece are moribund firms kept alive by government assistance. The assistance is typically provided by banks in the form of external financing under pressure from the government anxious to minimize unemployment that would ensue if these firms are allowed to fail. The 1979 oil crisis, the entrance of Greece into the European Economic Community, and resulting competition, as well as the worldwide recessions in the 1980s brought about the mini-collapse of the industrial sector. Irresponsible lending policies of banks and the improper management of the capital structure by the firms were also, according to Theodossiou and Papoulias, contributing factors. The purpose of the study is to demonstrate, using a corporate failure prediction model developed by Theodossiou and Papoulias, that the prevailing state of problematic firms in Greece could have been anticipated years before the problem became an issue. The models employed are logit, probit and a Bayesian approach to discriminant analysis. In the Bayesian discriminant analysis, the coefficients are identical to those of traditional discriminant analysis. However, the discriminant score is scaled by an intercept in such a way that its distributional assumptions are invariant to either the sample size or the industries. Moreover, this technique is said to be free from the problem of heteroscedasticity and yield probabilities in the 0–1 interval.

The sample used by Theodossiou and Papoulias contained 33 failed firms and 68 non-failed firms for the year 1983. To adjust the timing of failure for the bankrupt firms kept alive by government interventions beyond their natural span of existence, the data for such firms was collected as of two years prior to the time their net worth became negative. For others, data was gathered for one year prior.

Theodossiou and Papoulias found that the performance scores generated by the three models were highly correlated and ranked the problematic firms similarly. Because the models appeared to be equivalent, they chose just the probit model for presenting the results. It was found that the probabilities of failure increased for the problematic firms from 0 in 1973–74 to more than 0.5 in the mid-1970s, with complete deterioration of performance of about two-thirds of the problematic firms in the sample by 1979.

While there is no doubt that the models anticipated the problematic firms quite well, the results would be more compelling had Theodossiou and Papoulias published the Type I accuracy of the models. A model may have 100 percent Type I accuracy, but if it has 0 Type II accuracy, then it is of no value.

ITALY

Cifarelli, Corielli and Forestieri (1988)

Cifarelli et al. propose a Bayesian variant to the classical discriminant analysis which takes explicit care of the uncertainty with which the parameters of the diagnostic distribution are known when classifications are made, in particular, in "out-of-sample" cases. The classical method uses an estimate density of future observables, whereas the method suggested by Cifarelli et al. uses a predictive density calculated using Bayes theorem.

The sample used to test develop the model came from a large Italian bank's loan portfolio. Unsound companies were selected among cases of formal declaration of bankruptcy. The sound firm sample was formed by a random selection from the bank loan portfolio, 14 financial ratios descriptive of growth, profitability, productivity, liquidity and financial structure were used. Cifarelli et al. report that the classification accuracy of the Bayesian model is very close to that obtained with different versions of the classical discriminant analysis model.

Altman, Marco and Varetto (1994)

Altman et al.'s study presents the results of two interesting innovations in the diagnosis of corporate financial distress (ch. 3 of this volume). The first is the use of a two-stage decision process employing two discriminant analysis models to fine tune the process used to grade companies into groups of healthy, vulnerable and unsound companies. The second innovation is the application of neural networks (NN) to solve the same problem. The study is also of interest because of Altman et al.'s access to a large and well-developed database of financial information on over 37,000 companies in Italy, as much as to the pooling of this data by a consortium of banks that have thereupon been able to use the diagnostic system developed for medium and small-sized businesses in Italy. After trying out various alternative approaches in NN modeling, Altman et al. conclude that the linear discriminant model compares well relative to NNs. The main advantages of the discriminant model being its consistency of performance and the modest cost in fine tuning the model. Having said that, Altman et al. state that NNs continue to hold promise especially in situations where the complexity of the problem can be handled well by the flexibility of NN systems and the capacity to structure them into simple, integrated families.

The study was carried out in the Centrale dei Bilanci (CB) in Turin, Italy. CB is an organization established by the Banca d'Italia, the Associazione Bancaria Italiana and over 40 leading banks and special credit institutions in Italy. CB develops and distributes tools for the member banks to use. One product was a linear discriminant analysis based model that is used in practice to improve credit analyst productivity by preselecting the credits and for monitoring the uniformity of the judgments made about businesses by the various branches of the bank.

The first part of the study describes the results of the new release of the system that improves on predictive accuracy by splitting the estimation/classification problems into two steps. In the first step, the two-group sample consists of healthy firms on the one hand, and unsound and vulnerable companies on the other. "Vulnerable" companies are those that are not at the point of being considered "Unsound" but are borderline cases. The second step was to develop another discriminant analysis model to classify the vulnerable companies on the one hand and the unsound companies on the other. Estimation of the model was done based on data 3 years prior to distress and tested on original and control (holdout) samples for 1 and 3 years prior. The results of the tests of the two models are as shown in table 4.9.

Table 4.9 Discriminant model results

	Test period	Healthy firms (%)	Unsound firms (%)
F1 discriminant model results			
Estimation sample 404 companies in each group			
Estimation period	T–3	90.3	86.4
Control period	T–1	92.8	96.5
Holdout sample (150 companies in each group)	T–1	90.3	95.1
F2 discriminant model results			
Estimation sample (404 companies in each group)			
Estimation period	T–3	99.0	60.1
Control period	T–1	97.8	82.7
Holdout sample (150 companies in each group)	T–1	96.8	81.0

NEURAL NETWORKS (NNS)

NNs consist of potentially large numbers of elementary processing units. Every unit is interconnected with other units and each is able to perform relatively simple calculations. The processing behavior of the network is derived from the collective behavior of the units each of which is capable of altering its responses to stimuli from the external environment as well as from the other neurons with which it is linked. Obviously, the change of response is the learning process that the NN goes through as revisions are introduced to the weightings that drive the response. NNs can range in complexity from the simple single-layer network to multi-layer networks. In general, the more complex the network, the greater is the promise that it will have a genuine capacity to solve a problem, but greater is the difficulty associated with understanding its some-times anomalous behavior. Also, more complex networks take longer to train.

The experiment with NNs progressed through four steps:

1 Attempt to replicate the scores generated by multiple discriminant analysis using ratios different from those used in discriminant analysis
   The objective in doing so was to verify the network's capacity to do at least as well as discriminant analysis but using a different set of ratios
2 Train the network using data three years prior and test it in one year prior data in its ability to separate the healthy and bankrupt companies
3 Attempt to integrate the knowledge implicit in observing the evolution of the various ratios and indicators over time
   In other words, teach the network to learn from both point-in-time data and trend data
4 Check the capacity of the network to separate the healthy, vulnerable and un-sound companies in the same way as the two-stage discriminant analysis models presented earlier

RESULTS

The best results were obtained with a three-layer network in replicating the scores generated by discriminant analysis. The initial layer of ten neurons, a second layer of four neurons and an output layer consisting of a single neuron (the layering of the network is expressed in shorthand as 10, 4, 1 network). The input consisted of ten financial ratios. The resulting profile after 1000 learning cycles on 808 companies was extremely close to the desired level.

In the second stage (classifying healthy and bankrupt companies) a 15, 4, 1 network provided the best recognition rate, i.e., classification accuracy of 97.7 percent for the healthy companies and 97 percent for the unsound companies. However Altman et al. noted two concerns with the network: it was able to obtain that accuracy using a much higher number of indicators, i.e., fifteen as opposed to nine used by discriminant ana-lysis. Second, its behavior became erratic as the learning progresses – initially the model makes rapid strides in its capacity to identify the groups but, as it moves forward, there are often points where its performance actually deteriorates. This led Altman et al. to suggest that NNs may suffer from "overfitting," a phenomenon encountered with quadratic discriminant functions that do very well in the development sample but fail in holdout testing.

In the third stage, Altman et al. fed the same ratios used in discriminant analysis to the NN using the argument that it is common for analysts and systems to receive a standard information base. The objective was to check the network's capacity to replic-ate the knowledge base produced by discriminant analysis, using the same inputs. The results of this, obtained using a 9, 5, 1 network are as shown in table 4.10.

Table 4.10 Comparison of classification rates: neural Network vs. linear discriminant analysis

Sample size = 404 in each group	Neural Network		Linear discriminant function (F1)	
	Healthy (%)	Unsound (%)	Healthy (%)	Unsound (%)
Estimation T–3 period	89.4	86.2	90.3	86.4
Control T–1 period	91.8	95.3	92.8	96.5

The next experiment involving the synthesis of historical information by the network also produced impressive classification results, but here again, the behavior of the network became at times unexplainable and unacceptable, such as frequent inversion of output values when the inputs were modified uniformly or in limited subsets.

In conclusion, Altman et al. note that while complex networks may produce better classification results, they take longer to train and are more difficult to control in terms of illogical behavior. However, they have shown enough promising features to provide an incentive for better implementation techniques and more creative testing.

JAPAN

In Japan, bankruptcies are concentrated in the small and medium-size firms, especially those that do not enjoy the protection of an affiliated group of companies. These groups, known as "Keiretsu," usually involve a lead commercial bank and a number of firms in diverse industries. Still, a number of larger firms listed on the first section of the Tokyo Stock Exchange have succumbed to the negative economic reality of failure. A comparison of the business failures in Japan and the USA may be made based on these statistics appearing in the *Failure Record* published by Dun & Bradstreet and *Tokyo Shoko Koshinso*, among others. There have been a number of studies concentrating on failure prediction in Japan – most were built prior to 1984. Although we will discuss just two, the reader can find reference and discussion to at least a half dozen more in Altman (1993).

Takahashi, Kurokawa and Watase (1979)

Using multiple discriminant analysis, over 130 measures on individual firms, 36 pairs of failed and non-failed manufacturing firms listed on the Tokyo Stock Exchange in the period 1962–76 and 17 different model types, Takahashi et al. have constructed a failure prediction model using the following measures:

- Net worth/Fixed assets
- Current liabilities/Assets
- Voluntary reserves plus unappropriated surplus/Total Assets
- Borrowed expenses (interest)/Sales
- Earned surplus
- Increase in residual value/Cash sales

- Ordinary profit/Total assets
- Value added (sales – variable costs)

Takahashi et al. suggest that their model could be more accurate than Altman's (1968) because of

1   its simultaneous consideration of data from one, two and three years prior to failure
2   its combination of ratios and absolute numbers from financial statements
3   its utilization of the cash basis of accounting from financial statements as well as the accrual base, and
4   its adjustment of the data when the firm's auditors express an opinion as to the limitations of the reported results (window dressing problem).

It was found that models with several years of data for each firm outperformed a similar model with data from only one year prior to failure. Further, absolute financial statement data contributed to the improved classification accuracy and data from financial reports prepared external to the firm on an accrual basis were more predictive than those prepared from an "investment effect" or cash basis method. Adjusting the data to account for auditor opinion, limitations improved the information content of the reported numbers and ratios. A holdout sample of four failed and 44 non-failed firms was tested with the selected model. The four failed firms went bankrupt in 1977, that is, the year after the last year used in the original model.

One problem with the above model might be the use of several years of data for the same firm in order to construct a model. Takahashi et al. apparently were aware of this problem but felt it was not serious. While this technique may be superior to the sometimes-advocated technique of utilizing several models, each based on a different year's data – e.g. Deakin (1972) – it still remains that the observations are not independent from each other. That is, while the 36 firms are independently drawn observations, the three years of data for each firm are not.

The accuracy of this model on the original and holdout samples was simulated based on various cutoff score criteria. The Type I error was found to be quite low for the original sample (range of 0.0–16.7 percent error rates) and virtually nil on the very small four-firm holdout failed firm sample. The Type II error rates ranged greatly, from 0.0–52.8 percent, indicating the tradeoff between Type I and Type 11 errors as one varies the cutoff score.

Takahashi et al. spend considerable effort to discuss the derivation of cutoff scores based on various assumptions of prior probabilities and cost of errors. In essence, they simulate various assumptions and leave the choice of a cutoff score up to the individual user.

Ko (1982)

Ko's sample included 41 pairs of bankrupt and non-bankrupt entities from 1960 through 1980. Several accounting corrections, adjustments, and transformations, in addition to variable trends, were applied to the data set in order to reduce the biases held to be inherent in conventional Japanese reporting practices. He compared the standard linear model design against a model with first-order interactions and also a quadratic model. He also examined a discriminant model using factor analysis for orthogonal variable transformation. On the basis of classification results, a five-variable linear independent model, without the orthogonal transformations, was selected as the best model; it yielded a 82.9 percent correct classification rate by Lachenbruch (1967) tests versus a 90.8 percent for the original sample set. It is interesting to note that the linear inter-action design appeared best on the basis of group separations potential, but not for classification accuracy.

Ko found, with respect to the variables of the model, that each sign was in agreement with each variable's economic meaning and that three of the variables are similar to those in Altman's 1968 model. They are: EBIT/sales, working capital/total debts, and market equity/total debts. A fourth variable in this model is an inventory turnover change ratio. His last ratio was the standard deviation of net income over four periods. The final standardized coefficient model is of the form

$$Z_j = 0.868X_1 + 0.198X_2 - 0.048X_3 + 0.436X_4 + 0.115X_5$$

where

X_1 = EBIT/Sales
X_2 = Inventory turnover two years prior/Inventory turnover three years prior
X_3 = Standard error of net income (four years)
X_4 = Working capital/Total debt
X_5 = Market value equity/Total debt
Z_j = Z-score (Japanese model)

The standardized form results in a zero cutoff score; that is, any score greater than zero indicates a healthy situation, with probability of classification of bankruptcy less than 0.5, and probabilities greater than 0.5 for negative scores.

Note: The further development and implementation of early warning systems in Japan has been surprisingly absent in the wake of the prolonged economic recession in the 1990s and early 2000s.

THE NETHERLANDS

Bilderbeek (1979)

Bilderbeek analyzed a sample of 38 firms which went bankrupt from 1950 through 1974, and 59 ongoing companies. They found that 85 firms had sufficient data for analysis. Bilderbeek analyzed 20 ratios within a stepwise discriminant framework and arrived at a five-variable model of the form:

$$Z = 0.45 - 5.03X_1 - 1.57X_2 + 4.55X_3 + 0.17X_4 + 0.15X_5$$

where

Z = Z-score (Netherlands, Bilderbeek)
X_1 = Retained earnings/Total assets
X_2 = Added value/Total assets
X_3 = Accounts payable/Sales
X_4 = Sales/Total assets
X_5 = Net profit/Equity

Two of the five signs (coefficients), X_4 and X_5, are positive and contrary to expectations since, for this model, negative scores indicate a healthy situation and positive scores indicate a failure classification. His model was based on observations over five reporting periods prior to failure and not on one-year intervals. His results were only mildly impressive, with accuracies ranging from 70 percent to 80 percent for one year prior and remaining surprisingly stable over a five-year period prior to failure. Bilderbeek explains that the stability is due to the fact that there are no liquidity variables and the stable role of the value added measure. Subsequent tests of Bilderbeek's model have been quite accurate (80 percent over five years). Apparently, several institutions are now using his model for practical purposes.

Van Frederikslust (1978)

Van Frederikslust's model included tests on a sample of 20 failed and a matched non-failed sample of observations for 1954 through 1974. All firms were quoted on the Netherlands Stock Exchange. In addition to the now traditional research structure, that is, linear discriminant, single year ratio, equal *a priori* probability of group membership assumptions, Van Frederikslust performed several other tests. Those included

1   looking at the development of ratios over time (temporal model) as well as analyzing ratio levels
2   varying the *a priori* assumption of group membership likelihood to conform with a specific user of the model (e.g., lending officer), and
3   varying the expected costs of the models, taking into consideration the specific user's utility for losses.

Van Frederikslust attempts to provide a theoretical discussion for his choice of variables. He concludes that traditional measures of firm performance, that is, liquidity, profitability, solvency, and variability of several of these categories, are the correct indicators. Industry affiliation and general economic variables are also thought to be important but are not included in his model. In fact, the primary model only contained two variables representing liquidity and profitability.

Van Frederikslust's primary model analyzed the level of ratios. His definition of failure included many different types but essentially involved the failure to pay fixed obligations. His sample included textile, metal processing, machinery, construction, retailing, and miscellaneous firms. The non-failed group (20) were randomly selected from the same industries, size categories (assets), and time periods as was the failed group. His first model was:

$$Z_{NF} = 0.5293 + 0.4488X_1 + 0.2863X_2$$

where

Z_{NF} = Z-score (Netherlands, Frederikslust)
X_1 = Liquidity ratio (external coverage)
X_2 = Profitability ratio (rate of return on equity)

Van Frederikslust distinguishes between the *internal coverage* ratio (Cash balance + Resources earned in the period/Short-term debt) and the *external coverage* ratio: Short-term debt in period t + Available short-term debt $(t-1)$. The external coverage measures what can be expected from the renewal of debt and additional debt. "Failure at moment (t) is completely determined by the values of internal and external coverage at that moment" (p. 35). Van Frederikslust uses only the external coverage measure in his "simple" model.

Separate models were developed for each year, as did Deakin (1972). The arguments for this are that a separate model is necessary to assess failure probabilities for different time periods and that the distributions of ratios vary over time. While we do not necessarily agree that separate models are desirable – indeed, they could be confusing – the discussion on timing of failure prediction is a useful one. The classification program utilized was actually a 0.1 multiple regression structure and not the discriminant analysis model used in most other studies. Fisher (1936) has shown that the coefficients of these structures are proportional when dealing with a two-group model.

The results for the one-period model indicate that the estimated chances of misclassification into the two groups are 5 percent for the failed group and 10 percent for the non-failed group. The expected accuracy falls as time prior to failure increases. For example, the error rates are 15 percent and 20 percent respectively for two years prior.

A revised model, analyzing the development of ratios over time, yielded an equation which utilized the liquidity ratio in the latest year before failure, the profitability ratio two years prior, the coefficient of variation of the liquidity ratio over a seven-year period, and the prediction error of the profitability ratio in the latest year before failure. Again, separate models were developed for each year prior to failure. Using Lachenbruch's procedure for estimating error rates, the results were quite similar to those of the first set of equations based on the two-variable "levels" ratios. Accuracies for earlier years did show slight improvements.

The Fire Scoring System – de Breed and Partners (1996)

A small consulting firm in the Netherlands recently developed specialized credit scoring models for specific industries in Holland. Utilizing discriminant analysis techniques, like many of the other studies discussed earlier, the unique aspect of these models is their specific industry orientation and the very large data bases of failed and un-failed companies maintained and updated. In 1996, the firm published a type of "Michelin Guide" for rating the health of Dutch companies, using a zero to four star system. Since the models are proprietary, we cannot comment further.

Spain

Fernández (1988)

Fernández's study describes an empirical model to objectively evaluate and screen credit applicants. The work consists of the determination of the model with two objectives:

1   to check the validity of financial ratios as prediction tools, and
2   to predict a firm's collapse.

The research sample consisted of 25 failed and 25 non-failed firms, with an additional 10 each being set aside for validation testing. Data pertaining to two years preceding the failure was collected. Only data pertaining to 1978–82 was permitted in order to eliminate the possible distortion caused by the natural changes in ratios caused by the business cycle. The ratios were examined using three techniques:

1   Univariate analysis
2   Factor analysis by principal components
3   Discriminant analysis

Fernández concludes that univariate analysis is not practical given the volume of the ratios to be considered and the possible interactions among the ratios. In addition, the univariate ratio analysis has to be performed in the context of the market in which the firm operates, thus the ratios show only relative position of the company. Lastly, multivariate ratios can improve analyst productivity and free him/her to concentrate on other equally important matters such as the credit terms, maturity, guarantees, etc.

When there are a large number of variables to be considered, principal component analysis is a way to eliminate the variables that carry the same information and reduce the observation to a handful of factors or "principal components." Each principal component is a linear combination of one or more of the underlying variables. The coefficient of the underlying variable in the factor equation is called the "factor loading." In this study the author conducted factor analysis in two ways:

1   without rotation of the factors, and
2   using varimax rotation to ensure the independence of the resulting factors.

The second way is believed to produce more desirable (i.e., stabler) results when used as independent variables in regression or discriminant analysis.

Fernández found that eight factors existed that account for 79.3 percent of the information contained in the initial set of ratios. Just two factors provide for 42.1 percent of the information. The eight factors are:

1   Capacity to repay the debts
2   Liquidity
3   Fixed assets financing
4   Efficiency of the firm
5   Rotation of fixed assets
6   Profitability of permanent funds

7   Structure of working capital
8   Structure of short-term debt

Fourteen ratios with a higher loading from the principal components were selected as input for the discriminant analysis procedure. A six-variable discriminant function emerged as the best, with an overall classification accuracy of 84 percent in the original sample:

$$Z_1 = -0.26830V_3 + 0.54666*V_4 + 0.55483*V_6 + 0.62925*V_9 - 0.514119*V_{12} + 0.43665*V_{17}$$

where

V_3 = (Permanent funds/Net fixed assets)/Industry value
V_4 = Quick ratio/Industry value
V_6 = Cash-flow/Current liabilities
V_9 = Return on investment
V_{12} = Earnings before taxes/sales
V_{17} = Cash-flow/sales

The results of the model on the development sample and the holdout sample are given in table 4.11. As expected, there is a slight drop in performance of the model in the holdout sample. Of greater concern is where the drop in performance is: normally the Type I accuracy will be maintained and the Type II accuracy will be lower. In this case, the Type I accuracy has dropped from 84 percent to 70 percent. Some follow-up analysis of the Type I and Type II errors by individual case might have been useful. Fernández compared the discriminant model using the underlying ratios (described in the foregoing) with a discriminant model using the factor scores and found that the percentage accuracy of classification was the same in both cases. This is an interesting result for future researchers.

Table 4.11 Classification results

Actual group	No of cases	Predicted Group Membership	
		1	2
Group 1	25	21 84.0%	4 16.0%
Group 2	25	4 16.0%	21 84.0%

Overall classification accuracy: 84.0%.

Briones, Marín and Cueto (1988)

Briones et al.'s study presents the results of empirical research undertaken to build a multivariate model to forecast the possible failure of financial institutions in Spain and their takeover by the monetary authorities or regulatory agencies.

During the period 1978–83, Spain underwent a serious crisis in its financial institutions. Roughly 47 percent of all Spanish banks failed during this period; 21.4 percent of the equity and 18.7 percent of the deposits were affected by the problem banks. Banco de Espana (the Spanish equivalent of the Federal Reserve) working through Fondo de Garantía de Depósitos (the Spanish equivalent of the Federal Deposit Insurance Corporation) carried out the resolution of the banks through "administrative solutions." Legal solutions such as bankruptcy procedures were not used for fear of causing a panic. A bank may thus be technically insolvent when it has a liquidity crisis or it may be definitively insolvent when there is negative net worth. Since a "failed" institution can operate indefinitely with assistance from the regulators, the authors have defined a bank to have failed if there an intervention by Fondo de Garantía Depósitos.

The sample consisted of 25 failed banks and an equal number of non-failed banks paired up based on the 5-year average size of deposits during the period prior to intervention. The data sources were Anuario Estadístico la Banca Privada published by the Consejo Superior Bancario and the memorandum of the Fondo de Garantía de Depósitos. Both a univariate and multivariate approach were used in classifying the failed and non-failed groups.

In the univariate approach, Briones et al. found that the mean values for the ratios maintain a logical correspondence (the actual mean values obtained are not mentioned in the study, however). They also found that standard deviations of the failed bank ratios generally tended to be higher. Profitability and liquidity measures were found to be the most significant variables for forecasting failures in a univariate analysis. The cutoff point for the individual ratio was fixed in a heuristic way, by a process of trial and error. The costs of Type I and Type II errors were assumed to be equal.

In the multivariate approach, discriminant analysis was used to develop models using data of j year prior as the development sample ($j = 1, 2, 3, 4, 5$) and testing the model on the data for the all the years j. Since the ratios for a bank tend to be correlated from one year to the next, the classification test on the other years does not constitute a true out-of-sample (holdout) test. Some of the classification results presented are nonsensical because if you used data for $j = 2$ to develop the model, you cannot test it on data of $j = 1$ because in real time that information would be non-existent; only $j = 3, 4$ and 5 would be!

The multiple discriminant analysis produced 3- and 4-variable models for each year prior, resulting in a total of ten alternative models to choose from. The comparison of the prediction accuracy using univariate analysis and the discriminant analysis showed that univariate analysis actually did better than the discriminant function in the first and the fifth year (table 4.12) – a surprising result. Most research using multivariate

Table 4.12 Overall accurate predictions – comparison of single ratios with discriminant functions

Years	Ratios (%)	Functions (%)
1	90/95	80/85
2	75/80	80/85
3	75/80	75/80
4	75/80	75/80
5	80/85	75/80

methods appears to come to the opposite conclusion because it is believed that the interaction or the substitution effects of one variable with others provide better information that if the variables are considered sequentially.

Briones et al. conclude that there is a close balance between the univariate ratio approach and the function approach, and that both types of analysis can be viewed as complementary.

More rigorous testing using a holdout sample will be needed to confirm that the univariate approach has predictive power comparable to the multivariate approach. Coming to this conclusion based solely on original sample test results is premature because of the sample bias in the results.

SWITZERLAND

While bankruptcy classification and its many implications have interested researchers in Germany for many years, the earliest major work published in German was performed in Switzerland by Weibel (1973). He constructed a sample of 36 failed Swiss firms from 1960 to 1971 and matched them to a like number of non-failed firms in terms of age, size, and line of business. Using univariate statistical parametric and non-parametric tests, Weibel analyzed ratios of these two groups in much the same way that Beaver (1967) did. He found that many of the individual ratios were non-normal and so he abandoned multivariate tests. [We have often referred (Altman et al., 1997) to the non-normality problem which exists in many economic and financial data sets but we prefer to test the robustness of models using such data rather than abandoning the tests. We do observe that some European researchers have found multivariate studies suspect due to the non-normality properties of financial measures.]

Out of 41 original ratios, Weibel selected 20 for dichotomous comparisons. He utilized cluster analysis to reduce collinearity and arrived at the conclusion that six ratios were especially effective in discriminating among the paired groups. Three ratios were types of liquidity measures with one (Near monetary resource assets – current liabilities/ Operating expenditures prior to depreciation) performing best. He also found that inventory turnover and debt/asset ratios were good individual predictors. He examined the overlapping range of individual ratios for the two groups and presented some *ad hoc* rules for identifying failures. He then divided the observations into three risk groups. The low-risk group had all six ratios in the interdecile range of good firms; high-risk firms had at least three ratios in the interdecile range of failed companies; and a final category was identified where the firm does not fall into either of the other two groupings. Weibel's results were quite accurate in the classification stage; we have no documentation on how his "model" performed on holdout tests and what has been the evolution of models in Switzerland since his original work.

ARGENTINA

Swanson and Tybout (1988)

In 1981, Swanson and Tybout analyzed the determinants of industrial bankruptcy on Argentina on three levels. First, the importance of macroeconomic variables on the business failures was considered. Real interest rate, credit stock, manufacturing output, real wage rate and the peso exchange rate were regressed on business failures, two variables at a time, using a multivariate regression with third-order polynomial distributed lag terms. Second, sectoral failure rates were examined to determine whether reform policies had a differential effect on highly protected industries. The data was divided into high-protection and low-protection industries, and the differential impact of economic policies was evaluated by adding the degree of protection as a dummy variable in a regression of the number of business failures against the real interest rate and credit stock. Swanson and Tybout then considered the firm-level anatomy of failure by creating a probit regression model on a sample of 19–22 failures and 190–324 survivors with measures of financial structure consisting of cash flow indices, firm financial structure variables, firm size and the degree of protection. The firm failure model was estimated for the pre-, post-, and maxi devaluation periods of the Argentinian peso, i.e., 1979–1981 and the period following 1981 respectively.

Following the military coup that ousted Isabel Peron in 1976, Argentina passed through a reform period. The reform started with selective tariff reductions. Soon, contractionary monetary policies and temporary wage and price controls were imposed to combat hyperinflation. In late 1978, an exchange rate regime was introduced. The end result of all these policies led to a maxi devaluation of the peso that threw the economy into a recession. Swanson and Tybout examine the effects of the reform polices with the hope that policy makers will evaluate future policy options in terms of the stress they place on the corporate sector.

Using quarterly data on the macroeconomic variables (24 data points), ten regressions were estimated using a different combination of two macro variables. Although the business failure *rate*, rather than the absolute number of business failures would have been more appropriate as the dependent variable, Swanson and Tybout did not have the data on the total numbers of businesses in each time period, and therefore they were forced to use the absolute number of failures. They also noted other shortcomings: limited size of the data sample, conceptual problems with measuring expected devaluation rates and the distortions in measuring the time of failure by lags in court processing time. They concluded, based on the results of the regressions, that of all the factors considered, interest rates and credit stocks are the most important factors in explaining business failures.

The second question examined by Swanson and Tybout is the issue of whether all industries were *uniformly* affected by the Argentine reforms. Their hypothesis was that the high-protection industries suffer considerably higher failure levels than the low-protection industries when the protection is reduced. Each subsample for the study consisted of 12 industries with data for 20 quarters. To account for interindustry difference in the number of firms, the logarithm of the number of establishments in the industry was included as an explanatory variable. Swanson and Tybout reported statistically significant evidence to support their hypothesis that high protection leads to higher failures when protection is removed.

To test their third question, i.e., what are the firm level variables that predict failure, Swanson and Tybout favored the use of a probit regression instead of discriminant analysis because of two stated reasons: that assumptions necessary for statistical inference are typically not satisfied and that the individual influences of the predictors cannot be isolated. The criticism of discriminant analysis was not compelling because Swanson and Tybout appeared to tolerate even more serious limitations caused by the smallness of the sample. Also the standardized discriminant function did show the relative importance of the variables.

The models were estimated for the pre-devaluation period and post-devaluation period. The final model contained ratios with total assets as the best normalizing variable (as opposed to total debt or net worth). The results ratios were the protection index, quick ratio, real financial cost, EBIT, Sales, Debt, Ln (Assets) and Foreign exchange.

In the post-devaluation period, the role of financial costs, foreign currency exposure and firm size became more marked as expected.

In both pre- and post-devaluation periods, the dummy variable for protection had the expected sign but was not statistically significant. Swanson and Tybout concluded based on this outcome, and because sectoral regressions reflected contrasts among firms not listed in stock exchange, that higher failure rates for protected firms were concentrated among smaller, privately held firms.

Although, by using probit regression, Swanson and Tybout could evaluate and present the statistical significance of individual variables, the published statistics (log-likelihood and the χ^2) do not tell us anything about the classification/misclassification accuracy among fails and non-fails respectively. In addition, the published results are in-sample values. Despite the problems with the data, this article is impressive in the broad sweep of the issues considered in both microeconomic terms and in explicitly modeling trade protection and foreign currency exposure. As we move further into the truly global economy, these variables take on added significance in assessing risk.

BRAZIL

Brazil is an example of an economy where the end result of a series of economic setbacks would put severe pressure on private enterprises. For example, tightening of credit for all firms, especially smaller ones, can jeopardize financial institutions and undermine government efforts to promote economic development. Most observers would agree that action to detect and avoid critical pressures of this type is highly desirable in an economy like Brazil, which has enjoyed extraordinary growth followed by severe inflation and maxi devaluations. And, as a result of the very recent significant reduction in inflation, banks are now making loans again and are therefore concerned with credit risk issues.

Altman, Baidya, and Ribeiro-Dias (1979)

Altman, Baidya, and Ribeiro-Dias examined two *a priori* groups of firms categorized as serious-problem (SP) and no-problem (NP) companies. A small number of variables were then calculated for each observation (firm) in each of the two samples. Data covered the period from one to three annual reporting statements prior to the problem date. The data from one year prior (and the corresponding year for the control sample) were then analyzed through the use of linear discriminant analysis.

The serious-problem firms were defined as those filing formal petitions for court-supervised liquidations, legal reorganizations in bankruptcy (*concordatas*), and out-of-court manifestations of serious problems. In all but two of the 23 serious-problem cases, the problem became manifest during the 30 months from January 1975 to June

1977. Industry categories represented include textiles, furniture, pulp and paper, retail stores, plastics, metallurgy, and others. The average asset size of the serious-problem firms was surprisingly high at 323 million cruzeiros (US $25–30 million). Therefore, the model, if accurate, has relevance over a wide range of companies in terms of size. The control (or no-problem) sample was actually somewhat smaller.

One or two firms were selected for the control sample from each of the same industrial categories as those represented by the serious-problem group, and data were gathered from the year corresponding to the year prior to the problem date. Since there were more than 30 industrial categories to choose from, the number of firms in each industrial group was often quite small. Whenever possible, privately owned, domestic companies were selected since Altman et al. felt that a state-owned or multinational affiliation reduced, in general, the possibility of failure.

The classification procedure used in this study was based on the failure model developed in the USA (Altman 1968), with modifications that allowed for consideration of Brazilian standards and reporting practices. In this Brazilian study, the same variables were utilized but X_2 and X_4 were modified. With respect to X_2, the retained earnings account on US balance sheets reflects the cumulative profits of a firm less any cash dividends paid out and stock dividends. In most instances, the small, young firm will be discriminated against because it has not had time to accumulate its earnings. In Brazil, however, due to different financial reporting practices and adjustments for inflation, there is no exact equivalent to retained earnings. The nearest translation to retained earnings is "*lucros suspetisos*," which refers to those earnings retained in the business after distribution of dividends. This amount is usually transferred, however, within a short time (perhaps two years) through stock dividends to the account known as capital.

In addition, reserves which were created to adjust for monetary correction on fixed assets and the maintenance of working capital were deducted from profits and thereby decreased those earnings which were reported to be retained in the firm. These reserves, however, increased both the assets and the firm's equity, and they too were transferred to capital. In essence, then, that amount of capital which represented funds contributed by the owners of the firm was the only part of equity that was not considered in the Brazilian equivalent to retained earnings. X_2 was calculated as: (Total equity – Capital contributed by shareholders (CCS))/Total assets.

A more precise expression of the numerator would be the cumulative yearly retained earnings plus the cumulative reserves created over the life of the firm, but this information is very difficult to obtain outside the firm and was not available to Altman et al.

Since most Brazilian firms' equity is not traded, there cannot be a variable which measures the market value of equity (number of shares outstanding times the latest market price). To derive the new values for X_4, the book value of equity (*patrimonio liquido*) was substituted and divided by the total liabilities. The remaining three variables were not adjusted, although Altman et al. were aware of the fact that certain financial expenses are also adjusted for inflation in Brazilian accounting.

EMPIRICAL RESULTS

The empirical results will be discussed in terms of two separate but quite similar models. The first model, referred to as Z_1, includes variables X_2 to X_5 (four measures) of the original Z-Score model. Model Z_1 does not include X_1 because the stepwise discriminant program indicated that it did not add any explanatory power to the model and the sign of the coefficient was contrary to intuitive logic. Once again, as so often is found in multivariate failure classification studies, the liquidity variable is not found to be particularly important. The second model, referred to as Z_2, does not include X_2, because X_2 is quite difficult to derive with just one set of financial statements and it is similar to X_4. Model Z_2 can therefore be applied without supplementary data.

The models were as follows:

$$Z_1 = 1.44 + 4.03X_2 + 2.25X_3 + 0.14X_4 + 0.42X_5$$
$$Z_2 = 1.84 - 0.51X_1 + 6.23X_3 + 0.71X_4 + 0.56X_5$$

In both cases, the critical cutoff score was zero. That is, any firm with a score greater than zero was classified as having a multivariate profile similar to that of continuing entities and those with a score less than zero were classified as having characteristics similar to those of entities which experienced serious problems.

Results from the two models were essentially identical based on one year prior data. Model Z_1 performed better for years 2 and 3; therefore, only the results of that model were discussed. Of the 58 firms in the combined two samples, seven were misclassified, yielding an overall accuracy of 88 percent. The Type I error (that of classifying a serious-problem firm as a continuing entity) was 13 percent (three out of 23 misclassified) and the Type 11 error (that of misclassifying a continuing entity) was slightly lower at 11.4 percent (four of 35). These results are impressive since they indicate that published financial data in Brazil, when correctly interpreted and rigorously analyzed, do indeed possess important information content.

Due to the potential upward bias involved in original sample classification results, further tests of the models were performed with several types of holdout or validation samples. The accuracy of the SP sample was unchanged after applying the Lachenbruch test. Several replication tests also showed high accuracy levels. Finally, the accuracy of the model was examined as the data become more remote from the serious problem date. The SP sample results, as expected, showed a drop in the accuracy of the models. Altman et al. utilized the weights from the model constructed with year 1 data and inserted the variable measures for years 2 and 3 prior to the SP date. Year 2 data provided accuracy of 84.2 percent (16 of 19 correct). Year 3 data provided lower accuracy of 77.8 percent (14 of 18 correct) classifications. Therefore, in only four cases were errors observed in classification based on data from three (or more in some cases) years prior to the SP date.

IMPLICATIONS OF RESULTS FOR BRAZIL

The implications and applications of models designed for assessing the potential for serious financial problems in firms are many. This is especially true in a developing country, where an epidemic of business failures could have drastic effects on the strength of the private sector and on the economy as a whole. Most observers of the Brazilian situation would agree on the merit of preserving an equilibrium among private enterprises, state-owned firms, and multinationals. Such equilibrium would be jeopardized if the domestic private sector were weakened by an escalation of liquidations. If a model such as the one suggested is used to identify potential problems, then in many cases preventive or rehabilitative action can be taken. This should involve a conscious internal effort, by the firms themselves, to prevent critical situations as soon as a potential problem is detected. Besides internal efforts, a program of financial and managerial assistance – more than likely from official external sources – is a potential outcome.

Many economists have argued that significant government assistance for the private sector is an unwise policy except where the system itself is jeopardized. One can rationalize government agencies' attempts to stabilize those industries where a significant public presence or national security is involved, for instance, commercial and savings banks or the steel industry. In developing countries, the distinction between high public interest sectors and the fragile private sector is more difficult to make, and limited early assistance is advocated.

FINLAND

Suominen (1988)

Suominen employs a multinomial logit model (MNL) to classify firms into two groups: failing and non-failing and to assess relative importance of each financial ratio variable. The second part of the study classifies failed firms further into two groups: firms failed within one year of prediction and firms that failed later. Both models employ the same set of three financial ratios indicative of profitability, liquidity and leverage. The ratios are:

PROF = (Quick flow – Direct taxes)/Total assets

where

Quick flow = (Net turnover – Materials and supplies – Wages and salaries – Rent and leases – Other expenses + Other revenues)

LIQU = Quick/Total assets

where

Quick = (Current assets – Inventories/Current liabilities)

and

LEVE = Liabilities/Total assets

Suominen favors the MNL technique, corrected for the constant term, because of concerns that the assumptions of equal co-variance matrices and normal distribution of the variables are not usually prevalent or tested when using discriminant analysis. In addition, the coefficients from a MNL model are easily testable. Suominen's sample consists of two sets of data. The first set covers the period 1964–73 and consists of 49 failed firms and 87 healthy firms, both from manufacturing industries. The second set consists of data for a different set of failed and healthy firms covering the period 1981–82.

The PROF ratio was not found to be significant in the models for one and two years prior to failure. In the three years prior model, only LEVE was significant. In the four

Table 4.13 Classification accuracy

Years prior	Type I accuracy (%)	Type II accuracy (%)	Type I accuracy (%)	Type II accuracy (%)
1	67–71	85–86	65–74	61–65
2	53–57	84	61	70
3	31–33	87–89	65	70
4	26	93–95		

years prior model, only LIQU was significant. The classification results on the first sample and the second sample are summarized in table 4.13. It should be noted that both results are for the sample space and not for holdouts.

The results of the one-year model are comparable to those obtained using discriminant analysis using the same variables. The Type I errors are reported to be fewer in the discriminant model, however.

The purpose behind the second part of the study is not entirely clear. Here the objective is to predict correctly the firms that failed within one year of the prediction as distinct from those failed later. The results suggest that the MNL model is able to classify the firms into the two groups with an overall accuracy as indicated in table 4.14 for the first and the second sample sets. Type I and Type II accuracy rates could not be reported here because this information is not available in the study.

Table 4.14 Classification accuracy

Years of failure	Accuracy (%)	
	Sample 1	Sample 2*
1 versus 2, 3, 4	73–75	65–70
2 versus 3, 4	60–67	57–65
3 versus 4	50–52	

* There are no firms with data extending beyond three years prior to failure.

INDIA

Bhatia (1988)

Bhatia has developed a discriminant analysis model for identifying "sick" companies. Sick companies in India refer to companies that continue to operate (or more accurately are *kept* in operation even after their economic value is in question) even after incurring losses. The definition used by the Industrial Development Bank of India for sickness is if a company suffers from any of the following ills:

- Cash losses for a period of two years, or if there is a continuous erosion of net worth, say 50 percent

- Four successive defaults on its debt service obligations
- Persistent irregularity in the use the credit lines
- Tax payments in arrears for one to two years

The sample consisted of 18 sick and 18 healthy companies all of which are publicly traded. Data used pertained to the period 1976–95. The healthy companies were paired with the sick ones based on the type of product and gross fixed assets. The companies were drawn from the cement, electrical, engineering, glass, paper and steel industries.

The seven ratios in the final discriminant function, along with the standardized discriminant function coefficient are presented in table 4.15.

The Type I accuracy was 87.1 percent and the Type II accuracy was 86.6 percent on the development sample. A holdout test was performed on 20 healthy companies and 28 sick companies. The test results generally validated the efficacy of the model.

Table 4.15 Discriminant function coefficients

	Standardized coefficient	Rank	Unstandardized coefficient
X_1 Current ratio	0.56939	2	1.64621
X_2 Stock of finished Goods/Sales	0.23186	6	0.03071
X_3 Profit after Tax/Net worth	0.34543	4	0.004271
X_4 Interest/Value of Output	0.50499	3	0.08169
X_5 Cash Flow/Total Debt	0.64154	1	0.05372
X_6 Working capital Management Ratio	0.14993	7	−0.007024
X_7 Sales/Total Assets	0.34498	5	0.006616

IRELAND

In Ireland, Cahill (1981) presents some exploratory work on a small sample of 11 bankrupt, listed companies covering the period from 1970 through 1980. Three primary issues are explored:

1 identification of those ratios which showed a significant deterioration as failure approaches
2 whether the auditors' reports expressed any reservations or uncertainty about the continuance of the firms as going concerns, and
3 whether there were any other unique aspects of the failed companies' conditions.

Cahill's analysis revealed a number of ratios indicating clear distress signals one year prior to failure. These ratios compared unfavorably with aggregate norms and ratios for the comparable industrial sector. Although several measures continued to show differences in earlier years, the signals were less clear in year 2 prior and it was difficult to detect strong signals from ratios prior to year 2.

Only one of the 11 auditors' reports was qualified on the basis of going concern. Five other less serious qualifications were present in the auditor's reports. Cahill speculates that the low frequency of auditor qualifications on a going concern basis was due to auditor reluctance and accounting convention in Ireland as well as their feeling of being part of a "small society." Altman and Izan (1981) observed similar circumstances in Australia. Still, according to Cahill, since deterioration was quite apparent, those close to the situation should have been aware of the seriousness and earlier remedial action taken or qualification given.

Unsuccessful merger activity and significant investment and asset expansion financed by debt were the major causes of Irish failures. Several of the firms continued to pay dividends right up to the year prior to failure. On the other hand, only one company actually made payments to unsecured creditors after insolvency, indicating that asset value had deteriorated beyond repair and only then was failure declared.

KOREA

Altman, Kim and Eom (1995)

As a growing and potentially overheated economy, Korea may be following in the footsteps of its neighbor, Japan, which had a period of rapid economic growth only to be followed by increased business failures. For this reason, Altman et al. suggest that a failure prediction model for Korea is timely, even given the current 1995 robustness of the South Korean economy. In particular, because of the increased deregulation and greater autonomy in decision making by financial institutions, the availability of predictive models is relevant.

The distress classification model described in this study consists of two versions: the K1 model is applicable for both public and private firms, whereas the K2 model, which uses the market value of equity in one of its ratios, may be used only for publicly traded firms.

Linear discriminant analysis was the technique used in building the model. The sample of failed firms consisted of 34 publicly traded industrial and trading companies with assets ranging from $13 million to $296 million. Failure and failure dates were defined based on technical insolvency or liquidation, whichever came first. Technical insolvency is defined as the condition when the credit of a company is no longer accepted. Most of the failures in the sample occurred in 1991–92. It is significant to note that 30 of the 34 distressed firms had their shares publicly traded only since 1988, and 23 of the 30 were listed during the explosion of new IPO listings in 1988 and 1989. For this reason, the results of the model may be of interest to investors and regulators of new issues in the Korean stock market.

Because the non-distressed group of firms tended to be significantly larger in size on average, the pairing of the healthy firm with the failed firm was based mainly on industry sector grouping. For 34 distressed firms, a larger sample of 61 non-failed entities was chosen, with the actual one-to-one pairing done by random selection from the universe of 61 firms during model building.

The time series analysis of the individual ratio averages revealed that some early warning financial indicators such as book value of equity to total liabilities do not behave in the same way as they do for US firms. This ratio, contrary to expectations, actually improves for failed firms until just before bankruptcy. However, the same ratio based on market value behaves as expected. For this reason, Altman et al. have proceeded with two different models: one employing the book equity leverage variable and the other with a market equity variable.

The criteria for selecting the final variable set were as follows:

1   High univariate significance test (see table 4.13)
2   Expected sign for all the model coefficients
3   Original (in-sample) and holdout (out-of-sample) test results
4   Reasonable accuracy levels over time

The K1 model had the following variables:

1   LOG (Total assets)
2   LOG (Sales/Total assets)
3   Retained earnings/Total assets
4   Book value of equity/Total liabilities

The classification results on the original sample for the K1 and K2 models are presented in table 4.16.

Table 4.16   Classification results: K-1 model

	No. of firms	% Correctly classified
Bankrupt firms		
Years prior to failure		
1	34	97.1
2	34	88.2
3	33	69.7
4	32	50.0
5	16	68.8
Non-bankrupt firms		
Year		
1988	57	77.2
1989	58	81.0
1990	59	83.1
1991	47	89.4
1992	29	93.1
Total	250	83.6

The K2 model contained the following ratios:

1   LOG (Total assets)
2   LOG (Sales/Total assets)
3   Retained earnings/Total assets
4   Market value of equity/Total liabilities

The classification results on the original sample for the K2 models are presented in table 4.17.

Table 4.17 Classification results: K-2 model

	No. of firms	% Correctly classified
Bankrupt firms		
Years prior to failure		
1	29	96.6
2	23	85.2
3	15	71.4
4	4	40.0
5	3	75.0
Non-bankrupt firms		
Year		
1988	40	75.0
1989	51	86.3
1990	57	86.0
1991	47	89.4
1992	29	93.1
Total	224	85.7

Altman et al. note two major limitations of these models. First, because of lack of data, they were unable to perform holdout testing. Second, the Type II accuracy of 70 percent is perceived to be rather low. Both these limitations would be removed if future tests of the model yield usable predictions.

Note: The subsequent financial crisis in Korea in 1997–2000 has provided a large number of business failures to test the above model. Such tests are currently being performed.

MALAYSIA

Bidin (1988)

The New Economic Policy launched by the Malaysian Government in the early 1980s was aimed at increasing and redistributing corporate ownership among the races in that country. The indigenous races in which the Malays form the majority have a dispropor-tionately small share of the corporate wealth. The government has set up a number of public corporations and enterprises to directly involve the indigenous races in terms of ownership and the development of managerial skills. Permodalan Nasional Berhad (PNB) is a corporation whose objective is to evaluate, select and acquire shares in cor-porations with good potential with the intention of ultimately selling them to a unit trust fund. PNB is thus an investment institution which has developed some expertise in the financial analysis and monitoring of the operations of companies. In 1985, the government entrusted PNB with the additional task of monitoring the performance of *all government companies*, not just those in PNB's portfolio. This led to the formation of CICU, the Central Information Collection Unit, the unit within PNB that performs this function. CICU is charged with the task of identifying companies in distress at an early stage so that the necessary remedial action may be taken by the authorities. A multivariate discriminant analysis model has been built with applicability mainly for manufacturing companies, and also for companies in the transportation and service sector.

The sample consisted of 21 companies known to have been in distress paired with financially sound companies which were entirely Malaysian with business activities in Malaysia. Forty-one ratios were defined for inclusion in the analysis. Stepwise selection yielded a discriminant function that had seven variables ranked by the level of contribution to the F statistic as shown in table 4.18.

Table 4.18 Discriminant function variables

Variable	R^2	F-statistic
R1 Operating profit/Total liabilities	0.5307	45.230
R2 Current assets/Current liabilities	0.3921	–
R3 EAIT/Paid-up capital	0.2388	–
R4 Sales/Working capital	0.2275	10.898
R5 Current assets – Stocks – Current liabilities/EBIT	0.1360	5.665
R6 Total shareholders' fund/Total liabilities	0.0333	3.181
R7 Ordinary shareholders' fund/Employment of capital	0.0795	2.935

Bidin presents three case studies where the PNB-Score was able to correctly predict the outcome in advance. He also noted that the test of the model on over 600 companies showed that the results predicted by the model were found to be relatively consistent with the actual performance of the companies. The model was very sensitive to the liabilities of the company, which is to be expected because failure is most often caused when the company's cash-flows are relative to its fixed debt commitments. The study does not present any information on Type II accuracy. It is also not clear whether the 600 companies tested are all problem companies or whether they included some healthy ones as well. A revised model is still actively used by PNB.

MEXICO

Altman et al. (1995)

Emerging markets credits should be initially analyzed in a manner similar to traditional analysis of US corporates. Once a quantitative risk assessment has emerged out of traditional analysis, it can then be modified by the qualitative assessments of an analyst for other risks, such as currency risk and industry risk characteristic of the industry itself as well as the firm's competitive position in that industry. It is not often possible to build a model specific to an emerging country based on a sample from the country itself because of lack of credit experience in that country. To deal with this problem, Altman et al. have modified the Altman Z-Score model and renamed the resulting model as the EMS model (Emerging Market Scoring Model); see chapter 5 in this volume.

The process of deriving the rating for a Mexican corporate credit is as follows:

1 EMS score is calculated and equivalent rating is obtained based on the calibration of the EMS scores with US bond rating equivalents.
2 The company's bond is then analyzed for the issuing firm's vulnerability to servicing its foreign currency denominated debt. This is based on the relationship between the non-local currency revenues minus costs compared to non-local currency expense and non-local currency revenues and non-local currency debt. Then the level of non-local currency cash flow is compared with the debt coming due in the next year. Depending on the degree of vulnerability seen by the analysis, the rating is adjusted downward.
3 The rating is further adjusted downward (the credit is seen as riskier) if the company is in an industry considered to be relatively riskier.
4 The rating is further adjusted up or down depending on the dominance of the firm's position in its industry.
5 If the debt has special features such as collateral or a bona fide guarantor, the rating is adjusted accordingly.

For relative value analysis, the corresponding US corporates' credit spread is added to the sovereign bond's option adjusted spread. Only a handful of the Mexican companies are rated by the rating agencies. Thus the risk assessments such as those provided by EMS are often the only reliable indicators of credit risk to overseas investors in Mexico. Altman et al. report that the ratings have proven accurate in anticipating both downgrades (Grupo Synkro in May 1995) and upgrades (Aeromexico in July 1995).

Note: The EMS model was tested on post-1995 defaulting companies with a 100% accuracy in predicting default of the emerging market and issuing firms.

SINGAPORE

Singapore is a dynamic and growing economy which has attracted a large amount of foreign investment. A business failure prediction model is justified both for preserving Singapore's image as a major financial center and as a way to assist rational investment in Singapore companies by investors and creditors.

Ta and Seah (1981)

The study by Ta and Seah examines 24 financial ratios using linear discriminant function analysis.

The failed firm sample consists of 22 firms with failure dates in the period 1975–83. The failure characteristics of the firms in the sample are as follows: 9 percent went into receivership, 18 percent went into creditors' voluntary liquidation, while the rest were involuntary 'winding up' by the order of the court. The matched sample consists of 21 non-failed entities. Only industrial and commercial firms are considered in the samples. The mean asset size of the firms in the sample is $89.5 million. The data sources for the sample are:

- Singapore Registry of Companies and Businesses
- Singapore Stock Exchange
- National University of Singapore's Financial Database

The discriminant analysis process produced a 4-variable model:

- Total debt/Equity
- Profit before tax/Sales
- Profit before tax/Equity
- Interest payment/Profit before interest and taxes

The results of the model on the original sample and a validation (holdout) sample are reported in table 4.19. The results for the original sample were based on data from one year prior to failure. The validation test results were for one and two years prior.

Although the sample size is relatively small, the results of the model were fairly good, and its performance was assured as quality data was available on a larger number of Singapore companies.

Table 4.19   Summary of results

Prediction Horizon	Original sample			Holdout sample		
	Type I accuracy (%)	Type II accuracy (%)	Overall accuracy (%)	Type I accuracy (%)	Type II accuracy (%)	Overall accuracy (%)
1 year prior	77.3	93.5	86.8	75.0	90.5	86.2
2 year prior				62.5	85.7	79.3

TURKEY

Unal (1988)

In this study, Unal argues in favor of conducting principal component and congruency analysis on the universe of financial ratios in order to reduce the dimensions of the variables selected and minimize multi-collinearity in the discriminant analysis by the use of highly correlated variables. This, in turn, leads to insufficient discriminating ability and possibly also lack of stability. His research on the Turkish Food sector employs these two techniques to reduce the number of variables that best separate failing and stable firms.

In the second phase, cluster analysis, principal factor analysis and Q factor analysis were conducted to determine the basic financial ratios that will appear in the early warning model. Varimax rotation was applied to the principal factors to obtain a more meaningful interpretation of the principal factors. The basic financial ratios that were obtained were then subjected to discriminant analysis to formulate a failure prediction model for the industry during the period 1979–84.

The failed firm sample consisted of 33 firms. The definition of a failed firm was

- one that reported continuous losses after a certain period of time
- firms whose capital profitability was below that provided by risk-free Government bonds
- those firms that had standing debts after the date they were due

- those firms that could not be considered successful because they did not exhibit a positive correlation between the ratios representing risk and profitability respectively.

Sixty-two firms registered in the Turkish Capital Market Roster were used in the study. The data comprised of 50 financial ratios.

Unal discusses the pros and cons of adjusting the financial numbers for inflation (i.e., use ratios derived from constant dollar data) versus using the nominal amounts. In the end, Unal used the nominal values because of the limited scope of the research. There are other limitations in a study of this nature, according to Unal. The first is the existence of correlation among the financial ratios. This can be addressed through factor analysis. The effect economic change brought about by the business cycle cannot be evaluated by looking at data for a narrow band of time. A time series analysis of data from 1979–84 was performed to take account of this problem. To address the question of the distribution of the financial ratios, normalcy tests were conducted on the ratios. Although the attempts to normalize through transformations of the non-normal ratios proved to be unsuccessful, the normalcy tests did bring about the rejection of outliers that appeared to cause right skewness in the sample data.

After conducting factor analysis to identify principal components, time series analysis to look for ratio stability, and cluster analysis and Q factor analysis to group "like" ratios, the final model was determined.

The ratios satisfying the normalcy conditions, low correlations, and stability were as follows:

- X_1: Earnings before income and tax/Total assets
- X_2: Net working capital/Sales
- X_3: Long-term debt/Total assets
- X_4: Total debt/Total assets
- X_5: Quick assets/Inventory
- X_6: Quick assets/Current debt

The standardized discriminant function coefficients and the discriminant function are as shown in table 4.20. The classification accuracy of the model on the development sample was 97 percent overall, with the same level of accuracy for Type I and II. Tests on data 2 years prior yielded a Type I accuracy of 91 percent and Type II accuracy of 93 percent. No holdout test results were reported.

Table 4.20 Discriminant function coefficients

Ratio	Coefficient	Coefficient (absolute value of the difference of the means)	The relative importance of the ratio (%)
X_1	18.11	5.4029	52.04
X_2	1.64	1.0365	9.98
X_3	−1.21	0.1078	1.04
X_4	1.21	0.1806	1.74
X_5	−0.96	0.3890	3.75
X_6	5.85	3.2663	31.45

Uruguay

Pascale (1988)

The economic situation in Uruguay has gone through a major transformation, starting from a period of deep economic intervention during 1950–74 that led to high inflation, low real growth and frequent balance of payments crises. Starting in 1974, there was gradual reduction in the controls for capital flows and the government intervention in economic affairs was reduced and a new tax policy implemented. The change in the economic environment provided a new set of shocks to Uruguayan firms because they had to face new market conditions, and decreased protection. It is in this setting that this model to predict financial problems in firms was developed.

The sample consisted of 44 failed firms (FPs; financial problems), and 41 healthy firms (NPs; no problems). The criterion for failure was any one of the following: liquidation, bankruptcy, (forbearance/restructuring) agreement with creditors, arrangements with bank syndicates or other financial backers which did not always involve special formalities but entailed substantial changes in financial structure and cessation of activities owing to financial problems. The firms were in food, beverage, footwear and apparel, leather, chemical and metal products. All the firms selected had no less than ten workers each, with most firms (both failed and healthy) employing 50 or more workers. Healthy firms were matched with failures based on size and industry, although an exact correspondence was not always possible due to lack of data. Both groups of firms were studied for the period from 1978 to 1982. Of the firms with problems, 77 percent experienced their difficulties in 1980 and 1981, and 11 percent in 1982.

The adjustments performed on the sample data are worth mentioning because normally nominal values of the ratios are used in such studies rather than those based on constant term or inflation-adjusted financials:

1　The data was cross checked with published reports.
2　All amounts were restated in a common currency.
3　Fixed assets were valued in accordance with tax regulations.
4　Current assets and liabilities in local currency were deflated by the wholesale price index applicable to the industry.
5　Investments other than fixed assets were deflated using the general consumer price index.
6　Fixed assets were computed at their value for tax purposes for the first year of data. In subsequent years, the adjustments to the value were deflated by the implicit price index for fixed gross investment.
7　Net worth was calculated in constant terms as the differences between assets and liabilities.
8　Sales were deflated using the wholesale price index for the industry.

The variables used in the model along with the means and univariate F statistics are presented in table 4.21.

The resulting discriminant function using the F value as the criterion to enter contained the following three variables.

Table 4.21 Means of the variables and significant tests

Variable	FP mean	NP mean	F
Asset turnover	1.11932	1.64829	16.39 7
Current ratio	1.02636	2.29415	39.59 4
Changes in working capital	0.03091	0.46927	4.514
Sales/Non-bank working capital	2.94295	4.78073	10.43 3
Leverage	1.33432	3.03975	54.26 0
Inventory/Bank debt	0.98568	4.58146	21.54 8
Bank debt/Total debt	1.68295	2.84097	8.735
Long-term debt/Total debt	0.07455	0.12659	2.912
(Accounts receivable + inventories)/accounts payable + spontaneous sources	3.85841	3.06780	2.070
Inventory turnover	3.90432	7.68439	16.65 6
Rate of return	−0.25068	0.23341	6.414
Sales/Debts	1.53454	4.67829	68.24 3
Net earnings/Total assets	−0.08705	0.10756	27.05 7

$F_{1.60}(0.05) = 4.00.$ $F_{1.120}(0.05) = 3.92.$ $F_{1.60}(0.01) = 7.08.$ $F_{1.120}(0.01) = 6.85.$

- Sales/Debts
- Net earnings/Total assets
- Long term debt/Total debt

The classification accuracy of the model in the original sample was 98 percent for Type I and 85 percent for Type II. In the Lachenbruch test, the corresponding values were 98 percent and 83 percent respectively. The Lachenbruch test (also sometimes called the "jackknife" test) is used to eliminate the sample bias, by estimating the model with one observation held out and then classifying that observation. This process is repeated as many times as there are cases which virtually eliminates any potential bias. Pascale performed holdout tests by validating the model with random subsamples. The classification accuracy in the holdout subsample ranged from 79 percent to 100 percent. Finally, the accuracy of the model was tested on data, two and three years prior to failure. The Type I accuracy for two and three years prior was 83 percent and the Type II accuracy was 79 percent for two years prior and 81 for three years prior, indicating that the model had an impressive ability to predict failure.

SUMMARY AND A FEW CONCLUSIONS

We have attempted to review and compare a relatively large number of empirical failure classification models from many countries. Much of the material is derived from little-known sources and as such we hope that the study will stimulate a greater transnational discussion. Indeed, as financial institutions and government agencies in countries such as Canada, the USA, Brazil, France, and England wrestle with the specter of large firm failures in the future, the knowledge that prior work has been done with respect to early warning models may help obviate the consequences or reduce the number of these failures.

We expect that the quality and reliability of models constructed in many of the afore-mentioned countries will improve

1   as the quality of information on companies is expanded and refined
2   as the number of business failures increases, thereby providing more data points for empirical analysis, and
3   as researchers and practitioners become more aware of the problems and potential of such models.

Where sufficient data do not exist for specific sector models, for instance, manufacturing, retailing, and service firms, the application of industry relative measures, e.g., like Altman and Izan (1981), can perhaps provide a satisfactory framework for meaningful analysis. Of course, this requires that government or private agencies build reliable industry data bases for comparison purposes.

REFERENCES

Altman, E. I., 1968, Financial Ratios, Discriminant Analysis and the Prediction Of Corporate Bankruptcy, *Journal of Finance* 23 (4), 589–609.

Altman, E. I. (ed.), 1984, International Corporate Failures Model, in Special Studies in Banking & Finance, *Journal of Banking & Finance*.

Altman, E. I., 1993, *Corporate Financial Distress*, John Wiley & Sons, New York. First edition published in 1983.

Altman, E. I. and H. Y. Izan, 1981, *Identifying Corporate Distress in Australia; An Industry Relative Analysis*, Australian Graduate School of Management, Sydney.

Altman, E. I. and M. Lavallee, 1981, Business Failure Classification in Canada, *Journal of Business Administration*, Summer.

Altman, E. I., T. Baidya, and L. M. Riberio-Dias, 1979, Assessing Potential Financial Problems of Firms in Brazil, *Journal of International Business Studies*, Fall.

Altman, E. I., R. G. Haldeman, and P. Narayanan, 1977, ZETA analysis: A New Model to Identify Bankruptcy Risk of Corporations, *Journal of Banking and Finance* 1 (1), 29–51.

Altman, E. I., J. M. Hartzell, and M. B. Peck, 1995, *Emerging Markets Corporate Bonds Scoring System – Mexican 1995 Review and 1996 Outlook*, New York: Salomon Brothers Inc.

Altman, E. I., D. W. Kim, and Y. H. Eom, 1995, Failure Prediction: Evidence from Korea, *Journal of International Financial Management and Accounting* 6 (3), 230–49.

Altman, E. I., G. Marco, and F. Varetto, 1994, Corporate distress diagnosis: Comparisons using linear discriminant analysis and neural networks (the Italian experience), *Journal of Banking and Finance* 18, 505–29.

Altman, E. I., M. Margaine, M. Schlosser, and P. Vernimmen, 1973, Statistical Credit Analysis in The Textile Industry; A French Experience, *Journal of Financial and Quantitative Analysis*, March.

Argenti, J., 1983, *Predicting Corporate Failure*, Institute of Chartered Accountants in England and Wales.

Baetge, J., M. Muss, and H. Niehaus, 1988, The Use Of Statistical Analysis to Identify the Financial Strength of Corporations in Germany, *Studies in Banking & Finance* 7, 183–96.

Beaver, W., 1967, Financial Ratios as Predictors of Failures, *Empirical Research in Accounting*, Selected Studies, Supplement to the Journal of Accounting Research, January.

Beerman, K., 1976, *Possible Ways to Predict Capital Losses With Annual Financial Statements*, Dusseldorf, University of Dusseldorf.

Bhatia, U., 1988, Predicting Corporate Sickness in India, *Studies in Banking & Finance* 7, 57–71.

Bidin, A. R., 1988, The development of a predictive model (PNB-Score) for evaluating performance of companies owned by the Government of Malaysia, *Studies in Banking & Finance* 7, 91–103.

Bilderbeek, J., 1979, An Empirical Study of the Predictive Ability of Financial Ratios in the Netherlands, *Zeitschrift fur Betriebswirtschaft* 5, May.

Bontemps, P., 1981, *Credit Scoring for Risk*, Paris, Credit National.

Brigham, G. and M. Ehrhardt, 2001, *Financial Management: Theory and Practice*, Dryden Press.

Briones, J. J., J. L. Martin Marin, and M. J. Vazquez Cueto, 1988, Forecasting bank failures: The Spanish case, *Studies in Banking & Finance* 7, 127–39.

Cahill, E., 1981, Irish Listed Company Failure Ratios, Accounts and Auditors' Opinions, *Journal of Irish Business and Administration Research*, April.

Castagna, A. D. and Z. P. Matolcsy, 1982, The Prediction of Corporate Failure; Testing the Australian Experience, *Australian Journal of Management*, June, 35.

Cifarelli, D. M., F. Corielli, and G. Forestieri, 1988, Business Failure Analysis: A Bayesian Approach with Italian Firm Data, *Studies in Banking & Finance* 7, 73–89.

Collongues, Y., 1977, Ratios, Financiers et Prevision des failites des Petites et Moyennes Enterprises (Financial ratios and Forecasting of Small and Medium Size Enterprises), *Review Banque* 365.

Deakin, E., 1972, A Discriminant Analysis of Predictors of Business Failure, *Journal of Accounting Research*, March.

De Breed and Partners, 1996, The Netherlands, Publicity Document.

Earl, M. J. and D. Marais, 1982, Predicting Corporate Failure in the U.K. Using Discriminant Analysis, *Accounting and Business Research*.

Fernandez, A. I., 1988, A Spanish model for credit risk classification, *Studies in Banking & Finance* 7, 115–25.

Fischer, J. 1981, Forecasting Company Failure by the Use of Non-Numeric Data, EIASM Workshop on Bank Planning Models, Brussels, 6 April 1981.

Fisher, R. A., 1956, The Use of Multiple Measurements in Taxonomic Problems, *Annals of Eugenics*, VII, September, 179–88.

Gebhardt, G., 1980, Insolvency Prediction Based on Annual Financial Statements According to The Company Law – An Assessment of the Reform of Annual Statements by the Law of 1965 from the View of External Addresses, in H. Besters, et al., eds., *Bochumer Beitrage Zur Untennehmungs und Unternehmens-forschung, Vol 22* (Wiesbaden).

Gloubos, G. and T. Grammatikos, 1988, The success of bankruptcy prediction models in Greece, *Studies in Banking & Finance* 7, 37–46.

Izan, H. Y., 1984, Corporate distress in Australia, 1984, *Journal of Banking and Finance* 8 (2), 303–20.

Joy, O. and J. Tollefson, 1975, On the Financial Applications of Discriminant Analysis, *JFQA*, December.

Knight, R. M., 1979, The Determination of Failure in Canadian Firms, ASA Meetings of Canada, Saskatoon, May 28–30, 1979, University Of Western Ontario Working Paper, May.

Ko, C. J., 1982, A Delineation of Corporate Appraisal Models and Classification of Bankruptcy Firms in Japan, Thesis (New York University).

Lachenbruch, Peter A., 1967, An Almost Unbiased Method of Obtaining Confidence Intervals for the Probability of Misclassification in Discriminant Analysis, *Biometrics*, 23.

Lincoln, M. 1984, An Empirical Study of the Usefulness Of Accounting Ratios to Describe Levels of Insolvency Risk, *Journal of Banking and Finance* 8 (2), June.

Mader, F., 1975, Les Ratios et l'analyse du risque (Ratios and Analysis of Risk), *Analyse Financiere*, Zeme Trimestre.

Mader, F., 1979, Un Enchantillon d'Enterprises en Difficulte (A sample of Enterprises in Difficulty), *Journee des Centrales der Bilans* (Journal of the Central Balance Sheet Section of the Banque de France).

Marais, D. A. J., 1979, A Method of Quantifying Companies' Relative Financial Strength, Working Paper No. 4 (Bank of England, London).

Pascale, R., 1988, A Multivariate Model to Predict Firm Financial Problems: The Case of Uruguay, *Studies in Banking & Finance* 7, 171–82.

Ross, S., R. Westerfield and J. Jaffe, 1999, Corporate Finance, 5th edn, Irwin, McGraw-Hill.

Suominen, S. I., 1988, The prediction of bankruptcy in Finland, *Studies in Banking & Finance* 7, 27–36.

Swanson, E. and J. Tybout, 1988, Industrial bankruptcy determinants in Argentina, *Studies in Banking & Finance* 7, 1–25.

Ta, H. P. and L. H. Seah, 1981, Business failure prediction in Singapore, *Studies in Banking & Finance* 7, 105–13. Reprinted in Altman (1988).

Taffler R. J., 1976, Finding Those Firms in Danger, *Accounting Age*, 16 July.

Taffler, R. J., 1982, Forecasting Company Failure in the U.K. Using Discriminant Analysis and Financial Ratios Data, *Journal of Royal Statistical Society*.

Taffler, R. and L. Houston, 1980, How to Identify Failing Companies Before It is Too Late, *Professional Administration*, April.

Taffler, R. J. and H. Tisshaw, 1977, Going, Going, Going – Four Factors Which Predict, *Accountancy*, 50.

Takahashi, K., Y. Kurokawa, and K. Watase, 1979, Corporate bankruptcy prediction in Japan, *Journal of Banking and Finance* 8 (2), 229–247. Reprinted in Altman (1984).

Tamari, M., 1964, Financial ratios as a means of forecasting bankruptcy, *Economic Review* (Bank of Israel, Jerusalem).

Theodossiou, P. and C. Papoulias, 1988, Problematic firms in Greece: An evaluation using corporate failure prediction models, *Studies in Banking & Finance* 7, 47–55.

Unal, T., 1988, An early warning model for predicting firm failure in Turkey, *Studies in Banking & Finance* 7, 141–70.

van Frederikslust, R. A. I., 1978, *Predictability of Corporate Failure*, Leiden; Martinus Nijhoff Social Science Division.

von Stein, J. H., 1968, *Identifying Endangered Firms*, (Hohenheim University, Stuttgart-Hohenheim). Reprinted in Altman (1984).

von Stein, J. H. and W. Ziegler, 1984, The Prognosis and Surveillance of Risks from Commercial Credit Borrowers, *Journal of Banking and Finance* 8 (2), 249–68.

Weibel, P. F., 1973, *The Value Of Criteria To Judge Credit Worthiness In The Lending Of Banks*, (Bern/Stuttgart).

Weinrich, G., 1978, *Predicting Credit Worthiness, Directions of Credit Operations by Risk Class*, Galder, Weisbaden.

5 | Emerging Market Corporate Bonds – A Scoring System

with John Hartzell and Matthew Peck

EMERGING MARKET SCORE MODEL (EMS MODEL)

The emerging market scoring model (EMS model) for rating emerging markets credits is based first on a fundamental financial review derived from a quantitative risk model; and second, by our analyst assessments of specific credit risks in order arrive at a final analyst modified rating. This rating can then be utilized by the investor, after considering the appropriate sovereign yield spread, to assess equivalent bond ratings and intrinsic values.

The foundation of the EMS model is an enhancement of Edward I. Altman's Z-Score model, described in the body of this report (and in chapter 1 of this volume), resulting in an EM score and its associated bond rating equivalent.

The EM Score's rating equivalent is then modified based on three critical factors:

1　the firm's vulnerability to currency devaluation
2　its industry affiliation, and
3　its competitive position in the industry.

Unique features of the specific bond issue should also be considered. These subjective modifications are an important complement to the EM score.

The resulting analyst modified rating is compared to the actual bond rating (if any). Where no agency rating exists, our modified analyst rating is a means to assess credit quality and relative value both to credits within a country and to US corporates. These results are listed in table 5.1 for Mexican corporates. The results are based on year-end 1994 financials and will be updated as new information becomes available. The implied yield spread based on the analyst modified rating can be observed from the US

Table 5.1   Mexican corporate issuers – EM scores and modified ratings

Company	Industry	EM score	Bond-rating equivalent	Modified rating	Ratings M/S&P/O&P
Aeromexico	Airlines	–4.42	D	D	NR/NR/NR
Apasco	Cement	8.48	AAA	A	Ba2/NR/NR
CCM	Supermarkets	4.78	BB–	B+	NR/NR/NR
Cemex	Cement	5.67	BBB–	BBB–	Ba3/BB/BB
Cydsa	Chemicals	4.67	BB–	B+	NR/NR/NR
DESC	Conglomerate	4.23	B	BB+	NR/NR/NR
Empresas ICA	Construction	5.96	BBB	BB	B1/BB–/B+
Femsa	Bottling	6.37	A–	BBB+	NR/NR/NR
Gemex	Bottling	5.40	BB+	BB+	Ba3/NR/NR
GIDUSA (Durango)	Paper and Forest Products	4.61	B+	BB	B1/BB–/NR
GMD	Construction	4.85	BB	B–	B3/NR/NR
Gruma	Food Processing	5.56	BBB–	BBB+	NR/NR/NR
Grupo Dina	Auto Manufacturing	5.54	BBB–	BB+	NR/NR/B
Hylsamex	Steel	5.51	BBB–	BB–	NR/NR/NR
IMSA	Steel	5.45	BBB–	BB–	NR/NR/NR
Kimberly-Clark de Mexico	Paper and Forest Products	8.96	AAA	AA	NR/NR/NR
Liverpool	Retail	9.85	AAA	A+	NR/NR/NR
Moderna	Conglomerate	5.28	BB+	BB+	NR/NR/NR
Ponderosa	Paper and Forest Products	6.64	A	BB	NR/NR/NR
San Luis	Autoparts	2.69	CCC	CCC–	NR/NR/NR
Sidek	Conglomerate	4.68	BB–	B	NR/NR/CCC
Simec	Steel	4.42	B+	B–	NR/NR/CCC
Situr	Hotel and Tourism	5.17	BB+	B	NR/NR/CCC
Synkro	Textile/Apparel	1.59	CCC–	CCC	NR/NR/NR
TAMSA	Steel Pipes	3.34	CCC+	B	NR/NR/NR
TELMEX	Telecommunications	9.57	AAA	AA–	NR/NR/NR
Televisa	Cable and Media	7.29	AA	BBB+	Ba2/NR/NR
TMM	Shipping	5.34	BB+	BB+	Ba2/BB–/NR
Vitro	Glass	5.18	BB+	BB	Ba2/NR/NR

NR: No rating. M Moody's. S&P Standard & Poor's. D&P Duff & Phelps.
Note: Ratings are for senior long-term foreign debt unless otherwise specified. EM Scores were calculated using fiscal year end 1994 financials.
Source: Salomon Brothers Inc.

corporate bond market. Steps 1 through 6 (pages 133–7) outline the process by which we use the EM score to reach an analyst modified rating.

Note that our analyst modified rating is not constrained in any manner by the so-called "sovereign-ceiling." We do advocate, however, factoring in the appropriate current sovereign yield spread differential between the emerging market country and comparable duration US Treasuries. In most cases, the full sovereign "haircut" should be added to the stand-alone issuer spread. There are instances, however, where the full sovereign spread is not appropriate because of unique attributes of the issuer or the issuer's sovereign affiliation. For example, investor portfolio considerations may swell the demand for a firm in a key industry, such as telecommunications. Or, the sovereign's huge supply of outstanding debt relative to investor demand may widen that security's spread *vis-à-vis* a more modest supply of a particularly attractive corporate bond. The resulting spread may indeed be below that of the sovereign as a result of technical factors rather than fundamental credit characteristics.

Step 1: US Bond Rating Equivalent

Score each bond by its EM score and classify it relative to its stand-alone US bond rating equivalent. See table 5.2 for each EM score variable's US bond rating equivalent, and table 5.3 and figure 5.1 for the overall EM scores' rating equivalents.

Emerging markets corporate credits should initially be analyzed in a manner similar to traditional analysis of US corporates. This involves the examination of measures of performance in such a manner as to establish a rating equivalent of the particular issuer. Instead of using a new *ad hoc* system, which may not be based on a rigorous analytical examination of credit worthiness, we will use an established and well-tested system. Since it is not yet possible to build such a model from a sample of emerging market credits, we suggest testing the applicability of a modified version of the original Z-score model. It is based on a comparative profile of bankrupt and non-bankrupt US manufacturers, however, our modification can be applied to nonmanufacturing, industrial firms and for private and public entities.

The original Z-Score model is based on at least two data sources that make it inappropriate to use for all emerging markets corporates. It requires the firm to have publicly traded equity and it is primarily for manufacturers. In more than 25 years of experience in building, testing and using credit scoring models for a variety of purposes, the original model has been enhanced to make it applicable for private companies and nonmanufacturers. The resulting model, which is the foundation for our EMS model approach, is of the form:

Table 5.2 Average EM-score variables by bond rating – US industrials 1994

Bond rating	(x_1) Working capital/total assets	(x_2) Retained earnings/total assets	(x_3) Oper. income/total assets	(x_4) Stockholder's equity/total liabilities
AAA	0.175	0.470	0.187	1.120
AA*	0.150	0.450	0.166	1.085
AA–	0.142	0.439	0.150	1.025
A+	0.138	0.359	0.114	0.970
A	0.127	0.350	0.107	0.866
A–	0.120	0.276	0.099	0.755
BBB+	0.114	0.226	0.088	0.701
BBB	0.103	0.184	0.080	0.636
BBB–	0.081	0.065	0.075	0.546
BB+	0.065	0.040	0.070	0.444
BB	0.060	(0.031)	0.065	0.328
BB–	0.055	(0.040)	0.062	0.305
B+	0.050	(0.091)	0.055	0.287
B	0.040	(0.149)	0.050	0.272
B–	0.025	(0.200)	0.045	0.169
CCC+	0.010	(0.307)	0.025	(0.052)
CCC	(0.044)	(0.321)	0.015	(0.099)
CCC–	(0.052)	(0.561)	(0.025)	(0.256)
D	(0.068)	(0.716)	(0.045)	(0.325)

* There were insufficient data points to calculate the average AA+ ratio.
Source: In-Depth Data Corp. Results are based on over 750 US industrial corporates with rated bonds outstanding; 1994 data.

Table 5.3   US bond rating equivalent based on EM score

US equivalent rating	Average EM score	Sample size
AAA	8.15	8
AA+	7.60	–
AA	7.30	18
AA–	7.00	15
A+	6.85	24
A	6.65	42
A–	6.40	38
BBB+	6.25	38
BBB	5.85	59
BBB–	5.65	52
BB+	5.25	34
BB	4.95	25
BB–	4.75	65
B+	4.50	78
B	4.15	115
B–	3.75	95
CCC+	3.20	23
CCC	2.50	10
CCC–	1.75	6
D	0	14

Source: In-Depth Data Corp. Average based on over 750 US industrial corporates with rated debt outstanding; 1994 data.

Figure 5.1   Equivalent bond rating

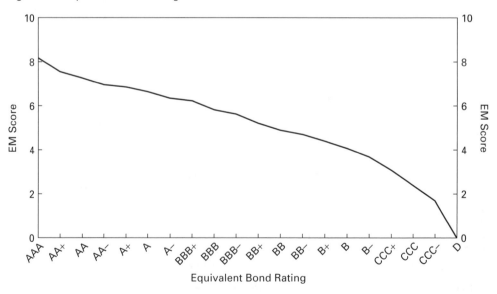

Source: In-Depth Data Corp. Average based on over 750 US industrial corporates with rated debt outstanding; 1994 data.

$$\text{EM score} = 6.56(X_1) + 3.26(X_2) + 6.72(X_3) + 1.05(X_4) + 3.25$$

where

$+X_1$ = Working capital/Total assets
$+X_2$ = Retained earnings/Total assets
$+X_3$ = Operating income/Total assets
$+X_4$ = Book value equity/Total liabilities

The constant term in the model (3.25) enables us to standardize the analysis so that a default equivalent rating (D) is consistent with a score of zero or below.

Major accounting differences between the emerging market country and the US must be factored into the data used in the calculations of our measures. For example, our calculation of retained earnings is based on the sum of retained earnings and capital reserve, the surplus (deficiency) on restatement of assets, and the net income (loss) for the current period.

The model has been tested on samples of both nonmanufacturers and manufacturers in the US and its accuracy and reliability have remained high. We have also carefully calibrated the variables and the resulting score with US bond rating equivalents. These equivalents, given in tables 5.2 and 5.3 and graphed in figure 5.1, are based on a sample of more than 750 US firms with rated bonds outstanding.

Step 2: Adjusted Bond Rating for ForEx Currency Devaluation Vulnerability

Each bond is analyzed as to the issuing firm's vulnerability to problems in servicing its foreign currency denominated debt. Vulnerability is assessed based on the relationship between nonlocal currency revenues minus costs compared to nonlocal currency interest expense, and nonlocal currency revenues versus nonlocal currency debt. Finally, the level of cash is compared with the debt coming due in the next year.

If the firm has high (weak) vulnerability, that is, low or zero nonlocal currency revenues and/or low or zero revenues/debt, and/or a substantial amount of foreign currency debt coming due with little cash liquidity, then the bond rating equivalent in Step 1 is lowered by a full rating class, such as, BB+ to B+. There is no upgrade for a low (strong) vulnerability and a one notch (BB+ to BB) reduction for a neutral vulnerability assessment.

Step 3: Adjusted for Industry

The original (Step 1) bond rating equivalent is compared to Salomon's generic industry safety rating equivalent in table 5.4. For up to each full letter grade difference between the two ratings, Step 2's bond rating equivalent is adjusted up or down by one notch. For example, if the rating from Step 1 is BBB and the industry's rating is BBB−, BB+, or BB, then the adjustment is one notch down; if the difference is more than one full rating class but less than two full ratings, there is a two-notch adjustment. Finally, the industry environment in the specific emerging market country is factored into the analysis.

Table 5.4   Average credit safety of industry groups – Salomon Brothers

	Average sector credit safety
Telecommunication	High A
Independent Finance	High A
Natural Gas Utilities	High A
Beverages	High A
High Quality Electric Utilities	High A
Railroads	High A
Food Processing	Mid A
Bottling	Mid A
Domestic Bank Holding	Low A
Tobacco	Low A
Medium-Quality Electric Utilities	Low A
Consumer Products Industry	Low A
H.G. Diversified Mfg./Conglomerates	Low A
Leasing	Low A
Auto Manufacturers	Low A
Chemicals	Low A
Energy	Low A
Natural Gas Pipelines	High BBB
Paper/Forest Products	Mid BBB
Retail	Mid BBB
P&C Insurance	Mid BBB
Aerospace/Defense	Mid BBB
Information/Data Technology	Mid BBB
Supermarkets	High BB
Cable and Media	High BB
Vehicle Parts	High BB
Textile/Apparel	High BB
Low-Quality Electric Utilities	Mid BB
Gaming	Mid BB
Restaurants	Mid BB
Construction	Mid BB
Hotel/Leisure	Mid BB
Low Quality Manufacturing	Mid BB
Airlines	Low BB
Metals	High B

Source: Adapted from Six-Month Credit Quality Overview, *Salomon Brothers Inc, January 18, 1995.*

Step 4: Adjusted for Competitive Position

Step 3's rating is adjusted up (or down) one notch if the firm is a dominant (or not) company in its industry or if it is a domestic power in terms of size, political influence and quality of management. It is possible that the consensus competitive position result is neutral (no change in rating).

Step 5: Special Debt Issue Features

If the particular debt issue has unique features, such as collateral or a bona fide, high-quality guarantor, then the issue should be upgraded accordingly.

Step 6: Comparison to the Sovereign Spread

The analyst modified rating is then compared to what US corporate bonds of the same rating are currently selling for. The US corporate credit quality spread is then added to the appropriate option adjusted spread of the sovereign bond.

How to Use the EMS Model

Unique Features of the EMS Model

An important distinction must be made between this model and the original Z-Score model. First, this model, referred to by Altman as the Z″ Score Model, is applicable for nonmanufactures and private firms in addition to manufactures and public firms. Second, the model applies our analysts' subjective measures of credit strength as outlined in Steps 2 through 5.

It is important to remember that the stand-alone rating generated in Step 1 is based on the specific operating performance and financial characteristics of the company. The analyst modified rating likely will change with the operating environment within which a company functions. For US firms in mature industries, this environment does not typically change dramatically. For Mexican firms, however, their respective operating environments are subject to major changes. Outlined below are some of the unique characteristics of the operating environments for Mexican firms.

FOREIGN EXCHANGE RISK

One of the largest credit risks facing Mexican Eurobond issuers at this time is their nonlocal currency debt service capacity. Two critical factors affecting a firm's debt service capacity are their export revenues and nonpeso cost structure. The extraordinary political and economic events of the last year have undoubtedly raised the default risk of Mexican companies. Firms with low export revenues have become particularly vulnerable to exchange risk, given their dollar liabilities and associated debt service. In addition, those firms with a high percentage of raw materials sourced from abroad have experienced reduced margins and debt service capacity.

ACCOUNTING ANOMALIES

The high inflation environment in Mexico precludes Mexican firms from the standard credit analysis applied to US companies (the original Z-score model was for US companies only). For example, the impact of noncash foreign exchange losses on pretax earnings is dramatic for Mexican firms. Analysis of retained earnings and the book equity, and therefore leverage ratios of Mexican firms, is subject to more careful analysis and appropriate adjustments.

GOVERNMENT INTERVENTION

The Mexican Government has recently proactively supported certain sectors of the Mexican economy in order to prevent default. Examples of this include the support of the banking system through programs like Procapte; the facilitation of providing short-term financing for Grupo Sidek (the Mexican conglomerate which defaulted, and subsequently made payment, on its commercial paper); and the government's renegotiation of construction sector concessions. Despite its recent support of the private sector, the Mexican Government's continuing presence in crisis situations cannot be assumed with certainty.

BANK FINANCING ENVIRONMENT

Short-term financing has become prohibitively expensive in Mexico. With interest rates for short-term financing above 80 percent and Cetes rates still at levels of approximately 60 percent, Mexican firms cannot economically access short-term capital. Historically, Mexican firms maintained high levels of short-term liabilities to finance working capital, in part, because longer-term financing was unavailable given Mexico's high inflation rate. The current government support of the banking system has enabled many banks to avoid liquidity problems since the devaluation. However, the Government's continuing support of the banking system in the future, while highly likely, cannot be guaranteed.

MARKET SHARE DOMINANCE

Most of the Mexican Eurobond issuers represent the largest of Mexican companies. Most of these companies were either owned by the Government prior to the late 1980s and subsequently privatized, or they were controlled by wealthy families for decades. Therefore, most Mexican Eurobond issuers have typically dominated their respective markets. With the advent of NAFTA, and the economic weakness brought about since the devaluation, we expect Mexican firms will see greater competition and shrinking market shares in the future.

Our analyst modified rating embodies these particular Mexican credit features. Together with timely sovereign and economic research, we can adjust the analyst modified rating to incorporate changes in the Mexican economic and corporate landscape. We will be updating the results of the EMS Model regularly.

Applying the Analyst Modified Rating to the Current Market

The analyst modified rating reported in table 5.1 should be used to evaluate whether current market levels for bonds appropriately reflect the credit risk implied by the rating. Since the devaluation, the Mexican corporate market has traded with extreme volatility. Market levels have often been driven by technical factors (more sellers than buyers) rather than fundamental creditworthiness. If the Mexican macroeconomic environment stabilizes, we expect the corporate market to continue its recent recovery. The analyst modified rating should be used to provide a clear measure of relative credit risk independent of market technicals.

The EMS Model is not a Bankruptcy Predictor

The EMS Model is not a predictor of emerging markets company bankruptcy for two reasons. First, the current issuers of Mexican Eurobonds have not experienced defaults on their dollar Eurobond liabilities since they issued their debt (nearly all of the Eurobonds have been issued within the last five years). Second, the unique characteristics of the Mexican political and economic environment make bankruptcy prediction more difficult than that for US firms. The Mexican Government's potential involvement in the corporate restructuring process is a variable which cannot be reasonably built into the model. Our model is a means to estimate equivalent bond ratings and intrinsic fixed income values.

CONCLUSION

The EMS model should be used to assess relative value among credits in the inefficient trading environment for emerging markets credits. The model is flexible, allowing for future modifications depending on the operating and financial environment and sovereign risk.

Note: The author of this volume has found that the EMS model is also relevant and accurate in assessing the default risk of US non-financial, non-manufacturing firms, both public and private, as well as manufacturing companies.

6 | Managing a Return to Financial Health

with James K. La Fleur

When Jim La Fleur took the helm at GTI, it was a company hovering on the edge of bankruptcy. By using the Altman Bankruptcy Predictor Model in an active way to set strategy, La Fleur was able to return the company to a sound going concern. This is a case report of a marriage of an academically developed model and a corporate strategy designed to manage a financial turnaround.

Statistically verified predictive models have long been used in the study of business. Generally, these models are developed by scientists and tested by "observers," who do not interact with, or influence, the measurements of the model. Consequently, the models, when valid, have predicted events with satisfactory accuracy, and thereby enjoy a reasonable degree of confidence among business analysts.

This "passive" use of predictive models overlooks the possibility of using them actively. In the "active" use of a predictive model, the role of the observer is shifted to that of a "participant." For example, a manager may use a predictive model that relates to business affairs of a company by deliberately attempting to influence the model's measurements. The manager, acting as a participant – rather than as an observer – makes decisions suggested by the parameters of the model to control the prediction of the model.

In the specific case we will discuss, the Altman Bankruptcy Predictor Model was used actively to manage the financial turnaround of a company, GTI Corporation, that was on the verge of bankruptcy.[1] A series of management decisions were made over a

[1] Michael Ball of *Inc. Magazine* has written about GTI in the context of a small business management ("Z Factor: Rescue by the Numbers," *Inc. Magazine*, Dec. 1980, pp. 45–59). C. Hofer has written about turnaround situations in general ("Turnaround Strategies," *The Journal of Business Strategy*, Summer 1980, pp. 19–31).

period of five years to foil the model's prediction of bankruptcy. These decisions, many of which were specifically motivated by considering their effect on the financial ratios in the model, led directly to the recovery of the company and the establishment of a firm financial base.

The success in the active use of this specific model suggests that it may be worthwhile to consider the "active approach" to the use of other appropriate predictive models.

PREDICTING BANKRUPTCY WITH THE Z-SCORE

Working with an original sample of bankrupt manufacturing firms and a control sample of healthy entities, Altman (1968) utilized a combination of traditional financial ratio analysis and a rather sophisticated statistical technique known as discriminant analysis to construct and test a financial model for assessing the likelihood that a firm would go bankrupt. The model combined five financial measures utilizing both reported accounting and stock market variables to objectively arrive at an overall measure of corporate health. Developed in 1968, the model has proven to be remarkably durable and is still accepted as an important indicator for analysts and decision makers in many spheres of work. Where it had not been tested and verified is in the application of its underlying theory for the very firms that are being examined. This article attempts to fill the gap.

Discriminant analysis is a multivariate technique that analyzes the characteristics (e.g., financial ratios) of two or more populations or groups (e.g., corporations) in order to identify and weight the important measures that will most accurately classify the original observations into their identified groups. These groupings are qualitative in nature (e.g., bankrupt vs. non-bankrupt, Aaa vs. A rated bonds). The trick is to maximize the classification accuracy of the original test observations and to test the model on many relevant types of holdout or test samples, which are utilized to verify the statistical reliability of the model. The final test relates to the old adage that the "proof is in the eating." That is, how well has the model predicted the fate of observed companies in periods after the model was developed?

The Altman Z-Score model is a linear analysis in that five measures are objectively weighted and summed up to arrive at an overall score that then becomes the basis for classification of firms into one of the *a priori* groupings. As an example, figure 6.1 shows a two-variable analysis where measures of profitability and liquidity are plotted for a sample of healthy (X) and sick (O) firms. The discriminant model selects the appropriate weights which will separate as far as possible the distance between the average values of each group while at the same time minimizing the statistical distance of each observation (the individual X's and O's) and its own group mean. Each observation is then "projected" on the line (AB) which best discriminates between the two groups.[2]

---

[2] For a technical explanation of the procedure and discriminant analysis in general, see W. Cooley and P. Lohnes, *Multivariate Procedures for the Behavioral Sciences* (New York: John Wiley, 1962); Edward I. Altman, *Corporate Bankruptcy in America* (Lexington, Mass.: D. C. Heath, 1971); R. Eisenbeis and R. Avery, *Discriminant Analysis and Classification Procedures: Theory and Applications* (Lexington, Mass.: D. C. Heath, 1972). For the application of classification techniques to business, banking, and finance, see Edward I. Altman, R. Avery, R. Eisenbeis, and J. Sinkey, *Application of Classification Techniques to Business, Banking and Finance* (Greenwich, Conn.: JAI Press, 1981).

Figure 6.1 Linear discriminant analysis: An example

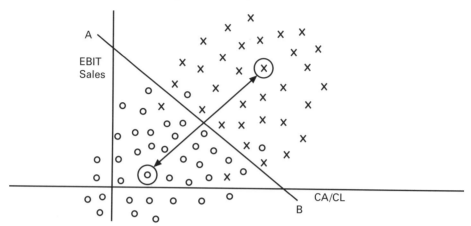

O = Bankrupt firms   X = non-bankrupt firms   Ⓞ = group mean   Ⓧ = group mean

The Bankruptcy Predictor Formula (Z) is a relatively straightforward equation

$$Z = 1.2X_1 + 1.4X_2 + 3.3X_3 + 0.6X_4 + 1.0X_5$$

where

Z = overall index of corporate health
X_1 = working capital divided by total assets
X_2 = retained earnings divided by total assets
X_3 = earnings before interests and taxes divided by total assets
X_4 = market value of equity divided by book value of total liabilities
X_5 = sales divided by total assets

Each of these financial ratios is defined in appendix A, where the information content of the ratio and its insertion into the formula is described.

If ratios calculated from a company's financial statement and stock market results are inserted into the formula, a single number will result, which typically has a range from –5 to +10. Scores above 10 are possible, primarily, if the firm's market value of equity is high combined with relatively small amounts of total liabilities. The range of Z-Scores achieved by firms in Altman's original sample of 33 bankrupt and 33 carefully matched healthy firms showed that all firms which scored below 1.8 were classified as bankrupt and did actually go bankrupt. Those above 3.0 were classified as healthy and remained continuing entities. Scores between 1.8 and 3.0 are classified into a gray area, which indicates less clearly the firm's ultimate fate. In all cases, the higher the Z-Score, the healthier the firm and the lower probability of failure. Figure 6.2 shows the three zones referred to as safe, gray, and bankrupt, along with the Z-Score for GTI Corporation for the period of 1972 through 1979.[3]

---

[3]   This model was developed for manufacturing firms, and no claim is made about its expected accuracy for other types of companies. Models such as Zeta (Edward I. Altman, R. Haldeman, and P. Narayanan, "Zeta

Figure 6.2 GTI's 1972–79 Z-Score curve with annual EPS notations

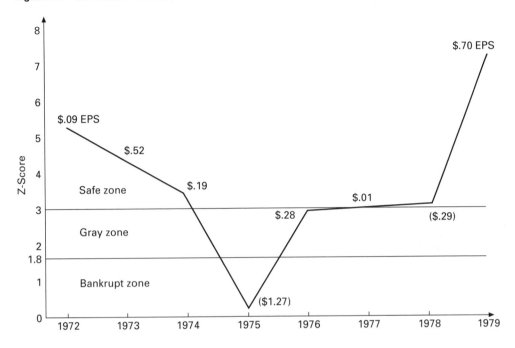

The Bankruptcy Predictor has proven consistently accurate over the period of time since its development. The original bankrupt and non-bankrupt samples and an independent sample of additional bankrupt firms displayed accuracy of 95 percent based on data from approximately one year prior to failure. The accuracy dropped to 72 percent based on two-year prior data. Subsequent tests on firms that have gone bankrupt since 1968 have shown an accuracy level of 82–85 percent.

One can observe an overall deterioration in the average Z-Score for all US manufacturing companies from the mid-1960s to the present. Firms have become more risky, their average return on investment has shrunk, and the stock market's assessment of the value of equity relative to increased debt has also deteriorated. In other words, the average US company has become more risky, according to the model, than it was over a decade ago. That is good reason for companies to make a careful assessment of strengths and weaknesses in today's highly competitive and high fixed charges environment.

APPLICATIONS OF THE BANKRUPTCY PREDICTOR

In the twelve years since the bankruptcy model was first developed, various types of practitioners have employed the model for distinctly different objectives:

Analysis, A New Model to Identify Bankruptcy Risk of Corporations," *Journal of Banking and Finance*, June 1977, pp. 29–54) and Gamblers Ruin (J. Wilcox, "The Gamblers Ruin Approach to Business Risk," *Sloan Management Review*, Autumn 1976) claim broader applicability but are proprietary and less easy to use by practitioners armed only with a firm's financial statements, stock price, and a hand-held calculator.

- Credit analysis (e.g., accept vs. reject) and loan review for financial institutions
- Investment analysis (e.g., money manager and investment banker applications)
- Analytical auditing analysis (e.g., going concern assessment)
- Legal analysis (e.g., prudent man and failing company doctrine defenses)
- Merger target analysis (e.g., both before and during reorganization)

It is beyond the scope of this article to discuss each of these application areas, but they all have one thing in common. They are being used by individuals external to the firms being analyzed. Altman did indicate in his original works that potential application of the Z-Score approach is to objectively assess a firm's own strengths and weaknesses. This could be done at a particular point in time and over time via a trend analysis. Reference was also made to the use of the model internally for accounts receivable management, the analogue to commercial bank credit analysis.

What Altman did not indicate was what management could do with the results of the model once the indication was that a firm was headed toward bankruptcy, that is, that its overall financial profile was consistent with other firms which had gone bankrupt in the past. It took GTI Corporation, and specifically the management strategy formulated and implemented by Jim La Fleur, to turn the model "inside out" and show its ability to help shape business strategy to avert bankruptcy.

WHAT THE Z-SCORE TOLD GTI

When Jim La Fleur took charge of the company, GTI had a $4.4 million net worth and had experienced a $5.6 million decrease in working capital during the previous half year. The company was losing money, overburdened by debt, and nearly devoid of cash.

Noticing an article in *Boardroom Reports* about Professor Altman and the Z-Score, La Fleur saw the potential application of the bankruptcy predictor to the problem at hand.

Plugging in the preliminary numbers for the five ratios, La Fleur put the Altman predictor to work for GTI: The resulting Z-Score was 0.7. At that level, the Altman predictor forecast almost certain bankruptcy. When more accurate numbers were inserted into the Z-Score formula, it fell even lower, to 0.38, about half the earlier calculation. The prediction was grave.

A Tool for Recovery

Despite its portent of doom, the Z-Score was also seen as a management tool for recovery. Clearly, the predictor's five financial ratios, the X ratios, were the key to the Z-Score movement, either up or down. While the previous management had followed an inadvertent strategy, which decreased the ratios and caused the Z-Score to fall, GTI's new management decided to reverse the plunge by deliberate management action to increase the X ratios.

Inherent in the Altman Predictor was the message that underutilized assets could be a major contributor to the deterioration of a company's financial condition. Such deterioration had taken place at GTI over several years. The company's total assets had grown far out of proportion to other financial factors.

By using retrospective analysis, La Fleur concluded that the Z-Score could have predicted GTI's turn toward financial distress. For example, historical data showed that GTI's Z-Score started to dive precipitously two years earlier in 1973 in spite of an increase in earnings per share to $.52 at the end of 1973 from $.09 in 1972. The retrospective Z-Score slide became even steeper in 1974, as GTI dropped at year-end to $.19 in earnings per share. Thus, GTI's Z-Score had been falling for several years, as shown in figure 5.2, even during periods when company's profits were rising. That was further proof of the predictor's validity and suggested its ability to help set strategy to guide the company's recovery.

The Effects of Growth Fever

For more than two years previously, as a member of the board of directors, La Fleur had cautioned against what appeared to be overaggressive policies of debt and expansion by GTI's operating management. The warnings, unfortunately, had little effect.

Along with most of the industry, GTI had succumbed through the 1960s to a highly competitive growth fever. During those years, many managers focused almost entirely on their P&L statements. They were willing to borrow what was necessary to increase sales and profits. With stock values rising, they expected to obtain very favorable equity funding in the future to pay off the accumulated debt. That strategy served well until economic downturns of 1969 and 1972. Then, with profits falling, many companies had trouble servicing the debt that had looked so easy to handle a few years earlier. But GTI, like many others, continued pursuing the same strategy, despite changed economic conditions. That worked for a while.

But early in 1975, GTI started losing money. Before that profit slide could be stopped, GTI's 1975 net loss accumulated to over $2.6 million on sales of $12 million, a painful loss of $1.27 per share.

Taking Quick Action

Then, during the month of May, a member of the audit committee discovered information indicating that the figures for the first quarter of 1975 were reported incorrectly. As the evidence developed during the ensuing audit committee meetings, it was obvious that the company's problems were serious. GTI's auditing firm began a thorough reexamination of the company's first-quarter activities. The auditors quickly confirmed that there was, indeed, a material discrepancy in the figures and set to work revising first-quarter figures.

As chairman of the audit committee, La Fleur contacted the SEC, disclosing the discrepancy and promising to define and correct it. He also asked the American Stock Exchange to halt trading of the company's stock. By finding the reporting errors quickly, GTI had the stock back in trading in less than ten days. No delisting of the stock ever occurred, and the company even received compliments from some observers on its rapid self-policing action.

At that point, GTI's board of directors chose a new executive team, asking La Fleur to become part of management and take over as chairman and chief executive officer. Having observed GTI going into debt to finance its operations over several previous years, even with record sales and profits on paper, La Fleur determined to find the underlying problems. It didn't take long.

Inventory, out of control, revealed itself as a major contributor to the company's ballooning assets. In many instances, returned goods had been set aside and not properly accounted for. Adding to that difficulty, work-in-process was grossly out of proportion to sales.

Genesis of Strategy

From this new evidence of excess assets, a recovery strategy began to emerge. It was to find ways to decrease GTI's total assets without seriously reducing the other factors in the numerators of the Z-Scores X ratios: working capital, retained earnings, earnings before interest and taxes, market value of equity, and sales. GTI started looking for assets that were not being employed effectively – that is, not earning money. When identified, such assets were sold and the proceeds used to reduce the company's debt. The effect was a decrease in the denominators of all five X ratios simultaneously. GTI's Z-Score rose accordingly.

While the Altman Predictor was originally designed for an observer's analysis of a company's condition, GTI used it as an aid to managing company affairs. The Altman Predictor actually became an element of active strategy to avoid GTI's impending bankruptcy.

Having evolved the strategy, La Fleur began to implement the action to eliminate GTI's excess assets. Excess inventory was sold as quickly as possible, even at scrap value in some cases.

Stopping the Cash Bleed

In quick order, GTI's plunge was slowed by stanching its cash bleed. The staffs at two unprofitable West Coast plants were sliced to a skeleton crew within ten days, and the corporate staff at headquarters was pared from thirty-two to six. A year earlier, with company profits at $1.5 million, the corporate staff expense had been over $1 million! All capital programs were frozen. Only the most critical production needs, repair, and maintenance were authorized. GTI asked its creditors for additional short-term credit, then pushed strenuously ahead on its collections. Inventories were placed under strict control. Taking effect, these measures got cash and expenses under control and improved debt service capability.

Reducing costs further took more analysis. A management function/location matrix, a "job-versus-cost" grid, was constructed for each of GTI's plants. The grid showed each executive's job, what work was performed, and how much that job cost the company. When overlaps or duplications were found, jobs were consolidated.

Finding Lost Profits

Employees were also involved in the turnaround. A simple questionnaire was handed out to the 250 employees of GTI's largest plant in Saegertown, Pennsylvania, asking their opinions on why the plant was no longer profitable. The implied question, of course, was about the underutilized assets that had depressed GTI's Z-Score. The employees knew what was wrong. They were specific about how to improve the use of their machines. Many of the suggestions were implemented, and productivity improved.

Several weeks later, similar questions were asked at GTI's plant in Hadley, Pennsylvania. The employee responses resulted in changing the plant's organization from functional to product line, another move that more effectively employed the company's assets. Because they participated in the changes, the plant's employees really worked to make the reorganization succeed. After a few weeks, the plant began to return to profitability.

Those profits were the forerunner of profits that would be produced in other parts of the company as time went on. The Z-Score, while it did not jump as a result of those profits, did begin to react. By mid-1976, after slanting down for three years, the Z-Score bottomed out and started up. GTI began turning the corner.

Selling Off a Product Line

Though cost reduction and increased profits had eased the problems, GTI needed stronger recovery actions. The function/location matrix analysis was extended to include products and was used to rate product profitability throughout the company. Plans were made to eliminate the losers and strengthen the winners. As a result, late in 1976, GTI sold one of its major underutilized assets. GTI's Crystal Base product line had appeared fairly strong, but the product matrix analysis presented a different view. Crystal bases were not complementary to GTI's other products, and though the line was marginally profitable in the past, demand for its products was likely to decrease. The line also apeared to need a great deal of capital to be competitive in the future.

The cash generated by the sale of the Crystal Base product line was used to reduce debt. The consequent simultaneous decrease of both total assets and debt produced a dramatic effect. The Z-Score leaped from under 1.0 to 2.95. In one transaction, GTI zoomed all the way into the Altman Predictor's safe zone.

Although, to outside observers, the company did not appear to turn around for another year and a half, La Fleur felt the firm was on the road to recovery with the sale of the Crystal Base product line. The company had come from almost certain bankruptcy to the stage where it could begin contemplating new products. In less than eighteen months, the Z-Score had climbed from 0.38, in the near-death bankrupt zone, almost all the way to the Z-Score's safe zone.

With heightened confidence in the Altman Predictor, GTI started working to put the Z-Score firmly in the safe zone. Since the company's improving stability and profitability were corroborating the Z-Score approach, GTI's headquarters staff began figuring how a proposed new product or financial transaction would affect the rising Z-Score. Further, GTI extended the product evaluation matrix from simple profit and loss to multiyear projections of return on assets. This involved taking a hard look at projected working capital and capital expenditure requirements product by product. This analysis established what costs would be if the company attempted to expand within its current markets.

Progress in Operations

While doing this planning, GTI continued to make progress on the operations side, finishing 1976 with $0.28 earnings per share and an increasing Z-Score as well. In 1977, earnings sagged to $0.01 per share; but with an improving overall financial condition,

GTI's Z-Score continued gradually to rise. The company even bought out a competitor's glass seal product line with notes simply secured by the acquired assets – with negligible adverse impact on the Z-Score.

Then in 1978, GTI boosted its Z-Score again by shutting down an entire division, which made ceramic capacitors, and selling its assets. That transaction, again based on the strategy of selling underutilized assets to pay off debt, occurred later than it should have. This was a case of emotion interfering with a rational, proven strategy. La Fleur was swayed toward saving this technically interesting product line, though the Z-Score strategy consistently suggested disposal. Though delayed, the difficult disposal decision finally was made.

As a result of the closing of the Capacitor Division and the sale of its assets, GTI's 1978 bottom line sustained a $.29 per share loss, but the Z-Score increased automatically as the company paid off more debt. As anticipated, operating profits continued to gain throughout the year, paving the way for a strong 1979. Once again, the asset-reduction strategy had worked.

Into the Safe Zone

Since then, GTI's Z-Score has continued climbing, rising through the Altman safe zone, as 1979 pretax profits reached $1.9 million and $.70 per share on sales of $21 million. From a balance sheet viewpoint, GTI's strategy, in five years, had decreased the debt to equity ratio from 128 percent to 30 percent, and increased stockholders' equity from $3.5 million to $4.7 million. These and other comparative figures for 1975 and 1979 are shown in table 6.1. Currently, the Z-Score is over 7.0, a level ten times higher than it

Table 6.1 Getting GTI into the safe zone

	1975	1979
Comparative balance sheet ($ in millions)		
Current assets	5.1	5.3
Total assets	9.6	8.3
Current liabilities	3.7	2.5
Total liabilities	6.1	3.6
Equity	3.5	4.7
Total liabilities and equity	9.6	8.3
Comparative income statement ($ in millions)		
Net sales	12	21
Cost of goods sold	11	15
Gross profit	1	6
S G & A	(3.5)	(4.1)
Other expenses	(.5)	0
Profit (loss) before taxes	(3.0)	1.9
Miscellaneous financial factors ($ in millions)		
Working capital	1.4	2.8
Market value of equity	1	15*
Debt/equity	128%	30%
Current ratio	1.38	2.10
Acid ratio	.78	1.29

* *1980 high.*

was at the time of the first use of the Altman Predictor. GTI is today a financially sound company pursuing new avenues to controlled growth. In major part, that success came about from implementing a financial strategy suggested by the Altman Bankruptcy Predictor Model.

CONCLUSION

The authors believe that certain predictive models offer opportunities to be used as management tools. Supporting that view, GTI's employment of the Altman Bankruptcy Predictor has been described as a specific illustration of how an ordinarily passive model can be used actively with substantial success.

With emphasis made on prudent product selection and use, managers are encouraged to search out and review predictive models that relate to their company's activities. Improved business strategies could well result.

APPENDIX: Z-SCORE MODEL DESCRIPTION

$$X_1 = \frac{\text{Working capital}}{\text{Total assets}}$$

Frequently found in studies of corporate problems, this is a measure of the net liquid assets of the firm relative to the total capitalization. Working capital is defined as the difference between current assets and current liabilities. Liquidity and size characteristics are explicitly considered. Ordinarily, a firm experiencing consistent operating losses will have shrinking current assets in relation to total assets.

$$X_2 = \frac{\text{Retained earnings}}{\text{Total assets}}$$

This is a measure of cumulative profitability over time, and the balance sheet figure is used. The age of a firm is implicitly considered in this ratio. For example, a relatively young firm will probably show a low RE/TA ratio because it has not had time to build up its cumulative profits. Therefore, it may be argued that the young firm is somewhat discriminated against in this analysis, and its chance of being classified as bankrupt is relatively higher than another, older firm. But this is precisely the situation in the real world. The incidence of failure is much higher in a firm's earlier years; over 50 percent of firms that fail do so in the first five years of existence. It should be noted that the retained-earnings account is subject to manipulation via corporate quasi reorganizations and stock dividend declarations. It is conceivable that a bias would be created by a substantial reorganization or stock dividend.

$$X_3 = \frac{\text{Earnings before interest and taxes}}{\text{Total assets}}$$

This ratio is calculated by dividing the total assets of a firm into its earnings before interest and tax reductions. In essence, it is a measure of the true productivity of the firm's assets, abstracting from any tax or leverage factors. Since a firm's ultimate existence is based on the earning power of its assets, this ratio appears to be particularly appropriate for studies dealing with corporate failure. Furthermore, insolvency in a bankruptcy sense occurs when the total liabilities exceed a fair valuation of the firm's assets with value determined by the earning power of the assets.

$$X_4 = \frac{\text{Market value of equity}}{\text{Book value of total liabilities}}$$

Equity is measured by the combined market value of all shares of stock, preferred and common, while liabilities include both current and long-term. Book values of preferred and common stockholders' equity may be substituted for market values when the latter is not available. The substitution of book values, especially for the common stock component, should be recognized as a proxy without statistical verification, since the model was built using market values (price × shares outstanding). The measure shows how much the firm's assets can decline in value (measured by market value of equity plus debt) before the liabilities exceed the assets and the firm becomes insolvent. For example, a company with a market value of its equity of $1,000 and debt of $500 could experience a two-thirds drop in asset value before insolvency. However, the same firm with $250 in equity will be insolvent if its drop is only one-third in value.

$$X_5 = \frac{\text{Sales}}{\text{Total assets}}$$

The capital-turnover ratio is a standard financial ratio illustrating the sales-generating ability of the firm's assets. It is one measure of management's capability in dealing with competitive conditions.

It should be noted that variables X_1, X_2, X_3 and X_4 should be inserted into the model as *decimal fractions*; for example, a working capital/total assets of 20 percent should be written as 0.20. The variable X_5, however, is usually a ratio *greater than unity*; for example, where sales are twice as large as assets, the ratio is written as 2.0.

Note also that the weights of each of the five ratios are not identical to those found in the original Altman article[4] since the ratios in the original paper were specified differently. The reader is referred to the original article only for an in-depth description of the model.

---

[4]   Edward I. Altman. "Financial Ratios Discriminant Analysis and the Prediction of Corporate Bankruptcy," *Journal of Finance*, Sept. 1968, pp. 589–609.

7 | Valuation, Loss Reserves, and Pricing of Commercial Loans

The need for banks and other lending institutions to establish a framework to value their loans made to both publicly and privately held firms has never been more important. For one thing, banks are selling loans to other banks with increasing frequency. And distressed bank loan sales are now a common occurrence, as nonbank investors provide an additional demand. Also, domestic and foreign banks are becoming increasingly comfortable with distressed loan transactions.

RECENT DEVELOPMENTS IN LOAN DISCLOSURE

Recent actions by the Financial Accounting Standards Board (FASB) will probably require the revaluation of many financial assets, including commercial and industrial loans when they are impaired. It is the opinion of some observers that most debt and equity securities will be required to be marked-to-market with the resulting gains or losses becoming a separate component of equity.[1]

Loans, on the other hand, will only be affected when the creditworthiness of the borrower deteriorates substantially. The resulting deduction from equity due to the implementation of new reporting rules can, however, be quite substantial. Many practitioners fault the intended changes; the banking industry, in particular, is quite negative, citing the rules' unnecessary, uncertain, subjective, and costly nature.

Impaired and Nonaccruing Loan Valuation

It should be noted that impaired or nonaccruing loan valuation is not conceived by the FASB to be based on a mark-to-market or fair valuation concept. Impaired or non-

---

[1]   Pat McConnell, "Mark-to-Market: The FASB Changes Direction Again," *Accounting Issues*, July 16, 1992.

accruing loan valuation is to be based on a present value of expected recovery when the discount rate is the original effective yield on loans that are restructured or charged off without a formal restructuring. As time passes, the discount rate does not change on either of these types of loans.

With the increasing tendency for banks to actually sell distressed loans, there will be more pressure to mark-to-market such assets. Indeed, my research in 1992 found that the volume of distressed loan sales was probably in the $2–3 billion range in 1991–92, and the outlook was for further increases as banks and investors became more comfortable with the transactions. Also, partial sales of distressed firms' loans automatically provide a market-value estimate for the remaining loan amount.[2]

Since the size of the distressed and defaulted loan market was estimated to be more than $100 billion in 1992, the importance of valuing such loans goes far beyond reporting regulations.

SFAS No. 114: Loan Impairment

SFAS No. 114, "Accounting by Creditors for Impairment of a Loan," specifies how a loss should be calculated and recorded for both problem and restructured loans. It is an attempt to present consistent guidance to lenders, but I feel it simply substitutes a number of new alternatives for old ones. If the present value of the loan's future cash flow, discounted at the original loan's contractual interest rate, is less than the balance, a loss is recorded (bad debt expense and a credit to the allowance). In the event of a subsequent reduction in the present value, due to either the passage of time or a change in cash flow, further changes in bad debt expense and allowance are necessary. If the present value increases, interest income is credited.

The rule also permits the use of a loan's market price or the fair value of collateral in lieu of discounting cash flow. Since these measures reflect interest rate changes and the present value calculation does not, the alternative measures are not truly comparable. The new reporting requirement does not apply to such instruments as consumer installment notes, credit cards, residential mortgages, loans already carried at lower cost or market value on the balance sheet, and debt securities held for sale accounted for at market value under SFAS No. 115.

In the final analysis, while the present value technique is appropriate in many instances, this method will continue to be subjectively and inconsistently applied as long as banks use arbitrary and subjective techniques to estimate risk-adjusted cash flow. This article suggests an approach to the process using current interest rate criteria and rigorous estimates of expected losses.

No doubt, the new requirements will be both annoying and costly for financial institutions. But changes of the types noted above, or ones with modifications, are sure to be eventually installed. This reality can and should provide the motivation for active changes on the part of banking and nonbanking institutions, for example, insurance companies. Indeed, most money center banks have already estimated the impact of fair-value accounting compared to cost in their 1992 annual reports. In an analysis of

---

[2] Edward I. Altman, "The Market for Distressed Securities and Bank Loans," *Foothill Report II* (Los Angeles: The Foothill Corporation, October 1992).

nine large banks, Cutler and Daley found that in every case, the fair-value estimate is slightly greater than the historical cost for the aggregate of loans.[3]

A Suggested Approach for Loan Valuation

For mark-to-market valuations, actual market quotes on the assets are the best evidence of value. However, the process becomes far more difficult for illiquid assets when market quotes are either unavailable or difficult to ascertain. If market quotes are not available, new standards suggest methods to calculate the net present value of estimated future cash flow using a discount rate commensurate with the risks involved. Until just recently, several pieces of the technology puzzle for performing discounted cash flow (DCF) analysis for valuation and pricing of loans did not exist.

By combining unbiased and accurate assessments of the probability, severity, and timing of defaults, the banking analyst and valuation officer now have the complete tool kit for both DCF and loan reserve estimation. In this article, I propose a rigorous, yet practical, method to value loans of all credit qualities and, in so doing, also present an alternative to the new regulations for impaired loans.

This methodology is particularly relevant when market quotes are unavailable. The method of valuation requires a three-step process:

1. Estimation of default rates and losses associated with known credit standards
2. Objective measurement of borrowers' credit quality that is consistent with those credit standards
3. Modeling the expected cash flow from each loan

A number of prior works on distress classification and prediction models now can be combined with related mortality/default studies to provide important guidelines in the commercial lending process.[4] The following discussion will outline a proposal for the steps and linkages that can achieve a logical analytical approach to these important decisions.

Step 1: Estimating Default Rates and Losses

The first critical step in commercial loan valuation is calculating a reliable estimation of default rates associated with known credit standards. Bond ratings are the most visible and respected measure of credit quality. Objective evidence suggests that the standards of credit quality used by the major rating agencies have been relatively consistent over long periods of time. Starting in the mid-1980s, a substantial amount of data have been collected, and analyses of bond defaults and losses have been performed. Several researchers have published reports of default rates associated with bond ratings for

---

[3] C. Cutler and D. Daley, "Statement of Financial Accounting Standards No. 107: Disclosures about Fair Value of Financial Instruments," Working Paper, Bankruptcy and Reorganization Seminar, Stern School of Business, Executive Program, New York University, May 1993.

[4] Edward Altman, Robert Haldeman, and P. Narayanan, "ZETA® Analysis: A New Model to Identify Bankruptcy Risk of Corporations," *Journal of Banking and Finance*, June 1, 1977, pp. 29–54.

publicly traded bonds. Relying on the apparent stability of rating definitions, actuarial techniques have been applied to the bond's actual default experience. First presented in 1988, cumulative mortality rate and loss schedules have now been updated through 1991. These studies concentrated on Standard & Poor's (S&P) and Moody's Investor's Service data. Studies based on S&P data analyzed original issue bond ratings, while analyses of Moody's data looked at mortalities of seasoned bond issuers.

Mortality Rates and Losses for Publicly Traded Bonds

In my article "Measuring Corporate Bond Mortality and Performance," I utilized the notion that default rates for specific one-year periods are measured on the basis of defaults in that interval in relation to some base population at the start of that same period.[5] The calculation, however, becomes more complex when we begin with a specific cohort group, such as a bond-rating category, and track that group's performance for multiple time periods. Because the original population can change over time as a result of a number of different events, we consider mortalities, rather than defaults, in relation to a survival population. The mortality rate is the expected cumulative default rate over time. Similar to the concept of mortality rates used by the insurance industry in establishing life insurance premiums for individuals, mortality rate calculations consider default rates from "birth" to specified periods after issuance. Bonds can exit from the original population by means of at least five different events: defaults, exchanges, calls, sinking funds, and maturities.

The individual mortality rate for each year or *marginal mortality rate* (MMR) is calculated as follows:

$$(MMR)_{(t)} = \frac{\text{value of defaulting debt in year } (t)}{\text{value of the population at the start of the year } (t)}$$

We can measure the *cumulative mortality rate* (CMR) over a specific time period by subtracting the product of the surviving populations of each of the previous years from 1.

$$CMR_{(T)} = 1 - \prod_{t=1}^{T} SR_t$$

where $CMR_{(T)}$ is the cumulative mortality rate, $SR_{(t)}$ is the survival rate in (t); $1 - MMR_{(t)}$

The individual year MMR for each bond rating is based on a compilation of that year's mortality measured from issuance. For example, all of the one-year mortalities are combined for a sample period such as 1970–1991, to arrive at the one-year rate. All of the second-year mortalities are combined to get the two-year rate, and so forth.

The mortality rate is a value-weighted rate for the particular year after issuance, rather than an unweighted average. If we were simply to average each of the year-one

[5] Edward Altman, "Measuring Corporate Bond Mortality and Performance," *Journal of Finance*, September 1989, pp. 909–22; Douglas Lucas and John Lonski, "Corporate Bond Defaults and Default Rates 1970–1990," *Moody's Special Report*, 1991; Jerome Fons, Andrew Kimball, and Dennis Girault, "Corporate Bond Defaults and Default Rates 1970–1991," *Moody's Special Report*, January 1992.

rates or year-two rates, for example, our results would be susceptible to significant specific-year bias. The weighted-average technique correctly biases the results toward the larger-issue years.

After establishing mortality rates stratified by the original bond rating of publicly issued bonds, the measures are adjusted for the actual losses incurred on defaulting and distressed exchange issues. These losses include the difference between the purchase price and the price that the investor could have sold the bond for just after default plus the loss of one coupon payment, which would have been paid if the issue had not defaulted. In essence, mortality losses are calculated by original rating and for specific time periods after issuance.

Tables 7.1 and 7.2 list the marginal and cumulative mortality rates and mortality losses for publicly issued bonds from 1971 through 1991. For example, B-rated bonds experienced a three-year cumulative mortality of 14.90 percent (which computes into an approximate rate of 5 percent per year). The comparable cumulative *loss* rate is 10.81 percent.

In tables 7.1 and 7.2 we can observe that for most bond rating categories, the annual mortality rates and losses increase in the first three years of a bond's life and then tend to level off after the third year for both investment-grade and noninvestment-grade bonds. This implies an aging effect, but only in the first three years or so, for publicly traded debt.[6] For bank loans of relatively short-term maturity, these relationships are very important.

Adjustments for Seniority

The mortality rates and losses indicated in tables 7.1 and 7.2 are for all defaults regardless of the priority of the issue. Therefore, senior secured and unsecured bonds are lumped together with subordinated issues of various types. While it is true that most original issue investment grade bonds are senior in priority and *pari passu* (equal in priority) with senior bank loans (unless stated otherwise) and most noninvestment grade bonds are junior in priority, lumping all bonds together will somewhat distort the relevance of our results for bank loan valuation analysis.

We adjust the mortality loss results in table 7.2 in the following manner. First, we note that the initial recovery rate on defaults (price just after default) can be broken down by seniority and priority.[7] These data for the period 1985–91 are shown in table 7.3. From this table, we can observe that senior secured and senior unsecured recovery rates were 0.605 and 0.523 respectively. The weighted average recovery rate for all 205 senior bond issues was 0.539 compared with 0.392 for all 486 defaulting issues, including junior priority bonds. The ratio of senior bond recovery rates to that of all issues is therefore 1.375 (0.539 divided by 0.392).

I utilize this recovery ratio of senior bonds to all issues in the adjustment of mortality losses. This adjustment process, while not difficult, is complex due to the number of calculations and assumptions.

---

[6] For more information read Edward I. Altman, "Revisiting the High Yield Debt Market," *Financial Management*, Summer 1992.

[7] Edward I. Altman, "Defaults and Returns on High Yield Bonds: Through 1991," *High Yield Securities Research Report* (Merrill Lynch & Co., March 6, 1992).

Table 7.1 Mortality rates by original rating (1971–91 experience)

Rating		Years after issuance									
		1	2	3	4	5	6	7	8	9	10
AAA	Yearly	0.00%	0.00%	0.00%	0.00%	0.00%	0.12%	0.05%	0.00%	0.00%	0.00%
	Cumulative	0.00%	0.00%	0.00%	0.00%	0.00%	0.12%	0.17%	0.17%	0.17%	0.17%
AA	Yearly	0.00%	0.00%	1.09%	0.32%	0.11%	0.00%	0.19%	0.00%	0.08%	0.09%
	Cumulative	0.00%	0.00%	1.09%	1.41%	1.52%	1.52%	1.71%	1.71%	1.79%	1.87%
A	Yearly	0.00%	0.19%	0.26%	0.31%	0.17%	0.04%	0.42%	0.24%	0.17%	0.00%
	Cumulative	0.00%	0.19%	0.45%	0.76%	0.93%	0.97%	1.08%	1.32%	1.49%	1.49%
BBB	Yearly	0.10%	1.00%	0.42%	0.52%	0.70%	0.19%	1.09%	0.00%	0.13%	0.75%
	Cumulative	0.10%	1.10%	1.51%	2.03%	2.72%	2.90%	3.96%	3.96%	4.09%	4.81%
BB	Yearly	0.00%	0.91%	3.66%	1.93%	2.78%	1.27%	4.33%	3.96%	0.00%	2.66%
	Cumulative	0.00%	0.91%	4.53%	6.37%	8.97%	10.13%	14.02%	14.02%	14.02%	16.31%
B	Yearly	1.72%	4.67%	9.16%	5.61%	6.64%	2.65%	4.24%	2.88%	5.07%	3.58%
	Cumulative	1.72%	6.31%	14.90%	19.67%	25.00%	26.99%	30.09%	32.10%	35.54%	37.85%
CCC	Yearly	1.55%	14.84%	11.74%	9.23%	3.82%	3.86%	1.54%	N/A	N/A	N/A
	Cumulative	1.55%	16.16%	26.01%	32.84%	35.40%	37.90%	38.85%	N/A	N/A	N/A

Source: Edward I. Altman, "Revisiting the High Yield Debt Market," Financial Management, Summer 1992.

Table 7.2 Mortality losses by original rating (1971–91 experience)

Rating		1	2	3	4	5	6	7	8	9	10
						Years after issuance					
AAA	Yearly	0.00%	0.00%	0.00%	0.00%	0.00%	0.01%	0.03%	0.00%	0.00%	0.00%
	Cumulative	0.00%	0.00%	0.00%	0.00%	0.00%	0.01%	0.05%	0.05%	0.05%	0.05%
AA	Yearly	0.00%	0.00%	0.20%	0.12%	0.02%	0.00%	0.10%	0.00%	0.05%	0.05%
	Cumulative	0.00%	0.00%	0.20%	0.32%	0.34%	0.34%	0.43%	0.43%	0.48%	0.53%
A	Yearly	0.00%	0.03%	0.05%	0.19%	0.13%	0.02%	0.05%	0.15%	0.12%	0.00%
	Cumulative	0.00%	0.03%	0.08%	0.27%	0.40%	0.42%	0.47%	0.62%	0.74%	0.74%
BBB	Yearly	0.07%	0.61%	0.24%	0.36%	0.21%	0.11%	0.84%	0.00%	0.07%	0.50%
	Cumulative	0.07%	0.68%	0.92%	1.27%	1.48%	1.59%	2.41%	2.41%	2.48%	2.98%
BB	Yearly	0.00%	0.61%	2.95%	1.48%	1.85%	0.84%	4.08%	0.00%	0.00%	2.10%
	Cumulative	0.00%	0.61%	3.54%	4.97%	6.73%	7.51%	11.29%	11.29%	11.29%	13.15%
B	Yearly	0.79%	2.81%	7.50%	4.12%	5.59%	2.06%	3.21%	2.20%	3.01%	2.55%
	Cumulative	0.79%	3.58%	10.81%	14.48%	19.26%	20.92%	23.46%	25.15%	27.40%	29.25%
CCC	Yearly	1.24%	13.67%	9.60%	7.57%	3.01%	2.88%	1.38%	N/A	N/A	N/A
	Cumulative	1.24%	14.74%	22.92%	28.76%	30.90%	32.89%	33.82%	N/A	N/A	N/A

Source: Edward I. Altman, "Revisiting the High Yield Debt Market," Financial Management, Summer 1992.

Table 7.3 Average recovery prices on defaulted debt by seniority (per $100 face amount)

Year	Senior Secured		Senior Unsecured		Senior Subordinated		Subordinated Cash pay		Subordinated Noncash pay
1991	54.50	(02)	58.15	(62)	34.62	(21)	20.28	(35)	21.06 (04)
1990	35.04	(07)	32.02	(27)	24.04	(28)	17.93	(17)	18.99 (12)
1989	82.69	(09)	53.70	(16)	19.60	(21)	23.95	(30)	None
1988	67.96	(13)	41.99	(19)	30.70	(10)	35.27	(20)	None
1987	12.00	(01)	70.52	(29)	53.50	(10)	40.54	(07)	None
1986	48.32	(07)	37.09	(08)	37.74	(10)	31.58	(34)	None
1985	74.25	(02)	34.81	(03)	36.18	(07)	41.45	(15)	None
Average 1985–1991	$60.50	(41)	$52.32	(164)	$32.72	(107)	$29.37	(158)	$19.01 (16)
Average of all issues	$39.24	(486)							

Source: Edward I. Altman, "Defaults and Returns on High Yield Bonds: Through 1991,"
High Yield Securities Research Report, *Merril Lynch & Co., March 6, 1992.*

Adjustment Using Recovery Ratio

First, we observe the weighted average recovery price of defaulted issues over the past two decades stratified by their original bond rating. Note the number of observations is shown in column 1 and the average recovery results in column 2 of table 7.4. Since we can assume that most original issue bonds that receive an investment-grade rating from S&P are senior in priority, we do not need to utilize the senior-to-all-issue ratio of 1.376 for the top four ratings. For non-investment grade issues, however, we adjust the recovery rates upward for their implied senior debt equivalent recoveries (column 4). We then calculate, in column 5, the implied senior debt loss rate by subtracting the recovery rate from one and adding the lost semiannual coupon, which would have been received if the bond had not defaulted. The lost coupon is assumed to increase as the original rating deteriorates, as indicated in the notes to table 7.4.

The final mortality loss adjustment step uses, as an example, the third-year mortality rate in column 6 multiplied by the implied senior bond loss rate in column 5 to arrive at the senior bond mortality loss rate shown in column 7. Hence, the senior bond expected cumulative mortality loss rate for B-rated bonds after three years is 8.97 percent versus the 10.81 percent rate for all bonds listed earlier in table 7.2. We will utilize this result in a valuation analysis example that follows. The same adjustment procedure can be used for any original bond rating and for any maturity.

Expected Mortalities for Seasoned Loans

The mortality rate and loss statistics essentially trace new issues and provide cumulative expected losses for various holding periods after issuance. As such, a seasoned loan's expected losses cannot directly be estimated. Therefore, we utilize the Moody's default studies, noted earlier, for seasoned bonds. Moody's results differ from the above in two ways:

Table 7.4 Adjusting mortality loss rates for senior debt equivalent

Original rating	(1) N	(2) Average price after default	(3) Ratio of senior issue recovery rates to all issues	(4) Implied senior bond recovery rate	(5) Implied senior bond loss rate[1]	(6) Third year mortality rate[2]	(7) Adjusted senior bond mortality loss rate[3]
AAA	5	.794	–	.794	.246	0.00%	0.00%
AA	20	.821	–	.821	.222	1.09%	0.24%
A	49	.606	–	.606	.439	0.45%	0.20%
BBB	51	.455	–	.455	.593	1.51%	0.89%
BB	38	.297	1.376	.409	.644	4.33%	2.92%
B	233	.332	1.376	.456	.602	14.90%	8.97%
CC	64	.228	1.376	.314	.749	26.01%	19.48%

[1] Recovery plus loss of semiannual coupon payment; assumes 0.25% semiannual coupon increment for investment grade bonds and 0.50% for noninvestment grades for each lower bond rating starting from AAA = .04; for example, AAA = 1 − .794 + .04 = .246.
[2] From Figure 1; includes bonds of varying seniority.
[3] Column 5 × column 6.

1   They measure defaulting issuers and not the dollar amount of issues, that is, the number of defaults is compared with the number of issuers rated in a certain category for a given period of time.

2   Moody's combines issuers whose bonds are of different ages into a single measure. For example, when the average cumulative default rate for three years is calculated, the rating three years prior to default is observed, regardless of the age of the bond at that three-year prior point. As such, seasoned bonds of various ages are combined.

Table 7.5 compares Moody's average cumulative default rates with my cumulative mortality rates for 1, 3, 5, and 10 years. Note that the results are quite different for one-year rates but converge as the holding period increases. This convergence is expected since very young bonds have little or no defaults in the first year, while one-year default rates of seasoned, older bonds are more likely. For longer periods (three or more years), the distinction between new and seasoned bonds would appear to be small. Indeed, the 5- and 10-year comparisons are very close.[8]

Finally, Moody's does not calculate default losses, although they do list the average recovery price just after default by seniority over the period 1974–91, which is similar to data in table 7.3.

Interestingly, the overall average for Moody's entire sample of 605 bonds was $39.22, almost identical to the data in table 7.3 of $39.24 for the shorter 1985–91 period. We could attempt to interpret the various Moody's tables to infer a default loss for specific seasoned bonds, although the result would not be precise since coupon rates are not included and Moody's procedure combines bonds of all ages.

Table 7.5 Comparing average cumulative default/mortality rates for various horizon holding periods

	1-year		3-years		5-years		10-years	
	Altman (%)	Moody's (%)	Altman (%)	Moody's (%)	Altman (%)	Moody's (%)	Altman (%)	Moody's (%)
Aaa	0.0	0.0	0.0	0.0	0.0	0.2	0.2	0.9
Aa	0.0	0.0	1.1	0.1	1.5	0.4	1.9	1.1
A	0.0	0.0	0.5	0.3	0.9	0.7	1.5	2.2
Baa	0.1	0.2	1.5	1.0	2.7	2.1	4.8	5.1
Ba	0.0	2.0	4.5	7.3	9.0	11.9	16.3	18.7
B	1.7	8.8	14.9	19.9	25.0	26.9	37.9	35.8

Altman data based on market values of new issues only (1971–97).
Moody's data based on number of issuers including issuers whose bonds are of various ages (1970–97).

[8]   Note that Moody's does not report results for the Caa category, while my study does indicate S&P CCC results. While all rating categories above Caa/CCC are roughly comparable between Moody's and S&P, there is a distinct difference for the Cs. A Caa for Moody's is virtually, or sometimes actually, in default, while a CCC for S&P is very weak but not nearly as hopeless as the Moody's designation. Hence, we will only compare the B and above categories.

STEP 2: THE CREDIT-RATING LINK

The second critical step in valuation and pricing of loans is to objectively estimate the appropriate credit rating. Subjective or gut level credit ratings are fraught with problems. First, bankers have a number of biases and may tend to overrate their borrowers' credit quality. For seasoned loans, the fact that they "liked" the companies enough to lend to them is a potential biasing factor. Second, while most banks have their own internal rating systems, they are rarely linked specifically to public bond ratings and are often inconsistently applied across geographical areas and economic sectors.

The unbiased link between company-specific risk factors and bond ratings can be provided by a credit-rating process such as the ZETA® Risk Control System.[9] This technique combines company financial data into a unique index value that corresponds to an equivalent bond rating, as shown in table 7.6. Note that the average ZETA® scores for bonds of different ratings are given for the period 1983–92. For example, the average S&P A-rated bond for the 10-year period ending in 1992 had an average ZETA score of 5.4 and the average B-rated bond's equivalent score was –1.8.

An objectively determined credit rating provides the link between default/mortality loss estimates and "fair" valuation. Financial statement data are the basis for the ZETA® equivalent bond ratings, and the ratings are, in turn, the basis for selecting the appropriate default loss estimates. These expected default loss rates are then used to establish adequate loss reserves on commercial loans as well as for modifying each individual loan's expected cash flow.

Table 7.6 Average ZETA scores by rating and rating category

	Average (1983–92)	1992*	1991	1990	1989	1988	1987	1986	1985	1984	1983
AAA	9.00	7.80	8.18	7.94	7.81	8.76	8.95	8.78	9.95	11.01	10.80
AA	7.25	7.29	7.35	7.12	7.08	7.25	7.02	6.82	7.55	7.48	7.58
A	5.40	5.47	5.28	5.36	5.48	5.87	5.29	5.19	5.34	5.47	5.20
BBB	2.83	2.16	2.09	2.56	2.80	3.25	2.94	2.87	3.26	3.51	2.83
BB	0.35	(0.61)	(0.86)	(0.71)	0.03	0.85	0.59	1.47	1.08	0.86	0.78
B	(1.80)	(2.47)	(1.97)	(2.19)	(2.02)	(1.53)	(1.70)	(0.59)	(1.88)	(2.08)	(1.56)
CCC	(5.95)	(4.72)	(6.27)	(6.16)	(5.74)	(8.19)	(6.27)	(8.36)	(5.24)	(4.35)	(4.23)
NR	2.47	1.37	1.62	1.52	2.15	3.30	2.40	2.83	4.20	4.52	0.82

* AAA Industrial Average = 10.82 (Not including AAA public utilities).
Source: Zeta Services Inc., Bond Rating Analysis Book.

STEP 3: LOAN CASH FLOW ESTIMATES

When making the final decision as to a loan's valuation, or indeed whether or not to lend to applicants, the analysis must integrate the promised cash flow, adjusted for expected losses, with the terms and conditions of the loan. Such items as maturities,

---

[9] Edward I. Altman, Robert Haldeman and P. Narayanan, "ZETA® Analysis: A New Model to Identify Bankruptcy Risk of Corporations", *Journal of Banking and Finance*, June 1, 1977, pp. 29–54.

nominal or variable interest rates, cost of funds for the bank, up-front fees, prepayment penalties, and collateral must all be considered. The resulting cash flow should be discounted by the appropriate interest rate to arrive at a present or "fair" value that is consistent with existing market conditions. A likely candidate for the discount rate is the bank's overall cost of funds or its cost of capital.[10] If the loan's present value minus the amount of funds to be loaned to the applicant is positive, then the loan would appear to be acceptable. This assumes that the loan is considered in isolation of the existing portfolio of loans or any related bank policy on diversification.[11] See table 7.7 for an example showing this series of steps to assist in the valuation, loss reserves, and pricing decisions.

Table 7.7 Example of valuation, loss reserves, and pricing*

Period	Promised cash flow	Expected loss rate	Expected cash flow	Discount factor	Present value expected cash flow
0	($1,000,000)	0.00%	($1,000,000)	0.0000	($1,000,000)
1	110,000	1.04%	108,856	0.9259	100,790
2	110,000	3.80%	105,820	0.8573	90,719
3	1,110,000	8.97%	1,010,433	0.7938	802,081
					($ 6,410)

* Given: Loan Amount = $1 million.
          Loan Type = Unsecured, interest only until maturity.
          Maturity = 3 years.
          Interest Rate = Simple 11%, payable annually at end of year.
          Zeta Score = –1.8 (S&P B-rating equivalent).
          Cost of Funds = 8% (Discount Rate).

The fair net present value of the loan in the example shown in table 7.7 is –$6,410. The expected cash flow is determined by reducing the promised annual interest payments ($110,000) and principal repayment ($1 million) by the adjusted cumulative loss rates shown in table 7.4. The negative net present value indicates that this loan is slightly unacceptable at the time of the initial analysis. Either charging a 1 percent fee up front or increasing the interest rate by 1 percent per year would result in a positive net present value and an acceptable loan. It is interesting to consider that if the loan's credit quality were equivalent to a CCC-rated bond, then the fair net present value would be about –$107,000 and the loan would probably be rejected. Of course, banks sometimes accept loans despite the fact that if the loans were analyzed in isolation of other factors, the credits would not appear to be profitable. Other factors mitigating the rejection decision might include ancillary fees, preserving relationships with clients, and market penetration and diversification objectives.

[10] The FASB does use the current cost of funds for restructured loan valuation but retains the original effective rate. It is unclear why the current rate is not the relevant one regardless of the status of the loan.
[11] See Paul Bennett, "Applying Portfolio Theory to Global Bank Lending," *Journal of Banking and Finance* 8 (1984), pp. 153–69 for a discussion of a bank's lending portfolio policy from a diversification and covariance viewpoint and R. S. Chirinko and G. D. Guill, "A Framework for Assessing Credit Risk in Depository Institutions: Toward Regulatory Reform," *Journal of Banking and Finance* 15, (1991), pp. 785–804, for an analysis of the importance of covariation between loans in the portfolio. The latter's emphasis is on the relevance of diversification for the bank regulator, while the former is related primarily to the bank's decisions.

Still, a precise and accurate profitability analysis is critical when deciding if other factors could outweigh the numerically determined initial decision.

LOSS RESERVES

Loss reserves would equal the sum of the present values of the annual loss rates multiplied by the promised cash flow. These reserves would be reduced if the loan performs as promised over time. In the example, the initial loss reserve would equal $83,679. (This is calculated as the sum of the three years' present values of expected losses: $1,059, $3,584, and $79,036.)

If, after one year, the borrower's credit quality changes, for example, to a BB-rated bond rating equivalent, then the analysis would change to a seasoned loan with two years of maturity remaining (data permitting). Of course, the present value influence changes as the loan approaches maturity, regardless of the credit quality.

Finally, if the loan becomes nonperforming, that is, the equivalent of a defaulted loan, then the expected recovery amount should be determined by the specific attributes of the loan, such as its security, if any, seniority, and so forth. An unsecured senior loan of uncertain recovery would be assigned the average recovery of senior bonds, as indicated in tables 7.3 and 7.4.

Discount Rate

The question of the appropriate discount rate to use in the present value procedure is conceptually interesting and complex. Although slight variations in the rate chosen will have little effect on the valuation of a short-term loan, if the initial effective rate is several percentage points different from the current rate, the resulting present value can be substantially affected. I have chosen the bank's cost of capital as the discount rate, rather than the original rate, or a risk-free rate, or a rate that further adjusts for the individual attributes of each loan. While the procedures outlined earlier adjust the promised cash flow for expected losses, there still remains the risk of a distribution of possible outcomes around expected values.

CONCLUSION

The procedure described in this article provides a rigorous approach for the valuation of nonpublicly traded assets. I have concentrated on bank loans, but the procedure is equally valid for other private placements and can be used by nonbank financial institutions as well. The approach is potentially useful for assets in liquid and illiquid markets, but the payoff would seem to be especially great in the latter.[12]

With respect to the FASB's fair-value reporting requirement, banks now have a basis for making sophisticated estimates for impaired loans made to privately held firms as well as publicly held ones. I advocate its use for all loans, however, not just impaired or

---

[12] See D. L. Kao, 1993, "Illiquid Securities: Issues of Pricing and Performance Measurement," *Financial Analysts Journal*, March/April, 28–35.

nonaccruing. In addition, pricing decisions are also inherent in the methodology. For example, we could solve for the nominal interest rate that would result in a net present value of zero on the loan – a type of break-even analysis.

Expected loss rates are implicit in the valuation analysis. As such, the procedure is a valid tool for setting aside capital reserves for expected losses.

Mortality loss estimates, based on loss experience in the public bond market, are already being used by high-yield, fixed-income investors, particularly insurance companies that are comfortable with such a methodology. It would seem that private placement valuation of insurance companies and other institutions is a natural extension of the bank loan application.

Indeed, a new study by the Society of Actuaries focuses on the credit risk exposure of insurance company private placements, and the results will no doubt shed some light on default rates in this nonliquid market.[13]

---

[13] *Credit Risk Event Loss Experience: Private Placement Bonds* (Chicago: Society of Actuaries, 1993).

8 | An Economic and Statistical Analysis of The Failing Company Doctrine

with Laurie S. Goodman

I INTRODUCTION

At a time when growing anti-merger pressures exist in Congress and in the nation's regulatory agencies, we find it important to investigate means in which preferential treatment can be legally administered to foster a merger. One of these preferences, known as the Failing Company Doctrine (FCD), is an antitrust defense which is utilized to justify an otherwise illegal merger due to the failing nature of one of the parties. One of the conditions of the doctrine is the lack of any other good faith purchaser. There are two factors in the FCD defense which must be considered. The first is that an anticompetitive merger will generate social costs to society. These must be contrasted with the social costs of bankruptcy, both direct and indirect, avoided by permitting the merger.

In traditional applications of the FCD, beginning with precedent setting *International Shoe vs. FTC*[1] (1930), the cases have involved a qualitative analysis of the merger's impact, on a type of hierarchal level. First, anticompetitive effects are assessed and if these appear not to be significant, then the benefits inherent in saving the failing firm are seriously considered. We believe that the merits of the FCD defense should be evaluated on a simultaneous basis with the costs. Optimally, the potential merger should be allowed only if the social costs of the anticompetitive behavior are less than the social costs of business failure.

In this paper, we present a methodology for assessing these relative costs and also statistical documentation of a number of FCD cases. In section II, the background of the FCD is presented, allowing us to better understand its potential future role. In the following two sections, we discuss the social costs of failure and the social costs of anticompetitive behavior presenting our analysis in a form so as to suggest a methodology

---

[1] *International Shoe vs. F.T.C.*, 280 US 291 (1930).

for assessing the tradeoff in these two costs. Section V explores the question of what is a failing firm in terms of the way the courts have appraised the situation. We will suggest an objective test, which is prominent in the finance literature, for estimating failure probabilities and compare the court's decisions with this test. The final section presents our conclusions.

II Background of the Failing Company Doctrine

We have noted in our introductory comments that a failing company defense is a doctrine. The term "doctrine" is, in our opinion, an elaboration of an evolutionary process which to this day is poorly understood and inconsistently interpreted by almost everyone involved. The landmark[2] Supreme Court case, *International Shoe v. FTC* (1930) ruled in favor of that proposed merger when the Court concluded that there was only very limited competition between the two firms and that the other firm, McElwain, was in very serious financial trouble without any hope of reversing the trend. The FTC did offer two alternatives – additional borrowings or reorganization under the Bankruptcy Act, but since the Court felt that no substantial lessening of competition would result, the merger was allowed.[3] Indeed, procompetitive benefits were attributed and it is still not clear just how much of an impact the failing company argument had on the decision.

The interpretations of the International Shoe case are many, ranging from the FCD as an absolute defense in merger litigation to the more likely interpretation that an acquisition of a failing company may violate the Clayton Act but still be allowed in order to avoid injurious consequences. This is known as the "rule of reason" concept which enables the Court to utilize a degree of subjective sensitivity to the facts of each case. Our reading of the subsequent failing company case histories leads us to conclude that the degree of anticompetitive consequences is usually the overriding concern with token acknowledgment and little analysis of the social costs of bankruptcy.

There are two major requirements for the invocation of the FCD; namely that the company be failing and that there be no other good faith purchaser. Both of these requirements have been characterized by ambiguity. In the case of the lack of any other

---

[2] There were two cases prior to the International Shoe Case which invoked the failing company argument. In *American Press vs. US* (1916) and in *US Steel vs. US* (1923), the failing company argument was successful in sanctioning the merger but no significant anticompetitive issues were presented.

[3] The relevant passage from 280 US 291 (1930) is:

> In light of the case thus disclosed of a corporation with resources so depleted and the prospect of rehabilitation so remote that it faced the grave probability of a business failure with resulting loss to its stockholders and injury to the communities where its plants were operated, we hold that the purchase of its capital stock by a competitor (there being no other prospective purchaser), not with a purpose to lessen competition, but to facilitate the accumulated business of the purchaser and with the effect of mitigating seriously injurious consequences otherwise probable, is not in contemplation of law prejudicial to the public and does not substantially lessen competition or restrain commerce within the intent of the Clayton Act.

good faith purchaser, the courts have never analyzed how much the failing company must forego in terms of opportunity cost to preserve competition. In section III, we will see that the failing company will be worth more to a rival than to a noncompeting firm. The issue is, then, at what point does the non-competing offerer become a "good faith purchaser." Should an offer of half as much with no anticompetitive impact be considered a bona-fide offer? The court has recently ruled that "A company invoking the defense has the burden of showing that . . . it tried and failed to merge with a company other than the acquiring one".[4] This allows for the possibility that talks could have broken down because of the failure to agree on the terms of the offer. The same line of reasoning would be applicable where another potential purchaser is also a competitor but it possesses a smaller share of the market than does the petitioning competitor, hence lower social costs would result from the merger. Our analysis will assume that there are no other good faith purchasers. Clearly, however, the issue of what constitutes a bona-fide offer must be addressed in every court decision.

The issue concerning "what is a failing firm" has received more attention. Bauman (1965) notes that the court has held "that a company does not have to be actually in a state of bankruptcy to be exempt from section 7 provisions;" and that "it is sufficient to be heading in that direction with the probability that bankruptcy will ensue." Blum (1974b) notes that the courts have not been consistent in their definition of what is a failing firm. We will pursue this issue further in section V.

While the FCD has been utilized in numerous circumstances, it is impossible to locate a case where a merger decision rested solely on the fact that the company was failing. In fact, Bock (1969) found that the conditions under which a company can acquire a failing company without risking challenge had been steadily narrowed by the courts in the late 1960s and speculated that the merger alternative for companies that cannot survive will be problematic especially for strong acquiring companies and for acquired companies accounting for substantial shares of concentrated markets.

There are infrequent examples of demonstrated concern for bankruptcy costs although even in cases where it did manifest, it was not clear whether the decision was economically motivated. Perhaps the prime example is a situation which did not reach the courts for analysis and interpretation. In 1978, Attorney General Griffin Bell sanctioned the merger of Ling Temco Vought and Lykes Corp. Both firms have major steel manufacturing subsidiaries (the seventh and eighth largest producers) with the Youngstown Steet & Tube's subsidiary of Lykes apparently on the road to failure. Overruling disagreement from the Justice Department, Bell decided that, despite the potential for serious anticompetitive consequences in the steel industry, the merger would not be contested. "In justifying his action, he invoked the so-called 'failing company' defense under the antimerger law . . ." (Adams, 1978).

The results of FCD defense are not usually so positive for the acquiring company especially when the court decides the issue. Table 8.1 lists 17 such cases and in only four (24 percent) did the court allow the merger to proceed – one being the landmark case discussed earlier. In most of these cases, anticompetitive consequences ruled the decision and rarely, if ever, do we observe a rigorous articulation of the tradeoff

---

[4] 94 S. Ct. 1186 (1974) as cited by Rothberg (1979).

Table 8.1 Sample of companies that have used the failing company defense (exclusive of financial institutions)

Name	Failing Company	Allowed	Type of company	Year
Arden Publishing	Citizen Publishing	No	Private	1940
Blatz Brewery Co.	Pabst Brewery Inc.	No	Public	1958
Brown Shoe Co.	Kinney Shoe Co.	No	Public	1962
Continental Oil Co.	Malco Refineries Inc.	No	Subsidiary	1959
Crown Zellerbach	St. Helens	No	Public	1961
Dean Foods	Bowman Dairy Corp.	No	Private	1966
Diebold	Herring–Hall–Marvin	No	Private	1958
El Paso Natural Gas	Pacific NW Pipeline	Yes	Public	1964
Erie Sand and Gravel	Sandisky Corp.	No	Subsidiary	1961
Farm Journal Inc.	Country Gentlemen	No	Private	1956
International Shoe	McElwain Shoe	Yes	Public	1923
Md. and Va. Milk Prod.	Richmond Dairy	Yes	Private	1957
Pabst Brewing Co.	Carling National Breweries	No	Public	
Pillsbury Mills	Ballard & Ballard	No	Public	1960
United Airlines	Capital Airlines	Yes	Public	1962
US Steel	Certified Industries	No	Public	1964
Von's Grocery Inc.	Shopping Bag Food Store	No	Public	1966
Recent related cases				
Lancaster Colony	Federal Glass Division[1] (Federal Paper Board)	No	Public	1978
Jones & Laughlin (Ling-Temco Vought)	Youngstown Sheet & Tube (Lykes Corp.)	Yes	Public	1978
Schmidt's Beer	Schaefer Beer[2]	No	Public	1978
White Consolidated[2,3]	White Motor Co.	Yes	Public	1976

[1] Was not litigated.
[2] The two firms involved were the contestants – no federal agencies involved.
[3] White Consolidated dropped the case but the Justice Dept. would not have contested.

in costs. Table 8.1 also lists four recent instances where the FCD was invoked in a non-traditional setting.[5] The sample listed in table 8.1 is not meant to be comprehensive but it does represent our best effort to find relevant cases.

It might be of interest to track the existence of these firms, especially to see what happened to those "failing" firms where the merger was disallowed or dissolved. While our search of corporate records did not always reveal definitive results, it appears that of the ten publicly held failing firms which were divested or not allowed to merge, the following occurred: three firms or divisions were later dissolved or were liquidated (Ballard & Ballard, Certified Industries, and the Federal Glass Division of Federal

---

[5] For example, *Schaefer Beer vs. Schmidt's Beer* (1978) involved an unsuccessful attempt by the defendant to purchase controlling interest securities in the plaintiff. The foundations of Schmidt's case were that Schaefer was a failing company and that the merger would also not result in meaningful anticompetitive behavior. The court ruled, however, that while it was "indisputable that Schaefer is experiencing difficulties" the firm was not failing since it could still be rehabilitated and that its principal creditor had not categorized the outstanding debt as being in default and considered the firm "viable" (*NY Times*, 1978). Very little, if any, discussion in the case addressed the bankruptcy cost question although it was clear that the probability of failure was quite high.

Paper Board); five are still in existence in some form; in two cases we simply could not find any company records. We cannot draw any definitive conclusions from these results but, in a few cases, the court's or regulatory agency's decision helped to determine the fate of the failing firm.

We conclude that, in most cases involving the FCD defense, the court and the prosecuting agencies have not been persuaded by the numerical evaluation, cost-tradeoff framework but have relied principally on a qualitative assessment of the anticompetitive ramifications of the merger. This was perhaps most clearly articulated by Chairman Dixon of the FTC in his statement about the proposed acquisition by the United State's Steel's Atlas Cement division of Certified Industries, Inc. (1968).[6] As the dissenting opinion illustrates, however, the issues are not clear and bankruptcy costs are at least given some mention as a potentially important factor.

III   SOCIAL COSTS OF FAILURE

The social costs of business failure consist of two types: direct and indirect costs. The direct costs include the so-called bankruptcy costs to the firm, e.g., internal incremental administrative costs, legal and accountant's fees, and expert appraisal of assets. The indirect costs, i.e., costs borne by society due to the firm's bankrupt condition, include the lost profit opportunities of the firm; the unemployment benefits; government insurance payments, if any, on unfunded pension liabilities owed to laid-off employees; the cost to suppliers; and other multiplier effects caused by these disruptions.[7] One should also include the lost consumer surplus from the goods that are no longer produced by the bankrupt firm's plant. The direct and indirect costs can be quite large. For instance, in the current Chrysler Corporation crisis, Treasury estimates that "bankruptcy could cost taxpayers $2.75 billion and result in 75,000 to 100,000 lost jobs in the next two years" (*NY Times*, November 9, 1979). No breakdown as to those costs was given.

The losses incurred by the firm's bondholders and stockholders are already included in the indirect bankruptcy costs, i.e., the costs involved with lost opportunities of the firm due to the bankruptcy *condition*. These costs – namely lost revenues, profits, and investment opportunities – could be significant and should be reflected in the market value of securities after the bankruptcy announcement. One estimate (Altman, 1971) is that the negative announcement effect on equity prices could be as much as 25 percent of the price one month prior to bankruptcy.

The direct and indirect costs are difficult to measure with various opinions in the literature as to their size and importance. Warner (1977) finds that for 11 railroad

---

[6]   Despite his acknowledgement that Certified was failing, he held that "neither International Shoe nor the legislative history of Clayton 7, as amended, forced the Commission to exempt the acquisition of a 'failing' company from the requirements of the law." Commissioner Elman took exception to this ruling, however, and felt that it could be argued that a failing company exemption is justifiable on strict antitrust grounds as a means for facilitating withdrawal from the market of seriously inefficient firms. In addition, he said that public policy is not necessarily served by requiring businesses to sell their assets in a forced sale at distressed prices. See Bock (1969) for a more in-depth discussion of this case.

[7]   Warner (1977) notes that another indirect cost might be the higher compensation necessary for managers of highly levered firms due to the greater probability of failure and subsequent unemployment. His railroad industry's results did not support this hypothesis, however.

bankruptcies, direct costs are 1 percent of the firm's market value 84 months before the bankruptcy petition date and 5.3 percent of the market value at the time of the bankruptcy. These totals include only the monies paid to lawyers, accountants, professional consultants, expert witnesses and the bankruptcy trustee. They do not explicitly include the cost of foregone economic opportunities or the value of managerial time spent administering the bankruptcy. To some extent, however, the drop in market value as bankruptcy is announced partially incorporates these costs. Warner's tentative conclusions are that bankruptcy costs are relatively small but he does caution that his study is based on a very limited sample in a regulated industry. In addition, potentially important indirect costs are not considered.

Baxter (1967) finds that, for personal bankruptcies, costs average 20 percent of assets. Stanley and Girth (1971) report a figure similar to Baxter. Van Horne (1976) estimates that bankruptcy costs are quite high for relatively small corporations. Haugen and Senbet (1978) argue that bankruptcy costs are fairly insignificant although liquidation costs may well be high because all costs associated with liquidation are unrelated to the state of the firm (bankrupt or non-bankrupt). A bankrupt firm need not be liquidated; it may be reorganized and continue. It must be noted that if bankrupt firms opt for reorganization rather than liquidation, it has been estimated that the chances are three out of four that the firm will ultimately be liquidated and incur the costs of liquidation.[8] Furthermore, the foregone opportunities in reorganization may be significant; a Chapter XI proceeding took an average of two years and a Chapter X reorganization an average of five years.[9] Even though the magnitude of the direct bankruptcy costs are in dispute, it appears that these costs are substantially greater in a failure situation than if the firm were merged into a healthier entity.

With respect to indirect bankruptcy costs, the supplier to a failed company must find alternative outlets for its product. The product might not be worth as much in the alternative outlet as in its original use. There may be situations in which the failed company is the major outlet of a particular supplier and the value of the product in alternative uses is so low that it does not pay to produce it. Hence, the supplier may also be forced to liquidate and the direct and indirect costs of this liquidation must be included.

The cost of unemployment benefits and the regional multiplier effects can be enormous. For example, International Shoe wanted to merge with the McElwain Company in 1921. Liquidation for McElwain would have caused extensive employee layoffs in an already depressed New England. McElwain was the largest employer in two cities and the second largest in three others, accounting for 20 percent of the inhabitants in these five cities. The further unemployment caused by these layoffs would have been significant.

Pension liabilities, now payable, which include unfunded prior service costs to employees plus unfunded vested benefits, are potentially significant indirect costs should a firm have to close its doors and where eventual payment from government insurance is

---

[8] Anne Calamosca (1978). Our own assessment is that the 75 percent figure is on the high side and we feel that while a majority of cases will end up in liquidation, many will be successfully reorganized, especially the larger firms, e.g. United Merchants and Mfg. (1977–78).
[9] Calamosca (1978). Also see Altman (1971, ch. 6). The new Bankruptcy Code (1979) seeks to reduce the time in reorganization under the new Chapter 11.

required. Since the enactment of ERISA (1974), firms have become painfully aware of their obligations. For example, unfunded vested benefits alone amounted to more than 100 percent of net worth of Lockheed and LTV Corporation in 1978 and over 50 percent of the net worth of Bethlehem Steel, TWA, and Chrysler Corporation.

Finally, there is lost consumer surplus from not being able to purchase goods from the shut-down plant. This loss results since the price of the goods which were produced by the plant will now be higher due to restricted supply. Consumer surplus is created because buyers are paying the marginal price for all units, not their reservation price for each unit. When the price goes up, there will be less consumer surplus as some individuals who, at the old price bought the good and obtained some surplus, now find that it is above their reservation price. In a world of atomistic competition, these losses would not arise as firms have no influence on price. One of the objectives of antitrust litigation is to eliminate the drop in consumer surplus.[10]

In general, we would expect indirect costs of firms to be substantial as the failing company must be fairly large to generate a complaint from a government agency.

IV   Social Costs of Anticompetitive Behavior

The costs of anticompetitive behavior are always mentioned, but rarely measured carefully in FCD cases. We show that the expected costs of anticompetitive behavior depend on both the market structure of the industry and the probability of default of the "failing" company.

---

[10]   The concept behind the lost consumer surplus is straightforward. Assume the plant is producing widgets. (Assume also that income effects from widgets are zero so that the ordinary and compensated demand curves coincide.) If the plant liquidates, there will be fewer widgets produced and their price will rise. This is shown as a rise from $<p_0, q_0>$ to $<p_1, q_1>$.

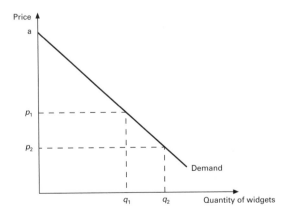

The consumer surplus before the liquidation was the triangular area $<a, p_0, q_0>$. This is the surplus gained because the consumers only have to pay the marginal price for all the units, when they would be willing to pay more for the first few widgets. After liquidation, consumer surplus is the area $<a, p_1, q_1>$. Thus consumer surplus has decreased by an amount $<p_1, p_0, q_0, q_1>$.

In a situation in which there are only two firms in the industry and one is failing, allowing a merger will be beneficial rather than detrimental to the public. The intuition is that since the healthy firm will soon have a monopoly anyway, allowing the monopolist to acquire another plant will allow him to increase output and hence lower prices.[11]

This can best be illustrated by comparing a duopolist with a multi-plant monopolist and a single-plant monopolist. For simplicity, we shall assume a linear demand curve and quadratic cost functions. We define

$$q_1 = \text{quantity produced by firm 1}$$
$$q_2 = \text{quantity produced by firm 2}$$
$$\text{Price} = p = A - B(q_1 + q_2) \qquad A, B > 0$$
$$\text{Cost in firm 1} = C_1 = a_1 q_1 + b_1 q_1^2 \qquad a_1, b_1 \geq 0$$
$$\text{Cost in firm 2} = C_2 = a_2 q_2 + b_2 q_2^2 \qquad a_2, b_2 \geq 0$$

Let us first consider the equilibrium output for Cournot duopolists. In Cournot equilibrium, we seek a situation where, if each company takes the other's output as given, neither desires to alter his output. The profits of the duopolists are

$$\pi_1 = Aq_1 - B(q_1 + q_2)q_1 - a_1 q_1 - b_1 q_1^2$$
$$\pi_2 = Aq_2 - B(q_1 + q_2)q_2 - a_2 q_2 - b_2 q_2^2$$

To find the equilibrium, we first differentiate and then express each duopolist's output as a function of his rival's output. The expression is called the reaction function. Thus the reaction functions for our problem are:

$$q_1 = \frac{A - a_1}{2(B + b_1)} - \frac{B}{2(B + b_1)} q_2$$

$$q_2 = \frac{A - a_2}{2(B + b_2)} - \frac{B}{2(B + b_2)} q_1$$

We want to find a $<q_1, q_2>$ combination which satisfies both reaction functions. Substituting and solving, it can be shown

$$q_1^{**} = \frac{2(B + b_2)(A - a_1) - B(A - a_2)}{4(B + b_1)(B + b_2) - B^2} \tag{1}$$

$$q_2^{**} = \frac{2(B + b_1)(A - a_2) - B(A - a_1)}{4(B + b_1)(B + b_2) - B^2} \tag{2}$$

---

[11]   This was the situation in a type of FCD defense which actually preceded the landmark *International Show vs. US* case. In the *American Press Association Union vs. US* (1916) the plaintiff and Western Newspaper Union represented a duopoly in their relevant market. The court ruled in favor of the merger since it was clear that the directors of American Press were planning to dispose of their principal plate plant assets if the merger was not allowed and the joinder of these companies would probably not injure the public because even if the sale were disallowed, Western would still survive as a monopolist capable of buying up the plant piecemeal. Finally, it was felt that a law designed to shield the public from injury (Sherman Antitrust Act) should not be construed to compel the public to suffer an injury.

In the duopoly solution, each actor equates his marginal cost to his marginal revenue. Since the marginal revenue will be lower to the duopolist with the higher output, the marginal costs of the two duopolists will not necessarily be the same.

If one of the duopolists is failing, say company 2, and the two companies are allowed to merge by invoking the FCD, producing a multi-plant monopoly, the equilibrium solution will be the same as if the two duopolists had colluded. Industry profit is

$$\pi = \pi_1 + \pi_2 = Aq_1 + Aq_2 - B(q_1 + q_2)^2 - a_1q_1 - b_1q_1^2 - a_2q_2 - b_2q_2^2$$

We differentiate and solve for optimal production in each plant:

$$q_1^* = \frac{Ab_2 - Ba_1 + Ba_2 - a_1b_2}{2Bb_1 + 2Bb_2 + 2b_1b_2} \tag{3}$$

$$q_2^* = \frac{Ab_1 + Ba_1 - Ba_2 - a_2b_1}{2Bb_1 + 2Bb_2 + 2b_1b_2} \tag{4}$$

Total profit will always be at least as large with a multi-plant monopolist as with a duopolist. The former always has the option of acting like a pair of duopolists. This explains why the failing company will be worth more to the rival company than to any other purchaser.

It can also be shown that the total production under duopoly is always greater than the total production under monopoly and the price is always lower under duopoly.[12] Thus, monopoly does impose a larger dead weight loss (DWL) to society than duopoly. However, if company 2 is failing, the relevant choice is between a single-plant monopolist and a two-plant monopolist.

Consider the case of a single-plant monopolist:

$$\pi_1 = Aq_1 - Bq_1^2 - a_1q_1 - b_1q_1^2$$

Solving we find

$$q_1' = \frac{A - a_1}{2B + 2b_1} \tag{5}$$

We want to compare q_1' as given in equation (5) to $q_1^* + q_2^*$ as given in equations (3) and (4). Consider first the case in which $b_1 = 0$ and $b_2 > 0$; that is, the marginal costs of production in plant 1 are constant while those in plant 2 are increasing. Output will be identical with a single-plant or multi-plant monopoly, i.e., $q_1^* + q_2^* = q_1'$.[13] The intuition is that in the two-plant situation, plant 2 is used until the marginal costs of production

---

12 The intuition is that the marginal revenue from production of an extra unit is higher from a duopolist than from a monopolist. Thus marginal revenue equals marginal cost at a greater quantity and a lower price. For a rigorous proof, see Cournot (1963).

13 With $b_1 = 0$, $q_1^* + q_2^*$ from equations (3) and (4) simplifies to

$$\frac{A - a_1}{2B} = q$$

are equal to those in plant 1, then plant 1 is used for all additional production. Since the marginal revenue curves are the same for the multi-plant or single-plant monoplist, the result follows. There will, however, be a larger DWL by not having plant 2 in operation of $q_2^* > 0$. This is illustrated in figure 8.1.

MC_1 is the marginal cost curve with only plant 1 in operation. MC_{12} is the marginal cost curve with both plants in operation. The social cost to society from a multi-plant monopolist is the cost generated because output is restricted and hence the marginal cost of production is less than the demand; that is, people would have been willing to purchase goods for more than they cost to produce. The single-plant monopolist generates this cost as well as the opportunity cost of not producing goods in a cost-efficient manner.

If $b_1 > 0$ and $b_2 \geq 0$, output will be lower in the case of a single-plant monopolist than with a multi-plant monopolist. This can be seen by reference to figure 8.2.

(p_1, q_1) is the price–quantity combination with only plant 1. (p_{12}, q_{12}) is the price–quantity combination with both plants. With two plants, the output is higher and the price is lower. The DWL to society from a single-plant monopolist is that generated by the multi-plant monopolist plus the social cost of further restriction of output as well as the opportunity cost of not producing goods in a cost-efficient manner. The DWL to society is considerably lower if the duopolist is able to acquire its failing rival.[14] The effect is compounded if there are economies of scale in multi-plant operations.

Figure 8.1 Monopolistic dead weight losses

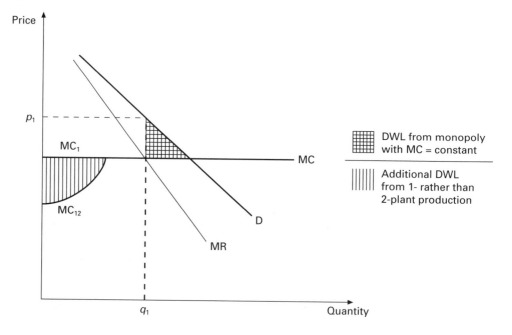

---

[14]   If the failing firm is one that legitimately should go out of business – i.e., no matter how efficiently it is operated, in the long run, it cannot cover its fixed costs and make a profit – no other firm, whether a rival firm or a new entrant would want to acquire it.

Figure 8.2 Single vs multi-plant dead weight losses

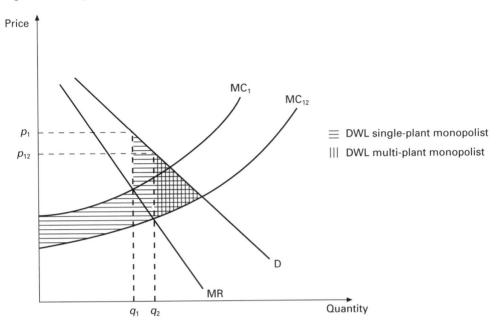

In this duopoly case, the surviving monopolist has merely acquired additional plant capacity. One might ask why we must petition for an exemption to the antitrust doctrine when there are at least two other ways in which the firm can gain additional plant capacity, i.e., buying assets at auction and building a new plant. Buying the assets at auction is conceptually equivalent to merging. In realization of this, the Cellar-Kefauver Act of 1950 closed the loophole which allowed immunity if consolidation was accomplished through the consolidation of assets.

It is possible that a rival company may wish to purchase an existing plant and may be unwilling to build a new plant. If the healthy firm builds a new plant, it must anticipate that the incremental earnings are sufficient to cover the fixed and variable costs of running the plant as well as earning its cost of capital. If the purchase price is less than the new building costs, the firm will be willing to merge but not necessarily to build a new plant. Thus, the FCD defense generates a social benefit because it is not possible to duplicate its effects either through the purchase of the "failing" company's assets or the construction of new plant capacity.

We now relax the assumption that the failing company will fail with a probability equal to 1 and return to our duopoly where one of the firms is a probable failing company. There will be an anticompetitive effect if equation 6 holds.

$$(1 - PF)DWL_{duopoly} + (PF)DWL_{SPM} < DWL_{MPM} \qquad (6)$$

where

PF = probability of failure
DWL = dead weight loss

DWL$_{SPM}$ = dead weight loss from a single-plant monopolist
DWL$_{MPM}$ = dead weight loss from a multi-plant monopolist

With three or more firms in the industry, the anticompetitive impact depends on the market structure. Consider first the case in which there are three firms in the industry of roughly equal power and one of these is failing. If this firm fails, we will be left with a duopoly. If we allow one of the rival companies to merge with the failing company, we will still have a duopoly. One of the duopolists will have additional plant capacity. Earlier we observed that each duopolist equates marginal cost with marginal revenue. Acquiring an additional plant will allow one of the duopolists to lower marginal cost, and hence it appears output will be increased.

Consider now a case in which there are three firms in the industry, one with 15 percent of the market, one with 50 percent and the failing firm with 35 percent. If the large firm was allowed to take over the failing firm, it would have 85 percent of the market. Thus the large firm may act like a monopolist and the other firm may act like a price-taker. If the firm failed and the market shares were prorated, the small firm would have 22 percent of the market and the large firm would have 78 percent. The large firm would look less overbearing. In this type of case, the anticompetitive impact deserves further notice. The issue is: "At what relative market shares do two duopolists begin to act like a monopolist and a price-taker?"

The same analogy occurs if there were four or more firms in an industry. In an industry with firms of roughly equal size, if one of the firms will fail with a probability equal to 1, allowing one of the rival companies to acquire it imposes an advantage rather than a cost on society. This is not necessarily true if the probability of failure is less than 1 or if the firms are of such unequal size that because of the takeover some of the smaller firms begin to act as price-takers rather than oligopolists.

V EVALUATING THE PROBABILITY OF FAILURE

One of the problems in evaluating the FCD defense is the ambiguous nature of the term "failing firm." Interpretations cover a range of opinions from "movement in the direction of failure" (Bauman, 1965) to the implied rigid interpretation that "a firm is not failing because its debt is not as yet in default," e.g., *Shaefer Beer vs. Schmidt's Beer* (1978). In fact, there is no single definition and no single set of characteristics that one can use to unequivocally distinguish a healthy firm from a failing entity. We have shown that the failing potential of a firm, i.e., the probability of failure, plays an important role in any determination of *expected* costs of bankruptcy. The latter, in our opinion, must be factored into any rigorous FCD analysis. Such terms as depleted assets, remote rehabilitation chances, and grave probability of failure sprinkle the case histories without much precision. While we agree that subjective interpretation of the facts must play an important role in the eventual court decision, significant progress in the literature on business failure classification and prediction can assist this process.

The most important attempts at quantifying the probability of failure involve relatively sophisticated multivariate, statistical investigations based on comparison of test observations with profiles of bankrupt vs. non-bankrupt entities. These works, usually employing linear or quadratic discriminant analyses, e.g. Altman (1968, 1973, 1976, 1977), Deakin (1972, 1977), Sinkey (1975), Wilcox (1971, 1973) and most directly

Table 8.2 Merger court cases and Z-Score failure determination

Failing company	Merger allowed?	Year prior[1] Z-Score	Probability of bankrupt classification[2]	Prediction
Ballard & Ballard	No	5.262	0.04	N
Capital Airlines	Yes	0.769	0.92	F
Certified Industries[3]	No	1.240	0.86	F*
Kinney Shoes	No	5.708	0.02	N
McElwain Shoes	Yes	0.951	0.90	F
Pabst Brewery	No	3.083	0.38	N
Shopping Bag Stores	No	4.953	0.05	N
St. Helens	No	2.958	0.41	N
Schaefer Beer	No	1.368	0.84	F*
Lykes Corp. (Youngstown Sheet and Tube)	Yes	1.093	0.87	F

Prediction: F = predict failure; N = predict no failure.
* Inconsistent classification.
[1] Year prior to the anti-trust case date.
[2] Based on results of the original model.
[3] Subsequently liquidated.

relevant by Blum (1974a, b), attempt to analyze financial statement and security market information so that failure probabilities can be estimated. An important attribute of these studies is the objective, almost unbiased nature of the analysis. Table 8.2 illustrates the application of one of these models (Altman, 1968) to a list of firms claimed to be "failing" among FCD cases. The model allows us to estimate the probability of failure (table 8.2) based on a comparison of a particular firm's financial profile with that of representative failed vs. non-failed entities. Note that in eight of the ten instances, the model "agrees" with the decision as to whether or not to allow the merger[15] – agrees in the sense of the probability of failure; no attempt is made to assess the expected value of the costs.

This model, which was developed after most of the cases noted in table 8.2, is only presented as indicative of the types of statistical analyses which can be applied in FCD cases. Of course, the decision should be based on many other ingredients, as we have noted in our formal model, but we feel that such statistical methodologies and models can substantially assist the process.

VI CONCLUSION

This paper has explored a "doctrine" which has been in the legal-economic framework of antitrust policy for over half a century. Despite the seemingly venerable nature of the FCD, it is our conjecture that the principles behind its invocation are not well

---

[15] In one case, Certified Industries, the merger was not allowed and the firm was subsequently liquidated. The Z-Score model classified the firm as a high potential failure (F), its eventual fate.

understood and inconsistently applied in the courts. We have attempted to specify the application of the FCD in a rigorous, rational framework.

We argue that the FCD should be upheld if the combined social costs of firm failure are greater than the anticompetitive effects of a merger. From our analysis, it is clear that whether or not the FCD should be invoked cannot be determined by the probability of failure alone or whether there is a significant anticompetitive effect. For example, a firm with a high chance of failure may have low social costs of bankruptcy and a medium anticompetitive impact. The merger, in this case, might be disallowed despite the FCD defense. On the other hand, a merger involving a firm with a relatively low chance of failure, high bankruptcy costs, and low anticompetitive impact, may be allowed on the basis of the "doctrine".

Inherent in any failing company analysis is the question of just what constitutes a failing firm or, more practically, how do we assess the probability of failure. Perhaps the existing ambiguity of an operational definition of failing has deterred the courts from seriously considering bankruptcy costs in a rigorous manner. We have attempted to define this probability unambiguously based on a financial-statistical failure classification model.

The outlook for the FCD's role in the courts is still unclear but we have observed that the regulatory agencies are acutely concerned with its application. Growing anti-merger efforts in Congress and increased insolvency risk pressures on more and larger firms, combined with a revival of the merger movement in many industries in the late 1970s, makes failing company analysis perhaps more relevant than ever before.

REFERENCES

Adams, W., "Merging Sick Giants." *New York Times*, August 8, 1978.
Altman, E., "Financial Ratios, Discriminant Analysis and the Prediction of Corporate Bankruptcy." *Journal of Finance*, September 1968, 23(4), 589–610.
——, *Corporate Bankruptcy in America*. D. C. Heath & Company, Lexington, MA., 1971.
——, "Predicting Railroad Bankruptcies in America." *Bell Journal of Economics and Management Science* 4, Spring 1973, 184–211.
——, "A Financial Early Warning System for Over-the-Counter Broker Deals." *Journal of Finance*, September 1976.
——, "Predicting Performance in the S and L Industry." *Journal of Monetary Economics*, October 1977.
Bauman, J. K., "The Impact of the Failing Company Doctrine in the F.T.C.'s Premerger Clearance Program." *Syracuse Law Review* 19, 1965.
Baxter, Nevins, "Leverage, Risk of Ruin and the Cost of Capital." *Journal of Finance*, September, 1967: pp. 395–404.
Blum, Mark P., "The Failing Company Doctrine." *Boston College Industrial and Commercial Review* 16, 1974a.
——, "Failing Company Discriminant Analysis." *Journal of Accounting Research* 12 (1), Spring 1974b.
Bock, Betty, "The Failing 'Failing' Company Justification for a Merger." *The Conference Board* 26, 1969.
Calamosca, A., "Congressional Battle Over Bankruptcy." *New York Times*, March 3, 1978.
Cournot, Augustin, *Researches Into the Mathematical Principles of the Theory of Wealth*. (Translated by Nathaniel T. Bacon), Homewood: Irwin, 1963.
Deakin, Edward, "A Discriminant Analysis of Predictors of Failure." *Journal of Accounting Research*, Spring 1972.

——, "Business Failure Prediction: An Empirical Analysis." in *Financial Crises*, Edited by E. Altman and A. Sametz, John Wiley, 1977.

Haugen, Robert and Senbet, L., "The Insignificance of Bankruptcy Costs on the Theory of Optimal Capital Structure." *Journal of Finance*, May 1978.

International Shoe vs. FTC, 280 US 291 (1930).

Rothberg, B., *The Failing Company Doctrine*, unpublished MBA Thesis, New York University, Summer 1979.

"Schaefer Wins a Round." *New York Times*, December 6, 1978.

Sinkey, J., "A Multivariate Statistical Analysis of the Characteristics of Problem Banks." *Journal of Finance*, March 1975.

Stanley, David T., and Marjorie Girth, *Bankruptcy: Problem, Process, Reform*. Washington, DC: The Brookings Institution, 1971.

Van Horne, James, "Optimal Initiation of Bankruptcy Proceedings by Debtholders." *Journal of Finance*, June 1976.

Warner, Jerold, "Bankruptcy Costs: Some Evidence." *Journal of Finance*, May 1977.

Wilcox, J., "A Gambler's Ruin Prediction of Business Failure Using Accounting Data." *Sloan Management Review*, Spring 1971.

——, "A Prediction of Business Failure Using Accounting Data." *Empirical Research in Accounting: Selected Studies*, 1973.

Part II: Credit Risk Management

9 | Credit-Risk Measurement and Management: The Ironic Challenge in the Next Decade

with John B. Caouette and Paul Narayanan

Interest in and concern with credit-risk management is escalating, despite historically low US default rates and losses in the loan and corporate bond markets. One reason is that lending institutions are increasingly comfortable with transacting their assets in counter-party arrangements whereby credit-risk exposure is shifted. This motivation has helped to stimulate the congruence of several important ingredients for the sophisticated treatment of corporate credit evaluation and management, including stand-alone valuation techniques, portfolio-management approaches, comprehensive and reliable relevant data-bases, and the growth in credit-derivative and other types of credit-insurance structures. We expect these dynamic forces to continue for the next several years. Combined with more fundamental credit concerns in Asia and Latin America, credit-risk management is the next great risk management challenge for the coming years.[1]

The US economy has been strong for more than six years, and most of the world's stock markets have been booming for a substantial period, reflecting impressive corporate growth and low interest rates. As a result, credit markets in most parts of the world, with some conspicuous exceptions (e.g., Japan, South Korea, Switzerland, and some parts of Southeast Asia and Latin America), have been in a benign state, especially in 1997. Indeed, nonperforming bank loans as a percentage of total loans and the default rate on leverage loans and low-quality junk bonds have been well below 2 percent for the 1994–97 period, compared with an average nonperforming loan rate of close to 4 percent from 1988 to 1993, and an average annual default rate of 3.6 percent for high-yield (junk) bonds for the 1971–96 period (Altman and Kishore, 1997). With these positive credit market statistics, why are we now (1998) experiencing dynamic revolutionary changes in the interest in and concern with credit-risk management and integrated techniques to assess both the stand-alone and portfolio aspects of corporate credit?

---

[1] This article is based on Caouette et al. (1998).

The answer, we believe, is that lending institutions, primarily commercial banks, have reached a certain maturation stage whereby they no longer simply want to make loans (buy) and hold them either to maturity or charge-off. Stimulated by pressures from regulators, dynamic trading markets, and internal return on equity objectives, banks are increasingly willing to consider transacting their assets in counterparty arrangements whereby the credit-risk exposure is shifted with the reduction in total risk of the original lender. Because the markets in which credit assets are hedged or sold are quite young, still fairly illiquid, and probably inefficient, banks and their counterparties are struggling to amass the information and analytical foundation for valuing the underlying assets in some form of meaningful risk–return framework.

This motivation has helped to stimulate the congruent coming of age of four important ingredients for the sophisticated treatment of corporate credit evaluation and management:

- Stand-alone valuation techniques
- Attempts to resolve the portfolio credit-risk problem
- Comprehensive and fairly reliable relevant databases
- The advent and impressive early growth in the structuring and trading of credit-risk derivatives and various types of credit insurance and guarantees

By being more sophisticated in the assessment and laying off of credit-risk-related securities and assets, financial institutions can be more aggressive in the creation and trading of new products (e.g., structured instruments). Before addressing these points, one should examine the economic environment that both predates and now surrounds the current surge of interest and activity in credit-risk issues.

CREDIT-RISK MANAGEMENT AND THE ECONOMIC ENVIRONMENT

The assertion that market practitioners in the late 1990s are placing strong emphasis on credit-risk management does not imply that interest was nonexistent or even low in the past. Indeed, this matter received significant attention throughout most of the world with the structural increase in defaults in the late 1980s and early 1990s. The USA led the way with record bank loan and public corporate bond defaults caused by many ill-fated, highly leveraged restructurings of the mid- and late 1980s, an economic recession, and the inability of marginal firms to refinance their obligations. The junk bond default rate jumped to more than 10 percent in 1990 and 1991, and many skeptics argued that high-credit-risk markets, such as leveraged bank lending and junk bond financing, were likely to disappear. (This surmise proved to be far from the reality, as new issuance in both of these lending markets has reached record levels in each of the past few years.) Indeed, in 1996, high-yield public bond issuance was $66 billion and leveraged loan (low-quality) new-issue volume reached $135 billion (and 1997 totals are far greater, with junk bond issuance likely to exceed $100 billion). Specific sector problems (e.g., in real estate, retailing, deregulated finance, and transport) compounded the default problems of the early 1990s.

Although these events heightened concern about established credit-management techniques and the lack of a meaningful credit culture within the world's largest and most sophisticated financial institutions, we did not as yet witness a pervasive interest in the creation and evaluation of new valuation techniques. What we observed was the occasional stand-alone valuation model, continued refinement of some relevant default databases (first established in the mid-1980s), and surveys by regulators and consultants of existing techniques. The surveys invariably reached the conclusion that credit cultures of financial institutions and their lending strategies needed to be rethought and possibly redesigned (see, e.g., Wuffli and Hunt 1993).

These calls for reassessment have come at a time of increased competition in lending markets as more-varied types of firms are intermediating credit. Corporations no longer need to go to many different types of institutions for their complex borrowing needs. Banks are underwriting credits of all maturities, and securities firms are making loans, as well as underwriting bonds. The concept of a one-stop financial conglomerate has arrived, and with it the reduction of profit margins on traditional lending as the markets become more competitive.

On the demand side, some investors in credit instruments are trying to enhance their yields by switching to nontraditional markets, such as emerging market debt and asset-backed vehicles, as well as moving down the credit-quality spectrum. In addition to the greater risk that investors are now willing to take, the low interest rate environment creates greater vulnerability to market risk and, combined with credit-risk migration concerns (i.e., the risk that a firm's credit rating will drift downward), can result in mark-to-market losses, even if default incidence continues to be low. When defaults do increase, as they invariably will in the near future, these concerns will escalate.[2]

STAND-ALONE RISK PROCEDURES

The foundation for any comprehensive treatment of a credit portfolio of loans and/or bonds is the initial assessment of the risk of each asset in the portfolio on a stand-alone basis. If the analysis is faulty or incomplete as to the default and credit migration risk of the underlying entity, then no matter how sophisticated the portfolio algorithm, the end result will be of little use. Stand-alone credit-risk measurement involves a growing array of analytical techniques from univariate, qualitatively weighted quantitative systems, and qualitative variable credit-scoring systems to an increasing number of more sophisticated procedures. These other approaches have included multi-variate regression, discriminant and logit statistical models, models based on contingent claims and market price proxies for asset value coverage of debt obligations, and finally, artificial intelligence procedures to either predict default or replicate the bond-rating results of established bond-rating agencies. The latter objective is critical because it is directly related to one of the caveats of any credit-evaluation system: Regardless of the credit-scoring system used, the results should be linked to capital market indicators and experience. We suggest that the appropriate capital market indicators are bond ratings, not because we believe that the rating agencies have the best models and results with respect to default likelihoods, but because the relevant databases on default and migration risk patterns are primarily based on the bond rating of the underlying credit. Hence, if the data that we use are based on ratings, then the scoring system should also be tied to ratings.

---

[2] In a recent report, we estimated that US public bond defaults will approximate $22 billion (face value) in the 1997–99 period. See Altman et al. (1997).

We have mentioned several times the notion of credit-risk migration. In essence, the ultimate negative migration is from some initial state to a default (i.e., from a performing asset to one that either has missed a periodic interest payment or for which a distressed restructuring is accomplished whereby the creditor receives a lower interest payment, an extension of the time period for repayment, and/or a more risky claim on the asset than the initial contract specified). In addition, credit risk involves the possibility that the inherent risk of the asset migrates to a lower quality level, thereby resulting in lower security values in a mark-to-market pricing environment.

The final ingredient of the credit-risk assessment of individual loans/bonds is the loss to the creditor if the asset's quality deteriorates or if it actually defaults. This step mainly involves assessing the impact of the recovery level given a default, although the impact of a change in credit quality on the security's value is also relevant. The recovery rate concept is extremely important, but it is given small, if any, consideration in traditional bond-rating systems. (Some rating agencies adjust for expected recoveries by reducing the senior unsecured bond-rating equivalent for bonds of lower seniority levels and explicitly consider recovery levels in their bank loan rating programs. Other agencies state that recoveries are explicitly considered.) On the other hand, financial institutions of all types and the rating agencies themselves now realize that the recovery on defaulted assets plays an important role in assessing credit-risk loss, and we can expect increased research and resources to be spent on the empirical investigation of historical recovery experience, particularly of nonpublicly traded private debt.[3]

To summarize, the standalone, individual asset ingredient in credit-risk management systems involves credit-scoring procedures, assessments of negative-event probabilities, and the consequent losses given these negative migration or default events. Although, for many years, we have been emphasizing the important link between credit-scoring procedures and capital market experience, an institution that ties its scoring system to its own portfolio's historical experience is certainly justified in using its own files to assess risk and losses. The experience of the bank, however, or several banks that agree to pool their data, must be rich enough in terms of statistical quantity and data reliability to provide meaningful future estimates.

Portfolio Models

The return distribution on risky debt assets is not nearly as normal as it is on equities. Whereas the debt investor is usually limited to the promised yield or slightly higher returns (given positive credit migration), the potential downside is total. The expected return distribution is, therefore, skewed toward lower-than-promised returns with a fairly large (fat) tail at default levels. Hence, traditional mean return–variance of return models are not appropriate, although they may be robust enough to use over short (e.g., one month or one quarter) measurement periods.

---

[3] Many studies have documented the recovery experience on corporate bonds, including Altman and Eberhart (1994), Altman and Kishore (1996), Carty and Lieberman (1997), and Standard & Poor's Corporation (1997). Moody's Investors Service also has estimated the recovery rate on a small sample of defaulted corporate bank loans in Carty and Lieberman (1996). A study by Altman and Suggitt (1997) documents the recent default rate experience on bank commercial and industrial loans.

The search for alternative portfolio schemes seems to be heading either in the direction of Monte Carlo simulation results of possible returns on a credit portfolio to help the credit-risk decision maker or in the direction of the use of a proxy measure of risk, other than the variance of return, in a return–risk trade-off measure. One proxy that has received increased attention of late is the *unexpected loss* on individual loans or portfolios of loans based on some estimated distribution around the expected loss. In this approach, the expected loss estimate can be used in adjusting the promised yield to obtain the expected return. The unexpected loss is a by-product of this analysis and is an outcome that requires capital reserves. In all portfolio models, however, the illusive ingredient is to properly and reliably estimate risky-event correlations between assets. Little agreement exists as to how this estimate should be achieved, although meaningful attempts are being made by analyzing the time-series correlations of rating series, equity prices, or variables that explain equity prices and/or defaults.[4]

DATABASES

In both the stand-alone and portfolio treatment of fixed-income assets, the solutions are dependent on the methodology used and the data inputs to the models. Among the most important data inputs are the expected default rates and migration (drift) patterns from the asset's initial credit rating. Fairly comprehensive databases exist on these inputs, the criteria being the bond rating from Moody's Investors Service or Standard & Poor's Corporation, either from original issuance or based on a basket of bonds at some point in time and then observed for subsequent years. Databases are available covering default and migration experience back to at least 1970.[5]

In addition to default and migration rates, a third important input is the recovery rate on defaults, for which the critical distinguishing feature of the bond or loan is its seniority. Although data for recoveries on bonds are fairly comprehensive, data for recoveries on defaulted bank loans are quite inferior, and this statistic needs more study. Although financial institutions may choose to use their own databases rather than rely on rating agency inputs, the reality is that few institutions have extensive historical data that are based on the credit-scoring system currently in place. Hence, reliance on public data is likely to be the route that most decision makers will take, at least in the near future.

CREDIT-RISK DERIVATIVES AND CREDIT-ENHANCEMENT MECHANISMS

The final factor related to the increased motivation for creating sophisticated credit evaluation and management techniques is the advent and impressive early growth in the credit-risk derivative and the corporate credit-enhancement/financial guarantee markets.

---

[4] Some recent analytical models have been promoted by McQuown (1994), J. P. Morgan & Company (1997), McKinsey & Co. (1997), Credit Suisse Financial Products (1997), and Altman and Saunders (1998).
[5] See Altman and Kao (1992), Carty and Fons (1993), and Standard & Poor's Corporation (1997). Altman and Waldman (1997) compare and contrast these three rating migration databases.

Selling a credit asset outright is no longer necessary if, for some reason, the original lender no longer wants to assume the credit risk. Relatively simple and also more complex financial instruments are being devised to set up a type of insurance mechanism for transferring the risk of default and also the risk of migration in the case of total-return derivatives. These instruments have created new and dynamic counterparty exposures.

The credit-derivative market is growing as banks, securities firms, corporations, and other institutions seek to hedge their credit exposures or realign their lending portfolios. In the past five years, this market has grown considerably, with many of the major securities firms providing liquidity by immediately finding willing counterparties or taking on the insurance risk themselves, confident that a counterparty will soon be found (Parsley 1996 and McDermott 1997). The derivative seller provides insurance against any event (e.g., default) that changes the value of the underlying asset. In all of these cases, the relationship between the original borrower or lender is preserved.

Financial guarantees provide, in some cases, a leaner, less ambiguous form of a credit derivative because no question arises of a change in ownership of the asset if some credit event occurs. The guarantor simply pays off the original lender based on some predetermined formula. This arrangement is particularly useful in the case of a nontransferable loan.

The seller-counterparties in credit-risk derivative transactions, or the more traditional credit insurance providers, are increasingly mindful of managing and trading their own credit portfolios. Hence, these institutions are particularly interested in techniques that combine the stand-alone and portfolio aspects of their revenue-based assets. The credit-risk derivative and credit-enhancement markets have been improving, and will continue to improve, the credit market's liquidity and vice versa. This development, in turn, will require more accountability and transparency of asset values and will also motivate attempts to price the products more profitably.

CONCLUSION

We are witnessing an impressive escalation in analytical resources devoted to more-effective management of credit risk. This development comes at a time when credit-related losses in the USA and many other countries are historically very low. The primary motivating factors include refinements of traditional techniques to evaluate the default likelihood of individual assets, new analytical solutions to credit portfolio management, larger and improved databases to translate risk ratings into expected losses, and the dynamics of market mechanisms such as credit-derivative and other credit-enhancement techniques. When and if defaults increase in the near future, we can expect even more refinements and perhaps further breakthroughs in credit portfolio management.

REFERENCES

Altman, E., and A. Eberhart. 1994. "Do Seniority Provisions Protect Bondholders' Investment?" *Journal of Portfolio Management* 20 (4) (Summer): 67–75.

Altman, E., and D. L. Kao. 1992. "The Implications of Corporate Bond Ratings Drift." *Financial Analysts Journal* 48 (3), (May/June): 64–75.

Altman, E., and V. Kishore. 1996. "Almost Everything You Wanted to Know about Recoveries on Defaulted Bonds." *Financial Analysts Journal* 52 (6), (November/December): 57–64.

——. 1997. "Defaults and Returns on High-Yield Bonds: Analysis through 1997." Special report, New York University Salomon Center (January).

Altman, E., and A. Saunders. 1998. "Credit Risk Measurement over the Last 20 Years." *Journal of Banking and Finance* 21 (10/11), 1721–42.

Altman, E., and H. Suggitt. 1997. "Default Rates in the Syndicated Bank Loan Market: 1991–1997." Special report, New York University Salomon Center (Fall).

Altman, E., and R. Waldman. 1997. "Rating Migration of Corporate Bonds' Comparative Results and Investor/Lender Implications." Salomon Brothers Inc (May 13).

Altman, E., S. Schimpf, and J. Seltzer. 1997. "The Investment Performance of Defaulted Bonds and Bank Loans and Market Outlook." Special report, New York University Salomon Center (January).

Carty, L., and J. Fons. 1993. "Measuring Changes in Credit Quality." Special report, Moody's Investors Service (November).

Carty, L., and D. Lieberman. 1996. "Defaulted Bank Loan Recoveries." Special report, Moody's Investors Service (November).

——. 1997. "Corporate Bond Defaults and Default Rates, 1938–1996." Special report, Moody's Investors Service (January).

Caouette, J., E. Altman, and P. Narayanan. 1998. *Managing Credit Risk: The Next Great Financial Challenge*. John Wiley & Sons.

Credit Suisse Financial Products. 1997. "CreditRisk$^+$." Research report, Credit Suisse Financial Products.

J. P. Morgan & Company. 1997. "CreditMetrics." J. P. Morgan & Company (April).

McDermott, R. 1997. "The Long Awaited Arrival of Credit Derivatives." *Derivatives Strategy* (January 21): 19–25.

McKinsey & Co. 1997. "Credit View." Research report, McKinsey & Co.

McQuown, J. 1994. "All That Counts Is Diversification." Publicity document, KMV Corporation.

Parsley, M. 1996. "The Launch of a New Market: Credit Derivatives." *Euromoney* (March): 28–33.

Standard & Poor's Corporation. 1997. "Ratings Performance 1996: Stability and Transition." Special report, Standard & Poor's Corporation (February).

Wuffli, P., and D. Hunt. 1993. "Fixing the Credit Problem." *McKinsey Quarterly* 2, McKinsey & Co.

10 | Credit Risk Measurement: Developments Over the Last 20 Years

with Anthony Saunders

1 INTRODUCTION

Credit risk measurement has evolved dramatically over the last 20 years in response to a number of secular forces that have made its measurement more important than ever before. Among these forces have been:

   (i)   a worldwide structural increase in the number of bankruptcies
   (ii)   a trend towards disintermediation by the highest quality and largest borrowers
   (iii)   more competitive margins on loans
   (iv)   a declining value of real assets (and thus collateral) in many markets, and
   (v)   a dramatic growth of off-balance sheet instruments with inherent default risk exposure (see, e.g. McKinsey, 1993), including credit risk derivatives.

In response to these forces academics and practitioners alike have responded by:

   (i)   developing new and more sophisticated credit-scoring/early-warning systems
   (ii)   moving away from only analyzing the credit risk of individual loans and securities towards developing measures of credit concentration risk (such as the measurement of portfolio risk of fixed income securities), where the assessment of credit risk plays a central role
   (iii)   developing new models to price credit risk, such as the risk adjusted return on capital models (RAROC), and
   (iv)   developing models to measure better the credit risk of off-balance sheet instruments.

In this paper, we trace key developments in credit risk measurement over the past two decades and show how many of these developments have been reflected in papers that have been published in the *Journal of Banking and Finance* over this period. In addition, we explore a new approach, and provide some empirical examples to measure the credit risk of risky debt portfolios (or credit concentration risk).

2 CREDIT RISK MEASUREMENT

2.1 Expert Systems and Subjective Analysis

It is probably fair to say that 20 years ago most financial institutions (FIs) relied virtually exclusively on subjective analysis or so-called banker "expert" systems to assess the credit risk on corporate loans. Essentially, bankers used information on various borrower characteristics – such as borrower character (reputation), capital (leverage), capacity (volatility of earnings) and collateral, the so-called 4 "Cs" of credit, to reach a largely subjective judgement (i.e., that of an expert) as to whether or not to grant credit. In a recent paper, Sommerville and Taffler (1995) show that in the context of the *Institutional Investor's* rating of LDC indebtedness (based on bankers' subjective ratings), that:

(a) bankers tend to be overly pessimistic about the credit risk of LDCs and
(b) multivariate credit-scoring systems (see below) tend to outperform such expert systems.

Perhaps, not surprisingly, FIs themselves have increasingly moved away from subjective/expert systems over the past 20 years towards systems that are more objectively based.

2.2 Accounting Based Credit-Scoring Systems

In univariate accounting based credit-scoring systems, the FI decision-maker compares various key accounting ratios of potential borrowers with industry or group norms. When using multivariate models, the key accounting variables are combined and weighted to produce either a credit risk score or a probability of default measure. If the credit risk score, or probability, attains a value above a critical benchmark, a loan applicant is either rejected or subjected to increased scrutiny.

In terms of sheer number of articles, developments and tests of models in this area have dominated the credit risk measurement literature in the *Journal of Banking and Finance* and in other scholarly journals. In addition to a significant number of individual articles on the subject, the *Journal of Banking and Finance* published two special issues (*Journal of Banking and Finance*, 1984, 1988) on the application of distress prediction models internationally. Indeed, international models have been developed in over 25 countries (Altman and Narayanan, 1997).

There are at least four methodological approaches to developing multivariate credit-scoring systems:

(i) the linear probability model
(ii) the logit model

(iii)   the probit model, and
(iv)   the discriminant analysis model.

By far the dominant methodologies, in terms of *Journal of Banking and Finance* publications, have been discriminant analysis followed by logit analysis. In our inaugural issue (*Journal of Banking and Finance*, June 1977), Altman et al. (1977) developed the now commonly used and referenced ZETA® discriminant model. Stripped to its bare essentials, the most common form of discriminant analysis seeks to find a linear function of accounting and market variables that best distinguishes between two loan borrower classification groups: repayment and non-repayment. This requires an analysis of a set of variables to maximize the between-group variance while minimizing the within-group variance among these variables. Similarly, logit analysis uses a set of accounting variables to predict the probability of borrower default, assuming that the probability of default is logistically distributed i.e., the cumulative probability of default takes a logistic functional form and is, by definition, constrained to fall between 0 and 1.

Martin (1977) used both logit and discriminant analysis to predict bank failures in the 1975–76 period, when 23 banks failed. Both models gave similar classifications in terms of identifying failures/non-failures. West (1985) used the logit model (along with factor analysis) to measure the financial condition of FIs and to assign to them a probability of being a problem bank. Interestingly, the factors identified by the logit model are similar to the CAMEL rating components used by bank examiners. Platt and Platt (1991a) use the logit model to test whether industry relative accounting ratios, rather than simple firm specific accounting ratios, are better predictors of corporate bankruptcy. In general, the industry relative accounting ratio model outperformed the unadjusted model. (Similar findings to this have been found in the context of relative accounting ratio based discriminant analysis models (Izan, 1984).) Lawrence et al. (1992) use the logit model to predict the probability of default on mobile home loans. They find that payment history is by far the most important predictor of default. Smith and Lawrence (1995) use a logit model to find the variables that offer the best prediction of a loan moving into a default state (calculated from a Markov model of default probabilities).

Finally, as noted earlier, by far the largest number of multivariate accounting based credit-scoring models have been based on discriminant analysis models. Altman et al. (1977) investigate the predictive performance of a seven-variable discriminant analysis model (that includes the market value of equity as one variable). A private firm version of this model also exists. In general, the seven-variable model – the so-called "ZETA® model" – is shown to improve upon Altman's (1968) earlier five-variable model. Also, Scott (1981) compares a number of these empirical models with a theoretically sound approach. He concludes that the ZETA® model most closely approximates his theoretical bankruptcy construct. A large number of other mainly international applications of discriminant analysis credit-related models are to be found in the two special issues of the *Journal of Banking and Finance* on credit risk, mentioned above.

2.3   *Other (Newer) Models of Credit Risk Measurement*

While in many cases multivariate accounting based credit-scoring models have been shown to perform quite well over many different time periods and across many different countries, they have been subject to at least three criticisms. First, that being predominantly based on book value accounting data (which in turn is measured at discrete intervals), these models may fail to pick up more subtle and fast-moving changes in borrower conditions, i.e., those that would be reflected in capital market data and values. Second, the world is inherently nonlinear, such that linear discriminant analysis and the linear probability models may fail to forecast as accurately as those that relax the underlying assumption of linearity among explanatory variables. Third, the credit-scoring bankruptcy prediction models, described in section 2.2, are often only tenuously linked to an underlying theoretical model. As such, there have been a number of new approaches – most of an exploratory nature – that have been proposed as alternatives to traditional credit-scoring and bankruptcy prediction models.

A class of bankruptcy models with a strong theoretical underpinning are "risk of ruin" models. At its most simple level, a firm goes bankrupt when the market (liquidation) value of its assets (A) falls below its debt obligations to outside creditors (B). Models of this type can be found in Wilcox (1973), Scott (1981) and Santomero and Vinso (1977). As was recognized by Scott, the risk of ruin model is in many respects similar to the option pricing models (OPM) of Black and Scholes (1973), as well as those of Merton (1974) and Hull and White (1995). In the Black–Scholes–Merton model, the probability of a firm going bankrupt depends crucially on the beginning period market value of that firm's assets (A) relative to its outside debt (B), as well as the volatility of the market value of a firm's assets (σ_A). The ideas of the risk of ruin/OPM models have gained increasing credence in the commercial area. A current example is the KMV (1993) and Kealhofer (1996) model. In the KMV model, crucial inputs into the estimation of the probability of default are A and σ_A, both of which have to be estimated. The underlying constructs are two theoretical relationships. First is the OPM model, where the value of equity can be viewed as a call option on the value of a firm's assets. Second, is the theoretical link between the observable volatility of a firm's equity value and its (unobservable) asset value volatility. Implied values for both A and σ_A can therefore be imputed for all publicly traded companies with adequate stock return data. Moreover, given any initial values of A and B (short-term debt outstanding), and a calculated value for the diffusion of asset values over time (σ_A), an expected default frequency (EDF) can be calculated for each borrowing firm. That is, default occurs in some future period when (or if) the value of a firm's assets falls below its outstanding (short-term) debt obligations. That is, the normalized area of the future distribution of asset values which falls below B. In actual practice, KMV uses an empirically based "distance from default" measure based on how many standard deviations A values are currently above B, and what percentage of firms actually went bankrupt within one-year with A values that many standard deviations above B.

Major concerns of the OPM type default models are

(i) whether the volatility of a firm's stock price can be used as an accurate proxy to derive the expected or implied variability in asset values and
(ii) the efficacy of using a comparable, or proxy, analysis necessary for non-publicly traded equity companies.

A second, newer class of models, with strong theoretical underpinnings, are those that seek to impute implied probabilities of default from the term structure of yield spreads between default free and risky corporate securities. An early version of this approach can be found in Jonkhart (1979) with a more elaborate version being presented by Iben and Litterman (1989). These models derive implied forward rates on risk-free and risky bonds, and use these rates to extract the "markets" expectation of default at different times in the future. Important assumptions underlying this approach include:

(i) that the expectations theory of interest rates holds
(ii) transaction costs are small
(iii) calls, sinking fund and other option features are absent, and
(iv) discount bond yield curves exist or can be extracted from coupon bearing yield curves.

Many of these assumptions are questionable.

A third, capital market based model is the mortality rate model of Altman (1988, 1989) and the aging approach of Asquith et al. (1989). These mortality-default rate models seek to derive actuarial-type probabilities of default from past data on bond defaults by credit grade and years to maturity. All of the rating agencies have adopted and modified the mortality approach (Moody's, 1990; Standard and Poor's, 1991) and now routinely utilize it in their structured financial instrument analyses (McElravey and Shah, 1996).

Such models have the potential to be extended to an analysis of the default/mortality of loans, but have been hampered by the lack of a loan default data base of sufficient size. For example, McAllister and Mingo (1994) estimate that to develop very stable estimates of default probabilities, an FI would need some 20,000–30,000 "names" in its data base. Very few FIs worldwide come even remotely close to approaching this number of potential borrowers. This many explain a number of current initiatives in the USA, among the larger banks, to develop a shared national data base of historic mortality loss rates on loans (a current project of Robert Morris Associates, Philadelphia, PA).

A fourth, newer approach is the application of neural network analysis to the credit risk classification problem. Essentially, neural network analysis is similar to nonlinear discriminant analysis, in that it drops the assumption that variables entering into the bankruptcy prediction function are linearly and independently related. Specifically, neural network models of credit risk explore potentially "hidden" correlations among the predictive variables which are then entered as additional explanatory variables in the nonlinear bankruptcy prediction function. Applications of neural networks in distress prediction analysis include Altman et al.'s (1994) application to corporate distress prediction in Italy, Coats and Fant's (1993) application to corporate distress prediction in the USA and several studies summarized in Trippi and Turban (1996). A commercial model of rating replication using neural networks is available from Standard & Poor's (Credit Model®).

The major criticism of the neural network approach is its *ad hoc* theoretical foundation and the "fishing expedition" nature by which hidden correlations among the explanatory variables are identified. Also, in a comparison test, Altman et al. (1994) concluded that the neural network approach did not materially improve on the linear discriminant structure.

2.4 Measures of the Credit Risk of Off-Balance Sheet Instruments

Perhaps one of the most profound developments over the past 20 years has been the expansion in off-balance sheet instruments – such as swaps, options, forwards, futures, etc. – in FIs' portfolios (Jagtiani et al., 1995; Brewer and Koppenhaver, 1992; Saunders, 1997) as well as credit risk derivatives (default insurance). Along with the expansion of these instruments has come concerns regarding default risk properties. This has, in turn, been reflected in the BIS risk-based capital ratios finally imposed in 1992, requiring banks to hold capital reserves to cover both the current and future replacement costs of such instruments, should default occur.

The probability of default on off-balance sheet instruments issued by a counter-party can, in principle, be measured in the same fashion as on-balance sheet loans since a necessary condition for default by a counter-party to an off-balance sheet contract is that the party is in financial distress, i.e., the models of sections 2.1–2.3 can be applied.

However, there are a number of subtle differences between the default risk on loans and over-the-counter (OTC), off-balance sheet instruments. First, even if the counter-party is in financial distress, it will only default on out-of-the-money contracts. That is, it will seek to enforce all in-the-money contracts. This potential "cherry picking" incentive has been recognized by the market through increased use of master netting agreements, where losses on defaulted contracts can be offset against contracts that are in the money to the defaulting counter-party. Second, for any given probability of default, the amount lost on default is usually less for off-balance sheet instruments than for loans. A lender can lose all the principal and interest on a loan, while by comparison for an interest rate swap of the same notional principal size, losses are confined to the present-value difference between the fixed and expected future cash flows on the swap (e.g., as implied by the forward rate curve).

2.5   Measures of Credit Concentration Risk

Increasingly, FIs have recognized the need to measure credit concentration risk as well as the credit risk on individual loans. The early approaches to concentration risk analysis were based either on:

1   subjective analysis (the expert's feel as to a maximum percentage of loans to allocate to an economic sector or geographic location, e.g., an SIC code or Latin America)
2   on limiting exposure in an area to a certain percent of capital (e.g., 10 percent) or
3   on migration analysis, measuring the transition probabilities of relatively homogenous loans, in a given pool, moving from current to any number of possible default states, varying from 30 days overdue to charge-off.

With respect to migration analysis, the usual methodology employed to estimate transition probabilities has been the Markovian stable or unstable model (Altman and Kao, 1992). In an earlier article in the *Journal of Banking and Finance*, Bennett (1984) presented rating migration of bank assets in a pioneering portfolio risk discussion. He emphasized the need for a common risk rating system for all bank assets, including corporate, country, consumer loans and loans to other banks. Migration analysis plays a critical role in the recent Credit Metrics® (1997) approach.

More recently, the potential for applying modern portfolio theory (MPT) to loans and other fixed income instruments has been recognized. One attempt at applying MPT was that of Chirinko and Guill (1991). Their approach required the use of a macro econometric model of the US economy to generate future possible states of the world and thus SIC sector loan payoffs (loss rates). From the distribution of such loss rates, means, variances and covariances could be calculated and an efficient loan portfolio constructed (defined at the level of SIC code aggregation).

In the remainder of this paper, we discuss an alternative portfolio theory based approach for analyzing the optimal composition of fixed income (either bond or loan) portfolios.

3   Fixed Income Portfolio Analysis

Since the pioneering work of Markowitz (1959), portfolio theory has been applied to common stocks. The traditional objectives of maximizing returns for given levels of risk or minimizing risk for given levels of return have guided efforts to achieve effective diversification of portfolios. Such concepts as individual stock and portfolio betas to indicate risk levels and to calculate efficient frontiers, with optimal weightings of the portfolio's member stocks, are now common parlance among investment professionals and in textbooks (Elton and Gruber, 1995). This is not to say that these concepts are widely used to the exclusion of more traditional industrial sector, geographical location, size, or some other diversification strategy. The necessary data in terms of historical returns and correlations of returns between individual stocks are usually available to perform the portfolio optimization analysis.

One might expect that these very same techniques would (and could) be applied to the fixed income area involving corporate and government bonds and even to bank loans. There has been, however, very little published work in the bond area[1] and a recent survey of practices by commercial banks found fragmented and untested efforts.[2] The objective of effective risk reducing methods is, however, a major pre-occupation of FIs, with bank loan research departments and regulators spending considerable resources to reduce the likelihood of major loan losses that jeopardize the very existence of the lending institution. Recent bank failures attributed to huge loan losses in the USA, Japan, Europe and Latin America have raised the level of concern. Still, conceptually sound diversification techniques have eluded most bank and bond portfolio managers, probably for valid reasons. And, despite recent analytical attempts, e.g., Credit Metrics® (1997), effective portfolio management techniques of loans/bonds is still, in our opinion, an unresolved area.

It is the objective of this section of our paper to outline a method that will avoid the major data and analytical pitfalls that have plagued fixed income portfolio efforts, and to provide a sound and empirically feasible portfolio approach. Our empirical examples will involve corporate bonds but we feel confident that the methodology is applicable as well to commercial and industrial loans.

---

[1]   Platt and Platt (1991b) did some preliminary work for high yield "junk bond" portfolios by introducing a linear programming algorithm which maximized yield-to-maturity subject to a constraint as to the level of default risk and the degree of diversification. To our knowledge, however, corporate bond portfolio managers have not utilized this concept and continue to invest based on traditional industry, size, and credit rating criteria.

[2]   The survey of McAllister and Mingo (1994) concluded that commercial banks were experimenting with a number of different techniques but few had been implemented or had impacted corporate lending practices.

3.1 Return–Risk Framework

The classic mean variance of return framework is not valid for long-term, fixed income portfolio strategies. The problem does not lie in the expected return measure on individual assets, but in the distribution of possible returns. While the fixed income investor can lose all or most of the investment in the event of default, positive returns are limited. This problem is mitigated when the measurement period of returns is relatively short, e.g., monthly, and the likely variance of returns is small and more normal. We will return to measures of portfolio risk both for short-term returns and the more challenging buy-and-hold, long-term strategy.

3.2 Return Measurement

The measurement of expected portfolio return is actually quite straightforward for fixed income bond and loan assets. The investor (or FI) is promised a fixed return (yield-to-maturity or yield-to-worst) over time and should subtract, from this promised yield, the expected losses from default of the issuer. For certain measurement periods, the return will also be influenced by changes in interest rates but we will assume, for purposes of exposition, that these changes are random with an expected capital gain of zero. Likewise, we acknowledge that investors can infer capital gains or losses from the yield curve and also from whether the bonds are trading at a premium or discount from par.

The expected annual return is therefore

$$EAR = YTM - EAL \tag{1}$$

where EAR is the Expected annual return, YTM the Yield-to-maturity (or Yield-to-worst) and EAL the Expected annual loss.

We derive the EAL from prior work on bond mortality rates and losses (Altman, 1988, 1989). Each bond is analyzed based on its initial (or existing)[3] bond rating which implies an expected rate of default for up to ten (or longer) years after issuance. Tables 10.1 and 10.2 list cumulative mortality rates and cumulative mortality losses, respectively, covering the period 1971–94.[4] Table 10.3 annualizes these mortality rates and losses. So, for example, a 10-year BB (S&P rated) bond has an expected annual loss of 91 basis points per year. If the newly issued BB rated bond has a promised yield of 9.0 percent with a spread of 2.0 percent over 7.0 percent risk-free US Treasury bonds, then the expected return is 8.09 percent per year, or a risk premium of 109 basis points over the risk-free rate. If our measurement periods were quarterly returns instead of annual, then the expected return would be about 2.025 percent per quarter. Again, our expected return measure is focused primarily on credit risk changes and not on yield curve implications.

---

[3] The measurement of expected defaults for existing bonds compared to newly issued ones is essentially the same for bonds with maturities of at least five years. Moody's and S&P publish data on existing baskets of bonds by rating without regard to age. Their results and ours essentially converge after year four (Altman, 1992).

[4] For updated data through 1996, see Altman and Kishore (1997).

Table 10.1 Mortality rates by original rating:[a] 1971–94 (years after issuance)

Rating		1 (%)	2 (%)	3 (%)	4 (%)	5 (%)	6 (%)	7 (%)	8 (%)	9 (%)	10 (%)
AAA	Yearly	0.00	0.00	0.00	0.00	0.08	0.00	0.00	0.00	0.00	0.00
	Cumulative	0.00	0.00	0.00	0.00	0.08	0.08	0.08	0.08	0.08	0.08
AA	Yearly	0.00	0.05	1.06	0.09	0.00	0.00	0.01	0.00	0.06	0.04
	Cumulative	0.00	0.05	1.11	1.20	1.20	1.20	1.20	1.20	1.26	1.30
A	Yearly	0.00	0.19	0.07	0.21	0.06	0.06	0.20	0.19	0.00	0.00
	Cumulative	0.00	0.19	0.26	0.47	0.53	0.59	0.78	0.98	0.98	0.98
BBB	Yearly	0.41	0.25	0.32	0.55	0.89	0.39	0.09	0.00	0.59	0.23
	Cumulative	0.41	0.66	0.97	1.51	2.39	2.77	2.86	2.86	3.44	3.66
BB	Yearly	0.50	0.58	4.15	4.84	1.13	0.33	0.94	0.23	0.64	0.58
	Cumulative	0.50	1.08	5.19	9.78	10.79	11.26	13.64	13.87	14.55	15.21
B	Yearly	1.59	7.12	6.80	7.29	3.40	3.40	2.80	2.13	2.83	3.43
	Cumulative	1.59	8.60	14.82	21.02	23.71	28.21	30.22	31.70	33.63	35.91
CCC	Yearly	8.32	10.69	18.53	10.26	9.18	5.56	2.49	2.97	12.28	1.35
	Cumulative	8.32	18.13	33.30	40.14	45.63	48.66	49.94	51.42	57.39	58.31

[a] Rated by S&P at issuance.
Source: Altman and Kishore (1995).

Table 10.2 Mortality losses by original rating:[a] 1971–94 (years after issuance)

Rating		1 (%)	2 (%)	3 (%)	4 (%)	5 (%)	6 (%)	7 (%)	8 (%)	9 (%)	10 (%)
AAA	Yearly	0.00	0.00	0.00	0.00	0.08	0.00	0.00	0.00	0.00	0.00
	Cumulative	0.00	0.00	0.00	0.00	0.08	0.08	0.08	0.08	0.08	0.08
AA	Yearly	0.00	0.02	0.21	0.03	0.00	0.00	0.01	0.00	0.04	0.02
	Cumulative	0.00	0.02	0.23	0.26	0.26	0.26	0.26	0.26	0.30	0.32
A	Yearly	0.00	0.03	0.02	0.15	0.06	0.03	0.11	0.13	0.00	0.00
	Cumulative	0.00	0.03	0.05	0.20	0.26	0.29	0.40	0.52	0.52	0.52
BBB	Yearly	0.27	0.10	0.21	0.26	0.36	0.30	0.06	0.00	0.41	0.14
	Cumulative	0.27	0.37	0.58	0.84	1.19	1.49	1.55	1.55	1.95	2.08
BB	Yearly	0.26	0.26	3.34	2.14	0.70	0.33	0.94	0.23	0.64	0.58
	Cumulative	0.26	0.51	3.84	5.90	6.56	6.86	7.74	7.95	8.54	9.07
B	Yearly	0.83	5.12	5.02	5.95	2.44	3.93	2.06	1.64	1.98	1.59
	Cumulative	0.83	5.90	10.63	15.95	18.00	21.22	22.84	24.11	25.61	26.79
CCC	Yearly	7.22	8.87	15.30	6.82	6.76	3.29	2.49	0.91	8.35	1.25
	Cumulative	7.22	15.45	28.39	33.27	37.78	39.83	41.33	41.87	47.47	47.61

[a] Rated by S&P at issuance.
Source: Altman and Kishore (1995).

The latter is obviously more relevant to government bond portfolios.

The problem of measuring expected returns for commercial loans is a bit more complex. Since most loans do not have a risk rating attached by the rating agencies,[5] the loan portfolio analyst must utilize a proxy measure. We advocate using the bank's own risk rating system, or a rating replication system, as long as each of the internal

---

[5] The rating agencies will rate loans by their private placement service but these were relatively few in number in 1995. In 2001, however, loan ratings are the rule rather than the exception for most syndicated and other large loans.

Table 10.3 Annualized cumulative default rates and annualized cumulative mortality loss rates (1971–94)

Original rating/Year	1 (%)	2 (%)	3 (%)	4 (%)	5 (%)	6 (%)	7 (%)	8 (%)	9 (%)	10 (%)
Annualized cumulative default rates										
AAA	0.00	0.00	0.00	0.00	0.01	0.01	0.01	0.01	0.01	0.01
AA	0.00	0.00	0.27	0.27	0.22	0.19	0.16	0.14	0.13	0.12
A	0.00	0.05	0.08	0.11	0.10	0.09	0.10	0.11	0.10	0.09
BBB	0.04	0.27	0.26	0.33	0.37	0.40	0.44	0.39	0.35	0.37
BB	0.00	0.35	1.26	1.44	2.10	1.91	2.02	1.81	1.68	1.59
B	0.99	2.14	4.61	5.01	5.14	4.71	4.58	4.25	3.97	4.09
CCC	2.24	8.35	11.75	10.50	9.87	9.78	8.82	8.07	7.21	8.35
Annualized cumulative mortality loss rates										
AAA	0.00	0.00	0.00	0.00	0.00	0.00	0.00	0.00	0.00	0.00
AA	0.00	0.00	0.05	0.06	0.05	0.04	0.04	0.03	0.03	0.03
A	0.00	0.01	0.01	0.04	0.05	0.04	0.05	0.05	0.05	0.05
BBB	0.03	0.15	0.15	0.20	0.19	0.20	0.24	0.22	0.19	0.21
BB	0.00	0.20	0.86	1.01	1.22	1.11	1.09	0.98	0.94	0.91
B	0.42	1.23	3.29	3.64	3.81	3.46	3.36	3.12	2.91	2.89
CCC	1.51	7.19	9.79	8.69	7.82	7.57	6.87	6.13	7.06	7.25

Source: Calculation on data from Tables 10.1 and 10.2.

ratings is linked with the public bond ratings, e.g., those used by Altman, Moody's or S&P in their cumulative default studies.

We will also show that these proxy risk measures, either from internal systems or from commercially available systems,[6] are critical ingredients in the compilation of historical correlations of risk and return measures between assets in the portfolio. The expected portfolio return (R_p) is therefore based on each asset's expected annual return, weighted by the proportion (X_i) of each loan/bond relative to the total portfolio, where

$$R_p = \sum_{i=1}^{N} X_i EAR_i \tag{2}$$

3.3 Portfolio Risk and Efficient Frontiers Using Returns

The classic mean return-variance portfolio framework is given in (3) when we utilize a short holding period, e.g., monthly or quarterly, and historical data exist for the requisite period to calculate correlation of returns among the loans/bonds

$$V_p = \sum_{i=1}^{N} \sum_{j=1}^{N} X_i X_j \sigma_i \sigma_j \rho_{ij} \tag{3}$$

---

[6] Such systems as ZETA Services (Hoboken, NJ) and KMV Corporation (San Francisco, CA) are available to assign ratings and expected defaults to all companies, whether or not they have public debt outstanding. See our earlier discussions of these models in Sections 2.2 and 2.3.

where V_p is the variance (risk) of the portfolio, X_i the proportion of the portfolio invested in bond issue i, σ_i the standard deviation of the return for the sample period for bond issue i, and ρ_{ij} the correlation coefficient of the quarterly returns for bonds i and j.

For example, if returns on all assets exist for 60 months or 20 quarters, then the correlations are meaningful and the classic efficient frontier can be calculated. Figure 10.1 shows an efficient frontier, i.e., maximization of expected return for given levels of risk or minimization of risk (variance of returns) for given levels of return, for a hypothetical high yield bond portfolio. The objective is to maximize the high yield portfolio ratio (HYPR) for given levels of risk or return. Note that an existing portfolio with a HYPR of 5.0 can be improved to 6.67 holding risk constant or to 10.0 holding return constant.

Figure 10.1 The HYPR approach for risk–return assessment

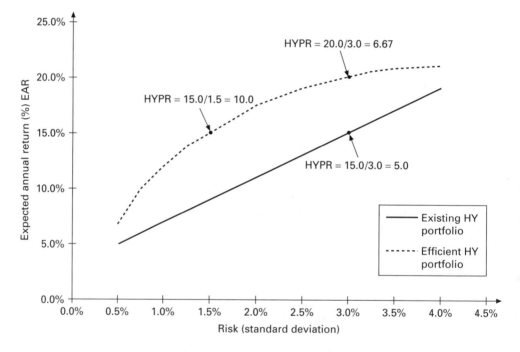

Our HYPR is a variation on the so-called Sharpe ratio, first introduced as a reward-to-variability ratio by Sharpe (1966), later popularized as the Sharpe Index or Sharpe ratio by many, e.g., Morningstar (1993), and finally generalized and expanded to cover a broader range of applications by Sharpe (1994). Most often applied to measuring the performance of equity mutual funds, this ratio captures the average differential return ($\bar{d}$) between a fund's return (R_F) and an appropriate benchmark (R_B) and the standard deviation (σ_d) of the differences over the period. As such, it captures the average differential return per unit of risk (standard deviation), assuming the appropriate risk measure is the variance of returns.

The only other applications of a version of the Sharpe ratio to fixed income asset portfolios and derivatives were proposed in unpublished manuscripts by McQuown

(1994) and Kealhofer (1996). They utilize a risk of default model developed by KMV (see section 2.3) which itself is based (indirectly) on the level, variability and correlations of the stock prices of the existing and potential companies in the portfolio. Our fixed income asset portfolio model has many similarities to that of McQuown, with the major difference being the measure of default risk in the model (see our earlier discussion of the Z and ZETA® risk measures and KMV's EDF approach).

We agree with McQuown and Kealhofer that the risk of any individual bond/loan as well as the entire portfolio itself is a measure that incorporates the *unexpected loss*. We will return to the concept of unexpected losses shortly.

Figure 10.2 shows an efficient frontier based on a potential portfolio of 10 high yield corporate bonds utilizing actual quarterly returns from the five-year period 1991–95. The efficient portfolio compared to the equally weighted one shows considerable improvement in the return-risk tradeoff. For example, the HYPR goes from about 0.67 (2.0/3.0) to 1.14 (2.0/1.75) for the same expected return and to 1.0 (3.0/3.0) for the same variance of return. Note also the link between the risk-free rate at about 1.5 percent per quarter and the tangent line to the efficient frontier, indicating various proportions of risky vs. risk-free fixed income assets. The efficient frontier, calculated without any constraint as to the number of issues in the portfolio, involved eight of the possible ten high yield bonds. And, when we constrain the model such that no issue can be greater than 15 percent of the portfolio, the actual number of issues was either seven or eight depending upon the different expected returns (shown later in table 10.5).

Figure 10.2 Efficient high yield bond portfolio, using quarterly returns (10 issues)

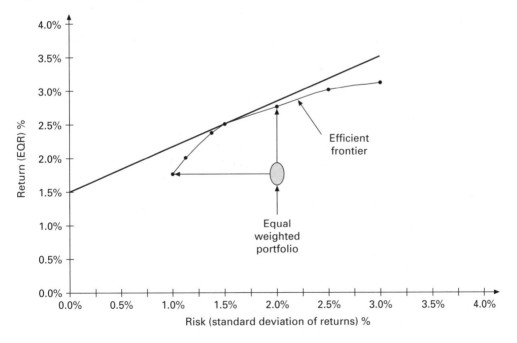

3.4 *Portfolio Risk and Efficient Frontiers Using an Alternative Risk Measure*

The reality of the bond and loan markets is that even if one was comfortable with the distribution qualities of returns, the need to analyze a reasonably large number of potential assets precludes the use of the classic mean-variance of return framework. Specifically, there simply is insufficient historical high yield bond return and loan return data to compute correlations. The same problem would be true if, instead of using return correlations, which can vary due to maturity differences between bonds, we utilized the correlation of the duration of each bond with other bonds and with the overall index of bonds to calculate

(i) the correlation between bonds and
(ii) the variance of the portfolio.

Other sample selection problems include the change in maturities of individual bonds over the measurement period and the exclusion of bonds that defaulted in the past.

We analyzed the potential to use returns or durations in the high yield corporate debt market and, out of almost 600 bond issues that existed as of year-end 1995, less than forty had 20 quarters of historical data. If we add to this scenario our other conceptual concerns, as indicated above, it is simply not appropriate (theoretically or empirically) to utilize the variance of return as the measure of the portfolio's risk.

An alternative risk measure, one that is critical to most bank and fixed income portfolio managers, is *unexpected loss* from defaults. Recall that we adjusted the promised yield for expected losses. Therefore, the risk is the downside in the event that the expected losses underestimate actual losses.[7] In addition, unexpected losses are the cornerstone measure in the determination of appropriate reserves against bank capital in the RAROC approach adopted by many banks.

Our suggested approach for determining unexpected losses is to utilize a variation of the Z-Score model, called the Z″-Score model (Altman, 1993) to assign a bond rating equivalent to each of the loans/bonds that could possibly enter the portfolio.[8] As noted earlier, these scores and rating equivalents can then be used to estimate expected losses over time. If we then observe the standard deviation around the expected losses, we have a procedure to estimate unexpected losses. For example, the expected loss on a BB rated equivalent 10 year bond is 91 basis points per year (table 10.3). The standard deviation around this expected value was computed to be 2.65 percent, or 265 basis points per year. The standard deviation is computed from the individual issuance years' (independent) observations that were used to calculate the cumulative mortality losses. For example, there are 24 one-year default losses, for bonds issued in a certain rating class, over the 1971–95 period, i.e., 1971 issued bonds defaulting in 1972, 1972 issued bonds defaulting in 1973, etc. In the same way, there are 23 two-year cumulative loss data points, 22 three-year loss observations, etc., up to 15 ten-year observations.

---

[7] This idea is similar to the use of the semi-variance measure of returns, whereby the analyst is concerned only with the return below the mean.

[8] The Z″-Score model is a four-variable version of the Z-Score approach. It was designed to reduce distortions in credit scores for firms in different industries. We have also found this model extremely effective in assessing the credit risk of corporate bonds in the emerging market arena (Altman et al., 1995).

As noted above, the model used here is the Z''-Score, risk rating model, indicated in eqn (4) with the bond rating equivalents shown in table 10.4.[9]

$$Z''\text{-Score} = 6.56(X_1) + 3.26(X_2) + 6.72(X_3) + 1.05(X_4) + 3.25 \tag{4}$$

where X_1 is the Working capital/Total assets, X_2 the Retained earnings/Total assets, X_3 the EBIT/Total assets and X_4 the Equity (book value)/Total liabilities.

Table 10.4   US bond rating equivalent, based on Z''-Score

US equivalent rating	Average Z''-Score	Sample size
AAA	8.15	8
AA+	7.60	–
AA	7.30	18
AA–	7.00	15
A+	6.85	24
A	6.65	42
A–	6.40	38
BBB+	6.25	38
BBB	5.85	59
BBB–	5.65	52
BB+	5.25	34
BB	4.95	25
BB–	4.75	65
B+	4.50	78
B	4.15	115
B–	3.75	95
CCC+	3.20	23
CCC	2.50	10
CCC–	1.75	6
D	0.00	14

Average based on over 750 US industrial corporates with rated debt outstanding; 1994 data.
Source: In-Depth Data Corporation.

3.5   *Portfolio Risk*

The formula for our portfolio risk measure is given by

$$UAL_p = \sum_{i=1}^{N}\sum_{j=1}^{N} X_i X_j \sigma_i \sigma_j \rho_{ij} \tag{5}$$

The measure UAL_p is the unexpected loss on the portfolio consisting of measures of individual asset unexpected losses (σ_i, σ_j) and the correlation (ρ_{ij}) of unexpected losses

---

[9]   To standardize our bond rating equivalent analysis, we add a constant term of 3.25 to the model; scores of zero (0) indicating a D (default) rating and positive scores indicating ratings above D. The actual bond rating equivalents are derived from a sample of over 750 US corporate bonds with average scores for each rating category.

over the sample measurement period. Again, these unexpected losses are based on the standard deviation of annual expected losses for the bond rating equivalents calculated at each quarterly interval.[10]

All that is necessary is that the issuing firm (or borrower) was operating for the entire sample period, e.g., five years, and had quarterly financial statements. The actual bonds/loans did not have to be outstanding in the period, as is necessary when returns and variance of returns are used. Since the actual debt issue may not have been outstanding during the entire measurement period, leverage measures will likely also vary over time. Still, we expect to capture most of the covariance of default risk between firms.

3.6 *Empirical Results*

We ran the portfolio optimizer program[11] on the same 10-bond portfolio analyzed earlier, this time using the Z''-Score bond rating equivalents and their associated expected and unexpected losses, instead of returns. Figure 10.3 shows the efficient frontier compared to an equal weighted portfolio. As we observed earlier, the efficient frontier indicates considerably improved HYPRs. For example, the return/risk ratio of just above 0.50 for the equal weighted 10-bond portfolio can be improved to 1.60 (2.00/1.25) at the 2.00 percent quarterly return level and to about 1.00 for the same risk (3.75 percent) level.

Table 10.5 shows the portfolio weights for the efficient frontier portfolio using both returns and risk (unexpected losses) when the individual weights are constrained at a maximum of 15 percent of the portfolio.[12] This is for the 1.75 percent quarterly expected return. Note that both portfolios utilize eight of the ten bonds and very similar weightings. Indeed, seven of the eight bonds appear in both portfolios. These results are comforting in that the unexpected loss derived from the Z''-Score is an alternative risk measure. Our small sample test results are encouraging and indicate that this type of portfolio approach is potentially quite feasible for fixed income assets. The important factor in our analysis is that credit risk management plays a critical role in the process.

We should note clearly that these are preliminary findings. Subsequent conceptual refinements and larger sample empirical tests are necessary to gain experience and confidence with this portfolio technique for fixed income assets (including loans).

---

[10] We do recognize that our measure of covariance is potentially biased in two ways. First, estimates of individual firms' debt unexpected losses are derived from empirical data on bonds from a given bond rating class and, as such, will probably understate the risk of loss from individual firm defaults. On the other hand, the covariance of default losses between two firms' debt is based on the joint probability of both defaulting at the same time. If the default decision of each firm is viewed as 0,1, i.e., as a binomial distribution, then the appropriate covariance or correlation should be calculated from a joint density function of two underlying binomial distributions. Our measure, however, assumes a normal density function for returns and thus returns are jointly, normally distributed for each firm which could result in a higher aggregate measure of portfolio risk. As such, the two biases neutralize each other to some extent although it is difficult to assess the relative magnitude of each.
[11] Using a double precision, linear constrained optimization program (DLCONG).
[12] The unconstrained weighting results yielded efficient portfolios of between five and eight individual bonds with some weightings of over 30 percent. These high weights would not be prudent for most portfolio managers.

Figure 10.3 Efficient high yield bond portfolio, using EMS scores, 10 issues

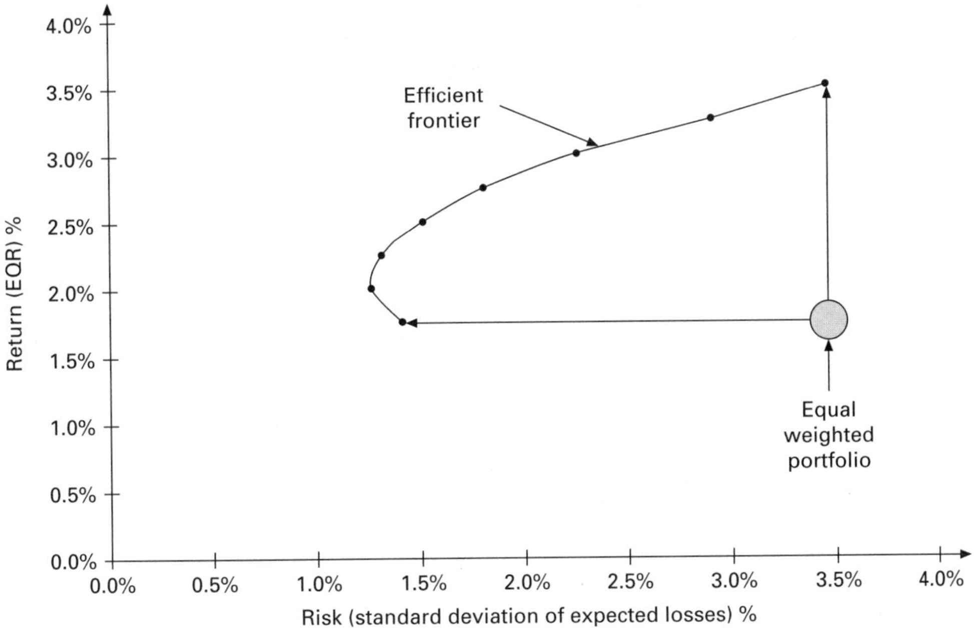

Table 10.5 Portfolio weights using two different measures of risk and return

Company ticker	Weights using Z"-Scores	Weights using returns (quarterly)
AS	0.0000	0.1065
BOR	0.0776	0.0000
CGP	0.1500	0.1500
CQB	0.1500	0.1500
FA	0.0000	0.0000
IMD	0.1500	0.1351
RHR	0.1500	0.1209
STO	0.1500	0.1500
USG	0.1500	0.1500
WS	0.0224	0.0376

Return = 1.75%, constrained to 15% maximum weights.

4 SUMMARY AND CONCLUSION

In this paper, we have sought to accomplish two objectives. In sections 1 and 2 we traced the development of credit risk measurement techniques over the past 20 years and showed how many of these developments have been mirrored in published articles in the JBF. In section 3, we developed a new approach to measuring the return risk tradeoff in portfolios of risky debt instruments, whether bonds or loans. In particular, we showed that this new approach added much promise to the complex problem of estimating the optimal composition of loan/bond portfolios.

Clearly, over the next 20 years, one can foresee significant improvements in data bases on historical default rates and loan returns. With the development of such data bases will come new and exciting approaches to measuring the ever present credit risk problems facing FI managers.

REFERENCES

Altman, E. I., 1968. Financial ratios discriminant analysis and the prediction of corporate bankruptcy. *Journal of Finance* 589–609.

Altman, E. I., 1988. *Default Risk, Mortality Rates, and the Performance of Corporate Bonds.* Research Foundation, Institute of Chartered Financial Analysts, Charlottesville, VA.

Altman, E. I., 1989. Measuring corporate bond mortality and performance. *Journal of Finance* September, 909–22.

Altman, E. I., 1992. Revisiting the high yield debt market. *Financial Management* Summer, 78–92.

Altman, E. I., 1993. *Corporate Financial Distress and Bankruptcy*, 2nd ed. Wiley, New York.

Altman, E. I., Haldeman, R., and Narayanan, P., 1977. Zeta analysis: A new model to identify bankruptcy risk of corporations. *Journal of Banking and Finance* 11, 29–54.

Altman, E. I., Hartzell, J., and Peck, M., 1995. *A Scoring System for Emerging Market Corporate Debt*. Salomon Brothers, 15 May.

Altman, E. I., and Kao, D. L., 1992. The implications of corporate bond rating drift. *Financial Analysts Journal* May/June, 64–75.

Altman, E. I., and Kishore, V., 1995. *Default and returns in the high yield debt market, 1991– 1995*, NYU Salomon Center Special Report.

Altman, E. I., and Kishore, V., 1997. *Default and returns in the high yield debt market, 1991– 1996*, NYU Salomon Center Special Report.

Altman, E. I., Marco, G., and Varetto, F., 1994. Corporate distress diagnosis: Comparisons using linear discriminant analysis and neural networks (The Italian Experience), *Journal of Banking and Finance* 18(3), 505–29.

Altman, E. I., and Narayanan, P., 1997. Business Failure Classification Models: An International Survey. In: Choi, F. (ed.), *International Accounting*, 2nd ed. Wiley, New York.

Asquith, P., Mullins Jr., D. W., and Wolff, E. D., 1989. Original issue high yield bonds: Aging analysis of defaults, exchanges and calls. *Journal of Finance* 44(4), 923–53.

Bennett, P., 1984. Applying portfolio theory to global bank lending. *Journal of Banking and Finance* 18(8), 153–69.

Black, F., and Scholes, M., 1973. The pricing of options and corporate liabilities. *Journal of Political Economy* 81, 637–59.

Brewer, E., and Koppenhaver, G. D., 1992. The impact of standby letters of credit on bank risk: A note. *Journal of Banking and Finance* 16(7), 1037–46.

Chirinko, R. S., and Guill, G. D., 1991. A framework for assessing credit risk in depository institutions: Toward regulatory reform. *Journal of Banking and Finance* 15, 785–804.

Coats, P., and Fant, L., 1993. Recognizing financial distress patterns using a neural network tool. *Financial Management* 22(3), 142–55.

Credit Metrics®, 1997. J. P. Morgan & Co., New York (April 3).

Elton, E., and Gruber, M., 1995. *Modern Portfolio Theory and Investment Analysis*, 5th ed. Wiley, New York.

Hull, J., and White, A., 1995. The impact of default risk on the prices of options and other derivative securities. *Journal of Banking and Finance* 19(2), 299–322.

Iben, T., and Litterman, R., 1989. Corporate bond valuation and the term structure of credit spreads. *Journal of Portfolio Management*, Spring, 52–64.

Izan, H. Y., 1984. Corporate distress in Australia. *Journal of Banking and Finance* 8(2), 303–20.

Jagtiani, J., Saunders, A., and Udell, G., 1995. The effect of bank capital requirements on bank off-balance sheet financing. *Journal of Banking and Finance* 19(4), 647–58.

Jonkhart, M., 1979. On the term structure of interest rates and the risk of default. *Journal of Banking and Finance* 3(3), 253–62.

Journal of Banking and Finance, 1984. Special Issue on "Company and Country Risk Models" 151–387.

Journal of Banking and Finance, 1988. Supplement Studies in Banking and Finance, "International Business Failure Prediction Models".

Kealhofer, S., 1996. Measuring Default Risk in Portfolios of Derivatives. Mimeo KMV Corporation, San Francisco, CA.

KMV Corporation, 1993. *Credit Monitor Overview*, San Francisco, Ca, USA.

Lawrence, E.L., Smith, S., and Rhoades, M., 1992. An analysis of default risk in mobile home credit. *Journal of Banking and Finance* 16(2), 299–312.

McAllister, P., and Mingo, J. J., 1994. Commercial loan risk management, credit-scoring and pricing: The need for a new shared data base. *Journal of Commercial Bank Lending* 76(9), 6–20.

McElravey, J. N., and Shah, V., 1996. *Rating Cash Flow Collateralized Bond Obligations*. Special Report, Asset Backed Securities, Duff and Phelps Credit Rating Co., Chicago, IL, USA.

McKinsey, 1993. Special report on "The new world of financial services" *The McKinsey Quarterly*, Number 2.

McQuown, J., 1994. *All that counts is diversification: In bank asset portfolio management*. IMI Bank Loan Portfolio Management Conference, May 11.

Markowitz, H., 1959. *Portfolio Selection: Efficient Diversification of Investments*, Wiley, New York.

Martin, D., 1977. Early warning of bank failure: A logit regression approach. *Journal of Banking and Finance* 13, 249–76.

Merton, R., 1974. On the pricing of corporate debt. *Journal of Finance* 29, 449–70.

Moody's Special Report, 1990. *Corporate Bond Defaults and Default Rates, 1970–1989*, April.

Morningstar Mutual Funds User's Guide, 1993. Chicago, Morningstar, Inc.

Platt, H. D., and Platt, M. B., 1991a. A note on the use of industry-relative ratios in bankruptcy prediction. *Journal of Banking and Finance* 15(7), 1183–94.

Platt, H. D., and Platt, M. B., 1991b. A linear programming approach to bond portfolio selection. *Economic Financial Computing*, Spring 71–84.

Santomero, A., and Vinso, J., 1977. Estimating the probability of failure for firms in the banking system. *Journal of Banking and Finance* 1(1), 185–206.

Saunders, A., 1997. *Financial Institutions Management: A Modern Perspective*, 2nd ed. Irwin, Homewood, IL.

Scott, J., 1981. The probability of bankruptcy: A comparison of empirical predictions and theoretical models. *Journal of Banking and Finance*, September, 317–44.

Sharpe, W., 1966. Mutual fund performance. *Journal of Business* January, 111–138.

Sharpe, W., 1994. The Sharpe Ratio. *Journal of Portfolio Management* Fall, 49–58.

Smith, L. D., and Lawrence, E., 1995. Forecasting losses on a liquidating long-term loan portfolio. *Journal of Banking and Finance* 19(6), 959–85.

Sommerville, R. A., and Taffler, R. J., 1995. Banker judgement versus formal forecasting models: The case of country risk assessment. *Journal of Banking and Finance* 17(2), 281–97.

Standard and Poor's, 1991. Corporate Bond Default Study. *Credit Week*, September 16.

Trippi, R., and Turban, E., 1996. *Neural Networks in Finance and Investing*, revised ed. Irwin, Homewood, IL.

West, R. C., 1985. A factor-analytic approach to bank condition. *Journal of Banking and Finance* 8(2), 253–66.

Wilcox, J. W., 1973. A Prediction of business failure using accounting data. *Journal of Accounting Research*, 11(2), 163–79.

11 | Measuring Corporate Bond Mortality and Performance

The recent emergence of the high-yield corporate debt market in the USA has intensified interest in the relation between expected yield spreads of bonds of various credit quality and expected losses from defaults. In addition to default risk, investors also consider the effects of the two other major risk dimensions of investing in fixed-interest instruments, i.e., interest rate risk and liquidity risk. The interaction among the three dimensions of risk has raised the analytic content of fixed-income assessment to an increasingly sophisticated level. The analysis of default risk, however, has probably been the area of most concern and empirical measurement over the years since the initial pioneering work by Hickman (1958).

The appropriate measure of default risk and the accuracy of its measurement are critical in the pricing of debt instruments, in the measurement of their performance, and in the assessment of market efficiency. Analysts have concentrated their efforts on measuring the default rate for finite periods of time – for example, one year – and then averaging the annual rates for longer periods. In almost all previous studies, the rate of default has been measured simply as the value of defaulting issues for some specific population of debt compared with the value of bonds outstanding that could have defaulted. Annual default rates are then usually compared with observed promised yield spreads in order to assess the attractiveness of particular bonds or classes of bonds. A corollary approach is to compare default rates with ex post returns to assess whether investors were compensated for the risks they bear.

This study seeks to explore further the notion of default risk by developing an alternative way of measuring that risk and utilizes this measure to assess the performance of fixed-income investment strategies over the entire spectrum of credit-quality classes. Our approach seeks to measure the expected mortality of bonds in a manner similar to that used by actuaries in assessing human mortality. Our use of the term mortality refers specifically to a life expectancy or survival rate for various periods of time after issuance. Although it is informative to measure default rates and losses based on the average annual rate method, that traditional technique has at least two deficiencies. It fails to consider that there are other ways in which a bond dies, namely redemptions from calls, sinking funds, and maturation. Therefore, it fails to consider the surviving population of bonds; nor does it answer the question of the probability of default for various time periods in the future on the basis of an issue's specific attributes at issuance, summarized into its bond rating. This study does explicitly consider the surviving population as the relevant basis or denominator in the default calculation and addresses the initial default assessment by the following questions. Given an issue's initial bond rating:

1 What is the estimated probability of default and loss from default over a specific time horizon of one year, two years, three years, or N years?
2 What are the estimates of the cumulative annual mortality rates and losses for various time frames as well as the marginal rates for specific one-year periods?
3 Given estimates of cumulative mortality losses suffered by investors and expected return spreads earned on the surviving population of bonds, what were the net return spreads earned or lost in comparison with returns on risk-free securities?

This paper is organized as follows. In section I we review prior studies in the default risk area. In section II we expand on traditional measures of default rates and losses. The new concept of mortality rates is then presented in section III, indicating what we believe to be a more comprehensive and meaningful measure. Section IV presents empirical results including new-issue volume by bond rating, adjusted mortality rates and losses, and, finally, net return spreads received by investors in different risk categories of bonds. The final section reviews the paper's implications.

I PRIOR STUDIES

Previous works in the area of default were of three general kinds. The first example, which might be called Hickman-style (1958) reports, usually presents statistics on annual default rates and actual returns to bond holders over various time frames.

A second kind of study emphasizes the default risk potential of individual-company debt by examining the determinants of risk premiums over risk-free securities, e.g., Fisher (1959), or by constructing univariate (Beaver, 1966) or multivariate classification models (Altman (1968) and others) based on the combination of micro-finance measures and statistical classification techniques. Variants on those models were based on the gambler's ruin concept (Wilcox, 1971), recursive partitioning techniques (Frydman et al., 1985), and market indicators of survival (Queen and Roll, 1987). The latter study is particularly relevant because it emphasizes the distinction between favorable and unfavorable disappearance. Our measure of mortality of bonds has similar qualities in that we adjust the population for various kinds of redemptions.

Finally, a study by Fons (1987) attempts to combine observed pricing and the inherent default risk premium with estimates of corporate bond default experience. He incorporates default experience measured by Altman and Nammacher (1985, 1987) and others with a risk-neutral investment strategy – that is, where the only factor that matters is the return distribution of debt with no relevance for volatility or liquidity factors. Fons did not believe, however, that default rates on particular bond-rating classes could be meaningfully addressed because the ratings are not permanent designations. Yet, it does appear to be relevant to measure losses to investors by original investment in specific bond-rating categories.

II TRADITIONAL MEASURES OF DEFAULT RATES AND LOSSES

The corporate debt market has pretty much accepted the distinction between the so-called investment-grade and non-investment-grade categories. At the same time, bonds receive more precise ratings, with four classes of investment-grade debt and essentially three classes of lower quality junk bonds. Despite the finer distinctions, all published analytical works concentrate on either the entire corporate-bond universe or just the high-yield, non-investment-grade sector. Default rates are calculated on an average annual basis, with individual rates for each year combined with rates for other years, over some longer time horizon to form the estimate for the average annual rate.[1] Our own results show that the average annual default rate, measured in the traditional way, for the period 1978–87 was 1.86 percent per year. See Altman (1989) for the complete year-by-year results.

A Default Losses

The more relevant default statistic for investors is not the rate of default but the amount lost from defaults.[2] Altman and Nammacher (1987) measured the amount lost from defaults by tracking the price for the defaulting issue just after default and assuming that the investor had purchased the issue at par value and sold the issue just after default. The investor also is assumed to lose one coupon payment. The average annual default loss over the sample period has been approximately 1.2 percent per year. That lower percentage of loss compared with default rates stems from the fact that defaulting debt, on average, sells for approximately 40 percent of par at the end of the defaulting month.

III THE MORTALITY RATE CONCEPT

We retain the notion that default rates for individual periods – yearly, for example – are measured on the basis of defaults in the period in relation to some base population in that same period. The calculation, however, becomes more complex when we begin with a specific cohort group such as a bond-rating category and track that group's

---

[1] The rate for each year is based on the dollar amount of defaulting issues in that year divided by the total population outstanding as of some point during that year.

[2] An additional item of importance is the amount lost not just from defaults but also from other crisis situations, such as distressed exchange issues. Fridson et al. (1988) did look at the loss on distressed exchange issues as well as losses from defaults and found that the overall average annual loss for the period 1978–87 was 1.88 percent. Their base and reference population was only original-issue high-yield debt.

performance for multiple time periods. Because the original population can change over time as a result of a number of different events, we consider mortalities in relation to a survival population and then input the defaults to calculate mortality rates. Bonds can exit from the original population by means of at least four different events: defaults, calls, sinking funds, and maturities.

The individual mortality rate for each year (marginal mortality rate = MMR) is calculated by

$$\text{MMR}_{(t)} = \frac{\text{total value of defaulting debt in the year}\,(t)}{\text{total value of the population of bonds at the start of the year}\,(t)}$$

We then measure the cumulative mortality rate (CMR) over a specific time period $(1, 2, \ldots, T$ years) by subtracting the product of the surviving populations of each of the previous years from one (1.0), that is,

$$\text{CMR}_{(T)} = 1 - \prod_{t=1}^{T} \text{SR}_t$$

where

$$\text{CMR}_{(T)} = \text{cumulative mortality rate in } (T)$$
$$\text{SR}_{(t)} = \text{survival rate in } (t);\ 1 - \text{MMR}_{(t)}$$

The individual year marginal mortality rates for each bond rating are based on a compilation of that year's mortality measured from issuance. For example, all of the one-year mortalities are combined for the seventeen-year sample period to arrive at the one-year rate; all of the second-year mortalities are combined to get the two-year rate, etc.

The mortality rate is a value-weighted rate for the particular year after issuance, rather than an unweighted average. If we were simply to average each of the year-one rates, year-two rates, etc., our results would be susceptible to significant specific-year bias. If, for example, the amount of new issues is very small and the defaults emanating from that year are high in relation to the amount issued, the unweighted average could be improperly affected. Our weighted-average technique correctly biases the results toward the larger-issue years, especially the more recent years.

IV EMPIRICAL RESULTS

Table 11.1 lists the dollar amount, by bond rating, issued for the period 1971–86 according to statistics complied from *Standard & Poor's Bond Guide*. Note that investment-grade categories dominated new listings over much of the sample period. During the 1971–81 period, the below-investment-grade sector showed small, relatively consistent BB-rated issues ranging from a low of $20 million in 1975 to a high of $579 million in 1977. Since 1982, however, BB new issues exceeded $1 billion each year. Single-B debt had small, sporadic new issues from 1971 to 1976. Since 1977, volume has picked up, with more than $500 million issued in 1977, more than $1 billion issued in

Table 11.1 Corporate bond total new issue amounts by S&P bond rating, 1971–86 ($ million)

Bond rating	1971	1972	1973	1974	1975	1976	1977	1978	1979	1980	1981	1982	1983	1984	1985	1986
AAA	5,125	3,179	4,046	7,420	11,348	9,907	11,046	7,967	10,400	10,109	11,835	6,197	3,920	2,350	9,016	14,438
AA	5,467	4,332	3,670	8,797	9,654	9,560	7,494	7,374	5,910	10,497	11,748	14,597	14,110	18,291	23,223	46,978
A	6,688	4,745	4,254	8,388	12,752	8,103	5,236	5,330	6,489	12,195	12,432	13,315	5,516	12,252	23,381	34,173
BBB	2,139	1,198	937	1,248	2,367	2,938	1,558	1,513	1,225	2,595	3,900	5,738	5,827	5,194	11,068	21,993
BB	292	258	105	250	20	397	579	408	359	418	290	1,378	2,894	4,698	2,041	7,098
						(10)	(15)	(10)	(8)	(9)	(6)	(16)	(24)	(23)	(23)	(37)
B	112	101	140	18	27	59	526	1,029	917	879	894	1,122	3,713	6,485	5,945	21,260
						(3)	(17)	(39)	(33)	(28)	(15)	(24)	(46)	(68)	(77)	(133)
CCC	0	0	0	0	14	75	78	34	91	25	0	145	285	1,901	1,668	4,668
						(1)	(5)	(1)	(3)	(1)	(0)	(2)	(5)	(9)	(14)	(40)
Total rated	19,823	13,813	13,152	26,121	36,182	31,039	26,517	23,655	25,391	36,718	41,099	42,492	36,205	51,171	76,342	150,608

Number of issues of low-rated bonds are in parentheses. Data are from S&P's Bond Guides, Annual and Monthly.

1978, more than $6 billion in 1984–85, and over $21 billion in 1986.[3] The number of issues in each year is also indicated for the junk bond sector (lower three categories of ratings) since 1977, showing its impressive growth.

A Mortality Rates

The data in table 11.2 show our mortality rate computations, adjusted for redemptions and defaults, for the entire period 1971–87. The data include individual year and cumulative mortalities for up to ten years after issuance. It is possible to list the data for beyond ten years, but the number of observations obviously diminishes as the number of years after issuance increases.

The relative results across cohort groups are pretty much in line with expectations, with the mortality rates very low for the higher-rated bonds and increasing for lower rated issues. For example, AAA-rated debt had a zero mortality rate for the first five years after issuance and then only 0.13 percent from six to ten years (due to Texaco's 1987 bond default). AA-rated and A-rated debt mortalities reached just 2.46 percent and 0.93 percent, respectively, over a ten-year period. The mortality rates for BBB and lower bonds begin to increase almost immediately after issuance, with BBB (the lowest

Table 11.2 Adjusted mortality rates by original S&P bond rating covering defaults and issues (1971–87)

	Years after issuance									
Original rating	1	2	3	4	5	6	7	8	9	10
AAA										
Yearly	0.00%	0.00%	0.00%	0.00%	0.00%	0.13%	0.00%	0.00%	0.00%	0.00%
Cumulative	0.00%	0.00%	0.00%	0.00%	0.00%	0.13%	0.13%	0.13%	0.13%	0.13%
AA										
Yearly	0.00%	0.00%	1.81%	0.39%	0.14%	0.00%	0.00%	0.00%	0.13%	0.00%
Cumulative	0.00%	0.00%	1.81%	2.20%	2.33%	2.33%	2.33%	2.33%	2.46%	2.46%
A										
Yearly	0.00%	0.31%	0.39%	0.00%	0.00%	0.06%	0.12%	0.00%	0.04%	0.00%
Cumulative	0.00%	0.31%	0.71%	0.71%	0.71%	0.77%	0.89%	0.89%	0.93%	0.93%
BBB										
Yearly	0.04%	0.25%	0.17%	0.00%	0.45%	0.00%	0.17%	0.00%	0.23%	0.84%
Cumulative	0.04%	0.29%	0.46%	0.46%	0.91%	0.91%	1.07%	1.07%	1.30%	2.12%
BB										
Yearly	0.00%	0.62%	0.64%	0.31%	0.29%	4.88%	0.00%	0.00%	0.00%	0.00%
Cumulative	0.00%	0.62%	1.25%	1.56%	1.84%	6.64%	6.64%	6.64%	6.64%	6.64%
B										
Yearly	1.98%	0.92%	0.74%	4.24%	4.16%	4.98%	3.62%	4.03%	8.47%	4.33%
Cumulative	1.98%	2.88%	3.60%	7.69%	11.53%	15.94%	18.98%	22.24%	28.83%	31.91%
CCC										
Yearly	2.99%	2.88%	3.97%	22.87%	1.37%	N/A	N/A	N/A	N/A	N/A
Cumulative	2.99%	5.78%	9.52%	30.22%	31.17%	N/A	N/A	N/A	N/A	N/A

Mortality rates are adjusted for defaults and redemptions. Data were derived from S&P's Bond Guide.

---

[3] Nonrated debt is not included in our formal analysis because the risk nature of those issues appears to have shifted over the years, with the most recent data probably dominated by low-rated equivalent securities. The earlier nonrated debt data appear to have included all risk types.

investment-grade debt level) showing a cumulative rate of 0.91 percent after five years and 2.12 percent after ten years.

The single-B mortality rates were relatively high throughout the period, particularly in the later years. The marginal mortality rates are fairly constant after year three. The single-B-rated debt, however, had relatively small issue amounts throughout the 1970s, and, when we calculate mortality rates for seven to ten years after issuance, the number of observations is quite small. For example, years 1971–77 are the only years contributing to our ten-year results, 1971–78 to nine-year results, and so on. Hence, we emphasize that the longer term mortality results should be analyzed with considerable caution with respect to expectations about future mortality rates and return spreads.[4] Despite the high cumulative mortality rate, we will show that the net return to investors in B-rated bonds remains very attractive.

The results for five years after issuance do provide more observations, but they took lack results for new issues in the most recent, high-growth years (1982–87). The five-year cumulative rate of 11.5 percent for B-rated debt might also be considered to be surprisingly high, but is it really? Consider that the average annual default rate calculated in the traditional way is 1.86 percent per year for the period 1978–87. If we simply sum the one-year rates, the result is 9.30 percent for five years compared with our CMR of 11.5 percent. In addition, the traditional default rates are calculated on the basis of the population on June 30, while our mortality rates use survival population data from the start of each year. Therefore, the "old" way probably understates default rates somewhat. As for the six- to ten-year results, only time will tell if the relatively large marginal one-year rates, especially for the ninth year, continue in the future.[5]

Since we adjust the population for all redemptions as well as defaults, the mortality rates listed in table 11.2 will be higher than if the population data were unadjusted. For example, the B-rated cumulative mortality rate, unadjusted for redemptions, was 27.4 percent for ten years. I believe that both the adjusted and unadjusted methods of calculating the results are meaningful. The mortality figures over time should adjust for changing population size, while the unadjusted data could be helpful in examining the probability of default of a particular rating category from a given year's issuance. Strictly speaking, however, the unadjusted figures are not "rates." For a more in-depth discussion of this and a presentation of the entire unadjusted default amounts, see Altman (1989).

B Losses

As in the previous discussion on traditional measurements of default, the loss to investors from defaults is of paramount importance. In our ensuing analysis of net return

---

[4] In addition, the later year results could be biased since a portion of the original population of bonds will be redeemed by then. If more creditworthy firms tended to be called earlier than more risky ones, then the later year mortality rates would be biased upward. Our results, however, did not show a great deal of difference when we did not exclude redemptions. (Results without redemptions are available from the author.)

[5] If we begin our analysis in 1976, rather than in 1971, the five-year B-rated cumulative rate is slightly higher at 11.7 percent; the eight-year rate is 23.7 percent; and the ten-year rate is 36.4 percent. The latter is due to the relatively high nine- and ten-year defaults of 1977 new issues ($85.5 million and $26.7 million, respectively, from the $526 million issued).

spreads for each category of bond rating, we use the actual recovery amount for which investors were able to sell the defaulting issue and also assume that one coupon payment was lost. The average recovery rate was slightly below 40 percent of par.

We did look at the relation between individual bond ratings at issuance and the subsequent average price that could be realized upon default and found essentially that no relationship existed. Table 11.3 lists those results and shows that the average retention rate was actually 44.6 percent including Texaco (39.2 percent without Texaco). Note that there is virtually no correlation between initial bond rating and average price after default.

There also does not appear to be a correlation between the price after default and the number of years that a bond is in existence before default (table 11.4). Therefore, while the marginal default rate is relatively low in the first three years after issuance (table 11.2), the recovery rate is unaffected by the age of the issue.

Table 11.3 Average price after default by original bond rating (1971–87)

Original rating	Average price after default (per $100)	Number of observations
AAA	78.67	5
AA	79.29	13
A	45.90	19
BBB	45.30	22
BB	35.71	13
B	42.56	64
CCC	41.15	12
C	10.00	2
NR	31.18	23
Arithmetic average or total	44.58	173

Data are from S&P Bond Guides, 1971–87.

Table 11.4 Average price after default by number of years after issuance (1971–87)

Number of years after issuance	Average price after default (per $100)	Number of observations
<1	45.41	10
1–2	44.74	19
2–3	63.43	27
3–4	38.97	18
4–5	41.70	17
5–6	50.46	15
6–7	43.50	11
7–8	37.17	6
8–9	28.33	6
9–10	43.52	7
>10	44.45	34

Data are from S&P Bond Guides, 1971–87.

C   Net Return Performance

An important dimension to our analysis is the ability to track performance of bonds from issuance, across bond ratings and over relevant time horizons. This analysis enables us to compare the performance of various risky bond categories with default risk-free US Treasury securities. By factoring into the analysis *actual* losses from defaults and yield spreads over Treasuries, a more complete analysis results. We calculate actual return-spread performance, but the algorithm used is sufficiently robust to handle any set of assumptions on the variables analyzed.

Table 11.5 and figure 11.1 present the return spread results across bond ratings over the sample period 1971–87. The spreads, expressed in terms of basis points compounded over a ten-year investment horizon, are based on actual yield spreads (table 11.6) for the 18-year period. The average yield spreads were 0.47 percent (AAA), 0.81 percent (AA), 1.08 percent (A), 1.77 percent (BBB), 3.05 percent (BB), 4.09 percent (B), and 7.07 percent (CCC).[6]

The body of table 11.5 represents returns realized above what would have been earned on risk-free Treasuries, measured in basis points. Table 11.5 uses actual long-term Treasury coupon rates, yield spreads at birth for the different rating categories, the sale of defaulted debt, the loss of one coupon payment, and the reinvestment of cash flows at the then prevailing interest rates for that boundrating group. Cash flows are reinvested from coupon payments on the surviving population as well as the reinvestment of sinking funds, calls, and the recovery from defaulted debt. The results assume no capital gains or losses over the measurement period, and the investor follows a buy-and-hold strategy for the various horizons.

Table 11.5   Return spreads earned by corporate bonds over Treasury bonds (measured in basis points (bp) compounded over time)

Years after issuance	Bond rating at issuance						
	AAA	AA	A	BBB	BB	B	CCC
1	45	76	104	171	326	382	519
2	100	168	223	366	684	861	1,174
3	165	243	367	609	1,129	1,460	2,062
4	246	359	556	923	1,710	1,746	496
5	344	515	782	1,250	2,419	2,160	1,561
6	457	710	1,047	1,700	2,648	2,676	NA
7	598	949	1,366	2,286	3,585	3,365	NA
8	772	1,246	1,778	2,911	4,725	4,058	NA
9	987	1,591	2,278	3,721	6,073	3,673	NA
10	1,245	2,028	2,885	4,577	7,637	4,467	NA

Return spreads are based on compound returns net of losses incurred from defaults. They reflect actual mortality rates and reinvestment rates derived from S&P's Bond Guide *and a number of securities firms.*

[6]   In an earlier version of this paper (Altman, 1988), we assumed yield spreads of 0.50, 1.0, 1.5, 2.0, 3.0, 4.0, and 5.0 percent for AAA, AA, A, etc., respectively. Except for the CCC rate, the actual average yield spreads (table 11.6) are quite similar to these assumptions.

Figure 11.1 Realized return spreads on net investment in corporate bonds over risk-free governments

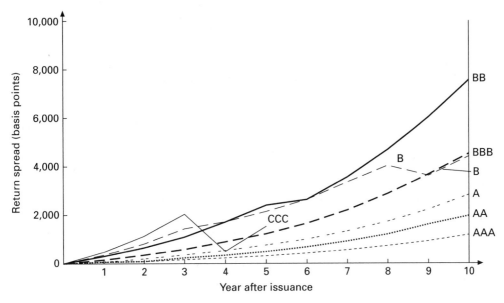

Return spreads are based on compounding cash flows received from coupon payments, redemptions, and default recoveries. Cash flows were reinvested in the same bond-rating class at prevailing interest rates at that time. Data points are from table 11.5.

Table 11.6 Yield to maturity on various bond rating categories: 1973–87 (yield is the average for the twelve monthly rates)

Year	Treasury Bond	AAA	AA	A	BBB	BB	B	CCC
1973	7.15	7.56	7.71	7.87	8.40	NR*	NR	NR
1974	8.13	8.33	8.56	8.65	9.37	NR	NR	NR
1975	8.28	8.64	8.89	9.31	10.12	NR	NR	NR
1976	7.88	8.36	8.37	8.81	9.45	NR	NR	NR
1977	7.76	8.12	8.34	8.48	8.87	NR	NR	NR
1978	8.57	8.74	8.93	9.05	9.53	NR	NR	NR
1979	9.27	9.53	9.80	10.01	10.62	11.66	13.16	NR
1980	11.22	11.66	12.02	12.31	13.09	14.15	14.98	NR
1981	13.20	13.91	14.32	14.60	15.50	16.54	17.33	NR
1982	12.51	13.32	13.73	14.19	15.45	16.32	17.76	21.86
1983	11.09	11.66	11.86	12.17	12.79	13.63	14.61	18.62
1984	12.34	12.43	12.94	13.25	13.97	14.99	15.53	17.71
1985	10.74	10.94	11.41	11.66	12.16	13.65	14.52	16.75
1986	8.16	9.02	9.40	9.64	10.19	11.79	12.82	15.98
1987	8.76	9.32	9.66	9.92	10.42	11.46	12.96	16.12

* NR = not relevant due to small samples and unreliable data.
Data are from S&P's Bond Guide supplemented by data from a number of securities industry firms, including Shearson Lehman for Treasury bonds and Drexel Burnham Lambert, Merrill Lynch, and Salomon Brothers for high-yield bonds.

Results show that AAA-rated bonds can be expected to earn 45 basis points (0.45 percent) *more* than Treasuries over one year (two semiannual coupon payments) and 1245 basis points after ten years. BB-rated bonds earn 326 basis points more than Treasuries after one year and an impressive 7637 basis points after ten years. Another way to put this is that an investment of $100 would return $76.37 more than Treasuries over ten years.

Of interest is that, for the first three years after issuance, the lower the bond rating the higher the net return spread, with triple-C- and single-B-rated bonds doing best. In the fourth year, the B-rated bonds do best as the CCC's drop off. After the fourth year, however, the BB-rated category begins to dominate (except in the sixth year) while the B-rated bonds lose ground. That crossover is illustrated in figure 11.1. For all holding periods, all bond types do well and have positive spreads over Treasuries.

As indicated, the historical average 4.09 percent yield spread for B-rated debt provides an ample cushion to compensate for losses, but the performance relative to the BB-rated category is inferior in the later years. This changes, however, if we adjust our initial yield spread assumptions to reflect different market conditions, assuming the same default experience. For example, in the period October 1987 to early 1988, yield spreads on single-B rated bonds jumped to over 5.5 percent. Under this assumption, the resulting net return spreads over Treasuries are higher for the lower rated bonds, with B-rated debt dominating all others for the entire ten-year time frame. (These results are available from the author.)

V IMPLICATIONS

The results indicate the expected adjusted mortality rates and losses, cumulated for a number of years after issuance, for all bond-rating categories. Despite somewhat higher than expected cumulative mortality rates over long holding periods, return spreads on all corporate bonds are positive, with impressive results for the high-yield, low-grade categories. If the analyst wishes to use higher (or lower) than historical mortality rates to reflect a number of macro- and microeconomic uncertainties or different yield spread assumptions, that is certainly feasible.

Why do we observe such relatively consistent positive return spreads for all rating categories? The results show that investors have been more than satisfactorily compensated for investing in high-risk securities. Indeed, if expected default losses are fully discounted in the prices (and yields) of securities, our return spread results should be insignificantly different from zero. The fact that the spreads are so positive has a number of possible explanations, none of them easily corroborated.

One possible explanation is that the fixed-income market has been mispricing corporate debt issues and the discrepancy has persisted, perhaps because of the lack of appropriate information. That implies market inefficiency. If default losses are consistently lower than yield spreads and this comparison is the only relevant determinant of future yield spreads, inefficiency is a reasonable conclusion.

If all other things are not equal, however, for determining yield spreads on corporate bonds, then the market inefficiency conclusion is difficult to reach. For example, liquidity risk is often mentioned as important to price determination. If liquidity risk increases with lower bond ratings, then the excess returns noted earlier may in part be the returns necessary to bear this risk. Indeed, during the post-October 19, 1987 period, poor liquidity was cited as one cause of the precipitous drop in common stock prices and the rise in yields of certain high-yield debt issues.

The other risk element that is not isolated in our study is interest rate or reinvestment risk. Actual returns on bonds are obviously affected by interest rate changes. Our results include actual reinvestment rates over time, and we have not factored in any capital gains or losses, assuming a buy-and-hold strategy for investors. Blume and Keim (1987) and Altman and Nammacher (1985) have shown, however, that, if anything, lower grade bonds have lower volatility from interest rate changes than risk-free, lower coupon Treasuries.

Another explanation of the persistent positive return spreads attributed to lower-rated bonds is the variability of retention values after default. Our observation of a recovery rate of an average of about 40 percent of par value just after default is an expected value. Investors might require positive spreads based on the possibility that retention values will be below the 40 percent average. In addition, the 40 percent retention is relevant only for a portfolio of defaulting bonds. An investor may not be well diversified and may be vulnerable to higher than average mortality losses on specific issues. Therefore, if the market prices low-quality issues as individual investments and not as portfolios, required spreads are likely to be higher than is perhaps necessary. On the other hand, if defaults are correlated with market returns, risks may not be as diversifiable as we assume to be the case for equities.

Investors might also be restricted in relation to the risk class of possible investments, thereby creating an artificial barrier to supply–demand equilibrium. For instance, certain institutions are prohibited from investing in low-grade bonds or are limited in the amount that they can invest in such securities. That reduces demand and inflates yield and possibly return spreads.

REFERENCES

Altman, Edward I., 1968, Financial ratios, discriminant analysis and the prediction of corporate bankruptcy, *Journal of Finance* 23, 589–609.
——, 1988, Measuring corporate bond mortality and performance, Working Paper, New York University, February.
——, 1989, *Default Risk, Mortality Rates and the Performance of Corporate Bonds: 1970–1988* (Foundation for Research of the Institute for Chartered Financial Analysts, Charlottesville, VA).
—— and Scott A. Nammacher, 1985, The default rate experience on high yield corporate debt, Morgan Stanley & Co., Inc. (March) and *Financial Analysts Journal* 41, July–August, 12–25.
—— and Scott A. Nammacher, 1987, *Investing in Junk Bonds: Inside the High Yield Debt Market* (John Wiley, New York).
Beaver, William, 1966, Financial ratios as predictors of failure, *Empirical Research in Accounting*, selected studies, supplement to the *Journal of Accounting Research* 4, 71–111.
Blume, Marshall E. and Donald B. Keim, 1987, Risk and return characteristics of lower grade bonds, *Financial Analysts Journal* 43, July–August, 26–33.
Fisher, Lawrence, 1959, Determinants of risk premiums on corporate bonds, *Journal of Political Economy* 67, 217–37.
Fons, Jerome S., 1987, The default premium and corporate bond experience, *Journal of Finance* 42, 81–97.
Fridson, Martin S., Fritz Wahl, and Steven B. Jones, 1988, New techniques for analyzing default risk, *High Performance* January, 4–11.

Frydman, Halina, Edward I. Altman, and Duen-Li Kao, 1985, Introducing recursive partitioning analysis to financial analysis: The case of financial distress classification, *Journal of Finance* 40, 269–91.

Hickman, W. Braddock, 1958, *Corporate Bond Quality and Investor Experience* (Princeton University Press, Princeton, NJ and the National Bureau of Economic Research, New York).

Queen, Maggie and Richard Roll, 1987, Firm mortality: Using market indicators to predict survival, *Financial Analysts Journal* 43, May–June, 9–26.

Wilcox, Jerrod W., 1971, A gamblers ruin prediction of business failure using accounting data, *Sloan Management Review* 12, 1–10.

12 | Default Rates in the Syndicated Bank Loan Market: A Mortality Analysis

with Heather J. Suggitt

1 INTRODUCTION: THE IMPORTANCE OF DEFAULT RATES

Credit risk management is perhaps the next great challenge in risk management for financial institutions. We have observed (Altman et al., 1998; Caouette et al., 1998) that despite benign default conditions in many economies of the world in recent years, the financial community has promoted credit risk management to center stage in their efforts to understand, and even profit from, credit events and products. Several large financial institutions have developed elaborate models of stand-alone and portfolio analysis of credit instruments, primarily corporate bonds and loans, to promote efficient management and the trading of these assets and their derivatives.[1] This trend, combined with the obvious current importance of credit risk in Asia and Latin America, accounts for its global concern.

The most fundamental aspect of credit risk models is the rating of the underlying credit asset and the associated expected and unexpected risk migration patterns. The concept of rating drift, or migration,[2] encompasses the change in credit quality in any direction from some initial state. The most important and costly negative migration is to default. This is certainly true for a buy and hold strategy but also for the trading of credit assets or their derivatives. Combined with recoveries on defaulted assets, default rate estimates permit the investor to quantify the expected loss from the individual

---

[1] For example, J. P. Morgan's CreditMetrics® (1997), Credit Suisse Financial Product's CreditRisk+® (1997), and McKinsey and Company's Creditview® (1997) have attempted to integrate large, complex data bases with theoretical and empirical strategies that involve models to motivate the trading of corporate loans and other credit assets. And, the International Swaps and Derivatives Association (1998) has commented on the relationship between regulatory capital and credit risk.

[2] See Altman and Kao (1991, 1992), Lucas and Lonski (1992); Carty and Lieberman (1997a) and S&P (1998) for estimates of rating drift and their implications. Caouette et al. (1998) summarize and compare these studies.

assets and the entire portfolio. (The latter focus also requires estimates of correlations among credit assets). Finally, volatility estimates of default rates and recoveries can provide information for the assessment of unexpected losses.

2   PRIOR DEFAULT RATE ANALYSIS

Most of the prior empirical work on corporate defaults has concentrated on publicly traded bonds. From Hickman's (1958) original analysis, to Altman and Nammacher's (1985, 1987) junk bond studies, to Altman (1989) and Asquith et al.'s (1989) mortality or aging analysis, to the rating agencies (Moody's, 1991–1998[3] and Standard & Poor's, 1992–1998)[4] analyses and to Altman & Kishore's (1991–1998) updates, the data have tracked annual default rates as well as cumulative rates on those bonds that received ratings from the agencies. The necessary ingredients of published credit ratings and historically observable, comprehensive and verifiable default data have enabled analysts to assess the risk of default on corporate bonds with a reasonable amount of precision.

The Society of Actuaries (1996) has examined default and recovery rates on insurance company private placements investments and Carey (1998) estimated default, loss severity, and average loss rates for a sample of privately placed bonds held by 13 insurance companies over the period 1986–92. The vast majority were obligations of US corporations and his sample covered about 25 percent of all private placements. His estimates, to which we will return, were essentially one-year default and loss rates, and comparisons were made with one-year default rates of publicly issued corporate bonds.

3   THE DEFAULT DATA GAP

A major credit asset class that has heretofore remained unanalyzed with respect to default rates is commercial bank loans. The domestic US market for commercial and industrial bank loans is approximately $1 trillion. Although most banks still practice the traditional "buy and hold" investment strategy for loans, increasingly we find loans being traded like securities. Therefore, not only do bank credit analysts and loan underwriters need information on expected defaults, but the emergence of loans as tradable, securitizable and hedgeable underlying assets has motivated the search for more precise estimates of risk.

The major stumbling block for measuring default risk on various levels of loan credit quality is the "private" nature of the market. The two primary ingredients for measuring default risk (ratings and known defaults) are far more difficult to assemble for this market than is the case for publicly traded rated bonds. Even individual banks will have problems assembling relevant default statistics since their current internal rating systems are probably quite new, having been revised over the years. Since loan portfolios vary from bank to bank, even if a few banks have reasonable default data and consistent rating systems, it would be inappropriate to generalize these results for the entire market – if the banks were willing to share their data.

---

[3]   See, for example, Moody's (1998a) cohort group study.
[4]   S&P periodically updates their static pool analysis; see, for example, their January 1998 report.

4 DEFAULT RECOVERIES

The highly aggregated nature of loan default rate or charge-off data reflects the difficulty of estimating rates both in terms of precise credit ratings and the timing, or aging effect. Instead, research in the bank loan default market has been restricted, up to now, to the *default recovery* component of the default risk measure (see table 12.1 for results from several loan recovery studies). Carty and Lieberman (1996) of Moody's measured the recovery rate on a small sample (58) of bank loans. Based on the secondary market prices for defaulted syndicated senior-secured bank loans, the average recovery rate was 71 percent of face value. In the same study, a larger sample (229) of mostly small and medium-sized loans experienced an average recovery rate of 79 percent, based on a present value of cash flows methodology.

Table 12.1 Default recovery rates on public bonds and private bank loans by seniority (percent of face value)

Seniority	Moody's (1986–97)[a]			Altman (1978–97) and others		
	No.	Mean (%)	Standard deviation (%)	No.	Mean (%)	Standard deviation (%)
Sr. secured loans (PV based)	178[c]	87	23	831[d]	65.31	–
Sr. unsecured loans (PV based)	19[c]	79	27			
Sr. secured and unsecured loans (price based)	98[c]	70	21	60[e]	82.00	–
Sr. secured public bonds	57[a]	63.45	26.21	93[b]	58.67	23.00
Sr. unsecured public bonds	156[a]	47.54	26.29	237[b]	48.87	26.62
Sr. sub. public bonds	166[a]	38.28	24.74	192[b]	34.99	24.97
Subordinated public bonds	119[a]	28.29	20.09	219[b]	31.71	22.53
Jr. (Disc) sub. public bonds	8[a]	14.66	8.67	36[b]	20.71	17.64
All public bonds	506[a]	41.25	26.55	777[b]	40.55	25.87

[a] *Carty and Lieberman (1997b).*
[b] *Altman and Kishore (1998).*
[c] *Carty et al. (1998).*
[d] *Asarnow and Edwards (1995) (senior secured and unsecured loans).*
[e] *Grossman et al. (1997), Absolute, not present value, prices.*

In their most recent update, Moody's (1998b) concluded that the overall recovery rate on bankrupt bank loans averaged 87 percent on senior secured loans (178 loans) and 79 percent for senior unsecured loans (19 loans). These recoveries are measured by the present value, as of the bankruptcy date, of actual payouts associated with the resolution of the bankruptcy as a percentage of the principal and interest due as of the filing date. They use the contractual lending rate as the discount rate. Average recovery rates varied by type of bankruptcy (prepackaged vs. regular) and by collateral type. Regular Chapter 11 bankruptcies and those associated with subsidiaries stock as collateral, as opposed to accounts receivables/cash/inventory collateral, achieved lower recovery. When recoveries were measured based on market pricing, as opposed to the present value of cash flows, the average post-default loan price was 70 percent. Regardless of the measurement method, the standard deviation of recoveries (based on the number of observations in each study) was in the 25 percent range.

Another default recovery study by Asarnow and Edwards (1995) examined a sample of 831 defaulted (classified as doubtful or non-performing) Citibank loans over the period 1971–93 and concluded that the recovery rate on this sample of secured and non-secured loans was 65 percent – again on a present value basis with the reference date being the date of "default" classification. The above recoveries are all higher than comparable rates in the corporate bond market for senior secured as well as unsecured securities of all seniorities. Finally, a recent study by Fitch (Grossman et al., 1997), concluded that loan recoveries on 60 distressed syndicated loans was 82 percent (absolute value just after emergence from distressed condition) while the recovery on senior subordinated debt of the same issuers was 42 percent, 39 percent for subordinated bonds. For a smaller sample of 14 international loans, the recovery rate was 68 percent.

To estimate the expected and unexpected loss from loan defaults, both the probability of default and the expected recovery are necessary. This study fills the vacuum with respect to the former estimate.

5   FILLING THE GAP – DEFAULT RATES ON SYNDICATED LOANS

We measure the default rate experience in the broadly syndicated, bank loan market. We will concentrate on commercial loans of at least $100 million in size for which there was an original rating assigned to the loan by one or more of the major rating agencies or an implied rating could be assigned. The sample period of loan issuance is from January 1, 1991 through the end of 1996 and covers the entire population of "rated" syndicated loans that were originated during that period. Ratings on bank loans have gradually been solicited and paid for by corporations, primarily since early 1995 when Moody's announced its intention to rate large loans. Starting in April 1995, Moody's has steadily increased its coverage of bank loan ratings to $311 billion based on over 1300 facilities (December 1997). S&P has also rated bank loans since 1995 and as of December 1997 covers 588 facilities totaling $358 billion (Bavaria, 1997). The syndicated bank loan market has evolved over the past several years into a highly liquid source of financing for medium and large US corporations. Syndicated loans, i.e., loans originated by one bank and sold either in its entirety or, more typically, in pieces to other banks and non-bank intermediaries, e.g., loan mutual funds, experienced an increase in volume of almost 500 percent over the seven year period 1991–97, with originations growing from $234 billion in 1991 to $1.1 trillion in 1997 (figure 12.1). And, the leveraged loan segment (interest rates of at least 125 basis points over LIBOR) of the syndicated market had a new issue volume of almost $200 billion in 1997 and $263 billion in 1998, compared to just $28 billion in 1993. This reflects the enormous capital needs for US corporations combined with refinancing opportunities as interest rates continued to shrink. Banks have been able and willing to supply loans during this generally favorable interest rate and low credit risk period. The growth rate of leveraged syndicated bank loans has paralleled a similar growth in the high yield corporate bond market.

In recent years, the syndicated loan market has become more complex and increasingly difficult to distinguish from the traditionally more transparent corporate bond market. Investors are now willing to consider syndicated loans as a substitute or complement to

Figure 12.1 Syndicated and leveraged loan volume: 1991–97

Overall volume
(US$ billions)

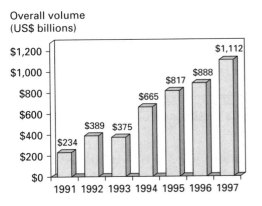

Leveraged volume
(US$ billions)

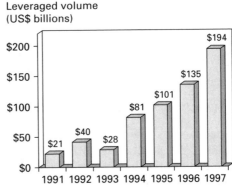

Source: Loan Pricing Corporation.

bonds in their debt portfolios and loan trading is now commonly found (Miller, 1998). Hence, the additional motivation to compare all corporate debt, i.e., loans as well as bonds and mortgages, on a risk-adjusted basis. The expected loss from default is a key ingredient in this comparative evaluation.

Such new investors as "Prime Funds" – closed-end mutual funds providing a variable rate of return to retail investors – and collateralized loan obligations (CLOs) – special purpose vehicles that use proceeds from high and low grade capital market issues to purchase pools of syndicated loans – have impacted the market in a major way by providing liquidity and demanding more and better information from what heretofore was a closed, private placement market.

6 LEVERAGED LOANS

As noted above, an important segment of the large, syndicated loan market is the higher yielding, high risk group known as "leveraged" loans. We are particularly interested in this segment because it is likely that all, or most, of the subsequent defaults will originate in this segment. These loans are typically senior-secured, LIBOR-based floating rate, quarterly coupon instruments, which combine relatively low-cost or zero-cost prepayment options, relatively wide interest rate margins with, in some cases, strong covenant and collateral protection. They are usually divided into two tranches – one for banks and the other for other financial institutions, such as insurance companies, specialized mutual funds, hedge funds and derivative structures.

As of June 1998, the main features for the two tranches of leveraged loans are listed in table 12.2. Despite these differences in spread, fees and maturity, the two branches are pari-passu with each other in the case of distressed restructuring or default. As such, the non-bank investors are less permanent and not as "close-to" the underlying issuer, in terms of monitoring and other typical bank loan relationships. Hence, these loans are, in most cases, equivalent to public bonds and subject to an "arm's-length" relationship in case of problems. Since non-bank creditors are equal in priority with the

Table 12.2 Features of leveraged loans (June 1998)

	Pro-rata tranches	Institutional tranches
Investors	Mostly banks	Mostly institutional investors
Typical spread	L + 100–250	L + 150–350
New-issue fees	0.1–0.5%	0.00–0.25%
Term	5–7 years	6–10 years
Amortization	Aggressive	Back-end loaded

Source: Portfolio Management Data Corporation, Miller (1998) now part of Standard & Poor's.

banks, the negotiating process in distressed situations is subject to less strategic motivations than the here-to-fore bank relationship priorities. In 1998, it was estimated that as many as 75 institutional investors participated in the leveraged loan market (Miller, 1998).

Given the benign situation concerning defaults in the last five years, annual returns (net of defaults) of syndicated leveraged loans have been quite good, ranging between 8 percent to almost 12 percent a year in the 1972–97 period. These returns, combined with very low comparative volatility measures, result in a very favorable Sharpe ratio.[5] Correlations with other credit assets and equities are quite low, as well.

One of the characteristics of the leveraged loan market that is relevant to our analysis of default rates is the degree that issuing firms utilize bank debt *vis-à-vis* public debt (bonds). As we will discuss at a later point, default rates are a function both of the amount of the default and the relevant exposures in each credit quality category. And, in our subsequent comparison of loan vs. bond default rates, it will be demonstrated that rating categories with the same *number* of defaults can have different mortality rates due to differing default *amounts* and differing *exposures*.

7 Loan Ratings

One of the important factors motivating increased secondary trading of syndicated loans is the recent emergence of bank loan ratings and vice versa. Moody's states that it will rate loans in order to stimulate loan trading if the loan commitment is likely to be "drawn," i.e., used by the borrower, that there is enough information available to express an opinion of risk, and the loan is capable of being traded either through assignment or participation (Lustig et al., 1996). In most cases, the loan is rated prior to its syndication with a preliminary or prospective rating in case the terms of the underwriting change prior to closing.

With this enormous amount of new, large loan exposures comes the obvious questions of risk management. And, just as in the corporate bond market, the "investor" in bank loans must be concerned with three types of risk, i.e., interest rate, liquidity and default risk. Recently, credit terms have reacted to the highly competitive bank loan market and interest rate spreads in the 1995–97 period have narrowed. Hence, there is

---

[5] We are fully aware that Sharpe ratios assume lognormal return distributions, which are typically not evident for high default risk, fixed or floating rate, credit assets. Still, the ratio is instructive.

even a greater need of late for more and better information on all levels of risk, with the key void being default probabilities measured in a precise and meaningful way.

Currently, there is no comprehensive study of bank loan defaults for borrowings of different credit quality. At best, there are estimates of loan charge-offs, e.g., the annual survey published by *Robert Morris & Associates*, for the system as a whole or for broad segments of the market and also for individual banks. Indeed, charge-offs as a percentage of outstandings have averaged less than 2 percent per year over the period 1991–96 in the so-called leveraged loan market. Barnish et al. (1997) discuss how sponsors, issuers, and investors interact in this higher risk segment of the syndicated loan market. Our analysis concentrates on the entire risk spectrum of the syndicated loan market in terms of the issuers' initial rating.

8 SAMPLE DATA

Our sample includes all "rated" syndicated loan commitments in the USA of $100 million or greater between 1 January 1991 and 31 December 1996. We restricted our analysis to loans greater than $100 million since the issuing firm was more likely to have public debt outstanding than if we also included smaller size loans from smaller companies. The importance of our issuing firms having public bonds as well as bank debt outstanding in the first few years of our sample period will be explained below. Also, our database (from Loan Pricing Corporation) included 100 percent of the syndicated loans over $100 million but did not include smaller loans in any known proportion to total small loans. The initial sample of these syndicated loans included 5856 commitments of which we were able to find or assign ratings on 4069 from 2184 different borrowers. Aggregate facilities totalled to $2.4 trillion (table 12.3). The sample only included loans that could have defaulted.[6] As noted earlier, Moody's only began rating most large corporate loans in early 1995. This mostly explains why our sample was 70.0 percent of the total syndicated loans in the study period. We have no reason to believe, however, that the excluded loans were not representative of those included since all were major corporate borrowers and differed only in that they did not have public bonds outstanding at the time of the loan's issuance.

We used either the actual loan rating from Moody's or the implied senior unsecured rating based on the public bond rating of outstanding bonds of the same company. The assigned ratings were used mainly for the 1991–94 period. Our convention was to use the same rating as the bond if the company had an outstanding senior unsecured bond, or to add one "notch" if the bond was subordinated and investment grade or two notches if the subordinated bond was rated non-investment grade.[7] For example, if a subordinated bond is rated Ba3, we assigned a Ba1 rating to the loan. We are aware that Moody's does not treat loans of companies that have bonds outstanding in this conventional manner – indeed, they specifically state that they do not (Lustig et al., 1996; Moody's, 1998b) since loans typically have higher recovery rates. While we agree

---

[6] There were 17 debtor-in-possession, post Chapter 11 financings of firms already in default that were not included.
[7] Since the early 1980s, the rating agencies have added subgrades, or notches, to their major category bond ratings. Each major category, e.g., Ba, has three subgrades, Ba1, Ba2 and Ba3 or, in the case of S&P ratings, BB+, BB, and BB–.

Table 12.3 Aggregate loan default data: 1991–96 (US syndicated loan ≥ $100 million)

Original rating	Aaa	Aa	A	Baa	Ba	B	Caa
Defaults by issues							
Number of issues	96	250	1,003	1,120	1,036	537	27
Number of issues defaulted	0	0	1	1	17	24	5
Percentage of total defaulted issues	0.00	0.00	2.08	2.08	35.42	50.00	10.42
Number of issues defaults relative to total issues (%)	0.00	0.00	0.10	0.09	1.64	4.47	18.52
Defaults by issuers							
Number of issuers	33	122	463	545	638	366	17
Number of issuers defaulted	0	0	1	1	8	17	4
Percentage of total defaulted issuers	0.00	0.00	3.23	3.23	25.81	54.84	12.90
Number of issues defaults relative to total issuers (%)	0.00	0.00	0.22	0.18	1.25	4.64	23.53
Defaults by amount							
Total issuance ($millions)	93,731	277,106	836,927	626,808	408,209	154,046	5,087
Issue amount defaulted ($millions)	0	0	400	250	3,815	7,013	1,136
Percentage of total default amount	0.00	0.00	3.17	1.98	30.25	55.59	9.01
Defaults as percentage of total issuance	0.00	0.00	0.05	0.04	0.98	4.55	22.34

that this "notching" procedure does not always capture the exact difference, in every case, between loans and bonds, including expected recoveries at default, we feel that our approach is reasonable and adds little bias to the study.

Although our study uses Moody's ratings as the benchmark, and Moody's states that it does not have an explicit notching convention consistent with our approach, we are convinced that our results are still quite representative and robust.[8] For one thing, S&P does use the convention that we have adopted and the differences between S&P and Moody's ratings are extremely small.[9] To test this, we compared Moody's and S&P ratings on a random selection of 300 bond issues and found that in about 50 percent of the cases, the ratings were identical and in almost 90 percent (269 of the 300 issues) the two agencies had ratings either identical or within one notch. We also aggregated all bonds within a major rating category in our default rate calculations, e.g., B1, B2 and B3 are all categorized as B's. Hence, mis-rating by one notch, if in fact we did misrate the issue, will usually not impact our results and certainly not in any systematic way (see discussion below).

There are other reasons for our notching convention. We are informed that 60 percent of all syndicated bank loans had, in fact, been rated two notches higher than the same company's subordinated bond; 31 percent were rated three notches higher and the remainder (9 percent) were evenly divided between one or four notches higher (Lustig et al., 1996; Moody's, 1988b). Also, in a recent compilation, Bavaria (1997) at S&P found that only about 10 percent of the bank loans received a rating higher than the underlying corporate senior bond equivalent. Finally, since neither Moody's, S&P or we actually rated the loan in the pre-1995 period, we had no choice but to adopt a "shadow" rating approach.

The information on each loan included is the loan date, borrower name, facility size, description, tenor (maturity period), purpose of the deal and rating at the time of issuance. Sources of the information were from the *Loan Pricing Corporation Data Base, Moody's Investors Service's* Global Credit Research Bank Loan Ratings, *Credit Suisse First Boston's* syndicated finance research desk and the list of public bond defaults and Chapter 11 bankruptcies from the *NYU Salomon Center's* defaulted bond and bankruptcy files.[10]

Table 12.4 indicates that 60 percent of the syndicated loans were rated investment grade (2461/4069) from 53 percent of the borrowers (1163/2184). The vast majority of these deals were rated A or Baa. The non-investment grade loan dollars accounted for the remaining 40 percent (47 percent of all borrowers) with the dominant categories

---

[8] Indeed, practitioners who have studied this notching convention (Fridson and Garman, 1998) have explicitly stated that "Notching for companies has tended to follow a rule of thumb. The subordinated debt has typically been rated two notches lower than the senior debt. . . . By a similar rule of thumb, a one notch differential usually has prevailed when the senior debt has carried an investment grade rating and that despite recent attempts by the rating agencies to add more flexibility to its notching, it remains the case that subordinated debt is almost always notched to the fullest extent, which is generally two notches down from the Company's highest rating".

[9] We did not use S&P ratings since Moody's had more loan ratings than S&P in the study period (perhaps no longer the case in 1999) and our database did not have the S&P rating indicated. It would have been possible to get the S&P ratings, if they existed, and in future work we will include both agencies' ratings as our benchmarks of risk category at issuance.

[10] The NYU Salomon Center's default files include all US corporate bond defaults from 1971–99, numbering over 800 defaulting issues and the list of bankruptcies includes virtually all with liabilities greater than $100 million.

Table 12.4 Loan data by year (1991–96) and by rating (US syndicated loans ≥ $100 million)

Original rating	Aaa	Aa	A	Baa	Ba	B	Caa	Total
1991								
Total issuance ($millions)	8,357	20,598	59,727	33,504	27,556	7,989	906	158,638
No. of issues	8	22	82	91	70	29	5	307
No. of issuers	7	22	78	87	68	28	4	292
1992								
Total issuance ($millions)	10,937	22,225	54,882	62,419	34,489	29,525	261	214,775
No. of issues	12	24	116	142	105	64	1	464
No. of issuers	12	24	109	134	102	59	1	441
1993								
Total issuance ($millions)	18,110	37,295	120,701	93,431	46,200	27,521	1,265	342,523
No. of issues	18	38	168	168	145	85	7	625
No. of issuers	15	37	162	163	139	82	5	603
1994								
Total issuance ($millions)	14,915	56,739	176,328	144,856	79,499	21,130	635	494,156
No. of issues	19	60	228	237	181	95	5	825
No. of issuers	18	59	227	232	178	95	5	814
1995								
Total issuance ($millions)	18,004	67,079	205,797	156,316	90,966	25,502	610	564,275
No. of issues	21	53	210	263	233	114	4	898
No. of issuers	20	53	209	259	229	109	4	883
1996								
Total issuance ($millions)	25,372	73,116	219,492	136,282	129,498	42,378	1,410	627,548
No. of issues	18	51	201	219	302	150	5	946
No. of issuers	1	50	200	216	298	148	5	934

being Ba and B. Loans clustering around the investment/non-investment grade inter-section were the most common rating classes. Total new issuance in our sample ranged from $158 billion in 1991, steadily increasing to $628 billion in 1996. Our sample rep-resents about 70 percent of the new issuance over the sample period.

9 DEFAULT/MORTALITY RATE METHODOLOGY

The primary focus of this study is to measure the default rate on large, syndicated commercial loans. Our unique data base enables us to measure, for the first time, the expected default of loans on a quarterly and annual basis. Our default estimates will be based on both dollar amount and number of issuers, and we aggregate all defaults into major rating categories, i.e., not by notches.[11] For both population bases, we have utilized the mortality rate methodology, first introduced by Altman (1988, 1989). This actuarial based technique adjusts for changes over time in the size of the original sample based on defaults, calls, and scheduled redemptions. The specific calculation for marginal loan mortality rates (MLMR) and cumulative loan mortality rates (CLMR) are

$$\mathrm{MLMR}_t = \frac{\text{Dollar (or issuer number) of loans defaulting in period } t}{\text{Dollar (or issuer number) of loans at start of period } t}$$

and

$$\mathrm{CLMR}_t = 1 - [\Pi\mathrm{SR}_t]$$

where SR_t = survival rate in period $t = 1 - \mathrm{MLMR}_t$.

It should be made explicitly clear that we are measuring the marginal and cumulative mortality rates for loans with specific original ratings over the relevant time periods after issuance. As such, we can assess the aging effect of loan defaults, for both quar-terly and annual periods, as of the time of the loan's origination. While this method is consistent with actuarial theory, it is different from the cohort (Moody's) and static pool (S&P) approaches utilized by the rating agencies for estimating bond defaults.[12] Even if we desired to measure loan defaults on a cohort/static pool basis, we could not do so in this study since we do not have access to the complete rating history of our loan sample.

We observe quarterly default/mortality rates since the tenor (maturity period) is relatively short for loans and also due to the relatively short sample period (6 years). This is the first default study to utilize a horizon of less than one year. We also estimate annual mortality rates and compare these results with publicly traded bond mortality rates over the same sample period (1991–96).

---

[11] Data by notches does exist but is not discussed here due to the reduced amounts in many of the subgrades.
[12] These approaches measure the proportion of issuers that default from different bond rating classes as of some initial date regardless of the age of the bond. For example, all Ba bond issuers as of 1 January 1995 are observed as to their default frequency in subsequent periods. See Moody's (1998a) and S&P (1998) for details and results. The three approaches for measuring corporate bond defaults, as well as rating migration pat-terns, are discussed and contrasted in Caouette et al. (1998).

10 FINDINGS

The total number of new loan facilities in our sample was 4069, representing 2184 borrowers and $2.4 trillion in commitments (table 12.3). Of the 4069 deals, 48 defaulted by our terminal date (31 March 1997). Therefore, total defaults were 1.18 percent of those loans issued. There were $ 12.6 billion of defaults (0.53 percent of the $2.4 trillion of new loans).

The breakdown of aggregate default rates by original rating is given in table 12.5. These aggregate default rates, by dollar amount, number of borrowers and number of issues, regardless of the timing of defaults, are listed in the same table. Only the Baa class had an aggregate default rate which was lower than its higher rated neighbor (A). Since both the A and Baa loans had only one default in the sample period, this difference is attributable to the sizes of the single data points relative to total issuance.

Table 12.5 Loan default rates by issue size, number of issuers and number of issues

Original rating	Default rates by		
	Dollar amount (%)	No. of issuers (%)	No. of issues (%)
Aaa	0.00	0.00	0.00
Aa	0.00	0.00	0.00
A	0.05	0.22	0.10
Baa	0.04	0.18	0.09
Ba	0.93	1.25	1.64
B	4.55	4.64	4.47
Caa	22.34	23.53	18.52

11 MORTALITY RATES BASED ON FACE VALUE AMOUNTS

While aggregate default rates by original rating provide some relevant data, the more important data for decision makers involves the expected default over time. Our mortality rate structure, discussed earlier, not only measures the marginal and cumulative rates over time but provides us with specific results for the syndicated loan market that can be directly compared with results for the publicly traded corporate bond market. Since the effective tenor of bank loans (probably less than 18 months) is short relative to bonds, we also calculated our results in quarterly, as well as annual, periods from the date of the original loan commitment. The comparable bond data is only available on an annual basis. Hence, we cannot compare bonds and loans on a quarterly basis. The quarterly results are available only from Altman and Suggitt (1997).

Table 12.6 shows the annual syndicated loan mortality rate on a marginal and cumulative basis for new issuance loans and bonds in the 1991–96 period.[13] As noted earlier,

[13] Defaulted loans are tracked through the first quarter of 1997 while defaulted bonds are based on defaults through the end of 1996. Both series will be updated for defaults as data becomes available. The bond mortality rates for the period 1971–96 were derived from a special computation from the Altman and Kishore (1998) study. Note that the bond mortality rates are based on S&P ratings, which have the same notching convention for senior vs. subordinated loans that we used.

Table 12.6 Comparison of syndicated bank loan vs. corporate bond mortality rates based on original issuance principal amounts (1991–96)

		1 year		2 years		3 years		4 years		5 years	
		Bank (%)	Bond (%)	Bank (%)	Bond (%)	Bank (%)	Bond (%)	Bank (%)	Bond (%)	Bank (%)	Bond (%)
Aaa	Marginal	0.00	0.00	0.00	0.00	0.00	0.00	0.00	0.00	0.00	0.00
	Cumulative	0.00	0.00	0.00	0.00	0.00	0.00	0.00	0.00	0.00	0.00
Aa	Marginal	0.00	0.00	0.00	0.00	0.00	0.00	0.00	0.00	0.00	0.00
	Cumulative	0.00	0.00	0.00	0.00	0.00	0.00	0.00	0.00	0.00	0.00
A	Marginal	0.00	0.00	0.12	0.00	0.00	0.00	0.00	0.00	0.00	0.05
	Cumulative	0.00	0.00	0.12	0.00	0.12	0.00	0.12	0.00	0.12	0.05
Baa	Marginal	0.04	0.00	0.00	0.00	0.00	0.00	0.00	0.54	0.00	0.00
	Cumulative	0.04	0.00	0.04	0.00	0.04	0.00	0.04	0.54	0.04	0.54
Ba	Marginal	0.17	0.00	0.60	0.38	0.60	2.30	0.97	1.80	4.89	0.00
	Cumulative	0.17	0.00	0.77	0.38	1.36	2.67	2.32	4.42	7.10	4.42
B	Marginal	2.30	0.81	1.86	1.97	2.59	4.99	1.79	1.76	1.86	0.00
	Cumulative	2.30	0.81	4.11	2.76	6.60	7.61	8.27	9.24	9.97	0.24
Caa	Marginal	15.24	2.65	7.44	3.09	13.03	4.55	0.00	21.72	0.00	0.00
	Cumulative	15.24	2.65	21.55	5.66	31.77	9.95	31.77	29.51	31.77	29.51

Source: Author's computations for loans, and a special run from data collected and computed from Altman and Kishore (1998) for bonds.

we recognize that the period 1991–96 involves below average default activity for newly issued debt in both the loan and bond markets and we will return to this theme shortly. This relatively benign credit risk period is the same, however, for both markets.

We observe a zero mortality rate up to five years for both loans and bonds in Aaa and Aa classes. There is a very small five-year mortality rate for A and Baa loans and bonds. The timing of the one default for A rated loans and bonds[14] was dependent upon when the defaulted debt was issued (the second year for the bank loan and the fifth year for the bond). The same was true for the Baa loan (Petrie Stores) which defaulted within one year of issuance. As expected, the loan mortality rates for the non-investment grade categories increase substantially with the five-year cumulative loan mortality rates rising to 7.10 percent, 9.97 percent and 31.77 percent for Ba, B and Caa respectively.

With the exception of Ba loans, we find the five-year "junk-loan" cumulative mortality rates remarkably similar to the cumulative "junk bond" mortality rates. And the Ba differential is due to an abnormally large default amount in the fifth year when three Ba loans defaulted amounting to $690 million. Of course, there were some default rate timing differences between loans and bonds that can be observed. For example, the B-rated bank loan first and fifth years' marginal rates were higher while the third year's experience was the opposite. The second and fourth years' rates were very similar. By the fifth year, however, both loans and bonds originally rated B suffered cumulative mortality rates between nine and ten percent. The cumulative five-year results, based on dollar amount of issuance, indicate that the mortality rates are remarkably similar for the publicly traded bond and the syndicated bank loan markets.

---

[14] Dow Corning's $400 million default.

It is also important to compare our loan vs. bond mortality rates for the first few years after issuance, especially since the average loan's effective maturity, adjusting for pre-payments by borrowers, is about 18 months.[15] We observe (in table 12.6 for issues, and also table 12.7 for issuers) that the marginal mortality rates for loans are, for the most part, higher than for bonds in years one, two, and three. The exceptions are in year two, where the B-rated marginal loan and bond *issue* mortality rates are about the same (1.86 percent vs. 1.97 percent) and in year three the B-rated bond issue rate is greater than the bank loan issue rate (4.99 percent vs. 2.59 percent). Indeed, it is primarily because of the relatively high third year marginal bond mortality rate, that the four- and five-year cumulative rates for B's are essentially the same for bond and bank loan issues. Note that the cumulative loan *issuer* rate (table 12.7) is considerably higher than the *issue* rate for loans (table 12.6) for just about all periods. We do not, however, have issuer *bond* rates as a comparative statistic.

The above implies that the bank loan mortality rates appear to be higher than comparable bond mortality rates in the first two years after issuance – an important comparison for the shorter maturity loans. And, we are more confident about the shorter time horizon results, since we have far more data points in our one- and two-year mortality rate calculations than for the four- and five-year rates (see table 12.4 where we observe that there were only 70 Ba and 29 B new issues in 1991 contributing to our five-year rate calculation vs. over 1000 Ba- and over 500 B-rated issues contributing to our one-year mortality rates). Whether these differences will persist when default rates in general rise and revert to mean average rates, is a question that we will not be able to examine for at least a few more years.

Table 12.7 Syndicated bank loan issuer mortality rates based on number of issuers (1991–96) years after issue

		1 year (%)	2 years (%)	3 years (%)	4 years (%)	5 years (%)
Aaa	Marginal	0.00	0.00	0.00	0.00	0.00
	Cumulative	0.00	0.00	0.00	0.00	0.00
Aa	Marginal	0.00	0.00	0.00	0.00	0.00
	Cumulative	0.00	0.00	0.00	0.00	0.00
A	Marginal	0.00	0.48	0.00	0.00	0.00
	Cumulative	0.00	0.48	0.48	0.48	0.48
Baa	Marginal	0.18	0.00	0.00	0.00	0.00
	Cumulative	0.18	0.18	0.18	0.18	0.18
Ba	Marginal	0.31	1.05	1.05	2.47	9.38
	Cumulative	0.31	1.36	2.40	4.81	13.73
B	Marginal	1.37	3.78	5.93	2.08	4.35
	Cumulative	1.37	5.10	10.73	12.59	16.39
Caa	Marginal	17.65	9.09	25.00	0.00	0.00
	Cumulative	17.65	25.13	43.85	43.85	43.85

Source: Author's computations.

[15] This average life of syndicated bank loans is an estimate based on our discussions with market practitioners. As far as we know, there is no published study on average *de-facto* maturities since the market for bank loans is still predominantly non-public.

In contrast to our findings of higher loan default rates compared to bonds, Carey (1998) concluded that insurance company private placements performed better, i.e., lower overall average default loss rates, than comparable Moody's and S&P public bond default loss statistics. For private placements spanning all rating categories, he found that the loss rate in the first year was 0.39 percent vs. 1.16 percent for bonds. These loss rate comparisons were not consistent, however, across all rating categories. For example, the BB private placement loss rate was 1.53 percent vs. 0.83 percent for public bonds. Indeed, only the B- and CCC-rated loss rates were higher for public bonds. While private placements have average maturities and *de-facto* lives more similar to bonds than to loans, Carey asserts that the former are similar to loans in that both are monitored more closely by the lending institution than are the more distant public bond owners. Despite this monitoring factor, our results show higher loan default rates, especially in the earlier years.

12   AGING EFFECTS

The marginal mortality rate results and its information content concerning the aging effect of corporate loan default rates is not conclusive. In the case of the Ba class, there does appear to be a clear aging effect. We observe a relatively low first year rate (0.17 percent), followed by increasing marginal rates up to 4.89 percent in the fifth year. The quarterly results show this too, although there are many quarters with a zero default rate. The B rating class marginal rates, however, are fairly steady over the entire five-year post-issuance period, ranging from 1.79 percent to 2.59 percent. The Caa class has too few observations to make any definitive statement. The investment grade classes have virtually a zero default rate so there is no opportunity to observe an aging effect.

13   MORTALITY RATES BASED ON ISSUERS

Our prior discussion focused on dollar based mortality rates. Table 12.7 depicts the annual mortality rates based on the percentage of original number of issuing companies with loan commitments. The issuer base is used by Moody's and S&P in their bond default rate computations. Since these agencies do not measure default rates from original issuance and since there is not a continuous rating series for our loan data base, we cannot compare our results directly to those published by the agencies for bonds. Still, loan mortality rates by issuer and credit rating will be useful information to banks and other investors who are concerned with borrower rates as well as dollar exposures.

One generalization about cumulative issuer mortality rates is that they are consistently higher than comparable rates for dollar weighted mortality rates. For example, the five-year issuer based cumulative rate for Ba loans is 13.73 percent vs. 7.10 percent for dollar based Ba loans (tables 12.6 and 12.7) and 16.39 percent vs. 9.97 percent for B-rated loans. Except for the Aaa and Aa ratings, which are zero, the issuer rates are higher for all categories. This implies that defaults are proportionally greater for smaller syndicated loans and lower for larger ones. All of this is relative since the minimum loan size in our data base was $100 million. And, when we are dealing with a relatively small number of defaulting issuers, the addition or subtraction of a few defaults can make a substantial difference.

14 SAMPLE FIRM BIAS

One relevant concern with our empirical analysis and the way we construct our sample is whether one should be surprised with our findings given the loan and bond overlap of the defaulting firms and also the issuing entities. In other words, does one learn any useful insights from our conclusions above and beyond what might be construed based on a cursory consideration of the sample design?

For several reasons, our mortality results do add considerable new information, despite our findings that loan and bond default rates are quite similar. For one thing, about 50 percent of our loan issuing sample of firms are rated by Moody's, whether or not the firm is also an issuer of bonds and already has a bond rating. The other 50 percent of the loans are assigned a rating class based on their outstanding bond rating. If we require a complete sample of loans with independent ratings assigned by Moody's, we would have to wait about two more years to be able to calculate a five-year cumulative default rate. In the interim, credit risk analysts who desire estimates of default and loss rates on bank loans would continue to rely upon the only available data – rates based on bond ratings.

Another relevant consideration is to understand that mortality rates are based on the face value of defaults relative to the total face value that was issued, in a certain rating class, and had survived up to the default year. Even if the sample of defaults and issuing firms were identical, the mortality rates would only be the same if the underlying issuing sample had the same ratio of bank loans to bonds as the sample of firms that default. An example will illustrate this point. A firm, in the Ba class, defaults with $300 million of bank debt and $100 million of bonds (a 3:1 ratio). If the total relevant Ba loan population is $30 billion, then this firm's contribution to the Ba loan mortality rate is 1.0 percent ($0.30/$30.0). If the total relevant Ba sample of bonds was $20 billion, then the same firm's contribution to the Ba bond default rate would be 0.50 percent ($0.10/$20.0) – quite a difference between the two contributions even though it was the same firm.

In order to investigate this potential loan/bond ratio bias for our mortality analysis, we observed the ratio of bank to non-bank debt for the entire leveraged loan population from 1991 to 1996 – based on a compilation from *Portfolio Management Data Corporation* – with a similar ratio from the defaulted firm sample (the latter consists of the 31 issuers). Leveraged loans seemed to be the relevant population since almost all loans that default were non-investment grade (see table 12.3). The average bank loan to non-bank debt (mainly bonds) ratio for all leveraged loans over the six-year study period was 1.24, with a range of annual values from 1.08 to 1.40. For our sample of defaulted loans, however, the ratio of bank loans to non-bank debt was only 0.48 – a significant difference showing that defaulted bank loan companies have a great deal less bank debt as a percentage of total debt than do all companies with syndicated leveraged loans.

15 SAMPLE PERIOD BIAS

As noted earlier, our sample period for syndicated loan default analysis is restricted to a relatively benign credit cycle and is therefore probably not indicative of what investors might expect over several complete credit cycles. We can attempt to assess the degree of bias by observing the annual bond default rate comparisons in the 1991–96 period vs. a longer time period from 1971 to 1996, as well as the bond mortality rates in these two periods. Comparable loan data does not exist.

As can be seen from table 12.8, the weighted average annual default rates on high yield bonds in the US have averaged 3.05 percent for the period 1971–98; the annual rates are weighted by the amount outstanding. Since there were relatively few new

Table 12.8 Historical default rates – straight bonds only excluding defaulted issues from par value outstanding 1971–98 ($ millions)

Year	Par value outstanding[a]	Par value defaults	Default rates (%)	Standard deviation (%)
1998	$465,500	$7,464	1.603	
1997	$335,400	$4,200	1.252	
1996	$271,000	$3,336	1.231	
1995	$240,000	$4,551	1.896	
1994	$235,000	$3,418	1.454	
1993	$206,907	$2,287	1.105	
1992	$163,000	$5,545	3.402	
1991	$183,600	$18,862	10.273	
1990	$181,000	$18,354	10.140	
1989	$189,258	$8,110	4.285	
1988	$148,187	$3,944	2.662	
1987	$129,557	$7,486	5.778	
1986	$90,243	$3,156	3.497	
1985	$58,088	$992	1.708	
1984	$40,939	$344	0.840	
1983	$27,492	$301	1.095	
1982	$18,109	$577	3.186	
1981	$17,115	$27	0.158	
1980	$14,935	$224	1.500	
1979	$10,356	$20	0.193	
1978	$8,946	$119	1.330	
1977	$8,157	$381	4.671	
1976	$7,735	$30	0.388	
1975	$7,471	$204	2.731	
1974	$10,894	$123	1.129	
1973	$7,824	$49	0.626	
1972	$6,928	$193	2.786	
1971	$6,602	$82	1.242	
Arithmetic average default rate	1971–1998		2.577	2.515
	1978–1998		2.790	2.753
	1985–1998		3.592	2.999
Weighted average default rate[b]	1971–1998		3.054	3.308
	1978–1998		3.075	2.890
	1985–1998		3.166	2.921
Median annual default rate	1971–1998		1.552	

Source: Authors' compilation and various dealer estimates.
[a] *As of mid-year.*
[b] *Weighted by par value of amount outstanding for each year.*

issue bonds or large loans in 1991, it probably does not make sense to include 1991's enormous bond default rate (10.27 percent) in our sample period comparison with the longer period's default rate. Indeed, virtually all of the defaults in 1991 came from bonds issued in earlier years. The weighted average annual high yield bond default rate for the 1992–96 period is 1.72 percent, about one-half of the 3.61 percent rate in the 1971–96 period.[16] The median rates comparison is closer with 1.60 percent for the longer period and 1.23 percent for the shorter 1992–96 period.

Comparative cumulative bond mortality rates for 1991–96 vs. 1971–96, shown in table 12.9, confirm the considerably lower default incidence in the former shorter period. This can be seen most clearly when comparing the fourth or fifth years' cumulative mortality rates. It appears from the fifth year comparison that the more recent six-year period of our loan default study experienced a cumulative mortality rate of between one-third to one-half the rate of the longer period. For example, the more recent period's BB rated bonds had a rate of about one-half of the longer period (4.4 percent vs. 9.1 percent) while the BBB- and B-rated issues had about a one-third comparative default incidence.

If our long-term vs. short-term comparative results for bonds are indicative of the longer-term loan cumulative default rates, then our syndicated loan five-year cumulative default rates could range from 14 percent to 20 percent for Ba loans and 20 percent to 30 percent for single-B loans. Of course, it is difficult to be precise about long-term loan default rates since the number of defaults in the 1992–97 period was quite low. Still, the total number of newly committed loans exceeded 4000, a substantial sample. The analyst should consider these data characteristics when extrapolating the shorter period's results for loans, based on the bond market's recent and long-term comparative experience.

16 CONCLUSIONS

This report is the first step in assessing annual and cumulative default rates on large, rated, syndicated commercial loans. Due to data availability constraints on newly committed loan facilities where it was also feasible to get implied or actual ratings, we have necessarily restricted our analysis to a relatively short six-year period, 1991–96. Our results show a cumulative default rate which is probably relatively low compared to what rates can be expected to be over credit cycles that include higher charge-offs and losses. We do find, however, that cumulative default rates on loans were quite similar to comparably rated corporate bonds in our sample period for maturities of four and five years, but it appears that the loan-default rates for the first two years after issuance are somewhat higher than comparable bond default rates. Hence, loan portfolio managers, regulators and others concerned with credit risk management and appropriate value at risk measures should treat the existing data bases that report only on bond default rates quite gingerly and with an understanding that loan default expectations may vary some from what they have been inputting into their transition matrices.

With the primary and secondary loan trading market growing significantly of late and with the many new instruments that include loans as part of the structured finance or asset-derivative pools, assessments of expected default rates by rating and by age

---

[16] If we included 1991, the weighted average rate would be 2.92 percent for 1991–96.

Table 12.9 Cumulative bond mortality rates for 1991–96 vs. 1971–96

Original rating	1 year		2 years		3 years		4 years		5 years	
	1991–96	1971–96	1991–96	1971–96	1991–96	1971–96	1991–96	1971–96	1991–96	1971–96
AAA	0.00	0.00	0.00	0.00	0.00	0.00	0.00	0.00	0.00	0.00
AA	0.00	0.00	0.00	0.00	0.00	0.00	0.00	0.00	0.00	0.00
A	0.00	0.00	0.00	0.00	0.00	0.05	0.00	0.19	0.05	0.27
BBB	0.00	0.03	0.00	0.42	0.00	0.82	0.54	1.49	0.54	1.88
BB	0.00	0.44	0.38	1.41	2.67	4.77	4.42	6.47	4.42	9.09
B	0.81	1.41	2.76	5.65	7.61	12.51	9.24	18.58	9.24	24.33
CCC	2.65	2.46	5.66	18.62	9.95	33.02	29.51	41.17	29.51	43.82

Source: Author's computations.

of the loan become even more important. The traditional tradeoff between risk and returns can now be assessed more completely for the heretofore non-transparent syndicated loan market.

This study's implications must be analyzed within the context that the sample period was relatively short and, although it included over 4000 loans, the number of observations in each rating class is much less. Also, the credit cycle over the sample period was relatively benign. The actual number of defaults, therefore, was quite low. As we update these results over time, they will become even more relevant for decision makers in the syndicated loan market. In addition, we have not concentrated on the unique relationship patterns that exist for loan customers and their bankers vs. the more distanced relationship between bondholders and issuers. We feel that these differences are becoming smaller as the syndicated leveraged loan market becomes more of a multi-institutional one and less like the more traditional private loan market. Finally, additional work needs to be done for the small and medium-sized loan market which, we believe, will also become more liquid and security-like in the future.

REFERENCES

Altman, E., 1988. *Default risk, mortality rates and the performance of corporate bonds: 1970–1986*. Foundation for Research of the Institute of Chartered Financial Analysts (now the AIMR), Charlottesville, VA.

Altman, E., 1989. Measuring corporate bond mortality and performance. *The Journal of Finance*, September, 909–22.

Altman, E., Caouette, J., and Narayanan, P., 1998. Managing credit risk: The ironic challenge in the next decade. *Financial Analysts Journal*, January/February, 7–11 and in: *Managing Credit Risk: The Next Great Financial Challenge*, Wiley, New York, 1998.

Altman, E., and Nammacher, S., 1985. The default rate experience of high yield corporate debt. *The Financial Analysts Journal*, July/August, 25–41.

Altman, E., and Nammacher, S., 1987. *Investing in Junk Bonds*. Wiley, New York.

Altman, E., and Kao, D. L., 1991. *Corporate Bond Rating Drift: An Examination of Rating Agency Credit Quality Changes*. AIMR, Charlottesville, VA.

Altman, E., and Kao, D. L., 1992. The implications of corporate bond rating drift. *The Financial Analysts Journal*, May/June, 64–75.

Altman, E., and Kishore, V., 1998. *Default rates and returns in the high yield debt market, 1971 – Annually from 1991–1997*. New York University, Salomon Center.

Altman, E., and Suggitt, H., 1997. *Default rates in the syndicated bank loan market, WP # S-97-39*. NYU Salomon Center.

Asarnow, E., and Edwards, D., 1995. Measuring loss on defaulted bank loans: A 24 yr study. *The Journal of Commercial Lending*, March, 11–19.

Asquith, P., Mullins, D., and Wolff, E., 1989. Original issue high yield bonds: Aging analysis of defaults, exchanges and calls. *The Journal of Finance*, September, 923–52.

Barnish, K., Miller, S., and Rushmore, M., 1997. The new leveraged loan syndication market. *The Journal of Applied Corporate Finance* 10 (1), 79–86.

Bavaria, S., 1997. Bankruptcy rating volume continues to climb, In: Proceedings of the High Yield Bond and Bank Loan Ratings. *Standard and Poor's*, Second Quarter, 58–60.

Caouette, J., Altman, E., and Narayanan, P., 1998. *Managing Credit Risk: The Next Great Financial Challenge*. Wiley, New York.

Carey, M., 1998. Credit risk in private debt portfolios. *Journal of Finance* LIII (4), 1363–87.

Carty, L., and Lieberman, D., 1996. Defaulted bank loan recoveries. *Moody's Investors Service*, November.

Carty, L., and Lieberman, D., 1997a. Corporate bond defaults and default rates. *Moody's Investors Service*, July.

Carty, L., and Lieberman, D., 1997b. Moody's rating migration and credit quality correlation, 1920–1996. *Moody's Special Report*, July.

Carty, L. et al., 1998. Moody's Special Report, January.

CreditMetrics®, 1997. J. P. Morgan, N.Y., April 2, 1997.

CreditRisk+®, 1997. Credit Suisse Financial Products, October 1997.

Credit Portfolio View®, 1997. McKinsey, New York, Zurich.

Fridson, M., and Garman, C., 1998. Valuing like-rated senior and subordinated debt, EXTRA CREDIT, Merrill Lynch. Reprinted in: Barnhill, T., Maxwell, W., Shenkman, M. (eds.), *High Yield Bonds*, Irwin, Boston, MA, 1999.

Grossman, R., Brennan, W., and Vento, J., 1997. Syndicated bank loan recovery study. *Structured Finance Credit Facilities Report*, Fitch IBCA, October 22.

Hickman, W. B., 1958. *Corporate Bond Quality and Investor Experience.* Princeton University Press, Princeton, NJ.

International Swaps and Dealers Association, 1998. *Credit Risk and Regulatory Capital.* London and New York, March.

Lucas, D., and Lonski, J., 1992. Changes in corporate credit quality: 1970–1990. *The Journal of Fixed Income*, March, 7–14.

Lustig, J., Guinee, C., Weston, M. D., and Dornnermuth, M., 1996. Bank loan ratings: Pricing implications. *Moody's Rating Approach*, June, 12–15.

Miller, S., 1998. Leveraged loans. NYSSA High Yield Bond Seminar, June 18 and EXTRA CREDIT, Merrill Lynch, May/June 1999.

Moody's, 1998a. Historical default rates of corporate bond issues, 1920–1997 (L. Carty et al., January), Annual Studies since 1991.

Moody's, 1998b. Bankrupt bank loan recoveries, June.

Society of Actuaries, 1996. *1986–1992 Credit risk loss experience study: Private placement bonds.* Asset Risk Experience Committee and Private Placement Sub-Committee of the Society of Actuaries, Schaumberg, IL.

Standard & Poor's 1998. *Ratings Performance 1997: Stability and Transition.* New York, January, Annual Studies.

13 Almost Everything You Wanted to Know About Recoveries on Defaulted Bonds

with Vellore M. Kishore

This study documents, for the first time, the severity of bond defaults stratified by Standard Industrial Classification sector and by debt seniority. The highest average recoveries came from public utilities (70 percent) and chemical, petroleum, and related products (63 percent). The differences between those sectors and all the rest are statistically significant, even when adjusted for seniority. The original rating of a bond issue as investment grade or below investment grade has virtually no effect on recoveries once seniority is accounted for. In addition, neither the size of the issue nor the time to default from its original date of issuance has any association with the recovery rate. These results should provide important information for investors as well as analysts.

Perhaps the most critical analytical factor that determines required yields on risky corporate debt is the expected default probability and the severity of default. Bond-rating agencies focus almost exclusively on the probability of default and the timeliness of payment of interest and principal in their assigned risk categories. A fairly standard rule of thumb, however, reduces the rating of a firm's subordinate bond issues by two notches compared with its senior issues if the senior bond is below investment grade and by one notch if it is investment grade. This *ad hoc* adjustment is more than likely based on the expectation that the junior bonds will recover less than the more senior issues. Recently, the rating agencies have explicitly incorporated severity of default expectations in their private placement and structured finance analytics.

The severity issue, based on default recoveries, affects the expected loss from defaults and has been highlighted both in traditional calculations and in aging and mortality rate approaches. The term "recovery" can refer to the price of the bonds at the time of default or their value at the end of the distressed–reorganization period. In this study, we examined the recovery experience at default.[1] Recovery rates for defaulted bonds perhaps now share equal importance with default rate expectations and hence deserve increased scrutiny. We continue that scrutiny by focusing on the industry affiliation of the defaulted debtor and, where possible, the seniority of the issue within each industry.

The reason industry affiliation is likely to be important is that the business activity of an enterprise dictates the types of assets and the competitive conditions of firms within different industrial sectors. Assuming the equality of other factors such as leverage structure, the more tangible and liquid the assets, the higher their liquidation value and, hence, the higher the expected price of the debt securities in a distressed situation. In addition, in certain industries, the more certain the future earnings of the distressed entity, the higher the enterprise value and its debt component. For example, the asset structure and regulatory environment of public utilities bodes for better recovery rates than those of industries that operate in a highly competitive environment and have little or no tangible assets. Because these factors need to be assessed in the pricing of debt securities throughout their duration – from original issuance and most definitely in a distressed situation – the actual recovery experience by industry and priority is likely to be useful and welcome information.

RECOVERY RATES BY SENIORITY

The ability to sell publicly held and traded bonds just after default at positive values has always been an attractive attribute. For decades, average prices at default have been calculated at approximately 40 cents on the dollar (Hickman 1958). Indeed, this average overall recovery rate persists today. The arithmetic average recovery rate on a sample of more than 700 defaulting bond issues from 1978 to 1995 was $41.70 per $100 face value.[2] As table 13.1 shows, however, seniority does play the expected important role: Senior secured debt averages about 58 percent of face value; senior unsecured, 48 percent; senior subordinate, 34 percent; and junior subordinate, about 31 percent.

[1] Altman and Eberhart (1994) observed recoveries at the confirmation of the Chapter 11 filing (or at liquidation) and found that the most-senior bonds recovered significantly more at default than less senior bonds and also performed significantly better from default to confirmation and emergence. This finding is perhaps surprising because one would expect that the market would properly discount the junior bonds at default and that the post-default return experience would be about the same for junior bonds as for those with senior priority – especially because the variance of returns was about the same for each class of bonds.

[2] It should be noted that our defaulted bond sample includes bonds that at issuance were investment grade (25 percent) and noninvestment grade (75 percent).

Table 13.1 Weighted-average recovery rates per $100 face value on defaulted debt by seniority, 1978–95

Default year	Senior secured		Senior unsecured		Senior subordinated		Subordinated		Discount/Zero coupon	
	Number	Recovery rate	Number	Recovery rate	Number	Recovery rate	Number	Recovery rate	Number	Recovery rate
1995	5	$44.64	9	$50.50	17	$39.01	1	$20.00	1	$17.50
1994	5	48.66	8	51.14	5	19.81	3	37.04	1	5.00
1993	2	55.75	7	33.38	10	51.50	9	28.38	4	31.75
1992	15	59.85	8	35.61	17	58.20	22	49.13	5	19.82
1991	4	44.12	69	55.84	37	31.91	38	24.30	9	27.89
1990	12	32.18	31	29.02	38	25.01	24	18.83	11	15.63
1989	9	82.69	16	53.70	21	19.60	30	23.95	0	—
1988	13	67.96	19	41.99	10	30.70	20	35.27	0	—
1987	4	90.68	17	72.02	6	56.24	4	35.25	0	—
1986	8	48.32	11	37.72	7	35.20	30	33.39	0	—
1985	2	74.25	3	34.81	7	36.18	15	41.45	0	—
1984	4	53.42	1	50.50	2	65.88	7	44.68	0	—
1983	1	71.00	3	67.72	0	—	4	41.79	0	—
1982	0	—	16	39.31	0	—	4	32.91	0	—
1981	1	72.00	0	—	0	—	0	—	0	—
1980	0	—	2	26.71	0	—	2	16.63	0	—
1979	0	—	0	—	0	—	1	31.00	0	—
1978	0	—	1	60.00	0	—	0	—	0	—
Total/average	85	57.89	221	47.65	177	34.38	214	31.34	31	21.66
Median		51.04		40.65		27.86		31.96		18.66
Standard deviation		22.99		26.71		25.08		22.42		18.35

RECOVERY RATES BY INDUSTRY

We first stratified our sample of 696 defaulted bond issues into 61 groups by three-digit Standard Industrial Classification (SIC) codes.[3] A firm was assigned an SIC code corresponding to the product group that accounts for its greatest value of sales. Many of the sectors (14) included 20 or more observations, the majority of codes (47) had fewer than 20, and a large number had fewer than 10 observations. The weighted and unweighted (by dollar amount outstanding) recovery rates at default for those 61 sectors are shown in table 13.2.

We cannot feel very comfortable with table 2's summary averages because many sectors have so few data points and also because measures of variance are not meaningful. As a result, we combined a number of the three-digit SIC codes into logical groups to arrive at a reduced number of reasonable aggregations. Table 13.3 shows aggregate recovery prices per $100 for 18 industry categories, most of which have more than 20 observations each (some have more than 50 observations). The highest arithmetic average recoveries came from public utilities (70 percent) and from chemicals, petroleum, and related products (63 percent). The difference in the recovery rates of these two industrial aggregations compared with all the rest is quite large. Next came heavy machinery and electrical instruments, business and personal services, food, wholesale and retail trade, diversified manufacturing and casino, hotel, and recreation (all exceeding 40 percent). The remaining industrial sectors, with the exception of lodging, hospital, and nursing facilities (26 percent), had recovery rates in the 30–40 percent range. Weighted-average recoveries showed similar patterns with a few exceptions; for example, chemicals and related products actually exceeded utilities, and the lowest category had weighted recovery rates of less than 20 percent.[4]

Although the remaining industrial categories listed may appear to be fairly tightly clustered in the 30–40 percent recovery range, in reality, recoveries in the high 40 percent range are quite distant and significantly higher in many cases than those in the low 30 percent range. Machinery, instruments, and related products; business and personal services; and food product companies have recovered considerably more than, for example, drilling companies and textile/apparel firms.[5]

Table 13.3 also lists, by industry, standard deviations of the average recovery rates. Most are in the 20–28 percent range. Public utilities, which have the highest recovery rates, are among the lowest in variance. Textile and apparel manufacturers and mining and petroleum drilling both have low average recoveries and relatively low variance. In

[3] These SIC codes are from Standard & Poor's Compustat and Securities Data Company's compilations and may be different from industrial classifications found in other data sources. Indeed, Kahle and Walkling (1996) found that nearly 80 percent of the four-digit classification (the most finely separated categories) is different between Compustat and the CRSP stock data files; about 50 percent of the differences were found at the three-digit level and 36 percent at the two-digit level. Other sources of SIC codes are Lexis, the SEC Directory, the Million Dollar Directory, and the Value Line Investment Survey. Kahle and Walkling, after a controlled experiment, concluded that Compustat's SIC codes tend to outperform the CRSP codes, despite the fact that Compustat does not provide historical information about firms' industry affiliations.

[4] The weighted recoveries were 80 percent for the chemicals group and 65 percent for public utilities. The relatively high price and size of Texaco's defaulting issues were primarily responsible for this reversal in averages.

[5] We were somewhat surprised that services (personal and business) recovered more than 46 percent of face value. This sector's sample size was quite small, however, and had a few outliers.

Table 13.2 Recovery rates by industry: Defaulted bonds, 1971–95

SIC Code	Industry	Number of Observations	Recovery rate Average	Recovery rate Weighted
492	Gas utilities	25	$81.75	$90.42
150	Construction contracting	1	71.00	71.00
616	Mortgage banks	4	67.60	49.80
290	Petroleum and energy products	23	67.29	84.18
730	Personal business services – computer	3	64.87	70.90
491	Electric utilities	29	62.57	51.43
560	Apparel and accessory stores	1	61.00	61.00
790	Recreation services	10	59.00	60.70
280	Chemicals and allied products	6	58.00	61.63
470	Transportation services	5	52.73	43.16
350	Machinery (except electric)	20	50.54	49.95
300	Rubber and plastic products	6	49.96	56.55
500	Wholesale and retail trade	7	49.54	52.00
610	Finance companies	3	49.50	53.91
380	Instruments and related products	2	49.38	49.30
770	Casino hotels	11	48.91	44.22
609	Noncredit institutions	12	48.75	54.76
520	Retail trade	2	48.50	47.56
390	Manufacturing, miscellaneous	6	47.40	51.18
260	Paper and allied products	6	46.83	44.37
270	Printing and publishing	8	46.77	47.76
330	Steel and metal products	32	46.07	42.92
360	Electrical and electronic equipment	14	46.06	35.90
200	Food and related – manufacturing	18	45.28	37.40
208	Beverage bottlers	1	44.50	44.50
496	Steam and air conditioning supply	2	44.00	43.99
420	Trucking	4	43.63	40.59
620	Financial services	7	42.07	36.46
100	Mining	10	40.69	33.34
410	Bus transit	1	40.50	40.50
998	Diversified manufacturing	14	40.11	23.64
450	Air transportation	39	39.50	41.25
483	Radio and TV broadcasting	32	38.97	39.81
720	Laundry service	2	38.50	39.31
220	Textile and mill products	18	37.22	38.52
590	Retail miscellaneous	20	36.95	38.37
780	Movie production	15	35.00	35.41
540	Food stores	21	34.47	26.68
650	Real estate	34	34.21	27.93
320	Building materials	26	32.31	25.25
340	Fabricated metal products	10	32.15	24.62
130	Oil and gas drilling	33	31.54	31.91
580	Eating and drinking places	3	31.50	38.74
630	Insurance	10	31.48	35.17
530	Department stores	37	30.69	27.99
533	Variety stores	5	30.33	18.28
370	Transportation equipment	8	30.28	40.77
602	Commercial banks	22	29.33	21.60
510	Wholesale trade – nondurable goods	3	28.08	34.15
800	Hospitals and nursing facilities	11	26.89	18.47
482	Telegraph and related communications	10	26.43	34.85
701	Lodging places	11	26.09	22.12
230	Apparel and related products	13	23.96	26.13
570	Furniture, furnishings and equipment stores	2	23.00	23.20
632	Hospitals and medical services	3	22.50	31.41
670	Investment funds and trusts	2	20.82	28.21
138	Oil and gas field services	2	19.07	19.08
310	Leather products	1	13.00	13.00
250	Furniture	3	9.50	11.59
603	Savings institutions	6	9.25	19.68
240	Wood and related products	1	5.00	5.00

[Total number of observations is 696 although data here sums to 686.]

Table 13.3 Recovery rates by industry: Defaulted bonds by 3-digit SIC code, 1971–95

Industry	SIC Code[a]	Number of observations	Recovery rate			
			Average	Weighted	Median	Standard deviation
Public utilities	490	56	$70.47	$65.48	$79.07	$19.46
Chemicals, petroleum, rubber, and plastic products	280, 290, 300	35	62.73	80.39	71.88	27.10
Machinery, instruments, and related products	350, 360, 380	36	48.74	44.75	47.50	20.13
Services – business and personal	470, 632, 720, 730	14	46.23	50.01	41.50	25.03
Food and kindred products	200	18	45.28	37.40	41.50	21.67
Wholesale and retail trade	500, 510, 520	12	44.00	48.90	37.32	22.14
Diversified manufacturing	390, 998	20	42.29	29.49	33.88	24.98
Casino, hotel, and recreation	770, 790	21	40.15	39.74	28.00	25.66
Building materials, metals, and fabricated products	320, 330, 340	68	38.76	29.64	37.75	22.86
Transportation and transportation equipment	370, 410, 420, 450	52	38.42	41.12	37.13	27.98
Communication, broadcasting, movie production, printing, and publishing	270, 480, 780	65	37.08	39.34	34.50	20.79
Financial institutions	600, 610, 620, 630, 670	66	35.69	35.44	32.15	25.72
Construction and real estate	150, 650	35	35.27	28.58	24.00	28.69
General merchandise stores	530, 540, 560, 570, 580, 590	89	33.16	29.35	30.00	20.47
Mining and petroleum drilling	100, 130	45	33.02	31.83	32.00	18.01
Textile and apparel products	220, 230	31	31.66	33.72	31.13	15.24
Wood, paper, and leather products	240, 250, 260, 310	11	29.77	24.30	18.25	24.38
Lodging, hospitals, and nursing facilities	700 through 890	22	26.49	19.61	16.00	22.65
Total		696	41.00	39.11	36.25	25.56

[a] For example, 490 includes 490 through 499; 280 includes 280 through 289; and 700 includes 700 through 709.

general, variability is quite high relative to the mean recovery price, indicating that knowledge of specific issuer characteristics is still important.

TESTING FOR STATISTICAL SIGNIFICANCE

Public utilities and chemicals, petroleum, and plastics manufacturers experienced much higher recovery rates than did the rest of the industrial sectors. Also, senior bonds recovered more than junior bonds. The higher recoveries in certain industries might be explained by a greater preponderance of senior secured bonds or senior unsecured bonds in the higher-recovery sectors. Table 13.4 lists recovery prices by seniority within the 18 industrial categories.[6] According to this table, public utilities, for example, appear

Table 13.4 Recovery rates by industry and seniority: Defaulted bonds, 1971–95

Industry	Number of observations	Recovery rate Average	Recovery rate Weighted
Mining and petroleum drilling			
Senior secured	1	$71.00	$71.03
Senior unsecured	9	43.60	37.37
Senior subordinated	12	37.78	36.51
Subordinated	21	25.41	27.48
Discount and zero coupon	2	17.75	19.84
Construction and real estate			
Senior secured	1	40.00	40.00
Senior unsecured	12	41.91	39.16
Senior subordinated	10	37.31	24.59
Subordinated	12	26.52	22.79
Food and kindred products			
Senior unsecured	6	54.42	48.27
Senior subordinated	6	31.00	36.22
Subordinated	6	50.42	36.68
Textile and apparel products			
Senior unsecured	8	34.47	36.24
Senior subordinated	14	31.65	36.56
Subordinated	6	28.25	24.80
Discount and zero coupon	3	31.00	32.51
Wood, paper, and leather products, and publishing			
Senior unsecured	3	47.33	58.54
Senior subordinated	8	36.63	27.32
Subordinated	5	44.33	47.14
Discount and zero coupon	3	15.00	8.27
Chemicals, petroleum, rubber, and plastic products			
Senior secured	6	75.04	89.17
Senior unsecured	16	71.91	81.71
Senior subordinated	7	63.07	77.81
Subordinated	6	25.54	31.46
Building materials, metals, and fabricated products			
Senior secured	7	48.33	47.66
Senior unsecured	20	44.23	36.55
Senior subordinated	9	44.08	33.02
Subordinated	28	35.39	31.83
Discount and zero coupon	4	6.31	7.15

[6] Although we include discounted/zero-coupon bonds in our compilation, this category is less meaningful because it can encompass several of the seniority classes (e.g., senior subordinated or subordinated zero-coupon bonds).

Table 13.4 (cont'd)

| | | Recovery rate | |
Industry	Number of observations	Average	Weighted
Machinery, instruments, and related products			
Senior unsecured	11	$47.55	$51.36
Senior subordinated	8	58.41	35.40
Subordinated	15	44.75	41.60
Discount and zero coupon	2	46.50	50.52
Diversified manufacturing			
Senior unsecured	3	85.71	82.37
Senior subordinated	7	36.73	29.33
Subordinated	10	33.16	21.58
Transportation and transportation equipment			
Senior secured	14	55.72	58.12
Senior unsecured	22	30.83	36.28
Senior subordinated	8	45.81	48.02
Subordinated	8	21.60	15.00
Services – business and personal			
Senior secured	6	56.61	54.37
Senior subordinated	6	35.18	47.96
Subordinated	2	48.25	43.06
Communications, broadcasting, and movie production			
Senior secured	2	36.88	38.64
Senior unsecured	12	34.97	53.73
Senior subordinated	13	39.77	38.10
Subordinated	21	33.16	35.56
Discount and zero coupon	9	36.61	38.16
Public utilities			
Senior secured	21	64.42	59.64
Senior unsecured	32	77.74	71.53
Subordinated	2	44.00	43.99
Discount and zero coupon	1	17.75	17.75
Wholesale and retail trade			
Senior unsecured	2	39.00	33.50
Senior subordinated	2	76.45	69.18
Subordinated	7	37.88	47.17
Discount and zero coupon	1	32.00	32.00
General merchandise stores			
Senior unsecured	26	44.55	45.59
Senior subordinated	27	36.37	30.20
Subordinated	26	25.95	28.83
Discount and zero coupon	10	13.67	10.18
Financial institutions			
Senior secured	6	49.20	52.70
Senior unsecured	37	38.68	42.70
Senior subordinated	12	29.70	30.78
Subordinated	11	24.81	21.28
Lodging, hospitals, and nursing facilities			
Senior unsecured	4	20.50	19.39
Senior subordinated	8	26.75	15.49
Subordinated	9	28.08	18.63
Discount and zero coupon	1	34.00	34.00
Casino, hotel, and recreation			
Senior secured	10	40.78	37.18
Senior unsecured	1	100.00	100.00
Senior subordinated	5	34.20	44.59
Subordinated	4	26.13	26.22
Discount and zero coupon	1	60.00	60.00
Total	696	41.00	39.11

to have the vast majority of their bonds in the senior classes (53/56 = 95 percent). Chemicals and related industries have a lower senior priority ratio (63 percent), which is still higher than most, but not all, others.

Table 13.5 compares the average recovery prices of senior secured public utility issues ($64.42) and of senior secured chemical industry issues ($75.04) with all other senior secured debt ($56.59). The same test was applied to the senior unsecured class in the two industries (with recovery prices of $77.74 and $71.91, respectively) and versus all other senior unsecured defaults ($42.56 and $45.76).

The results show that the differences between public utilities and all other industries and between chemicals and all other groups are significant at the 1% or 5% level; that is, the observed differences did not happen by chance and are not determined by seniority. We thus concluded that the nature of the firms' assets and the industry's competitive structure, and perhaps other industry-related variables, explain differential recovery rates.

RECOVERY RATES BY SENIORITY AND ORIGINAL CREDIT RATING

Does a defaulting issue's original bond rating play any role in the recovery rate? One might expect that because a bond issue is almost always below investment grade just prior to default, its original rating should play no role in determining its recovery rate.[7] If, however, firms affiliated with certain industries have a greater preponderance of higher-rated, senior secured, and senior unsecured original debt, then one might expect higher recovery rates. An obvious example of this structure would be public utilities, and indeed, utilities do recover more than other sectors.

The comparison of the average recovery price for high-rated, investment-grade original issues versus low-rated, non-investment-grade issues, presented in table 13.6, shows clearly that original rating, at least in terms of the broad investment-grade versus junk-bond categories, has no effect on recoveries once seniority is taken into account. Although this finding is perhaps consistent with intuition and expected values, it is counter to what was observed when the original rating was not stratified by seniority.

The time between origination date and default date also has no effect on the recovery rate (Altman and Kishore 1996). We also tested for the association between the size of an issue (face value), stratified by seniority, and the default recovery rate. We found absolutely no statistical association between size and recovery rate.

CONCLUSION

We have documented average recovery rates on defaulted bonds stratified by industry and also by seniority. Aggregated by three-digit SIC codes, the results show similar recovery rates for a large number of industries, although great differences occur in a

---

[7] In an earlier study (Altman and Kishore 1996), we observed that about 6 percent of bonds that defaulted had an investment-grade rating six months prior to default but that for the bond to be investment grade just prior to default is very rare (perhaps in just two or three cases during the past 25 years).

Table 13.5 Significance test for selected industry vs. aggregate recovery rates by seniority

Industry group/Seniority	Industry group			Entire sample[a]			
	Number of observations	Average price ($)	Standard deviation ($)	Number of observations	Average price ($)	Standard deviation ($)	t-Test[b]
Public utilities							
Senior secured	21	64.42	14.03	64	55.75	25.17	1.98*
Senior unsecured	32	77.74	18.06	189	42.56	24.89	9.59**
Chemicals, petroleum, rubber, and plastics							
Senior secured	6	75.04	25.83	79	56.59	22.16	1.70*
Senior unsecured	16	71.91	18.41	205	45.76	26.52	5.27**
Senior subordinated	7	63.07	25.74	170	33.20	24.45	3.01**

[a] From Table 13.1, excluding observations from the particular industrial group(s) being tested.

[b] $t = \dfrac{\overline{X}_1 - \overline{X}_2}{\sqrt{\dfrac{\text{Std Dev}_1^2}{N_1} + \dfrac{\text{Std Dev}_2^2}{N_2}}}$

* Significant at the 5% level.
** Significant at the 1% level.

Table 13.6 Recovery rates by seniority and original bond rating, 1971–95

Seniority	Number of observations	Recovery rate			
		Average price	Weighted price	Median price	Standard deviation
Senior secured					
Investment grade	16	$54.80	$48.58	$55.82	$15.11
Noninvestment grade	58	56.42	56.82	50.50	24.93
Senior unsecured					
Investment grade	49	48.20	41.34	40.00	30.63
Noninvestment grade	175	48.73	55.61	42.50	25.64
Senior subordinated					
Investment grade	26	32.74	37.26	29.75	20.43
Noninvestment grade	136	39.93	35.01	32.00	25.67
Subordinated					
Investment grade	63	31.89	33.97	30.00	18.75
Noninvestment grade	136	31.67	27.58	28.40	21.07
Discount and zero coupon					
Investment grade	7	24.14	23.57	23.50	10.79
Noninvestment grade	30	24.42	17.21	19.90	19.14
Total	696	41.00	39.11	36.25	25.56

few sectors. We did not calculate default rates by industry, which would require assembling new issue and cumulative totals of amounts outstanding stratified by accepted definitions of industries. We intend to pursue this compilation in a subsequent study.

REFERENCES

Altman, E. I., and Allan C. Eberhart. 1994. "Do Seniority Provisions Protect Bondholders' Investments?" *Journal of Portfolio Management* 20 (4), (Summer), 67–75.
Altman, E. I., and Vellore M. Kishore. 1996. "Defaults and Returns on High Yield Bonds: Analysis through 1995." New York University Salomon Center Special Report.
——. 1987. *Investing in Junk Bonds.* New York: John Wiley & Sons.
Hickman, W. Braddock. 1958. *Corporate Bond Quality and Investor Experience.* Princeton, NJ: Princeton University Press.
Kahle, Kathleen, and Ralph Walkling. 1996. "The Impact of Industry Classification on Financial Research." Working paper, Ohio State University, College of Business (February).

14 Do Seniority Provisions Protect Bondholders' Investments?

Lenders need not fear expropriation.

with Allan C. Eberhart

A number of recent studies document that violations of the absolute priority rule (APR) are commonplace and can be of large magnitude. The APR states that senior creditors should be fully compensated before junior creditors receive a payoff, and that junior creditors should be paid in full before shareholders receive any portion of the bankrupt firm's value.

Studies finding that the rule is violated about 75 percent of the time include Betker (1992b), Eberhart et al. (1990), Eberhart and Sweeney (1992), Fabozzi et al. (1993), Franks and Torous (1989), Hotchkiss (1993), LoPucki and Whitford (1990), Weiss (1990), and White (1989). All these studies note that the lowest-priority claimants – i.e., the shareholders – benefit from APR violations.[1]

Estimates of the percentage of firm value that shareholders receive in violation of the rule range from 2.4 percent (Betker, 1992b) to 7.6 percent (Eberhart et al., 1990). Junior creditors, though, can be helped or harmed by APR violations.[2]

Departures from the APR have a potentially pernicious effect on the ability of firms to borrow money. If seniority provisions in bond contracts are routinely violated by the bankruptcy court, their value may be negligible. Jensen (1991) forcefully argues that APR violations are harmful. He posits that senior creditors may respond to deviations from the APR by refusing to lend to risky firms for fear of expropriation.

---

[1] The term "benefit" perhaps should be placed in quotation marks because it implies a wealth transfer. As we discuss in this article, however, the capital markets appear to anticipate APR violations as well as other influences on the bankruptcy emergence payoffs to securityholders. Eberhart and Senbet (1993) show that anticipated APR violations can be beneficial in reducing the risk incentive for financially distressed firms.

[2] For example, Eberhart and Sweeney (1993) show that the Wickes' 9% convertible subordinated debenture holders received over $449.93 less per $1,000 face value bond than they would have received if the APR had been followed. On the other hand, they also note that the Baldwin United 10% subordinated debenture holders collected over $576 more per $1,000 face value bond than they were entitled to under the APR.

One response to Jensen's argument is that as long as lenders anticipate the possibility (and the size) of a departure from the APR, they should not be averse to lending to high-risk firms because they will be compensated with a lower price/higher yield. In other words, in an efficient market investors are protected against expropriation.

Overall, the empirical evidence supports the efficient market hypothesis at the time firms default or file for Chapter 11. This implies that investors who purchase a firm's bond at this time pay an appropriate (i.e., efficient) price. It does not imply (although it is by no means inconsistent) that, at the time the bonds are issued, the market prices these bonds efficiently.

The market for distressed securities is dominated by sophisticated institutional investors called "vultures" who specialize in these securities; Altman (1991) estimates that there are at least sixty institutional investors and many broker/dealers who specialize in distressed and defaulted securities. The proportion of informed investors who purchase bonds at issuance is likely to be smaller.

To the extent this is true, there is a greater chance that, for example, senior bond prices at issuance do not reflect the potential dilution of seniority provisions in states of default. That is, investors may be overpaying for seniority provisions that they believe will offer more protection against the severity of default (i.e., the magnitude of the loss in states of default) than an informed investor would expect.[3]

This study investigates the efficiency of the market for bonds of firms that default and subsequently file for Chapter 11. To the best of our knowledge, our sample of 91 firms with 232 bonds that filed for and emerged from Chapter 11 between January 1980 and July 1992 is larger and more recent than for any other sample in this area.

We conduct two types of tests with this sample. First, we test the efficiency of these bonds as of the default date. Unlike previous researchers, we test for efficiency within each priority category. For the statistically most reliable sample, the results are generally supportive of efficiency.

Our second and more important test focuses on the efficiency of bond prices at issuance. Because we have, ex post, chosen those bonds that went into bankruptcy, we cannot conduct traditional efficiency tests. Rather we attempt to answer the question: Do seniority provisions protect bondholders' investments? In other words, do investors receive compensation for the seniority provisions they pay a premium for at issuance? If not, this suggests that, for example, senior bonds are overpriced at issuance.

We answer this question by documenting the losses that bankrupt firms' bondholders experience over the entire life of the bond. We find that, on average, higher seniority is associated with higher payoffs at emergence, providing evidence (albeit indirect) that the bonds are efficiently priced at issuance.

LITERATURE REVIEW

Studies of the market for distressed securities by Warner (1977), Betker (1992a), and Eberhart and Sweeney (1992) report results that, overall, are supportive of efficiency. Other studies that find support for efficiency in this market include Eberhart et al.

---

[3] For some more recent evidence on the probability and/or severity of default, see Altman (1989, 1992), Altman and Kao (1991), Fons et al. (1993), and Lucas and Lonski (1992).

(1990) and Gilson et al. (1990). Branch and Ray (1992) provide a complete discussion of investing in bankrupt firm securities.

Warner (1977) finds that the average cumulative abnormal return (ACAR) for a sample of bankrupt railroad bonds is generally insignificantly different from zero (during the bankruptcy period). He concludes therefore that the market is efficient.

Betker (1992a) also reports that the ACAR for his sample of bankrupt firms' stocks and bonds is generally insignificantly different from zero. His study covers returns through 1990 for post-1978 Bankruptcy Code filings (so do Eberhart and Sweeney (1992)). He segregates bonds into secured versus unsecured categories, but does not analyze different priority bondholders within the unsecured class (e.g., senior versus junior, etc.).

Eberhart and Sweeney (1992) test the efficient market hypothesis for a sample of bankrupt firm bonds using the ACAR and price-unbiasedness tests. This latter test asks if the actual return for each bond during the bankruptcy period, cross-sectionally regressed on the bond's expected rate of return, falls along a 45-degree line. The authors demonstrate that this can be a more powerful test of efficiency than the ACAR test. Overall, their results support efficiency. In a more recent study, Eberhart and Sweeney (1993) note that although APR violations may not bias distressed security prices, they can introduce additional noise (i.e., uncertainty about a security's intrinsic value).

A working paper by Datta and Iskander (1992) analyzes daily price changes for bankrupt firm stocks and bonds. Although some of these results are consistent with our results, this study has a very small sample size (under 30 issues). Hradsky and Long (1989) provide an analysis of the post-default monthly performance of bonds for up to 24 months after default. For a comparison of the new versus the old Bankruptcy Code, see Bradley and Rosenzweig (1992) and Altman (1993a).

Our study provides further insight into the degree of efficiency in the market for distressed securities by testing for abnormal performance during the default period for each category of bond. As mentioned earlier, we also include more recent defaults than previous studies.

DATA AND METHODOLOGY

Data

The sample is composed of 91 firms (with 232 bonds) that defaulted, filed for Chapter 11, and completed a bankruptcy/reorganization between January 1980 and July 1992. We collected information on the coupon and seniority of each bond as well as the issue price, the price just after default, and the price/payoff of the debt securities upon emergence from Chapter 11.[4]

Our pricing sources include: Standard & Poor's *Bond Guide*; *Capital Changes Reporter*; OTC dealers' quotes (bid); *The Wall Street Journal*; *The Bankruptcy Datasource*; Standard & Poor's *Daily Stock Price Record*; annual reports, 10–Ks, 8–Ks, and investor files. For a small number of issues (eight), we use data from T. Rowe Price Associates,

---

[4] Although the confirmation date can precede the emergence date, they are often the same date. Thus, we use the terms interchangeably. More generally, these dates represent the completion of the bankruptcy process, as some of these firms were liquidated or acquired.

which did an internal study of defaulted bond investor performance. Broker dealers' quotes are from B.D.S. Securities, Merrill Lynch & Co., and Salomon Brothers. Our sample represents the vast majority of defaulting issues in the sample period that have gone through the entire bankruptcy/reorganization process, and probably well over 90 percent of relevant defaulting dollars.[5]

The subordinated category is the largest portion of the sample (38 percent; 89 issues), with senior-unsecured next (33 percent; 76 issues). The vast majority of issues are straight (non-convertible) (189; 81.5 percent). Only five issues are original-issue, discounted, non-cash-pay bonds.

The average time spent in Chapter 11 is 1.97 years, which is slightly longer than what Altman (1993a) reports. Note that the time from default to emergence is slightly longer than from bankruptcy to emergence because some firms default on debt issues prior to the actual Chapter 11 filing. (Because the default date and Chapter 11 filing date are often the same, we use the phrases default period, Chapter 11 period, and reorganization period interchangeably.)

Post-Default Performance of Bonds

We measure the performance of 202 defaulting issues from the end of the default month to the completion of the Chapter 11 period.[6] Specifically, we calculate the ACARs by adjusting the raw return of each defaulting issue for the comparable-period performance on an index of high-yield "junk" bonds. The latter is represented by the returns on the "BlumeKeim Low Rated Bond Index" (Blume and Keim (1987) and Blume et al. (1991)).[7]

The ACAR test is a test of whether the average actual return ($\bar{R}$) equals the average expected rate of return ($\overline{ER}$):

$$ACAR = \bar{R} - \overline{ER}$$

$$= \left(\frac{1}{N}\right) \sum_{i=1}^{N} R_{i,T_i} - \left(\frac{1}{N}\right) \sum_{i=1}^{N} R_{i,T_i}$$

$$= \left(\frac{1}{N}\right) \sum_{i=1}^{N} CAR_{i,T_i} \tag{1}$$

[5] Over the period January 1980–July 1992, approximately 610 corporate debt issues defaulted from about 350 different firms. As of July 1992, at least 280 issues from over 140 firms were still being reorganized and had not emerged from Chapter 11; see Merrill Lynch (1993a, 1993b) for a discussion of issues trading while under Chapter 11. In addition, at least 45 of the defaulting issues from 30 firms were restructured outside the confines of the bankruptcy court or for some other reason did not file for Chapter 11 protection. Therefore, our 232-issue and 91-firm sample represents at least 80 percent of the defaulting issues, and our 91 firms represent over 50 percent of the eligible defaulting companies that emerged from Chapter 11 in the sample period.

[6] This sample is slightly smaller than the 232 issues because of missing price data at default on 30 issues.

[7] The correlation coefficient between monthly returns on the Merrill Lynch Master Index of High Yield Debt Securities and the Altman–Merrill Lynch Index of Defaulted Debt Securities is 0.595 for the period 1987–92 (Altman, 1993b). But the two indexes are totally independent with respect to their bond issue sample.

where

R_{i,T_i} = actual rate of return for bond i over T_i months (expressed in monthly returns)

ER_{i,T_i} = expected rate of return for bond i over T_i months (expressed in monthly returns)

CAR_{i,T_i} = cumulative abnormal return for bond i (expressed in monthly returns)

N = sample size

T_i = number of months from default to emergence from Chapter 11 for bond i.

We express each CAR in terms of monthly returns because there are large cross-sectional differences in the amount of time each firm spends in default.[8] To test the statistical significance of the ACAR, we use a simple t-statistic based on the cross-sectional variation in the CARs.

Loss Measures

We calculate three loss measures to measure the degree of protection that seniority provisions offer:

$$L_1 = \frac{P_c - P_o}{P_o} \tag{2}$$

$$L_2 = \frac{P_c - [P_o + FI]}{P_o} \tag{3}$$

$$L_3 = \frac{P_c - [P_o + FI + IFI]}{P_o} \tag{4}$$

where

L_1, L_2, and L_3 = the three loss calculations

P_o = original issue price

P_c = price/payoff at confirmation

FI = forgone interest during the reorganization period including one-half lost coupon at default, not including reinvestment of the interest

IFI = interest on FI

L_1 is the most straightforward measure of the lost principal from original issuance purchase until the end of the reorganization period. L_2 considers the opportunity cost of holding a debt security during an investment period when no interest is being paid.

[8] Specifically,

$$R_{i,T_i} = (P_{T_i}/P_d)^{1/T_i} - 1$$

and $ER_{i,T}$ is the average monthly rate of return on the market (i.e., the Blume–Keim Junk Bond Index).

For our calculations, we use the coupon amount on the specific issue as the forgone interest. Finally, L_3 also encompasses lost return on reinvestment of the interest that would have been received if the bond had not defaulted.[9] Of course, $L_1 > L_2 > L_3$; the L_1 loss (gain) is "less severe" than L_2, which is "less severe" than L_3.

Sample Selection Bias Issues

Our sample of defaulted bonds is limited to those of issuers that eventually filed for Chapter 11. Curing default outside Chapter 11 has been shown to be a less costly way to resolve financial distress (Gilson et al., 1990). Consistent with this finding is the observation by Betker (1992a) that bonds experience negative reactions to Chapter 11 announcements.

Hence, the sample of defaulted bonds that did not go through Chapter 11 likely experienced higher returns; this suggests that our measure of average returns during the default period may be biased downward. This insight is important to keep in mind when interpreting the efficiency results. (This bias is likely greater than the possible opposite bias in our default period sample, which analyzes thirty fewer issues than the sample covering returns/losses from issuance to emergence.)

EMPIRICAL RESULTS

Prices at Issuance and Emergence

Table 14.1 shows the average issuance price and the average payoff at emergence for the overall sample and each priority class. Note that the average initial price (P_o) is (with the exception of discounted bonds) close to but not equal to 100; that is, 100 percent of the bond's face value. These average values range from a high of 99.67 for secured bonds to 95 for senior-subordinated bonds. The overall sample average is

Table 14.1 Average bond price at issuance and average emergence payoff

Debt issue type	Sample size	Issuance price (P_o)	Emergence payoff (P_c)
Overall sample	232	96.33	50.46
Non-convertible	189	95.83	56.91
Convertible	43	98.52	22.12
Overall sample by seniority			
Secured	24	99.67	100.91
Senior	76	98.85	76.94
Senior-subordinated	38	95.00	23.30
Subordinated (cash-pay)	89	96.19	28.41
Subordinated (non-cash-pay)	5	54.88	4.78

[9] We calculate interest on interest at 8 percent. Ideally, we would use a rate that changes with market conditions (and thus reflects the true opportunity cost of the interest), but the magnitude of these amounts involves such a small portion of the loss measure that we consider our approximation reasonable.

96.33. It should be noted that 84 of the 232-bond sample (38 percent) have initial prices less than face value, including the five discounted bonds; five issues have initial prices greater than face value.

The overall average emergence payoff is 50.46; approximately 50 cents on the dollar. For the sample of bonds with prices at default (202 issues), the average price just after default is 38.44 (shown in table 14.2).

The average emergence payoff sorted by seniority shows the highest average value recorded for secured bonds (100.91) followed by 76.94 for senior bonds and just 4.78 for non-cash-pay subordinated debt.[10] The one exception to this hierarchy is the senior-subordinated average of just 23.30 versus 28.41 for subordinated issues. This is explained by the fact that the firms represented for each of these two categories are not identical.

Hence, we also calculate the average prices for those firms that have *both* senior-subordinated and subordinated debt outstanding, and we then find the expected ordering (for the 20 senior-subordinated bonds the average P_c is 22.62; for the 28 subordinated bonds the average P_c is 10.75).[11] Although the loss measures discussed below make a stronger case for the value of seniority, these results are consistent with the notion that investors pay an appropriate price for higher priority.

Table 14.2   Average bond price at default and average emergence payoff

Debt issue type	Sample size	Issuance price (P_d)	Emergence payoff (P_c)
Overall sample	202	38.44	52.57
Non-convertible	171	41.16	57.16
Convertible	31	23.41	27.25
Overall sample by seniority			
Secured	23	69.36	102.24
Senior	68	46.02	77.78
Senior-subordinated	32	25.69	21.32
Subordinated (cash-pay)	74	29.80	30.71
Subordinated (non-cash-pay)	5	2.48	4.78

Efficiency Tests at Default

Table 14.2 lists the average prices at default (P_d) and at emergence (P_c) for the subsample of 202 bonds with prices available at default. Note that for many, but not all, priorities and types of issues, as well as the entire sample of 202 defaulted issues, the average price at the end of the reorganization period is greater than the average price at default; this is what we would expect in an efficient market.

[10]   The average emergence/confirmation price for straight, non-convertible senior bonds is 81.05, about 4 more than the sample of senior bonds that includes convertibles (five issues).
[11]   When we update our results through September 1993, the sample size increases to 321 bonds (152 firms). The senior-secured and senior-unsecured average payoffs at confirmation/emergence drop substantially to 88.79 and 58.2, respectively (the senior-subordinated and junior-subordinated remain virtually unchanged). These changes are driven by the Continental Airlines bonds. When these bonds are removed, the results are qualitatively similar. These results are available from the authors.

We find one exception, however; the average emergence payoff to the senior-subordinated bonds (21.32) is lower than the average default price (25.69). This suggests the bonds are overpriced at default.

On the other hand, the secured and senior bond samples appear to have done exceptionally well, at least with respect to absolute price differences. Of course, these comparisons provide only informal evidence on the efficiency of defaulted bond prices.

Table 14.3 presents the excess return (i.e., ACAR) results. The overall sample average excess returns are significantly negative (-1.29 percent, $t = -2.49$). The average excess returns to the secured, subordinated (cash-pay), and convertible bonds are also significantly negative; this suggests these bonds are systematically overpriced at default. The median returns, however, are generally much lower in magnitude. Because extreme outliers are not unusual in this sample, the median return results are a better indicator of "typical performance."

These results include multiple debt issues for a number of companies. For example, the 23 secured observations were issued by just 8 companies; the 64 straight senior bonds by 31 companies; the 30 straight senior-subordinated bonds by 26 companies; and the 49 straight subordinated issues by 37 companies. The positive correlation among bonds from the same firm causes the t-statistics to be biased toward larger magnitudes.

To circumvent this problem, we calculate the equal-weighted average return among bonds from the same firm (Warga and Welch, 1993). These independent excess return results are shown in table 14.4 and, overall, are supportive of efficiency.

Table 14.3 Efficiency tests for sample of all bonds

Debt issue type	Sample size	Monthly excess returns (%) (ACARs)			
		Mean	Median	Standard deviation	t-test
Overall sample	202	(1.29)	0.14	7.35	(2.49)
Non-convertible	171	(0.67)	0.38	6.56	(1.34)
Convertible	31	(4.73)	(2.22)	10.03	(2.63)
Overall sample by seniority					
Secured	23	1.23	(1.14)	1.99	2.96
Senior	68	0.60	1.07	5.43	0.91
Senior-subordinated	32	(1.88)	(2.41)	7.76	(1.37)
Subordinated (cash-pay)	74	(3.95)	(1.40)	8.65	(3.93)
Subordinated (non-cash-pay)	5	4.34	1.85	7.32	1.33

Table 14.4 Efficiency tests for independent sample

Debt issue type	Sample size	Monthly returns (%)		
		Absolute	Excess	t-test
Secured	8	2.07	1.46	1.49
Senior	33	0.81	0.01	0.01
Senior-subordinated	27	(1.45)	(2.12)	(1.37)
Subordinated (cash-pay)	54	(4.16)	(4.67)	(4.03)
Subordinated (non-cash-pay)	4	6.16	4.99	1.24

The subordinated-straight bonds are the only exception, as they display negative and significant returns of −4.16 percent (t = −4.03). Although this suggests these bonds are overpriced at default, the inefficiency is probably not exploitable because we have not accounted for the transaction costs, which are likely to be high. Moreover, the implied arbitrage strategy is to short-sell these bonds; given the negative average reaction to default announcements (Betker, 1992a), implementing this strategy may be impossible.

Loss Measures

Table 14.5 summarizes the average and median results for the three loss measures. In the majority of cases (164 issues; 70.7 percent), we use actual market values for the payoff upon emergence. For the cases where market values are not available, we use the stated book values of the package of securities exchanged for the old debt.

The results using the 164-issue sample where only market values are available are qualitatively similar to the results with our larger sample. Some average results showed lower losses with the reduced sample, however. For example, L_1 for senior bonds is −7.30 percent versus −22.1 percent for the larger sample.

For all defaulted bond investors, the average L_1 is −48.38 percent (median = −65.6 percent). In fact, many issues suffer virtually a 100 percent loss, and 53 issues suffer L_1 losses of over 90 percent. Also, the range of values is high; for example, the range for L_1 is +74.1 percent to −100 percent.

The average L_2 and L_3 for the entire sample are considerably lower (greater losses) than the L_1 figure, with L_2 = −79.8 percent and L_3 = −83.4 percent. Median losses are also again lower than the mean (L_2 = −91.6 percent and L_3 = −92.6 percent). Therefore, average losses to investors almost double when one includes the lost opportunities for an issue that trades "flat" (i.e., without interest).

The importance of lost interest in a bankruptcy/reorganization is clearly demonstrated for a firm where there are some issues that accrue interest and others that do not during the reorganization. For example, in the LTV Corp. bankruptcy, all the LTV issues were unsecured and were trading flat, while several of the firm's Youngstown

Table 14.5 Three loss measures

Debt issue type	Sample size	L_1 (%) mean	L_1 (%) median	L_2 (%) mean	L_2 (%) median	L_3 (%) mean	L_3 (%) median
Overall sample	232	(48.38)	(65.60)	(79.81)	(91.57)	(83.37)	(92.64)
Non-Convertible	189	(41.70)	(49.00)	(74.42)	(83.53)	(78.07)	(85.10)
Convertible	43	(77.75)	(90.00)	(103.51)	(112.71)	(106.66)	(113.12)
Overall sample by seniority							
Secured	24	1.68	(0.75)	(32.15)	(29.73)	(36.29)	(33.49)
Senior	76	(22.05)	(12.59)	(52.57)	(39.10)	(56.51)	(41.46)
Senior-subordinated	38	(75.13)	(86.04)	(109.51)	(113.97)	(113.09)	(116.38)
Subordinated (cash-pay)	89	(70.58)	(79.57)	(99.54)	(106.62)	(102.59)	(108.36)
Subordinated (non-cash-pay)	5	(90.38)	(91.38)	(145.74)	(133.91)	(149.44)	(137.23)

Sheet & Tube subsidiary bonds were secured and had interest accruing during the seven years of reorganization. When LTV emerged from Chapter 11 in July 1993, the unsecured parent company bonds were selling for about 26 cents on the dollar, while the two Youngstown bonds were over $160 per $100 face value. Of course, the price of the latter bonds would be less than par value if not for the accrued interest.

These results underscore one of the many potential benefits of a shortened bankruptcy process (i.e., the possibility of lower losses). See Altman (1993a) and LoPucki (1993) for a discussion of the average time in bankruptcy.

Loss by Seniority

The L_1, L_2, and L_3 losses by seniority are also shown in table 14.5. Secured bonds (24 issues) show an average L_1 of 1.68 percent, although the median is slightly negative (−0.8 percent). When we adjust for lost interest and also lost interest on interest, though, the secured bonds incur average returns of −32.2 percent (L_2) and −36.3 percent (L_3). Some of the secured bonds are sold "flat," although in a few cases their prices reflect post-petition accrued interest, e.g., Public Service Corporation of New Hampshire. L_1 values are a modest −22.1 percent for senior bonds, although the L_2 and L_3 rates are significantly greater at −52.6 percent and −56.5 percent, respectively.

Lower-priority senior-subordinated and subordinated bond issues do quite poorly, with L_1 losses of 75.1 percent and 70.6 percent, respectively. When we include forgone interest, the senior-subordinated bonds incur losses of 109.5 percent (L_2) and 113.1 percent (L_3). The comparable loss rates for subordinated bonds are slightly less.[12] Again, if you stratify these two samples with firms that have *both* senior-subordinated and subordinated debt outstanding, the anomaly disappears, i.e., the senior-subordinated bond L_1 is −76.4 percent versus −87.4 percent for subordinated bonds.

Table 14.5 also lists our results for convertible bonds versus straight debt. The convertible bonds, which have more equity-like features, do somewhat worse than their straight-debt counterparts. Losses due to the equity-like features are neutralized, however, by the lower average coupon rate for convertibles. This is because L_2 and L_3 are affected by the lower coupon, but our measures ignore the fact that convertibles have the lower coupon in the first place due to the conversion features of the bonds. Hence, by accounting for the lost coupon payments only from the default date, we are underestimating the loss to convertibles *vis-à-vis* non-convertible issues.

As noted above, the L_1 experience of senior-secured debt is slightly positive and modestly negative for the senior-unsecured class. The L_1 loss percentage for all subordinated bonds, however, is about 50 percentage points worse than the loss for senior-unsecured bonds (−70.6 percent versus −22.1 percent). These results clearly show that despite the existence of widespread – and potentially large – APR violations, higher seniority, *ceteris paribus*, leads to greater protection of a bondholder's investment (i.e., lower losses/higher payoffs at emergence from Chapter 11). This is consistent with the efficient pricing of bonds at issuance, because bondholders pay a premium for the higher seniority.

---

[12]   This anomaly is possible because the senior-subordinated bonds were issued during periods of high interest rates; thus, their higher average coupon rate increases the magnitude of L_2 and L_3.

SUMMARY AND CONCLUSIONS

The dramatic rise in debt ratios for many firms during the 1980s has been followed by an equally dramatic rise in the number of firms filing for bankruptcy in the late 1980s and early 1990s (Altman, 1991). Some resulting research shows that absolute priority rule (APR) violations occur in approximately 75 percent of Chapter 11 bankruptcy cases, and that these violations can be considerable.

The regularity and frequency of APR violations has led some observers to argue that they may make lenders hesitant to lend to anything less than stellar credit rating firms for fear of expropriation. If the market is efficient, however, lenders need not fear expropriation, because they are compensated for any possible dilution of their priority in case of a bankruptcy with a lower purchase price/higher yield.

This study conducts two tests of efficiency of the market for bonds of firms that default and subsequently file for Chapter 11. Our sample is composed of 91 firms (with 232 bonds) that defaulted, filed for Chapter 11, and emerged from Chapter 11 between January 1980 and July 1992. Our first test focuses on the efficiency of these bonds as of the default date. Some of the results within priority categories suggest that bonds are overpriced at the time of default. The results with the statistically most reliable sample, however, generally support efficiency.

Our second and more important test focuses on the efficiency of bond prices at issuance. Because we have, ex post, chosen bonds that went into bankruptcy, we cannot conduct traditional efficiency tests. Rather we provide some indirect evidence on efficiency by calculating the extent to which seniority provisions protect bondholders' investments. Specifically, we document the losses bankrupt firm bondholders experience over the entire life of the bond. We find that bonds with seniority provisions receive significantly higher payoffs (lower losses) at emergence than subordinated bonds, providing indirect evidence that the bonds are efficiently priced at issuance.

REFERENCES

Altman, E. "Default Risk, Mortality Rates and the Performance of Corporate Bonds." *Journal of Finance*, September 1989, 909–22.

——. *Distressed Securities*. Chicago, IL: Probus Publishing Co., 1991.

——. "Revisiting the High Yield Debt Market." *Financial Management*, Summer 1992, 78–92.

——. "Evaluating the Chapter 11 Bankruptcy-Reorganization Process." *Columbia Business Law Review*, No. 1 (1993a), 1–25.

——. "The Performance of Defaulted Debt Securities: 1987–1991." *Financial Analysts Journal*, May/June 1993b.

Altman, E., and D. L. Kao. "Corporate Bond Rating Drift: An Examination of Rating Agency Credit Quality Changes Over Time." Charlottesville, VA: Research Foundation of the Chartered Financial Analysts Federation, 1991.

Betker, B. "An Analysis of the Returns to Stockholders and Bondholders in a Chapter 11 Reorganization." Working Paper, The Ohio State University, 1992a.

——. "Equity's Bargaining Power and Deviations from Absolute Priority in Chapter 11 Bankruptcies." Working Paper, The Ohio State University, 1992b.

Blume, M., and D. Keim. "Lower Grade Bonds: Their Risks and Returns." *Financial Analysts Journal*, July/August 1987, 26–33.

Blume, M., D. Keim, and S. Patel. "Returns and Volatility of Low Grade Bonds." *Journal of Finance*, 46 (March 1991), 49–74.

Bradley, M., and M. Rosenzweig. "The Untenable Case for Chapter 11." *Yale Law Journal*, March 1992, 1043–95.

Branch, B., and H. Ray. *Bankruptcy Investing*. Chicago, IL: Dearborn Press, 1992.

Datta, S., and M. Iskander. "The Valuable Effects of Chapter 11 Bankruptcy Filing on Different Classes of Security Holders: An Empirical Investigation." Working Paper, Northern Illinois University, July 1992.

Eberhart, A., W. Moore, and R. Roenfeldt. "Security Pricing and Deviations from the Absolute Priority Rule in Bankruptcy Proceedings." *Journal of Finance*, 45 (December 1990), 1457–69.

Eberhart, A., and L. Senbet. "Absolute Priority Rule Violations and Risk Incentives for Financially Distressed Firms." *Financial Management*, 22 (Autumn 1993), 101–16.

Eberhart, A., and R. Sweeney. "Does the Bond Market Predict Bankruptcy Settlements?" *Journal of Finance*, 47 (July 1992), 943–80.

——. "Noise: The Case of the Market for Bankrupt Firms' Securities." Working Paper, New York University and Georgetown University, 1993.

Fabozzi, F., J. Howe, T. Makabe, and T. Sudo. "Recent Evidence on the Distribution Patterns in Chapter 11 Reorganizations." *Journal of Fixed Income*, March 1993.

Fons, J., L. Carty, and D. Girault. "Corporate Bond Defaults and Default Rates, 1970–1991." *Moody's Special Report*, January 1993.

Franks, J., and W. Torous. "An Empirical Investigation of US Firms in Reorganization." *Journal of Finance*, 44 (July 1989), 769–97.

Gilson, Stuart C., Kose John, and Larry H. P. Lang. "Troubled Debt Restructurings: An Empirical Study of Private Reorganization of Firms in Default." *Journal of Financial Economics*, 27 (October 1990), 315–54.

Hotchkiss, Edith S. "The Post-Bankruptcy Performance of Firms Emerging from Chapter 11." Unpublished Dissertation, New York University, 1993.

Hradsky, Gregory T., and Robert D. Long. "High-Yield Default Losses and the Return Performance of Bankrupt Debt." *Financial Analysts Journal*, 1989, 38–49.

Jensen, Michael C. "Corporate Control and the Politics of Finance." *Journal of Applied Corporate Finance*, 4 (Spring 1991), 13–33.

LoPucki, L. "The Trouble with Chapter 11." *University of Wisconsin Law Review*, June 1993.

LoPucki, L., and W. Whitford. "Bargaining Over Equity's Share in Reorganization of Large Publicly Held Companies." *University of Pennsylvania Law Review*, November 1990, 125–96.

——. "Corporate Bond Default Rates." In S. Levine, ed., *Investing in Bankruptcies and Turnarounds*. New York: Harper Business, 1991.

Lucas, D., and J. Lonski. "Changes in Corporate Credit Quality." *Journal of Fixed Income*, March 1992, 7–14.

Merrill Lynch. "Defaulted Bonds: Supply, Demand and Investment Performance." High Yield Securities Research, 1993a.

——. "Defaults and Returns on High Yield Bonds: Analysis Through 1992." High Yield Securities Research, 1993b.

Warga, A., and I. Welch. "Bondholder Losses in Leveraged Buyouts." *Review of Financial Studies*. 1993, March.

Warner, Jerold B. "Bankruptcy, Absolute Priority, and the Pricing of Risky Debt Claims." *Journal of Financial Economics*, 4 (1977), 239–76.

Weiss, L. "Bankruptcy Costs and Violations of Claims Priority." *Journal of Financial Economics*, 27 (October 1990), 285–314.

White, Michelle. "The Corporate Bankruptcy Decision." *Journal of Economic Perspectives*, 3 (Spring 1989), 129–51.

15 | Aggregate Influences on Business Failure Rates

INTRODUCTION

The business failure phenomenon has received increased attention in the literature in the last decade. In recent years (the early 1980s), over 40,000 firms per year petitioned the courts to liquidate or to reorganize under the bankruptcy act. A good deal of the recent interest in business failures has resulted from the number of large firms which have succumbed to this negative economic reality. Prior to 1970, firms with assets of more than $25 million almost never failed. Since 1970, more than 35 nonfinancial firms with assets over $125 million have failed, topped by the Penn Central debacle. The costs to society of large firm bankruptcies have been cited and debated in the popular press; frequently mentioned are Chrysler Corp.'s problems and government loan guarantees (1979–81), and more recently the International Harvester crisis.

The importance of microeconomic issues and the attendant large number of analytical studies have obscured the relevance and influence of macroeconomic influences on the business failure phenomenon. It is argued, however, that certain aggregate measures and macroeconomic conditions are closely associated with the causes of business failure and contribute to the fact that marginally continuing enterprises are forced to declare bankruptcy or are unable to continue as going concerns.

The primary purpose of this chapter is to examine the aggregate economic influences on business failure experience. We will primarily be concerned with the failure rate in the USA, that is, the number of business failures recorded per 10,000 firms covered by Dun & Bradstreet (the most comprehensive and continuous failure time series). A quarterly, first difference, distributed lag regression model is constructed to achieve our objectives. In doing so, we will be guided by some rather intuitive economic relationships and the work performed by the National Bureau of Economic Research in the area of business cycle analysis and economic indicators. Business failure had been classified as a fairly consistent leading indicator of recessions and somewhat less reliable, but still leading, for recovery periods. However, it no longer is considered one of the nation's leading indicators. The work discussed in this chapter has formed the basis of my econometric business failure rate forecasts found in *Business Week* (March 24, 1980, p. 98, and April 29, 1982, p. 20).

I am aware of just a few published studies relating to macroeconomic influences on bankruptcies in the USA: Noto and Zimmerman (1981), and, for Britain and Japan, Cumming and Saini (1981). For more details of the work discussed below, see Altman (1980).

Variable Specification

We will attempt to analyze the change in aggregate business failure experience in the USAs. Our dependent variable will be the change in the business failure rate (BFR) as compiled by Dun & Bradstreet over the period 1951–78. For statistical reasons, discussed later, we specify the model in a first difference form.

The primary theme which will guide us in our choice of explanatory variables is exacerbating pressures on the marginal firm, that is, what conditions, at the aggregate level, can be expected to impact upon a firm's propensity to continue. The following categories of aggregate economic behavior are specified as potentially revealing indicators of business failure:

1   Economic growth activity
2   Credit availability or money market activity
3   Capital market activity
4   Business population characteristics
5   Price level changes

Economic Growth

Interest in business failure is usually heightened during periods of economic stress. Stress is most devastating to vulnerable entities, and we can expect that business failure and low or negative economic growth are closely associated economic series. Figure 15.1 presents quarterly BFRs from 1950 through the last quarter of 1981. Recessionary periods are indicated as well, and we observe increases in failure rates during these phases.

Sales and earnings of individual enterprises are directly related to overall business activity, and we should expect a negative correlation between series which reflect the nation's economic health and business failures. A related factor is the timing specification between economic activity and failure. On the one hand, we might specify that business failures will lead to changes in aggregate activity since the failure rate has often been referred to as a leading indicator of business cycle changes. On the other hand, we would also expect that the accumulation of negative aggregate activity will heighten pressures on all firms, particularly on those most vulnerable. Therefore, a distributed-lag model could provide a more effective structural specification.

The two series chosen to reflect economic growth are real GNP and corporate profits. Both are aggregate series which indicate total sales and profit experience of the individual entities which make up the market. Growth in GNP is traditionally viewed as an

Figure 15.1   BFR per 10,000 firms: Quarterly 1950–81

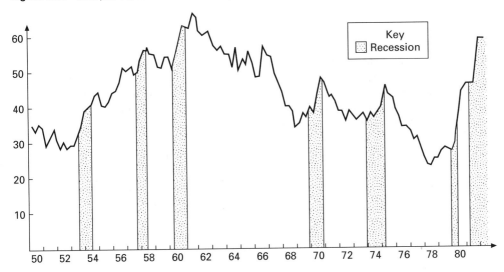

Source: Dun & Bradstreet, *Business Failure Record* and *Dun's Review*.

overall indicator of national economic health and an important measuring tool for economic analysts. The relationship between corporate profits and failures is well documented in business cycle measurement. Conditions leading to a change in profits are logically related to failures since a slight drop in profits to the marginal firm is often critical to its continued existence.

Money Market and Credit Conditions

One of the more likely current economic debates concerns the effect that the nation's monetary stock has on our economic conditions. In the case of the potential failing firm the argument is quite clear. Money, or more specifically credit availability and its cost, most certainly does matter. The typical chain of events in a failing firm begins with operating difficulties manifesting in losses and/or deteriorating market share. The firm's vulnerability is often magnified by relatively high financial and/or operating leverage structures. Since the capital markets are usually unavailable to firms whose solvency is threatened (see discussion below), and suppliers may be reluctant to increase their exposure, a critical source of credit is commercial banks. Regardless of how poorly a firm is performing, it seldom is "motivated" to declare bankruptcy as long as liquidity is sufficient or credit is available. Therefore, we can expect that the propensity to fail will be increased during periods of relatively tight credit conditions *vis-à-vis* periods of easy credit.

Compounding this problem is the seemingly discriminatory policy against smaller concerns during periods of tight money. Since the great majority of failures are small firms, the so-called small business "credit rationing" effect, which is alleged to occur during tight money conditions, is potentially an important influence on the total failure experience of US businesses. The hypothesized relationship between credit availability and business failures is therefore inverse. Measures which we choose to reflect credit and liquidity conditions are the nation's monetary stock, free reserves, and interest rates.

Credit conditions are affected by the combined forces of supply and demand for funds as well as the monetary policy being pursued by the Federal Reserve System. In this chapter, we attempt to observe an economic consequence of adjusting the money supply. Previously mentioned reasons for attempting to adjust the supply of money and credit concern overall economic growth goals, the containment of price inflation, and balance of payments problems. Related to the overall consequence of shifts in money supply are the costs (or gains) of increasing (decreasing) business failures. Whether or not monetary policy manifestations are associated with individual firm failures will be examined. Cumming and Saini (1981) found that the interest cost burden was statistically significant for Japan and the UK, indicating that restrictive monetary policy may be an important determinant of bankruptcy change.

The two other cited measures of money market conditions – free reserves and interest rates – are probably less consistent in their relationship to credit conditions. Both may be looked upon as transmitters of Federal Reserve action. We did examine these measures as well.

Investor Expectations

The potential failing firm is not likely to take the necessary steps of voluntary failure "declaration" if the future appears hopeful. This is logical whether the optimism is manifest internally or from forces external to the firm. One sector of external influence is the investment community's expectations which are reflected in the prices paid for financial asset ownership. The relationship between common stock prices and business failures is predicated on both empirical and theoretical grounds. Empirically, business cycle analysts had, for many years, reported that business failures and stock prices were both leading indicators of cyclical turning points. The fact that we observe these two aggregate series moving together periodically, with both indicating changes in future economic activity, is interesting but not necessarily indicative of a causal relationship. Both are likely to be related to a third factor – expected economic conditions – and therefore their mutual association is not clearly direct.

A case could be made for a more direct relationship between stock prices and failures if we consider that the definition of insolvency in bankruptcy is the situation where the firm's liabilities exceed the economic value of its assets. An accurate indicator of just how much of a fall in asset value is necessary before this insolvency situation is manifest is the market value of the equity in a firm as a percentage of its debt (MV/D). A MV/D ratio of 0.25 indicates that the company's asset values can only fall 20 percent before insolvency occurs. The argument here is that market values, in a fairly accurate way, reflect economic values. A drop in the growth of overall stock prices affects most firms, but it can be crucial to the existence of a marginal firm. The failure symptoms may have been present in the firm for some time, yet the decision to liquidate or reorganize in bankruptcy is rarely invoked while the firm's equity is still selling at some tangible positive value. Therefore, the drop in stock price to some negligible value is the "immediate" cause of failure. This is more likely to occur in a bear market than in more favorable stock market conditions. We utilize the MV/D measure again in the Z-score model.

In order to reflect overall stock market performance, we choose the change in the Standard & Poor (S&P) index of stock prices. The major reasons for this choice are the relative comprehensiveness of this index and the availability of quarterly observations during the entire post-World War II period. Since most firms that fail are not listed corporations, the use of the S&P index is a proxy for investor expectations. Also, the S&P index is the one utilized by the National Bureau of Economic Research as one of their economic indicators.

A second type of investor expectation variable which may have some relationship with business failures is a risk premium measure. All financial instruments except risk-free assets contain an element of risk which is reflected in the yield which investors require. The difference between this yield and the risk-free rate is the risk premium, and the more risky the security, the greater the risk premium. Although we do observe a stable ordinal relationship between rates of return on various risky assets over time, this by no means implies that the yield differential is numerically stable. Indeed, we find greater fluctuations in yield in the relatively high-risk securities.

The above phenomenon is possibly reflected in the relationship between the yield on the highest grade corporate fixed-income bonds and the yield on more risky bonds. We have chosen the differential between *Moody's* Aaa and Baa bonds. During stable times, we hypothesize that this differential is relatively small, and it increases as investors become less optimistic as to the ability of some firms to fulfill their financial obligations. While the credit risk component of all *rates* is expected to rise as future conditions become less certain, the expected increase in that component rate on the more risky securities is greater. Therefore, the absolute differential should increase during, or perhaps slightly before, periods of increased uncertainty. Since we also expect to experience an increase in failure rates in these periods, the hypothesized relationship between our "risk premium" variable and the failure series is positive. We are aware that risk premiums may be associated with several of the other explanatory variables specified earlier and do not expect that all will appear together in our multivariate model.

Business Population Statistics

The time series association between the change in business failures and the change in business population statistics is both obvious and somewhat subtle. On the one hand, increased business formation can be thought of as coincident with positive profit expectations. We would expect that the failure *rate* would diminish due to fewer failures and a larger business population. The later *coincident* association would probably preclude econometric interpretation since the dependent and independent variables would be impacted simultaneously. Still, when we observe the frequency distribution of failures with respect to the age of the firm, aggregate data show quite clearly that over one-half of all failures occur within a firm's first five years and almost one-third within three years. The young firm is usually a marginal operation and is one type of vulnerable entity which we are concerned with in this study.

On closer inspection, we find that there is a relative distribution of failures versus age of the firm which is quite interesting (figure 15.2). It takes some time for a firm actually to fail, and so failures of firms in their *initial year* are relatively infrequent (1 percent of all failing firms go out of business in their first year). The second year, however, shows a marked increase in failure propensity to 10.5 percent and the third year the rate is

Figure 15.2 Frequency distribution of failures versus age of the firm

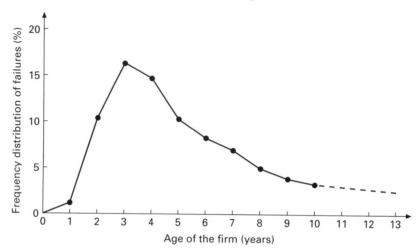

16 percent. We observe a rather flat but high propensity to fail until the firm's seventh year, and then the frequency tails off. As one would expect, at some point the older the firm the less likely it is to fail since it has an established position. In our econometric examination to follow, we will include the change in new business formation as one of our potentially important explanatory variables, but the lagged relationship between it and the change in failure rate will not be coincident at its beginning point. That is, we postulate that new business formation leads business failures by a substantial amount of time. The relatively large net business formation rate in 1976 through 1979 may have contributed to the rise in failures from 1980 into 1982.

Price Level Changes

In recent years, the nation's most disturbing economic problem has been the rate of inflation. Despite the debilitating overall effects of consistent and sizable price level increases, a case can be made for their "positive" short-term impact upon a firm's propensity to survive; that is, increases in prices, especially unanticipated increases, tend to be inversely correlated with failure rates.

Poorly managed companies may be kept afloat for a longer period of time during unanticipated price increases since these firms tend to be highly leveraged and are able to repay their debts with "cheaper" money. This so-called net monetary debtor-creditor theory could have accounted for lower failure rates, for example, in the late 1970s and it might continue, *ceteris paribus*, as long as lenders settle for interest charges which eventually prove to be lower than the rate of inflation. (There are indications that interest rates in early 1980, e.g., prime rates over 20 percent, were adjusting for recent past underestimates.)

It can also be argued that inflation helps marginal companies by reducing competitiveness and protecting inefficiency. Price level increases are more easily passed through to the consumer during rising price level periods and perhaps can aid the firm selling inferior goods. Reported profits of all firms appear more attractive due to "inventory earnings" and depreciation rates are unrealistically low – hence higher earnings. To the extent that lending institutions assess these earnings in their credit analysis, the chance of a favorable extension of credit is perhaps greater.

ECONOMETRIC STRUCTURE OF THE MODEL

Aggregate influences on the business failure rate will be analyzed within first difference, quarterly, regression models with emphasis on the distributed lag properties of a number of explanatory variables. The specified structure of the model will combine both first-degree and second-degree polynomials (Almon, 1965) of the form

$$Y_t = \alpha + \beta(W_0\Delta X_t + W_1\Delta X_{t-1} + W_2\Delta X_{t-2} \cdots W_n\Delta X_{t-n}) + \varepsilon_t$$

for a set of independent variables X, assuming that

$$W_i = C_0 + C_1 i + C_2 i^2 \qquad i = 0, 1, 2, 3, \ldots, n$$

where

Y_t = change in the BFR in period t
X_1 = percentage change in real GNP (RLGNP)
X_2 = percentage change in the money supply (M2)
X_3 = percentage change in the S&P index
X_4 = percentage change in new business formation (NEWINC)

We use percentage changes for our independent variables to adjust for scale effects over time.

Before examining our estimated results, we should discuss the nature of the model's structure. We do expect that our specified explanatory variables will have a significant coincident association with the BFR, but there is likely to be greater information inherent in cumulative or distributed lag structure. Firms usually fail after a number of internal and external pressures build up and finally the fragile entity bursts.

While a geometric lag, that is, a declining set of lagged weights, is quite useful, it is limited in its range of potential uses. The more general polynomial distributed lag structure assumes that the lagged weights can be specified by a continuous function. The polynomial function can be approximated by evaluating the function at discrete points in time. We might assume, for example, that $W_i = C_0 + C_1 i + C_2 i^2$ (second degree) for RLGNP and that $i = 0, 1, 2, 3, 4, 5$ (six quarters of observations starting from period zero and going to five quarters prior to the failure rate observation quarter) with $W_i = 0$ for both i less than 0 (future RLGNP) and "greater" than 5 (more remote than $t - 5$). The choice of the number of lag periods depends essentially on the nature of the problem specified, so that rules of thumb are not available. It is quite common to vary the degree of polynomial and the length of the lag where no precise theory exists. In our case, we first estimate second-degree polynomial equations for each independent variable specification (univariate analysis) and observe the structure, amount, and significance of the various lagged periods parameters.

EMPIRICAL RESULTS

Univariate Structure

We start by estimating the univariate BFR relationships for four prime independent variables of the form

$$Y_t = \sum_{i=0}^{n-1} W(i) X_{j,t-1}$$

where

$Y_t = \Delta$BFR in t
$X_j = \Delta$ independent variable j
i = quarterly designation
$n = 7$
w = weight

We utilized a second-degree polynomial in each case although higher degrees allow greater flexibility in structure of the lag pattern. The results are illustrated in table 15.1.

As expected, we find a negative correlation among each of the first three variables RLGNP, M2, and S&P and the BFR. The parameters conform to the second degree form and the significance level for the parameters of $t(0) \rightarrow t - 3$ is for the most part at the 0.05 level (or better) and in only one case at the 0.10 level. In each case, except the M2 variable, the significance level is highest in the coincident period t_0 and slowly falls until the fourth lag $(t - 3)$; thereafter the weights are insignificant and/or show changes

Table 15.1 Quarterly distributed lag parameters – failure rate model: 1951–78 (univariate models); Dependent variable = Δ failure rate (t_0).

Independent variable	R^2	F-test	D–W	Distributed lag parameters[a]						
				t_0	t_{-1}	t_{-2}	t_{-3}	t_{-4}	t_{-5}	t_{-6}
% Δ Real GNP	0.096	5.59	2.22	−0.123	−0.190	−0.201	−0.155	−0.052	0.106	0.321
				(−2.53)	(−2.43)	(−2.25)	(−1.81)	(−0.67)	(1.13)	(2.13)
% Δ M$_2$	0.093	5.40	2.19	−0.162	−0.259	−0.289	−0.254	−0.153	0.015	0.248
				(−2.95)	(−3.03)	(−3.16)	(−3.28)	(−2.53)	(0.16)	(1.36)
% Δ S&P	0.085	4.85	2.08	−0.029	−0.044	−0.046	−0.035	−0.011	0.027	0.078
				(−2.80)	(−2.68)	(−2.45)	(−1.93)	(−0.64)	(1.39)	(1.57)
% Δ NEWINC	0.110	6.50	2.15	−0.028	−0.041	−0.040	−0.024	0.007	0.053	0.114
				(−2.15)	(−1.94)	(−1.59)	(−0.95)	(0.32)	(2.30)	(2.44)

[a] t-statistics in parentheses.
All series are seasonally adjusted with the exception of the S&P Index. Data sources for quarterly GNP, S&P, and money supply are respectively: National Income and Product Accounts of the United States and Survey of Current Business (US Department of Commerce); S&P Trade and Securities Statistics: and the Federal Reserve Bulletin. The latter source presents the most recent revised series of money supply data and reflects adjustments for eurodollar transactions, recent benchmarks, and seasonal factors. Quarterly failure rate and number of enterprises data are available in Dun's Statistic Review until 1957 and in Dun's Review and the Failure Record thereafter.

in sign. The M2 variable's significance level actually increases in $t - 1$, $t - 2$, and $t - 3$, indicating that the change in money supply is probably a leading indicator of the change in BFRs.

The NEWINC variable also performed as expected, but the results and interpretation are quite different from the other three measures. We do find a significant negative correlation in quarters $t(0)$ and $t - 1$, but this could be explained simply by the impact of the change in new incorporations on the number of firms covered by D&B: hence, everything held equal, the failure rate will fall as the number of firms increase in any one period. We also find that the sign change in NEWINC in period $t - 4$ is followed by highly significant t-values in periods $t - 5$ and $t - 6$, indicating that the more distant lagged positive association between BFR and NEWINC could be due to the failure concept explored earlier. In fact, we find the expected positive correlation continuing for many more quarters after $t - 6$.

Overshooting

We observe that, after several quarters of the expected correlation between RLGNP, M2, and S&P and the BFR, the sign changes and the opposite correlation manifests. While this type of overshooting will be helpful in specifying our multivariate lagged structure, it is difficult to explain the relationship conceptually. However, since the proper interpretation of lagged weights is to sum them, it seems reasonable that, at some point, the signs will change. We already explained why NEWINC in prior periods can be expected to affect failure rates in current periods and, as noted above, we observe this "positive" effect continuing well beyond $t - 6$. We will exploit this finding in our multivariate specification.

The explanatory power (R^2) of our individual variables are all in the 0.09–0.11 range with significant (at the 0.01 level) F-ratios. The Durbin–Watson test does not indicate serial correlation. We find that the change in business failures is negatively correlated with percentage changes in overall activity (RLGNP), money supply (M2), and the general stock market behavior (S&P) and positively related (with a year's lag) to changes in the new business incorporation rate (NEWINC).

Variables Not Included

We found that the RLGNP variable had a slightly higher negative correlation with the BFR than did corporate profits. This was a bit surprising since conditions which lead to changes in corporate profits are also related to business failure. Other aggregate variables not utilized but on which we ran tests on both a univariate and a multivariate basis were the unemployment rate (business conditions), Federal Reserve discount rate, free reserves, the prime rate (interest rates and credit conditions), and the difference between the corporate AAA and BBB rates (market risk premium). All of the not-included variables displayed the expected signs but did not add explanatory power when added to the multivariate model or substituted for similar indicators.

We experienced some problems when we attempted to measure the impact of changes in the inflation rate (GNP price deflator) on changes in the BFR over the period 1950–79. Not surprisingly, we do not observe any significant or meaningful association over most of the sample period since the first 20 years plus are distinguished by relatively stable price levels. We do, however, observe a highly significant (in terms of R^2) correlation in the most recent years, 1971–79 (2nd quarter) as the economy has changed to a more unstable and accelerating inflationary period. This is indicated in table 15.2, which shows the univariate results for GNPDFL for various subsample periods as well as the entire period.

Note that, although the entire and the most recent period's distributed lag structure are the familiar second degree form with some overshooting (sign changing from positive to negative), the period 1961–70 shows the reserve situation. Since the model's temporal nature is not consistent, we do not include here the price level change variable in our multivariate results for the entire sample period. One should not, however, ignore the potential of this variable to be a meaningful one in the future.

Table 15.2 Distributed lag structure – inflationary effects on failure rates (various sample periods)

Sample period	R^2	F-test	D–W	t_0	t_{-1}	t_{-2}	t_{-3}	t_{-4}	t_{-5}
1950–71	0.016	0.87	2.04	0.119	0.157	0.110	−0.011	−2.17	−5.04
				(0.80)	(0.75)	(0.62)	(−0.12)	(−1.27)	(−1.11)
1950–60	0.003	0.05	1.69	−0.087	0.148	0.183	0.192	0.175	0.132
				(0.22)	(0.25)	(0.27)	(0.31)	(0.29)	(0.15)
1961–70	0.059	1.16	2.46	−0.417	−0.514	−0.289	0.257	1.125	2.314
				(−0.62)	(−0.55)	(0.36)	(0.67)	(1.30)	(1.05)
1971–79	0.125	2.06	2.44	0.298	0.421	0.368	0.140	−0.263	−0.842
				(1.98)	(1.94)	(1.82)	(1.04)	(−1.39)	(−1.90)

Dependent variable = Δ failure rate (t_0), independent variable = Δ GNPDFL.

Multivariate Results

The combined model for explaining aggregate failure rate experience in the USA, 1951–78, is illustrated in table 15.3 and is of the form

$$\text{BFR}_t = a_0 + a_1 \% \, \Delta \, \text{S\&P}_{t-1} + \sum_{i=0}^{3} W(i) \% \, \Delta \, \text{RLGNP}_{t-i}$$

$$+ \sum_{i=0}^{3} W(i) \% \, \Delta M2_{t-1} + \sum_{i=3}^{10} W(i) \% \, \Delta \, \text{NEWINC}_{t-i}$$

The BFR, therefore, is a function of the percentage change in real GNP, M2, S&P, and new incorporations. The first two variables are specified in a four-quarter distributed lag structure with the starting point in the coincident period with Δ BFR. The NEWINC variable's starting point is, however, $t − 3$, and the number of lagged quarters is eight since a more sustained impact on failure rates is observed. All distributed lag forms assume that the lag weights outside the interval are zero. In addition, one other variable (S&P)$_t$ is specified. A simple one-period lag proved slightly more significant than a distributed lag form for the S&P variable in the multivariate run.

Table 15.3 BFR model (1951–78): Quarterly distributed lag specification (multivariate model)

Independent variable	t_0	t_{-1}	t_{-2}	t_{-3}	t_{-4}	t_{-5}	t_{-6}	t_{-7}	t_{-8}	t_{-9}	t_{-10}
Constant	0.506 (0.70)										
% Δ S&P		−0.099 (−2.19)									
% Δ Real GNP	−0.114 (−1.07)	−0.131 (−1.09)	−0.050 (−0.68)	0.128 (0.52)							
% Δ M₂	−0.226 (−1.85)	−0.283 (−1.88)	−0.168 (−1.81)	0.116 (0.43)							
% Δ NEWINC				0.020 (1.77)	0.036 (1.88)	0.048 (2.01)	0.055 (2.18)	0.058 (2.39)	0.058 (2.55)	0.053 (2.26)	0.043 (1.44)

Dependent variable = Δ failure rate (t_0); t-statistic in parentheses.
Test results in equation: Adj. $R^2 = 0.26$; F-Test = 4.85; D–W = 2.31; N = 112.

The overall results (table 15.3) are quite encouraging, with the expected cumulative sign for all parameters, significant coefficients for many of the parameters of each distributed-lag variable, and relatively good explanatory power. The $R^2 = 0.26$ is fairly good in view of the nature of the aggregation problem, that is, cumulating a series of microeconomic failure events to get an aggregate figure for the economy.

In order to assess the expected impact of these macroeconomic changes on BFR, one would cumulate the various lag parameters' products with their appropriate variables. In this way, one could, for example, estimate the effects of diminished GNP activity, reductions in credit availability, and changes in stock prices on the propensity of firms to fail. If, for instance, we expect real GNP to fall by 2 percent per quarter for the next four quarters, money supply to drop by 4 percent per quarter, and stock prices to remain fairly constant, than one could trace out the cumulative effects in BFRs.

In fact, we have done this with some consensus estimates of GNP, S&P, and M2 behavior for 1980 combined with actual 1979 and 1978 statistics, and our overall estimate was for the BFR to rise to approximately 36–40 per 10,000 firms from the 1979 level of 28 per 10,000 (an increase of at least 25 percent). Translated into the number of business bankruptcies filings, we expected a record number of filings in 1980 and 1981 (*Business Week*, March 25, 1980, pp. 104–8). In fact, filings did break all records in both 1980 (36,411) and 1981 (over 47,000). In the case of the failure rate, the 1980 figure was 42 (slightly above our estimate).

SUMMARY AND IMPLICATIONS

The purpose of this analysis is to examine the influences of aggregate economic conditions on the BFR experience. The period 1951 through 1978 was chosen, and a set of explanatory variables reflecting various macroeconomic pressures was examined within a first difference, distributed lag regression structure. Findings indicate that a firm's propensity to fail is heightened due to the cumulative effects of reduced real economic growth, stock market performance, money supply growth, and business formation. The latter variable was found to have a more remote but rather important and lengthy lagged association with the failure rate.

The implications of these findings relate both to macroeconomic conditions and to the marginal firm itself. Although we do not advocate that the expected impact on business failures should be the prime consideration when deciding on the nation's fiscal and monetary policies, we should still be cognizant of the effects on the marginal enterprise.

On the micro side, if a firm finds its very existence in a tenuous state and the aggregate economic conditions indicate increased failure pressures, then drastic preventive measures should be implemented – if possible and if deemed desirable. For instance, the alternative to eventual failure and perhaps liquidation may be to seek a merger with a sound company, or perhaps the firm should declare bankruptcy and attempt to reorganize. These decisions, if made early enough, may salvage the economic value of the firm's assets if the problems are temporary and not chronic. Of course, if the value of the firm as a going concern is less than its liquidation value, then early liquidation in the face of expected continued micro and macro pressures would be expedient.

The results indicate the potential to combine selected aggregate economic variables with the unique microeconomic characteristics of specific firms in order to explain and predict individual business failures more efficiently. It should be made clear, however, that statistical models for classifying and predicting individual firm business failures cannot directly utilize macroeconomic measures as additional explanatory variables. This is due to the traditional paired sample approach whereby non-bankrupt firms are matched, usually by industry and *year*, to bankrupt firms. Therefore, the values of macroeconomic variables will be identical in both groups and no discriminatory power will be achieved. Where macroeconomic *expectations* could be extremely important is in the choice of appropriate prior probabilities of failure. This level is useful in adjusting the optimum cutoff score for micro bankruptcy prediction models.

REFERENCES

Almon, S., 1965, A Distributed Lag Between Capital Appropriations and Expenditures, *Econometrica*, January.

Altman, E. I., 1980, Commercial Bank Lending: Process, Credit Scoring and Costs of Errors in Lending, *Journal of Financial and Qualitative Analysis*, November.

Cumming, C. and K. Saini, 1981, The Macroeconomic Determinants of Corporate Bankruptcies in Japan and the U.K., Federal Reserve Bank of New York, December.

Noto, N. A. and D. Zimmerman, 1981, A Comparison of Failure and Liability Trends, Report no. 81-36E, Congressional Research Service, 30 January 1981.

16 | An Analysis and Critique of the BIS Proposal on Capital Adequacy and Ratings

with Anthony Saunders*

1 INTRODUCTION

In June 1999, the BIS released its long awaited proposal on reform of the 8 percent risk-based capital ratio for credit risk that has been in effect since 1993.[1] The 8 percent ratio has been criticized on at least three major grounds. First, it gives an equal risk-weighting to all corporate credits whether of high or low credit quality. Second, it fails to incorporate potential capital savings from credit (loan) portfolio diversification. The latter is a result of its simple additive nature. And third, it has led to extensive regulatory capital arbitrage which adds to the riskiness of bank asset portfolios.

In its June 1999 draft, the BIS proposed a three-stage reform process.[2] In the first stage, the 8 percent risk based ratio (where all loans receive the same 100 percent risk-weighting) would be replaced by weightings based on the external credit agency rating of the borrower (we discuss this proposal in more detail in section 2). In the second stage, at some unspecified time in the future, when some sophisticated banks have developed their own internal rating systems for loans, a transformation may be made to calculating capital requirements based on a bank's allocation of its loans to the various grades/ratings in its own internal loan rating system. Finally, in the third stage, given appropriate model and data base development and testing, some banks may be

* The authors wish to thank several individuals from Standard & Poor's and Moody's for their data assistance. The computational assistance of Vellore Vishore and Sreedar Bharath are also acknowledged as well as the coordination by Robyn Vanterpool. The opinions presented are solely of the authors.

[1] The 8 percent ratio was phased-in over the 1988–92 period, following the 1988 Basel Accord. Some countries have actually adopted a capital adequacy ratio of over 8 percent (e.g., Brazil uses 11 percent). In all cases, the level of capital is to help to ensure a bank's solvency against unexpected losses.

[2] The original discussion period for the proposal ran until March 2000. After several revisions, the final plan is expected by 2002, to be implemented by 2005.

able to use their own internal credit risk models to calculate capital requirements. Importantly, these internal models allow for portfolio diversification effects.

A number of issues have been raised about stages two and three of the reform proposal, e.g., how will the internal rating systems of different banks – especially if they continue to develop independently of each other – be grouped into some standardized set of capital risk weights; that is will a rating of 1 for Citigroup be the same as a 1 for BankAmerica or will a rating of 1 for a bank in the USA be equivalent to a 1 for a bank in Germany?[3] Also, what is the appropriate mapping of the internal rating model with external ratings? While these are important issues, this paper concentrates on the first stage of the proposal. In particular, we raise a number of concerns (backed by data) regarding the use of rating agencies' rating systems in a reformed capital adequacy system in the manner that the 1999 BIS proposal stipulates.

Section 2 of this paper briefly outlines the BIS stage-one proposal. Section 3 presents some empirical evidence that questions the proposal and shows that similar "risk-shifting" incentives (i.e., regulatory capital arbitrage) exist under the new plan as under the current 8 percent risk-based capital ratio. These empirical tests are supplemented by simulations on sample data to better assess expected and unexpected losses from actual bond portfolios. We will show that the current Basel "one size fits all" approach is not sufficiently modified in the new approach. Finally, section 4 provides our recommendation to enlarge the number of "buckets" with different risk weightings to better approximate actual loss experience and risk categories.

2 THE BIS STAGE 1 PROPOSAL

Table 16.1 shows the proposed reform of the 8 percent ratio in stage 1 of the new plan. As noted in the introduction, currently all corporate loans have the same 100 percent risk-weight (for risk adjusted assets) implying the same minimum capital requirement

Table 16.1 Proposed BIS risk weighting system for bank loan credits

Claim	Assessment (%)					
	AAA to AA–	A+ to A–	BBB+ to BBB–	BB+ to B–	Below B–	Unrated
Sovereigns	0	20	50	100	150	100
Banks						
Option 1[a]	20	50	100	100	150	100
Option 2[b]	20	50	50[c]	100[c]	150	50[c]
Corporates	20	100	100	100	150	100

[a] Risk weighting based on risk weighting of sovereign in which the bank is incorporated.
[b] Risk weighting based on the assessment of the individual bank.
[c] Claims on banks of a short original maturity, for example less than six months, would receive a weighting that is one category more favorable than the usual risk weight on the banks' longer term debt.

[3] See W. Tracey and M. Carey (1998) for a discussion and survey of banks' internal ratings systems. A more recent discussion paper by the Basel Committee on Banking Supervision (2000) examines the range of banks' internal rating systems.

(e.g., 8 percent). Under the new proposal, corporate borrowers rated AAA to AA– by S&P, or the equivalent authorized rating agencies (see table 16.2), will have a risk weight of 20 percent. This implies a capital ratio of 0.2 × 8 percent i.e. 1.6 percent – much lower than at present for "high quality" loans. In what follows, we shall label this category "bucket 1." For corporate borrowers rated A+ to B–, the risk weight will remain at 100 percent, i.e., they will continue to have a capital ratio of 8 percent; we will call this group of borrowers "bucket 2." For those borrowers rated below B–, the risk weighting increases to 150 percent, implying a capital ratio of 1.5 × 8 percent i.e. 12 percent. It might be noted that, somewhat paradoxically, unrated corporate borrowers are given a lower 100 percent risk-weight and thus an 8 percent capital requirement. A similar, but less broad bucketing approach is adopted for sovereigns and banks. In particular, the current system of a zero risk-weight for OECD countries and a 100 percent risk-weight for all other countries is replaced by four new buckets based on agency ratings.

In section 3, we use data on bond ratings, defaults and loss rates to more closely examine the three-bucket approach for corporate borrowers. We do this with two questions in mind. First, does this approach lead to bank capital reserves rising prior to recessions, i.e., before the realization of loan losses typically occurs – as should happen under an "ideal" system? In particular, a well-designed regulatory system should see capital rising during periods of high profitability and earnings for banks (which normally coincides with periods of business expansions) and falling during recessions as "unexpected losses" are written off against capital. At the very least, the size of the capital reserve should be coincident with the business cycle even if it does not lead it.

Second, does the bucketing system make economic sense? That is, how homogeneous in terms of risk are the different buckets? For example, bucket 2 encompasses both investment grade debt (A and BBB) as well as below investment grade debt (BB and B). Moreover, if they are not homogeneous, what relative risk-weighting scheme would these data suggest?

Table 16.2 Rating agencies extreme credit quality categories

Credit assessment institution	Very high quality assessment	Very low quality assessment
Fitch IBCA	AA– and above	Below B–
Moody's	Aa3 and above	Below B3
Standard & Poor's	AA– and above	Below B–
Export insurance agencies	1	7

Source: Basel Committee on Bank Supervision (June 1999).

3 EMPIRICAL RESULTS

In this section, we use data from Moody's and S&P's and from the NYU Salomon Center's data base on Corporate bond defaults[4] and losses on defaults in order to gain insight into these two questions.

---

[4] The data includes defaults on straight (non-convertible) corporate bonds over the period 1971–99, rating and prices on the defaulting issues at birth, one year and one month prior to default as well as just after default.

3.1   The Lead-Lag Relationship of Capital Reserves – Procyclicality

As discussed above, ideally, capital reserves for unexpected losses should be accumulated during periods of high bank profitability and business expansion. Banks find it
much more difficult, if not impossible, to add substantially to their capital reserves
when profits are low and the economy is in recession. And, reserves should be adequate
prior to, not after defaults and losses increase.

In figure 16.1, we have used Moody's bond ratings to group bonds outstanding over
the March 1989 to March 1999 period into the three buckets implied by the Moody's
equivalents to the S&P ratings shown in table 16.1. The period 1989–91 is a period of
recession while the period of the current expansion begins post-1992. Although these
data include only one recession, they are representative of a number of recent critiques
that have found that rating agencies move slowly and their ratings are often inflexible.
As a result, external ratings' ability to predict default with a long (if any) lead has been
questioned. Indeed, figure 16.1 suggests that a capital adequacy system built around
traditional agency ratings might even follow, rather than lead, the business cycle. As
can be seen, the proportion of bonds in bucket 2 appear to fall continuously over the
March 1989 to March 1991 period, while those in buckets 1 and 3 appear to rise
continuously. Specifically, the proportion of bonds in bucket 3, with the 150 percent
risk-weight, peaks in September 1991, near the end of the recession rather than at the
beginning. Figure 16.2 shows a similar result for S&P ratings. As can be seen, while the
percentage of bonds in bucket 3 is small, its proportion still rises over the 1990–91
period. If risk-weights and capital requirements were tied to these buckets, this could
have meant (had the new proposal been in effect during the 1989–91 recession) that some
banks would have had to build up their minimum reserve requirements during the recession with a peak minimum capital ratio being achieved at or near the recession's end.[5]

Figure 16.1   Proportion of bonds in different BIS proposed buckets (1989–98)

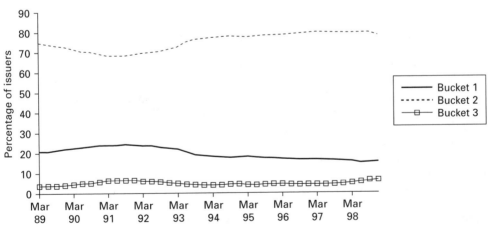

Source: Moody's Investor Services, New York.

---

[5]   The years 1990 and 1991 saw defaults rise dramatically in both the corporate loan and bond markets.
Indeed, corporate bond default rates in each of those years were over 10 percent of the outstanding bonds at
the start of each year (see Altman et al., 1999).

Figure 16.2 Proportion of bonds in different BIS proposed buckets (1989–98)

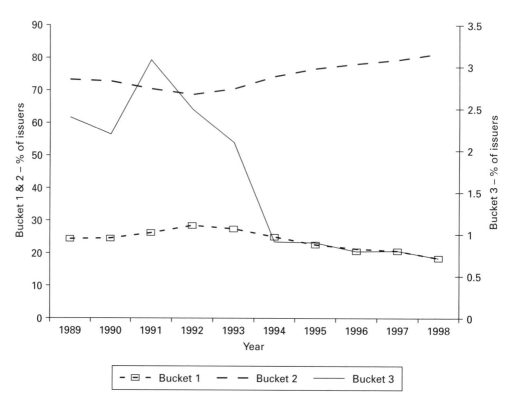

Source: S&P's, New York.

That is, rather than leading the recession, minimum capital requirements would have been lagging it and also the rising wave of loan defaults.

This suggests that alternatives to the rating agencies' bucket approach be assessed. For example, there are a number of rating and default forecasting approaches that have been developed in the last decade. These include ones by Jonsson and Fridson (1996), Moody's (1999), and Altman (1989). The first two utilize the existing rating proportions and add macroeconomic variables to the forecasting regression. The latter assumes a stable default aging frequency by original rating, and forecasts defaults based on the previous 30 years of default aging experience, in essence a regression-to-the-mean approach.

A second possibility is that the individual issuers of loans be subjected to a micro-default probability model and the aggregate of this bottom-up approach be assessed for expected and unexpected (capital) losses of the loan portfolio. Approaches with this objective include equity value option models (expected default frequencies) and multivariate models which involve financial statement and market equity variables.[6]

A final idea exploits the use of credit spreads to define the buckets. It can be empirically demonstrated that credit spreads were particularly accurate forecasters of subsequent

[6] A survey of these methods can be found in Altman and Saunders (1997).

default rates at the start of 1990 and again at the start of 1991.[7] The credit spread indicator is a commonly used barometer of risk in financial systems and for economic cycles by both the government and banks.

Table 16.3 Annual returns, yields and spreads on 10-year Treasury (TREAS) and high yield (HY) bonds* (1978–99)

Year	Return (%)			Promised yield (%)		
	HY	TREAS	Spread	HY	TREAS	Spread
1999	1.73	(8.41)	10.14	11.41	6.44	4.97
1998	4.04	12.77	(8.73)	10.04	4.65	5.39
1997	14.27	11.16	3.11	9.20	5.75	3.45
1996	11.24	0.04	11.20	9.58	6.42	3.16
1995	22.40	23.58	(1.18)	9.76	5.58	4.18
1994	(2.55)	(8.29)	5.74	11.50	7.83	3.67
1993	18.33	12.08	6.25	9.08	5.80	3.28
1992	18.29	6.50	11.79	10.44	6.69	3.75
1991	43.23	17.18	26.05	12.56	6.70	5.86
1990	(8.46)	6.88	(15.34)	18.57	8.07	10.50
1989	1.98	16.72	(14.74)	15.17	7.93	7.24
1988	15.25	6.34	8.91	13.70	9.15	4.55
1987	4.57	(2.67)	7.24	13.89	8.83	5.06
1986	16.50	24.08	(7.58)	12.67	7.21	5.46
1985	26.08	31.54	(5.46)	13.50	8.99	4.51
1984	8.50	14.82	(6.32)	14.97	11.87	3.10
1983	21.80	2.23	19.57	15.74	10.70	5.04
1982	32.45	42.08	(9.63)	17.84	13.86	3.98
1981	7.56	0.48	7.08	15.97	12.08	3.89
1980	(1.00)	(2.96)	1.96	13.46	10.23	3.23
1979	3.69	(0.86)	4.55	12.07	9.13	2.94
1978	7.57	(1.11)	8.68	10.92	8.11	2.81
Arithmetic annual average						
1978–1999	12.16	9.28	2.88	12.82	8.27	4.35
Compound annual average						
1978–1999	11.54	8.58	2.96			

* End of year yields.
Source: Salomon Smith Barney Inc.'s High Yield Composite Index; Altman et al. (2000).

3.2 Bucket Risk Homogeneity

To analyze the second question, bucket risk homogeneity, we examined data on bond issues (and issuers) over the 1981–99 (September) period. Our focus of attention was

[7] On 31 December 1989 the yield-spread between high yield corporate bonds and ten-year US Treasury bonds was 7.24 percent and one year later it was 10.50 percent (table 16.3). These were the highest levels for several decades and the subsequent annual default rates (10.1 percent and 10.3 percent) were the highest default rates on high yield "junk" bonds ever recorded. It should be noted that the highest dollar amount of defaults ($23.5 billion) in this market, perhaps in the commercial loan market as well, occurred in the most recent year (1999), see Altman et al. (2000). Of course, the sizes of these markets are much greater in 1999 than in the early 1990s. Still recent default experience highlights the cyclical nature of default rates and marks the end of the benign credit cycle of most of the 1990s.

the degree of homogeneity (heterogeneity) of unexpected loss rates over the sample period. Following most approaches of economic capital and loan loss reserve calculations, loan loss reserves are meant to cover expected (or mean) losses while economic capital reserves are meant to cover unexpected losses.

To undertake this study, we collected data on bond issues and issuers that did and did not default, the ratings of those defaulting issues one year prior to default, the price and coupon of the bonds one year prior to default and the price of the bonds just after default. The price (and coupon) one year prior to default (P_{t-1} and C_{t-1}) and the price (and lost coupon) on default (P_t and C_t) allowed us to calculate a loss rate for each bond default, i.e.,

$$\frac{P_t - \left(P_{t-1} + \dfrac{C_{t-1}}{2} \right)}{P_{t-1}}$$

The total number of defaulting bonds over the 18-year sample period, for which we had full price and rating information, was 588. For an additional 104 bonds, we only had the rating and not the price, one year prior to default. For these bonds, we assumed that their default experience mirrored the distribution of losses of the bonds in each rating class for which we did have loss data. Finally, there were over 100 bonds that were unrated and for which we had no price data. We placed them in the unrated category (see table 16.1). Since we are only looking at the relative loss experience for rated bonds, these unrated bonds played no further part in our study.

We then applied a number of models to calculate unexpected loss rates (or "economic" capital requirements) for bonds of different ratings one year prior to default,[8] so as to calculate loss rates at various confidence intervals. Three distribution models were used to initially calculate loss rates:

   (i)   a normal distribution
   (ii) the actual distribution, and
   (iii) a Poisson distribution (with a stable mean).

The first two models are similar to those used in J. P. Morgan's CreditMetrics® and the third is a simplified version of the model assumed in CSFP's CreditRisk⁺®. Tables 16.4–9 show the results for the full sample period for rating classes A through CCC and below. Note that BIS bucket 2 is represented here by the ratings A, BBB, BB and B and bucket 3 is represented by the CCC and lower category. Bucket 1 is not shown because of non-existent defaults in the AAA to AA ratings range at one year prior to default.

In addition, we carried out a set of Monte-Carlo simulations. Since most formal credit-risk models – such as CreditMetrics® and CreditRisk⁺® – contain certain parametric assumptions (e.g., about correlations) embedded in their structures, these formal models' results reflect, in part, these untested assumptions. Monte-Carlo simulations, by contrast, allow estimation of the size of losses in the tail of loan loss distributions conditional only on assumptions made about the composition of bank portfolios. In

---

[8] The one-year horizon is consistent with the horizon adopted by most internal credit risk models.

the simulations, we follow Carey (1998) and look at a number of portfolios. The first reflects the allocation for US life insurance company privately placed bonds. In this allocation, approximately 13 percent are below investment grade. The second reflects the suggested allocation by Carey for US banks' commercial loan portfolios. This reflects, on average, a much lower credit quality than that adopted by life insurers, with some 50 percent being below investment grade. In addition to these two portfolios, we look at loss distributions for portfolios that contain respectively only AAA, AA and A bonds (portfolio 3), BBB bonds (portfolio 4), BB bonds (portfolio 5), B bonds (portfolio 6) and CCC and lower (portfolio 7).

In conducting the Monte-Carlo simulation, a portfolio aggregate size is chosen (here $1 billion) and assets are drawn at random subject to the composition of the portfolios conforming to the representative portfolios discussed above (until the target aggregate portfolio size is reached). The loss rate on the portfolio is then calculated. For each portfolio (1–7), the simulation is repeated 50,000 times and the frequency distribution of losses forms an estimate of the relevant loss distribution. From that loss distribution, loss rates at different quantiles can be analyzed, and by implication the capital reserves needed to absorb the level of unexpected losses are determined. Unexpected losses are the difference between the loss rate at a given quantile and the mean, or expected, loss rate.

3.3 Empirical Results of Loss Distributions

Table 16.4 shows that, for A-rated bonds, 12,115 issuers did not default over this period, while seven A-rated issuers defaulted within one year of being rated A. Of the seven, two defaults had a loss rate in the 1 percent to 10 percent range, two had loss rates in the 11 percent to 20 percent range, two had loss rates in the 21 percent to 30 percent range and one had a loss rate in the 51 percent to 60 percent range. The mean loss rate (the expected loan loss reserve) for the entire A-rated sample was 0.012 percent. Recall, we do not observe any one year losses for AAA or AA rated bonds; hence, no tables are presented.

For capital or unexpected loss calculations, different quantiles were used to describe extreme losses. The more conservative the banker or the regulator, the higher the quantile chosen. For the normal distribution, we calculated the 95% (1.64485σ), 99% (2.32634σ) and 99.97% (3.431925σ) unexpected loss rates. As can be seen for single A bonds, these unexpected loss rates were respectively 1.021 percent, 1.448 percent and 2.142 percent. These are well below the current 8 percent capital requirement (actually quite close to the proposed guideline for AAA/AA credits). However, as is well known, the loss distribution of loans is highly non-normal, so the second calculation, also shown in table 16.4, uses the actual distribution of bond losses. To calculate a particular quantile's loss rate involves counting backwards under the actual default distribution and finding the loss rate coincident with the default that just matches the quantile. For example, to find the unexpected loss rate consistent with the 99.97% quantile (i.e., where capital is sufficiently large to meet all but 3 losses out of 10,000),[9] we calculate that 0.03 percent of 12,122 is 3.6 issuers. We then count backwards under the

---

[9] Alternatively, where the bank will have sufficient capital to survive all but 3 years out of the next 10,000 years.

Table 16.4 Frequency distribution of losses (principal and coupon), (1981–9/1999) by rating one year before default (normal and actual loss distributions)

Range of Default Losses	Midpoint	A	BBB	BB	B	CCC & Lower	Total
0	0	12,115	7,529	5,311	4,997	294	30,246
0.01–0.10	0.05	2	26	11	81	43	163
0.11–0.20	0.15	2	16	15	89	18	140
0.21–0.30	0.25	2	4	18	81	36	141
0.31–0.40	0.35	0	1	8	62	24	95
0.41–0.50	0.45	0	0	8	29	24	61
0.51–0.60	0.55	1	0	3	17	18	39
0.61–0.70	0.65	0	0	1	10	21	32
0.71–0.80	0.75	0	0	0	2	5	7
0.81–0.90	0.85	0	0	0	4	6	10
0.91–0.94	0.92	0	0	0	0	0	0
0.95–0.98	0.96	0	0	0	0	1	1
0.99	0.99	0	0	0	0	0	0
1	1	0	0	0	0	3	3
Total		12,122	7,576	5,375	5,372	493	30,938
Mean		0.012%	0.067%	0.298%	1.734%	14.079%	0.598%
Median		0.000%	0.000%	0.000%	0.000%	0.000%	0.000%
St.Dev		0.628%	1.027%	3.181%	8.066%	29.890%	5.001%
3.43192σ–E(L)		2.142%	3.458%	10.619%	25.947%	88.501%	16.566%
2.32634σ–E(L)		1.448%	2.323%	7.102%	17.030%	55.455%	11.037%
1.64485σ–E(L)		1.021%	1.623%	2.051%	11.533%	35.085%	7.628%
99.97%		14.988% 3.6	24.933% 2.3	54.702% 1.6	83.266% 1.6	85.921% 0.1	84.402% 9.3
99.00%		0.000% 121.2	0.000% 75.8	4.702% 53.8	43.266% 53.7	70.921% 4.9	24.402% 309.4
95.00%		0.000% 606.1	0.000% 378.8	0.000% 268.8	13.266% 268.6	50.921% 24.7	0.000% 1546.9

Source: S&P's NYU Salomon Center Default Data Base.

A-rated bond distribution and find that 3.6 defaults are coincident with a loss range of 11–20 percent. In all cases, we take the mid-point of the loss range (here 15 percent) to reflect the unexpected loss. To net out the loan loss reserve, we deduct from 15 percent the expected or mean loss rate (here 0.012 percent) to get an unexpected loss rate at the 99.97% quantile of 14.988 percent. This is clearly much larger than the current 8 percent ratio of the BIS. Note, however, at the less conservative quantiles of 99% and 95%, the unexpected loss rates (and hence capital ratios) are actually zero.

Table 16.4 carries out a similar exercise to the one discussed above for BBB, BB, B and CCC (and lower) bonds. In addition, a "total" column aggregates across all of the rating classes.[10]

We can use these calculations to examine the degree of homogeneity (heterogeneity) across the four rating grades A, BBB, BB and B entering into bucket 2. Using the 99th percentile, or its equivalent, as a standard for comparison, we can see that, under the normal distribution assumption, the capital requirements for the four ratings classes are respectively 1.448 percent, 2.323 percent, 7.102 percent and 17.030 percent. Even under the highly unrealistic assumption of normally distributed loss rates, B-rated bonds' risk is more than ten times that of A-rated bonds.[11] Looking at the actual distribution of losses at the 99th percentile, a similar degree of heterogeneity emerges. Specifically, the capital requirements are respectively 0 percent, 0 percent, 4.702 percent and 43.266 percent, indicating a very clear distinction between unexpected loss rates of investment grade borrowers (those rated A and BBB) and below investment grade borrowers (those rated BB and B). Thus, table 16.4 suggests that if we use external rating agency buckets, as the current proposal suggests, for capital requirement risk-weights, the degree of granularity is far too coarse.

Finally, what can be said about the relative risk weightings of buckets 2 and 3? Under the BIS proposal, bucket 2 has a 100 percent risk-weight while bucket 3 has a 150 percent risk-weight – implying that loans in bucket 3 are $1\frac{1}{2}$ times "more default risky" than those in bucket 2. As can be seen from table 16.4, even where we use, for bucket 2, the lowest rating grade (B), and unexpected loss rates are used to compare with bucket 3 loss rates, the *normal* distribution suggests a risk-weighting ratio of 3.26 times (i.e., 55.455 percent divided by 17.030 percent) at the 99% level. The equivalent 99% relative risk-weighting was 1.64 times using the *actual* distribution. Of course, these relative risk-weightings are far larger when either A, BBB, or BB are used to compare to loss rates in bucket 3. Overall, these results suggest that, for the new BIS proposal, the degree of a loan's credit risk in bucket 3 may be relatively underpriced (under capitalized) to that of a loan in bucket 2.

3.4 Robustness Checks

We decided to carry out a number of additional robustness checks to examine how the degree of heterogeneity in bucket 2 changes under "alternative" assumptions. In

---

[10] Interestingly, the total mean or expected loss rate of 0.598 percent is quite close to the level of banks' average loan loss reserve holdings in recent years.

[11] This compares to an expected loss rate ratio of about 100 times greater for B vs. A-rated bonds; see the cumulative loss rates in Altman et al. (1999). For example, the five-year cumulative loss rate for bonds rated A upon issuance is 0.12 percent, while the B-rated bonds' loss rate is 13.9 percent. The fifth year's marginal (one year) loss rate is 0.04 percent for A-rated bonds compared to 3.36 percent for B-rated bonds.

Table 16.5 Frequency distribution of losses (principal and coupon), (1981–9/1999) by rating one year before default (normal and actual loss distributions) (Based on number of issuers)

Range of Default Losses	Midpoint	A	BBB	BB	B	CCC & Lower	Total
0	0	12,115	7,529	5,311	4,997	294	30,246
0.01–0.10	0.05	0	0	0	14	4	18
0.11–0.20	0.15	2	1	0	11	8	22
0.21–0.30	0.25	0	1	1	18	11	31
0.31–0.40	0.35	0	1	5	19	11	36
0.41–0.50	0.45	0	1	2	22	11	36
0.51–0.60	0.55	0	3	3	32	9	47
0.61–0.70	0.65	0	0	3	33	17	53
0.71–0.80	0.75	0	4	1	28	12	45
0.81–0.90	0.85	0	0	1	19	7	27
0.91–0.94	0.92	0	0	2	11	1	14
0.95–0.98	0.96	0	0	1	1	2	4
0.99	0.99	0	1	0	0	0	1
1	1	0	0	0	0	0	0
Total Default		2	12	19	208	93	334
Total Non-Default		12,115	7,529	5,311	4,997	294	30,246
Total		12,117	7,541	5,330	5,205	387	30,580
Mean		0.002%	0.091%	0.205%	2.126%	12.078%	0.574%
Median		0.000%	0.000%	0.000%	0.000%	0.000%	0.000%
St.Dev		0.193%	2.454%	3.658%	11.529%	24.521%	6.028%
3.43192σ-E(L)		0.659%	8.332%	12.351%	37.440%	72.077%	20.114%
2.32634σ-E(L)		0.446%	5.619%	8.306%	24.694%	44.967%	13.450%
1.64485σ-E(L)		0.314%	3.946%	5.813%	16.837%	28.256%	9.342%
99.97%		0.000% 3.6	74.909% 2.3	91.795%	89.874% 1.6	83.922% 0.1	91.426% 9.5
99.00%		0.000% 121.2	0.000% 75.4	0.000%	72.874% 52.1	72.922% 3.9	14.426% 305.8
95.00%		0.000% 605.9	0.000% 377.1	0.000%	0.000% 260.3	62.922% 19.4	0.000% 1529.0

Source: Standard & Poor's, NYU Salomon Center Default Data Base.

table 16.5, we recognize that table 16.4's findings are biased towards finding higher capital ratios and may be confounding loan losses with bond losses (the latter is what we actually measure). Both biases occur, in part, because for non-defaulters we have used the number of issuers (i.e., implicitly assuming one bond per issuer), while the defaults reflect the number of defaulted issues (i.e., one issuer may default on a number of bonds).[12] This bias is corrected in table 16.5 where we only analyze the loss rate on the most senior bond or note of each defaulting issuer. As a result, the total number of defaults falls from 692 to 334.[13] This has the additional advantage of making bonds look more like loans, since most bank loans have covenants and/or collateral backing that make them highly senior in the debt repayment structure – especially on default.

Again, we find a considerable degree of heterogeneity persisting. For example, at the 99% quantile (2.3264σ), and assuming the normal distribution, the unexpected loss rates vary widely: i.e., 0.446 percent (A), 5.619 percent (BBB), 8.306 percent (BB), 24.694 percent (B). At the same 99% quantile, under the actual distribution, the unexpected loss rates are respectively 0 percent, 0 percent, 0 percent, and 72.874 percent.

Table 16.6 repeats a similar exercise as table 16.5 but assumes defaults follow a Poisson distribution with a stable mean.[14] For bucket 2, the simple Poisson model produces similar results as those in tables 16.4 and 16.5. In particular, the unexpected loss rates at the 99% quantile are respectively: 0 percent (A), 0 percent (BBB), 0.205 percent (BB) and 17.011 percent (B).

Finally, table 16.7 repeats a similar exercise to those above except that it replaces the number of issuers in the no default category with an estimate of the number of issues.[15] This considerably increases the number of non-defaults and reduces the mean or expected loss rate. The unexpected loss rates are also affected because of the larger total sample size. As can be seen from table 16.7, however, using estimated issues instead of issuers for the non-defaulting class leaves the basic conclusions unchanged. Specifically, again using the 99% quantile, the unexpected loss rate under the normal distribution is 0.604 percent for A-rated borrowers versus 9.550 percent for B-rated borrowers, while using the actual distribution the relative unexpected loss rates for A versus B are respectively 0 percent versus 33.912 percent. Table 16.8 shows a similar "lack of granularity" using the Poisson distribution. In this case, 0 percent versus 8.704 percent.[16]

[12] The rating agencies only report the number of issuers for each grade rating category in each of the years in our sample period. See, for example, table 16 in S&P (1999).

[13] The most senior bond is defined as the one with the highest price one-year prior to default.

[14] The CreditRisk$^{+®}$ model assumes defaults follow a Poisson distribution around a shifting mean. Specifically, the mean default rate is assumed to follow a gamma distribution. The Poisson distribution is a simple distribution in that its mean equals its variance. Assuming a stable mean will tend to underestimate the "fat-tailedness" of the distribution and thus unexpected loss rates will be understated.

[15] This was done by taking three monthly samples (for December 1987, December 1992 and February 1999) on the number of issues per issuer from S&P bond guides, calculating an average number of issues per defaulting issuer in each rating category and multiplying the number of issuers row in table 1 by the resulting average number of issues per issuer.

[16] Similar conclusions, regarding the relative risk weights of buckets 2 and 3, to those discussed earlier are also reached by analyzing tables 16.5 through 16.8. The large risk-weighting differences between rating classes (and lower) are particularly evident.

Table 16.6 Frequency distribution of losses (principal and coupon), (1981–9/1999) by rating one year before default (normal and actual loss distributions) (Based on number of issuers) – Poisson process for defaults

Range of Default Losses	Midpoint	A	BBB	BB	B	CCC & Lower	Total
0	0	12,115	7,529	5,311	4,997	294	30,246
0.01–0.10	0.05	0	0	0	14	4	18
0.11–0.20	0.15	2	1	0	11	8	22
0.21–0.30	0.25	0	1	1	18	11	31
0.31–0.40	0.35	0	1	5	19	11	36
0.41–0.50	0.45	0	1	2	22	11	36
0.51–0.60	0.55	0	3	3	32	9	47
0.61–0.70	0.65	0	0	3	33	17	53
0.71–0.80	0.75	0	4	1	28	12	45
0.81–0.90	0.85	0	0	1	19	7	27
0.91–0.94	0.92	0	0	2	11	7	14
0.95–0.98	0.96	0	0	1	1	2	4
0.99	0.99	0	1	0	0	0	1
1	1	0	0	0	0	0	0
Total Default		2	12	19	208	93	334
Total Non-Default		12,115	7,529	5,311	4,997	294	30,246
Total		12,117	7,541	5,330	5,205	387	30,580
Mean		0.002%	0.091%	0.205%	2.126%	12.078%	0.574%
Median		0.000%	0.000%	0.000%	0.000%	0.000%	0.000%
St.Dev		0.193%	2.454%	3.658%	11.529%	24.521%	6.028%
99.97%		0.000%	0.091%	0.409%	23.391%	495.178%	2.869%
99.00%		0.000%	0.000%	0.205%	17.011%	410.636%	1.721%
95.00%		0.000%	0.000%	0.000%	12.759%	374.403%	1.148%
default rate m per 100 loans in the portfolio		0.017	0.159	0.356	3.996	24.031	1.092
		99.997% (1)	99.965% (2)	99.949% (3)	99.976% (12)	99.979% (42)	99.979% (6)
		99.178% (0)	99.194% (0)	99.421% (2)	99.671% (9)	99.182% (35)	99.001% (4)
		99.178% (0)	99.194% (0)	94.972% (1)	96.975% (7)	96.454% (32)	94.921% (3)

Source: Standard & Poor's NYU Salomon Center Default Data Base.

Table 16.7 Frequency distribution of losses (principal and coupon), (1981–9/1999) by rating one year before default (normal and actual loss distributions) (Based on number of issues)

Range of Default Losses	Midpoint	A	BBB	BB	B	CCC & Lower	Total
0	0	67,507	34,525	12,137	8,187	487	122,843
0.01–0.10	0.05	2	26	11	81	43	163
0.11–0.20	0.15	2	16	15	89	18	140
0.21–0.30	0.25	2	4	18	81	36	141
0.31–0.40	0.35	0	1	8	62	24	95
0.41–0.50	0.45	0	0	8	29	24	61
0.51–0.60	0.55	1	0	3	17	18	39
0.61–0.70	0.65	0	0	1	10	21	32
0.71–0.80	0.75	0	0	0	2	5	7
0.81–0.90	0.85	0	0	0	4	6	10
0.91–0.94	0.92	0	0	0	0	0	0
0.95–0.98	0.96	0	0	0	0	1	1
0.99	0.99	0	0	0	0	0	0
1	1	0	0	0	0	3	3
Total Default		7	47	64	375	199	692
Total Non-Default		67,507	34,525	12,137	8,187	487	122,843
Total		67,514	34,572	12,201	8,562	686	123,535
Mean		0.002%	0.015%	0.131%	1.088%	10.118%	0.150%
Median		0.000%	0.000%	0.000%	0.000%	0.000%	0.000%
St.Dev		0.261%	0.286%	1.421%	4.573%	20.549%	2.488%
3.43192σ-E(L)		0.892%	0.967%	4.747%	14.605%	60.406%	8.390%
2.32634σ-E(L)		0.604%	0.651%	3.176%	9.550%	37.687%	5.639%
1.64485σ-E(L)		0.427%	0.456%	2.207%	6.434%	23.683%	3.943%
99.97%		0.000% / 20.3	0.000% / 10.4	54.869% / 3.7	83.912% / 2.6	89.882% / 0.2	64.850% / 37.1
99.00%		0.000% / 675.1	0.000% / 345.7	0.000% / 122.0	33.912% / 85.6	74.882% / 6.9	0.000% / 1235.4
95.00%		0.000% / 3375.7	0.000% / 1728.6	0.000% / 610.1	0.000% / 428.1	54.882% / 34.3	0.000% / 6176.8

Source: Standard & Poor's, NYU Salomon Center Default Data Base.

Table 16.8 Frequency distribution of losses (principal and coupon), (1981–9/1999) by rating one year before default (normal and actual loss distributions) (Based on number of issues) – Poisson process for default

Range of Default Losses	Midpoint	A	BBB	BB	B	CCC & Lower	Total
0	0	67,507	34,525	12,137	8,187	487	122,843
0.01–0.10	0.05	2	26	11	81	43	163
0.11–0.20	0.15	2	16	15	89	18	140
0.21–0.30	0.25	2	4	18	81	36	141
0.31–0.40	0.35	0	1	8	62	24	95
0.41–0.50	0.45	0	0	8	29	24	61
0.51–0.60	0.55	1	0	3	17	18	39
0.61–0.70	0.65	0	0	1	10	21	32
0.71–0.80	0.75	0	0	0	2	5	7
0.81–0.90	0.85	0	0	0	4	6	10
0.91–0.94	0.92	0	0	0	0	0	0
0.95–0.98	0.96	0	0	0	0	1	1
0.99	0.99	0	0	0	0	0	0
1	1	0	0	0	0	3	3
Total		7	47	64	375	199	692
Total Non-Default		67,507	34,525	12,137	8,187	487	122,843
Total		67,514	34,572	12,201	8,562	686	123,535
Mean		0.002%	0.015%	0.131%	1.088%	10.118%	0.150%
Median		0.000%	0.000%	0.000%	0.000%	0.000%	0.000%
St.Dev		0.261%	0.286%	1.421%	4.573%	20.549%	2.488%
3.43192σ–E(L)		0.892%	0.967%	4.747%	14.605%	60.406%	8.390%
2.32634σ–E(L)		0.604%	0.651%	3.176%	9.550%	37.687%	5.639%
1.64485σ–E(L)		0.427%	0.456%	2.207%	6.434%	23.683%	3.943%
99.97%		0.000%	1 0.015%	2 0.393%	4 13.055%	49 485.668%	4 0.449%
99.00%		0.000%	0 0.000%	1 0.262%	3 8.704%	42 414.841%	3 0.300%
95.00%		0.000%	0 0.000%	0 0.131%	2 7.616%	38 374.369%	2 0.150%
default rate m per 100 loans in the portfolio		0.010	0.136	0.525	4.380	29.009	0.560
		99.996%	99.971%	99.979%	99.967%	99.979%	99.987%
		99.115%	99.288%	99.792%	99.629%	99.037%	99.862%
		99.115%	99.303%	98.368%	97.098%	94.853%	98.790%

Source: Standard & Poor's, NYU Salomon Center Default Data Base.

3.5   Simulation Results

Table 16.9 looks at the loss rates generated from Monte-Carlo simulations of the seven different portfolios discussed earlier (US life insurer-type portfolio, US bank-type portfolio, and different agency ratings). Each loss distribution is based on 50,000 simulations and an aggregate portfolio size of $1 billion. In recent years, $1 billion in asset size has been viewed as representative of medium-size US banks.[17]

From table 16.9, it can be seen that at the 99% quantile, the unexpected loss rates suggest capital requirements much lower than 8 percent in all cases, even the most risky rating class. For the insurance company portfolio (portfolio 1), the unexpected loss rate (99% loss rate minus the mean loss rate) suggests a capital ratio of

$$0.673\% - 0.109\% = 0.564\%$$

For the riskier bank loan portfolio (portfolio 2), the implied capital ratio is 1.077 percent. Looking at the question of bucket homogeneity, which is the key focus of this paper, it can be seen that unexpected loss rates for BBB vs. BB vs. B differ significantly, i.e., specifically, 0.235 percent vs. 0.769 percent vs. 1.765 percent.[18] The simulation results clearly show that the unexpected loss rate of the investment grade components (A and BBB) of bucket 2 is much lower than the below investment grade components of bucket 2 (BB and B). Even for the CCC and lower portfolio (bucket 3) the unexpected loss rate is

$$15.2\% - 10.119\% = 5.08\%$$

This may imply that the suggested BIS capital ratio for bucket 3 (12%) is perhaps too high.[19] Overall, the Monte-Carlo simulations confirm the results of the parametric approaches discussed in tables 16.4–8 – especially the heterogeneity of bucket 2.

Table 16.9   Monte-Carlo simulation of loss rates using data 1981–6/1999

| Portfolio | Portfolio size ($b) | mean | Simulated loss rates (%) Confidence Level | | | | | |
			95%	97.5%	99%	99.5%	99.9%	99.95%
1. 13% < BBB (P.P.)	1.00	0.109	0.468	0.55	0.673	0.767	1.007	1.112
2. 50% < BBB (Loans)	1.00	0.409	1.106	1.28	1.486	1.657	2	2.18
3. AAA, AA, A	1.00	0.003	0	0	0.05	0.25	0.55	0.55
4. BBB	1.00	0.015	0.15	0.15	0.25	0.3	0.4	0.4
5. BB	1.00	0.131	0.55	0.7	0.9	1	1.25	1.35
6. B	1.00	1.085	2.2	2.5	2.85	3.05	3.6	3.8
7. CCC & lower	1.00	10.119	13.6	14.35	15.2	15.95	17.1	17.56

[17]   Interestingly, the results of our simulations were quite insensitive to asset portfolio size assumptions beyond the $1 billion size range.

[18]   In this test, A was combined with AA and AAA to be comparable with the Carey (1998) paper.

[19]   This assumes that appropriate reserves for the high expected losses (e.g., over 10 percent) are deducted from the profit and loss accounts.

4   SUMMARY AND PROPOSAL

This paper has examined two specific aspects of stage 1 of the BIS's proposed reforms to the risk-based capital ratio. It has been argued that relying on "traditional" agency ratings could produce cyclically lagging rather than leading capital requirements, resulting in an enhanced rather than reduced degree of instability in the banking and financial system. In addition, even if risk-weights were to be tied to traditional agency ratings, the current bucketing proposal lacks a sufficient degree of granularity. In particular, lumping A and BBB (investment grade borrowers) together with BB and B (below investment grade borrowers) severely misprices risk within that bucket and calls, at a minimum, for that bucket to be split into two.

Table 16.10 repeats the calculations of table 16.5, but groups together A and BBB for comparison with BB and B. If we take the most conservative regulatory view and require capital to be sufficient to meet the 99.97% quantile test, then we can calculate some relative risk-weightings as examples for a split bucket 2. Specifically, in table 16.10, which is based on senior bond defaults (the bond default data that most closely resembles loans), we observe 14 defaults out of 19,658 observations in the A/BBB

Table 16.10   Frequency distribution of losses (principal and coupon), (1981–9/1999) by rating one year before default (normal and actual loss distributions) (Based on number of issuers)

Range of Default Losses	Midpoint	A & BBB		BB & B		CCC & Lower		Total	
0	0	19,644		10,308		294		30,246	
0.01–0.10	0.05	0		14		4		18	
0.11–0.20	0.15	3		11		8		22	
0.21–0.30	0.25	1		19		11		31	
0.31–0.40	0.35	1		24		11		36	
0.41–0.50	0.45	1		24		11		36	
0.51–0.60	0.55	3		35		9		47	
0.61–0.70	0.65	0		36		17		53	
0.71–0.80	0.75	4		29		12		45	
0.81–0.90	0.85	0		20		7		27	
0.91–0.94	0.92	0		13		1		14	
0.95–0.98	0.96	0		2		2		4	
0.99	0.99	1		0		0		1	
1	1	0		0		0		0	
Total Default		14		227		93		334	
Total Non-Default		19,644		10,308		294		30,246	
Total		19,658		10,535		387		30,580	
Mean		0.036%		1.154%		12.078%		0.574%	
Median		0.000%		0.000%		0.000%		0.000%	
St.Dev		1.528%		8.565%		24.521%		6.028%	
3.43192σ-E(L)		5.208%		28.240%		72.077%		20.114%	
2.32634σ-E(L)		3.519%		18.771%		44.967%		13.450%	
1.64485σ-E(L)		2.477%		12.934%		28.256%		9.342%	
99.97%		54.964%	5.9	90.846%	3.2	83.922%	0.1	91.426%	9.2
99.00%		0.000%	196.6	53.846%	105.4	72.922%	3.9	14.426%	305.8
95.00%		0.000%	982.9	0.000%	526.8	62.922%	19.4	0.000%	1529.0

Source: Standard & Poor's, NYU Salomon Center Default Data Base.

investment grade bucket and 227 out of 10,535 in the non-investment grade BB/B bucket within the one-year time horizon. At the 99.97% level, for the actual distribution results, the ratio of unexpected losses between the two buckets is 1.65 (90.846/54.96). Under the normal distribution assumption for all levels of confidence (95% to 99.97%), the ratio is about 5.4 (e.g., 28.240/5.208 for 3.43σ or the 99.97% quantile).[20] Hence, we find a considerable difference in risk between these buckets, as expected. The CCC and lower bucket is considerably more risky under the normal distribution assumption – about 2.5 times the BB/B bucket.[21] Since the CCC and lower category has so few observations (387), we cannot be as confident as we would like to be about its exact risk compared to other buckets.

4.1 A Revised Bucket Proposal

A bucket system with four categories, and with a weighting system something like that shown in table 16.11, would accomplish much of what the BIS proposal is attempting to do, and also comes closer to capturing the reality of actual relative default losses by ratings.

We constructed this table based on the following logic. We felt constrained to choose a non-zero weighting for the first bucket (AAA/AA), although our results (over the last 19 years) clearly show that no defaults have actually taken place within one year for bonds in these two highest ratings. The choice of 10 percent for bucket 1 is therefore arbitrary but still less than the BIS proposal's 20 percent. A second consideration was that we felt it appropriate to give the new BB/B non-investment grade bucket a full 100 percent weighting.[22] This left us with a decision as to the appropriate A/BBB classification. We decided to use a ratio of about 3.33 to 1 when comparing the BB/B bucket with this A/BBB bucket. This is about the midpoint between the normal distribution and actual distribution's results at the 99.97% quantile (1.65 and 5.40), Hence, the designation of 30 percent for our bucket 2. Note that this 30 percent weighting is considerably lower than the BIS proposal and the 100 percent weighting for bucket 3 is the same as their earlier proposal. Finally, we adopt the same 150 percent weighting for below B-credits (bucket 4).

Table 16.11 An alternative risk weighting proposal for bank corporate loans

	AAA to AA–	A+ to BBB–	BB+ to B–	Below
Corporates	10%	30%	100%	150%

[20] The 99.97% level is actually not shown but is essentially identical to the 99.9% level.
[21] The results for the CCC and lower bucket were about the same as the BB/B for the actual distribution, since both were near the maximum loss possible at the 99.97% level.
[22] One could actually argue for a higher weighting in this bucket but this would almost surely cutoff most lending to firms in this bucket – a bucket which we believe now represents a very high proportion of current loans outstanding.

4.2   The Unrated Class

Note that we do not propose any specific weighting for the category "unrated." We feel that the appropriate weighting system that bank regulators sanction will be based on a combination of external and internal ratings. Using internal ratings obviates the need for an "unrated" class since banks should be rating all customers. Also, the currently proposed BIS unrated class is essentially a classification that assumes no clear risk analysis. That is not very helpful in a world where most assets are unrated by external rating agencies; hence, the inevitable sanctioning of internal systems.

4.3   Final Comment

We are aware that our proposals are not perfect, but they appear to resemble more closely the existing data on unexpected losses. Although we do not expect regulatory capital arbitrage to cease completely, we are convinced that it will be reduced with our modifications and will bring regulatory capital closer to economic capital estimates.

REFERENCES

Altman, E. I., "Measuring Corporate Bond Mortality and Performance" *Journal of Finance* XLIV (4), September 1989, 909–22.
Altman, E. I., and A. Saunders, "Credit Risk Measurement: Developments Over the Last 20 Years," *Journal of Banking & Finance* (11), 1997, 1721–42.
Altman, E. I., D. Cooke and V. Kishore, "Defaults and Returns on High Yield Bonds: Analysis through 1998 & Default Outlook for 1999–2001," *NYU Salomon Center Special Report*, January 1999, updated in January 2000.
Basel Committee on Banking Supervision, "A New Capital Adequacy Framework," Basle, June 1999.
Basel Committee on Banking Supervision, "Range of Practice in Banks' Internal Ratings Systems," Basel, January 2000.
Carey, M., "Credit Risk in Private Debt Portfolios," *Journal of Finance*, August 1998, 1363–87.
CreditMetrics, J. P. Morgan, April 1997.
Credit Suisse Financial Products, *Credit Risk+: A Credit Risk Measurement Framework*, London, 1997.
Jonsson J. G. and M. Fridson "Forecasting Default Rates on High Yield Bonds," *Journal of Fixed Income*, June 1996.
Moody's "Predicting Default Rates: A Forecasting Model for Moody's Issuer-Based Default Rates," *Special Comment*, Global Credit Research, August 1999.
Standard & Poor's, "Rating Performance 1998: Stability & Transition," *S&P Special Report*, March 1999.
Tracey, W. and M. Carey, "Credit Rating Systems at large US Banks," Federal Reserve Bulletin, November 1998, and *Journal of Banking & Finance* 24, 2000, 167–201.

Part III: High Yield "Junk" Bonds and Distressed Securities

17 | The Default Rate Experience on High-Yield Corporate Debt*

with Scott A. Nammacher

Recent (1978–83) net returns on high-yield, low-rated debt have been impressive, averaging 490–580 basis points above the long-term government bond index. But low-rated "junk" bonds pose a risk of default not present in the higher-rated segment of the bond market.

The authors divided the par value of defaulting debt by total low-rated straight debt outstanding to arrive at an estimate of the default rate for high-yield bonds (excluding Johns Manville, which had the only defaulting debt rated investment grade just prior to the default date). For the 1974–84 period, this averaged 1.52 percent (or 152 basis points) annually. Year-to-year variations in the rate were substantial. Furthermore, default experience differed across various industry segments. Railroads and REITs were particularly vulnerable to default in the past, although they are unlikely to represent a large portion of future defaults. Retailer, electronic/computer, airline, and oil and gas defaults have become more common in recent years.

Losses from default are actually lower than the default rate alone implies. Defaulted bonds traded, on average, at 41 percent of par shortly after default. After accounting for the bonds' retained value and the loss of interest, the average reduction in return to the investor who had purchased the bonds at par would have been in the range of 96–100 basis points annually.

---

* This article was the first in a series of studies by Dr. Altman which monitor the default experience of high-yield bonds. See chapters 23 and 24 for updated studies.

Rising interest rates and the rapid expansion of the high-yield corporate debt market since the late 1970s have led a wide variety of financial institutions to explore the relative attractions of lower-rated securities. In addition to promised superior yields and returns, the high-yield (or "junk") sector now offers considerable liquidity and diversification potential.

According to some estimates, total high-yield debt outstanding was close to $75 billion by the end of 1984.[1] As table 17.1 shows, *low-rated, public, nonconvertible debt* grew from under $10 billion in 1978 to almost $42 billion in mid-1984. By 1984, this segment represented 11.2 percent of the total corporate straight debt market, versus just 3.8 percent in 1978. In 1984 alone, nearly $15 billion in straight high-yield financing was issued.[2] This market's size, growth rate and yield potential make it an increasingly important investment area.

High-yield bonds have experienced healthy return premiums over investment grade securities, but they have also experienced substantial defaults. Without a reliable measure of past losses from defaults, investors cannot intelligently estimate the net returns over time on high-yield bonds. This article provides an in-depth and comprehensive look at the default experience since the dramatic growth of the high-yield bond market began.

Table 17.1   Public straight debt outstanding, 1970–84 (millions of dollars)

		Low-rated debt[b]			
Year	*Average par value public straight debt outstanding over year ($)*[a]	*Straight public debt ($)*	*% of public st. debt*	*Amount outstanding per issuer ($)*	*Amount outstanding per issue ($)*
1984	317,100 (Est.)	41,700	11.2	125	49
1983	339,850	28,223	8.3	93	39
1982	320,850	18,536	5.8	69	33
1981	303,800	17,363	5.7	62	32
1980	282,000	15,125	5.4	59	31
1979	260,600	10,675	4.1	47	30
1978	245,000	9,401	3.8	49	30
1977	228,500	8,479	3.7	46	27
1976	209,900	8,015	3.8	41	27
1975	187,900	7,720	4.1	41	27
1974	167,000[c]	11,101[d]	6.6	59	35
1973	154,800	8,082	5.2	45	29
1972	145,700	7,106	4.9	45	29
1971	132,500	6,643	5.0	45	29
1970	116,200	6,996	6.0	48	32

[a] *Source: Salomon Brothers Inc – average of beginning and ending years' figures (1975–84).*
[b] *Source:* Standard & Poor's Bond Guide *and* Moody's Bond Record, *July issue of each year. Defaulted railroads excluded. Also includes nonrated debt equivalent to rated debt for low-rated firms.*
[c] *Estimates for 1973 and earlier based on linear regression of this column vs. the Federal Reserve's Corporate Bonds Outstanding figures (*Federal Reserve Bulletin*).*
[d] *Includes $2.7 billion in Con Edison debt.*

[1]   Drexel, Burnham & Lambert, *High Yield Newsletter* (Los Angeles), October 1984.
[2]   See E. I. Altman and S. Nammacher's high-yield bond studies, Morgan Stanley & Co. Incorporated, 1985.

MEASURING THE DEFAULT EXPERIENCE

Most past studies of the default experience of US corporate debt have dealt with the entire public corporate debt market, estimated to be over $400 billion at the end of 1984.[3] These studies noted that the total default rate of US corporate debt ranged from 0.03 percent during 1960–67 to 3.2 percent during 1930–39. Table 17.2 summarizes a number of disparate studies of the default experience since 1900. Because the bases used are not identical and the degree of comprehensiveness is not always clear, these results are not directly comparable.

The appropriate base for calculating the default rate for corporate debt seems to us to be the low-rated straight debt market. If the strategy entails investing in this sector (and nearly all defaults occur here), then the relevant rate should be based on this sector's issues. Bonds rated investment grade (BBB-/Baa3 or higher) just prior to default rarely default. Out of 130 defaulting debt issues from the 15-year period 1970–84, only four had a rating of BBB-/Baa3 or higher six months prior to default.[4] (Johns Manville had the only A rating.)

It could be argued that a more relevant default rate base would be low-rated public straight debt *less* utilities, because defaults have occurred only in the nonutility segment. This base, being a smaller one (see table 17.3), would result in higher default rates. In recent years, however, downgraded utilities have become a large segment of the high-yield straight debt area; in 1984, utilities accounted for 23 percent of this market. Although there have been no utility defaults to date, the notion is not nearly as

Table 17.2 Corporate debt default rates, 1900–84

Period	Total corporate debt default rate (%)
1900–09	0.90
1910–19	2.00
1920–29	1.00
1930–39	3.20
1940–49	0.40
1950–59	0.04
1960–67	0.03
1968–77	0.16
1978–84	0.07

Source: W. B. Hickman, Corporate Bond Quality and Investor Experience *(Princeton, New Jersey: Princeton University Press, 1958); T. R. Atkinson,* Trends in Corporate Bond Quality *(New York: National Bureau of Economic Research, 1967); J. D. Fitzpatrick and J. T. Severiens, "Hickman Revisited: The Case for Junk Bonds,"* The Journal of Portfolio Management, Summer *1978, J. H. Hill and L. A. Post,* The 1977–78 Lower-Rated Debt Market: Selectivity, High Yields, Opportunity *(New York: Smith Barney Harris Upham & Co., December 1978); and table 17.6.*

[3] See W. B. Hickman, *Corporate Bond Quality and Investor Experience* (Princeton, New Jersey: Princeton University Press, 1958); T. R. Atkinson, *Trends in Corporate Bond Quality* (New York: National Bureau of Economic Research, 1967); H. J. Hill and L. A. Post, *The 1977–78 Lower-Rated Debt Market: Selectivity, High Yields, Opportunity* (New York: Smith Barney Harris Upham & Co., December 1978).

[4] We have data on 125 defaulting companies from 1970 to 1984 and have prior rating data on 130 of the issues. Railroad issues were excluded.

Table 17.3 Low-rated public straight debt outstanding less utilities (millions of dollars)

Year	Low-rated debt less utilities ($)[a]	% of total public straight debt[b]	Amount outstanding per issuer ($)	Amount outstanding per issue ($)
1984	32,120	8.6	101	51
1983	22,167	6.5	76	40
1982	16,111	5.0	62	35
1981	15,010	4.9	56	35
1980	12,807	4.5	52	34
1979	10,031	3.8	47	30
1978	8,995	3.7	49	31
1977	7,548	3.3	47	31
1976	7,024	3.3	42	29
1975	6,971	3.7	43	30
1974	7,445	4.5	45	32
1973	7,195	4.6	42	32
1972	6,245	4.3	45	31
1971	5,935	4.5	45	31
1970	6,448	5.5	48	32

[a] *Source:* Standard & Poor's Bond Guide *and* Moody's Bond Record, *July issue of each year. Defaulted railroads excluded. Also includes nonrated debt equivalent to rated debt for low-rated firms.*

[b] *See table 17.1 for total public straight debt dollar amounts.*

inconceivable as it formerly was. On balance, the increased risk and size of the utility market, plus the need to use a consistent base over time, warrant the inclusion of the utility sector in the default rate base.

The outstanding amounts in this study were calculated using July issues of *Standard & Poor's Bond Guide* and *Moody's Bond Record.* Various prior studies have used different points in the year for calculating the amount outstanding base. If we had used year-end totals instead of mid-year amounts, the default rate for 1974–84 would be 10–15 basis points lower than our estimate. We used mid-year figures, however, because technical defaults on any new issues cannot take place before the initial coupon payments are due (barring bankruptcy or defaults on other issues). This means semiannual coupon bonds issued after June could not generally default (by missing a coupon payment) until the next calendar year. The dollars outstanding for each default came from the bond guides for the month when the firm fell into a DDD or lower rating category or, where no rating was found, the bankruptcy filing date.[5] Where amounts outstanding were not available, annual reports and *Moody's Industrial Manuals* were consulted.

THE RESULTS

Tables 17.4 through 17.7 document the default experience for the period 1970–84. That 15-year period witnessed the default of over $3.6 billion of straight debt and $5.3 billion of total debt (see table 17.4 and figure 17.1). [Appendix A to the original article

[5] The DDD rating is no longer used by S&P's. In cases where amounts outstanding differed, S&P's out-standings were used.

Table 17.4 Public corporate debt defaulting on interest and/or principal: 1970–84 (millions of dollars)

Year of default	Straight debt ($)	Convertible debt ($)	Total debt in default ($)
1984	344.16	279.95	624.11
1983	301.08	111.55	412.63
1982	752.34	243.29	995.63
1981	27.00	52.61	79.61
1980	224.11	31.60	255.71
1979	20.00	10.70	30.70
1978	118.90	73.30	192.20
1977	380.57	74.21	454.78
1976	29.51	83.99	113.50
1975	204.10	115.63	319.73
1974	122.82	165.87	288.69
1973	49.07	150.84	199.91
1972	193.25	79.34	272.59
1971	82.00	42.90	124.90
1970	796.71	135.81	932.52
Total	3,645.62	1,651.59	5,297.21

Figure 17.1 Public straight debt defaulting, par value at default (millions of dollars)

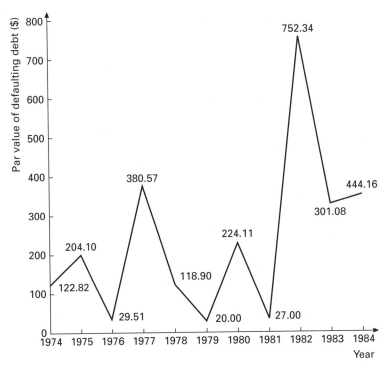

Table 17.5   Historical default rates – all ratings (millions of dollars)

Year	Par value straight & convertible public debt outstanding ($)[a]	Par value all public defaults ($)	Default rate (%)	Par value public straight debt outstanding ($)[a]	Par value straight debt defaulted ($)	Default rate (%)
1984	413,200 (Est.)	624.11	0.151	391,700 (Est.)	344.16	0.088
1983	372,900	412.63	0.111	350,500	301.08	0.086
1982	352,300	995.63	0.283	329,200	752.34	0.228
1981	331,400	79.61	0.023	312,500	27.00	0.009
1980	311,900	255.71	0.082	295,100	224.11	0.076
1979	281,700	30.70	0.011	269,900	20.00	0.007
1978	258,600	192.20	0.074	252,200	118.90	0.047
1977	248,300	454.78	0.183	237,800	380.57	0.160
1976	229,100	113.50	0.049	219,200	29.51	0.013
1975	209,900	319.73	0.152	200,600	204.10	0.102
1974	183,500	288.69	0.157	175,200	122.82	0.070
1973	162,900[b]	199.91	0.123	158,800[b]	49.07	0.031
1972	154,400	272.59	0.176	150,900	193.25	0.128
1971	143,000	124.90	0.087	140,500	82.00	0.058
1970	125,500	932.52	0.743	124,400	796.71	0.640

	Average Default Rate 1970 to 1984:	0.160%		0.116%
	Average Default Rate 1974 to 1984:	**0.116%**		**0.080%**
	Average Default Rate 1978 to 1984:	0.105%		0.077%

[a] *Source: Salomon Brothers Inc. These numbers are year-end outstanding amounts.*
[b] *Estimates for 1973 and earlier based on linear regression of this column vs. the Federal Reserve's Corporate Bonds Outstanding figures (Federal Reserve Bulletin).*

provided a comprehensive list of the 125 firms (65 of which had public straight debt) that defaulted, the dates of default and the aggregate amounts of defaulted debt per company.][6]

In calculating the default rate, the relevant period seems to us to be 1974–84. The straight low-rated debt market from 1970 to 1977 was made up primarily of declining, ex-investment grade firms. Few, if any, new issues were rated less than BBB, and there was limited liquidity and interest in the low-rated area. The more modern era of high-yield investing began in the late 1970s, when low-rated new issuers appeared and the market began to expand.

Although the market had not changed appreciably by 1974, the first of two major recessions (1974–75 and 1981–82) had begun. Including both recessions gives a more realistic view of the default experience, as these downturns conceivably represent the magnitude of economic shocks that could recur in the future. Also, the bulk of the railroad defaults had occurred by 1974. For these reasons, we believe 1974 to be an appropriate starting point for measuring default rates relevant to today's marketplace. It should be noted that the 1974–84 default experience is similar to the more recent period 1978–84 (see table 17.6), when the market began to expand rapidly.

From 1974 to 1984, the default rate on straight low-rated debt ranged from 0.155 of 1 percent in 1981 to 4.488 percent in 1977, with the average annual rate being 1.60 per-

---

[6]   Where possible, we have combined subsidiaries with parent company defaults. The actual number of defaulting issuers would be greater if the subsidiaries were listed separately.

Table 17.6 Historical default rates – low-rated straight debt only[a] (millions of dollars)

Year	Par value outstanding with utilities ($)[b]	Par value defaulted ($)	Default rate (%)	Par value public outstanding less utilities ($)[b]	Default rate (%)
1984	41,700	344.16	0.825	32,120	1.071
1983	28,233	301.08	1.066	22,167	1.358
1982	18,536	752.34	4.059[c]	16,111	4.670
1981	17,362	27.00	0.155	15,010	0.180
1980	15,126	224.11	1.482	12,807	1.750
1979	10,675	20.00	0.187	10,031	0.199
1978	9,401	118.90	1.265	8,995	1.322
1977	8,479	380.57	4.488	7,548	5.042
1976	8,015	29.51	0.368	7,024	0.420
1975	7,720	204.10	2.644	6,971	2.928
1974	11,101[c]	22.82	1.106	7,445	1.650
1973	8,082	49.07	0.607	7,195	0.682
1972	7,106	193.25	2.719	6,245	3.094
1971	6,643	82.00	1.234	5,935	1.382
1970	6,996	796.71	11.388	6,448	12.356
	Average Default Rate 1970 to 1984:		2.240%		2.540%
	Average Default Rate 1974 to 1984:		**1.604%[d]**		**1.872%**
	Average Default Rate 1978 to 1984:		1.291%		1.507%

[a] *Issues rated below Baa3 by Moody's or BBB by Standard & Poor's. Includes nonrated debt of issuers with other equivalently rated issues.*
[b] *Source: Standard & Poor's Bond Guide and Moody's Bond Record, July issue of each year.*
[c] *Includes almost $2.7 billion of Consolidated Edison Co. debt.*
[d] *Excluding Johns Manville, the default rate for 1982 was 3.115 percent and it was 1.518 percent for the 1974–84 period.*

cent of par value (table 17.6 and figure 17.2). One might argue that, because Johns Manville was investment grade at the time of default, it should not be included. If its two issues were excluded, the default rate would be 1.52 percent. The rate using the nonutility base would be 1.87 percent for the same period. Traditional analysis using total public straight debt outstanding as a base results in a default rate of 0.08 of 1 percent, or about 1/20th of what we view as the relevant rate.

Some analysts have commented that the appropriate base to use as a measure of the high-yield straight debt population would be all debt, including nonrated issues. The latter, it has been argued, probably represented 10–20 percent of the high-yield market in our sample period. If this additional debt had been included, the default rate for the 1974–84 period would be lowered to between 1.27 and 1.38 percent. But inclusion of nonrated, high-yield debt seems to us to be somewhat arbitrary, especially since some types of exchange obligations may not be traded for very long. Still, it is an issue worth considering.

We do not subscribe to the suggestion that only debt that was originally issued as high yield should be counted in the default rate calculation. The so-called "fallen angels," we believe, should also be considered when computing the default rate experience.

The straight debt default rate for the entire period 1970–84 was 2.24 percent. This rate is considerably higher than the aforementioned levels because of the 1970 Penn Central default. With Penn Central, the default rate for 1970 was 11.4 percent. Without

Figure 17.2 Public straight debt default rate as percentage of high-yield debt outstanding

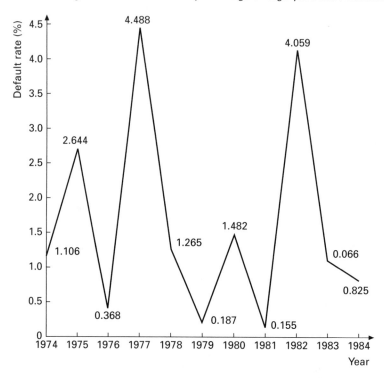

it, the 1970 rate falls to 2.5 percent (almost all of which is accounted for by other railroads). The 15-year average default rate without Penn Central was 1.65 percent.[7]

The number of firms that defaulted over the 1974–84 period ranged from 17 in 1982 to three in both 1979 and 1981 (table 17.7 and figure 17.3). The 1982 totals for both number of firms and dollar amounts are the high points for the 1970–84 period, barely nosing out 1970. Three large firms (Johns Manville, Wickes/Gamble Skogmo and Braniff Airlines) represented 76 percent of the defaulting straight debt in 1982.

The number of firms defaulting relative to the number of issuers with outstanding high-yield debt may also be of interest to investors. Table 17.8 lists the approximate number of high-yield straight debt issuers for each year of the 15-year period. It also highlights the default rate in issuer terms. The number of issuers outstanding increased from 145 in 1970 to 190 in 1978 and to 335 in 1984. The average percentage of defaulting issuers ranged from 0.4 percent in 1979 to 4.4 percent in 1982. Over the 1970–84 period, the issuer default rate was 2.0 percent. (It held at 2.0 percent for 1974–84 and fell to 1.8 percent for 1978–84.) The issuer default rate appears to drop as the number of issuers increases. Nevertheless, the *issuer default rate* is high relative to the *dollar default rate*.

---

[7] J. D. Fitzpatrick and J. T. Severiens ("Hickman Revisited: The Case for Junk Bonds," *The Journal of Portfolio Management*, Summer 1978) estimated the default rate on debt rated BB/Ba and B for the period 1965–75 to be 0.8 percent.

Table 17.7 Number of companies with public debt defaulting[a]

Year	Non-railroad companies	Major railroads
1984	12	
1983	14	
1982	17	
1981	3	
1980	5	
1979	3	
1978	5	
1977	8	1
1976	7	
1975	7	1
1974	11	
1973	9	1
1972	3	1
1971	4	1
1970	9	5
Total	117[b]	10[b]

[a] Includes straight and convertible defaults.
[b] Includes one of two companies that defaulted twice over period.

Figure 17.3 Number of companies defaulting on publicly held debt

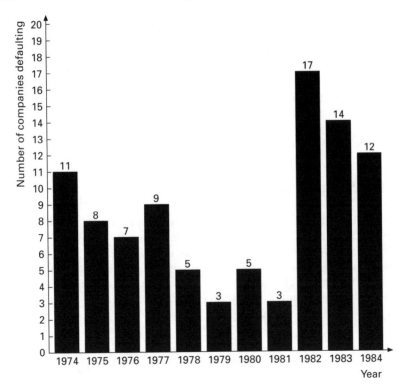

Table 17.8   Percentage of low-rated firms in default – straight debt only

Year	Number of low-rated firms	Number of firms in default*	% in default
1984	335	6	1.8
1983	305	9	2.9
1982	270	12	4.4
1981	280	2	0.7
1980	255	3	1.2
1979	230	1	0.4
1978	190	2	1.0
1977	185	8	4.3
1976	195	2	1.0
1975	190	4	2.1
1974	190	5	2.6
1973	180	3	1.7
1972	160	2	1.2
1971	150	1	0.7
1970	145	5	3.4

Average Percentage 1970 to 1984:   2.0%
Average Percentage 1974 to 1984:   2.0%
Average Percentage 1978 to 1984:   1.8%

* Public straight debt defaults only.

Although the issuer default rate is dropping, the number of dollars defaulting per issuer is increasing. Figure 17.4 shows the yearly average defaults per issuer, which ranged from a low of $14 million in 1981 to $75 million in 1980. The average over the 1974–84 period was $42 million per default. We anticipate this average will continue to increase in the future as the debt outstanding per company increases.

It should be noted that the total dollars and firms in default are conservative (i.e., high) estimates from the investor's viewpoint. At least 14 of these defaulting firms did not actually file for bankruptcy. In several cases, interest was paid in arrears at a later date either by the firm or by a firm purchasing the defaulted entity. In others, agreements were reached with creditors to restructure the debt.

IMPACT ON ANNUAL RETURNS

One might conclude that an investor with a portfolio of representative high-yield bonds suffered an average annual loss of 152 basis points from the total annual return of the portfolio over the 1974–84 period. This average default rate would be the relevant loss only if the security's value fell to zero upon news of the default and the investor liquidated after having purchased at par. In fact, the prices of debt issues immediately after default can be substantial. We found the average price to be 41 percent of par value.[8] If the investor sold the bonds just after bankruptcy, the actual loss would have

---

[8]   This is based on a study of 56 straight defaulted debt issues with the price taken at the end of the month in which either default or bankruptcy occurred (whichever came first). This finding is consistent with the 40–43 percent range found by Hickman (*Corporate Bond Quality, op. cit.*) for defaults from 1900 to 1943.

Figure 17.4   Average $ defaulting per company (for public straight debt only), based on par value at default (millions of dollars)

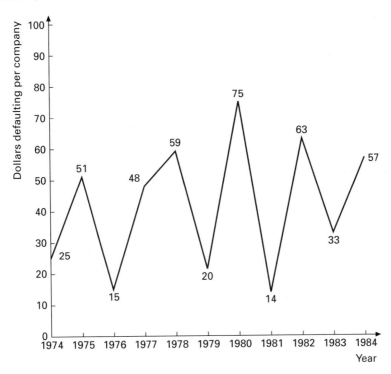

been 59 percent of par value, plus roughly one-half the annual coupon amount, assuming purchase at par.

Our estimate of the loss is based on retention of 41 percent of par value, less approximately one-half the annual coupon. We subtract the semiannual coupon (which we estimate at between 4 and 7 percent) because defaults usually occur when a coupon payment is due. This results in an annual loss of 96–100 basis points from returns:

100% – 41% = 59% loss of par value
0.59 × 152 = 89.7 basis point par value loss
plus
0.04 × 152 = 6.1 basis point coupon loss *to*
0.07 × 152 = 10.6 *basis point coupon loss* 95.8 to 100.3 annual loss in returns

Again, this assumes that the investor purchased at par – a relevant assumption for some groups (e.g., unit trust bond funds) but not for others (e.g., investors in distressed firms). For example, the average price of our 56 bonds was 56.3 percent of par one year prior to default, indicating a 27.2 percent drop in price over the year prior to default. Purchasing at this date and price level would have significantly reduced the basis point loss from defaults, compared to purchasing at par.

The average price of defaulting straight debt securities the month prior to bankruptcy or default was 50.1 percent of par. This indicates an 18.2 percent drop in value over the critical one month period prior to default. One might consider this the bond default announcement effect. Prior investigations into the announcement effect on common stock prices indicate that the drop in the equity price of bankrupt companies is substantially greater than that for debt.[9]

Holding a market basket (reconstituted at the end of each year) of straight high-yield bonds versus holding the equivalent of Shearson Lehman's Long Term Government Bond Index, from 31 December 1977 to 31 December 1983 would have resulted in an annual compound return spread of over 580 basis points in favor of the high-yield bond portfolio.[10] This premium is net of defaults.[11] Thus, although the 96 to 100 basis point default cost indicates risk in the high-yield straight debt area, the net returns from this sector are substantial and will undoubtedly continue to attract investors.

CHARACTERISTICS OF DEFAULTING FIRMS

Table 17.9 lists the original issue ratings of straight and convertible bonds that subsequently defaulted. Although only 8 percent (nine of 112 issues) of the defaulting bonds were originally rated A or better, a total of 34 (over 30 percent) were originally rated investment grade. These "fallen angels" demonstrate that firms can deteriorate from solid credits into bankruptcy or default. The largest percentage (36 percent) of defaulting bonds were originally rated B.

It is perhaps more relevant to assess the bond ratings as default approached. Rather than riding a bond all the way down, the portfolio manager can usually sell the security when its rating drops below some threshold level. Table 17.9 also shows defaulting

Table 17.9 Rating distribution of defaulting issues at various points prior to default*

Original rating	AAA	AA	A	BBB	BB	B	CCC	CC	TOTAL
Number	0	2	7	25	21	40	17	0	112
Percentage	0%	1.8%	6.2%	22.3%	18.8%	35.7%	15.2%	0%	100%
Rating one year prior	AAA	AA	A	BBB	BB	B	CCC	CC	TOTAL
Number	0	0	2	11	14	53	43	7	130
Percentage	0%	0%	1.5%	8.5%	10.8%	40.8%	33.1%	5.3%	100%
Rating six months prior	AAA	AA	A	BBB	BB	B	CCC	CC	TOTAL
Number	0	0	2	2	10	51	53	12	130
Percentage	0%	0%	1.5%	1.5%	7.7%	39.2%	40.8%	9.2%	100%

* Includes convertibles and straight debt issues. Excludes railroad issues. Ratings from Standard & Poor's Bond Guide.

[9] The drop for equities ranges from the 25 percent found by Altman ("Bankrupt Firms' Equity Securities as An Investment Alternative," *Financial Analysts Journal*, July/August 1969) to the 35–50 percent found by Clark and Weinstein, *Journal of Finance*, May 1984.

[10] Total compound returns for the period were 91.6 percent for the high-yield portfolio and 38.8 percent for the government index. The return spread is sensitive to starting and ending dates, however. For the six-year period from 31 March 1978 to 31 March 1984, the spread was 490 basis points. If we extend the period to the end of 1984, the spread drops to just below 400 basis points.

[11] The sample default rate was 1.50 percent for this six-year period. Our price data base did not run through 1984.

bond ratings 12 months and six months prior to default. The average rating is, as expected, lower than the original issue rating. Thirteen of 130 (10 percent) were rated investment grade (BBB-/Baa3 or above) one year prior to default, and four of 130 (3 percent) were investment grade at just six months prior to default. The percentages for straight debt only were 16.1 and 4.4 percent, respectively. Finally, only Manville's debt was investment grade one month prior to filing. In summary, virtually all the recent bond issue defaults were in the speculative or high-yield (junk) categories just prior to default.

INDUSTRY ANALYSIS

Table 17.10 [and Appendix B of the original article] break out defaults by industry sector for 1970–84. Railroad, retail and financial service companies had the largest proportional shares of the total (straight *and* convertible debt) dollar amounts defaulted. Including convertible defaults, the electronics/computer/communications sector had the largest *number* of firms defaulting.

In the straight debt default area, transportation companies were again well represented – including nine major railroads. Given the small number of extant railroads, the expected frequency of future defaults in this sector is low; the most recent major rail default was in 1977. Over the entire 15-year period, though, the aggregate amount of publicly traded railroad debt defaulting accounted for almost 35 percent of the total straight debt defaulted. Penn Central alone accounted for 49 percent of those dollars.

Table 17.10 Public debt defaults by industry sector, 1970–84 (million of dollars)

	Number of companies	Straight debt ($)	% of Total straight[a]	Convertible debt ($)	Total in default ($)	% of total[a]
Industrial						
Retailers	14	458.04	12.6	211.87	669.91	12.6
General Mfg.	15	340.55	9.3	139.63	480.18	9.1
Elect./Computer & Commn.	20	200.79	5.5	273.58	474.37	9.0
Oil & Gas	13	185.44	5.1	267.95	453.39	8.6
Real Estate – Const., Supplies	11	82.83	2.3	114.46	197.29	3.7
Misc. Industrials	11	189.40	5.2	133.26	322.66	6.1
Total Industrial:	84	1,457.05	40.0	1,140.75	2,597.80	49.0
Transportation						
Railroads	9	1,260.22	34.6	31.10	1,291.32	24.4
Airlines/Cargo	6	206.54	5.7	96.49	303.03	5.7
Sea Lines	2	0.00	0.0	110.00	110.00	2.1
Trucks/Motor Carriers	3	48.31	1.3	9.75	58.06	1.1
Total Transportation:	20	1,515.07	41.6	247.34	1,762.41	33.3
Finance						
Financial Serv.	9	393.79	10.8	164.04	557.83	. 10.5
REITs	12	279.71	7.7	99.46	379.17	7.2
Total Finance:	21	673.50	18.5	263.50	937.00	17.7
TOTAL DEFAULTS:	125[b]	3,645.62	100	1,651.59	5,297.21	100

[a] *Numbers may not add up because of rounding errors.*
[b] *Does not include multiple defaults by same firm (two firms defaulted twice).*

Retailers and financial service companies represent 12.6 and 10.8 percent of defaulted debt, respectively. Again, one company in each area represented a significant amount of the total. Wickes/Gamble Skogmo and its credit subsidiary represented 57 percent of the retail sector's defaults, while Itel (a leasing firm) represented 47 percent of the financial services sector's defaults.

Finance company defaults, particularly the REITs in the mid-1970s, were numerous. Although the number of future REIT defaults is not likely to be high, given the much diminished pool to draw from, the dynamic and increasingly competitive nature of the finance industry portends an increasing number of bankruptcies and, perhaps, bond defaults. Currently, however, few large financial institutions tap the public debt markets; most rely on short-term paper, public agency borrowing and deposits.

Recent years have witnessed relatively more retailing, electronics/computer, oil and gas, and airline defaults. Over time, however, the most vulnerable sectors change, and it is difficult at best to project these trends into the future.

DEFAULTS AND BUSINESS FAILURES

The business failure rate and bankruptcy filing experience of firms in the US reached record post-Depression levels in 1983 (see table 17.11).[12] Aggregate GNP data show that 1982 was the depth of the most recent recession, a fact reflected in our default data. It is difficult, however, to establish a clear connection between aggregate business failure rates in the USA and corporate default rates (see table 17.6).

Table 17.11   Bankruptcy and business failure statistics in the USA, 1974–84

Year	Number of business bankruptcy filings[a]	Yearly % change	Business failures[b]	Yearly % change	Business failure rates[c]	Yearly % change
1984	62,170	(11)	26,950	(14)	95(Est.)	(14)
1983	69,818	24	31,334	26	110	24
1982	56,423	19	24,908	46	89	46
1981	47,414	30	17,041	45	61	45
1980	36,513	24	11,742	55	42	50
1979	29,500	(3)	7,564	14	28	17
1978	30,528	(5)	6,619	(16)	24	(14)
1977	32,189	(9)	7,919	(18)	28	(20)
1976	35,201	17	9,628	(16)	35	(19)
1975	30,130	45	11,432	15	43	13
1974	20,747	19	9,915	6	38	6

[a] Source: Administrative Office of Bankruptcy Courts, Division of Bankruptcy Statistics. Fiscal year ends June.
[b] Source: Dun & Bradstreet's (NYC), Business Failure Statistics.
[c] Dun & Bradstreet changed its reporting system in 1984 and no longer reports the failure rate (failures per 10,000 listed companies); 1984 statistics estimated by E. Altman (NYU).

[12]   Published by Dun & Bradstreet (*The 1982 Dun & Bradstreet Business Failure Record* (New York: Economic Analysis Department of Dun & Bradstreet, 1983)), the failure rate is the number of companies involved in court proceedings or voluntary actions involving loss to creditors divided by the companies followed by D&B. The rate itself is the number of failures per 10,000 companies.

In some years, the directional change from the prior year is fairly consistent between these two seemingly related series. In 1982, for example, the business failure rate and number of bankruptcies in the US rose significantly, while the total and especially the low-rated corporate default rate increased dramatically. Other recent "consistent" years include 1975 (up), 1976 (down), 1978 (down), 1980 (up) and 1984 (down). In contrast, 1977, 1979, 1981 and 1983 do not show this consistent pattern.

The failure rate in any one year is not especially meaningful for estimating defaults of publicly held company debt. We need to look at a number of years for a better picture of the failure-default relation. It appears to us that the changing, less regulated structure of the US economy portends relatively high business failure rates in the future, and wider fluctuations in bond defaults.

IMPLICATIONS FOR INVESTORS

The default rate experience of high-yield corporate debt, particularly in the last decade and a half, indicates an average annual default rate of 1.52 percent – an extremely risky scenario. A portfolio with a buy-and-hold strategy can expect a fairly rapid deterioration of its capital base, especially if coupon income is paid out to investors. On the other hand, returns on low-quality debt portfolios have been very impressive, even after defaults.

Cautious investors may use hedging strategies to reduce the risks, as well as the returns, on high-yield portfolios. Alternatively, they might search the high-yield universe for more acceptable risk–return relations. Either way, reductions in return variations due to default should result.

18 | A Yield Premium Model for the High-Yield Debt Market

with Joseph C. Bencivenga

One of the venerable and important questions regarding investing in fixed-income securities markets is whether the level of promised returns is sufficient to compensate investors for the inherent risks of that market. For high-yield bond investors, the primary risk is default on the interest and principal of the companies that constitute their portfolios. One of the other major risks confronting investors in corporate bonds involves interest rate movements.[1] This risk is either lower for high-coupon, high-yield bonds or, at worst, similar to that of default-risk-free US Treasuries when the duration of the risky portfolio is matched. Liquidity risk, the last of the traditional risk categories, has never been rigorously derived or measured for risky bonds, although clearly it is higher for noninvestment-grade bonds than for either high-grade or Treasury bonds.

This article presents a simple approach to determining whether the high-yield debt market is rich or poor at any point in time. We use the break-even-yield (BEY) concept to measure the premium, if any, that investors can expect to receive over the yield that would leave them equally as well off compared with default-risk-free bonds. We assumed first that future default rates will essentially be identical to the historical average during the past 24 years (1971–94). A by-product of this model determines what the market's *implied default rate expectation* is, given the existing yield spread over comparable-duration Treasuries. We analyzed, for the first time, premiums and implied default rates for each of the bond-rating categories in the high-yield market (BB, B, CCC) and also made comparisons with the BBB market. Finally, we explored whether the model has any predictive value with respect to subsequent cumulative returns.

---

[1] See E. Altman and S. Nammacher, *Investing in Junk Bonds* (New York: John Wiley & Sons, 1987).

THE BREAK-EVEN-YIELD CONCEPT

The promised yield on a bond should compensate the investor for the expected and unexpected risk of default, the timing of the default, and the severity of the default. The latter refers to the recovery rate should the issue default and the bond is either sold immediately or held until the company emerges from Chapter 11 reorganization. The percentage loss from default is increased by the opportunity loss because of the defaulting bond's nonpayment of the semiannual coupon. The promised yield to an investor required to break even relative to risk-free, comparable-duration US Treasuries, including assumptions about expected default and recovery rates, is specified as

$$BEY_t = \frac{R_{f,t} + D_f(1 - \text{Rec}) + (D_f \times \text{HYC}/2)}{1 - D_f},$$

where

BEY_t = break-even yield in period t
$R_{f,t}$ = risk-free yield to maturity on benchmark US Treasury bonds in t
D_f = default rate assumption (either *implied*, *expected*, or based on *historical rates*)
Rec = recovery rate assumption upon default
HYC = average coupon rate on defaulted bonds (HY = high yield)

Note that the BEY must compensate the investor for the risk-free rate, the loss from defaults (including lost interest), and the fact that the *performing* bonds' proportion in the market $(1 - D_f)$ is the source of the BEY.

Table 18.1 shows the BEY under various assumptions about expected annual default rates (from 1 percent to 8 percent), the recovery rate after default (30 percent to 50 percent of face value), the coupon rates on defaulting bonds (12 percent), and the yield on US T-bonds (7.6 percent). For example, if the investor expects an annual default rate of 4 percent and a 40 percent average recovery rate, the BEY at that point would be 10.67 percent. The yield used for long-term T-bonds was matched by duration to the high-yield bond market's yield-to-worst rate.

Table 18.1 Break-even conditions for total returns on high-yield bonds versus US Treasury bonds

Expected default rate (%)	Default loss recovery rate (%)			Required yield on high-yield debt (%) recovery rate		
	30%	40%	50%	30%	40%	50%
1	0.76	0.66	0.56	8.44	8.34	8.24
2	1.52	1.32	1.12	9.31	9.10	8.90
4	3.04	2.64	2.24	11.08	10.67	10.25
5	3.80	3.30	2.80	12.00	11.47	10.95
6	4.56	3.96	3.36	12.94	12.30	11.66
8	6.08	5.28	4.48	14.87	14.00	13.13

The assumptions are that the bonds are 12 percent high-yield coupon bonds and the US T-bond rate is 7.6 percent.

If the actual yield on all high-yield bonds were 11.47 percent, then from table 18.1, the *implied* default rate in the market would be 5 percent. The investor who *expects* a 4 percent long-term default rate and a 40 percent recovery rate would be receiving an 80 basis point premium (11.47 percent – 10.67 percent). The premium is specified as PREM = AHY – BEY, where AHY is the actual yield on high-yield bonds and BEY is the break-even yield, given the expected default rate.

HISTORICAL DEFAULT RATE: ALL HIGH-YIELD BONDS

If the historic average annual high-yield default rate is to be used as a benchmark for future rates, there are at least two ways to estimate that rate. The so-called traditional approach compares the par value of defaults in any calendar year with the annual amount outstanding at the start of the year (or the midpoint) in order to calculate that year's annual default rate. Table 18.2 shows these calculations for the 1971–94 period. The population base does not include the amount of bonds that have defaulted in prior years but are still being traded. Over the 24-year sample period, the weighted (by amount outstanding) average default rate has been approximately 4.1 percent a year with a 3.4 percent standard deviation. The median rate, however, was only 1.6 percent a year. This time series includes two years when the rate was in excess of 10 percent (1990 and 1991) and five years when the annual rate was less than 1 percent.

Table 18.3 shows recovery rates, by seniority of bonds, for a sample of 600 defaulted bonds. The overall average (unweighted) recovery rate is $40.93 per $100 par value, or a recovery rate of about 40 percent.

These values – a 4.1 percent average annual default rate and a 40 percent average recovery rate – were used in the initial calculations of the BEY for the overall high market. Later estimates of expected default rates were consistent with current market dynamics.

DEFAULT RATE ASSUMPTIONS BY BOND-RATING CATEGORY

The prior analysis assumes the investor owns the market portfolio of high-yield bonds and does not differentiate by bond-rating category. Although actual default rates for the different rating categories of bonds conceivably could be calculated using the traditional approach, the result would be flawed because of the small sample sizes for certain categories in specific years and because the data have not been carefully assembled over the years for this purpose.

A superior way to estimate default rates by rating category, a method that also captures the aging effect of defaults for bonds from when they were first issued to up to ten years after issuance, is the market-weighted mortality rate approach.[2] This method,

---

[2] For more details, see E. Altman, "Measuring Corporate Bond Mortality and Performance," *The Journal of Finance* 44 (4), (September 1989): 909–22. Similar approaches are found in P. Asquith, D. Mullins, and E. Wolff, "Original Issue High Yield Bonds: Aging Analysis of Defaults, Exchanges and Calls," *The Journal of Finance* 44 (4), (September 1989): 923–52; D. Lucas and S. Douglas, "Corporate Bond Defaults and Default Rates 1970–90," *Moody's Special Report*, January 1991 and subsequent reports published by Moody's in January of each year; and C. Y. Wang, "Corporate Bond Default Study," *Creditweek*, Standard & Poor's, (September 16, 1991): 1–5. S&P's latest report was in *Creditweek*, May 1, 1995. In the latter two studies, the default rates were based on the number of issuers rather than market values. In addition, bonds of all ages were lumped into each rating category.

Table 18.2 Historical default rates

Year	Par value outstanding[a] ($millions)	Par value defaults ($millions)	Default rates (%)
1994	235,000	3,418[b,c]	1.454[b,c]
1993	206,907	2,287	1.105
1992	163,000	5,545	3.402
1991	183,600	18,862	10.273
1990	181,000	18,354	10.140
1989	189,258	8,110	4.285
1988	148,187	3,944	2.662
1987	129,557	7,486[d]	5.778[d]
1986	90,243	3,156	3.497
1985	58,088	992	1.708
1984	40,939	344	0.840
1983	27,492	301	1.095
1982	18,109	577	3.186
1981	17,115	27	0.158
1980	14,935	224	1.500
1979	10,356	20	0.193
1978	8,946	119	1.330
1977	8,157	381	4.671
1976	7,735	30	0.388
1975	7,471	204	2.731
1974	10,894	123	1.129
1973	7,824	49	0.626
1972	6,928	193	2.786
1971	6,602	82	1.242
Arithmetic-average default rate			
1971–94			2.758
			(2.672)
1978–94			3.095
			(2.976)
1985–94			4.431
			(3.177)
Weighted-average default rate[e]			
1971–94			4.108
			(3.424)
1978–94			4.282
			(3.438)
1985–94			4.553
			(3.404)
Median annual default rate			
1971–94			1.604

Data are for straight debt only. Numbers in parentheses are standard deviations.
[a] Excludes defaulted issues.
[b] Includes Grand Union debt of $1,631 million and Trans World Airlines debt of $231 million in 1994 defaults; if both were not included, the default rate would be 0.64 percent.
[c] Amount of defaults in 1994 adjusted for accreted values of two Grand Union issues and the original discounted trading values of the two TWA issues.
[d] $1,841.7 million without Texaco, Inc., Texaco Capital, and Texaco N.V. The default rate is 1.345 percent.
[e] Weighted by par value of amount outstanding for each year.

based on insurance actuarial techniques, measures marginal and cumulative mortality rates by bond rating for ten years after issuance. Table 18.4 shows annual and cumulative mortality rates for all major rating classes based on the default experience from 1971 to 1993. Figure 18.1 shows annualized mortality rates for each rating class from

Table 18.3   Average recovery rates on defaulted debt per $100 face amount, by seniority

Year	Secured		Senior		Senior subordinated		Cash pay		Subordinated Non-cash pay	
1994	$48.66	(5)	$51.14	(8)	$19.81	(5)	$37.04	(3)	$5.00	(1)
1993	55.75	(2)	33.38	(7)	51.50	(10)[a]	28.38	(9)	none	
1992	59.85	(15)[b]	35.61	(8)	58.20	(17)	49.13	(22)	15.00	(2)
1991	54.50	(2)	58.15	(62)[c]	34.62	(21)	20.28	(35)	21.06	(4)
1990	35.04	(7)	32.02	(27)	24.04	(28)	17.93	(17)	18.99	(12)
1989	82.69	(9)	53.70	(16)	19.60	(21)	23.95	(30)	none	
1988	67.96	(13)	41.99	(19)	30.70	(10)	35.27	(20)	none	
1987	12.00	(1)	70.52	(29)[d]	53.50	(10)	40.54	(7)	none	
1986	48.32	(7)	37.09	(8)	37.74	(10)	31.58	(34)	none	
1985	74.25	(2)	34.81	(3)	36.18	(7)	41.45	(15)	none	
Average	$59.26	(63)	$50.81	(187)	$36.48	(139)	$30.55	(192)	$18.73	(19)
Average all issues	$40.93	(600)								

Number of issues in parentheses. Prices are as of the end of the default month.
[a] *Includes two issues of Mesa. Without Mesa, recovery would be $38.13.*
[b] *All 15 issues are El Paso Electric.*
[c] *Includes 23 issues of Columbia Gas. Without these issues, the recovery rate was $43.30.*
[d] *Without Texaco, the 1987 recovery rate was $29.77.*

Table 18.4   Annual and cumulative bond mortality rates by original rating and number of years after issuance, 1971–93 (percentages)

Rating		Years after issuance									
		1	2	3	4	5	6	7	8	9	10
AAA	Yearly	0.00	0.00	0.00	0.00	0.00	0.11	0.04	0.00	0.00	0.00
	Cumulative	0.00	0.00	0.00	0.00	0.00	0.11	0.16	0.16	0.16	0.16
AA	Yearly	0.00	0.00	1.01	0.30	0.10	0.00	0.14	0.00	0.07	0.10
	Cumulative	0.00	0.00	1.01	1.30	1.41	1.41	1.55	1.55	1.62	1.72
A	Yearly	0.00	0.15	0.23	0.28	0.15	0.03	0.10	0.21	0.18	0.00
	Cumulative	0.00	0.15	0.38	0.66	0.80	0.84	0.93	1.14	1.32	1.32
BBB	Yearly	0.06	0.85	0.38	0.65	0.58	0.82	0.79	0.00	0.12	0.63
	Cumulative	0.06	0.92	1.29	1.93	2.50	3.30	4.06	4.06	4.18	4.78
BB	Yearly	0.00	0.75	4.35	2.03	2.64	1.07	3.15	0.00	0.00	2.81
	Cumulative	0.00	0.75	5.07	7.00	9.45	10.42	13.24	13.24	13.24	15.68
B	Yearly	1.51	4.57	10.02	5.30	6.45	5.98	3.29	2.87	2.75	1.56
	Cumulative	1.51	6.02	15.44	19.92	25.08	29.56	31.88	33.83	35.65	36.65
CCC	Yearly	1.51	14.84	14.77	8.90	3.30	3.77	0.71	NA	NA	NA
	Cumulative	1.51	16.12	28.51	34.88	37.02	39.40	39.83	NA	NA	NA

NA = not available.

Figure 18.1 Annualized cumulative default rates

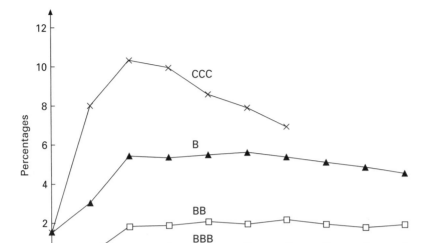

BBB to CCC. Note that although all rating categories show a positive mortality rate aging effect for the first three or four years, the marginal rates tend to level off after that point.

With the exception of CCC-rated bonds, the tenth year's annualized cumulative mortality rate is used as the historic benchmark. These rates are as follows:

BBB = 49 basis points
BB = 169 basis points
B = 446 basis points
CCC = 750 basis points[3]

When we calculated mortality rates for 1994, the effect on results from 1971 to 1993 was minimal.[4] Indeed, all rates were slightly lower; for example, the annualized mortality rate for B-rated bonds was 435 basis points and for BB was 164.

Analysts are not restricted to selecting the historic average annual mortality rate as the expected rate for the future. Indeed, we will argue at a later point that a somewhat lower rate is certainly a reasonable alternative assumption for 1995 and beyond.

Recovery rates by bond rating do not seem to vary much in any systematic way for bonds originally rated BBB and below. Hence, we used the venerable 40 percent recovery rate in all of our calculations. Analysts can change assumptions, however, according to their own expectations and according to the seniority makeup of their portfolios. For example, for a portfolio composed of all senior unsecured bonds, one might expect

---

[3] This rate is an approximation because we do not have a sufficient ten-year history of CCC new issuance.
[4] See E. Altman and V. Kishore, "Defaults and Returns on High Yield Bonds: Analysis Through 1994," *NYU Salomon Center Report*, January 1995.

recovery rates of about 50 percent (table 18.3) should the issues default. Indeed, in today's high-yield market, senior bonds are more prominent than they were in the past.

BREAK-EVEN-YIELD AND PREMIUM CALCULATIONS (1988–94)

Our data set for calculating break-even yields and premiums starts on 31 December 1988, and ends on 31 January 1995 (six years of monthly data). For the average coupon payment lost upon default, we used the actual average coupon loss for each year, as shown in table 18.5. For several other variables in the BEY calculation, we used the actual yields at the point in time of the calculation, that is, the yields-to-worst on bonds for the entire market and on bonds in each rating class, and the comparable-duration risk-free rate. We used one assumption throughout the entire sample period, however, for the annualized mortality rate and the recovery rate.

Table 18.6 shows selected monthly BEY and market premiums for all high-yield bonds. In addition to the historic average default rate, 4.1 percent, we varied the assumption about the annualized default rate to include 2 percent and 3 percent rates.

In all cases, the annual market yield premiums are positive, indicating that investors are being "promised," or are requiring, a rate of return greater than what is necessary to break even with Treasury bond investments, assuming that future annual default rates will be equal to the historic average over time. As shown in table 18.6, the premium for all high-yield bonds (using the 4.1 percent default rate) was 121 basis points in December 1988, and it steadily rose to 752 basis points in January 1991.[5] At that time, the market-implied default rate was an astounding 13.08 percent, based on a yield spread over Treasuries of 1,118 basis points! Although the December 1990 and January 1991 implied default rates expectations of the market seem extraordinarily high, recall that the actual default rate in 1990 exceeded 10 percent (table 18.2). So, at that time, investors were implicitly expecting about 3 percent more than the previous year's default rate (13.08 percent versus 10.27 percent). The premium was 7.50–8.00 percent over the BEY, however, using the historic average annual default rate assumption.

From the 8.00 percent high point of December 1990, the premium dropped swiftly to 7.52 percent one month later, and it was considerably lower one year later (2.71

Table 18.5 Average defaulted coupon rates by bond rating, 1988–94 (percentages)

Year	All high-yield	BBB	BB	B	CCC
1988	11.91	10.83	12.74	12.95	15.00
1989	13.40	10.48	11.85	13.32	15.06
1990	12.94	10.77	12.68	13.49	13.69
1991	11.59	10.48	12.44	12.82	14.49
1992	12.32	9.16	10.97	13.53	15.50
1993	12.98	8.42	11.03	12.66	12.75
1994	11.56	8.67	11.75	12.15	12.69

[5] Indeed, the premium was as high as 800 basis points in December 1990.

Table 18.6 Market premium calculations for the high-yield market for various default rate assumptions, selected dates, 1988–95 (percentages, except as noted)

Date	All high-yield	Treasury yield	Spread (bps)	Implied default rate	Breakeven yield at 2%	Market premium	Breakeven yield at 3%	Market premium	Breakeven yield at 4.1%	Market premium
Dec 30, '88	13.56	9.14	442	5.56	10.67	2.89	11.46	2.10	12.35	1.21
Jan 31, '89	13.53	9.00	453	5.65	10.54	2.99	11.34	2.19	12.24	1.29
Jan 31, '90	15.44	8.39	705	8.61	9.92	5.52	10.71	4.73	11.59	3.85
Jan 31, '91	18.33	7.67	1,066	12.67	9.17	9.16	9.94	8.39	10.81	7.52
Jan 31, '92	11.94	6.14	580	7.43	7.62	4.32	8.38	3.56	9.23	2.71
Jan 29, '93	10.10	5.31	479	6.25	6.78	3.32	7.53	2.57	8.38	1.72
Jan 31, '94	8.75	5.14	361	4.84	6.59	2.16	7.33	1.42	8.17	0.58
Jan 31, '95	11.39	7.58	381	4.94	9.08	2.31	9.85	1.54	10.72	0.67

percent). The downward trend in market premiums continued, hitting its low point of 0.26 percent in February 1994. The premium was 0.67 percent as of 31 January 1995.

The premium varies not only because of changes in the high-yield market's yield but also because of changes in the risk-free rate. For example, in February 1994, when the premium reached its lowest level in our six-year period, the drop from the previous month's level (0.58 percent) was primarily attributable to the sizeable increase in the risk-free Treasury rate in that month (from 5.14 percent to 5.67 percent). Because the Treasury yield increased by more than the high-yield market's yield did (i.e., the spread narrowed), the implied default rate actually fell in February 1994.

RESULTS BY BOND RATING

Figure 18.2 shows the implied default rates for bonds with different bond ratings, and figure 18.3 graphs the market premiums over time by bond rating. As expected, for the change in implied default rates, the correlation over time between the various rating classes is extremely high. For example, in January 1991, the implied annual default rates (figure 18.2) were 3.62 percent, 7.34 percent, 13.02 percent, and 22.54 percent for the BBB, BB, B, and CCC classes, respectively. Actually, the peak implied default rates for some of the rating classes varied by only a month or two around the January 1991 date.

Figure 18.2 Implied default rates

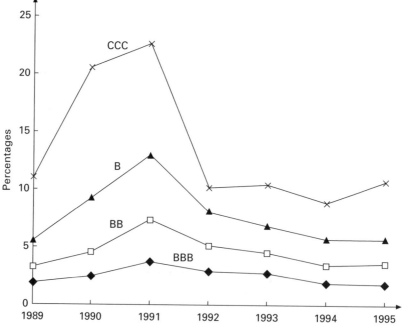

Note: Dates as at 31 Jan for all years except 29 Jan in 1993. This figure shows the implied default rates for the years 1989 through 1995. It does not depict the interim monthly data points.

Figure 18.3 Market premium by rating class (1989–95)

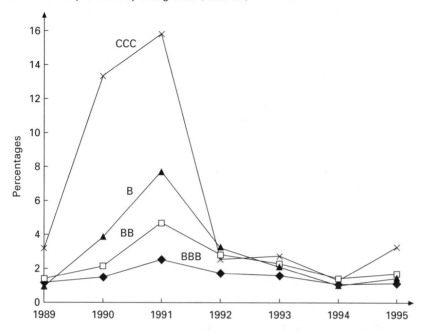

Note: Dates as at 31 Jan for all years except 29 Jan 1993. This figure shows the implied default rates for the years 1989 through 1995. It does not depict the interim monthly data points.

The range of BB market premiums (figure 18.3) was between 107 basis points in February 1994 to a high of 457 basis points in January 1991. The single-B premium was as low as 60 basis points in February 1994 (and also in October 1994) and was almost 800 basis points in January 1991.

CORRELATION ANALYSIS – PREMIUMS AND RETURNS

One of the important implications of the yield premium model is the relationship between the market premium at a point in time and subsequent returns. If the premium is positive, then return spreads, on average, should be positive over subsequent time horizons.

We analyzed the premium–return relationship for 3-, 6-, and 12-month horizons throughout the six-year sample period. We used cumulative compounded total rates of return over these three horizons for the market as a whole and for the individual bond-rating classes. Because the cumulative return for any horizon should not be overlapping, the initial sample size was limited to 24, 12, and 6 observations for the 3-, 6-, and 12-month returns, respectively.

For all of our tests (except for the three-month horizons and those for the CCC-rating class), the premium–return relationship was positive at statistically significant levels. Nevertheless, the explanatory power of the yield premium measure is not overwhelming because many other factors influence short-term returns and also the sample period includes the highly unusual 1990–91 period, when returns were very volatile with record negative (1990) and positive (1991) performances.

The correlation coefficients between the yield premium and subsequent 6- and 12-month cumulative monthly returns are shown in table 18.7. These correlations are all quite high, except for the CCC group, indicating a substantial statistical association.

Table 18.7 Correlation between yield premiums and 6- and 12-month returns, by bond rating

Rating group	12 months	6 months
High-yield market	0.75	0.61
BB	0.71	0.69
B	0.77	0.65
CCC	0.36	0.19
BBB	0.60	0.36

THE REGRESSION SPECIFICATION

Our conceptual yield premium model specifies a break-even condition relative to risk-free bonds when the yield spread on a class of *performing* bonds is just sufficient to compensate the investor for expected default losses. Therefore, one might expect that a zero current yield premium is consistent with expected returns equal to the risk-free rate, i.e., a zero return spread. Using this theory, the model can be specified as

$$Y_{i,T} = R_f + b_i(\mathrm{YP}_{i,t}) + e_i$$

or

$$Y_{i,T} - R_f = b_i(\mathrm{YP}_{i,t}) + e_i,$$

where

$Y_{i,T}$ = actual compound return of bond-rating class i in period $(t + 1)$ to $(t + 6)$ [or $(t + 1)$ to $(t + 12)$]
R_f = risk-free rate as of t on comparable-duration Treasuries
$\mathrm{YP}_{i,t}$ = yield premium as of t
b_i = slope
e_i = error term

Assuming no change in interest rates during the relevant horizon period, the return on the equivalent-duration risk-free bond portfolio should equal the Treasury bond's promised yield. Return above this rate is specified as a function of the calculated yield premium on the class of risky bonds.

Because in specifying the regression, we forced the intercept to equal zero, the return spread is a simple function of the prior yield premium. Not only does the zero intercept conform with our theory but also, when we did not constrain the intercept to be zero, the intercept coefficient was found to be insignificantly different from zero.

We regressed the yield premium (explanatory variable) on the return spread (actual return minus the risk-free rate) for both the 12-month and 6-month return data for all rating classes and the overall high-yield market. Table 18.8 lists the regression results for the high-yield market as a whole and for the triple-B, double-B, single-B and triple-C rating classes. For the high-yield market, we assumed that expected default rates were equal to the historic average rate, 4.1 percent. In addition, we regressed the model on the high-yield market assuming an annual default rate of 2 percent. We simulated expected returns using this lower default rate assumption because the high-yield market in 1995 appears to be of better quality and lower risk than at almost any time in the recent past; it is certainly less risky than the market of the mid- and late 1980s, when the highly leveraged and extremely high-priced corporate restructurings (e.g., LBOs) took place.[6] These risky financings resulted in the so-called bad cohort issuances, which

Table 18.8 Yield premium versus subsequent return (regression analysis results, 1988–94)

		Investment horizon	
Rating class	Coefficient	12 months	6 months
All high-yield debt 4.1% default rate	Regression coefficient	2.795	1.442
	t-test	1.920	2.670
	Significance level	0.100*	0.020**
	R^2	0.420	0.390
All high-yield debt 2.0% default rate	Regression coefficient	1.805	0.973
	t-test	1.850	2.030
	Significance level	0.120	0.060
	R^2	0.330	0.270
BB bonds	Regression coefficient	2.336	1.248
	t-test	2.550	2.970
	Significance level	0.050	0.010
	R^2	0.560	0.450
B bonds	Regression coefficient	3.048	1.557
	t-test	2.090	2.240
	Significance level	0.090	0.040
	R^2	0.470	0.310
CCC bonds	Regression coefficient	0.829	0.219
	t-test	0.520	0.300
	Significance level	0.620	0.760
	R^2	0.050	0.010

This table lists the size of the coefficient relating the level of the yield premium with the subsequent compounded return. The relevant t-test and level of significance indicates the level of confidence inherent in the correlation. The R^2 measures the proportion of the change in return explained by the change in yield premium. The adjusted R^2, although somewhat lower, is not reported because the regression has only one explanatory variable.
* Significant at the 0.90 confidence interval or better.
** Significant at the 0.95 confidence interval or better.

[6] A few attempts have been made to forecast default rates. Several are reviewed in J. Jonsson and M. Fridson, "Forecasting Default Rates on High Yield Bonds," *EXTRA C.R.E.D.I.T.*, Merrill Lynch Global Securities Research and Economic Group (March/April 1995): 11–28.

eventually manifested into the record default years of 1990 and 1991. Indeed, except for these two years, in only three years of the past 25 did the annual default rate exceed the historic average of 4.1 percent. In one of those years (1987), the default rate would have been considerably lower if not for the Texaco bankruptcy, and, in the other two years (1977 and 1989), the rates were both below 5.0 percent.

Our return forecasts assume that interest rates do not change in the forecast period. Relatively large fluctuations of rates will affect all returns, however, affecting both the actual returns and the spreads. For the high-yield market, assuming the historic default rate of 4.1 percent and a 40 percent recovery rate, the 12-month return results are

$$\text{Return spread} = 2.795(\text{YP})$$

and

$$\text{Return} = \text{Risk-free rate} + 2.795(\text{YP})$$

For the 2 percent default rate assumption (perhaps a more reasonable estimate in 1995), the return result is

$$\text{Return} = R_f + 1.805(\text{YP})$$

So, as of 1 February 1995, when the risk-free rate was 7.58 percent, the yield premiums of 0.67 percent and 2.31 percent for the 4.1 percent and 2.0 percent default rate assumptions result in a one-year expected return of 9.45 percent and 11.75 percent, respectively. Thus, the lower default rate assumption results in a higher estimate of future returns.

The explanatory power (R^2) of the regressions shown in table 18.8 is quite high, except for the CCC-rating class. The six-month slope parameters, linking the yield premium with subsequent returns, are for the most part significant at the 0.05 or 0.01 level. Although the 12-month regression parameter is slightly less significant than that for the 6-month horizon, the overall market's yield premium explained 39 percent and 42 percent of the change in the actual subsequent 12-month return (compared with 39 percent for the 6-month horizon). Similar results can be observed for the individual rating classes, with particularly impressive explanatory power for the BB and B classes. Recall, however, that we only have, at this point, 12 6-month return observations and 6 12-month returns. As we continue to monitor these models, the number of observations will increase, giving us even more confidence in the results.

Conclusion

The simple yield premium model based on a break-even high-yield debt market concept presents evidence that a combination of default rate and recovery analysis and current market yields can be used to assess the richness of the corporate bond market and even to forecast returns for various segments of the market. As more data become available, these relationships can be observed and measured even more precisely.

19 | Should We Regulate Junk Bonds?

The recent indictments against Drexel Burnham Lambert and several of its employees and the huge RJR Nabisco takeover have rekindled interest in banning or restricting high-yielding "junk bonds." These low-grade, fixed income securities have grown dramatically and now represent almost one-quarter of the total corporate, publicly traded bond market, with over $180 billion outstanding. Rather than cripple or kill junk bonds, which have valuable uses in America, we should provide adequate safeguards for them and other risky assets. And we should encourage equity financing, rather than discourage debt.

Financial institution regulators are wrestling with the so-called "moral-hazard" issue, whereby the government provides deposit insurance for institutions, such as S&Ls, whose health and safety could be in jeopardy if they purchase junk bond assets in lieu of traditional investments. Legislators and the Federal Reserve Board are rethinking the evils of junk-bond-financed takeovers, even going to the extreme of contemplating the elimination of the tax-deductibility of interest expense on high-coupon, low-rated bonds, in effect viewing them as equivalent to preferred stock, rather than debt.

Should we be concerned about the issuance of increasing proportions of debt – and, in particular, by its use in financing major restructurings? Should federally insured institutions be restricted from investing in high-yield bonds? For that matter, how emotionally charged is the term "junk bonds" itself? Can it be said of them, as Juliet said of Romeo, "tis but thy name that is my enemy"?

In my opinion, junk bonds play an important role in our financial system. They have been around in various forms for well over 60 years, financing major capital expenditures of emerging and established firms. Were it not for their use in the controversial, but legitimate, restructuring of corporate America, they would be much less controversial today.

Removing the tax-deductibility of the interest payments on such bonds would be a monumental blunder. It would weaken our nation's ability to compete with foreign firms, which not only use far more leverage than US firms, but also benefit from tax subsidies on common and preferred stock dividends. If Congress wants to be constructive, then it should consider the fact that the current system of taxing stock dividends at both the corporate and the personal level is punitive and serves to reduce the incentive for firms to issue new equity securities.

It would make more sense to give investors a tax break on common dividends than to eliminate tax-deductibility of interest payments. Instead of taxing 100 percent of cash dividends, for example, stockholders could receive a tax reduction of, say, 50 percent of the cash dividends received. Of course, the huge government deficit hinders such constructive tax changes to the extent that they reduce tax revenues. Congress would need some courage to promulgate such a change at this juncture, but the benefits would become evident in a very short time.

INSURANCE COMPANY AND THRIFT HOLDINGS

Insurance companies are a major investor in high-yield bonds, with holdings of publicly traded debt in excess of $40 billion. Still, life insurance companies in some states are allowed to invest only a set proportion of their assets in high-yield bonds, while other risky or riskier assets are not regulated.

Thrifts, while holding less than 10 percent of total high-yield bonds outstanding, are perhaps even more susceptible than insurance companies to restrictive regulation, because of the taxpayers' liability implied by deposit insurance. Federally chartered thrifts can invest up to an arbitrarily determined 11 percent of assets in low-quality bonds. Such restrictions are misplaced, especially in view of the current state of the thrift industry.

Thrifts have squandered billions of dollars on unsuccessful real estate ventures and loans, poor asset-liability management, and an outdated and undercapitalized insurance system. As a result, over 1,000 S&Ls have disappeared in the last few years. The public and legislators should worry more about traditional banking practices and less about the growing number of S&Ls that are trimming back on real estate assets and venturing into newer areas like high-yield junk bonds. Rather than condemning such investments, we should applaud efforts by S&L investment committees to raise overall profitability by prudent, diversified, high-yield investing.

According to the Federal Home Loan Bank Board, about 150 S&Ls are now investing in high-yield bonds, and I expect this number to increase. I am not aware of any thrift institution that has failed because of losses from investments in marketable financial instruments. Higher-yielding assets make an institution more competitive, and through their returns, add to its capital base – a resource most financial institutions will need as they approach new capital standards in 1992.

Based on the historical return-risk performance of high-yield bond portfolios, it is difficult to support restriction arguments. High-yield junk bonds have outdistanced returns on risk-free and investment-grade fixed income securities over the last decade, with average annual returns to investors of about 12 percent. And this continues to be the case, despite periodic predictions of the market's downfall. A recent GAO-sponsored research study performed by Wharton Econometric Forecasting Associates concluded that, on a risk-adjusted basis, high-yield bonds ranked as one of the most profitable investments for thrifts, coming in second to credit card activities.

Of course, the future may not continue to approximate past performance, but that is the nature of any risky market. The appropriate way to handle uncertainty is to set aside adequate reserves and mandate other prudent policies, not to regulate arbitrarily.

ALTERNATIVES TO RESTRICTIONS

While there is no robust evidence of excessive risk in these investments, high-yield bonds nevertheless have a considerably higher historical default rate than investment-grade corporate debt securities. Rather than imposing restrictions on junk bond holdings, one possible solution would be to treat these and other security investments in the same way that traditional loans are handled. Traditional loans for real estate development, mortgages, commerce and industrial purposes sometimes do lead to default and loss of principal and interest to lenders. Capital reserves are thus set aside to cover expected loan losses. The problem of late has been inadequate reserves in these traditional areas and lack of effective diversification.

A policy of setting aside additional reserves would, of course, discourage investments in junk bonds by institutions that have a shaky capital base. But that is precisely the kind of institution that is now of such concern to public regulators. And setting clear guidelines for reserves and diversification would reduce industry uncertainty about arbitrary legislation and regulation and thus probably encourage some thrifts and insurance companies to invest in these high-risk, higher-return assets.

CAPITAL-RESERVES DETERMINATION

How much should thrift institutions set aside against possible losses? As one measure, the average yearly default rate on high-yield bonds between 1978 and 1988 was 1.90 percent. But *losses* to investors were considerably less – about 1.3 percent per year (about 1.6 percent per year in the last four years). This is because defaulted bonds have historically sold at an average rate of about 40 percent of par value after default – an important liquidity component of publicly traded bonds compared to other types of debt. (The recovery rate has been 50 percent in the 1985–88 period.)

Another guideline for determining reserves is to use an amount based on the "mortality" of corporate bonds over time, categorized by the original issuer's bond rating. I have estimated these mortalities and losses from default over the 1971–87 period; many financial institutions, particularly insurance companies, are very comfortable with the results. Reserves based on this concept result in average provisions similar to aggregate high-yield-debt default losses measured the traditional way, but they can be estimated more precisely according to the credit quality of each portfolio. (This analysis is available from the author.)

Many critics of historical-default-rate approaches point to the expectation that defaults will rise significantly during the next recession, especially with the recent amount of leveraged transactions. One cannot reject this thesis, but a calm, dispassionate analysis would reveal that even if the default rate reaches 10 percent in one or more recession years, the loss to investors is within acceptable limits – probably 6–7 percent per year. As promised yield spreads on high-yield bonds over Treasuries are close to 4.5 percent today, loss rates of 6.5 percent would result in net (loss) return spreads relative to default-risk-free Treasuries of a relatively small 2 percent. Of course, recession-level defaults might panic investors into selling the better high-yield bonds at just the wrong time, i.e., when prices are low relative to intrinsic values. This should be avoided.

If regulators treat risky investments like risky loans, then a 1.75–2.00 percent loss reserve per year would be appropriate for a diversified portfolio of high-yield bonds. These reserves are flexible and can be changed to reflect new conditions. Adequate diversification should also be stressed, because diversification can ensure average return and risk performance and help to reduce the possibility of unacceptable losses from defaulting securities. Faced with the requirement of loss reserves, investment managers, acting in concert with other thrift officers and with boards of directors, would be forced to consider whether the return from high-yield bonds justified the set-aside amount.

20 | The High Yield Bond Market: A Decade of Assessment, Comparing 1990 with 2000

There are some signs of similarity between the record default *rates* and yield spreads of 1990 and the record default *amounts* and increasing yield spreads of 2000.

Despite these recent stormy conditions and relatively poor returns for high yield bonds, there are several *significant differences* between 1990 and 2000 that lead us to conclude that default rates will peak in the coming quarters and not come close to 1990/1991 levels. And, subsequent returns and spreads, starting just prior to or after the peak, could be very attractive.

These differences include a much lower, although still high, distressed proportion of the high yield market; a very minor proportion of defaults recently that are the result of poorly conceived highly leveraged transactions (HLT) compared to the almost 50 percent contribution to defaults from HLTs in 1990–1992; and a much stronger economic scenario in 2000 than in 1990.

We expect default rates to peak at 5.5–6.0 percent in 2000 or 2001. (Note: Due to increased problems in the telecom industry and significant deterioration in the overall economic environment, the 2001 forecast is 8.5 percent.)

Ten years ago I wrote an article that reviewed the turbulent history of the high yield bond market, from its start in the mid-1970s through the collapse of the leveraged restructuring movement at the end of the 1980s (Altman, 1990). In the summer of 1990, when writing the piece, the high yield bond market was at a critical point in its development. In 1989, the amount of defaulting issues had reached a new high of $8 billion, representing 4.3 percent of the then $190 billion market. That default rate was almost twice the historical average of 2.2 percent from 1978–1988. And another $4.8 billion had already defaulted in the first six months of 1990. With defaults high and still rising, the yield spreads over Treasuries of high yield bonds had skyrocketed to more than 700 basis points and the new issue market had all but dried up. Drexel Burnham Lambert, by far the leading market maker and underwriter of these bonds, had recently filed for Chapter 11 bankruptcy and its guru, Michael Milken, had been indicted.

At that time, many market observers were pronouncing the junk bond market "finished." The conventional wisdom on the Street – and this was Wall Street, mind you, not just Main Street – was that high yield bonds had run their course and neither new investors nor issuers would "play in the junkyard" again. Part of the market's depressed condition, and the forecast of its demise, can be attributed to the US government's enactment in August of 1989 of FIRREA, which mandated that S&Ls no longer invest in low-grade bonds and sell their holdings by the end of 1993. The popular stigma attaching to "junk" bonds at that time was reinforced by a widely circulated academic study (by Harvard professors) that challenged the methods and findings of prior studies. The contention of that study, which became the focus of a *Wall Street Journal* article, was that past research had systematically underestimated the true default risk of high yield bonds.[1]

As a financial economist who had devoted considerable time to the study of high yield bonds, I was convinced that the market's problems were temporary.

> The system needs to be "cleansed" of the excesses of the past few years, especially with respect to highly leveraged restructuring and failed innovations such as deferred interest securities (DIBs and PIKs) and reset provisions. The next wave of junk bond issues – and there will almost certainly be one (although whether the issuers will be publicly or privately placed is not at all clear) – will reflect more conservative capital structures and financing strategies. Prices of leveraged transactions will come down and the proportion of equity underlying such levels will rise. (Altman, 1990, p. 95)

This paper shows that almost all of those predictions have become reality (though deferred-interest-bonds continue to be used in some instances). The default rates noted by Asquith and Mullins were not precursors of a permanent increase, as the authors suggested (in fact, default rates averaged less than 2 percent from 1992 to 1998). Perhaps most important, research shows that during the 1990s – and, indeed, over the entire 24-year life of the modern high yield market – investors have essentially gotten what they bargained for. They have earned a rate of return that, at roughly 300 basis

---

[1]   The Asquith et al. study ("Original Issue High Yield Bonds: Aging Analysis of Defaults, Exchanges and Calls," *The Journal of Finance*, September 1989) championed a type of aging methodology that Altman, in fact, had advocated earlier through a similar type of "mortality" analysis. (See E. Altman, "Measuring Corporate Bond Mortality and Performance," *Journal of Finance*, September 1988 and WP NYU Salomon Center, 1988). Mortality rates are updated annually (Altman and Waldman, 2000) and have become one of the standard measures in the market. The former (Asquith–Mullins approach) is no longer maintained. Both the aging and mortality analysis give similar results – results that, in fact, are not very different from more traditional measures in calculating annualized default rates. Indeed, an article by R. Forsythe in *Barron's* "Junk Defaults: Nothing New," (17 April 1989) that appeared just after the initial *WSJ* article (M. Winkler, "Junk Bonds are Taking Their Lumps," *The Wall Street Journal*, 15 April 1989, Section C, 1) was the most accurate of all the journalistic pieces and correctly reported that the mortality and aging approaches give very similar results.

points over the return on 10-year Treasuries, is commensurate with high yield bonds' intermediate level of risk (higher than that of investment grade bonds, but lower than that of common stocks).

Despite the facts, it must be acknowledged that many of the same phenomena observed in 1989–90 have again surfaced in 1999–2000. Default rates jumped to 4.15 percent in 1999 and the dollar amount of defaults reached a new high of $23.5 billion. And another $15.2 billion have already defaulted in the first six months of 2000, indicating a second consecutive record year of defaults – the same phenomena that first occurred in 1990. With defaults relatively high and showing no sign of declining, investors' required yield spread over Treasuries has risen to close to 7.0 percent as of 30 June 2000 (6.7 percent to be exact). The benign credit cycle of 1993–98, when the default rate was below 2.0 percent each year, has clearly given way to a more turbulent and stormy environment.

Thus, people who remember (or have studied) the state of the high yield market in 1990 may now be experiencing an uneasy sense of *déjà vu* after almost a decade of recovery and growth. But will the next 18 months turn out to be as difficult and tumultuous as in 1990–91? Will default rates again reach approximately 10 percent as in both 1990 and 1991? And, will the market almost cease to function? Or, will returns rebound to almost unbelievable returns of over 40 percent, as they did in 1991? What are the similarities and differences in this market, which has matured but is surely never dull?

Despite their similarities, it is my opinion that there are also sufficient differences between 1990 and 2000 to make this current market downturn, with heightened default worries, less severe and dramatic in terms of the magnitude of defaults and losses as well as the subsequent rebound in returns. I believe the deteriorating credit quality of recent years' new issuance will be flushed from the system in a short time, perhaps in 2–4 quarters,[2] with a default rate peak of 5.5–6.0 percent.

WHAT CAME NEXT

The story of the high yield bond market in the 1990s was one of a steep decline followed by an even more remarkable recovery. As shown in table 20.1, defaults escalated in 1990 and default rates in both 1990 and 1991 exceeded 10.0 percent of the market (much larger than the previous high of 5.8 percent in 1987). The total amount of debt defaulting in each of these two years was over $18 billion. Table 20.2 shows that yield spreads at the end of 1990 reached double-digit levels – which was also unprecedented. The pundits who predicted the demise of the market were looking like sages when total returns to high yield investors turned out to be −8.5 percent in 1990 (only the second year since 1978 that total returns were negative). And since Treasuries earned a positive 6.9 percent return that year, the return spread of high yield bonds was a shocking −15.4 percent. What's more, the poor performance of 1990 wiped out virtually all of the gains achieved by investors over the prior decade. At the end of 1990, the average historical annual return (starting from 1978, when the data were first compiled) to high yield investors had fallen from 11.65 percent, one year earlier, to

---

[2] Others are less sanguine and at least one of the major rating agencies (July Default Report, [Moody's] August 7, 2000) is predicting an 8.4 percent default rate by mid-2001 and another (S&P) is increasingly agitated with the current state of defaults. Our own forecast for 2001 increased to 8.5 percent.

Table 20.1 Historical default rates – straight bonds only excluding defaulted issues from par value outstanding 1971–2000 Q2 ($ millions)

Year	Par value outstanding ($)[a]	Par value defaults ($)	Default rates (%)
2Q 00	584,000	15,244	2.610
1999	567,400	23,532	4.147
1998	465,500	7,464	1.603
1997	335,400	4,200	1.252
1996	271,000	3,336	1.231
1995	240,000	4,551	1.896
1994	235,000	3,418	1.454
1993	206,907	2,287	1.105
1992	163,000	5,545	3.402
1991	183,600	18,862	10.273
1990	181,000	18,354	10.140
1989	189,258	8,110	4.285
1988	148,187	3,944	2.662
1987	129,557	7,486	5.778
1986	90,243	3,156	3.497
1985	58,088	992	1.708
1984	40,939	344	0.840
1983	27,492	301	1.095
1982	18,109	577	3.186
1981	17,115	27	0.158
1980	14,935	224	1.500
1979	10,356	20	0.193
1978	8,946	119	1.330
1977	8,157	381	4.671
1976	7,735	30	0.388
1975	7,471	204	2.731
1974	10,894	123	1.129
1973	7,824	49	0.626
1972	6,928	193	2.786
1971	6,602	82	1.242

			Standard deviation (%)
Arithmetic average default rate			
1971–1999		2.631	2.487
1978–1999		2.852	2.705
1985–1999		3.629	2.900
Weighted average default rate[b]			
1971–1999		3.224	2.902
1978–1999		3.244	2.681
1985–1999		3.327	2.696
Median annual default rate			
1971–1999		1.603	

[a] As of mid-year.
[b] Weighted by par value of amount outstanding for each year.
Source: Authors' Compilation and Salomon Smith Barney Estimates

Table 20.2 Annual returns, yields and spreads on 10-year Treasury (TREAS) and high yield (HY) bonds* (1978–2000 Q2)

| Year | Return (%) | | | Promised Yield (%) | | |
	HY	TREAS	Spread	HY	TREAS	Spread
2Q 00	(1.42)	5.32	(6.74)	12.73	6.03	6.70
1999	1.73	(8.41)	10.14	11.41	6.44	4.97
1998	4.04	12.77	(8.73)	10.04	4.65	5.39
1997	14.27	11.16	3.11	9.20	5.75	3.45
1996	11.24	0.04	11.20	9.58	6.42	3.16
1995	22.40	23.58	(1.18)	9.76	5.58	4.18
1994	(2.55)	(8.29)	5.74	11.50	7.83	3.67
1993	18.33	12.08	6.25	9.08	5.80	3.28
1992	18.29	6.50	11.79	10.44	6.69	3.75
1991	43.23	17.18	26.05	12.56	6.70	5.86
1990	(8.46)	6.88	(15.34)	18.57	8.07	10.50
1989	1.98	16.72	(14.74)	15.17	7.93	7.24
1988	15.25	6.34	8.91	13.70	9.15	4.55
1987	4.57	(2.67)	7.24	13.89	8.83	5.06
1986	16.50	24.08	(7.58)	12.67	7.21	5.46
1985	26.08	31.54	(5.46)	13.50	8.99	4.51
1984	8.50	14.82	(6.32)	14.97	11.87	3.10
1983	21.80	2.23	19.57	15.74	10.70	5.04
1982	32.45	42.08	(9.63)	17.84	13.86	3.98
1981	7.56	0.48	7.08	15.97	12.08	3.89
1980	(1.00)	(2.96)	1.96	13.46	10.23	3.23
1979	3.69	(0.86)	4.55	12.07	9.13	2.94
1978	7.57	(1.11)	8.68	10.92	8.11	2.81
Arithmetic annual average						
1978–1999	12.16	9.28	2.88	12.82	8.27	4.55
Compound annual average:						
1978–1999	11.54	8.58	2.96			

* End of year yields, except for 2000 (June 30).
Source: Salomon Smith Barney Inc.'s High Yield Composite and Treasury Indices.

9.96 percent per year and the return spread from 1.64 percent per year at the end of 1989 to a mere 0.19 percent per year – clearly inadequate compensation for the added risk of high yield bonds.

Then came the turning point in 1991. Despite a second consecutive year of a default rate over 10 percent, high yield investors earned a total return of 43.2 percent, the highest ever recorded in the history of the market (table 20.2). Investors realized that the worst was over and that the excesses of the 1980s had been purged. What remained were, for the most part, viable companies whose bonds, despite their low prices at the start of 1991, were not going to default. And, as the operating performance of these companies continued to improve, the prices of their bonds made a spectacular recovery. The relationship between default rates and total returns is shown in figure 20.1. There is a striking parallel between the increasing default rates in 1989–90 and 1999–2000; note the dip in returns in 1990 and 2000 and finally the resurgence in 1991. A similar dramatic increase occurred in 1995. Will there be a comparable resurgence in 2001?

Figure 20.1   High yield bond market default rates vs. returns

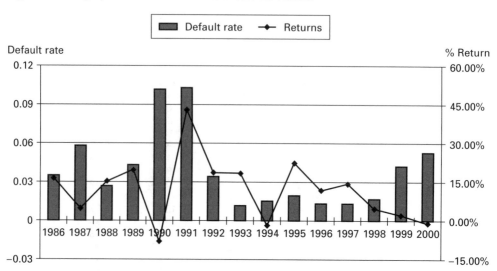

Source: E. Altman, NYU Salomon Center, Stern School of Business, and Salomon Smith Barney, Inc., first published in the *Wall Street Journal*, 10 July 2000.

Because of the high rates of default and almost complete cessation of the new issue market, the size of the high yield market had shrunk from its previous high of $189 billion in 1989 to $163 billion in the middle of 1992. Less than $1.4 billion of new issues were floated in 1990, down from an annual average of over $30 billion during the three-year period from 1987 to 1989. And, in spite of the high returns in 1991, the new issue market took longer to recover, with just under $10 billion issued in 1991. The growth in new issues since 1991, however, has been nothing short of spectacular, with over $100 billion of new issues in each of the last three years of the decade.[3] Moreover, from 1997 through 1999, new issuance of high yield bonds accounted for a substantial part of the total issuance of corporate bonds, representing over half of the bonds issued by indus-trial companies (that is, excluding financial firms and public utilities). At the end of the decade, about $600 billion of high yield bonds were outstanding, as compared to under $200 billion at the start of the decade – and this $600 billion today represents roughly a third of the entire corporate bond market in the US.

During the 1990s, the annual return spreads over Treasuries of high yield bonds returned from their near zero lowpoint at the end of 1990 to almost 3 percent per year by the end of the decade. As reported in table 20.2, total compound annual returns on high yield bonds for the 22-year period from 1978 through 1999 averaged 2.96 percent per year over the returns of 10-year US Treasuries. This means that a $1,000 invest-ment in high yield bonds in 1978 would have been worth over $11,000 at the end of 1999, as compared to just over $6,000 for 10-year treasuries. And if one subtracts the

[3] The vast majority of these new issues were brought to market using the "private" 144a mechanism (primarily because the private process is less cumbersome and time-consuming, although well over 90 percent of these do register with the SEC and become "public" within 90 days of issuance).

average annual losses from defaults,[4] of about 2 percent per year over the period 1978–99, from the average promised yield spread (4.55 percent) over that same period, the result (2.55 percent) is quite close to the realized return spread. Thus, one can attempt to predict future relative returns in the high yield market by comparing current yield spreads to actual losses from the primary risk component – defaults. A simple breakeven model uses this concept to estimate breakeven yields and yield premiums over Treasuries for high yield investors in the following years; see Altman and Bencivenga, ch. 18, this volume.

Besides its phenomenal growth in the US during the 1990s, the high yield bond market gathered its wings and went global, expanding into emerging markets such as Mexico and Brazil in 1992 and then into Western Europe in 1996. In 1999, $17.5 billion of high yield, non-investment grade bonds were issued in Europe – about the amount issued in the US in 1984. While there have as yet been no defaults by European issuers, they will begin to appear – defaults, after all, are a natural occurrence in this higher risk market. Emerging market high yield bonds now total about $100 billion, with the vast majority coming from Latin America. Defaults by emerging markets issuers began to show up with increased frequency in Latin America starting in 1996 and in Asia in the following year.

DETERIORATING CREDIT QUALITY IN RECENT YEARS

As stated earlier, the default rate in 1999 registered a sizeable increase from 1998, topping 4 percent for the first time since 1991 and well above the 1.6 percent rate of one year earlier. One of several apparent reasons for the increase in defaults in 1999 was the seeming deterioration in credit quality of new issuance in recent years. This is demonstrated by the significant increase in the percentage of bonds that defaulted in the first and second year after issuance. Indeed, over one quarter of a sample of 125 issues that defaulted in 1999 had been outstanding less than 12 months before they defaulted – and 55 percent had been outstanding less than 24 months (table 20.3). These percentages compare with just 4 percent and 20 percent from the period 1991–98, and 7.7 percent and 24.3 percent for 1971–99 (Grossman and Verde, 1999). Thus, there was a sizeable increase in the one- and two-year defaults in the 1999 group of defaults. For a sample of 91 defaults in the first six months of 2000, that proportion has dropped to 42 percent, but as much as 72 percent defaulted within 36 months. The latter figure is actually higher than in 1999 (67 percent).

To better understand these mortality statistics, however, it is important to analyze the purpose of the financing. Whether companies are using junk bonds to fund LBOs, growth opportunities, or just to refinance debt can tell us a good deal about whether these one- or two-year mortality results are truly symptomatic of a decline in credit quality or can be explained by other factors. We will return to the uses of new issue high yield financing at a later point.

To analyze this recent change in bond default morality, we gathered data on original issuance by S&P bond rating over the last decade (1990–99). As stated earlier, there was a sharp increase in high yield bond new issuance starting in 1997, with new issues

---

[4] The average annual loss rate adjusts the annual default rate for recoveries (price of the security just after default) plus the loss of a semi-annual coupon payment.

Table 20.3 Percentage defaults by year from issuance 1999 and 2000 1st half

	1999		*2000 1st half*	
Time	*# of issues*	*Percentage*	*# of issues*	*Percentage*
1st year	32	25.60	11	12.09
2nd year	37	29.60	27	29.67
3rd year	15	12.00	28	30.77
4th year	14	11.20	5	5.49
5th year	7	5.60	6	6.59
6th year	8	6.40	2	2.20
7th year	10	8.00	8	8.79
8th year	2	1.60	2	2.20
9th year	0	0.00	1	1.10
10th (+) year	0	0.00	1	1.10
Total	125	100.00	91	100.00

Sources: Authors' compilation, from Salomon Smith Barney reports by Peters and Altman (January and July, 2000).

exceeding $100 billion in each of the three years 1997–99. High yield new issuance as a percentage of all corporate bond issuance increased dramatically over the same three-year period. Within the high yield sector, the percentage of new issues rated B and CCC also increased.

The high yield bond industry's enthusiastic reception of new issues in the recent past and the apparent deterioration in credit quality needs to be monitored closely. At the start of 2000, I felt (and said in print) that investors would likely require additional promised yields to compensate them for the uncertainty about possible higher default rates in the next few years (much as banks set aside higher reserves for expected losses and capital allocations for unexpected losses). And the large spike in yield spreads during the first two quarters of 2000 seems to bear out these predictions.

OTHER REASONS FOR THE INCREASE IN DEFAULTS

In addition to the deterioration in credit quality and the earlier occurrence of defaults, at least four other factors contributed to the sizeable increase in 1999:

1 The recent increase in new issuance
2 The Russian default in 1998
3 A number of "sick" industries despite the economy's overall strength
4 Banks' reluctance to refinance or give additional waivers to the marginal firm

Because of the huge new issuance years during 1997–99, some increase in default rates is expected as these new issues age. In the absence of any other developments, two simple principles known as "regression to the mean" and the mortality of "aging" effect would have led us to expect both the default amounts and the default rate in 1999 to increase *vis-à-vis* the prior years'. Indeed, we predicted this increase, but underestimated the extent.

The surge in the default rate to over 4 percent was caused by additional factors. One important consideration, though difficult to document with statistics, is the ability of distressed firms to refinance their indebtedness. Refinancing occurred with increasing difficulty in the aftermath of Russia's default and the flight-to-quality that ensured. Without the Russian contagion, the default rate would most likely have been lower, as some companies that faced financial distress would have succeeded in renegotiating their debt claims.

In 1999, there were notable concentrations of defaults in a number of chronically or newly ailing industrial sectors. Such sectors as energy, retailing, communications, healthcare, leisure/entertainment, and shipping were hit hardest.[5]

The energy sector's difficulties reached their peak fairly early in 1999, while retailing and textiles have long experienced chronic problems. Industries such as communications and healthcare became new "leaders" in defaults, reflecting the frenetic new issuance in the former and the overcapacity and governmental changes in regulation of fees in the latter. In sum, despite a vigorous economy driven by technology and productivity growth, a number of sectors have been ailing, and going forward some will continue to flounder.

Finally, we have observed the increasing trend of banks and other lenders who are no longer willing to waive violations of covenants after just a few prior violations. Although this "evidence" is anecdotal, it is consistent with the marginal firm's difficulty in surviving in this hostile environment. A number of factors may be motivating banks to take a tougher stand on forgiveness of covenant violations. For one thing, there appears to be pressure from the FED in the last 12–18 months for banks to setup and record higher loss reserves and actual charge offs when bank profits are high. In other words, a pro-cyclical approach to loss reserves is inhibiting marginal firm survival. Coupled with some indications of a slowing of the US economy and higher interest rates, especially on lower quality issues, these factors are acting to increase the likelihood of defaults on bank loans and publicly held bonds.

THE DIFFERENCES BETWEEN NOW AND THEN

Although storm clouds hang over the high yield market in 2000, especially in view of recent default experience, the current situation is different in a number of important respects from a decade ago. Viewed from a purely statistical standpoint, 10 percent default rates in the near future are certainly possible, but not likely. Since the historic standard deviation of default rates around the average default rate of 3.2 percent is about 3.0 percent (table 20.1), statistical analysis would suggest there is something like a 2.5 percent probability of default rates returning to their 1990 and 1991 highs of over 9.0 percent (which is about two standard deviations above the mean). Interestingly, in the last 29 years (1971–99), there are two data points (about 7 percent) of default rates two standard errors above the mean.

The market, however, is not anticipating such a dire scenario, since yield spreads were 6.7 percent as of 30 June 2000, as compared to over 7.2 percent in mid-1990. One of the most important differences between 1990 and 2000, however, is the proportion of

---

[5] As points of reference, Grossman and Verde (1999) concluded that retail, insurance, supermarkets, drug stores, and textiles/furniture had the highest default rates in the 1991–98 period.

the market that is distressed. If distressed bonds are defined as those with a yield-to-worst at least 10 percent (1000 basis points) above the risk-free rate, 28 percent of high yield bond issues were in this precarious position at the end of 1990, as compared to 17 percent as of 30 June 2000 (figure 20.2). The proportion of high yield bonds that are distressed increased somewhat in July 2000. It's also important to recognize that a high percentage of those distressed issues in 1990 were the result of LBOs and other highly leveraged transactions (HLTs). Although HLTs made a comeback in the 1990s, they are far more conservatively financed today than their 1980s counterparts, with 25–35 percent equity, as compared to only about 10 percent in the late 1980s.

Table 20.4 shows defaults resulting from highly leveraged restructurings (LBOs and leveraged recaps) accounted for at least $19.7 billion in 1990–92; about 46 percent of total defaults in those years.[6] Indeed, in 1990, $7.9 billion of total defaults of $18.4 billion (43 percent) were from those ill-fated HLTs and $9.3 billion of $18.9 billion (49 percent) in 1991.

In contrast, the most recent years' results show that defaults from highly leveraged restructurings in 1999–2000 did not account for any material amount and the outlook is for this source to continue to not be very important. Table 20.5 shows the proportion of total new high yield bonds issued for a number of stated reasons, including acquisitions, leverage restructurings (e.g., LBOs), capital expenditure and other general corporate investments, and the refinancing of existing debt. The latter category has been the most important use of new debt financing every year since the data series began (1986–99). The levels of refinancing in 1997–99 are not exceptionally high – in

Figure 20.2 Distressed[a] and defaulted debt as a percentage of total high yield debt market

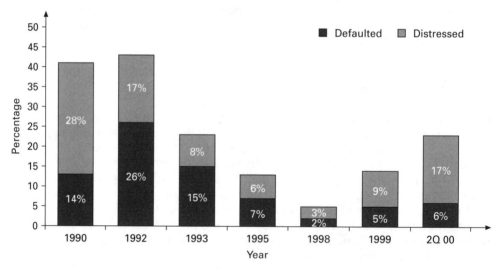

[a] Defined as yield-to-maturity spread greater than or equal to 1000bp over comparable Treasuries.
Source: Salomon Smith Barney and NYU Salomon Center.

[6] Data on LBO defaults is derived from *The Bankruptcy Almanac*, New Generation Research, Boston, MA and the NYU Salomon Center default database.

Table 20.4 Highly leveraged transactions that filed for Chapter 11 (1990–92)

Company	LBO date	Bankruptcy date	Confirmation date	Assets ($ mil.)	Sector	Default date	Face value O/S bonds ($ mil.)	Total defaults ($)	Percent HLT
Allied Stores Corp.	1986	1/15/1990	2/5/1992	3,502	Retail Department	1/15/1990	1,075		
Federated Dept. Stores	1988	1/15/1990	2/5/1992	7,913	Retail Department	1/15/1990	1,405		
Doskocil Cos., Inc.	1986	3/5/1990	9/26/1991	474	Meat Processing	2/1/1990	87		
Leaseway Transportation	1987	12/1/1992	6/30/1993	470	Auto & Freight Trans.	2/1/1990	193		
Servam Corp.	1987	10/20/1992	6/30/1993	293	Contract Foodservices	5/1/1990	132		
Greyhound Lines, Inc.	1987	6/4/1990	8/30/1991	593	Bus Transportation	5/15/1990	150		
Interco, Inc.	1988	1/24/1991	6/25/1992	1,148	Furniture & Shoes	6/15/1990	405		
Southland Corp.	1987	10/24/1990	2/21/1991	3,439	Convenience Stores	6/15/1990	1,643		
Community Newspapers	1987	2/25/1991	2/26/1992	440	Newspaper	7/1/1990	125		
Tracor, Inc.	1987	2/15/1991	12/6/1991	992	Defense Products	8/1/1990	458		
National Gypsum Co. (Aancor)	1986	10/28/1990	3/9/1993	1,444	Bldg. Supplies	10/26/1990	949		
Goldriver L.P. (Finance)	1988	2/21/1991	12/13/1991	138	Hotel & Casino	11/1/1990	118		
Interco, Inc.	1988	1/24/1991	6/25/1992	1,148	Furniture & Shoes	11/5/1990	537		
Days Inns of America	1988	9/27/1991	2/18/1992	596	Hotel Chain	11/12/1990	264		
Specialty Equip. Cos.	1988	12/24/1991	3/12/1992	493	Food Service Equip.	11/15/1990	150		
Harvard Industries	1988	5/2/1991	8/27/1992	533	Automotive Parts	11/26/1990	200		
Total HLT Defaulted Bonds 1990							**7,891**	**18,354**	**43.0**
Insilco Corp.	1988	1/13/1991	11/20/1992	1,105	Diversified Manuf.	1/15/1991	530		
E-II Holdings, Inc.	1987	7/15/1992	5/25/1993	2,141	Holding Co.	2/1/1991	1,241		
Trans World Airlines	1985	1/31/1992	8/11/1993	3,277	Passenger Airline	2/1/1991	1,356		
Hills Department Stores	1985	2/4/1991	9/13/1993	1,059	Discount Department	2/5/1991	229		
Carter Hawley Hale	1987	2/11/1991	9/14/1992	2,405	Department Stores	2/15/1991	350		
Charter Medical Corp.	1988	6/2/1992	7/8/1992	1,347	Hospital Management	2/15/1991	1,077		

Table 20.4 (cont'd)

Company	LBO date	Bankruptcy date	Confirmation date	Assets ($ mil.)	Sector	Default date	Face value O/S bonds ($ mil.)	Total defaults ($)	Percent HLT
Farley, Inc.	1988	9/24/1991	12/2/1992	2,408	Textiles & Metals	2/15/1991	500		
JPS Textile Group, Inc.	1988	2/7/1991	3/21/1991	621	Textiles	2/15/1991	360		
Morse Shoe, Inc.	1987	1/24/1991	12/23/1991	333	Footwear	3/15/1991	268		
Texas Supermarkets	1988	1/2/1992	9/29/1992	245	Supermarket Chain	5/1/1991	85		
Gaylord Container Corp.	1986	9/11/1992	10/16/1992	1,100	Container Board	5/15/1991	400		
Best Products Co., Inc.	1988	1/4/1991	5/31/1994	1,438	Discount Retail	6/1/1991	2		
Pay'N Pak Stores, Inc.	1987	9/21/1991	7/30/1992	326	Home Improvement	6/1/1991	110		
Gillett Holdings, Inc.	1987	6/25/1991	8/3/1992	986	Holding Co.	6/25/1991	632		
Memorex Telex Corp.	1988	1/6/1992	2/7/1992	1,643	Computers	7/16/1991	999		
Work Wear Corp.	1986	10/1/1991		107	Work Apparel	10/1/1991	100		
Gilbert/Robinson, Inc.	1989	11/26/1991	9/15/1992	265	Restaurant Chain	11/1/1991	85		
Zale Corp.	1986	1/23/1992	5/20/1993	1,789	Retail Jewelry Chain	12/1/1991	928		
Total HLT Defaulted Bonds 1991							**9,252**	**18,862**	**49.1**
Seaman Furniture Co.	1988	1/3/1992	10/14/1992	402	Retail Furniture	1/3/1992	74		
Macy (R.H.) & Co.	1986	1/27/1992	12/8/1994	4,812	Department Stores	1/27/1992	1,210		
Ladish Co., Inc.	1987	2/19/1993	4/6/1993	219	Metal Components	4/1/1992	110		
SPI Holdings, Inc.	1989	9/17/1992	10/29/1992	610	In-Room Movies	4/1/1992	296		
Envirodyne Industries	1989	1/7/1993	12/13/1993	1,086	Food pack. & Service	6/1/1992	459		
DR Holdings of DE	1990	8/26/1992	6/24/1993	1,150	Computers	8/17/1992	344		
Spreckels Industries, Inc.	1987	10/14/1992	8/14/1993	274	Holding Co.	9/15/1992	55		
Total HLT Defaulted Bonds 1992							**2,548**	**5,545**	**46.0**
Total LBO Defaults 1990–1992							**19,691**	**42,761**	**46.0**

Sources: *Bankruptcy Almanac, New Generation Research,* and *NYU Salomon Center Default Database.*

Table 20.5 Uses of high yield bond financing – new issues (1986–99)

Year	Acquisition financing	LBOs & recaps	Cap. exp. & gen'l. corp.	Refinancing debt	Other
1986	14%	27%	15%	44%	0%
1987	9%	36%	8%	45%	2%
1988	12%	32%	6%	50%	0%
1989	14%	38%	11%	36%	1%
1990	0%	0%	9%	91%	0%
1991	0%	3%	25%	70%	2%
1992	5%	6%	18%	68%	3%
1993[a]	6%	2%	16%	70%	4%
1994	15%	2%	31%	48%	4%
1995	19%	0%	23%	54%	4%
1996	21%	2%	30%	42%	5%
1997	18%	3%	35%	40%	4%
1998	19%	7%	29%	45%	0%
1999	23%	4%	26%	47%	0%

[a] *Percentages do not sum to 100 due to rounding errors.*
Source: Securities Data Corp., New York, 2000.

fact, they are below the average over this 14-year period. One reason for this is that, although Treasury rates did fall in these years from 1996 levels, the yields on high yield debt actually increased (see table 20.2) making refinancing actually more expensive. But even so, 40–45 percent of more than $100 billion of new issues in each year is a great deal of financing that did not provide new cash to issuers.

Overall, in recent years about 20 percent of high yield bond new issuance was used for acquisitions and only 4–5 percent for leveraged restructurings. This compares to 10–15 percent for acquisitions and well over 30 percent for LBOs and recapitalizations in the years leading up to the market's problems a decade ago. Since leveraged restructurings can lead to unsustainable levels of debt and possible financial distress, the new issue market was decidedly more risky in the earlier period.

To return to the proportion of the high yield market that is distressed, figure 20.2 shows that, in early 1990, the proportion of distressed and defaulted bonds was 42 percent, with 28 percent distressed (the total market includes defaulted bonds in this case). About one-third of the 28 percent actually defaulted in 1990 and again in 1991.[7] Incidentally, 5.7 percent of a market that is almost $600 billion works out to a default total of over $35 billion for the next 12 months. Moody's forecast of 8.4 percent,[8] on a somewhat smaller base, results in defaults of over $42 billion!

I believe that the default rate will be in the 5.5–6 percent range over the next 12 months and not reach the levels that Moody's and others are forecasting. And, I am persuaded by the market's dynamics in the past, that returns will be substantial after the peak of defaults – as figure 20.1's interesting dynamics indicate. Of course, it is difficult to forecast when the peak will occur. But it will occur, and the resulting recovery will probably be substantial, although not likely to achieve returns above 40 percent unless yield spreads first spike dramatically.

---

[7] I do not have data on the distressed proportion as of the end of 1990, but it was substantial.

[8] "July Default Report," Moody's Risk Management Services, D. Hamilton, Editor, August 7, 2000.

A Word on The Economy

The relationship between overall economic activity and default rates has always been tricky. Clearly, depressed economic growth and declining corporate profits and cash flows are related, in a negative sense, to default rates. But, the lead-lag relationship is not very stable over time, especially when dealing with quarterly or even annual data series. Still, it was clear that the economic recession at the start of the 1990s was an additional factor that helped to increase default rates to double-digit levels. Although there may be signs of economic growth slowing or declining as of mid-2000, virtually no economists are forecasting a recession in the next year or two. Indeed, the second quarter's growth in 2000 was surprisingly high and the continued robust growth in the economy is impressive. And, there are recent signs from the FED that interest rates are at or nearing a peak, at least until there are unmistakable signs of growing inflation rates.

A recent study by Osler and Hong, "Rapidly Rising Corporate Debt: Are Firms Now Vulnerable to an Economic Slowdown?" of the New York FED (June 2000), concludes that despite rapid growth in debt of US non-financial firms, the corporate sector is currently in good financial health. Their study, admittedly covering a broader group of firms in addition to high yield bond issuers, also concludes that the corporate bond sector would likely withstand a major stock market correction but a large rise in interest rates could bring corporate liquidity risk back to the relatively high levels common in the 1980s.

Conclusion

Is another crisis due, then? In my opinion, the high yield bond market will weather this downturn, just as it did in the early 1990s and again in the aftermath of Mexico's peso crisis in 1994–95. The present deterioration in credit quality will run its course, as investors refuse to continue providing capital to undercapitalized entities. New issue activities have already started to fall off somewhat in this retrenchment period. Defaults will probably continue at levels that, although unsettling, are not catastrophic – and yield spreads will possibly widen further. But, as long as the vast majority of issuing entities in the high yield market remain viable enterprises, the market for high yield bonds will retain its position as an important major source of finance for companies worldwide and a legitimate asset class for investors.

On balance, I do not foresee the same economic pressures on default rates in 2000 and 2001 as occurred a decade ago.

REFERENCES

Altman, E., 1990, Setting the Record Straight on Junk Bonds: A Review of Research on Default Rates and Returns, *Journal of Applied Corporate Finance*, Summer, 82–95.
Altman, E. and R. Waldman, 2000, *Defaults and Returns in the High Yield Bond Market*, Salomon Smith Barney, January.
Grossman R. and M. Verde, 1999, *High Yield Industry Default Risk*, December, FITCH/IBCA, New York.

21 The Implications of Corporate Bond Ratings Drift

with Duen-Li Kao

Examination of the ratings of over 7000 bonds issued in the 1970–88 period reveals that some 40 percent to 80 percent of bonds initially rated BB and above can be expected to experience at least one rating change in the 10 years following issuance. A-rated bonds appear to be more stable than AAA-rated bonds. BB-rated bonds (the highest "junk bond" category) are the least stable. Furthermore, bonds initially rated A and above have a greater tendency to be downgraded than to be upgraded. Among the investment grades, only bonds initially rated BBB tend to be upgraded more than they are downgraded. As for bonds originally rated non-investment-grade "junk," there does not appear to be a tendency toward either upgrades or downgrades in the sample period.

Results in two subperiods – 1970–79 and 1980–85 – reveal a tendency for a downgrade in rating to be followed by a second downgrade. That is, there is definite serial autocorrelation in ratings when the initial rating change was a downgrade; no autocorrelation is evident when the initial change was an upgrade. Investors may be able to use this information to enhance their bond portfolios' expected returns.

One of the most important indicators of a corporation's credit quality is the bond rating assigned to its outstanding, publicly traded indebtedness by independent rating agencies. Ratings were first developed in the USA in 1914 by Moody's and in 1922 by Poor's Corporation (predecessor of Standard & Poor's) and have evolved into a mini-industry comprised of at least four major firms in the US and a number of similar entities outside the USA. Debt ratings are also assigned by regulatory and quasiregulatory organizations such as the National Association of Insurance Commissioners (NAIC), which rates debt held by insurance companies.[1]

Bond ratings are usually first assigned to public debt at the time of issuance and are periodically reviewed by the rating companies. If deemed warranted, changes in ratings are assigned after the review. A change in a rating reflects the agency's assessment that the company's credit quality has improved (upgrade) or deteriorated (downgrade). A coincident effect, in some proximity to the date of the rating change, is a change in the price of the issue.[2] This article reports on an in-depth investigation of ratings changes (drift) over time.

Using Standard & Poor's bond ratings, we attempt to answer the following related questions:

- What has the ratings-change experience of corporate bonds been from time of issuance to 1–10 years following issuance?
- Was there a tendency for bonds of various initial ratings to be upgraded or downgraded over a 10-year post-issuance period?
- Did rating-change probabilities vary by time period of issuance?
- After a rating change, can one expect subsequent credit-quality changes of the same issue?
- What are the practical implications of ratings-change experience?

We investigate a large sample of over 7000 new bond issues. We analyze both major category rating changes (e.g., from AA to A or B to BB) and also intracategory changes (e.g., AA+ to AA−). Standard & Poor's added the plus and minus designations in 1974 to many of their rating categories.[3] The latter type of changes are analyzed only when we explore issues with at least two rating changes over time.

---

[1] A description of bond ratings and rating agencies can be found in E. I. Altman and D. L. Kao, *Corporate Bond Rating Drift: An Examination of Rating Agency Credit Quality Changes* (Charlottesville, VA: Association for Investment Management and Research, 1991); E. I. Altman and D. L. Kao, "Appendices to the ALMR Report on An Examination of Rating Agency Drift Over Time" (Working paper no. S-91-40, Salomon Center, New York University, 1991); and L. Ederington and J. Yawitz, "The Bond Rating Process," in E. Altman, ed., *Handbook of Financial Markets and Institutions* (New York: John Wiley & Sons, 1987).

[2] Studies of the impact of ratings changes on bond prices include P. Grier and S. Katz, "The Differential Effects of Bond Rating Changes Among Industrial and Public Utility Bonds by Maturity," *Journal of Business* 49 (1976); G. Hettenbouse and W. Satoris, "An Analysis of the Informational Value of Bond Rating Changes," *Quarterly Review of Economics and Business* 16 (1974); and M. Weinstein, "The Effect of A Rating Change Announcement on Bond Price, " *Journal of Financial Economics* 5 (1977). A study by D. Lucas and J. Lonski ("Changes in Corporate Credit Quality 1970–1990," *Moody's Special Report*, February 1991) is strictly descriptive, with little or no interpretive commentary and no attempt to model the ratings change experience. Our monograph (Altman and Kao, *Corporate Bond Rating Drift, op. cit*) reports on extensive modeling of the ratings drift experience using a technique known as Markov chains.

[3] The number of original categories changes from essentially seven (encompassing all major letter categories) to 20 (encompassing plus and minus categories). The intrarating process continued after its 1974 introduction and was completed in 1986, when Standard & Poor's added plus and minus to the CCC category.

RESEARCH AND DATA

We began with a large sample of over 9000 corporate bonds issued over the 19-year period 1 January 1970 to 30 September 1989. We then eliminated issues that were convertibles (1162 issues), in existence for less than one year (586) or were initially "non-rated" (284), ending up with a final sample of 7195 nonconvertible bonds. We examined the subsequent ratings of these bonds over a 10-year post-issuance period. Table 21.1 lists the number of bonds analyzed by original rating category with rating histories of from one to 10 years. Note that while 7195 issues had at least one year of experience, 1959 had a full 10 years of experience. In addition to the 7195-issue sample representing all economic sectors and all years, we analyzed rating histories for several subperiods – 1970–79, 1980–89, 1977–82, and 1983–89.[4]

After examining the 10-year rating-change experience of these corporate bonds, we looked at the subsequent behavior of issues that had undergone at least one downgrade or upgrade. After an issue has suffered one downgrade, will it be followed by a second rating change in the same direction? If so, an investor can take steps to enhance a bond portfolio's expected performance.

Time-Period Bias

Our results may be time-period-sensitive. Our study covers new issues from 1 January 1970 through 1988 and rating changes on those issues through September 1989. The first decade of the period was, in general, a rather positive one for bond-rating changes, both in terms of the stability of the initial ratings and the ratio of upgrades to downgrades. The second major subperiod, covering 1980–89, was less stable and had a greater frequency of downgrades than upgrades.

Table 21.1 Sample size of original bond issues by number of years of rating history

| Original rating | Number of years of rating history | | | | | | | | | |
	1	2	3	4	5	6	7	8	9	10
AAA	649	601	541	492	450	375	321	262	248	238
AA	1,917	1,744	1,510	1,230	1,048	875	759	649	611	576
A	2,410	2,194	1,938	1,644	1,429	1,251	1,096	969	891	831
BBB	1,090	950	807	636	514	397	335	287	245	217
BB	237	217	170	129	103	78	60	54	46	37
B	702	594	431	293	222	163	118	94	67	52
CCC	173	118	77	44	28	17	13	12	9	7
CC	13	11	9	3	1	1	1	1	1	1
C	1	1	0	0	0	0	0	0	0	0
D*	3	2	2	0	0	0	0	0	0	0
Total	7,195	6,440	5,485	4,471	3,795	3,157	2,703	2,318	2,117	1,959

* Issued in a distressed or defaulted restructuring.

[4] See Altman and Kao, *Corporate Bond Rating Drift, op. cit*, for ratings drift experience stratified by economic sectors. For more details on economic-sector experience, readers are encouraged to write to the New York University Salomon Center.

One could argue that the more recent subperiod reflects ratings drift more accurately and that the results for the entire sample period may thus not be indicative of the future. Given the enormous corporate debt burden built up in the mid- and late-1980s, on might reasonably expect an increase in downgrades and default risk. But such expectations do not necessarily apply to those issues brought to market before 1986 or after 1989. Indeed, there is reason to believe that, in the foreseeable future, new issues will be conservatively marketed, with a distinct bias toward more credit-worthy companies and their bonds. If this is true, then the experience of new issues in the late 1980s may not be representative of the ratings drift of new issues in the next decade. Finally, the initial rating assigned to a firm's bonds reflects the rating agency's best evaluation of the firm's risk; the propensity for a rating to change in the future should thus not be related to the bond's initial rating.

We believe that the entire 1970–89 period is the most representative of long-term ratings drift. This period includes several business cycles, both nuclear and non-nuclear incidents at public utilities, the growth of original-issue junk bonds and also a period when junk bonds were virtually nonexistent. And this overall period, obviously, includes our largest sample size.

RESULTS

Table 21.2 lists the ratings drift results for the full sample over selected post-issuance horizons. The number of observations in each rating category naturally diminishes as the number of years in the horizon increases. For example, 649 AAA issues had at least one year of experience, while 450 had at least five years and 238 had 10 years. The proportions of the issues that retained their initial bond ratings are listed on the diagonal in [each section of] the table.

The results can be analyzed in several ways. First, as expected, all rating categories show a continuously declining proportion of bonds retaining their initial rating as the investment horizon lengthens. We also find that AAA-rated issues had the greatest stability in terms of retaining their initial rating, up to five years after issuance. This is not surprising; an AAA bond can change in only one direction – down – while all other categories can be either upgraded or downgraded. Nevertheless, AAA-rated bonds exhibited a sizable propensity to be downgraded; only 69.8 percent of those issues with a five-year or longer history retained their top rating in the fifth year. Of the 238 issues that were in existence for 10 years, only 52.1 percent still had an AAA rating.

Interestingly, single-A bonds had higher 10-year stabilities (61.5 percent) than AAA issues. A-rated issues were actually the most stable category in years 5 through 10. The least stable category appears to be BB-rated issues, the highest of the so-called "junk bond" categories. Only 86.1 percent of these issues retained their initial rating after just one year of experience, and the proportion fell to 40.8 percent in year 5 and 21.6 percent in year 10.[5]

The entire transition matrix seems to indicate a somewhat symmetrical relation between the drop-off in stability as we move both down and up the rating scale and converge on

---

[5]   CCC-rated bonds had only seven observations after 10 years and the results are meaningless. We will not be concerned with the very small number of issues rated below CCC, which represent subordinated issues of senior bonds rated CCC. (Indeed, these issues were rated D, representing new issues exchanged for already defaulted ones.)

Table 21.2 Ratings drift results for all issues, 1970–89 (% of original issues by rating)

Obs.		AAA	AA	A	BBB	BB	B	CCC	CC	C	D
One year since issuance											
649	AAA	**94.3**	5.5	0.1	0.0	0.0	0.0	0.0	0.0	0.0	0.0
1,917	AA	0.7	**92.6**	6.4	0.2	0.1	0.1	0.0	0.0	0.0	0.0
2,410	A	0.0	2.6	**92.1**	4.7	0.3	0.2	0.0	0.0	0.0	0.0
1,090	BBB	0.0	0.0	5.5	**90.1**	2.9	1.1	0.1	0.0	0.0	0.3
237	BB	0.0	0.0	0.0	6.8	**86.1**	6.3	0.9	0.0	0.0	0.0
702	B	0.0	0.0	0.2	1.6	1.7	**94.0**	1.7	0.3	0.0	0.6
173	CCC	0.0	0.0	0.0	0.0	0.0	2.8	**92.5**	0.0	2.3	2.3
13	CC	0.0	0.0	0.0	0.0	0.0	0.0	0.0	**84.6**	15.4	0.0
1	C	0.0	0.0	0.0	0.0	0.0	0.0	0.0	0.0	–	0.0
3	D	0.0	0.0	0.0	0.0	0.0	0.0	0.0	0.0	0.0	–
Three years since issuance											
541	AAA	**81.0**	15.7	2.6	0.7	0.0	0.0	0.0	0.0	0.0	0.0
1,510	AA	2.0	**77.8**	17.5	2.0	0.2	0.1	0.1	0.0	0.0	0.3
1,938	A	0.3	6.9	**78.9**	12.0	1.3	0.7	0.0	0.0	0.0	0.0
807	BBB	0.3	0.7	14.6	**73.4**	7.0	2.1	0.7	0.0	0.0	1.2
170	BB	0.6	0.6	1.8	17.1	**62.9**	11.7	3.0	0.6	0.0	1.8
431	B	0.3	0.3	1.1	1.9	4.2	**75.4**	10.7	1.2	1.4	3.7
77	CCC	0.0	0.0	1.3	0.0	2.6	14.3	**66.3**	1.3	2.6	11.7
9	CC	0.0	0.0	0.0	0.0	0.0	11.1	11.1	**44.4**	0.0	33.3
0	C	0.0	0.0	0.0	0.0	0.0	0.0	0.0	0.0	–	0.0
2	D	0.0	0.0	0.0	0.0	0.0	0.0	0.0	0.0	0.0	–
Five years since issuance											
450	AAA	**69.8**	23.5	2.9	3.6	0.0	0.0	0.0	0.0	0.2	0.0
1,048	AA	2.5	**67.9**	22.8	5.2	1.1	0.3	0.1	0.0	0.0	0.0
1,429	A	0.4	9.2	**72.5**	15.2	1.9	0.7	0.0	0.0	0.0	0.1
514	BBB	0.4	1.6	19.6	**65.7**	7.6	1.7	1.9	0.0	0.0	1.4
103	BB	0.0	0.0	7.7	20.4	**40.8**	16.5	6.8	1.0	0.0	6.8
222	B	0.4	0.0	2.7	4.5	8.6	**59.9**	13.5	0.4	0.9	9.0
28	CCC	0.0	0.0	3.6	3.6	0.0	35.7	**28.6**	7.1	0.0	21.4
1	CC	0.0	0.0	0.0	0.0	0.0	0.0	0.0	–	0.0	0.0
0	C	0.0	0.0	0.0	0.0	0.0	0.0	0.0	0.0	–	0.0
0	D	0.0	0.0	0.0	0.0	0.0	0.0	0.0	0.0	0.0	–
Ten years since issuance											
238	AAA	**52.1**	35.7	7.1	4.6	0.0	0.4	0.0	0.0	0.0	0.0
576	AA	3.5	**46.7**	27.6	19.2	2.4	0.2	0.0	0.0	0.0	0.3
831	A	0.8	12.5	**61.5**	20.2	3.4	0.9	0.6	0.0	0.0	0.1
217	BBB	0.0	2.8	36.8	**43.3**	8.3	4.6	1.9	0.0	0.0	2.3
37	BB	0.0	0.0	10.8	27.0	**21.6**	13.5	18.9	2.7	0.0	5.4
52	B	1.9	0.0	7.7	9.6	5.7	**53.9**	9.6	0.0	0.0	11.5
7	CCC	0.0	0.0	0.0	0.0	0.0	0.0	**85.7**	0.0	0.0	14.3
1	CC	0.0	0.0	0.0	0.0	0.0	0.0	0.0	0.0	–	0.0
0	C	0.0	0.0	0.0	0.0	0.0	0.0	0.0	0.0	–	0.0
0	D	0.0	0.0	0.0	0.0	0.0	0.0	0.0	0.0	0.0	–

the BB rating. It is not perfectly symmetrical, however, as the single-B bonds tended to have greater stability than the CCCs and, after the second year, single-A issues had greater stability than AA issues. And, as noted above, the A-rated issues had the highest stability from year 5 on.

Upgrades vs. Downgrades

Perhaps of even greater interest than stability of rating is the propensity of a change in rating to be positive or negative. This observation can tell us something about expected change in the wealth and returns of bondholders. This is not a zero-sum game; one bond's upgrade is not another's downgrade. We would expect that the individual-year results will be sensitive to the general state of the economy.

We know that AAA-rated bonds can only be downgraded or remain the same. We found that, within five years, 30.2 percent of AAA bonds were downgraded – 23.5 percent to AA, 2.9 percent to A, 3.6 percent to BBB and one issue (0.2 percent) to below BBB (table 21.2). The results are perhaps even more dramatic for AA issues. While these bonds can be upgraded only to AAA, they can fall all the way to D. After five years, only 2.5 percent of the 1048 originally issued AAs saw their rating upgraded, while 29.5 percent were downgraded. For the 10-year horizon, 3.5 percent of the 576 AAs were upgraded, while 2.9 percent dropped all the way to junk-bond status, including the 0.3 percent that defaulted.

The most striking result is that bonds initially rated A and above have a greater propensity to be downgraded than to be upgraded, regardless of the investment horizon. And the downgrade-upgrade differential increases as the horizon increases. For example, A-rated bonds had 17.9 percent downgrades vs. 9.6 percent upgrades at five years and 25.2 percent downgrades vs. 13.3 percent upgrades at 10 years.

When we drop below A-rated bonds to BBBs, we observe, for the first time, that upgrades exceed downgrades for all horizons (e.g., 39.6 percent upgrades vs. 17.1 percent downgrades at 10 years). The category for which upgrades and downgrades were closest was BB-rated bonds (6.8 percent vs. 7.2 percent, 28.1 percent vs. 31.1 percent and 37.8 percent vs. 40.6 percent for 1-, 5- and 10-year horizons, respectively).

Single-B bonds have the least clear results, with upgrades leading downgrades for 1- and 10-year horizons, but downgrades leading upgrades for the 5-year horizon. Indeed, for this category, upgrades exceed downgrades in only the first and last (1- and 10-year) horizons.

Our main conclusion is that, for the 1970–89 period, the only rating category that clearly showed a greater propensity for upgrades than downgrades was the BBB class. As we will show, this propensity held even in the 1980s, when downgrades dominated upgrades in general. This result is consistent with Altman's finding that the BBB category realized the highest return spread over US Treasury bonds in the 1980s compared with all other corporate bond rating classes.[6] Furthermore, there does not appear to be a tendency for non-investment-grade original issues to be either upgraded or downgraded.[7]

Different Time Periods

The corporate bond market, like so many other financial systems, goes through distinct cycles of activity and performance. One of the most important for these risky securities

---

[6] See E. I. Altman, "How 1989 Changed the Hierarchy of Fixed Income Security Performance," *Financial Analysts Journal*, May/June 1990.

[7] See E. I. Altman and D. L. Kao, "Rating Drift of High Yield Bonds," *Journal of Fixed Income*, March 1992.

is the business cycle. It is reasonable to assume that aggregate economic activity will also be related to the incidence of rating changes. Upgrades can be expected to dominate when companies perform better as well as when the rating agencies perceive that performance will continue to improve. The opposite is likely with respect to downgrades. In some periods, however, counteracting forces can result in uncertainty about the direction of rating changes. Economic activity may be excellent while, at the same time, leverage is increasing. Earnings and cash inflows will thus be increasing as interest burdens swell, causing coverage ratios to move uncertainly.

In order to investigate the time dependence of rating changes, we broke our total sample period in half and observed changes in the 1970–79 and the 1980–89 subperiods. We also looked at the early stages of the junk bond market in 1977–82 and the later period of junk bond high growth in 1983–88.

The second 10-year period (1980s) had more bond issuances than the earlier period (4592 vs. 2603), reflecting the growth in fixed income securities as an attractive asset class for investors and the increasing use of leverage by corporate America. A reversal is likely to be the case in the early 1990s, as many companies deleverage, at least among the lowgrade issues.

Table 21.3 presents the one-year to five-year experience of bonds in the 1970–79 period and the 1980–89 period.[8] There was far less stability in ratings in the more recent 1980–88 issuance period, and this was true regardless of the bond rating or the specific year subsequent to the initial issuance. For example, one year after issuance, AAA-rated bonds retained their rating 97.4 percent of the time in the earlier sample period but only 91.6 percent of the time in the later period. At five years after issuance, 80.0 percent of AAAs retained their rating in the earlier sample period, but only 49.3 percent retained their rating in the later period. This was partially the result of a large number of nuclear-related public utility and commercial bank downgrades in the 1980s.

Examination of ratings changes in the two subperiods leads us to the following conclusions.

1 The incidence of downgrades was far more apparent in the 1980s than the 1970s, and this dominance was found in most, but not all, original-rating classes.

2 The lower-grade classes (below BBB) experienced a positive "balance of change" (upgrades/downgrades) for most of the 19-year sample period, but the balance reversed itself during the most recent 1983–88 subperiod.

3 The balance of change for investment-grade bonds rated A and above was extremely unfavorable throughout the entire sample period. Downgrades exceeded upgrades for every rating and every subperiod, and this was the case for the 1-, 3- and 5-year horizons.

4 The one exception to the upgrade vs. downgrade imbalance over the entire sample period, as well as the various subperiods, was the apparent excellent performance of the BBB class.

5 BB-rated bonds performed well, in terms of rating changes, except during the most recent 1983–88 subperiod.

6 There was a complete reversal in the CCC class between the 1970–79 period (upgrades dominated) and the 1983–88 period (downgrades dominate, especially for the 5-year horizon).

---

[8] The entire drift for both periods is given in Altman and Kao, *Corporate Bond Rating Drift, op. cit.*

Table 21.3 Comparative stability of ratings: New issues in 1970–79 vs. new issues in 1980–88

Rating	Years after issuance	1970–79 proportion unchanged (%)	1980–88 proportion unchanged (%)
AAA	1	97.4	91.6
	2	94.7	79.2
	3	92.1	66.9
	4	87.7	57.9
	5	80.0	49.3
AA	1	95.3	91.1
	2	87.5	83.1
	3	80.3	75.8
	4	73.1	71.8
	5	67.6	68.6
A	1	96.3	88.6
	2	92.3	76.9
	3	87.9	68.0
	4	83.1	62.2
	5	77.7	58.9
BBB	1	96.3	87.4
	2	93.6	76.8
	3	87.9	63.6
	4	80.9	56.8
	5	74.3	52.3
BB	1	98.6	81.0
	2	88.2	67.1
	3	70.1	58.3
	4	62.7	50.0
	5	46.9	30.8
B	1	97.5	93.3
	2	97.5	81.6
	3	82.5	72.7
	4	75.8	57.8
	5	68.7	50.5
CCC	1	100.0	91.6
	2	81.3	80.4
	3	46.7	71.0
	4	40.0	50.0
	5	35.7	21.4

WHAT CAN YOU EXPECT AFTER A RATING CHANGE?

A rating change some time after bond issuance is the norm rather than the exception. But after an initial rating upgrade or downgrade, what is the probability that there will be another change? If there is, is it likely to be in the same direction? In statistical terms, is there serial autocorrelation of multiple rating changes?

If there is significant autocorrelation of rating changes, then an initial change can tell us much about subsequent investment performance, especially if the expected holding period of the bond is less than maturity. An initial rating downgrade, for example, may imply that a second rating downgrade is likely, suggesting that subsequent performance will be inferior to what was "promised" or implicit in the yield at the time of the first rating change. The reverse – superior expected performance – will be the case for upgrades with positive autocorrelation or downgrades with expected negative autocorrelation.

Frequency

During the 1970–79 period there were 2603 new bond issues, of which 1984 (76.2 percent) experienced at least one subsequent rating change. When the sample period is expanded to 1970–85, the proportion of new issues that experienced at least one rating change rises slightly to 79.7 percent (3658/4592). For this segment of our investigation, we define a rating change as at least one "notch" up or down, where a notch can be intrarating – e.g., A to A– – or between ratings – e.g., A– to B–. In the 1970–79 period, 61.9 percent of the changes were downgrades and 38.1 percent upgrades. Downgrades increased to 64.4 percent for 1970–85.

Our initial results are for the two subperiods 1970–79 and 1980–85. Although the former period was almost twice as long as the latter, the number of issues that experienced a rating change was quite similar in the two periods – 1986 for the 1970s and 1672 for the six years of the 1980s. Tables 21.4 and 21.5 show the post-rating-change experience for those bonds that experienced an initial downgrade or upgrade in 1970–79. The data are broken down by economic sector and by initial full-letter rating. For 1970–79, 59.6 percent of those bonds that experienced an initial downgrade experienced a second downgrade (DD), compared with 23.4 percent that experienced a downgrade

Table 21.4 Rating change experience subsequent to an initial downgrade, 1970–79

Economic sector	Second change downgrade (DD)		Second change upgrade (DU)		No change (DN)		Total no.
	No.	%	No.	%	No.	%	
Industrial	248	54.7	86	19.0	119	26.3	453
Utility	413	62.6	182	27.6	65	9.8	660
Financial	69	69.7	12	12.1	18	18.2	99
Others	1	6.7	7	46.7	7	46.7	15
Total	731	59.6	287	23.4	209	17.0	1,227

Initial rating	Downgrade (DD)		Upgrade (DU)		No change (DN)		Total no.
	No.	%	No.	%	No.	%	
AAA	112	59.6	32	17.0	44	23.4	188
AA	296	68.0	79	18.2	60	13.8	433
A	246	54.9	135	30.1	67	15.0	448
BBB	44	52.4	33	39.3	7	8.3	84
BB	10	62.5	2	12.5	4	25.0	16
B	23	41.1	6	10.7	27	48.2	56
Total	731	59.6	287	23.4	209	17.0	1,227

Table 21.5   Rating change experience subsequent to an initial upgrade, 1970–79

Economic sector	Second change downgrade (UD)		Second change upgrade (UU)		No change (UN)		Total no.
	No.	%	No.	%	No.	%	
Industrial	122	37.9	119	37.0	81	25.2	322
Utility	80	30.2	101	38.1	84	31.7	265
Financial	62	42.5	50	34.2	34	23.3	146
Others	19	79.2	0	0.0	5	20.8	24
Total	283	37.4	270	35.7	204	26.9	757

Initial rating	Downgrade (UD)		Upgrade (UU)		No change (UN)		Total no.
	No.	%	No.	%	No.	%	
AAA	0	0.0	0	0.0	0	0.0	0
AA	74	66.1	8	7.1	30	26.8	112
A	120	32.3	140	37.7	111	29.9	371
BBB	56	33.3	70	41.7	42	25.0	168
BB	16	37.2	22	51.2	5	11.6	43
B	13	25.0	25	48.1	14	26.9	52
CCC	4	36.4	5	45.5	2	18.2	11
Total	283	37.4	270	35.7	204	26.9	757

followed by an upgrade (DU) and just 17.0 percent that did not experience any change after the initial one (DN). Initial upgrades were followed fairly equally by a second upgrade (UU = 35.7 percent), downgrade (UD = 37.4 percent) or no change (UN = 26.9 percent).

For 1980–85, 44.6 percent of those issues that were downgraded had a second downgrade, 17.6 percent had a downgrade followed by an upgrade, and 37.8 percent were unchanged. (The greater proportion of unchanged issues in 1980–85 versus 1970–79 in part reflects the truncation of the data in 1989.) Upgrades were followed by upgrades in 20.6 percent of the cases, by downgrades in 24.3 percent of the cases and by no change in 55.1 percent of the cases.

The above results indicate definite serial autocorrelation of ratings changes when the initial change was a downgrade but no autocorrelation when the initial change was an upgrade. Below we perform more definitive statistical tests using the longer new-issue sample period 1970–85.

Longer Periods

Of the 3658 new bonds issued from 1970 to 1985 that experienced at least one rating change, the majority (2514 or 68.7 percent) experienced a second rating change. Table 21.6 shows the ratio of the number of subsequent (second) ratings changes that were in the same direction as the first (i.e., DD or UU) to the number that were in the opposite direction (DU or UD). A ratio greater than 1.0 indicates serial correlation. Note that the ratios include only bonds that experienced a second change. For the 1717

Table 21.6 Relation of first bond rating change to subsequent change, 1970–85

	Ratio of second change given first change down				Ratio of second change given first change up			
	No. of issues				Number of issues			
	DD	DU	Ratio	Sign test	UU	UD	Ratio	Sign test
Economic sector								
Industrial	445	178	2.50	21.4*	162	170	0.95	−0.88
Utility	530	237	2.24	21.2*	140	111	1.26	3.66*
Financial	246	49	5.02	22.9*	100	92	1.09	1.15
Others	11	21	0.52	−3.5*	0	22	0.00	−9.38*
Initial rating								
AAA	165	45	3.67	16.6*	0	0	0.00	NA
AA	477	113	4.22	30.0*	8	92	0.09	−16.80*
A	386	202	1.91	15.2*	185	155	1.19	3.25*
BBB	101	85	1.19	2.3*	125	85	1.47	5.52*
BB	21	18	1.17	1.0	35	29	1.21	1.50
B	71	21	3.38	10.4*	41	29	1.41	2.87*
CCC	11	1	11.00	5.8*	8	5	1.60	1.66
Years to first change								
1	208	115	1.81	10.3*	61	62	0.98	−0.18
2	277	86	3.22	20.0*	85	81	1.05	0.62
3	172	61	2.82	14.5*	66	57	1.16	1.62
4	137	60	2.28	11.0*	53	46	1.15	1.41
5	107	44	2.43	10.3*	39	39	1.00	0.00
6	66	26	2.54	8.3*	23	19	1.21	1.23
7	54	17	3.18	8.8*	15	12	1.25	1.15
8	51	18	2.83	7.9*	6	23	0.26	−6.31*
9	36	11	3.27	7.3*	14	9	1.56	2.09*
> = 10	124	47	2.64	11.8*	40	47	0.85	−1.50
Total	1,232	485	2.54	36.1*	402	395	1.02	0.50

* Sign test is significant at 0.01 level.

bonds that had a rating change following an initial downgrade, the ratio of downgrades to upgrades (DD/DU) was 2.54.

The results are segmented by economic sector of the issuing companies, by initial bond rating and by the number of years it took for the first rating change to take place. Results are fairly similar, with a few exceptions, across sectors, across ratings and across years. The financial enterprises sector exhibits a much higher tendency toward serial autocorrelation than the industrials and utilities sectors. Also, the more extreme rating classes (AAA, AA, B and CCC) appear to have the highest positive autocorrelation. The sample sizes are quite small, however, for the latter two low-grade bond classes. The lower ratios for the middle range of rating classes – A, BBB and BB – give evidence for the mean-reversion hypothesis; that is, ratings will tend to drift toward the middle of the range of credit-quality ratings, but there will be less of a tendency for there to be a significant drift in either direction when the rating is at the mid-range at the onset.

The positive autocorrelation for initial downgrades analyzed by the period of time it took for the initial change to occur shows a fairly even pattern for all years.

Note that the ratio of upgrades to downgrades following an initial upgrade (UU vs. UD) is essentially 1.0, indicating no tendency for serial autocorrelation when the initial change is positive. We will have more to say later about this apparent difference between positive initial bond rating changes and initial downgrades.

We also analyzed the relation between the first and second ratings changes for individual issues stratified by the amount (number of notches) of the initial change. In this stratification, a change from B+ to B, for example, represents a single notch. For 51 percent of those issues with at least two ratings changes, the initial change was one notch. For 24 percent and 21 percent of the issues, the initial changes were two and three notches, respectively. The ratio results for this stratified sample were similar to those presented in table 21.6.

Significance Tests

We can test for

1   the probability that a second rating change will be the same as the first, given the possibility that the result could also be a reversal in rating change or no change or
2   the probability that, given a second change does take place, the change will be in the same direction as the first change.

We believe that the latter test is more appropriate for investors, because only an expected second rating change has definite implications for them. If an investor expects an initial downgrade to be followed by a second downgrade, for example, then he should probably sell (or not purchase) the bond – unless, of course, the expected yield after the initial change is satisfactory. The reverse is true if the investor expects a reversal of an initial downgrade. To test for the significance of our findings, we utilize the binomial sign test.[9]

The ratios given in table 21.6 are derived from the actual numerical results, also given in that table. For instance, the 2.54 DD/Du ratio is based on 1232 downgrades and 485 upgrades. The sign tests given in the last columns of the table show clearly that an initial downgrade can be expected to be followed by a subsequent downgrade. This finding is significant for all economic sector groupings (except the tiny "others" group) and virtually all initial rating classes. The only exception is the BB class, which had only slightly more downgrades than upgrades (1.17 ratio) and an insignificant sign test. For all economic sectors and initial rating classes combined, the sign tests are extremely significant (with a value of 36.1). The results hold regardless of the number of years it took for the first change to take place.

The results are not as clear when the initial change was an upgrade. The overall results indicate that serial correlation did not take place; the ratio of upgrades to downgrades is virtually equal to 1.0, and the sign test is insignificant. A few subgroupings, however,

---

[9]   The null hypothesis is that the probability of a second change given a first is 0.5 in either direction. The sign test examines the difference in outcomes of a second rating change in the same direction or a reversal.

do show significant positive serial correlation. These include the public utilities and the A, BBB and B-rated classes. Indeed, BBBs had 125 positive second changes following an initial upgrade, compared with 85 downgrades. But initial AAs showed a vast dominance of rating change reversal, given the initial upgrade.

Issues With More Than Two Changes

We now examine bond issues that experienced at least two rating changes in the same direction (up or down) and test for autocorrelation of the subsequent *third* rating change (if any). In the 1970–85 period, 1634 new issues had at least two rating changes in the same direction and 1107 of these had a third change. Are two downgrades (upgrades) likely to be followed by a third downgrade (upgrade)?

We found that 54.5 percent of those issues with two downgrades suffered a third in the same direction, while only 17.9 percent had a reversal (up) and the remaining 27.6 percent did not experience a third rating change (at least not through 1989). Therefore, the ratio of downgrades to upgrades, given two prior downgrades, was about 3 to 1. Recall that this ratio was 2.54 to 1.0 in our earlier results. The results here are thus even more significant.

The ratio of upgrades to downgrades given two initial upgrades was essentially one-to-one (27.1 percent/26.1 percent). The number of observations where the first two rating changes were positive was much smaller (402) than the observations with at least two downgrades (1232). In conclusion, the results are again quite significant for downgrades but not for upgrades.

Bias Correction

The above results could be biased because the period of observation had far more downgrades than upgrades. As noted above, in 1970–85, 64.4 percent of all first ratings changes were downgrades. It is perhaps not surprising, therefore, that the predominant second change that occurred either in that same 16-year period or in the next few years (1986–89, a period of even greater downgrade incidence) was also a downgrade. Table 21.7 presents adjusted results that account for possible time-period selection bias. To adjust, we subtract from the actual second downgrade experience (column 4) what could have been expected if one had known the aggregate first rating change experience for the same period. For example, we subtract the observed 64.4 percent initial downgrade proportion for the period 1970–85 (column 2) from the 71.8 percent second downgrade actual result (column 4) and test the difference (7.4 percent in column 8) to see whether it is significantly different from zero. These results also show significant positive serial autocorrelation for the entire sample as well as for industrial and financial companies and for all rating classes except AAs. The results are not significant, however, for utility downgrades.

Furthermore, the results for initial upgrades now exhibit positive autocorrelation as well. For example, an investor who knew that only 35.6 percent of initial changes were upgrades (column 3) and expected the same result for subsequent rating changes would have found that initial upgrades were followed by a second upgrade in 50.4 percent of the cases (column 7). The bias-corrected second upgrade experience of 14.8 percent

Table 21.7   Same-direction (autocorrelation) rating change experience adjusted for credit patterns (two rating changes for new issue 1970–85)

(1)	(2)	(3)	(4)	(5)	(6)	(7)	(8) (4)–(2)	(9) (7)–(3)
			Second rating change given first change (%)				Second change adjusted for first change (%)	
	First rating change (%)		First down		First up		First down	First up
	Downgrade	Upgrade	Down	Up	Down	Up	Second down	Second up
Economic sector								
Industrial	63.9	36.1	71.4	28.6	51.2	48.8	7.5	12.7
Finance	56.1	43.9	83.4	16.6	47.9	52.1	27.3	8.2
Utility	69.0	31.0	69.1	30.9	44.2	55.8	0.1	24.8
Other	67.7	32.3	34.4	65.6	100.0	0.0	N/R	N/R
Total	64.4	35.6	71.8	28.2	49.6	50.4	7.4	14.8
Initial bond rating								
AAA	100.0	0.0	78.6	21.4	N/R	N/R	N/R	N/R
AA	83.5	16.5	80.8	19.2	91.8	8.2	−2.6	−8.4
A	57.1	42.9	65.6	34.4	45.9	54.1	8.5	11.2
BBB	43.8	56.2	54.3	45.7	40.5	59.5	10.5	3.3
NIG	50.0	50.0	72.0	28.0	42.9	57.1	22.0	7.1
Total	64.4	35.6	71.8	28.2	49.6	50.4	7.3	14.8

N/R – Not relevant due to small sample size.
NIG – Non-Investment Grade.

(column 9) is easily significant, implying positive autocorrelation for upgrades adjusted for possible time-period bias.

We believe that the unadjusted results are more meaningful for investors. An investor simply cannot know, at the time of an initial rating change, the frequency distribution for all changes over the period. He can only know the experience up to that point. He may, of course, use that knowledge to predict subsequent ratings changes.[10]

Finally, correcting for anticipated ratings changes will be fruitful only to the extent that the price of a bond at the time of an initial change reflects the overall market's anticipation that a future rating change will take place in the same direction as and with the same probability that it did in the past. The market may believe, alternatively, that any observed rating change after the initial change will reflect the best estimate of the bond's credit quality, and that subsequent ratings changes will exhibit no autocorrelation.

PRACTICAL APPLICATIONS

Our findings have a number of practical implications for investment analysts, portfolio managers and rating agencies. They may be used

---

[10]   Markov-chain models such as those developed in Altman and Kao, *Corporate Bond Rating Drift, op. cit.,* may be helpful.

- as an early step in assessing the credit-quality risks of corporate bond investments
- to help bond actuaries and analysts to establish more precise loss reserves and capital allocations
- to establish guidelines for the construction of more precise finance obligations (e.g., collateralized bond obligations)
- to establish tolerance levels for aggregate changes in a portfolio's composition before liquidation procedures are enforced (the proportion of a portfolio that can fall to non-investment-grade levels, for example)
- to obtain better estimates of expected return performance for bond portfolios.

Knowledge of the past is useful in assessing future investment performance. The association between the historical performance of various bond rating classes and changes across rating classes is a meaningful analytic comparison. We have observed, for example, that BBB-class mutual funds outperformed all other rating categories in the 1980s, and we now find that BBB new issues had the most favorable experience in terms of upgrades versus downgrades in both the 1970s and 1980s.[11] The extension of bond-quality-rating changes to commercial bank loan portfolios is an important application outside of securities markets. Banks often assign credit ratings based on a loan's bond rating equivalent. Given evidence of bond-rating drift, loan-quality drift can also be assessed.

Of course, blind extrapolation of historical results into the future is unwise. The period examined in this article may be atypical of future environments. It is important to create different scenarios for performance analysis.

Loss Reserves and Structured Finance Obligations

Financial institutions usually have policies and procedures for setting aside reserves to cover anticipated losses from defaults on risky assets. Most of the analytical work in this area has centered on default rates and loss estimates using both traditional and mortality/aging approaches.[12] One can now also estimate one or more years of credit-rating transitions.

We advocate a "net" approach, which considers the effects of both expected upgrades and downgrades on expected losses. For example, the historical experience given in table 21.2 shows that new-issue A-rated and BBB-rated bonds had the one-year upgrade and downgrade experience presented in table 21.8. Combining the short-term gains and losses from these rating changes with expected losses from defaults (if any) should yield a more precise account of changes in a portfolio.

Our findings can also be extended to the collateralized bond obligation (CBO) market. This market has been growing rapidly and has attained sufficient status that the major rating agencies have set up special groups to evaluate CBOs. CBOs are based on explicit assumptions about the appropriate over-collateralization of amounts outstanding, where the collateral are risky obligations such as non-investment-grade bonds. CBO structures are often based on expected cash flows from the collateral, with a

---

[11] See Altman, "How 1989 Changed," *op. cit.*

[12] See E. I. Altman, *Default Risk, Mortality Rates, and the Performance of Corporate Bonds* (Charlottesville, VA: Research Foundation of the Institute of Chartered Financial Analysts, 1989) and *Journal of Finance*, September 1989.

Table 21.8   Rating change experience in one year

Magnitude of grade change	Percent market value of initial holdings	
	A	BBB
One upgrade	2.6	5.5
One downgrade	4.7	2.9
Net	−2.1	+2.6
Two upgrades	0.0	0.0
Two downgrades	0.3	1.1
Net	−0.3	−1.1
Three upgrades	0.0	0.0
Three downgrades	0.2	0.1
Net	−0.2	−0.1

number of "trigger" events calling for more collateral and cash flow assurances. One trigger mechanism that the creator of a CBO frequently includes is deterioration of the credit quality of the underlying collateral.

Rating agencies require conservative structural standards to assign a high invest-ment-grade rating (e.g., A or AA) to the safest, most senior tranche of a CBO. And if the CBO issue is insured, and the senior tranche receives an AAA rating, then the insurer requires conservative trigger mechanisms. For both agency and insurer, the credit quality of the portfolio is of primary concern, and they could use estimates of bond-rating changes in the CBO creation and review process.

Drift Tolerance

Financial institutions often have restricted or targeted risk levels for their investment portfolios. For instance, investment-grade bond funds may not be able to hold non-investment-grade bonds, including fallen angels, or they may be limited to holding a small percentage of these higher-risk assets. Our analysis and results can be used to estimate the proportion of original-issue, investment-grade bonds that will become non-investment-grade within, say, five years.

If, for example, a portfolio of original-issue, investment-grade bonds is held in the same proportions as the relative amounts listed in table 21.2 for year 1, then we can estimate the number of issues that will fall to a non-investment-grade (NIG) level within five years. Using a naive, simple extrapolation model, we observe that AAAs originally constituted 10.6 percent of the total (649/6066), AAs 31.6 percent, and so on. By the end of the fifth year, 4.0 percent of the portfolio had fallen to the NIG level, as table 21.9 shows. If the guideline for this investment fund is that no more than 5 percent of the portfolio can be fallen angels, then the manager can expect to be in accordance with the policy at the end of the fifth year.

For those who forecast the size of various segments of the corporate bond market (e.g., investment or non-investment grades), estimates of upgrades and downgrades can increase the accuracy of the forecast.

Table 21.9 Drift out of investment-grade ratings

Rating	Original proportions (%)	Fifth-year proportions (%)
AAA	10.7	8.5
AA	31.6	27.9
A	39.7	39.8
BBB	18.0	14.8
NIG	0.0	4.0
Total	100.0	100.0

Expected Portfolio Performance

One of the primary applications of our findings is to the prediction and evaluation of ratings drift over the expected holding period of a single bond or a portfolio of bonds. Table 21.10 presents a hypothetical portfolio used to illustrate this application. Assuming the investor's expected holding period is three years, table 21.11 presents ratings transition matrixes based on naive extrapolation of our observed ratings transitions. Because of the stationary nature of the naive model, estimated 3-year transition probabilities should be used for all the bonds, regardless of their ages. (If one adopts a nonstationary model, different 3-year transition matrixes will be applied to bonds according to the number of years since the bond was issued.)

The rating-transition probabilities shown in the top panel of the table are multiplied by the bond's weighting in the portfolio. Summing these weighted probabilities results in the portfolio's expected ratings distribution at the end of the 3-year holding period. Taking the probabilities of bond-rating drift into account results in an ending rating profile that differs from the beginning profile. AAAs, for example, drop from 25 percent of the portfolio to 21.2 percent, while As increase from 20.0 percent to 25.0 percent and the NIG class increases to 6.4 percent.

The future performance of corporate bonds typically varies with interest rate fluctuations and with expected defaults. Investors usually assume that the ratings of non-default bonds remain unchanged. Our evidence suggests that ratings drift can add substantially to the uncertainty of bond portfolio management. Because ratings changes result in an adjustment in the bond yield demanded by investors, drift alters the relative values and interest rate sensitivities of individual bonds. Consequently, it may affect

Table 21.10 Hypothetical portfolio

Bond No.	Bond Age (yrs)	Portfolio	
		Rating	Weighting (%)
1	New Issue	AAA	25
2	2	AA	40
3	5	A	20
4	3	BBB	10
5	1	NIG	5

Table 21.11 Estimating future rating distributions and total returns (3-year holding period)

Naive model estimation

	Beginning profile		Rating-transition probabilities (%)					
Bond Age	Rating Weights (%)	Bond Rating	AAA	AA	A	BBB	NIG	Ending rating weights (%)
0	25.0	AAA	81.0	15.7	2.6	0.7	0.0	21.2
2	40.0	AA	2.0	77.8	17.5	2.0	0.7	36.5
5	20.0	A	0.3	6.9	78.9	12.0	2.0	25.0
3	10.0	BBB	0.3	0.7	14.6	73.4	11.2	11.0
1	5.0	NIG	0.3	0.3	1.3	5.4	93.8	6.4

Bond yields and performance profiles

	Beginning profile		Expected total returns (%)				
Rating	Yields (%)	Expected ending yields (%)	AAA	AA	A	BBB	NIG
AAA	9.75	8.75	38.21	36.89	35.60	34.32	18.41
AA	10.00	9.00	38.99	37.97	36.96	35.96	23.23
A	10.25	9.25	37.67	37.21	36.76	36.31	30.26
BBB	10.50	9.50	41.74	40.89	40.04	39.20	28.33
NIG	13.00	13.00	65.43	64.15	62.89	61.64	44.91
T-Bond	9.25	8.25					

Total returns under various ratings-transition models

	Beginning profile		Expected returns (%) assuming		
Bond age	Rating weights (%)	Bond rating	Rating unchanged (%)	Naive-model transition (%)	T-Bond benchmark portfolio (%)
0	25.0	AAA	38.21	37.90	36.40
2	40.0	AA	37.97	37.67	35.19
5	20.0	A	36.76	36.65	32.97
3	10.0	BBB	39.20	38.14	34.51
1	5.0	NIG	44.91	46.21	35.82
Portfolio	100.0		38.26	38.00	35.01

how a portfolio manager implements investment strategies such as portfolio restructuring, optimization, bond swaps and duration management.

While a discussion of the implications of ratings drift to a full range of bond portfolio management practices is beyond the scope of this article, we can present an example of how estimated ratings transition matrixes can be incorporated into an analysis of expected total returns (price changes, coupon income and coupon reinvestments) of bonds over an assumed holding period.

The middle panel of table 21.11 presents credit yield curves and performance profiles over a three-year holding period. It assumes that

1 all five bonds were originally issued with a 10-year maturity and are purchased at par at various ages at the beginning of the expected 3-year investment horizon,
2 yields on bonds of all credit quality (except non-investment-grade issues) will decrease by 100 basis points by the end of the holding period,

3 yield spreads between adjacent investment-grade categories remain constant at 25 basis points, and
4 expected returns are based on the use of a naive ratings drift model estimated over 1970–89 (table 21.2).

The panel presents expected total returns over three years, given bond beginning and ending ratings. If the AAA-rated bond were downgraded to the AA category, for example, total return over the three-year period would be expected to be 36.89 percent – 1.32 percent less than if the AAAs were not downgraded.

Using the performance profile in the middle panel, the bottom panel of table 21.11 calculates total returns for these five hypothetical bonds and the entire portfolio, assuming that

1 ratings remain unchanged, or
2 ratings change according to historical patterns.

The expected total return is higher under the no-ratings-change scenario. Failure to consider bond ratings drift will overestimate the performances of both individual bonds and the entire portfolio. The expected performance of Treasury bonds with a comparable maturity is presented as a risk-free benchmark.

22 | Investing in Distressed Securities
The Anatomy of Defaulted Debt and Equities

The market for distressed firms' debt and equity securities has captured the interest and the imagination of the investment community like never before. Fueled by a substantial increase in the supply and diversity of bankrupt and near bankrupt companies and the perceived sizeable upside potential of securities selling at deeply discounted prices, investors are increasingly considering this area as one of the growth opportunities of the 1990s. The purpose of this study is to document and analyze this unique asset class, both in terms of a descriptive anatomy of the market's major characteristics and participants, as well as an analytical treatment of its pricing dynamics and performance attributes. While we refer to distressed securities as a market and an asset class, we are fully aware that these labels are premature due to the field's nascent condition and the lack of much rigorous research to date. In actuality, it is a market of securities of problem firms which afford opportunities if the problems are addressed successfully and where the current prices may be overdiscounted for the perceived problems.

Distressed securities can be defined narrowly as only those publicly held debt and equity securities of firms which have defaulted on their debt obligations and/or have filed for protection under Chapter 11 of the Bankruptcy Code. We estimate that the market value of these securities as of the start of 1990 was approximately $13 billion ($11.5 billion in debt), comprised of 178 different issuing firms.

A more comprehensive definition would also include those publicly held debt securities selling at sufficiently discounted prices so as to be yielding a minimum of 10 percent over comparable maturity US Treasury bonds (about 18 percent at the beginning of 1990). Viewed by this more liberal definition, at least $75 billion in par value of distressed and defaulted securities are outstanding, comprising several hundred issuers and over 600 issues. The market value of these public defaulted and distressed securities is probably about $45 billion. If one would also add the private debt with public registration rights, private bank debt and trade claims of defaulted and distressed companies, the relevant population for investor consideration increases substantially, perhaps by three to four times. Therefore, private defaulted claims add about another $75 billion, with an additional $150 billion in distressed debt bringing the total book value of defaulted and distressed securities and claims to about $300 billion. We estimate the market value of these securities and claims to be about $200 billion. A summary of these estimates is listed in table 22.1.

Following a descriptive and analytical treatment of investors and current developments, we will analyze the performance attributes of investing in distressed securities. While we do include equities, our focus will be on the performance of debt securities. We will also utilize information derived from a survey sent out to about 80 known, or thought to be known, investors in distressed securities. Our response rate was excellent, with 56 responses, giving us insights into the size and age of these entities, their investment focus, required and minimum rates of return criteria, and their outlook for opportunities in this area.

Table 22.1   Estimated public and private debt outstanding of defaulted and distressed firms (as of 31 January 1990)

	Book value ($ billions)	Market value ($ billions)	Market/book ratio
Publicly traded			
Defaulted debt	26.0	11.5	0.44
Distressed debt	50.0	33.0	0.66
Privately placed			
Defaulted debt	75.0	45.0	0.60
Distressed debt	150.0	112.5	0.75
Total Public & Private	301.0	202.0	0.67

SUPPLY OF DISTRESSED SECURITIES

Over the last 20 years, the American bankrupt company profile has been transformed from the small, undercapitalized distressed firm situation to a system which increasingly involves large and in some cases huge enterprises with complex asset and liability structures. In a sense, 1970 was a watershed year with Penn Central, Dolly Madison, and a few other relatively large companies filing for bankruptcy protection. There have been about 100 enterprises with over $120 million in liabilities that have filed for bankruptcy in the last 20 years (table 22.2). In the 1970s we experienced increasing numbers of sizeable business failures in retailing, REITs and railroads. In the early 1980s the severe inflationary-recession caused a consistently increasing number of failures including manufacturers, airlines, farmers, and service firms of all types followed by the energy industry collapse. The Business Failure Rate rose from a low of 24 per 10,000 firms followed by Dun & Bradstreet in 1978 to 110 per 10,000 firms in 1983 and reached a high of 120 in 1986 (table 22.3 and figure 22.1). One would have to go back to 1932 for a year when the failure rate exceeded 100 per 10,000. Clearly, the economy, while enjoying an unprecedented consecutive number of positive GNP growth years over the last eight years, has also seen an increasing vulnerability to distress of firms in all size categories. This is due to severe chronic problems in a number of industries, the oil industry collapse, increasing global competition, a record number of business

Table 22.2 Largest US bankruptcies (as of February 1990)

Company	Liabilities ($ in millions)	Bankruptcy date
Texaco, Inc. (Incl. Capital Subs.)	21,603	Apr-87
Campeau Corp. (Allied & Federated)	9,947	Jan-90
Lomas Financial Corp.	6,127	Sep-89
LTV Corp. (Incl. LTV Int'l NV)	4,700	Jul-86
Penn Central Transportation Co.	3,300	Jun-70
Eastern Airlines	3,196	Mar-89
Drexel Burnham Lambert	3,000	Feb-90
Wickes	2,000	Apr-82
Global Marine Inc.	1,800	Jan-86
ITEL	1,700	Jan-81
Public Service, New Hampshire	1,700	Jan-88
Baldwin-United	1,600	Sep-83
Integrated Resources	1,600	Feb-90
Revco Corp.	1,500	Jul-88
Placid Oil	1,488	Apr-85
McLean Industries	1,270	Nov-86
Hillsborough Holdings (Jim Walter)	1,204	Dec-89
Bell National	1,203	Aug-85
GHR Energy Corp.	1,200	Jan-83
L. J. Hooker	1,200	Aug-89
Manville Corp.	1,116	Aug-82
Braniff Airlines (1)	1,100	May-82
Continental Airlines	1,100	Sep-83
W. T. Grant	1,000	Oct-75
Charter Co.	976	Apr-85
Allegheny International	845	Feb-88
North American Car Corp.	841	Dec-84
Seatrain Lines	785	Feb-81
A. H. Robins	775	Aug-85
Penrod Drilling	764	Apr-85
Storage Technologies	695	Oct-84
Coral Petroleum	682	May-83
Nucorp Energy	615	Jul-82
Continental Mortgage Investors	607	Mar-76
Evans	600	Mar-85
Allis Chalmers	570	Jun-87
United Merchants & Manufacturing	552	Jul-77
Coleco Corp.	536	Jul-88
Maxicare Health Plans	535	Mar-89
AM International	510	Apr-82
OPM Leasing	505	Mar-81
Bevill Bresler Schullman	498	Apr-85
Smith International Inc.	484	Mar-86
Saxon Industries	461	Apr-82
Commonwealth Oil Refining Co.	421	Mar-78
W. Judd Kassuba	420	Dec-73
Erie Lackawanna Railroad	404	Jun-72
White Motor Corp.	399	Sep-80
Sambo's Restaurants	370	Jun-81
Investors Funding Corp.	370	Oct-74
Todd Shipyards	350	Aug-87
AMAREX	348	Dec-82
Food Fair Corp.	347	Oct-78

Table 22.2 (cont'd)

Company	Liabilities ($ in millions)	Bankruptcy date
Buttes Oil & Gas	337	Nov-85
Great American Mortgage & Trust	326	Mar-77
McLouth Steel	323	Dec-81
World of Wonder	312	Dec-87
MGF Oil	304	Dec-84
U.S. Financial Services	300	Jul-73
Hunt International	295	Apr-85
Radice	291	Feb-88
Chase Manhattan Mort. & Realty Tr.	290	Feb-79
Daylin, Inc.	250	Feb-75
Guardian Mortgage Investors	247	Mar-78
Waterman Steamship Corp.	242	Dec-83
Revere Copper & Brass	237	Oct-82
Air Florida System	221	Jul-84
Chicago, Rock Island & Pacific	221	Mar-75
Hellenic Lines, Ltd.	216	Dec-83
Wilson Foods	213	Apr-83
Lion Capital Group	212	Apr-84
KDT Industries	203	Aug-82
Equity Funding Corp. of America	200	Apr-73
De Laurentis Entertainment	198	Aug-88
Trial America Corporation	198	Jan-87
Interstate Stores, Inc.	190	May-74
Fidelity Mortgage Investors	187	Jan-75
HRT Industries	183	Nov-82
Technical Equities Corp.	180	Feb-85
Braniff Airlines (2)	178	Sep-89
Terex Corp.	176	Mar-83
Lionel Corp.	175	Feb-82
Omega, Alpha Corp.	175	Sep-74
Marion Corp.	175	Mar-83
Michigan General	170	Apr-87
Dart Drug Stores	169	Aug-89
U.N.R. Industries	165	Jul-82
Thatcher Glass	165	Dec-84
Towner Petroleum	163	Sep-84
Otasco Inc.	163	Nov-88
Dreco Energy	161	Jun-82
Reading Railroad	158	Nov-71
Anglo Energy	155	Nov-83
Boston & Maine Railroad	148	Dec-75
Westgate-California	144	Feb-74
Pizza Time Theatre	143	Mar-84
Cook United, Inc.	143	Oct-84
Colwell Mortgage & Trust	142	Feb-78
Phoenix Steel Corp.	137	Aug-83
Pacific Far East Lines	132	Jan-78
Allied Supermarkets	124	Jun-77
Penn-Dixie Industries	122	Apr-80

Table 22.3 Failure trends

	Number of failures	Total failure liabilities ($)	Failure rate per 10,000 listed concerns	Average liability per failure ($)
1927	23,146	520,105,000	106	22,471
1928	23,842	489,559,000	109	20,534
1929	22,909	483,252,000	104	21,094
1930	26,355	668,282,000	122	25,357
1931	28,285	736,310,000	133	26,032
1932	31,822	928,313,000	154	29,172
1933	19,859	457,520,000	100	23,038
1934	12,091	333,959,000	61	27,621
1935	12,244	310,580,000	62	25,366
1936	9,607	203,173,000	48	21,148
1937	9,490	183,253,000	46	19,310
1938	12,836	246,505,000	61	19,204
1939	14,768	182,520,000	70	12,359
1940	13,619	166,684,000	63	12,239
1941	11,848	136,104,000	55	11,488
1942	9,405	100,763,000	45	10,713
1943	3,221	45,339,000	16	14,076
1944	1,222	31,660,000	7	25,908
1945	809	30,225,000	4	37,361
1946	1,129	67,349,000	5	59,654
1947	3,474	204,612,000	14	58,898
1948	5,250	234,620,000	20	44,690
1949	9,246	308,109,000	34	33,323
1950	9,162	248,283,000	34	27,099
1951	8,058	259,547,000	31	32,210
1952	7,611	283,314,000	29	37,224
1953	8,862	394,153,000	33	44,477
1954	11,086	462,628,000	42	41,731
1955	10,969	449,380,000	42	40,968
1956	12,686	562,697,000	48	44,356
1957	13,739	615,293,000	52	44,784
1958	14,964	728,258,000	56	48,667
1959	14,053	692,808,000	52	49,300
1960	15,445	938,630,000	57	60,772
1961	17,075	1,090,123,000	64	63,843
1962	15,782	1,213,601,000	61	76,898
1963	14,374	1,352,593,000	56	94,100
1964	13,501	1,329,223,000	53	98,454
1965	13,514	1,321,666,000	53	97,800
1966	13,061	1,385,659,000	52	106,091
1967	12,364	1,265,227,000	49	102,332
1968	9,636	940,996,000	39	97,654
1969	9,154	1,142,113,000	37	124,767
1970	10,748	1,887,754,000	44	175,638
1971	10,326	1,916,929,000	42	185,641
1972	9,566	2,000,244,000	38	209,099
1973	9,345	2,298,606,000	36	245,972
1974	9,915	3,053,137,000	38	307,931
1975	11,432	4,380,170,000	43	383,150
1976	9,628	3,011,271,000	35	312,762

Table 22.3 *(cont'd)*

	Number of failures	Total failure liabilities ($)	Failure rate per 10,000 listed concerns	Average liability per failure ($)
1977	7,919	3,095,317,000	28	390,872
1978	6,619	2,656,006,000	24	401,270
1979	7,564	2,667,362,000	28	352,639
1980	11,742	4,635,080,000	42	394,744
1981	16,794	6,955,180,000	61	414,147
1982	24,908	15,610,792,000	88	626,738
1983	31,334	16,072,860,000	110	512,953
1984	52,078	29,268,646,871	107	562,016
1985	57,253	36,937,369,478	115	645,160
1986	61,616	44,723,991,601	120	725,850
1987	61,111	34,723,831,429	102	568,209
1988ᵖ	57,098	36,012,765,369	98	630,719

Due to statistical revision, data prior to 1984 are not directly comparable with the new series.
ᵖ Preliminary.

Figure 22.1 Number of failures

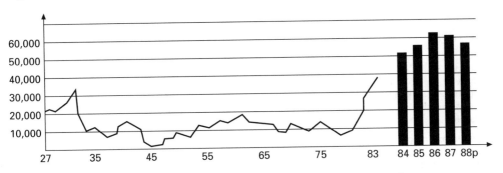

Source: The Dun & Bradstreet Corporation, *Business Failure Record*, 1988, p. 2.

start-ups, deregulation and the leverage excesses involving numerous corporate liability restructurings in the last few years.

The market for investing in distressed debt and equity securities has been growing dramatically with an outstanding market value of defaulted securities of about $13 billion as of January 1990 (table 22.4). The par value of the debt was about $26 billion. This compares with $4 billion in market value in 1984. The supply of defaulted debt has been swelled by over $24 billion par value of publicly traded straight debt in the last four years; $7.9 billion in 1989 alone and almost $4 billion in the first three months of 1990. Several billion dollars of defaulted convertible debt and equities in the last few years add to the total. And, the near term outlook bodes perhaps for even greater "growth."

While the par-value of such issues has increased substantially, a noticeable reduction in recovery rates on the sale of debt just after default, and deteriorating prices on some issues has tempered the market value growth, especially among the senior subordinated and subordinated debt issues. We estimate that the average recovery rate on senior,

senior subordinated and subordinated public debt was 55 percent, 32 percent and 32 percent, respectively, in the period 1985–89 but only about 23 percent for senior subordinated and subordinated debt in 1989 (table 22.5). The decline of recoveries on recent defaults of junior debt is probably due to the increased layers of debt and the general increase in the amount of indebtedness relative to asset values.

For several decades there has been curiosity and some interest for investors in bankrupt securities. Media stories of huge gains earned on bankrupt railroad and REIT securities and also on some equities, e.g., Toys-Я-Us, have fueled this attention. In

Table 22.4 Market value of securities (Companies in Chapter 11 reorganization and in default* 31 January 1990)

Security	Market value ($)
AMEX	
Bonds (19)	4,110,972,900
Convertible bonds (9)	356,894,550
Common stock (2)	33,634,500
Preferred stock (1)	678,100,875
Total (31)	5,179,602,825
Nasdaq (OTC)	
Bonds (101)	2,848,277,425
Convertible bonds (19)	85,177,200
Total (120)	2,933,454,625
NYSE	
Bonds (36)	3,885,197,588
Convertible bonds (13)	162,507,350
Common stock (11)	389,390,406
Preferred stock (6)	279,115,688
Total (66)	4,716,211,032
Total all exchanges (217)	12,829,268,482

Includes coupon bonds trading flat.
(number of companies)
Compilation: E. Altman and D. Chin, New York University, Stern School of Business.

Table 22.5 Recovery rates* on defaulted debt by seniority (1985–89)

Year	Secured		Senior		Senior subordinated		Subordinated	
1989	$82.69	(9)	$53.70	(16)	$21.53	(18)	$24.56	(29)
1988	67.96	(13)	41.59	(20)	29.23	(11)	36.42	(18)
1987	12.00	(1)	70.52**	(29)	51.22	(9)	40.54	(7)
1986	48.32	(7)	40.84	(7)	31.53	(8)	30.95	(33)
1985	74.25	(2)	34.81	(2)	36.18	(7)	41.45	(13)
Arith. Avg.	$66.451 (32)		$55.292** (74)		$31.614 (53)		$32.118 (100)	

(Number of issues)
Price per $100 of par value at end of default month.
***Without Texaco, 1987 Recovery = $29.77*
Arithmetic Average Senior Recovery = $43.11
Compilation by E. Altman & D. Chin, New York University.

addition to the interest of late caused by the sizeable increase in the breadth of this market, attention is being given by a relatively small number of professionals to deeply discounted but not defaulted debt issues and, even more intriguing, to the bank and trade debt claims of defaulted companies. Oftentimes, these issues have significant intrinsic value and potential profits.

In order to estimate the ratio of private to public debt, we examined the capital structures of 103 bankrupt firms. We found that this ratio was just under 4-to-1 for the entire sample and a bit over 3-to-1 for those firms (68) that had public debt outstanding. Among the large LBO defaults of late and for those expected to fail in the next few years, the ratio of bank debt to public debt is about 1.5-to-1, indicating that these defaults, caused mainly by leverage excesses, relied on public debt to a greater extent than did the more traditional business failure of the 1970s and early to mid-1980s. With several strata of senior and subordinated debt, the recovery rates after default on the most junior issues have declined.

DISTRESSED SECURITIES INVESTOR PROFILE

With the big increase in the supply of distressed securities and their likely continued growth, new investors and capital have been attracted. Our survey results indicate that there is at least $5 billion under active management by investment firms dedicated to the distressed securities field. Assorted other investors trade these securities, many times involuntarily. Of the responding companies that indicated their dollar commitment to distressed securities investing, the majority had $20–100 million under management. Many of these institutions are specialized groups of large money management firms. While as many as 12 invested less than $20 million and 13 are investing $100–300 million, there are just two with over $300 million dedicated to this area. A full list of investors is available in the complete report on this market.

The investors represent numerous types of organizations including private partnerships (the most common type), open-end mutual funds, closed-end funds, special groups within larger fund operations, broker-dealer pools of funds, departments of commercial and investment banks, arbitrageurs and other firms looking to take over distressed companies at bargain prices. In addition, there are always funds available from other investment vehicles which can be shifted to distressed securities purchases when opportunities present themselves. For instance, some LBO funds now seek out other vehicles as the highly leveraged restructuring movement is reduced in scope and relegated to smaller, privately financed deals.

The overwhelming majority of these investors specialize in debt securities with most investing 85–100 percent of their assets in debt. In many cases, however, the initial debt purchase will evolve into an equity interest in a distressed exchange issue or bankruptcy reorganization. In addition, over 80 percent (46 of 56) of the respondents indicated that they analyze and either invest in or are considering investing in the private debt of distressed companies.

Most investors have become somewhat more active in addition to continuing to operate under the traditional passive investment strategy. This indicates that they are more inclined now to seek either control of the restructuring process and even the company itself, as well as having an influence on the choice of management and setting the terms of the reorganization or the restructuring plan. This movement toward active, and even proactive, investing is one of the emerging trends in investments in general, and in particular, in the distressed securities field. A pre-packaged Chapter 11, e.g., Resorts International, is an example of this, as well as the creditor motivated plan of Coleco Industries.

An increasing number of firms are relative newcomers to the field. Of 56 respondents to our survey, eight were in business for less than one year and 19 for less than two years. A majority of portfolio managers of these new firms, however, had considerable experience in more established institutions before striking out with new institutions. While the number of new entities and inexperienced portfolio managers is troubling to certain established investors, experienced firms who have been in business for more than five years number an impressive 22 with seven in business for over 20 years.

RETURNS ON DISTRESSED SECURITIES

Just about anyone who has analyzed the distressed security market concludes that this is not a market for amateurs and that in order to attract new investment dollars, it is necessary to earn extraordinary returns. The risky nature of the business, the relatively poor liquidity of the issues and the costly skills required lead to high minimum required rates of return as hurdle rates. We queried our distressed investor sample as to their minimum and target rates of return. As expected, the target rates of return were, on average, higher than the minimum, although many respondents gave identical answers to both questions. The most common response was a target return of 30 percent and a minimum return of 20–25 percent. Indeed, 17 of 50 (about one-third) respondents had a 30 percent target return with the other two-thirds split fairly evenly below and above 30 percent. About two-thirds of the investors required a minimum rate of return of either 20 percent or 25 percent, with most of the remainder seeking higher returns.

INVESTMENT STRATEGIES

Along with the impressive increase in the market's size and diversity, perhaps the major interest in distressed public and private securities has developed from the reports of extremely attractive returns earned by a small number of astute investors. Despite the recent increase in new investors and capital, the formula for successful investing will continue to be a difficult set of fundamental valuation and technical legal-economic skills complemented by a patient and disciplined approach to asset management. These fundamentals are also important in the less efficient private bank and trade debt markets, although negotiating skills will also be rewarded.

Our examination of past studies and new tests shows that extraordinary gains over relevant alternative investment opportunities can be earned with a disciplined and careful credit and asset valuation strategy, concentrating on firms where the probability of successful reorganization or restructuring is high.

Several studies on bankrupt equity securities have shown that returns from firms achieving a successful reorganization were exceptionally high, but that for the entire sample the overall return was about equal to relevant equity opportunity costs. Indeed, in many cases the equity is essentially wiped out with the old creditors becoming the new equity holders. The sample variability of these equity returns was extremely high.

Results from the few defaulted debt studies available show that excess returns (total returns adjusted for opportunity returns in other risky debt markets) start to be negative from about 18 months prior to default, become very steeply negative five months before and tend to bottom out about six months after the default date. The excess returns then start to rise from month six to month 10, fall again from month 10 to 16 and then rise consistently to month 24 after default (figure 22.2). A strategy to buy just after default results in a positive excess return of about 7.5 percent over the two-year post-default period, but the excess return was about 16 percent from month six to 24. Distressed exchange debt issues also show good recoveries but only after the 17th month after the exchange.

Our new tests concentrate on distressed, not defaulted, debt whereby distressed is defined as a security with a current yield of 10 percent above comparable US Treasury bonds. In all, 310 issues qualified over an 11-year sample period, 1978–89. Incredibly over one-half of these distressed securities eventually defaulted. The key to successful investing is either to avoid as many defaults as possible or to invest in those which do default but are successfully reorganized. Indeed, a "blind" naive strategy of investing in all distressed bonds yields very poor returns, but avoiding the minefields brings substantial rewards.

Table 22.6 shows the results of some of our tests indicating absolute and excess (residual) returns on the naive strategy (panel A). Panel B shows the exceptionally high returns (29.7 percent, 67.6 percent and 90.3 percent for one-, two- and three-year periods) possible if all defaults are avoided. Panels C and D show the returns when using an objective credit evaluation scoring system to eliminate the most risky securities. We use the ZETA® credit evaluation system. Note the impressive results, revealing very positive absolute returns but, due to the small sample size, not always statistically significant residual returns.

These tests show that a prudent, disciplined credit approach can be successfully utilized in the distressed security arena. Techniques like ZETA® can be combined with other security selection approaches, including in-depth financial and legal analysis, to increase the relevant set of securities. Our tests do not, however, involve returns on securities allocated to the debt holders after a reorganization takes place, i.e., from a

Figure 22.2 Cumulative excess returns on defaults only, 1977–88

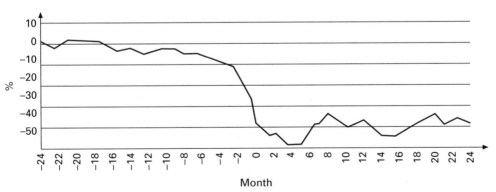

Source: G. Hradsky and R. Long, "High Yield Default Losses and the Return Performance of Bankrupt Debt," *Financial Analysts Journal*, July–August 1989, p. 46.

Table 22.6 Performance results for various strategies of investing in distressed debt securities (1978–89)

	Gross return (%)/Months after distress						Residual return (%)/Months After distress					
	6	12	18	24	30	36	6	12	18	24	30	36
A. Invest in all high yield spread issues												
Return	(7.2)	2.0	9.2	22.7	29.6	35.2	(14.1)	(15.2)	(16.4)	(9.7)	(12.5)	(18.1)
No. of Issues	310	251	199	160	114	83	310	251	199	160	114	83
Significant (.05)*							Yes	Yes	Yes	No	Yes	Yes
B. Invest in all non-defaulting high yield spread issues												
Return	7.1	29.7	45.4	67.6	80.2	90.3	0.4	10.5	14.8	30.1	28.6	26.8
No. of Issues	132	93	76	67	49	39	132	93	76	67	49	39
Significant (.05)*							No	Yes	Yes	Yes	Yes	Yes
C. Invest in positive ZETA® distressed high yield issues												
Return	15.4	23.6	45.7	43.2	68.1	79.1	3.1	1.1	15.1	8.1	22.1	22.7
No. of Issues	10	9	9	9	8	8	10	9	9	9	8	8
Significant (.05)*							No	No	No	No	No	No
D. Invest in ZETA® > –1 distressed high yield issues												
Return	17.6	24.2	37.3	44.9	68.4	72.9	5.4	1.0	7.9	9.8	20.7	23.8
No. of Issues	31	29	26	24	17	16	31	29	26	24	17	16
Significant (.05)*							No	No	No	No	Yes	No

$* t = \dfrac{\bar{x}}{\sigma/\sqrt{N}}$, at .05 level, approximately 2. Compilation: E. Altman & T. Ng, NYU Stern School of Business.

typical package of cash, debt and new equity. And, we utilize bond prices reported by the rating services in their bond publications. Due to poor liquidity in many of these issues, actual prices may differ.

We also constructed an index of defaulted debt securities, based on a market weighted basis. The index was based on an initial sample of 23 defaulted debt securities in January 1986 and increased to as much as 118 issues in late 1989. Investors in this market index of defaulted publicly traded debt received a compound annual return of 26 percent per year over the period 1986–89, despite a poor year in 1989. This was, coincidentally, about equal to our respondents' most frequent answer to the question regarding required rates of return on investments in distressed debt securities. In this four-year period, the larger issues did considerably better than the small ones (table 22.7). The performance of the defaulted debt index (DD) is illustrated in figure 22.3.

Table 22.7 Returns on defaulted debt securities indices (1986–89)

Period	Average number of securities	Annual return (marked weighted average) (%)	Annual return (marked weighted average)* (%)	Annual return (unweighted average) (%)
1986	51	12.7	12.7	−4.2
1987	61	53.0	38.9	26.0
1988	89	44.5	44.5	19.0
1989	106	2.4	−9.7	−16.5
1986–89				
Compound	77	26.3	20.0	4.7
Arithmetic	77	28.2	21.6	6.1

* Without Texaco and Public Service of New Hampshire issues.

Figure 22.3 Defaulted debt* (DD) performance vs. high yield debt** and S&P stock indices (1986–89)

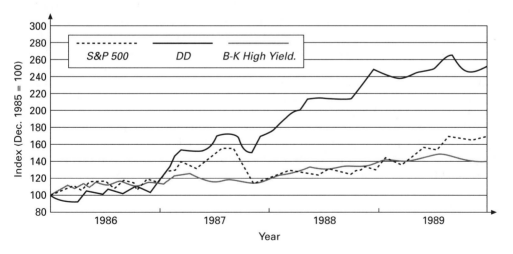

* Market Weighted Index
** Blume-Keim High Yield Index

The distressed securities index had relatively low correlations with other debt and equity returns indices. Attractive diversification attributes appear to be present for investors who combine distressed security investing with other asset classes. The correlations between our distressed index and several others are given in table 22.8. Note that all correlations were less than 0.5, some considerably less.

While no data exists for investment returns on private debt and trade claims, the supposition is reasonable that even higher returns are possible since the market is less efficient.

Table 22.8 Correlation matrix between defaulted debt security returns and various equity and high yield bond returns (Monthly Return Observations, 1986–89)

	Defaulted debt	S&P 500 equity	Value line equity	Blume–Keim (HY)	First Boston (HY)
Defaulted debt	1.00	0.25	0.47	0.37	0.42
S&P 500 equity	0.25	1.00	0.76	0.46	0.40
Value line equity	0.47	0.76	1.00	0.59	0.65
Blume–Keim (HY)	0.37	0.46	0.59	1.00	0.89
First Boston (HY)	0.42	0.40	0.65	0.89	1.00

Compilation: E. Altman & E. Katzman, NYU Stern School of Business.

MARKET IMPORTANCE AND OUTLOOK

The bankruptcy-reorganization system in the USA is a unique process, affording rehabilitative opportunities to distressed, yet productive, entities. The market for distressed firm securities reflects this process and, in a sense, monitors the system's performance. By providing continuous feedback as to the distressed company's progress, it actually helps to facilitate the allocation of new capital to the most promising uses. Investors, operating in their own best interest, are unwittingly contributing to this process.

The outlook for the future is somewhat mixed in the short run as the supply of new opportunities will likely exceed the amount of new capital allocated to distressed issues. This supply-demand situation has already contributed to some softening in prices in the last 14 months. Several distressed investors, however, have the impression that the relative number of promising new reorganizations is small with too much money chasing these situations. While this phenomenon may exist in the near term, this observer and the vast majority of our respondents expressed enthusiasm and optimism about future profit potential, especially in the longer run. In addition, the market for private bank and trade debt claims promises to provide excellent prospects. The key, as always, is to be able to select the successful reorganizations and undervalued securities.

23 Defaults and Returns on High Yield Bonds: Analysis Through 2000 and Default Outlook*

with Brenda Karlin

INTRODUCTION AND OVERVIEW

The year 2000 was one of the most difficult years for the high yield bond market in the USA since we began studying this market, a sample period of 30 years. Total returns were a dismal −5.68 percent, second only to the poorest absolute return year of 1990 (−8.46 percent) and the return spread of −20.13 percent was easily the worst in history. New issuance of high yield bonds dropped considerably from 1999's impressive level and was reduced to a trickle by the end of the year as promised yields soared to about 14.5 percent, almost 9.5 percent above the risk-free rate – again the highest since 1990.

Defaults registered its second straight record year in terms of absolute amounts and topped $30 billion for the first time. Still, the default rate, though rising to about 5.0 percent, was just half that of the record years of 1990 and 1991. Combined with a relatively low recovery rate of 26.4 percent, also second lowest to 1990, the default loss rate was 3.9 percent, above the weighted average annual rate of about 2.5 percent and about double the arithmetic average of about 2.0 percent per year. Average annual return spreads (above the risk-free rate) dropped to below 2.0 percent per year, still quite decent but almost a full percentage point per year less than just one year ago.

This report documents the high yield bond market's risk and return performance by presenting traditional and mortality default rate statistics and providing a matrix of performance data over the market's evolution and growth. Our analysis covers the 1971–2000 period for default and the 1978–2000 period for returns. In addition, we present our annual forecast of expected defaults. Although we expected high defaults in

* We wish to thank Chris McHugh of New Generation Research, Wilson Miranda, Sau Man Kam and Gabriella Petrucci of Salomon Smith Barney Inc. for their data assistance and also the many securities dealers for their price quotations. Finally, this report benefits from the assistance of Keith Cyrus, Aashish Mohan and Lourdes Tanglao of the NYU Salomon Center.

1999, we underestimated just how difficult the year would be as several new industries emerged as troubled, asbestos-related defaults reemerged after being dormant for many years and the flight to quality continued for the third year in a row (since August 1998).

For 2001, we are concerned about the proportion of the market that appears to be distressed and also a softening economy. We expect defaults to again set a record absolute level and perhaps rise to above $40 billion and the default rate to 6.5–7.0 percent. Although there are several parallels in 2000 to 1990, the default carnage is not expected to reach such a "lofty" rate as a decade earlier. When this becomes apparent in 2001, or perhaps even before the peak of defaults, we expect a reversal in total returns and return spreads. And, required yield spreads at the end of the year appear to be factoring in default rate expectations that are higher than we expect.

DEFAULT LEVELS AND RATES

In 2000, a record $30.25 billion of developed country high yield straight bonds defaulted or restructured under distressed conditions. This amount comprised 183 issues from 106 defaulting companies and resulted in a default rate of 5.07 percent. This compares to $23.5 billion on 149 issues from 100 companies in 1999. A list of 2000 defaults appears in table 23.1.[1] The 2000 default rate is somewhat higher than last year's rate (4.15 percent), above the historic weighted average annual rate from 1971–2000 of 3.48 percent per year (2.7 percent arithmetic average rate), and is also above the median annual rate (1.66 percent) over the same 30-year period (table 23.2 and figure 23.1). The face value of defaults reached record levels, topping the 1999 amount by almost $7 billion and exceeding 1991's previous record by almost $12 billion. Of course, the high yield market is now about three times larger than it was in 1991. The default rate calculation is based on a mid-year population of high yield bonds, estimated to be $597.2 billion. The default rate in 2000 provides a two-year string of record defaults and higher than average default rates, which followed a six-year period of below average rates. We will return shortly to a discussion of this sizeable increase.

Quarterly Defaults

In tables 23.3 and 23.4 and figure 23.2, we present default rates on a quarterly basis from 1990 to 2000. It can be observed that the quarterly default levels and rates in 2000 were consistently high (except perhaps in the third quarter) with the second and fourth quarters' levels at about $10 billion each; both were around 1.65 percent. As noted in our earlier reports, quarterly rates are usually not indicative of trends except possibly back in the 1990–91 period when default rates skyrocketed to record levels over several

---

[1] We do not include emerging market defaults in these calculations. All defaults were US, Canada, Australia, or offshore US dollar denominated issues from domestic companies. European company defaults, denominated in non-USD currencies totaling 738 million Euros are not included. If they were included as well as the Euro-High-Yield population of over $30 billion, the default rate would be 4.93 percent (see D. Newman and T. Crawley, *European High Yield Default Study – 2001*, Schroder Salomon Smith Barney (Europe), January 2001. In addition, consistent with our past approach, we do not include those issues that missed interest payments in 2000 but cured their delinquencies within the typical 30-day grace period and we indicate (table 23.1) those that missed their payment in December.

Table 23.1 2000 Defaulted corporate straight debt (by date of default)

Company	Bond issue	Coupon (%)	Maturity date	Outstanding amount ($ MM)	Default date
Altiva Financial Corporation	Subordinated Notes	12.500	12/1/02	31.0	1/1/00
Imperial Home Decor Group	Guaranteed Senior Subordinated Notes	11.00	3/15/08	125.0	1/5/00
PennCorp Financial Group, Inc.	Senior Subordinated Notes	9.250	12/15/03	150.0	1/10/00
Safety Components International, Inc.	Senior Subordinated Notes	10.125	7/15/07	90.0	1/15/00
Ameriserve – Ameriserve Foods, Inc.	Guaranteed Senior Notes	8.875	10/15/06	350.0	1/31/00
	Guaranteed Senior Subordinated Notes	10.125	7/15/07	500.0	1/31/00
Ameriserve – Ameriserve Financial[n]	Senior Secured Notes – Euro-Dollar	12.000	9/15/06	205.0	1/31/00
Ameriserve – Nebco Evans Holding Co.[a]	Senior Discount Notes	12.375	7/15/07	74.5	1/31/00
Phase Metrics, Inc.	Senior Notes	10.750	2/1/05	110.0	2/1/00
Paging Network, Inc.	Senior Subordinated Notes	8.875	2/1/06	300.0	2/1/00
	Senior Subordinated Notes	10.000	10/15/08	500.0	2/1/00
	Senior Subordinated Notes	10.125	8/1/07	400.0	2/1/00
Pen-Tab Industries, Inc.	Senior Subordinated Notes	10.875	2/1/07	75.0	2/1/00
Canadian Airlines	Senior Notes[b]	10.000	5/1/05	175.0	2/1/00
	Senior Notes	12.250	8/1/06	100.0	2/1/00
CellNet Data Systems	Senior Discount Notes[c]	0.000	6/15/05	223.3	2/4/00
	Senior Discount Notes[d]	0.000	10/1/07	452.6	2/4/00
Paracelsus Healthcare Corp.	Senior Subordinated Notes	10.000	8/15/06	325.0	2/15/00
Prime Succession, Inc.	Senior Subordinated Notes	10.750	8/15/04	100.0	2/15/00
Eagle Food Center, Inc.	Senior Notes	8.625	4/15/00	100.0	2/29/00
Superior National Insurance	Guaranteed Senior Notes	10.750	12/1/17	105.0	3/8/00
United Homes, Inc.	Debentures	11.000	3/15/05	6.8	3/9/00
LaRoche Industries, Inc.	Senior Subordinated Notes	9.500	9/15/07	175.0	3/15/00
Crown Vantage, Inc.	Senior Subordinated Notes	11.000	9/1/05	250.0	3/15/00
	Senior PIK Notes	11.450	12/31/07	110.1	3/15/00
President Casinos	Guaranteed Senior Notes	13.000	9/15/01	75.0	3/15/00
	Senior Secured Notes	12.000	9/15/01	25.0	3/15/00
Key Plastics, Inc.	Guaranteed Senior Subordinated Notes	10.250	3/15/07	125.0	3/23/00
ContiFinancial Corp.	Senior Notes	7.500	3/15/02	200.0	3/30/00
	Senior Notes	8.125	4/1/08	200.0	3/30/00
	Senior Notes	8.375	8/15/03	300.0	3/30/00
Genesis Health	Senior Subordinated Notes[e]	9.250	10/1/06	125.0	4/1/00
	Senior Subordinated Notes	9.750	6/15/05	120.0	4/1/00
	Senior Subordinated Notes	9.875	1/15/09	125.0	4/1/00
	First Mortgage Bonds	9.250	9/1/07	25.0	4/1/00

Table 23.1 (cont'd)

Company	Bond issue	Coupon (%)	Maturity date	Outstanding amount ($ MM)	Default date
Genesis Health – Multicare Co.	Senior Subordinated Notes	9.000	8/1/07	250.0	4/1/00
CHS Electronics, Inc.	Guaranteed Senior Notes	9.875	4/15/05	200.0	4/4/00
Vista Eyecare, Inc.	Senior Notes	12.750	10/15/05	125.0	4/5/00
Dimac Direct, Inc. – Dimac Holdings Corp.	Senior Subordinated Notes	12.500	10/1/08	100.0	4/6/00
Medical Resources, Inc.[s]	Senior Notes	7.770	2/20/05	75.0	4/7/00
Uniforet, Inc.[b]	Senior Secured Notes	11.125	10/15/06	125.0	4/10/00
Hedstrom Holdings, Inc.	Guaranteed Senior Subordinated Notes	10.000	6/1/07	110.0	4/11/00
	Senior Discount Notes[f]	0.000	6/1/09	36.5	4/11/00
Silver Cinemas International, Inc.	Senior Subordinated Notes	10.500	4/15/05	99.6	4/15/00
Employee Solutions	Guaranteed Senior Notes	10.000	10/15/04	85.0	4/15/00
Glenoit Corp.	Guaranteed Senior Subordinated Notes	11.000	4/15/07	100.0	4/15/00
United Artists Theatre	Senior Subordinated Notes	10.415[k]	10/15/07	50.0	4/15/00
	Senior Subordinated Notes	9.750	4/15/08	225.0	4/15/00
	Pass Thru Certs	9.300	7/1/15	107.7	4/15/00
Clark Material Handling Co.	Guaranteed Senior Notes	10.750	11/15/06	150.0	4/17/00
Zeta Consumer Products	Senior Notes	11.250	11/30/07	85.0	4/25/00
Kitty Hawk, Inc.	Senior Secured Notes	9.950	11/15/04	340.0	5/1/00
Pathmark Stores	Senior Subordinated Notes	9.625	5/1/03	438.8	5/1/00
	Junior Subordinated Notes	10.750	11/1/03	225.3	5/1/00
Packaging Resources	Senior Secured Notes	11.625	5/1/03	110.0	5/1/00
Stellex Technologies, Inc.	Senior Subordinated Notes	9.500	11/1/07	100.0	5/1/00
Cambridge Industries, Inc.	Senior Subordinated Notes	10.250	7/15/07	100.0	5/10/00
American Eco Corp.	Guaranteed Senior Notes	9.625	5/15/08	120.0	5/15/00
Sunterra Corp.	Senior Notes	9.250	5/15/06	140.0	5/16/00
	Senior Subordinated Notes	9.750	10/1/07	200.0	5/16/00
GST Telecommunications, Inc.	Senior Discount Notes[g]	0.000	5/1/08	370.4	5/17/00
	Senior Subordinated Accrual Notes[h]	12.750	11/15/07	165.3	5/17/00
	Senior Secured Notes	13.250	5/1/07	265.0	5/17/00
	Senior Discount Notes[i]	0.000	12/15/05	289.8	5/17/00
Morris Material Handling, Inc.	Guaranteed Senior Notes	9.500	4/1/08	200.0	5/17/00
Laidlaw, Inc.	Debentures[b]	6.500	5/1/05	200.0	5/18/00
	Debentures	6.650	10/1/04	225.0	5/18/00
	Debentures	6.700	5/1/08	100.0	5/18/00
	Debentures	6.720	10/1/27	200.0	5/18/00
	Notes	7.050	5/15/03	100.0	5/18/00

Company	Bond Type	Coupon	Maturity	Amount	Default Date
Laidlaw, Inc. (cont'd)	Notes	7.650	5/15/06	400.0	5/18/00
	Debentures	7.700	8/15/02	200.0	5/18/00
	Debentures	7.875	4/15/05	150.0	5/18/00
	Debentures	8.250	5/15/23	100.0	5/18/00
	Debentures	8.750	4/15/25	150.0	5/18/00
	Debentures – CAD[j]	8.500	12/16/02	66.7	5/18/00
	Debentures – CAD[j]	10.950	4/16/01	83.4	5/18/00
Safety-Kleen Corp.	Guaranteed Senior Notes	9.250	6/1/08	325.0	5/18/00
	Guaranteed Senior Notes	9.250	5/15/09	225.0	5/18/00
American Architectural Products Corp.	Senior Notes	11.750	12/1/07	125.0	6/1/00
Fine Air Services, Inc.	Guaranteed Senior Notes	9.875	6/1/08	200.0	6/1/00
Master Graphics – Premier Graphics, Inc.	Guaranteed Senior Notes	11.500	12/1/05	130.0	6/1/00
Mediq, Inc.	Senior Subordinated Notes	11.000	6/1/08	190.0	6/1/00
Mediq, Inc.[m]	Senior Discount Notes	0.000	6/1/09	87.0	6/1/00
Stage Stores – Specialty Retailers, Inc.	Guaranteed Senior Notes	8.500	7/15/05	200.0	6/1/00
	Guaranteed Senior Subordinated Notes	9.000	7/15/07	100.0	6/1/00
Stage Stores – 3 Bealls Holding Corp.	Notes	12.000	12/31/02	6.0	6/1/00
Iowa Select Farms	Senior Subordinated Notes	10.750	12/1/05	130.0	6/1/00
Cuddy Int'l Corp.	Senior Notes	10.750	12/1/07	75.0	6/1/00
Gothic Energy Corp.[l]	Senior Discount Notes	0.000	5/1/06	80.4	6/5/00
Safelite Glass Corp.	Senior Subordinated Notes, Ser. B	9.875	12/15/06	100.0	6/9/00
	Senior Subordinated Notes, Ser. D	9.875	12/15/06	55.0	6/9/00
Pathmark Stores	Subordinated Notes	11.625	6/15/02	199.0	6/15/00
	Subordinated Notes	12.625	6/15/02	95.8	6/15/00
	Senior Secured Notes	12.500	12/15/08	185.0	6/15/00
Bulong Operations[b]	Senior Notes	9.250	10/15/07	71.0	6/16/00
Flooring America, Inc.	Debentures	9.000	12/31/07	9.7	6/30/00
All Star Gas Corp.	Senior Notes	12.750	6/1/04	92.8	7/10/00
Waxman Industries, Inc.	Senior Notes	11.125	9/1/01	35.9	7/10/00
Waxman USA, Inc.	Senior Subordinated Notes	10.875	11/1/02	25.0	7/11/00
Reliant Building Products, Inc.	Senior Unsecured Notes	10.875	7/15/05	75.0	7/15/00
CNI Group, Inc.	Senior Secured Notes	12.875	7/15/04	127.2	7/15/00
All Star Gas Corp. – Empire Gas Corp.	Senior Subordinated Notes	9.375	2/1/09	198.0	8/1/00
Carmike Cinemas, Inc.	Unsecured Notes	7.400	2/15/02	100.0	8/1/00
Heilig-Meyers Co. – MacSaver Fin'l	Unsecured Notes	7.600	8/1/07	175.0	8/1/00
	Unsecured Notes	7.875	8/1/03	200.0	8/1/00
Tokheim Corp.	Senior Subordinated Notes[n]	11.375	8/1/08	8.3	8/1/00
	Guaranteed Senior Subordinated Notes	11.375	8/1/08	114.7	8/1/00
Globe Manufacturing Corp.	Guaranteed Senior Subordinated Notes	10.000	8/1/08	150.0	8/1/00
Globe Manufacturing Corp. – Globe Hldgs[o]	Senior Discount Notes	0.000	8/1/09	34.4	8/1/00

Table 23.1 (cont'd)

Company	Bood issue	Coupon (%)	Maturity date	Outstanding amount ($ MM)	Default date
Anacomp, Inc.	Senior Subordinated Notes, Ser. D	10.875	4/1/04	135.0	8/3/00
	Senior Subordinated Notes, Ser. B	10.875	4/1/04	200.0	8/3/00
Coram Healthcare Corp.[s]	Subordinated Notes	11.500	5/15/01	168.4	8/8/00
Anchor Advanced Products, Inc.	Senior Notes	11.750	4/1/04	50.0	8/8/00
Orbcomm Global LP	Senior Notes	14.000	8/15/04	170.0	8/15/00
Central European Media Enterprises, Ltd.	Senior Notes[q]	8.125	8/15/04	65.4	8/15/00
	Senior Notes	9.375	8/15/04	100.0	8/15/00
Styling Technology Corp.	Guaranteed Senior Subordinated Notes	10.875	7/1/08	100.0	8/31/00
Plainwell, Inc.	Senior Subordinated Notes; Ser. B	11.000	3/1/08	130.0	9/1/00
Amer Reefer Company, Ltd.	1st Mortgage Notes	10.250	3/1/08	100.0	9/1/00
AMF Bowling Worldwide	Guaranteed Senior Subordinated Notes	10.875	3/15/06	250.0	9/15/00
	Senior Discount Notes[p]	0.000	3/15/06	333.0	9/15/00
Resort at Summerlin	Senior Subordinated Notes	13.000	12/15/07	120.2	9/15/00
SFAC New Holdings	Senior Secured Discount Notes[t]	0.000	6/15/09	336.0	9/18/00
	Senior Notes	11.250	8/15/01	170.8	9/18/00
	Senior Subordinated Notes	13.250	8/15/03	201.0	9/18/00
Dyersburg Corp.	Guaranteed Senior Subordinated Notes	9.750	9/1/07	125.0	9/25/00
Galaxy Telecom L.P.	Senior Subordinated Notes	12.375	10/1/05	120.0	9/28/00
Kasper ASL, Ltd.	Senior Notes	13.000	3/31/04	110.0	9/30/00
Owens-Corning – Fiberglass[u]	Debentures	5.375	11/26/00	7.1	10/5/00
Owens Corning	Notes	7.000	3/15/09	250.0	10/5/00
Owens-Corning – Fiberglass[v]	Debentures	7.250	12/2/00	57.8	10/5/00
Owens Corning	Notes	7.500	5/1/05	300.0	10/5/00
	Bonds	7.500	8/1/18	400.0	10/5/00
	Notes	7.700	5/1/08	250.0	10/5/00
Owens-Corning – Fiberglass	Debentures	8.875	6/1/02	40.0	10/5/00
	Debentures	9.375	6/1/12	7.0	10/5/00
	Bonds	9.900	5/15/15	69.2	10/5/00
OC Funding BV	Guaranteed Subordinated Notes	10.000	6/1/01	42.4	10/5/00
Drypers Corp.	Senior Notes	10.250	6/15/07	145.0	10/10/00
Indesco International, Inc.	Senior Subordinated Notes	9.750	4/15/08	145.0	10/15/00
Compass Aerospace Corp.	Guaranteed Subordinated Notes; Ser. D	10.125	4/15/05	19.0	10/15/00
	Guaranteed Subordinated Notes; Ser. B	10.125	4/15/05	110.0	10/15/00
Talon Automotive Group, Inc.	Senior Subordinated Notes	9.675	5/1/08	120.0	11/1/00

Company	Bond Type	Coupon	Maturity	Amount	Date
Decora Industries, Inc.	Senior Secured Notes	11.000	5/1/05	112.8	11/1/00
Colorado Prime Corp.	Senior Notes	11.000	5/1/08	225.0	11/1/00
Global Health Sciences	Senior Notes	12.500	5/1/04	100.0	11/1/00
ICG Communications Corp. – ICG Holdings, Inc.	Senior Discount Notes	13.500	9/15/05	584.3	11/14/00
	Senior Discount Notes^w	0.000	5/1/06	521.6	11/14/00
	Senior Discount Notes^x	0.000	3/15/07	151.7	11/14/00
	Senior Discount Notes^y	0.000	2/15/08	394.0	11/14/00
	Senior Discount Notes^z	0.000	5/1/08	320.0	11/14/00
Pillowtex Corp.	Guaranteed Senior Subordinated Notes	10.000	11/15/06	125.0	11/14/00
	Guaranteed Senior Subordinated Notes	9.000	12/15/07	185.0	11/14/00
Sunbeam Corporation	Senior Discount Notes	0.000	5/15/01	3.2	11/15/00
Park 'N' View, Inc.	Senior Notes	13.000	5/15/08	75.0	11/15/00
Reliance Group Holdings, Inc.	Senior Notes	9.000	11/15/49	291.0	11/15/00
	Senior Subordinated Debentures	9.750	11/15/03	174.0	11/15/00
Lodestar Holdings, Inc.	Senior Notes	11.500	5/15/05	150.0	11/15/00
Wheeling-Pittsburgh Corp.	Senior Notes	9.250	11/15/07	274.5	11/16/00
	Senior Notes	10.500	4/15/05	302.0	11/16/00
Metal Management, Inc.	Senior Secured Notes	12.750	6/15/04	30.0	11/20/00
	Guaranteed Senior Subordinated Notes	10.000	5/15/08	180.0	11/20/00
	Senior Subordinated Notes	11.000	2/15/04	80.0	11/22/00
Big V Supermarkets	Guaranteed Senior Subordinated Notes	11.750	8/1/05	200.0	11/29/00
Lernout & Hauspie Speech Products N.V.	Senior Subordinated Notes	9.500	6/1/08	600.0	12/1/00
Regal Cinemas, Inc.*	Senior Subordinated Notes	11.500	12/1/06	52.0	12/4/00
Gorges/Quick-to-Fix Foods, Inc.	Senior Secured Notes	12.000	1/15/03	100.0	12/7/00
RBX Corp.	Guaranteed Senior Subordinated Notes	11.250	10/15/05	100.0	12/7/00
Regal Cinemas, Inc.*	Senior Subordinated Notes	8.875	12/15/10	200.0	12/15/00
Imperial Sugar Co.*	Guaranteed Senior Subordinated Notes	9.750	12/15/07	250.0	12/15/00
Quentra Networks – Diane Corp.	Debentures	11.250	1/1/02	1.3	12/15/00
Pioneer Americas Acquisition Corp.*	Senior Secured Notes	9.250	6/15/07	200.0	12/15/00
Worldtex, Inc.*	Senior Notes	9.625	12/15/07	175.0	12/15/00
Global Telesystems, Inc.	Senior Notes*^aa	10.875	6/15/08	150.0	12/15/00
	Senior Notes*^aa	11.000	6/15/08	68.6	12/15/00
Northwestern Steel & Wire Company	Senior Notes	9.500	6/15/01	115.0	12/15/00
Outboard Marine Corp.	Medium Term Notes	8.675	3/15/01	5.0	12/22/00
	Guaranteed Senior Notes	10.750	6/1/08	160.0	12/22/00
	Debentures	9.125	4/15/17	57.6	12/22/00
REV Holdings, Inc.	Senior Discount Notes	0.000	3/15/01	770.0	12/25/00
LTV Corp.	Guaranteed Senior Notes	8.200	9/15/07	300.0	12/29/00
	Guaranteed Senior Subordinated Notes	11.750	11/15/09	275.0	12/29/00
			Total	30,247.8	

Table 23.1 (cont'd)

Armstrong World defaulted on $50mm in commercial paper on 11/23/00. This triggered a cross-default with $450mm credit facility. Armstrong is not included in 2000 calculations because the company was still rated "investment grade" as of 9/30/00. As of 11/23/00, the company had $832.185mm in bonds outstanding.

* Coupon payment is under grace period.

a Zero coupon until 7/02, 12.375 percent thereafter. Face value $100.4 million. Accreted value at default $74.5 million. Subsidiary of Ameriserve Foods.

b Yankee Bond.

c Zero coupon until 6/15/00, 13 percent thereafter. Face value $235 million. Accreted value at default approximately $223.3 million.

d Zero coupon until 10/02, 14 percent thereafter. Face value $654.1 million. Accreted value at default $452.6 million.

e Forebearance granted until 6/30/00.

f Zero coupon until 6/02, 12 percent thereafter. Face value $44.612 million. Accreted value at default approximately $36.5 million.

g Zero coupon until 5/03, 10.5 percent thereafter. Face value $500 million. Accreted value at default $370.4 million.

h Outstanding amount includes $40.286 million accrued interest not paid-out in cash. Par value $125 million.

i Zero coupon until 12/00, 13.875 percent thereafter. Face value $312.448 million. Accreted value at default $289.8 million.

j Securities are denominated in Canadian dollars. Outstanding amounts are CAD$100million and CAD$125million, respectively. USD amount is based on 5/18 CAD spot rate of 1.499.

k Cpn rate is based on 3month LIBOR + 437.5bp. The business day following default, the coupon reset to 10.65625 percent.

l Zero coupon until 5/02, 14.125 percent thereafter. Face value $104 million. Accreted value at default $80.423.

m Zero coupon until 6/03, 13 percent thereafter. Face value $140.885 million. Accreted value at default $87.027.

n Euro-Dollar Market Issue.

o Zero coupon until 8/03, 14 percent thereafter. Face value $49.086 million. Accreted value at default approximately $34.424 million.

p Zero coupon until 3/01, 12.25 percent thereafter. Face value $451.5 million. Accreted value at default $333 million.

q Securities are denominated in Deutsche marks. Outstanding amount is DEM140million. USD amount is based on 8/15 spot rate of 2.1408.

s Private placement.

t Zero coupon until 6/04, 13 percent thereafter. Face value $569.636 million. Accreted value at default approximately $336.045 million.

u Securities are denominated in Swiss francs. Outstanding amount is CHF12.52million. USD amount is based on 10/05 spot rate of 1.7522.

v Securities are denominated in Deutsche marks. Outstanding amount is DEM130million. USD amount is based on 10/05 spot rate of 2.2501.

w Zero coupon until 5/01, 12.5 percent thereafter. Face value $550.300 million. Accreted value at default $521.611 million.

x Zero coupon until 3/02, 11.675 percent thereafter. Face value $176 million. Accreted value at default $151.724 million.

y Zero coupon until 2/03, 10 percent thereafter. Face value 490 million. Accreted value at default $393.970 million.

z Zero coupon until 5/03, 9.875 percent thereafter. Face value $405.250 million. Accreted value at default $320.040 million.

aa Securities are denominated in Deutsche marks. Outstanding amount is DEM150million. USD amount is based on 12/15 spot rate of 2.1858.

Table 23.2 Historical default rates – Straight bonds only excluding defaulted issues from par value outstanding 1971–2000 ($ millions)

Year	Par value outstanding[a] ($)	Par value defaults ($)	Default rates (%)
2000	597,200	30,248	5.065
1999	567,400	23,532	4.147
1998	465,500	7,464	1.603
1997	335,400	4,200	1.252
1996	271,000	3,336	1.231
1995	240,000	4,551	1.896
1994	235,000	3,418	1.454
1993	206,907	2,287	1.105
1992	163,000	5,545	3.402
1991	183,600	18,862	10.273
1990	181,000	18,354	10.140
1989	189,258	8,110	4.285
1988	148,187	3,944	2.662
1987	129,557	7,486	5.778
1986	90,243	3,156	3.497
1985	58,088	992	1.708
1984	40,939	344	0.840
1983	27,492	301	1.095
1982	18,109	577	3.186
1981	17,115	27	0.158
1980	14,935	224	1.500
1979	10,356	20	0.193
1978	8,946	119	1.330
1977	8,157	381	4.671
1976	7,735	30	0.388
1975	7,471	204	2.731
1974	10,894	123	1.129
1973	7,824	49	0.626
1972	6,928	193	2.786
1971	6,602	82	1.242

			Standard deviation (%)
Apithmetic average default rate			
1971–2000		2.713	2.484
1978–2000		2.948	2.683
1985–2000		3.719	2.829
Weighted average default rate[b]			
1971–2000		3.482	2.558
1978–2000		3.503	2.563
1985–2000		3.582	2.565
Median annual default rate			
1971–2000		1.656	

[a] As of mid-year.
[b] Weighted by par value of amount outstanding for each year.
Source: Authors' compilation and Salomon Smith Barney Estimates.

Figure 23.1 Historical default rates (1971–2000)

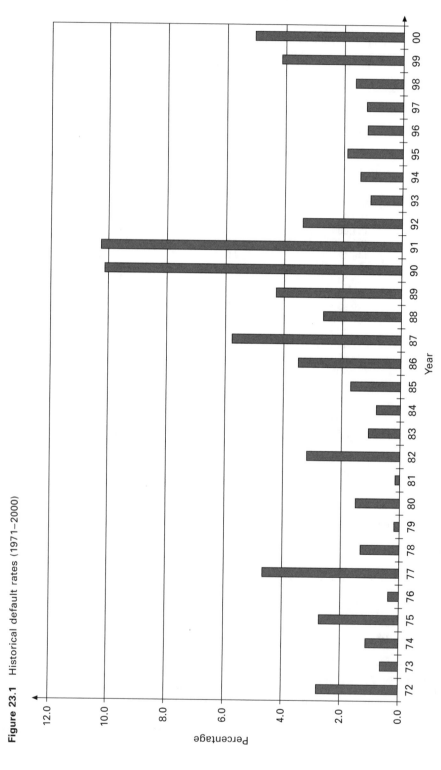

Source: Table 23.2

Table 23.3 Quarterly default rate comparison: Altman/SBC vs. Moody's high yield debt market 1990–2000

Quarter	Par value debt outstanding ($ billions)	Debt defaulted by quarter ($ billions)	Quarterly default rates (%)	Altman/SBC 12M moving average (%)	Moody's 12M moving average (%)
1990: 1Q	185.00	4.16	2.25		
2Q	185.00	2.51	1.36		
3Q	181.00	6.01	3.32		
4Q	181.00	5.67	3.13	10.06	8.83
		18.35			
1991: 1Q	182.00	8.74	4.80	12.61	10.62
2Q	182.00	2.75	1.51	12.77	11.57
3Q	183.00	5.01	2.74	12.18	10.58
4Q	183.00	2.36	1.29	10.34	9.65
		18.86			
1992: 1Q	183.20	3.33	1.82	7.35	7.17
2Q	151.10	1.26	0.83	6.67	5.55
3Q	163.00	0.37	0.23	4.16	4.69
4Q	151.89	0.59	0.39	3.26	3.94
		5.55			
1993: 1Q	193.23	0.38	0.20	1.65	3.78
2Q	193.23	1.33	0.69	1.50	3.23
3Q	206.91	0.05	0.03	1.30	3.08
4Q	190.42	0.52	0.27	1.19	3.06
		2.29			
1994: 1Q	232.60	0.67	0.29	1.28	2.49
2Q	230.00	0.16	0.07	0.65	1.44
3Q	235.00	0.41	0.17	0.80	2.18
4Q	235.00	2.18	0.93	1.46	1.93
		3.42			
1995: 1Q	240.00	0.17	0.07	1.24	1.20
2Q	240.00	1.68	0.70	1.88	2.17
3Q	240.00	0.98	0.41	2.11	2.41
4Q	240.00	1.72	0.72	1.90	3.30
		4.55			
1996: 1Q	255.00	0.44	0.17	2.00	3.48
2Q	255.00	0.89	0.35	1.64	2.86
3Q	271.00	0.41	0.15	1.39	2.19
4Q	271.00	1.59	0.59	1.26	1.66
		3.34			
1997: 1Q	296.00	1.85	0.63	1.71	1.60
2Q	318.40	0.60	0.19	1.55	1.61
3Q	335.40	1.48	0.44	1.84	2.27
4Q	335.40	0.27	0.08	1.34	2.03
		4.20			
1998: 1Q	379.00	2.37	0.63	1.34	2.38
2Q	425.70	1.22	0.29	1.43	3.01
3Q	465.50	1.62	0.35	1.34	2.73
4Q	481.60	2.26	0.47	1.73	3.46
		7.46			
1999: 1Q	515.00	4.76	0.92	2.03	3.89
2Q	537.20	8.42	1.57	3.31	4.74
3Q	567.40	5.24	0.92	3.88	5.89
4Q	580.00	5.11	0.88	4.30	5.51
		23.53			
2000: 1Q	584.00	5.96	1.02	4.39	5.64
2Q	595.60	9.95	1.67	4.50	5.43
3Q	597.50	4.32	0.72	4.30	5.13
4Q	608.15	10.02	1.65	5.06	6.02
		30.25			

Source: Altman (1990–2000), Salomon Smith Barney, and Moody's (New York).

Table 23.4   Comparing Altman/SBC moving average default rates with Moody's, 1990–2000

Absolute numbers		First differences		Percentage differences	
Altman 12M moving average (%)	Moody's 12M moving average (%)	Altman 12M moving average (%)	Moody's 12M moving average (%)	Altman 12M moving average (%)	Moody's 12M moving average (%)
10.06	8.83				
12.61	10.62	2.55	1.79	25.39	20.27
12.77	11.57	0.15	0.95	1.22	8.95
12.18	10.58	−0.58	−0.99	−4.56	−8.56
10.34	9.65	−1.84	−0.93	−15.13	−8.79
7.35	7.17	−2.99	−2.48	−28.89	−25.70
6.67	5.55	−0.68	−1.62	−9.25	−22.59
4.16	4.69	−2.51	−0.86	−37.62	−15.50
3.26	3.94	−0.90	−0.75	−21.57	−15.99
1.65	3.78	−1.62	−0.16	−49.55	−4.06
1.50	3.23	−0.14	−0.55	−8.64	−14.55
1.30	3.08	−0.20	−0.15	−13.39	−4.64
1.19	3.06	−0.12	−0.02	−9.05	−0.65
1.28	2.49	0.09	−0.57	7.62	−18.63
0.65	1.44	−0.62	−1.05	−48.68	−42.17
0.80	2.18	0.15	0.74	22.75	51.39
1.46	1.93	0.65	−0.25	81.40	−11.47
1.24	1.20	−0.22	−0.73	−14.77	−37.82
1.88	2.17	0.63	0.97	50.95	80.83
2.11	2.41	0.23	0.24	12.39	11.06
1.90	3.30	−0.21	0.89	−10.03	36.93
2.00	3.48	0.10	0.18	5.31	5.45
1.64	2.86	−0.35	−0.62	−17.64	−17.82
1.39	2.19	−0.26	−0.67	−15.51	−23.43
1.26	1.66	−0.13	−0.53	−9.21	−24.20
1.71	1.60	0.45	−0.06	35.86	−3.61
1.55	1.61	−0.16	0.01	−9.31	0.62
1.84	2.27	0.29	0.66	18.62	40.99
1.34	2.03	−0.51	−0.24	−27.54	−10.57
1.34	2.38	0.00	0.35	0.02	17.24
1.43	3.01	0.10	0.63	7.33	26.47
1.34	2.73	−0.09	−0.28	−6.55	−9.30
1.73	3.46	0.39	0.73	28.96	26.74
2.03	3.89	0.30	0.43	17.28	12.43
3.31	4.74	1.28	0.85	63.22	21.85
3.88	5.89	0.58	1.15	17.40	24.26
4.30	5.51	0.41	−0.38	10.65	−6.45
4.39	5.64	0.10	0.13	2.23	2.36
4.50	5.43	0.10	−0.21	2.34	−3.72
4.30	5.13	−0.20	−0.30	−4.44	−5.52
5.06	6.02	0.77	0.89	17.83	17.35

Regression statistics					
Multiple *R*	0.969785946		0.76820831		0.567898832
R^2	0.940484781		0.590144007		0.322509083
Adjusted R^2	0.93895875		0.579358323		0.304680375
Standard error	0.008448828		0.006061656		0.224030916
Observations	41		40		40

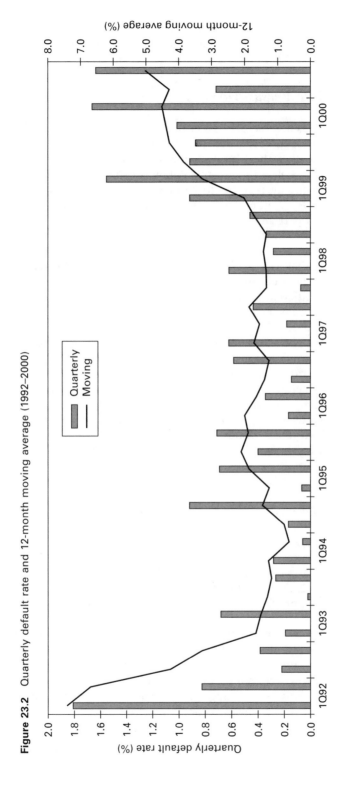

Figure 23.2 Quarterly default rate and 12-month moving average (1992–2000)

consecutive quarters. Yet in 2000, each quarter's default rate was greater than 1.0 percent (except in the third quarter) and showed a consistently higher level than any quarter since early in 1992 and the second quarter of 1999.

Our Default Rate Versus Moody's

There has been considerable discussion in recent years about how the Altman–NYU Salomon Center default rate calculations differ from Moody's (New York) results. Analysts point out that the Moody's rate, especially in recent years, is consistently higher. This can be seen in the last two columns of table 23.3. These results represent our 12-month moving average (or to be precise, last-four-quarter) default rates compared with Moody's 12-month moving average rate. One can observe that Moody's rate is, for the most part, higher since, essentially, 1992. The main reason for this is that the rating service firm includes emerging market corporate and quasi-municipal bond defaults while we do not. Our calculation essentially has been a domestic default rate calculation.[2] Note that Moody's ended the year 2000 at a 6.02 percent 12-month moving average rate compared to our 5.06 percent rate, about a 1 percent differential.

To analyze the differences in these two calculations, we constructed a moving four-quarter Altman/SC rate and compared it to Moody's 12-month moving averages, at the relevant quarterly dates. As noted above, Moody's rates are, for the most part, higher. But, when we ran a correlation of these absolute quarterly rates over the sample period (41 observations), we find (table 23.4) that the correlation is 0.97 and the R^2 (proportion of one default rate "explained" by the other) is a huge 0.94. Even when we ran the regression based on either first differences in the change in the quarterly default rates or the percentage change in the rates, the correlations were high (0.77 and 0.57 respectively). In other words, both default rate measures are depicting very similar trends and directions of default rates. Moody's predicted default rate of 9.5 percent by the end of 2001 is considerably higher, however, than our 6.5–7.0 percent rate (see discussion below).

DEFAULT LOSSES AND RECOVERY AT DEFAULT

Default losses also rose substantially in 2000 versus 1999 and 1998 (3.94 percent vs. 3.21 percent and 1.10 percent) and were substantially above the 1978–2000 average of 1.95 percent per year – 2.45 percent weighted (by the amount of bonds outstanding) average annual rate. Table 23.5 shows the 2000 loss rate, which includes the loss of half of the average annual coupon. Default losses for the last 23 years are shown in table 23.6.

The average recovery rate on the issues for which we had prices just after default was 26.4 percent, the lowest since 1990, far below the venerable 40–42 percent historical average recovery rate (table 23.6 and 23.7) and just below last year's figure (27.9 percent). This was less surprising this year than last, since the majority of the 164 defaulting issues with prices were subordinated (table 23.7). Still, the low recovery rate is important since it reflects supply and demand conditions for defaulted bonds and lower

---

[2] There are other differences in the two calculations, e.g., we do not include cured defaults, and their rated population is somewhat different, but these are minor compared to the emerging market bias.

Table 23.5 2000 Default loss rate

	%
Background data	
Average default rate 2000	5.065
Average price at default[a]	26.396
Average loss of principal	73.604
Average coupon payment	8.539
Default loss computation	
Default rate	5.065
× Loss of principal	73.604
Default loss of principal	3.728
Default rate	5.065
× Loss of $\frac{1}{2}$ coupon	4.269
Default loss of coupon	0.216
Default loss of principal and coupon	3.944

[a] If default date price is not available, end-of-month price is used.
Source: Authors' compilations and various dealer quotes.

Table 23.6 Default rates and losses[a] (1978–2000)

Year	Par value outstanding[a] ($ MMs)	Par value of default ($ MMs)	Default rate (%)	Weighted price after default ($)	Weighted coupon (%)	Default loss (%)
2000	597,200	30,248	5.06	26.4	8.54	3.94
1999	567,400	23,532	4.15	27.9	10.55	3.21
1998	465,500	7,464	1.60	35.9	9.46	1.10
1997	335,400	4,200	1.25	54.2	11.87	0.65
1996	271,000	3,336	1.23	51.9	8.92	0.65
1995	240,000	4,551	1.90	40.6	11.83	1.24
1994	235,000	3,418	1.45	39.4	10.25	0.96
1993	206,907	2,287	1.11	56.6	12.98	0.56
1992	163,000	5,545	3.40	50.1	12.32	1.91
1991	183,600	18,862	10.27	36.0	11.59	7.16
1990	181,000	18,354	10.14	23.4	12.94	8.42
1989	189,258	8,110	4.29	38.3	13.40	2.93
1988	148,187	3,944	2.66	43.6	11.91	1.66
1987	129,557	7,486	5.78	75.9	12.07	1.74
1986	90,243	3,156	3.50	34.5	10.61	2.48
1985	58,088	992	1.71	45.9	13.69	1.04
1984	40,939	344	0.84	48.6	12.23	0.48
1983	27,492	301	1.09	55.7	10.11	0.54
1982	18,109	577	3.19	38.6	9.61	2.11
1981	17,115	27	0.16	12.	15.75	0.15
1980	14,935	224	1.50	21.1	8.43	1.25
1979	10,356	20	0.19	31.	10.63	0.14
1978	8,946	119	1.33	60.	8.38	0.59
Arithmetic average 1978–2000			2.95	41.2	11.22	1.95
Weighted average 1978–2000			3.50			2.45

[a] Excludes defaulted issues.
Source: Tables 23.2 and 23.5.

Table 23.7 Weighted average recovery rates on defaulted debt by seniority per $100 face amount (1978–2000)

Default year	Senior secured		Senior unsecured		Senior subordinated		Subordinated		Discount and zero coupon		All seniorities	
	No.	$	No.	$	No.	$	No.	$	No.	$	No.	$
2000	13	39.58	47	25.40	61	25.96	26	26.62	17	23.61	164	25.83
1999	14	26.90	60	42.54	40	23.56	2	13.88	11	17.30	127	31.14
1998	6	70.38	21	39.57	6	17.54	0	0	1	17.00	34	37.27
1997	4	74.90	12	70.94	6	31.89	1	60.00	2	19.00	25	53.89
1996	4	59.08	4	50.11	9	48.99	4	44.23	3	11.99	24	51.91
1995	5	44.64	9	50.50	17	39.01	1	20.00	1	17.50	33	41.77
1994	5	48.66	8	51.14	5	19.81	3	37.04	1	5.00	22	39.44
1993	2	55.75	7	33.38	10	51.50	9	28.38	4	31.75	32	38.83
1992	15	59.85	8	35.61	17	58.20	22	49.13	5	19.82	67	50.03
1991	4	44.12	69	55.84	37	31.91	38	24.30	9	27.89	157	40.67
1990	12	32.18	31	29.02	38	25.01	24	18.83	11	15.63	116	24.66
1989	9	82.69	16	53.70	21	19.60	30	23.95			76	35.97
1988	13	67.96	19	41.99	10	30.70	20	35.27			62	43.45
1987	4	90.68	17	72.02	6	56.24	4	35.25			31	66.63
1986	8	48.32	11	37.72	7	35.20	30	33.39			56	36.60
1985	2	74.25	3	34.81	7	36.18	15	41.45			27	41.78
1984	4	53.42	1	50.50	2	65.88	7	44.68			14	50.62
1983	1	71.00	3	67.72			4	41.79			8	55.17
1982			16	39.31			4	32.91			20	38.03
1981	1	72.00									1	72.00
1980			2	26.71			2	16.63			4	21.67
1979							1	31.00			1	31.00
1978			1	60.00							1	60.00
Total/Average	126	53.73	365	44.28	299	31.27	247	31.03	65	20.83	1,102	37.17
Median		59.08		42.54		31.91		32.91		17.50		40.67

Source: Authors' compilation from various dealer quotes.

expected reorganization values. It is also consistent with our empirical observation of a strong negative correlation between concurrent levels of default and recovery rates.

Seventeen of the defaults were discount bonds, where we use accreted values as the base to determine recovery rates as well as in our default total and rate calculations. The number of discounted defaulting issues was the highest ever.

About 70 percent of all new issuance in the high yield market since 1991 has been senior in priority. But, the issuance of even more senior bank debt and secured bonds has lowered the priority of much of the defaulted public debt in the last two years, adding to the downward pressure on recovery rates. The much lower than average 1999 and 2000 recovery rates are a caution to investors who cannot assume that senior bonds will always result in above average recovery rates and junior bonds average recoveries. Table 23.7 lists the recovery rates (prices just after default) by seniority for 2000 and for the previous 22 years. For example, the senior secured recovery rate in 2000 was only 39.6 percent versus an historical average of more than 53.7 percent, and the senior unsecured average recovery rate slumped to just 25.4 percent compared to a two-decade average of close to 44 percent. All of the seniority levels recovered lower amounts in 2000 than the historical average, except for the discounted bond group, which represent bonds of all seniorities. The overall arithmetic average 23-year recovery rate dipped below 40 percent (37.2 percent) and is now based on 1102 issues (41.2 percent average, weighted by the amount outstanding in each year and a median rate of 40.7 percent).

Table 23.8 lists the average recovery at default stratified by original bond rating for the period 1971–2000. The weighted recoveries for the A-rated categories of bonds definitely show higher recovery rates than for non-investment grade debt, but the three non-investment-grade bond classes, and also BBB rated bonds, continue to show very little differences. This is also true after adjusting for seniority bias.

Table 23.9 lists the original Standard & Poor's ratings of defaulting issues, as well as the one year and six-months-prior to default ratings. Of the 1039 issues tabulated, 79.4 percent were original issue high yield bonds, and 20.6 percent were originally rated as investment grade but eventually defaulted; 9.0 percent of the defaulted issues were still rated investment grade one year before default and 7.6 percent six months prior (multiple issues from a few large high grade issuers, e.g., Columbia Gas System, however, accounted for a large proportion of the 12 and six-month-prior investment grade

Table 23.8 Average price after default by original bond rating (1971–2000)

Rating	No. of observations	Average price ($)	Median price* ($)	Std dev.* ($)	Minimum price ($)	Maximum price ($)
AAA	7	68.34	71.88	20.82	32.00	97.00
AA	20	59.59	54.25	24.59	17.80	99.88
A	65	62.07	62.00	24.86	10.50	100.00
BBB	117	37.54	46.00	23.79	2.00	103.00
BB	108	32.78	37.00	22.05	1.00	98.75
B	589	30.83	33.00	24.66	0.50	112.00
CCC	133	48.78	31.00	27.18	1.00	103.25
Total	1,039	48.56	36.50	25.76	0.50	112.00

* The median and standard deviation figures are from 1971–1999 only.
Source: Authors' compilation

defaults) and most of these were BBB. These twelve and six months prior statistics are up from last year's results since several BBB-rated bonds at these intervals did eventually default. This reflects the precipitous drops in credit quality, of late, of investment-grade bonds. And if the California public utility bonds default by 30 June 2001, those issues will add to the investment-grade original rating proportion, as well as the six-month and twelve-month categories when the bonds were rated AA– to A+.

Table 23.10 shows that the time it takes for an issue to default compared to its issuance date makes virtually no difference in the recovery rate. Most weighted recoveries by year after issuance are in the low to mid $30 range.

Table 23.9 Rating distribution of defaulted issues[a] at various points prior to default (1971–2000)

	Original rating		Rating six months prior to default		Rating one year prior to default	
	Number	%	Number	%	Number	%
AAA	5	0.5	0	0.0	0	0.0
AA	25	2.4	0	0.0	0	0.0
A	69	6.6	12	1.3	2	0.2
BBB	115	11.1	72	7.7	65	7.4
Total investment grade	214	20.6	84	9.0	67	7.6
BB	118	11.4	90	9.7	81	9.2
B	569	54.8	478	51.3	444	50.6
CCC	134	12.9	248	26.6	236	26.9
CC	4	0.4	22	2.4	43	4.9
C	0	0.0	8	0.9	7	0.8
D	0	0.0	1	0.1	0	0.0
Total noninvestment grade	825	79.4	847	91.0	811	92.4
Total	1,039	100	931	100	878	100

[a] Based on Standard & Poor's Bond Ratings.
Source: Authors' compilation.

Table 23.10 Average price at default by number of years after issuance (1971–2000)

Years to default	No. of observations	Average price ($)	Median price* ($)	Standard deviation*
1	81	32.30	31.75	24.45
2	183	30.60	31.30	22.30
3	194	29.97	34.31	25.83
4	150	36.36	39.00	24.90
5	124	34.44	36.50	27.30
6	92	49.90	36.25	26.33
7	62	36.92	37.75	24.16
8	39	30.80	27.50	27.07
9	20	36.01	33.00	27.34
10	28	28.83	32.00	22.78
All	973	34.61	35.00	25.15

* The median and standard deviation figures are from 1971–1999 only.
Source: Authors' compilation.

Deterioration in Original Issuance Credit Quality

One apparent reason for the sizeable amount of defaults in 2000 is the seeming deterioration in credit quality of new issuance in recent years. This is demonstrated by the significant increase in the percentage of bonds that defaulted in the first three years after issuance. From tables 23.11 and 23.12, we observe that in 2000, 19 of the 183 issues defaulted within 12 months (10 percent), 70 (38 percent) defaulted within 24 months and 126 (69 percent) within 36 months. This compares with 9 percent, 30

Table 23.11 Distribution of years to default from original issuance date (by year of default) (1989–2000)

	Years to default										
	1	*2*	*3*	*4*	*5*	*6*	*7*	*8*	*9*	*10*	*Total*
1989											
No. of issues	4	12	15	13	1	7	7	2	1	3	65
% of total	6	18	23	20	2	11	11	3	2	5	100
1990											
No. of issues	3	25	23	18	23	5	5	4	1	1	108
% of total	3	23	21	17	21	5	5	4	1	1	100
1991											
No. of issues	0	18	26	29	35	10	4	10	3	2	137
% of total	0	13	19	21	26	7	3	7	2	1	100
1992											
No. of issues	0	0	7	10	8	12	5	4	0	8	54
% of total	0	0	13	19	15	22	9	7	0	15	100
1993/1994											
No. of issues	3	6	5	2	4	8	7	0	0	2	37
% of total	8	16	14	5	11	22	19	0	0	5	100
1995											
No. of issues	1	9	7	3	1	2	2	2	4	1	32
% of total	3	28	22	9	3	6	6	6	13	3	100
1996											
No. of issues	2	3	3	8	1	5	0	0	0	2	24
% of total	8	13	13	33	4	21	0	0	0	8	100
1997											
No. of issues	5	4	4	9	3	0	0	0	0	0	25
% of total	20	16	16	36	12	0	0	0	0	0	100
1998											
No. of issues	2	5	10	3	10	2	1	0	0	0	33
% of total	6	15	30	9	30	6	3	0	0	0	100
1999											
No. of issues	32	37	15	14	7	8	10	2	0	0	125
% of total	26	30	12	11	6	6	8	2	0	0	100
2000											
No. of issues	19	51	56	14	13	5	12	4	3	6	183
% of total	10	28	31	8	7	3	7	2	2	3	100
1989–2000											
No. of issues	71	170	171	123	106	64	53	28	12	25	823
% of total	9	21	21	15	13	8	6	3	1	3	100

Source: Authors' compilation.

Table 23.12 Percentage defaults in 2000 by year from issuance

Time	# of issues	%
1st year	19	10
2nd year	51	28
3rd year	56	31
4th year	14	8
5th year	13	7
6th year	5	3
7th year	12	7
8th year	4	2
9th year	3	2
10th (+)year	6	3
Total	183	100.00

Source: Authors' compilation.

percent and 51 percent, respectively, for the 1971–2000 period (table 23.11) and about 4 percent, 17 percent and 20 percent for the 1991–1998 period.[3] Hence, a sizeable increase in 1-, 2- and 3-year defaults is observed in the 1999 and 2000 cohort. The 10 percent one-year proportion, however, is down from 1999 record of 26 percent.

We observe that in table 23.13 the 1999 new issue cohort had an approximate 0.49 percent (BBB), 1.50 percent (BB), 1.62 percent (B) and 63.11 percent (CCC) default rate,[4] which are higher than the one-year rates from 1971–2000 (see our mortality rate data in table 23.18 on page 407). These higher marginal default rates in 2000 are also manifested in the second and third years after issuance (1998 and 1997 cohorts), especially for all three B-rated categories. To better understand these statistics, however, we need to analyze the purpose of the financing (e.g., growth versus refinancing versus LBOs), to see if the 1–3 years aging results are symptomatic of credit quality drift or of other things.

Defaults in 1990 vs. 2000

In a prior study (Chapter 20, in this volume), we observed that defaults resulting from highly leveraged restructuring (LBOs, recaps, etc.) accounted for about $20 billion in 1990–92, about 46 percent of total defaults in those years. In contrast, the most recent years' results show that defaults from highly leveraged restructurings in 1999–2000 did not account for any material amount and the outlook is for this source to continue not to be very important. We assessed the proportion of total new high yield bonds issued for a number of stated reasons, including acquisitions, leveraged restructurings, capital expenditure and other general corporate investments, and the refinancing of existing debt. The latter category has been the most important use of new debt financing every year since our data series begins (1986–99). The levels of refinancing in 1997–99 are not

---

[3] R. Grossman and M. Verde, *High Yield Industry Default Risk*, December 1999, FITCH/IBCA, New York.
[4] The CCC default rate is based on a very low new issuance of $1.35 billion. The default amounts and rates are adjusted slightly for the fact that we could not locate an original issue rating on a small number of defaults.

Table 23.13 Year 2000 defaults by rating and age

Original rating	Defaults ($M)	# Issues	Amount issued ($M)	# Issues	Dollar default rate (%)	Issue default rate (%)*
One-year defaults – bonds issued 1999						
BBB	482.14	1	99,468.50	683	0.485	0.161
BB	439.59	2	29,311.80	160	1.500	1.375
B	973.92	5	60,108.60	295	1.620	1.864
CCC	853.20	3	1,352.00	7	63.106	47.143
Two-year defaults – bonds issued 1998						
A						
BBB	1,453.49	5	112,914.60	672	1.287	0.818
BB	1,147.68	5	44,569.10	209	2.575	2.632
B	6,445.16	34	73,427.00	450	8.778	8.311
CCC	116.28	1	7,976.90	39	1.458	2.821
Three-year defaults – bonds issued 1997						
A						
BBB	1,068.04	4	75,331.70	477	1.418	0.922
BB	1,296.14	5	28,674.30	176	4.520	3.125
B	6,094.10	27	67,450.30	425	9.035	6.988
CCC	183.40	1	2,846.30	18	6.443	6.111
Four-year defaults – bonds issued 1996						
A						
BBB	207.79	1	48,353.70	299	0.430	0.368
BB	311.69	1	17,420.20	114	1.789	0.965
B	3,102.98	14	36,339.10	220	8.539	7.000
CCC						
Five-year defaults – bonds issued 1995						
A						
BBB	599.35	4	37,877.60	267	1.582	1.648
BB						
B	2,375.09	8	16,806.40	102	14.132	8.627
CCC						

* With 10% adjustment to number of issues defaulted due to incomplete default sample.
Source: Authors' compilation, thomson Financial Securities Data.

exceptionally high – in fact, they are below the average over this 14-year period. One reason for this is that, although Treasury rates did fall in these years from 1996 levels, the yields on high yield debt actually increased, making refinancing more expensive. Even so, the refinancing proportion of 40–45 percent of the more than $100 billion of new issues in each year is a great deal of financing that did not provide new cash to the issuer.

Overall, we find that in recent years (1995–99), about 20 percent of high yield bond new issuance was used for acquisitions and only 4–5 percent for leveraged restructurings. This compares to 10–15 percent for acquisitions and well over 30 percent for LBOs and recapitalizations in the years leading up to the market's problems a decade ago. Since leveraged restructurings can lead to unsustainable levels of debt and possible financial distress, we feel that at least in terms of this important factor, the new issue market was decidedly more risky in the earlier period.

Still, the high yield bond industry's enthusiasm for new issuance in 1996–98, and the apparent deterioration in credit quality, needs to be monitored closely. No doubt, this deterioration in credit quality contributed to recent default growth, but the added factor of earlier defaults exacerbated the 1999–2000 numbers. Investors will need additional promised yields to expect to achieve return spreads comparable to the performance data of the past two decades (see our data involving return spreads, especially table 23.20 on page 408).

Other Reasons for the Increase in Defaults

In addition to the deterioration in credit quality and the earlier occurrence of defaults, a number of other factors contributed to the sizeable increase in 2000:

1 The increased dollar amount of recent new issuance
2 The vestige of Russia's default in 1998
3 A number of "sick" industries despite the economy's apparent overall strength (now being questioned for 2001)
4 Banks' reluctance to refinance marginal clients

We have already noted the huge new issuance years of 1997–99 and the expected increase in dollar defaults as these new issues age. This simple mortality idea is the primary basis for our forecasted default numbers and percentages, which we will discuss at a later point. If nothing else, a regression to the mean would have caused the 2000 default amounts and default rate to increase *vis-à-vis* prior years.

The increase in the bond default rate to more than 5 percent, however, was caused by additional factors. One intangible, but important, factor is the ability of distressed firms to refinance their indebtedness, especially with funding from the commercial banks. Refinancing occurred with increasing difficulty in the aftermath of Russia's default and the flight-to-quality that ensued. Although this occurrence is mainly anecdotal, we are convinced that, without the Russian contagion, the default rate would have been lower.

In 2000, bank loan defaults of rated loans (by S&P) were about $16 billion and Maden, Horowitz, and O'Connor estimate that bank loan defaults overall were $23 billion in 2000 and could reach $33 billion in 2001 (Salomon Smith Barney Equity Research: US report, 9 January 2001).

INDUSTRY DEFAULTS

We continue to observe pockets of defaults in either chronically or newly ailing industrial sectors. Table 23.14 lists the 2000 defaults by major industrial sector, as well as the industry default data since 1970. In 2000, in addition to general manufacturing and miscellaneous industries (23 and 34 defaulting issuers), such sectors as leisure/entertainment (9), communications (8), retailing (7), healthcare (6), real estate (6), and financial services (6) were most prominent. Some particularly hard hit categories were movie theatre chains and steel. Indeed, the former "industry" realized more than a 50 percent failure rate in recent years and the latter had two large Chapter 22's (LTV and Wheeling Pittsburgh). Hence, despite an ebullient economy for most of the year, driven by

Table 23.14 Corporate bond defaults by industry (number of companies)

Industry	1970–82	1983	1984	1985	1986	1987	1988	1989	1990	1991	1992	1993	1994	1995	1996	1997	1998	1999	2000	Total
Auto/motor carrier	3							3	3									1	1	11
Conglomerates	0							1	1	3	3	3		1					1	13
Energy	3	3	5	7	12	1	4	11	7	4	3	3	1	1	1	2	1		6	61
Financial services	4	1	1	1		2	4	4	8	14	3	2		2	1	5	6	1	9	67
Leisure/entertainment	0					2	4	4	5	2	3	3	4	3	1	5	5	8	9	62
General manufacturing	9	1	1	2	6	3	3	1	5	8	8	7	3	8	6	7	6	16	23	123
Health care	0					1	2		2	2	1	1		2			2	8	6	26
Miscellaneous industries	3	1	2	6	3	1		4	4	4	3	1	1	1		3	3	16	34	86
Real estate/construction	7		1	1		1	1	3	7	5	1	1	1	2	1	2	1	4	6	43
REIT	11	1									1									13
Retailing	6	1		6	3	2	1	2	6	15	6	4	5	6	3	6	6	12	7	86
Communications	7	2	2	1		3	1		3	4	1	1	3	2	2	1	6	11	8	59
Transportation (non auto)	4	2		1	1			1	1	2			2			2	1	8	5	30
Utilities						1	1				1				1	1				5
Total	57	12	12	19	23	15	24	26	47	62	34	22	19	28	15	29	37	98	106	685

technology and productivity growth, a number of sectors have been ailing, and some will continue to do so going forward. Others, like energy and shipping, which were big "contributors" in 1999, fell to just one default in each sector in 2000. As points of reference, Grossman and Verde concluded that retail, insurance, supermarkets, drug stores, and textiles/furniture had the highest default rates in the 1991–99 period.

Table 23.15 lists the 2000 defaults by more precise industry classifications for the individual defaulting issuers, and table 23.16 provides an update on the recovery rates by sector for 1971–2000.

Table 23.15   2000 defaults by industry

Company	Industry
All Star Gas Corp.	Retail – Propane Distribution
Altiva Financial Corporation	Finance – Consumer Loans
American Architectural Products Corp.	Miscellaneous Manufacturer
American Eco Corp.	Remediation Services
Ameriserve	Food – Wholesale/Distribution
Amer Reefer Company, Ltd.	Transport – Marine
Anchor Advanced Products, Inc.	Cosmetics & Toiletries
AMF Bowling Worldwide	Recreational Centers
Anacomp, Inc.	Computers – Memory Devices
Big V Supermarkets	Food-Retail
Bulong Operations	Metals/Minerals
Cambridge Industries, Inc.	Miscellaneous Manufacturer
Canadian Airlines	Airlines
Carmike Cinemas	Theatres
CellNet Data Systems	Wireless Equipment
Central European Media Enterprises, Ltd.	Television
CHS Electronics, Inc.	Distribution/Wholesale
Clark Material Handling Co.	Machinery – Construction & Mining
Colorado Prime Corp.	Diversified Mfg Op.
Compass Aerospace Corp.	Aerospace/Defense Equip.
ContiFinancial Corp.	Finance – Mtge Loan/Banker
Coram Healthcare Corp.	Health Care Services
Crown Vantage, Inc.	Paper & Related Products
Cuddy Int'l Corp.	Poultry
Decora Industries, Inc.	Miscellaneous Manufacturer
Dimac Direct, Inc.	Direct Marketing
Drypers Corp.	Cosmetics & Toiletries
Dyersburg Corp.	Textile – Products
Eagle Food Center, Inc.	Retail – Hypermarkets
Employee Solutions	Human Resources
Fine Air Services, Inc.	Transport – Air Freight
Flooring America, Inc.	Retail – Floor Coverings
Galaxy Telecom L.P.	Telecom Services
Genesis Health	Medical – Nursing Homes
Glenoit Corp.	Textile – Products
Global Health Sciences	Medical Products
Global Telesystems, Inc.	Telephone – Integrated
Globe Manufacturing Corp.	Textile – Products
GNI Group, Inc.	Hazardous Waste Disposal
Gothic Energy Corp.	Oil-US Royalty Trusts
GST Telecommunications, Inc.	Telecommunication Equip.
Hedstrom Holdings, Inc.	Miscellaneous Manufacturer
Heilig-Meyers Co. – Macsaver Fin'l	Finance – Consumer Loans
ICG Communications Corp.	Satellite Telecomm
Imperial Home Decor Group	Home Decoration Products
Imperial Sugar Company	Sugar
Indesco International, Inc.	Consumer Products – Misc
Iowa Select Farms	Agricultural Operations

Table 23.15 (cont'd)

Company	Industry
Kasper ASL, Ltd.	Apparel Manufacturers
Key Plastics, Inc.	Chemicals – Plastics
Kitty Hawk, Inc.	Transport – Air Freight
Laidlaw, Inc.	Transport-Services
LaRoche Industries, Inc.	Chemicals – Specialty
Lernout & Hauspie Speech Products N.V.	Communications Software
Lodestar Holdings, Inc.	Diversified Operations
LTV Corp.	Steel-Producers
Master Graphics – Premier Graphics, Inc.	Printing-Commercial
Medical Resources	Medical Laboratories
Mediq, Inc.	Medical Products
Metal Management, Inc.	Recycling
Morris Material Handling, Inc.	Bldg & Construct. Products
Northwestern Steel & Wire Company	Steel – Producers
Orbcomm Global LP	Telecom Services
Outboard Marine Corp.	Recreational Vehicles
Owens Corning	Bldg & Construct. Products
Packaging Resources	Containers – Paper/Plastic
Paging Network, Inc.	Wireless Equipment
Paracelsus Healthcare Corp.	Medical – Hospitals
Park 'N' View, Inc.	Retail-Misc/Diversified
Pathmark Stores	Food – Retail
PennCorp Financial Group, Inc.	Life/Health Insurance
Pen-Tab Industries, Inc.	Misc. Manufacturer
Phase Metrics	Data Processing/Mgmt.
Pillowtex Corp.	Textile-Apparel
Pioneer Americas Acquisition Corp.	Chemicals – Diversified
Plainwell, Inc.	Paper & Related Products
President Casinos	Gambling (Non-hotel)
Prime Succession, Inc.	Funeral Services
Quentra Networks, Inc. – Diane Corp.	Telecommunication Equip.
Gorges/Quick-to-Fix Foods, Inc.	Food-Misc/Diversified
RBX Group, Inc.	Misc. Manufacturer
Regal Cinemas, Inc.	Theatres
Reliance Group Holdings, Inc.	Property/Casualty Insurance
Reliant Building Products, Inc.	Prod – Doors & Windows
Resort at Summerlin	Resorts/Theme Parks
REV Holdings, Inc.	Cosmetics & Toiletries
Safelite Glass Corp.	Housewares
Safety Components International, Inc.	Misc. Manufacturer
Safety-Kleen Corp.	Non-Hazardous Waste Disposal
SFAC New Holdings	Food-Misc/Diversified
Silver Cinemas International, Inc.	Motion Pictures & Services
Stage Stores – Specialty Retailers, Inc.	Retail-Apparel/Shoe
Stellex Technologies	Aerospace/Defense
Styling Technology Corp.	Cosmetics & Toiletries
Sunbeam Corporation	Leisure&Rec Products
Sunterra Corp.	Resorts/Theme Parks
Superior National Insurance	Property/Casualty Insurance
Talon Automotive Group, Inc.	Auto/Trk Prts & Equip
Tokheim Corp.	Machinery – Gen'l Industry
Uniforet, Inc.	Building Prod. – Wood
United Artists Theatre	Motion Pictures & Services
United Homes, Inc.	Building – Res/Comm.
Vista Eyecare, Inc.	Retail – Vision Service Ctr
Waxman Industries, Inc.	Bldg&Construct Prod – Misc
Wheeling-Pittsburgh Corp.	Steel-Producers
Worldtex, Inc.	Textile – Apparel
Zeta Consumer Products	Containers – Paper/Plastic

Table 23.16 Weighted average recovery rates by industry (1971–2000)

Industry	Sample	Weighted avg. price ($)	Avg. price ($)	Price range ($) Low	Price range ($) High	Std dev. ($)	Median ($)
Mining	69	33.51	34.65	9.50	99.00	17.19	32.50
Food and kindred products, tobacco	37	43.73	47.38	10.00	98.00	25.50	44.50
Textile mill, apparel and related products	55	29.50	29.83	0.75	89.30	18.97	29.00
Lumber, wood products, furniture and fixtures, paper and allied products	20	26.70	30.07	2.00	75.00	22.90	27.50
Chemical, petroleum and energy, rubber, plastic & leather products	48	65.73	53.55	3.00	107.75	31.48	60.50
Stone, clay, glass, concrete, metals and fabricated products	85	26.61	35.77	1.75	101.50	24.35	30.00
Machinery, electrical, electronic and transportation equipment, instruments and related products	70	34.18	39.41	3.00	86.00	22.45	38.25
Miscellaneous and diversified manufacturing	12	36.26	34.09	0.75	88.00	29.89	31.19
Transportation (rail road, bus, air, water, freight), pipeline and transportation services	78	38.15	38.83	5.00	103.25	26.49	34.25
Printing and publishing, communication, and movie production	133	27.79	30.65	3.00	97.00	19.71	28.83
Utilities	62	54.77	67.01	2.00	99.88	23.15	77.38
Wholesale and retail trade	176	33.00	34.82	0.50	98.50	22.27	31.25
Finance, insurance and real estate	132	33.94	35.52	1.00	103.00	26.75	30.00
Services	98	38.14	39.73	0.75	112.00	29.87	34.50
Total	1,075	35.75	38.26	0.50	112.00	25.58	33.50

Source: Tables 23.1, 23.7 and 23.14.

RECOVERY RATES FOR COMMUNICATION COMPANIES

A great deal of attention of late has been given to recovery rate experience and expectations of recoveries for defaults in particular industrial sectors. This is particularly important for an industry such as the Communications sector, especially the telecommunication segment, which have been major issuers of new high yield bonds in recent years. These data are relevant not only for traditional investors (mutual and pension funds) in high yield debt, but also for specialized investors and insurers of such instruments as collateralized bond/loan obligations and writers of credit derivatives. Table 23.17 shows the default recovery experience for Communication firms on defaults since 1987, mostly in the last five years. Note that the weighted average recovery rate at default for 91 issues and 41 issuers was about 28 percent, with a standard deviation of about 20 percent. The relatively low recovery rate for communication defaults is indicative of recent overall recovery experience in the high yield bond market, perhaps reflecting low asset values.

If one wants to highlight specific segments within the Communications sector, the compilation in table 23.17 permits this. We intend to provide such analysis for other sectors in the future.

MORTALITY RATES AND LOSSES

Mortality rates and losses for 1971–2000 are reported in tables 23.18 and 23.19. Total defaulted issues that had a rating on issuance and a price at default were 953 and 845 respectively. The methodology for these calculations comes from Altman (1989).[5] It is interesting to note that bond calls in 2000 were again extremely low as interest rates in the high yield market increased throughout the year and the end of year promised yield to maturity on non-investment grade issues was 14.56 percent, compared to 11.41 percent one year earlier. Treasury bond yields decreased, however, over the same period, from 6.44 percent to 5.12 percent. As with actuarial insurance experience calculations, our mortality method measures default experience for major rating categories from the "birth" of the issue and is market value (not issuer) weighted. As such, it clearly adjusts for the aging bias, and the marginal default rate experience can also be analyzed. This becomes particularly relevant as we experience earlier defaulting issues, as has happened in 1999 and 2000.

As noted earlier, 2000 defaults were distinctive in their higher-than-average number and rate, as well as in their relatively early incidence. Indeed, in table 23.11 (page 395) we observe that for 2000 almost 70 percent of the defaults took place within three years of issuance. The early default phenomenon manifests clearly in our mortality rate compilations. We observe that the first, second and third year marginal rates of default for single B securities in the period 1971–2000 are 1.60 percent, 4.94 percent, and 5.95 percent respectively, compared with 1.58 percent, 3.92 percent and 4.88 percent for the period 1971–99 (Peters and Altman, 2000).[6] The same trend is observed in table 23.18

---

[5] E. Altman, "Measuring Corporate Bond Mortality and Performance," *Journal of Finance*, September 1989, pp. 909–22.
[6] G. Peters and E. Altman, *Defaults and Returns on High Yield Bonds: Analysis Through 1999 and Default Outlook for 2000–2001*, Salomon Smith Barney, 31 January 2000.

Table 23.17 Recovery rates for communications industry, 1987–2000

Issuer	Bond	Coupon	Issue size	Default date	Default price ($)
Western Union Telegraph	SF Deb 5/15/97	7.90	5.000	01/11/87	39.00
SCI Television	Sub Deb '99	17.50	128.000	01/08/89	20.00
	Sr ExtNts '90	15.50	200.000	01/08/89	65.00
	Sr Sr Deb '97	16.50	100.000	01/08/89	33.00
Metropolitan Broadcasting	Jr Sub Deb 9/30/06	16.50	70.200	12/10/89	57.75
	Sr Sub 9/30/06	13.25	65.000	12/10/89	84.50
Olympic Broadcasting	Sr Sub Deb '96	13.38	17.400	01/11/89	64.00
Univision Holdings	Sub Deb '99	13.38	105.000	01/02/90	37.00
	Sr Sub Disc Nts '98	0.00	160.000	01/02/90	65.00
Western Union Corp.	SF Debs 3/15/96	8.45	8.100	15/06/90	18.00
	SF Debs '8/15/98	8.10	7.700	15/06/90	20.88
	SF Debs 3/1/92	5.00	8.000	15/06/90	21.00
	SF Debs 12/1/97	9.25	1.400	15/06/90	22.50
	Sub Deb '97	10.75	14.500	15/06/90	19.50
Olympic Broadcasting	Sr Sr Deb '96	14.38	23.400	01/12/90	11.00
Price Communications	Sub Nts '96	13.00	93.000	15/01/91	7.88
	Sub Nts '95	11.75	52.500	15/02/91	6.50
Star Cable Vision	Sr Sub Debs '02	13.50	21.000	15/02/91	50.00
Price Communications	Sub Deb '00	14.63	66.600	15/03/91	6.50
Western Union Corp.	Sr Sec Rst Nts '12/15/92	19.25	201.700	15/06/91	39.25
Western Union Tel.	Notes '6/15/91	16.00	23.800	15/06/91	35.00
	SF Deb 10/1/08	13.25	30.300	15/06/91	27.00
Gillett Holdings	Sr Sr Deb 8/1/98	12.63	250.400	15/06/91	25.00
	Sr Nts E Zero cpn93	0.00	75.000	25/06/91	39.00
	Sub Deb 8/15/99	13.88	170.000	25/06/91	20.00
	Sr Nts F Zero cpn94	0.00	61.900	25/06/91	39.00
	Sr Nts D Zero cpn92	0.00	75.000	25/06/91	40.50
Burnham Broadcasting	Sub Deb '99	13.88	32.000	01/09/91	20.00
Western Union Tel.	Notes 3/15/94	13.63	6.300	15/09/91	22.13
Telemundo Group 46	Sr Zero Cpn Nts '8/15/93	0.00	55.000	15/01/92	46.00
Telemundo Group (John Blair)	Sub Debs '98	13.63	47.000	15/01/92	30.00
Telemundo Group 33	Sr Zero Cpn Nts '8/15/92	0.00	55.000	15/01/92	33.00
AR CableServices	Sub Deb 12/30/97	16.75	134.300	28/01/92	77.50

Company	Security	Coupon	Amount	Date	Price
SPI Holdings	Sub Debs '02	14.75	75.000	01/04/92	89.00
	Sr Sub Reset Nts'99	14.88	221.200	01/04/92	97.00
Telemundo Group	Jr Sub Dis Nts '01	12.00	21.300	15/05/92	15.00
Great American Comm Company	Sr Sub Notes '99	14.38	40.500	14/04/93	35.00
GACC Holding Company	Sr Nts '96	14.13	32.200	15/04/93	38.00
	Sr Nxt'd Rst Nts '95	20.50	4.600	15/04/93	36.00
Maryland Cable	Sr Sub Disc Nts '98	15.38	162.000	15/03/94	32.00
Spectravision	SrDiscNts'01	11.50	178.300	01/06/95	20.00
Spectravision	SrSubReset'95	11.65	313.400	01/06/95	7.00
Scott Cable Communications	SubDebs '01	12.25	50.000	15/02/96	65.50
Mobilemedia Communications	SrSubNts '11/07	9.38	250.000	01/11/96	54.20
	SrSubNts '12/03	10.25	210.000	01/11/96	44.19
In-Flight Phone Corp.	Senior Discount Notes	14.00	285.800	24/01/97	4.50
Australis Holdings	Senior Discount Notes	0.00	193.100	08/04/98	18.00
	Senior Discount Notes	0.00	80.200	08/04/98	33.00
Heartland Wireless Communications, Inc.	Senior Notes 4/15/03	13.00	100.000	15/04/98	30.00
	Senior Notes 10/15/04	14.00	125.000	15/04/98	28.50
American Telecasting	Senior Discount Notes	0.00	135.900	13/05/98	15.00
	Senior Discount Notes	0.00	141.000	13/05/98	19.60
Geotek Communications, Inc.	Senior Discount Notes	0.00	207.000	30/06/98	17.00
CAI Wireless Systems, Inc.	Senior Notes	12.25	275.000	30/07/98	24.00
CAI Wireless Systems, Inc.	Senior Notes	12.00	30.000	30/07/98	24.00
International Wireless Communications Hldgs	Senior Secured Discount Notes	0.00	139.000	03/09/98	10.00
Ionica Group PLC	Senior Notes	13.50	150.000	28/09/98	30.00
	Senior Discount Notes	0.00	250.000	28/09/98	3.00
PhoneTel Tech	Guaranteed Senior Notes	12.00	125.000	15/01/99	35.00
Telegroup, Inc.	Senior Discount Notes	0.00	85.600	10/02/99	34.00
Wireless One, Inc.	Senior Discount Notes	0.00	175.100	11/02/99	9.57
	Senior Notes	13.00	150.000	11/02/99	10.00
USN Communications	Senior Discount Notes	0.00	123.700	18/02/99	9.00
FWT, Inc.	Senior Subordinated Notes	9.88	105.000	16/04/99	7.00
Teletrac, Inc.	Senior Subordinated Notes	14.00	98.400	09/06/99	25.00
ICO Global Comm. Services, Inc.	Eurobonds	15.25	107.100	01/07/99	47.00
	Senior Notes	15.00	460.000	01/07/99	44.00
Iridium LLC/Capital Corp.	Senior Notes	11.25	5.600	15/07/99	19.00
	Senior Notes	13.00	0.300	15/07/99	19.00
	Senior Notes	10.88	350.000	15/07/99	19.00
	Senior Notes	14.00	500.000	15/07/99	19.00

Table 23.17 (cont'd)

Issuer	Bond	Coupon	Issue size	Default date	Default price ($)
TeleHub Network Services Corp.	Senior Unsecured Discount Notes	13.88	79.100	27/10/99	13.00
Optel, Inc.	Senior Notes	11.50	200.000	28/10/99	33.00
	Senior Notes	13.00	225.000	28/10/99	33.00
Paging Network, Inc.	Senior Subordinated Notes	10.00	500.000	01/02/00	39.70
	Senior Subordinated Notes	10.13	400.000	01/02/00	39.70
	Senior Subordinated Notes	8.88	300.000	01/02/00	39.70
CellNet Data Systems	Senior Discount Notes	0.00	452.600	04/02/00	17.34
	Senior Discount Notes	0.00	223.300	04/02/00	12.63
GST Telecommunications, Inc.	Senior Discount Notes	0.00	289.800	17/05/00	24.80
	Senior Subordinated Accrual Notes	12.75	165.300	17/05/00	6.75
	Senior Secured Notes	13.25	265.000	17/05/00	45.00
	Senior Discount Notes	0.00	370.400	17/05/00	56.70
Central Euro Media Entertainment	Senior Notes	8.13	65.396	15/08/00	30.00
	Senior Notes	9.38	100.000	15/08/00	35.00
Orbcomm Global LP	Senior Notes	14.00	170.000	15/08/00	15.00
ICG Communications Corp.	Senior Discount Notes	0.00	320.039	14/11/00	8.00
	Senior Discount Notes	0.00	393.970	14/11/00	8.00
	Senior Discount Notes	0.00	521.611	14/11/00	12.00
	Senior Discount Notes	13.50	584.300	14/11/00	12.00
	Senior Discount Notes	0.00	151.724	14/11/00	8.00
41 Firms/91 issues			14,098.340	Average price ($)	29.87
				Weighted average price ($)	28.08
				Standard deviation ($)	19.68

Source: Prior annual reports and various dealer quotes.

Table 23.18 Mortality rates (%) by original rating – all rated corporate bonds[a] (1971–2000)

		Years after issuance									
		1	2	3	4	5	6	7	8	9	10
AAA	Marginal	0.00	0.00	0.00	0.00	0.03	0.00	0.00	0.00	0.00	0.00
	Cumulative	0.00	0.00	0.00	0.00	0.03	0.03	0.03	0.03	0.03	0.03
AA	Marginal	0.00	0.00	0.35	0.19	0.00	0.00	0.00	0.00	0.03	0.02
	Cumulative	0.00	0.00	0.35	0.54	0.54	0.54	0.54	0.54	0.57	0.59
A	Marginal	0.00	0.00	0.02	0.07	0.03	0.08	0.05	0.09	0.06	0.00
	Cumulative	0.00	0.00	0.02	0.09	0.12	0.20	0.25	0.34	0.40	0.40
BBB	Marginal	0.12	0.48	0.55	0.59	0.56	0.58	0.72	0.15	0.05	0.26
	Cumulative	0.12	0.60	1.14	1.73	2.28	2.85	3.55	3.70	3.75	3.98
BB	Marginal	0.96	1.65	3.15	1.54	2.15	0.95	1.65	0.45	1.75	3.75
	Cumulative	0.96	2.59	6.50	7.12	9.12	9.98	11.47	11.87	13.41	16.66
B	Marginal	1.60	4.94	5.95	6.72	5.94	4.15	3.12	2.10	1.65	0.85
	Cumulative	1.60	6.46	12.03	17.85	22.73	25.94	28.25	29.76	30.92	31.51
CCC	Marginal	4.35	13.26	14.84	8.15	3.02	9.15	4.56	3.26	0.00	4.15
	Cumulative	4.35	17.03	31.00	36.62	38.53	44.15	46.70	48.44	48.44	50.58

[a] Rated by S&P at Issuance.
Based on 933 issues.
Source: Standard & Poor's (New York) and authors' compilation.

Table 23.19 Mortality losses (%) by original rating – all rated corporate bonds[a] (1971–2000)

		Years after issuance									
		1	2	3	4	5	6	7	8	9	10
AAA	Marginal	0.00	0.00	0.00	0.00	0.00	0.00	0.00	0.00	0.00	0.00
	Cumulative	0.00	0.00	0.00	0.00	0.00	0.00	0.00	0.00	0.00	0.00
AA	Marginal	0.00	0.00	0.06	0.06	0.00	0.00	0.00	0.00	0.02	0.02
	Cumulative	0.00	0.00	0.06	0.12	0.12	0.12	0.12	0.12	0.14	0.16
A	Marginal	0.00	0.00	0.01	0.04	0.02	0.05	0.02	0.04	0.04	0.00
	Cumulative	0.00	0.00	0.01	0.05	0.07	0.12	0.14	0.18	0.22	0.22
BBB	Marginal	0.10	0.35	0.37	0.36	0.42	0.43	0.50	0.10	0.04	0.18
	Cumulative	0.10	0.45	0.82	1.18	1.60	2.02	2.51	2.61	2.63	2.81
BB	Marginal	0.57	0.99	2.45	1.10	1.12	0.66	1.03	0.25	0.95	1.75
	Cumulative	0.57	1.55	3.96	5.02	6.08	6.69	7.68	7.89	8.77	10.37
B	Marginal	1.12	3.70	4.60	4.67	4.50	2.49	1.87	1.42	0.85	0.61
	Cumulative	1.12	4.78	9.16	13.40	17.30	19.36	20.87	21.97	22.65	23.12
CCC	Marginal	2.82	10.60	11.39	6.52	2.27	6.40	3.64	2.65	0.00	3.10
	Cumulative	2.82	13.12	23.02	28.04	29.67	34.17	36.57	38.25	38.25	40.16

[a] Rated by S&P at Issuance.
Based on 799 issues.
Source: Standard & Poor's (New York) and authors' compilation.

for BB defaults (0.96 percent, 1.65 percent and 3.15 percent versus 0.71 percent, 0.81 percent and 2.65 percent, measured last year). For BBB defaults, as well, this higher and earlier default trend is clearly observed.

We also note that there is a marked increase in the first three years' marginal and cumulative mortality rates in this current report. The same observations can be made for our mortality loss compilations in table 23.19. Again, the higher early mortality loss rates are a function primarily of earlier defaults but are also caused by lower recovery rates.

RETURNS AND RETURN SPREADS

Tables 23.20–22 and figure 23.3 document total returns and spreads on high yield bonds versus ten-year US Treasuries for the period 1978–2000, inclusive. Table 23.20 shows each year's absolute return and return spread as well as the promised yield to

Table 23.20 Annual returns, yields and spreads on 10-year Treasury (TREAS) and high yield (HY) bonds (1978–2000)

Year	Return (%)			Promised yield (%)*		
	HY	TREAS	Spread	HY	TREAS	Spread
2000	−5.68	14.45	−20.13	14.56	5.12	9.44
1999	1.73	−8.41	10.14	11.41	6.44	4.97
1998	4.04	12.77	−8.73	10.04	4.65	5.39
1997	14.27	11.16	3.11	9.20	5.75	3.45
1996	11.24	0.04	11.20	9.58	6.42	3.16
1995	22.40	23.58	−1.18	9.76	5.58	4.18
1994	−2.55	−8.29	5.74	11.50	7.83	3.67
1993	18.33	12.08	6.25	9.08	5.80	3.28
1992	18.29	6.50	11.79	10.44	6.69	3.75
1991	43.23	17.18	26.05	12.56	6.70	5.86
1990	−8.46	6.88	−15.34	18.57	8.07	10.50
1989	1.98	16.72	−14.74	15.17	7.93	7.24
1988	15.25	6.34	8.91	13.70	9.15	4.55
1987	4.57	−2.67	7.24	13.89	8.83	5.06
1986	16.50	24.08	−7.58	12.67	7.21	5.46
1985	26.08	31.54	−5.46	13.50	8.99	4.51
1984	8.50	14.82	−6.32	14.97	11.87	3.10
1983	21.80	2.23	19.57	15.74	10.70	5.04
1982	32.45	42.08	−9.63	17.84	13.86	3.98
1981	7.56	0.48	7.08	15.97	12.08	3.89
1980	−1.00	−2.96	1.96	13.46	10.23	3.23
1979	3.69	−0.86	4.55	12.07	9.13	2.94
1978	7.57	−1.11	8.68	10.92	8.11	2.81
Arithmetic annual average						
1978–2000	11.38	9.51	1.88	12.90	8.14	4.76
Compound annual average						
1978–2000	10.73	8.83	1.90			

* End of year yields.
Source: Salomon Smith Barney Inc.'s High Yield Composite Index.

Figure 23.3 Cumulative value of $1,000 investment: 1978–2000 high yield bonds vs. 10-year US T-bonds

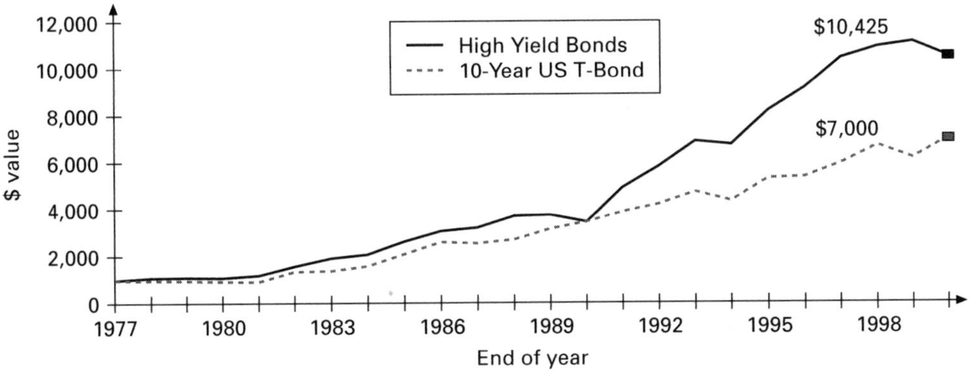

Source: Tables 23.21 and 23.22

maturity and yield spread at year-end. The high yield bond market's return spread over US Treasuries was a dismal −20.13 percent in 2000, bringing the arithmetic average annual spread for the last 23 years to 1.88 percent, versus 2.88 percent for data through 1999. The compound average annual spread, assuming reinvestment at the end of each year, is now 1.90 percent per year, versus 2.96 percent one year earlier. Hence, the low absolute returns on high yield bonds and the significant increase in returns on default risk-free ten-year Treasuries, 14.45 percent, resulted in the average historical return spread's falling by a full percentage point (100 bp) in one year. Tables 23.21 and 23.22 show these absolute and relative returns and spreads for various starting and ending years over the 1978–2000 period. And, figure 23.3 indicates that a $1,000 investment in high yield bonds would have aggregated to more than $10,425 by 2000, compared to $7,000 for ten-year Treasuries.

As noted above, high yield returns were exceptionally poor in 2000 and the yield spread versus ten-year Treasuries widened by almost 450 bp in just 12 months – from 4.97 percent to 9.44 percent (table 23.17). This change in spread of 447 bp is the largest increase for any annual period, including the 326 bp increase in 1990. Interest rates on high yield bonds averaged 18.57 percent at the end of 1990, however, compared to 14.56 percent in 2000. Clearly, the market is putting an enormous required risk premium on high yield bonds today, the primary cause of which is the market's concern about future default rates (see our breakeven discussion below) fueled by the observation of the record level of defaults in 2000, the sizeable increase in the distressed bond population to more than 30 percent of the high yield market as of 31 December 2000, and the uncertain state of the economy going forward. All of these things have caused an enormous liquidity and default risk premium imbedded to be in the required yield.

It should be noted that about 30 percent (132 bp) of the increase in yield spread in 2000 was owing to the *lowering* of the yield-to-maturity on ten-year US Treasuries as fixed-income investors fled-to-quality throughout the year and the supply/demand equation for long-term government bonds, like ten-year notes, changed dramatically

Table 23.21 Compound average annual returns of high yield bonds (%) (1978–2000)

Base period (Jan 1)	Terminal period (December 31)																						
	1978	1979	1980	1981	1982	1983	1984	1985	1986	1987	1988	1989	1990	1991	1992	1993	1994	1995	1996	1997	1998	1999	2000
1978	7.57	5.61	3.36	4.39	9.48	11.45	11.02	12.80	13.21	12.31	12.58	11.65	9.96	12.05	12.46	12.82	11.85	12.41	12.35	12.45	12.03	11.54	10.73
1979		3.69	1.32	3.36	9.97	12.24	11.61	13.57	13.93	12.85	13.09	12.03	10.16	12.41	12.82	13.18	12.12	12.70	12.62	12.71	12.26	11.73	10.88
1980			−1.00	3.19	12.14	14.48	13.26	15.30	15.47	14.05	14.18	12.90	10.77	13.17	13.55	13.89	12.71	13.29	13.17	13.23	12.73	12.15	11.82
1981				7.56	19.36	20.17	17.14	18.87	18.47	16.38	16.24	14.56	12.02	14.55	14.86	15.12	13.76	14.32	14.12	14.13	13.54	12.89	12.54
1982					32.45	27.01	20.52	21.88	20.79	17.92	17.53	15.47	12.53	15.27	15.54	15.77	14.25	14.81	14.57	14.55	13.91	13.19	12.83
1983						21.80	14.96	18.55	18.04	15.21	15.22	13.23	10.26	13.51	13.98	14.37	12.85	13.56	13.39	13.45	12.84	12.15	11.77
1984							8.50	16.96	16.81	13.62	13.94	11.86	8.70	12.51	13.14	13.65	12.07	12.90	12.77	12.88	12.26	11.57	11.17
1985								26.08	21.20	15.38	15.35	12.54	8.73	13.10	13.73	14.24	12.43	13.31	13.13	13.22	12.54	11.78	11.35
1986									16.50	10.37	11.98	9.39	5.56	11.07	12.07	12.84	11.01	12.10	12.02	12.21	11.56	10.83	10.36
1987										4.57	9.78	7.12	2.99	10.01	11.35	12.32	10.35	11.62	11.59	11.83	11.16	10.40	9.91
1988											15.25	8.41	2.47	11.42	12.76	13.67	11.20	12.54	12.39	12.58	11.78	10.90	10.36
1989												1.98	−3.38	10.17	12.14	13.35	10.53	12.16	12.04	12.29	11.43	10.51	9.93
1990													−8.46	14.50	15.75	16.39	12.33	13.95	13.56	13.65	12.54	11.41	10.76
1991														43.23	30.16	26.09	18.23	19.05	17.71	17.21	15.48	13.86	13.13
1992															18.29	18.31	10.90	13.67	13.18	13.36	11.98	10.64	9.84
1993																18.33	7.38	12.17	11.94	12.40	10.96	9.59	8.68
1994																	−2.55	9.21	9.89	10.97	9.54	8.20	7.15
1995																		22.40	16.69	15.88	12.80	10.49	9.21
1996																			11.24	12.74	9.77	7.70	6.14
1997																				14.27	9.04	6.54	4.49
1998																					4.04	2.88	−0.09
1999																						1.73	−4.05
2000																							−5.68

Source: Salomon Smith Barney Composite Index; Edward I. Altman, New York University Salomon Center.

Table 23.22 Compound annual return spreads between high yield and LT government bonds (%) (1978–2000)

Base period (Jan 1)	Terminal period (December 31)																						
	1978	1979	1980	1981	1982	1983	1984	1985	1986	1987	1988	1989	1990	1991	1992	1993	1994	1995	1996	1997	1998	1999	2000
1978	8.68	6.60	5.01	5.51	3.17	5.82	4.13	3.10	1.99	2.57	3.15	1.64	0.19	1.77	2.43	2.66	2.88	2.67	3.15	3.14	2.57	2.96	1.90
1979		4.55	3.23	4.48	1.71	5.22	3.32	2.23	1.08	1.84	2.55	0.94	-0.57	1.19	1.95	2.23	2.49	2.29	2.81	2.83	2.24	2.67	1.57
1980			1.96	4.45	0.67	5.39	3.05	1.79	0.51	1.46	2.30	0.54	-1.08	0.88	1.73	2.04	2.34	2.14	2.70	2.72	2.10	2.56	2.01
1981				7.08	-0.13	6.74	3.36	1.75	0.22	1.37	2.35	0.36	-1.43	0.77	1.70	2.05	2.36	2.15	2.75	2.77	2.42	2.60	2.05
1982					-9.63	6.49	1.93	0.18	-1.39	0.29	1.59	-0.58	-2.46	0.07	1.16	1.58	1.97	1.76	2.44	2.48	1.79	2.33	1.78
1983						19.57	6.62	2.97	0.39	1.94	3.13	0.49	-1.73	0.96	2.05	2.42	2.75	2.48	3.14	3.13	2.37	2.90	2.23
1984							-6.32	-5.94	-6.48	-2.59	-0.22	-2.73	-4.76	-1.40	0.08	0.68	1.23	1.04	1.87	1.96	1.22	1.86	1.18
1985								-5.46	-6.56	-1.30	1.34	-2.00	-4.50	-0.69	0.89	1.47	1.98	1.72	2.55	2.60	1.76	2.40	1.66
1986									-7.58	0.48	3.28	-1.26	-4.32	-0.00	1.67	2.22	2.68	2.33	3.18	3.17	2.24	2.88	2.00
1987										7.24	8.04	0.61	-3.61	1.38	3.08	3.51	3.84	3.34	4.16	4.06	2.98	3.61	2.58
1988											8.91	-3.00	-7.41	-0.24	2.15	2.82	3.31	2.80	3.78	3.71	2.56	3.28	2.23
1989												-14.74	-15.07	-3.32	0.44	1.58	2.38	1.93	3.14	3.14	1.93	2.77	1.64
1990													-15.34	2.59	5.68	5.82	5.82	4.76	5.73	5.41	3.80	4.52	3.21
1991														26.05	18.45	14.26	11.80	9.40	9.72	8.78	6.51	6.98	5.51
1992															11.79	9.06	7.84	5.83	6.94	6.32	4.14	4.98	3.23
1993																6.25	6.00	3.87	5.76	5.25	2.89	4.05	2.06
1994																	5.74	2.76	5.61	5.01	2.26	3.71	1.29
1995																		-1.18	5.50	4.69	1.22	3.23	0.78
1996																			11.20	7.29	1.93	4.17	0.51
1997																				3.11	-2.93	1.83	-2.58
1998																					-8.73	1.25	-5.82
1999																						10.14	-6.43
2000																							-20.13

Source: Salomon Smith Barney Composite Index; Edward I. Altman, New York University Salomon Center.

due to the budget surplus and unusually high redemptions.[7] In 1990, by contrast, interest rates on ten-year Treasuries actually increased slightly by 14 bp. That's a swing of 146 bp owing to monetary condition differences from a decade ago. If rates on ten-year Treasuries had not changed in either 1990 or 2000, the spread change would have been +315 bp in 2000 versus +338 bp in 1990.

To reflect on the almost 2 percent annual return spread advantage, one must assess whether this result is sufficient to compensate for both the higher liquidity risk of high yield bonds versus Treasuries and the fact that one might not achieve the average absolute return each year (11.38 percent). Although we see only four instances over the last 23 years of negative returns of high-yield bonds (table 23.20), it is clear, especially based on 2000 experience, that there is a possibility of unexpected losses, and investors must be compensated for this risk. Unexpected losses can occur in years of unexpected lackluster performance or when a portfolio is not well diversified and results fall short of average market performance.

Publicly regulated and insured financial institutions typically are required to allocate capital against unexpected loss possibilities while prudence guidelines for unregulated investors, such as mutual and pension funds, suggest professional standards for portfolio diversification and liquidity policies. Optimum portfolio analysis has recently become an important effort for the world's commercial banks in their trading and bank lending books[8] but little work has been published and tested for other credit asset portfolios, such as corporate bonds. As we noted last year, we expect that greater emphasis will be put on formal portfolio models for bond investors in the coming years.

BREAKEVEN AND RISK PREMIUM ANALYSIS

In a number of earlier papers, we have shown that a relatively simple analysis can be constructed that shows the breakeven yield (BEY) that investors must be promised in order to compensate for actual or expected default and recovery rates.[9] The end result is a comparison between actual yields at a point in time and the breakeven yield. This difference is the yield premium (if any) at any point in time (i.e., the amount to compensate investors for risks, other than expected default risk, e.g., liquidity, unexpected losses, flights to quality, etc).

Calculating the yield premium above the breakeven yield as of 31 December 2000, assuming a range of 4–10 percent default rates, various recovery rates, a risk-free rate of 5.12 percent, an average coupon of 10 percent and an average high yield-to-maturity rate of 14.56 percent (table 23.20), gives the results shown in table 23.23.

---

[7]   There are some observers who now question the usefulness of 10-year Notes as a benchmark for the default risk-free market owing to this supply vs. demand imbalance. We prefer to retain the same historical data series but need to point out the costs of doing so.

[8]   See A. Saunders, *Credit Risk Measurement*, John Wiley & Sons, New York, 1999 and J. Caouette, E. Altman and P. Narayanan, *Managing Credit Risk*, John Wiley & Sons, New York, 1998.

[9]   This formula is as follows:

$$\text{BEY} = \frac{R_f + D_f(1 - \text{Rec}) + (D_f x HYC/2)}{1 - D_f}$$

See Altman and Bencivenga (ch. 18, this volume).

Table 23.23 Breakeven yields and yield premiums for various assumptions of expected default and recovery rates (31 December 2000)

	Breakeven rates		Yield premiums	
Expected recovery rates (%)	30	40	30	40
Expected default rates				
4	8.46	8.04	6.10	6.52
5	9.34	8.81	5.22	5.75
6	10.23	9.60	4.33	4.96
7	11.15	10.40	3.41	4.16
8	12.09	11.22	2.47	3.34
9	13.04	12.05	1.52	2.51
10	14.02	12.91	0.54	1.65

Source: Authors' compilation.

We observe that if the market requires a risk premium above the breakeven rate of 2–3 percent, the implied default rate is 7.5–8.5 percent and a recovery rate of 30 percent. The 2–3 percent risk premium is selected to conform with historical total return spreads that have been earned by high yield investors over the last two decades – depending on whether the last year of our time series is 1999 or 2000. This analysis is sufficiently robust to accommodate more optimistic or pessimistic assumptions about expected default or recovery rates. Since we are expecting default rates in the next year or two to be in the 6.5–7.0 percent range, and a 30 percent recovery seems reasonable to us, the current yield premium seemed quite attractive relative to historic return spread performance. For example, a 7.0 percent default rate and a 30 percent recovery rate estimate results in a yield premium of 3.41 percent. Note that the yield premium jumps to 4.16 percent if we assume a 40 percent recovery rate.

DEFAULT FORECAST FOR 2001

Forecasting defaults is always a tricky exercise, but one that is necessary in order to understand the dynamics of a risky security market, like high yield bonds. One might try to forecast micro- and macro-economic variables,[10] as well as the term structure of default rates, or simply examine the historical experience that we can observe and therefore feel more confident about. We essentially embrace the latter methodology in our attempt to forecast default levels and rates. We also consider the size of the distressed bond market. Figure 23.4 shows the size of the distressed and defaulted bond market as a percentage of the high yield bond market from 1990–2000. We define distressed bonds, as we have since 1990, as those whose yield-to-maturity exceeds the ten-year Treasury Note by 10 percent (1000 bp). As shown in table 23.20, the spread for the entire market has widened dramatically in 2000 to 944 bp and the proportion greater than 1000 bp had grown to about 31 percent at the end of 2000. The proportion of distressed debt was just 9 percent one year earlier and 17 percent by mid-year. If US Treasuries had

[10] This is essentially Moody's approach (Moody's, 1999). The resulting expected default rate on all of their rated debt is 9.5 percent by the end of 2001 (revised up from 9.1 percent on 25 January 2001 from their year-end forecast).

Figure 23.4 Distressed* and default debt as a percentage of total high yield debt market

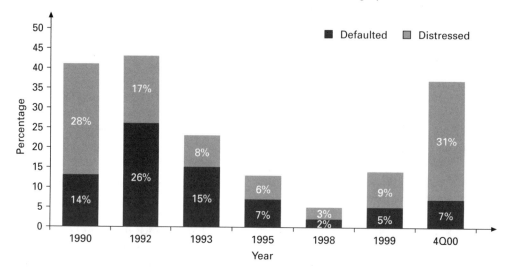

* Defined as yield-to-maturity spread ≥ 1000bp over comparable Treasuries.
Source: Salomon Smith Barney and NYU Salomon Center.

not *fallen* by 1.32 percent in 2000, the proportion of bonds with at least a 1000 bp spread would still have been very large, 27 percent, and comparable to the level in 1990.

To provide our forecast of default rates, we observe the amount of new issuance by initial bond rating over the last ten years and apply these amounts to the marginal mortality rates from table 23.18. We then consider the current market's distressed proportion (27–31 percent) and conclude that something like half of that cohort will default over the next two years. Combining these two methods results in a forecast of a 6.5–7.0 percent default rate in 2001.[11] This will add a considerable amount of debt to the defaulted debt segment, perhaps $42–45 billion – at least $12 billion more than in 2000. We expect that the size of the high yield bond market will swell by mid-2001 to perhaps $650 billion as we add the huge amount of new fallen angels to our base plus new issuance which picked up in early January 2001. Estimates are that as much as $70 billion of these bonds were downgraded to non-investment-grade status, most in the second half of 2000. Of course, a great deal will depend on the level of the economy and whether the nation enters a recession or not. A few very large defaults would swell our default numbers as well. For example, defaults by Finova, Southern California Edison, and Pacific G&E could increase our statistics considerably.[12]

---

[11] This is an increase of 1 percent over our midyear 2000 forecast, mainly owing to the increase in the size of the distressed market and the sudden vulnerability of heretofore investment grade public utilities and financial companies that have become fragile fallen angels.

[12] Indeed, Southern California Edison announced in mid-January that it had defaulted on its $32 billion line of Commercial Paper. If the bonds of these California electric and gas utilities default, they may add to our default totals. But, in reality, no high yield bond dedicated portfolios actually have invested in these bonds since they were downgraded only in early 2001. Indeed, Pacific G&E and Southern California Edison were AA- and A-rated as late as the end of 2000. Hence, these bonds do not appear in our high yield population at the end of the year and cannot be part of any first quarter 2001 default rate.

Size of the Defaulted and Distressed Debt Market

The current size of the defaulted and distressed debt markets is the largest we have ever recorded. Our estimate, shown in table 23.24 and figure 23.5, are that public defaulted bonds are about $47 billion face value and public distressed debt about $186 billion (assuming a 30 percent proportion on a $615 billion high yield bond market). We have revised our private to public debt ratio down from 2:1 to 1.8 due to more recent observations of defaulted firm balance sheets. Still, the enormous increase in defaulted and distressed bonds results in an estimate of more than $650 billion (face value) of public and private, defaulted and distressed debt. Our market value estimates are also extremely high although we reduced our estimates of the market to face value ratio to 25 percent (public defaults), 50 percent (public distressed), 60 percent (private defaults) and 75 percent (private distressed). All together, we estimate about a $400 billion (market value) defaulted and distressed debt market. Note that the 2000 estimates are more than double the amounts, for both face and market values, of the previous highest year (1990).

Table 23.24 Estimated face and market values of defaulted and distressed debt, 31 December 2000 ($ billions)

	Face value ($)	Market value ($)
Public debt		
Defaulted[a]	47.0	11.8 (.25×FV)
Distressed[b]	186.0	93.0 (.50×FV)
Total public	233.0	104.8
Private debt[c]		
Defaulted	84.6	50.8 (.60×FV)
Distressed	334.8	251.1 (.75×FV)
Total private	419.4	301.9
Total public and private	652.4	406.7

[a] Updated from 1998 and includes $23.5 billion of defaults in 1999 and $30.2 billion of defaults in 2000. The total is also adjusted for bonds that have emerged from Chapter 11 bankruptcies in 2000.
[b] Distressed debt is defined as YTM > 10 percent (1000 bps) above the Treasury 10-Year Bond Rate. This amount is estimated to be 31 percent of the high yield bond market ($600 billion).
[c] Assumes 1.8 : 1.0 ratio of private to public debt. Based on recent sample of defaulting company balance sheets in 1997–99 and several prior similar studies by the author.
Source: Estimated from Salomon Smith Barney's High Yield Bond DataBase, NYU Salomon Center Defaulted Bond DataBase, New Generation Research Corporation.

High Yield Market Returns

Estimates of returns for the coming year are also very difficult due to the many factors that could trigger a substantial turnaround or a continuation of the recent past downward spiral. Looking dispassionately at the aforementioned breakeven analysis (table 23.23) and the historical co-movement of default rates and total annual returns (figure 23.6), we actually were quite optimistic about returns in 2001, as long as default

Figure 23.5 Size of defaulted and distressed debt market exceeds record levels of early 1990s ($ billions)

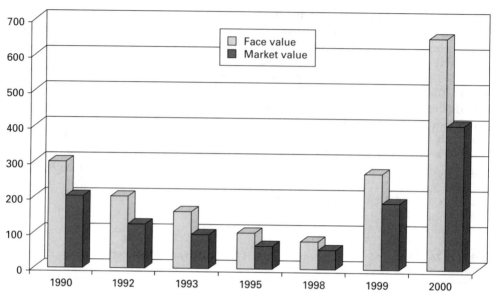

Source: E. Altman, NYU Salomon Center

Figure 23.6 High yield bond market default rates vs. returns

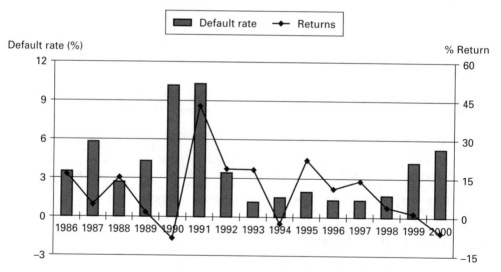

Source: E. Altman, NYU Salomon Center, Stern School of Business and Salomon Smith Barney, Inc.

rates do not exceed 8 percent this year. At 8 percent and a recovery rate of 30 percent, the yield-to-maturity of 14.56 (and the yield-to-worst of 13.75 percent) as of 31 December 2000 provided a substantial cushion over the breakeven rate. This "cushion," at 2.47 percent, compares quite closely with actual historical return spreads that investors have apparently been content with in the past. Since we are actually predicting lower default rates than 8 percent, the outlook is even more positive.

The average high yield bond market's yield spread tightened considerably in the first two weeks of January 2001, by about 60 bp, as returns have moved positively for the first time in a long time. We are quite sanguine about the possibility of another reversal as new bad news may manifest about defaults in general, or high-profile names becoming distressed or actually fail, or if the economy falters more than expected. If we look at the historical relationship (shown in figure 23.6), we could very well see a reversal similar to, although not as spectacular as, 1991, albeit with more volatility as the market has changed since the early 1990s. The question, of course, is when the reversal or turnaround will take place on a fairly consistent basis.

24 | Market Size and Investment Performance of Defaulted Bonds and Bank Loans: 1987–2000*

with Keith Cyrus

This report presents results and discussion of the investment performance of those bonds and bank loans that have defaulted on their scheduled payments to creditors and continue trading while the issuing firm attempts a financial reorganization. Monthly total return measures are compiled based on the Altman–NYU Salomon Center indexes of defaulted bonds and defaulted bank loans, as well as an index that combines bonds and loans. These returns are compared to the total returns of common stocks and high yield corporate bonds. Returns are based on our market-weighted indexes and presented for the past year (2000), as well as for the last 14 years (for bonds) and five years for bank loans. We also estimate the supply of defaulted debt in the USA in the public and private markets.

The year 2000 was a very poor year for investors in defaulted securities, although there were some bright spots and prospects. The Altman–NYU Salomon Center index of public defaulted bonds suffered its worst annual return performance in the entire history of our maintaining the index (14 years). Average return declined by slightly over 33 percent. Reasons for this precipitous decline were the severe imbalance of supply and demand for distressed debt, some chronically distressed industries, and the low

* The assistance of Brenda Karlin, Aashish Mohan and Lourdes C. Tanglao of the NYU Salomon Center and the many securities firms and distressed securities investors who provided us with price quotations and other data is appreciated. Special thanks to Gabriella Petrucci, Sau Man Kam and Wilson Miranda of Salomon Smith Barney for their data assistance. This article follows up that given in chapter 22.

perceived asset values of many of the newer defaulted and bankrupt companies. Finally, the dismal performance of the high yield bond market itself had a dampening effect on all risky debt, especially distressed debt.

Defaulted bank loans fared comparatively better, recording a more moderate decline of –6.59 percent. Except for the initial year (1996) of our bank loan index, performance has been lackluster in the past four years. Finally, the combined public bond and private bank loan index recorded an annual return in 2000 of –15.8 percent, resulting in a negative performance over the five years of the combined index calculation period. Comparative returns for the 14-year period (1987–2000) show that common stocks continued its number one asset class return/risk position. High yield bonds, while performing poorly in 2000 (–5.68 percent), maintained its average annual return advantage over defaulted bonds.

The two "bright" or positive factors related to the defaulted bond and bank loan markets in 2000 were the continued enormous increase in the supply of new defaulted issues and the record low average market-to-face value ratio of the index at the end of the year. The size of the index rose by more than 50 percent in number of issues and almost doubled in face value over the past twelve months as the default amount of high yield bonds reached a record high level in 2000 and the default rate went from 4.15 percent to over 5.0 percent (see our companion report on *Defaults and Returns in the High Yield Bond Market* [chapter 23 in this volume]). The market value of our defaulted bond index increased only modestly, however, as the average market-to-face value ratio declined to an all time low of 15.4 percent from 25.0 percent one year earlier.

Our estimate of the size of the distressed and defaulted debt markets, both public and private, increased dramatically to an astounding $640 billion face value and about $400 billion in market value.

INTRODUCTION

This report on the performance of defaulted bonds and bank loans presents our annual update and analysis. For in-depth discussions of the supply and demand elements of defaulted and distressed securities, as well as their performance and other attributes, see Altman (1991), (1993a and b), (1993–1999); Branch and Ray (1992); Altman and Eberhart (1994); Ward and Griepentrog (1993); Gilson (1995); Hotchkiss and Mooradian (1998); Reilly et al. (1998); and Eberhart et al. (1999). Despite the poor performance of defaulted bonds and bank loans in the last several years, we are confident that this "asset class" will continue to attract an increasing amount of new capital, and that the supply of distressed and defaulted securities will continue to grow – a phenomenon that manifested itself strongly over the past 24 months.

MONITORING PERFORMANCE

To monitor the performance of defaulted debt securities, a measure called the Altman–NYU Salomon Center defaulted bond index (A-NYU index) was developed in 1990.[1] The sample period of this index starts in January 1987 and, as of 31 December 2000, contained 129 issues (72 companies) with a market value of $4.3 billion and a face value of its component securities of $27.8 billion. This is a dramatic increase from the $1.4 and $5.5 billion amounts of two years ago, and $4.1 and 16.3 billion of last year. The number of issues in the index is considerably larger than in the recent past and is more reminiscent of the size of the index in the early 1990s. Indeed, the size of our index, in terms of face value of public defaulted bonds, is close to that of the early 1990s. The market value, however, is only slightly larger than it was one year ago. Table 24.1 shows the size of the index at year-end since its inception in December 1986. Note the variability in the number of issues from as low as 30 in 1986 to as high as 231 in 1992. In our report last year, we predicted that the size of the index, as measured by market values and number of issues, would continue to increase in the coming years as defaults would rise to record levels – and it did in a most spectacular way in 2000 as total bond defaults topped $30 billion, $6.7 billion more than the previous record year of one year earlier.

One measure of the defaulted bond market's current relative health, and also its potential, is the ratio of the aggregate market-to-face value of the component securities that comprise our indexes (last column of table 24.1). This ratio has ranged, at year-end, from a high of 0.74 in 1987 to its present low level of 0.15. In most years, this ratio varied between a fairly narrow range of about 0.40 to 0.52. Excellent returns in 1987

Table 24.1   Size of the Altman–NYU Salomon Center defaulted bond index (1986–2000)

Year end	Number of issues	Number of firms	Face value ($ billions)	Market value ($ billions)	Market-to-face ratio
1986	30	10	1.7	0.5	0.29
1987	53	18	5.7	4.2	0.74
1988	91	34	5.2	2.7	0.52
1989	111	35	8.7	3.4	0.39
1990	173	68	18.7	5.1	0.27
1991	207	80	19.6	6.1	0.31
1992	231	90	21.7	11.1	0.51
1993	151	77	11.8	5.8	0.49
1994	93	35	6.3	3.3	0.52
1995	50	27	5.0	2.3	0.46
1996	39	28	5.3	2.4	0.45
1997	37	26	5.9	2.7	0.46
1998	36	30	5.5	1.4	0.25
1999	83	60	16.3	4.1	0.25
2000	129	72	27.8	4.3	0.15

[1] This index, originally developed in Altman's Foothill Report (1990) is maintained and published on a monthly basis at the NYU Salomon Center of the Leonard N. Stern School of Business. It is available, along with data and reports on high yield debt default rates and performance, from the Center (212/998-0701 or 212/998-0709).

(38.0 percent) resulted in the market-to-face ratio increasing to 0.74, while the precipitous declines in 1989, 1990, 1998 and 2000 dropped the ratio to below 0.30. Although returns were so poor in 2000, we still believe in the eventual "regression to the mean" phenomenon. Therefore, 2000's year-end low of 0.15 bodes well for future increases in the ratio and high investment returns. The 2000 extremely low ratio is especially interesting in that newly defaulted bonds' price levels generally average about 40 percent of face value for all bonds and 50 percent for senior unsecured corporates. And, the majority of our 129 bond index issues are "senior" in priority. In 2000, the weighted average price of defaulting issues was about 26 percent of face value, so the bond index's market-to-face value ratio of 15 percent reflects the decline in both "seasoned" defaulted issues as well as the continued low initial prices at default.

The A-NYU index includes securities of companies at various stages of the reorganization process, either in bankruptcy or in a restructuring. Data on returns is compiled from just after default up to when the bankrupt firm either emerges from Chapter 11, is liquidated, or until the default is "cured" or resolved through an exchange. Distressed restructuring company securities are also included. The index includes issues of all seniorities, from senior-secured to junior-unsecured debt. A study by Altman and Eberhart (1994), updated by us for Standard & Poor's (Brand and Behar, 1998), assesses the performance of defaulted debt from the time of original issuance through default and then to emergence from bankruptcy. These studies concluded that the seniority of the issue is an extremely important determinant of the performance of defaulted debt for specific periods, not only from issuance to emergence but also from default to emergence. (Note that the A-NYU Index does not include convertible or international company issues.)

2000 Performance

As noted above, the Altman-NYU Salomon Center index of defaulted bonds performed very poorly in 2000, falling by 33.09 percent, continuing the recent lackluster performance (table 24.2). Returns were especially negative in the last quarter of the year (−23.4 percent), and the poor performance was across the board in terms of industrial sectors. The market also performed poorly in the second quarter of the year (except in June), falling by almost 10 percent, as the size of the index increased dramatically. The monthly returns for this past year, as well as for all of the prior 13 years, are shown in table 24.3. The index level fell from 247.0 at the end of 1999 to 165.3 at the end of 2000 (December 1986 = 100).

During 1999, there were several exceptionally poor months. There were five months with negative returns above 5 percent. There were no positive months greater than 5 percent and only two positive months overall. (See our later discussion on highly volatile months in table 24.9.) In contrast, the S&P 500 stock index, which also declined in 2000, had five monthly observations with returns or losses exceeding 5 percent in 2000, but two were positive months.

The overall performance of defaulted debt securities was again considerably lower than the total return of the S&P 500 common stock index (−9.11 percent – assuming reinvestment of dividends) and also below the Salomon Smith Barney high yield bond market index (−5.68 percent). Note, however, that all three of our risky security indexes posted negative performances in 2000. On the other hand, "relatively safe" ten-year US

Table 24.2 Altman–NYU Salomon Center defaulted bond index: Comparison of returns (1987–2000)

	Altman–NYU Salomon Center defaulted bond index (%)	S&P 500 stock index (%)	Salomon Smith Barney high yield market index (%)
Year			
1987	37.85	5.26	4.67
1988	26.49	16.61	13.47
1989	−22.78	31.68	2.75
1990	−17.08	−3.12	−7.04
1991	43.11	30.48	39.93
1992	15.39	7.62	17.86
1993	27.91	10.08	17.36
1994	6.66	1.32	−1.25
1995	11.26	37.56	19.71
1996	10.21	22.96	11.29
1997	−1.58	34.36	13.18
1998	−26.91	28.58	3.60
1999	11.34	20.98	1.74
2000	−33.09	−9.11	−5.68
1987–2000 arithmetic average (annual) rate	6.34	16.80	9.40
Standard deviation	23.99	14.97	12.33
1987–2000 compounded average (annual) rate	3.65	15.89	8.79
1987–2000 arithmetic average (monthly) rate	0.39	1.33	0.72
Standard deviation	4.25	4.40	1.80
1987–2000 compounded average (monthly) rate	0.30	1.24	0.70

Government securities performed very well, gaining 14.5 percent in 2000, as Treasury yields fell by 132 bps in the last 12 months.

Fourteen-Year Comparative Performance

In table 24.2, we observe the return on defaulted bonds as well as common stocks and high yield bonds for the entire fourteen-year sample period, 1987–2000. Note that the arithmetic average (6.34 percent per year) return for defaulted bonds is considerably less than the S&P 500 (16.80 percent) and also below the Salomon Smith Barney high yield bond market index (9.40 percent) for the same period. In five of the 14 years, defaulted bonds performed better than both of the other two indexes (all before 1995) while in seven years it performed the worst. And, the standard deviation of annual returns is largest for defaulted bonds. On a *monthly* basis, however, the volatility comparison (as measured by the standard deviation of returns) is considerably different with defaulted bond issues actually showing slightly lower volatility (4.25 percent) than common stocks (4.40 percent), but considerably higher than high yield bonds

Table 24.3 Altman–NYU Salomon Center index of defaulted public bonds and bank loans: Returns (1987–2000) and comparison with S&P 500 stock index and Salomon Smith Barney High Yield Market Index (December 1986 = 100)

Month	Public bond index	Public bond return (%)	Bank loan return (%)	S&P return (%)	SSMB-HYMI return (%)
Jan-87	109.80	9.80		13.47	
Feb-87	121.37	10.53		3.95	
Mar-87	125.95	3.77		2.89	
Apr-87	127.52	1.25		−0.89	
May-87	128.09	0.44		0.87	
Jun-87	131.80	2.90		5.05	
Jul-87	139.05	5.50		5.07	
Aug-87	139.77	0.52		3.73	
Sep-87	136.35	−2.45		−2.19	
Oct-87	124.19	−8.92		−21.54	
Nov-87	128.19	3.22		−8.24	
Dec-87	137.85	7.53		7.61	
Total 1987 return		37.85		5.26	
Jan-88	139.84	1.44		4.21	
Feb-88	147.45	5.44		4.66	
Mar-88	152.01	3.10		−3.09	
Apr-88	156.85	3.18		1.11	
May-88	155.42	−0.91		0.87	
Jun-88	166.94	7.41		4.59	
Jul-88	165.05	−1.14		−0.38	
Aug-88	160.40	−2.82		−3.40	
Sep-88	160.28	−0.07		4.26	
Oct-88	157.69	−1.61		2.78	
Nov-88	166.88	5.83		−1.43	
Dec-88	174.36	4.48		1.75	
Total 1988 return		26.49		16.61	
Jan-89	166.57	−4.47		7.32	1.75
Feb-89	159.93	−3.99		−2.49	0.43
Mar-89	159.60	−0.21		2.33	0.01
Apr-89	162.88	2.06		5.19	0.69
May-89	164.53	1.01		4.05	1.70
Jun-89	164.38	−0.09		−0.57	1.45
Jul-89	168.43	2.46		9.03	0.45
Aug-89	164.96	−2.06		1.96	−0.39
Sep-89	152.03	−7.84		−0.41	−1.62
Oct-89	139.26	−8.40		−2.32	−2.26
Nov-89	135.58	−2.64		2.04	0.37
Dec-89	134.64	−0.70		2.40	0.22
Total 1989 return		−22.78		31.68	2.75
Jan-90	130.72	−2.91		−6.71	−3.03
Feb-90	127.03	−2.83		1.29	−1.10
Mar-90	132.08	3.98		2.65	1.06
Apr-90	134.03	1.48		−2.50	−0.51
May-90	132.37	−1.23		9.75	2.63
Jun-90	130.12	−1.71		−0.68	1.86
Jul-90	133.09	2.29		−0.32	1.73
Aug-90	129.06	−3.03		−9.04	−3.87
Sep-90	125.21	−2.99		−4.87	−5.13
Oct-90	119.85	−4.28		−0.43	−3.54

Table 24.3 *(cont'd)*

Month	Public bond index	Public bond return (%)	Bank loan return (%)	S&P return (%)	SSMB-HYMI return (%)
Nov-90	116.63	−2.69		6.46	2.02
Dec-90	111.64	−4.27		2.79	1.01
Total 1990 return		−17.08		−3.12	−7.04
Jan-91	115.20	3.18		4.36	2.59
Feb-91	124.97	8.49		7.15	8.82
Mar-91	135.60	8.50		2.42	5.24
Apr-91	154.06	13.62		0.24	3.75
May-91	158.67	2.99		4.32	0.71
Jun-91	161.31	1.66		−4.58	2.10
Jul-91	169.99	5.39		4.66	2.85
Aug-91	167.79	−1.30		2.37	2.33
Sep-91	165.36	−1.45		−1.67	0.67
Oct-91	167.15	1.08		1.34	3.00
Nov-91	165.61	−0.92		−4.03	0.95
Dec-91	159.77	−3.53		11.44	1.34
Total 1991 return		43.11		30.48	39.93
Jan-92	171.04	7.06		−1.86	2.89
Feb-92	176.52	3.21		1.30	2.93
Mar-92	183.40	3.90		−1.95	1.48
Apr-92	182.90	−0.27		2.94	0.74
May-92	187.59	2.57		0.49	1.87
Jun-92	185.62	−1.05		−1.49	1.24
Jul-92	186.09	0.25		4.09	1.85
Aug-92	184.76	−0.72		−2.05	1.33
Sep-92	183.03	−0.93		1.18	0.93
Oct-92	181.53	−0.82		0.35	−1.22
Nov-92	180.79	−0.41		3.41	1.38
Dec-92	184.36	1.97		1.23	1.19
Total 1992 return		15.39		7.62	17.86
Jan-93	194.59	5.55		0.84	2.44
Feb-93	200.59	3.09		1.36	1.89
Mar-93	208.93	4.16		2.11	1.55
Apr-93	209.49	0.27		−2.42	0.77
May-93	214.81	2.54		2.68	1.38
Jun-93	218.68	1.80		0.29	2.23
Jul-93	224.26	2.55		−0.40	0.98
Aug-93	226.79	1.13		3.79	1.08
Sep-93	229.73	1.30		−0.77	0.24
Oct-93	231.21	0.64		2.07	1.94
Nov-93	235.27	1.76		−0.95	0.54
Dec-93	235.82	0.23		1.21	1.10
Total 1993 return		27.91		10.08	17.36
Jan-94	239.18	1.43		3.40	2.17
Feb-94	246.84	3.20		−2.71	−0.46
Mar-94	248.71	0.76		−4.36	−3.72
Apr-94	243.63	−2.04		1.28	−0.91
May-94	246.53	1.19		1.64	0.35
Jun-94	243.90	−1.06		−2.45	0.11
Jul-94	245.06	0.47		3.28	0.98
Aug-94	246.86	0.74		4.10	0.56

Table 24.3 (cont'd)

Month	Public bond index	Public bond return (%)	Bank loan return (%)	S&P return (%)	SSMB-HYMI return (%)
Sep-94	250.31	1.40		-2.45	-0.26
Oct-94	251.04	0.29		2.25	0.02
Nov-94	252.28	0.50		-3.64	-1.10
Dec-94	251.51	-0.30		1.48	1.12
Total 1994 return		6.66		1.32	-1.25
Jan-95	250.97	-0.22		2.59	1.44
Feb-95	256.42	2.17		3.90	3.33
Mar-95	267.27	4.23		2.95	1.04
Apr-95	267.51	0.09		2.95	2.35
May-95	282.02	5.42		4.00	2.98
Jun-95	281.51	-0.18		2.32	0.71
Jul-95	282.02	0.18		3.31	1.20
Aug-95	282.10	0.03		0.25	0.62
Sep-95	286.47	1.55		4.22	1.16
Oct-95	273.01	-4.70		-0.36	0.84
Nov-95	278.39	1.97		4.39	0.91
Dec-95	279.84	0.52		1.93	1.59
Total 1995 return		11.26		37.56	19.71
Jan-96	286.86	2.51	0.96	3.40	1.47
Feb-96	309.09	7.75	2.80	0.93	0.62
Mar-96	323.11	4.54	2.79	0.96	-0.50
Apr-96	329.51	1.98	-0.01	1.47	-0.03
May-96	333.71	1.28	4.87	2.58	0.56
Jun-96	344.77	3.31	3.76	0.38	0.77
Jul-96	340.99	-1.09	1.38	-4.42	0.65
Aug-96	341.81	0.24	-1.14	2.11	1.04
Sep-96	349.01	2.11	0.79	5.63	2.34
Oct-96	355.63	1.90	1.69	2.76	1.15
Nov-96	324.98	-8.62	0.37	7.56	1.92
Dec-96	308.40	-5.10	-0.10	-1.98	0.79
Total 1996 return		10.21	19.56	22.96	11.29
Jan-97	303.64	-1.54	1.88	6.25	0.75
Feb-97	308.02	1.44	2.40	0.78	1.70
Mar-97	313.37	1.74	0.77	-4.11	-1.03
Apr-97	306.69	-2.13	-6.63	5.97	0.71
May-97	307.03	0.11	-1.93	6.88	2.02
Jun-97	305.28	-0.57	3.60	4.48	1.69
Jul-97	304.59	-0.23	0.45	7.96	2.29
Aug-97	311.49	2.27	1.19	-5.60	0.25
Sep-97	316.60	1.64	2.41	5.48	1.75
Oct-97	315.20	-0.44	0.24	-3.34	0.80
Nov-97	311.57	-1.15	-0.41	4.63	0.51
Dec-97	303.53	-2.58	-1.82	1.72	1.05
Total 1997 return		-1.58	1.75	34.36	13.18
Jan-98	303.5	0.00	-0.38	1.11	2.26
Feb-98	309.5	1.96	-0.84	7.21	0.68
Mar-98	312.0	0.82	1.68	5.12	1.08
Apr-98	312.6	0.19	4.19	1.01	0.54
May-98	319.7	2.27	2.33	-1.72	0.27
Jun-98	318.8	-0.28	-0.99	4.06	0.22

Table 24.3 *(cont'd)*

Month	Public bond index	Public bond return (%)	Bank loan return (%)	S&P return (%)	SSMB-HYMI return (%)
Jul-98	322.5	1.15	−0.05	−1.07	0.80
Aug-98	263.6	−18.25	−6.26	−14.46	−6.70
Sep-98	234.1	−11.21	−6.16	6.41	1.23
Oct-98	211.9	−9.48	−7.88	8.13	−1.38
Nov-98	227.4	7.32	5.44	6.06	5.02
Dec-98	221.9	−2.43	−0.85	5.76	−0.07
Total 1998		−26.91	−10.22	28.58	3.60
Jan-99	222.3	0.22	3.59	4.18	1.50
Feb-99	231.0	3.91	−1.01	−3.11	−0.84
Mar-99	242.8	5.07	−1.70	4.00	0.85
Apr-99	269.8	11.15	2.91	3.87	2.09
May-99	266.7	−1.14	1.92	−2.36	−1.57
Jun-99	269.4	1.00	2.58	5.50	−0.22
Jul-99	279.5	3.75	1.31	−3.12	0.22
Aug-99	265.6	−4.96	−4.80	−0.50	−1.19
Sep-99	251.5	−5.33	1.29	−2.74	−0.76
Oct-99	233.5	−7.13	−2.64	6.33	−0.68
Nov-99	249.3	6.75	−2.31	2.04	1.57
Dec-99	247.0	−0.92	−0.12	5.89	0.84
Total 1999		11.34	0.65	20.98	1.74
Jan-00	255.7	3.50	3.64	−5.02	−0.83
Feb-00	253.1	−1.01	−2.27	−1.89	0.24
Mar-00	245.9	−2.86	−5.48	9.77	−2.03
Apr-00	232.0	−5.64	1.02	−3.01	0.40
May-00	219.3	−5.46	−0.08	−2.05	−1.39
Jun-00	221.9	1.16	−1.46	2.47	2.25
Jul-00	221.2	−0.32	0.38	−1.56	1.09
Aug-00	211.4	−3.96	−0.65	6.21	0.74
Sep-00	211.1	−0.64	0.86	−5.28	−1.07
Oct-00	196.5	−6.91	−0.71	−0.42	−2.96
Nov-00	176.6	−10.10	−1.39	−7.88	−4.09
Dec-00	165.3	−6.42	−0.39	0.49	2.04
Total 2000		−33.09	−6.59	−9.11	−5.68

(1.80 percent). This latter comparison is understandable since high yield bonds pay a fairly steady fixed interest component each month while defaulted bonds do not.

We also calculate the Sharpe ratio for each of our risky asset indexes. This ratio compares the excess performance (if any) of an asset class compared to default risk free Treasury bonds (in this case we use ten-year Treasuries) and then divide this excess return by a measure of the volatility of the asset class – the standard deviation. Again, the defaulted bond index performance compares unfavorably to the other two asset classes when we observe this measure of return/risk performance. The poorer relative Sharpe ratio measure is still evident when calculating monthly returns, but the differences are not as great.

Figure 24.1 graphs the monthly index levels for our three security classes for the entire sample period. We can observe that in March 1995, the S&P index level rose above the two others and remains solidly in that position. And, in mid-1997, the high yield bond index nudged the defaulted bond index out of second place.

Figure 24.1 Defaulted bond, stock, and high yield bond indices (1987–2000)

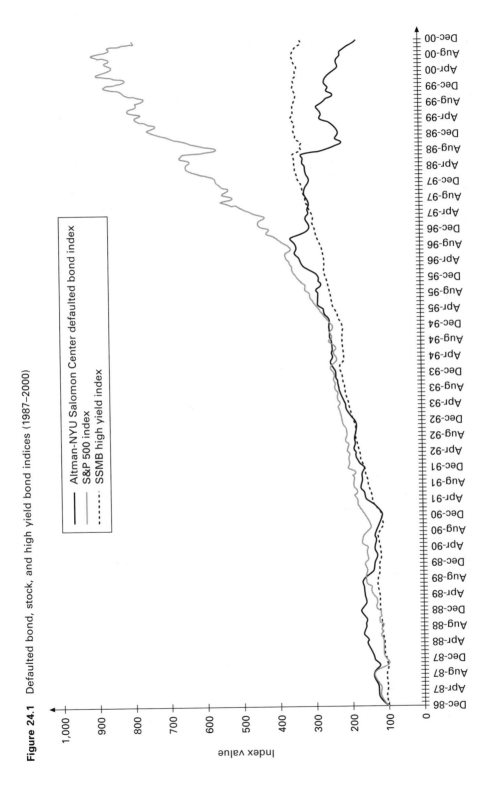

DIVERSIFICATION ATTRIBUTES: RISKY ASSET RETURNS CORRELATIONS

One of the potential strategies suggested by our analysis is to include defaulted debt in a larger portfolio of risky securities. A number of domestic pension funds and foreign portfolios have, in effect, taken this approach by allocating a proportion of their total investments to defaulted debt money managers. Almost all portfolio managers involved in the distressed market have been specialists in the sector, rather than investors in distressed bonds within broader-based portfolios. Therefore, the avenue of diversification appears to be primarily through the use of different investment managers. (There are some rare exceptions where a mutual fund combines investments in more traditional debt and equity securities with distressed securities). A number of "fund-of-funds" that have adopted this strategy have also chosen distressed securities managers with different styles including active, semi-active and passive approaches. A similar strategy, practiced by foreign closed-end funds, is to directly invest in a large number of private US distressed securities investment funds. Instead of diversifying across asset classes, these funds have a strategy of investing in distressed security managers with different approaches.

Table 24.4 demonstrates the correlation between the Altman–NYU defaulted bond index and the other two risky asset classes – common stocks and high yield bonds – for the last 14 years. We see that the monthly return correlation is only 26.6 percent between defaulted debt and S&P equities. This is down, somewhat, from 28.0 percent in the 1987–98 period but slightly higher than last year's 25.6 percent. Since defaulted debt holders usually end up owning the equity of the emerged Chapter 11 entity, unless they sell the debt just prior to emergence from restructuring, it is interesting to note the low correlation of returns between these two indexes. The quarterly correlations are slightly higher (31.0 percent).

The correlation between high yield bonds and defaulted bonds is fairly high at about 56.8 percent (monthly) and 59.9 percent (quarterly). Interestingly, the correlations between high yield bonds and our defaulted loan index (table 24.8) is significantly lower at 39.5 percent (monthly), while the correlation of loans and equities is actually negative, indicating an inverse relationship.

Table 24.4 Correlation of Altman–NYU Salomon Center indexes of defaulted bonds with other speculative securities indexes (1987–2000)

	Altman–NYU bond index (%)	S&P 500 stock index (%)	Salomon Smith Barney high yield index (%)
Correlation of monthly returns			
Altman–NYU bond index	100.00	26.56	56.75
S&P 500 stock index		100.00	51.83
Salomon Smith Barney high yield index			100.00
Correlation of quarterly returns			
Altman–NYU bond index	100.00	30.99	59.92
S&P 500 stock index		100.00	51.03
Salomon Smith Barney high yield index			100.00

We believe that the relatively high correlation of defaulted securities and risky bonds is partially a function of the operating performance of firms in general, the outlook for risky companies, and the overall confidence in the market for risky debt. Although these latter correlations are relatively high, it is also clear that the defaulted bond index is more volatile – in both good and bad years. Again, this is not surprising since high yield debt has a base return equal to the interest payments received in each period while virtually all defaulted bonds and most defaulted loans trade "flat" (without interest receipts). In addition, there is a great deal of uncertainty about what the reorganization plan will specify and how each class of creditors will be treated – not to mention the possibility that the end-result will be a liquidation. Finally, there are several critical event dates during a bankruptcy reorganization (i.e., bankruptcy filing, post-default financing, filing of a reorganization plan and the actual plan confirmation/liquidation) which can result in large swings in the price of debt issues.

We do observe that the relative volatility between defaulted bonds and equity returns, when measured on a monthly basis, puts the former in a much more favorable light. This implies a greater degree of autocorrelation (strings of gains or losses) that can exacerbate annual return levels and volatility but not monthly return variability.

DEFAULTED BANK LOAN PERFORMANCE

It is now quite common for distressed securities managers to invest in both distressed bonds and the private debt of defaulting companies – particularly bank debt. This coverage has been coincident with the loan market's increasing size and liquidity as market makers have devoted considerable resources to bank debt trading. We have attempted to fill the void of rigorous risk/return analysis by calculating an index of defaulted bank debt facilities, as well as a combined index of bonds and bank loans.

Our Altman–NYU Salomon Center index of defaulted bank loans is also a market weighted index comprised of US companies. The index started with 17 facilities as of December 1995 (table 24.5) and at the end of 2000 had 100 (up from just 45 one year earlier and 15 two years earlier). As of the end of 2000, the index had a face value of $26.9 billion and $13.6 billion in market value – a market-to-face value of 0.51, down from 0.53 last year, 0.63 two years ago and 0.71 three years ago. This compares with a 2000 market to face ratio of only 0.15 for our public bond index. Both the bonds' and bank loans' market-to-face ratio is at an all time low level. The bank loan index is comprised of only senior debt, much of which is secured; the bond index, discussed

Table 24.5 Size of the Altman–NYU Salomon Center defaulted bank loan index (1995–2000)

Year end	Number of issues	Number of firms	Face value ($ billions)	Market value ($ billions)	Market-to-face ratio
1995	17	14	2.9	2.0	0.69
1996	23	22	4.2	3.3	0.79
1997	18	15	3.4	2.4	0.71
1998	15	13	3.0	1.9	0.63
1999	45	23	12.9	6.8	0.53
2000	100	39	26.9	13.6	0.51

Table 24.6 Altman–NYU Salomon Center index of defaulted bank loans: Returns (1996–2000) and comparison with S&P 500 stock index and Salomon Smith Barney high yield market index (Base of 100 starting December 1995 for Altman Index)

Month	Bank loan index	Bank loan return (%)	Public bond return (%)	S&P return (%)	SSMB-HYMI return (%)
Jan-96	100.96	0.96	2.51	3.40	1.47
Feb-96	103.79	2.80	7.75	0.93	0.62
Mar-96	106.69	2.79	4.54	0.96	−0.50
Apr-96	106.68	−0.01	1.98	1.47	−0.03
May-96	111.88	4.87	1.28	2.58	0.56
Jun-96	116.08	3.76	3.31	0.38	0.77
Jul-96	117.68	1.38	−1.09	−4.42	0.65
Aug-96	116.34	−1.14	0.24	2.11	1.04
Sep-96	117.26	0.79	2.11	5.63	2.34
Oct-96	119.24	1.69	1.90	2.76	1.15
Nov-96	119.69	0.37	−8.62	7.56	1.92
Dec-96	119.56	−0.10	−5.10	−1.98	0.79
Total 1996 return		19.56	10.21	22.96	11.29
Jan-97	121.81	1.88	−1.54	6.25	0.75
Feb-97	124.73	2.40	1.44	0.78	1.70
Mar-97	125.69	0.77	1.74	−4.11	−1.03
Apr-97	117.36	−6.63	−2.13	5.97	0.71
May-97	115.10	−1.93	0.11	6.88	2.02
Jun-97	119.23	3.60	−0.57	4.48	1.69
Jul-97	119.77	0.45	−0.23	7.96	2.29
Aug-97	121.20	1.19	2.27	−5.60	0.25
Sep-97	124.12	2.41	1.64	5.48	1.75
Oct-97	124.42	0.24	−0.44	−3.34	0.80
Nov-97	123.90	−0.41	−1.15	4.63	0.51
Dec-97	121.65	−1.82	−2.58	1.72	1.05
Total 1997 return		1.75	−1.58	34.36	13.18
Jan-98	121.2	−0.38	0.00	1.11	2.26
Feb-98	120.2	−0.84	1.96	7.21	0.68
Mar-98	122.2	1.68	0.82	5.12	1.08
Apr-98	127.3	4.19	0.19	1.01	0.54
May-98	130.3	2.33	2.27	−1.72	0.27
Jun-98	129.0	−0.99	−0.28	4.06	0.22
Jul-98	128.9	−0.05	1.15	−1.07	0.80
Aug-98	120.8	−6.26	−18.25	−14.46	−6.70
Sep-98	113.4	−6.16	−11.21	6.41	1.23
Oct-98	104.5	−7.88	−9.48	8.13	−1.38
Nov-98	110.2	5.44	7.32	6.06	5.02
Dec-98	109.2	−0.85	−2.43	5.76	−0.07
Total 1998		−10.22	−26.91	28.58	3.60
Jan-99	113.1	3.59	0.22	4.18	1.50
Feb-99	112.0	−1.01	3.91	−3.11	−0.84
Mar-99	110.1	−1.70	5.07	4.00	0.85
Apr-99	113.3	2.91	11.15	3.87	2.09
May-99	115.5	1.92	−1.14	−2.36	−1.57
Jun-99	118.5	2.58	1.00	5.50	−0.22
Jul-99	120.0	1.31	3.75	−3.12	0.22
Aug-99	114.2	−4.80	−4.96	−0.50	−1.19
Sep-99	115.7	1.29	−5.33	−2.74	−0.76
Oct-99	112.7	−2.64	−7.13	6.33	−0.68

Table 24.6 *(cont'd)*

Month	Bank loan index	Bank loan return (%)	Public bond return (%)	S&P return (%)	SSMB-HYMI return (%)
Nov-99	110.1	−2.31	6.75	2.04	1.57
Dec-99	109.9	−0.12	−0.92	5.89	0.84
Total 1999		0.65	11.34	20.98	1.74
Jan-00	113.9	3.64	3.50	−5.02	−0.83
Feb-00	111.3	−2.27	−1.01	−1.89	0.24
Mar-00	105.2	−5.48	−2.86	9.77	−2.03
Apr-00	106.3	1.02	−5.64	−3.01	0.40
May-00	106.2	−0.08	−5.46	−2.05	−1.39
Jun-00	104.7	−1.46	1.16	2.47	2.25
Jul-00	105.1	0.38	−0.32	−1.56	1.09
Aug-00	104.4	−0.65	−3.96	6.21	0.74
Sep-00	105.3	0.86	−0.64	−5.28	−1.07
Oct-00	104.5	−0.71	−6.91	−0.42	−2.96
Nov-00	103.1	−1.39	−10.10	−7.88	−4.09
Dec-00	102.7	−0.39	−6.42	0.49	2.04
Total 2000		−6.59	−33.09	−9.11	−5.68

earlier, is a mix of senior and subordinated debt. As indicated, the 0.51 ratio is at the lowest level in the five-year history of our index and noticeably lower than what is typical for defaulted bank loans (Carty et al., 1998; Miller and Keisman, 1999).

The performance of our bank loan index was also poor in 2000, but relatively better than the defaulted bond and S&P 500 stock indexes, losing 6.59 percent. The index closed as of the end of 2000 at 102.7 (December 1995=100). Bank loans were far less volatile than defaulted bonds and did not suffer many extreme negative months, except in March when the bank loan index fell by 5.48 percent. In eight of the 12 months in 2000, our defaulted bond and bank loan indexes have the same sign (+ or −) in terms of monthly returns. The monthly defaulted bank loan index, from its inception to the present, is shown in table 24.6.

Table 24.7 shows that the five-year (1996–2000) defaulted bank loan average return was just barely positive at 1.03 percent per year, considerably below the stock market's incredible performance and also below that of high yield bonds. But, it was considerably above the defaulted bond index's negative return during this period. The annual standard deviations for defaulted loans was higher than high yield bonds but considerably lower than that of the stock market.

The correlation between our defaulted bank loan index and equity returns is actually negative (−7.4 percent, table 24.8) and just 39.5 percent with respect to the high yield bond index (compared to 56.2 percent for the defaulted bond vs. high yield bond indexes). Even the defaulted bond vs. defaulted bank loan index returns are, perhaps surprisingly, not very highly correlated at 58.7 percent (monthly returns). This measure is down slightly from one year earlier. While an almost 60 percent correlation is still fairly high, it is perhaps not as high as one would expect. This perhaps indicates that the monthly movements between bonds and bank loans are somewhat based on strategic desires as to the seniority of securities of specific firms and less a function of the overall outlook of the company.

Table 24.7 Altman–NYU Salomon Center bank loan index: Comparison of returns (1996–2000)

Year	Altman–NYU Salomon Center bank loan index (%)	S&P 500 stock index (%)	Salomon Smith Barney high yield market index (%)
1996	19.56	22.96	11.29
1997	1.75	34.36	13.18
1998	−10.22	28.58	3.60
1999	0.65	20.98	1.74
2000	−6.59	−9.11	−5.68
1996–2000 arithmetic average (annual) rate	1.03	19.55	4.83
Standard deviation	11.50	16.85	7.63
1996–2000 compounded average (annual) rate	0.53	18.49	4.60
1996–2000 arithmetic average (monthly) rate	0.08	1.53	0.39
Standard deviation	2.82	4.65	1.71
1996–2000 compounded average (monthly) rate	0.04	1.42	0.38

Table 24.8 Correlation of Altman–NYU Salomon Center indexes of defaulted loans with other speculative securities indexes (1996–2000)

	Altman–NYU loan index (%)	S&P 500 stock index (%)	Salomon Smith Barney high yield index (%)	Altman–NYU bond index (%)
Correlation of monthly returns				
Altman–NYU loan index	100.00	−7.41	39.51	58.68
S&P 500 stock index		100.00	56.12	18.53
Salomon Smith Barney high yield index			100.00	56.16
Altman–NYU bond index				100.00
Correlation of Quarterly Returns				
Altman–NYU loan index	100.00	11.11	36.15	72.65
S&P 500 stock index		100.00	76.29	45.60
Salomon Smith Barney high yield index			100.00	51.64
Altman–NYU bond index				100.00

CORRELATIONS IN EXCEPTIONAL MONTHS

The correlations listed in tables 24.4 and 24.8 are for the entire period 1987–2000. We thought it instructive to analyze the correlation between defaulted securities and equities, and the correlations between defaulted debt and high yield bonds, when the stock market performs exceptionally well or poorly. We selected an arbitrary criterion of ±5.0 percent monthly stock market return as a definition of an exceptional month. Over the 14-year sample period, there were 37 months when the stock market's performance exceeded this ±5 percent criteria (table 24.9). Note that there were six observations each in 1987 and 1997, none during the period 1992–95, seven in 1998, three in 1999, and five in 2000. Of these, August 1998 stands out as the biggest one-month decline for both the S&P index and our defaulted bond index.

The correlations calculated (not shown) from the data for the exceptional months are all considerably higher than the correlations when they are measured over the entire 14-year period. For example, our defaulted bond index had a 0.46 correlation with the

Table 24.9 Correlation between indexes given a change in S&P greater than 5%

Month	Bank loan index (%)	Bond index (%)	S&P 500 stock index (%)	Salomon Smith Barney high yield index (%)
Jan-87		9.80	13.47	2.83
Jun-87		2.90	5.05	1.38
Jul-87		5.50	5.07	0.54
Oct-87		−8.92	−21.54	−2.67
Nov-87		3.22	−8.24	2.53
Dec-87		7.53	7.61	1.33
Jan-89		−4.47	7.32	1.50
Apr-89		2.06	5.19	0.30
Jul-89		2.46	9.03	0.47
Jan-90		−2.91	−6.71	−3.03
May-90		−1.23	9.75	2.63
Aug-90		−3.03	−9.04	−3.87
Nov-90		−2.69	6.46	2.02
Feb-91		8.49	7.15	8.82
Dec-91		−3.53	11.44	1.34
Sep-96	0.79	2.11	5.63	2.34
Jan-97	1.88	−1.54	6.25	0.75
Apr-97	−6.63	−2.13	5.97	0.71
May-97	−1.93	0.11	6.88	2.02
Jul-97	0.45	−0.23	7.96	2.29
Aug-97	1.19	2.27	−5.60	0.25
Sep-97	2.41	1.64	5.48	1.75
Feb-98	−0.84	2.96	7.21	0.68
Mar-98	1.68	0.82	5.12	1.08
Aug-98	−6.27	−18.25	−14.46	−6.70
Sep-98	−6.16	−11.21	6.41	1.23
Oct-98	−7.88	−9.48	8.13	−1.38
Nov-98	5.44	7.32	6.06	5.02
Dec-98	−0.85	−2.43	5.76	−0.07
Jun-99	2.58	1.00	5.50	−0.22
Oct-99	−2.64	−7.13	6.33	−0.68
Dec-99	−0.12	−0.92	5.89	0.84
Jan-00	3.64	3.50	−5.02	−0.83
Mar-00	−5.48	−2.86	9.77	−2.03
Aug-00	−0.65	−3.96	6.21	0.74
Sep-00	0.86	−0.64	−5.28	−1.07
Nov-00	−1.39	−10.10	−7.88	−4.09

stock market compared to 0.27 for the entire period. And the S&P 500 stock index correlation with high yield bonds jumps from 0.52 to 0.62. This implies a type of contagion effect in these highly volatile months, i.e., the more liquid, and larger stock markets' extreme performance in these months impacts the performance of debt securities that are also perceived as risky but quite a bit less liquid. Despite the higher correlations during exceptional months, we also observe that in 17 of 37 months, the stock market and defaulted bond market moved in opposite directions. In the case of the six *negative* exceptional stock market months, the defaulted bond market increased in three instances and in only one instance (November 1987) did the high yield bond market increase.

Combined Bond and Bank Loan Index

We also calculated a combined defaulted securities index, which is calculated based on the market values and total returns of public bonds and private bank loans (table 24.10). The combined index return was −15.84 percent in 2000, causing the cumulative four-year index to drop to 84.2 (December 1995 = 100). With the three indexes, we now offer benchmark performance criteria for a more broadly defined defaulted securities market.

Size of the Defaulted and Distressed Debt Market

The year 2000 saw the size of the defaulted and distressed debt market grow to its largest size since we have been tracking this alternative investment asset class. The continued enormous amount of new defaulted bonds (over $30 billion in 2000, table 24.11) raised the total supply of defaulted bonds (net of emergences from Chapter 11) to $47 billion. Combined with the growth in the high yield distressed bond market (yield to maturity greater than 1000 basis over 10-year Treasuries) to 31 percent (figure 24.2), the total amount of defaulted and distressed *public bonds* outstanding grew to about $233 billion (table 24.12). If we assume that the average private to public debt ratio is 1.8:1 (down from 2:1 of recent years), the level of public and private defaulted and distressed debt grew to an all time high level of about $650 billion (face value). We scaled down our market value benchmarks to 0.25 and 0.50 of face values (*public* defaulted and distressed respectively) and 0.60 and 0.75 (*private* defaulted and distressed) so that the estimate of the market value of distressed and defaulted debt is just over $400 billion. The trend of these statistics, which shows the amazing growth in the last two years, can be seen in figure 24.3.

As for the future, we expect the market size of distressed and defaulted securities to continue to increase. The huge new issue supply of non-investment grade debt in the years 1996–99 should continue to result in an increase of default amounts next year, perhaps by as much as $40–45 billion. We also expect that the flow of capital into distressed debt funds will increase as investors see the potential, despite the recent dismal performance, of distressed securities. Although we do not expect the near-term default rates to approach the record years of 1990 and 1991, the net supply of distressed and defaulted issues will certainly increase.

The current level of 100 bank facilities from 40 companies in our index is already larger than at any time in the past. We anticipate that the market-to-face value ratio will rise from its current historically low level of 0.51. (In the interest of full disclosure,

Table 24.10 Combined Altman–NYU Salomon Center defaulted public bond and bank loan indexes (December 1995 = 100)

Date	Monthly level	Return (%)	Year-to-date return (%)
Dec-95	100.00		
Jan-96	101.8	1.80	1.80
Feb-96	107.1	5.21	7.09
Mar-96	111.1	3.71	11.05
Apr-96	112.2	1.04	12.23
May-96	115.7	3.13	15.74
Jun-96	119.8	3.53	19.82
Jul-96	119.8	0.02	19.84
Aug-96	119.0	−0.67	19.04
Sep-96	120.8	1.47	20.79
Oct-96	123.0	1.80	22.97
Nov-96	118.3	−3.80	18.29
Dec-96	**115.6**	**−2.26**	**15.62**
Jan-97	116.2	0.48	0.48
Feb-97	118.6	2.04	2.54
Mar-97	119.9	1.15	3.71
Apr-97	114.6	−4.39	−0.83
May-97	113.7	−0.85	−1.68
Jun-97	115.4	1.51	−0.19
Jul-97	115.6	0.19	−0.08
Aug-97	117.5	1.72	1.64
Sep-97	119.8	2.01	3.67
Oct-97	119.7	−0.13	3.54
Nov-97	118.7	−0.79	2.72
Dec-97	**116.1**	**−2.22**	**0.44**
Jan-98	115.9	−0.20	−0.20
Feb-98	116.3	0.38	0.18
Mar-98	117.8	1.32	1.50
Apr-98	121.0	2.67	4.21
May-98	123.8	2.31	6.61
Jun-98	123.0	−0.66	5.91
Jul-98	123.6	0.51	6.45
Aug-98	109.2	−11.67	−5.97
Sep-98	100.0	−8.37	−13.83
Oct-98	91.5	−8.52	−21.18
Nov-98	97.2	6.20	−16.29
Dec-98	**95.7**	**−1.51**	**−17.55**
Jan-99	97.6	1.97	1.97
Feb-99	98.4	0.78	2.77
Mar-99	99.2	0.84	3.63
Apr-99	105.5	6.31	10.16
May-99	105.9	0.45	10.66
Jun-99	107.7	1.66	12.49
Jul-99	110.4	2.49	15.29
Aug-99	105.0	−4.87	9.67
Sep-99	103.3	−1.58	7.94
Oct-99	98.8	−4.34	3.26
Nov-99	100.4	1.59	4.90
Dec-99	**100.0**	**−0.43**	**4.45**
Jan-00	103.6	3.59	3.59
Feb-00	101.7	−1.78	1.74
Mar-00	97.3	−4.31	−2.64
Apr-00	95.6	−1.80	−4.39
May-00	93.4	−2.26	−6.55
Jun-00	93.1	−0.41	−6.93
Jul-00	93.1	0.10	−6.85
Aug-00	91.3	−2.02	−8.73
Sep-00	91.4	0.13	−8.61
Oct-00	89.1	−2.51	−10.90
Nov-00	85.7	−3.77	−14.26
Dec-00	**84.2**	**−1.84**	**−15.84**

Table 24.11   Historical default rates – straight bonds only excluding defaulted issues from par value outstanding 1971–2000 ($ millions)

Year	Par value outstanding[a] ($)	Par value defaults ($)	Default rates (%)	
2000	597,200	30,248	5.065	
1999	567,400	23,532	4.147	
1998	465,500	7,464	1.603	
1997	335,400	4,200	1.252	
1996	271,000	3,336	1.231	
1995	240,000	4,551	1.896	
1994	235,000	3,418	1.454	
1993	206,907	2,287	1.105	
1992	163,000	5,545	3.402	
1991	183,600	18,862	10.273	
1990	181,000	18,354	10.140	
1989	189,258	8,110	4.285	
1988	148,187	3,944	2.662	
1987	129,557	7,486	5.778	
1986	90,243	3,156	3.497	
1985	58,088	992	1.708	
1984	40,939	344	0.840	
1983	27,492	301	1.095	
1982	18,109	577	3.186	
1981	17,115	27	0.158	
1980	14,935	224	1.500	
1979	10,356	20	0.193	
1978	8,946	119	1.330	
1977	8,157	381	4.671	
1976	7,735	30	0.388	
1975	7,471	204	2.731	
1974	10,894	123	1.129	
1973	7,824	49	0.626	
1972	6,928	193	2.786	
1971	6,602	82	1.242	
				Standard deviation (%)
Arithmetic average default rate				
1971–2000			2.713	2.484
1978–2000			2.948	2.683
1985–2000			3.719	2.829
Weighted average default rate[b]				
1971–2000			3.482	2.558
1978–2000			3.503	2.563
1985–2000			3.582	2.565
Median annual default rate				
1971–2000			1.656	

[a] As of mid-year.
[b] Weighted by par value of amount outstanding for each year.
Source: Authors' Compilation and Salomon Smith Barney Estimates.

Figure 24.2 Distressed* and defaulted debt as a percentage of total high yield debt market

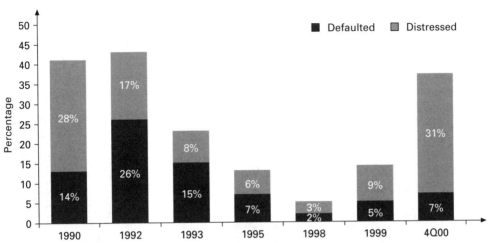

* Defined as yield-to-maturity spread ≥ 1000bp over comparable Treasuries
Source: Saloman Smith Barney and NYU Saloman Centre

Table 24.12 Estimated face and market values of defaulted and distressed debt, 31 December 2000 ($ billions)

	Face value ($)	Market value ($)
Public debt		
Defaulted[a]	47.0	11.8 (.25×FV)
Distressed[b]	186.0	93.0 (.50×FV)
Total public	233.0	104.8
Private debt[c]		
Defaulted	84.6	50.8 (.60×FV)
Distressed	334.8	251.1 (.75×FV)
Total private	419.4	301.9
Total public and private	**652.4**	**406.7**

[a] *Updated from 1998 and includes $23.5 billion of defaults in 1999 and $30.2 billion of defaults in 2000. The total is also adjusted for bonds that have emerged from Chapter 11 bankruptcies in 2000.*
[b] *Distressed debt is defined as YTM > 10 percent (1000 bps) above the Treasury 10-Year Bond Rate. This amount is estimated to be 31 percent of the high yield bond market ($600 billion).*
[c] *Assumes 1.8:1.0 ratio of private to public debt. Based on recent sample of defaulting company balance sheets in 1997–99 and several prior similar studies by the author.*
Source: Estimated from Salomon Smith Barney's High Yield Bond DataBase, NYU Salomon Center Defaulted Bond DataBase, New Generation Research Corporation.

Figure 24.3 Size of defaulted and distressed debt market exceeds record levels of early 1990s

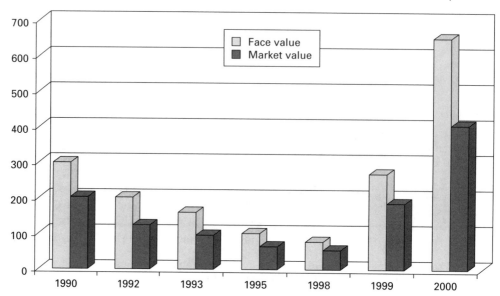

we said the same thing last year but the ratio actually fell slightly.) Unless history is not a good teacher, we expect the ratio to start its move back to more normal levels.

REFERENCES

Altman, E. I., *The Altman/Foothill Report on Investing in Distressed Securities: The Anatomy of Defaulted Debt and Equities*, April 1990 and *The Market for Distressed Securities and Bank Loans*, October 1992, Foothill Corporation, Los Angeles.

Altman, E. I., *Distressed Securities*, Probus Publishing, Chicago, 1991.

Altman, E. I., "Defaulted Bonds: Supply, Demand and Investment Performance, 1982–1992," *Financial Analysts Journal*, May/June 1993a, 55–60.

Altman, E. I., "Investment Performance of Defaulted Bonds and Bank Loans," Annual Reports, NYU Salomon Center, 1992–1998 (Annually 1993–1999).

Altman, E. I., *Corporate Financial Distress and Bankruptcy*, 2nd edn, John Wiley & Sons, New York, NY, 1993b.

Altman, E. I. and A. Eberhart, "Do Seniority Provisions Protect Bondholders' Investments?," *Journal of Portfolio Management*, Summer 1994, 67–75.

Branch, B. and H. Ray, *Bankruptcy Investing: How to Profit from Distressed Companies*, Dearborn Financial Publishing, 1992.

Brand, L. and R. Baehar, "Recoveries on Defaulted Bonds Tied to Seniority Rankings," in *Ratings Performance 1997: Stability and Transition*, Standard & Poor's, New York, August 1998.

Carty, L., D. Hamilton, S. Keenan, and P. Moss, *Bankrupt Loan Recoveries*, Moody's Investors Service, June 1998.

Eberhart, A. C., E. I. Altman, and R. Aggarwal, "The Equity Performance of Firms Emerging from Bankruptcy," NYU Salomon Center Working Paper #S-96-10, updated in 1997, and *Journal of Finance*, October 1999.

Gilson, S., "Investing in Distressed Situations: A Market Survey," *Financial Analysts Journal*, November/December 1995, 8–27.

Hotchkiss, E. and R. Mooradian, "Vulture Investors and the Markets For Control of Distressed Firms," *Journal of Finance*, 1998.

Miller, S. and D. Keisman, "Recovering Your Money: Insights into Losses from Defaults," *Credit Week*, Standard & Poor's, June 16, 1999, 29–34.

Reilly, F., D. Wright, and E. Altman, "Including Defaulted Bonds in the Capital Market Asset Spectrum," *Journal of Fixed Income* 8(3), December 1998, 33–48.

Ward, D. and G. Griepentrog, "Risk and Return in Defaulted Bonds," *Financial Analysts Journal*, May/June 1993, 61–5.

Part IV: Bankruptcy and Firm Valuation

25 | A Further Empirical Investigation of the Bankruptcy Cost Question

This paper presents an empirical investigation of the costs of bankruptcy. The relevance of bankruptcy costs remains as one of the major unresolved issues of financial theory. Empirical evidence, especially as to the amount of the *expected* bankruptcy costs and its consequent impact on optimum corporate capital structure is extremely sparse. If bankruptcy costs are relatively significant then it may be argued that, at some point, the expected value of these costs outweighs the tax benefit derived from increasing leverage and the firm will have reached its optimum capital structure point. An alternative view is that bankruptcy costs are relatively trivial and probably cannot explain capital structure decisions. At the extreme, one might argue that these costs are not even relevant to the cost of capital and capital structure decision and therefore should not be considered seriously.

This study assumes that the expected bankruptcy cost issue is relevant and that firms do recognize the probability of bankruptcy as an important ingredient when making operating and financial decisions. A simple model is presented for identifying and measuring the expected bankruptcy costs and, then, for a sample of retail and industrial firm failures in the USA, the following items are investigated:

1 *Direct bankruptcy costs* including legal, accounting, filing and other administrative costs
2 *Indirect bankruptcy costs*, namely the lost profits that a firm can be expected to suffer due to significant bankruptcy potential
3 *The probability of bankruptcy* for the sample firms

These items are combined to estimate the expected present value of bankruptcy costs which is compared with the expected present value of tax benefits from leverage.

I will attempt to measure the indirect costs using two related models, both of which estimate the abnormal or unexpected profit (loss) of bankrupt firms as the failure date becomes more imminent. It should be pointed out that indirect costs of bankruptcy, identified as relevant by many theorists, have never been measured. This is due to its opportunity cost nature and the difficulty in specifying and empirically measuring such costs.

I CONCEPTUAL ISSUES

The bankruptcy issue and its impact on capital structure can be traced back to the original Modigliani and Miller [21] work which did not explicitly consider bankruptcy costs in their formal model. They did, however (footnote 18), consider the possibility of temporary insolvency and they implicitly, at least, realized that bankruptcy is a reality which could be relevant. One component of bankruptcy costs which obviously can impact the firm's value and its cost of capital is the fact that payments must be made to third parties other than bondholders or owners. These direct costs of bankruptcy, e.g., filing fees, trustee expenses, legal and accounting fees, and other costs of reorganization or liquidation are deducted from the net asset value of the bankrupt firm in a liquidation or from the value of securities in a reorganization arrangement. These "deadweight" costs can consequently cause the value of the firm in bankruptcy to be less than the capitalized value of the expected cash flows of a continuing entity.

A number of researchers have attempted to specify the bankruptcy cost issue within the framework of capital structure and cost of capital assessment. An early discussion was provided by Baxter [4] and more sophisticated treatments have been offered by Stiglitz [30], Kraus and Litzenberger [18], Scott [26], and Kim [17]. Textbooks, such as Copeland and Weston [8, pp. 305–7], Brealey and Myers [5, pp. 384–9], and Brigham [6, pp. 659–64] have summarized these arguments.

There is by no means a consensus of opinion with respect to the theoretical relevancy of bankruptcy costs to firm valuation. Miller [20] introduces personal income taxes as well as corporate taxes as relevant and then analyzes, again, how leverage affects value. He attempts to show that the corporate tax rate, the personal tax rate on interest, and the personal tax rate on equity (dividends and capital gains) interact in such a way that the personal tax advantage of equity probably offsets the corporate tax advantages of debt. Hence, he concludes that there is an optimal capital structure for all firms in the aggregate but that one capital structure is as good as any other for an individual firm.

Other analysts have extended Miller's framework and have concluded that while there is still some tax advantage to the use of corporate debt, the advantages are less than were implied in the original Modigliani and Miller [22] tax treatment. For example, DeAngelo and Masulis [10, p. 4] argue that there does exist a unique interior optimum capital structure whereby the "market prices will capitalize personal and corporate taxes in such a way as to make bankruptcy costs a significant consideration in a tax benefit-leverage cost tradeoff." They argue that regardless of the size of bankruptcy costs, the market's relative prices of debt and equity will adjust so that the net tax advantage of debt is of the same magnitude as expected marginal default costs. Miller had argued that traditional models, which extol the bankruptcy costs argument, require unrealistically large expected marginal bankruptcy costs to offset the expected marginal corporate tax savings of debt.

A different line of reasoning is presented by Haugen and Senbet [15], who argue that the only relevant bankruptcy costs are attributable to liquidation, which is a capital budgeting decision that should be considered independent from the event of bankruptcy and therefore do not impact capital structure decisions. Titman [33], on the other hand, presents an analysis which shows that capital structure choice affects stockholder incentives to liquidate and also determines in which state the liquidation decision is transferred to bondholder's control, i.e., in bankruptcy. He also agrees that the liquidation decision can impose costs on customers, workers, and suppliers and that the agency relationship between these individuals and the firm can result in bankruptcy costs. Morris [23] attempts to develop the conditions under which an optimum capital structure would exist. He presents a model which includes the marginal expected bankruptcy costs which he claims strengthens the argument for the existence of an optimal structure but which are not absolutely necessary. His approach is to develop an expression for the present value of expected tax savings and bankruptcy costs and to analyze the first-order conditions for an optimum. I will also investigate the tradeoff between the expected bankruptcy costs and the expected tax benefit from interest on debt securities.

I will argue that, in addition to the costs of liquidation, there are other relevant costs including those which arise due to the process of bankruptcy (either liquidation or reorganization) and those due to the perceived significant potential of bankruptcy (lost opportunities and abnormal loss of sales and profits).

Despite arguments that bankruptcy costs are either immaterial, irrelevant, or unnecessary, many theorists and practitioners remain unconvinced. Brealey and Myers [5, p. 395] state this issue simply and clearly: "We do not know what the sum of direct and indirect costs of bankruptcy amounts to. We suspect it is a significant number particularly for large firms for which proceedings would be lengthy and complex."

When discussing the empirical evidence of bankruptcy costs, the work of Warner [34] is often cited. He concluded that the direct bankruptcy costs are insignificant. As I will discuss in the next section of this paper, Warner's conclusions are based on a narrow and incomplete definition of bankruptcy costs and examined for a very small and specialized sample. One of the primary purposes of this paper is to add to the empirical evidence on the size of bankruptcy costs in order to add insight for evaluating the bankruptcy cost/triviality argument.

II PRIOR EMPIRICAL FINDINGS

Unlike the frequent *conceptual* issues and debate surrounding the bankruptcy cost controversy, there is almost a total lack of empirical investigation.[1] The one exception to this dearth of information is the often cited work by Warner [34]. As such, his study has perhaps been overemphasized by others. Warner admits that his results are based on a narrowly defined bankruptcy cost definition and his small sample of railroad bankrupts is not necessarily indicative of the population of all firms. Still, his work is an important first step in setting out a methodology for measuring and evaluating bankruptcy-related costs.

Warner's study involved 11 railroads and investigated the so-called direct costs of bankruptcy. These process-related costs are documented by the railroad's regulatory agency (ICC) and are compared to the firm's total market value (debt and equity) for

---

[1] Titman [32] does present some evidence that the collateral effect discussed by Scott [27] is perhaps more important than the tax shield effect in explaining capital structure differences.

up to seven years prior to the bankruptcy petition date. Warner finds that the direct costs of bankruptcy averaged about 1 percent of market value seven years prior and rose to 5.3 percent market value just prior to the petition date. He infers that these percentages are relatively small and that the expected direct bankruptcy cost argument is not very helpful in assessing optimum capital structure decisions. Warner cautions that the costs are not small enough to be neglected completely in discussions of capital structure policy. But it would not seem unreasonable to conclude that for firms of the size under consideration "the expected direct costs of bankruptcy are unambiguously lower than the tax savings on debt to be expected at present tax rates in standard valuation models" [34, p. 345].

There are numerous problems with Warner's analysis and these are important given the degree to which others rely upon the study. Most important, is the total lack of specification and measurement of indirect costs (see below). In addition, his work essentially avoids the *expected* aspect of bankruptcy costs, although he does present a hypothetical example. He also finds that the average market value of his small, restricted sample of railroads falls continuously as bankruptcy approaches – from as much as seven years prior. This may be true for railroads, which take an excruciatingly long time to "die," but it is certainly not necessarily true for the vast majority of failing firms. This will be shown clearly in the following investigation of industrial failures. Understandably, Warner's empirical work does not specifically address the marginal character of the cost/benefit analysis of the capital structure decision and does not carefully consider time value elements.

Castanias [7] examines the relationship between failure rates and leverage measures for smaller firms in numerous lines of business and concludes that the capital structure irrelevance hypothesis is not consistent with his results. Based on nonparametric cross-sectional tests of bankruptcy risk and leverage, Castanias finds that firms that tend to have "high" failure rates also tend to have less debt. More important, his results are stated to be consistent with the thesis that "ex ante" default costs are large enough to induce the typical firm to hold an optimum mix of debt and equity, i.e., to influence debt policy. Like several other studies, Castanias concentrates on industry data and does not attempt to measure unique firm characteristics, nor indirect bankruptcy costs. Yet, he acknowledges that the indirect costs could be significant.

Indirect Bankruptcy Costs

Most important is the decision by Warner not to attempt measurement of the *indirect* costs of bankruptcy. Under this heading, I would include the opportunity costs of lost managerial energies. Warner lists managerial opportunity costs as a *direct* cost of bankruptcy but does not attempt to measure this illusive category. As such, Warner's measurement of direct costs underestimates his own definition. I have included lost managerial opportunities as part of the indirect costs. The latter usually are thought to include lost sales, lost profits, the higher cost of credit, or possibly the inability of the enterprise to obtain credit or issue securities to finance new opportunities. Robichek and Myers [25] referred to the lost investment opportunities as potentially sizeable and Myers [24] notes that a firm may pass up seemingly profitable investments if the benefits are perceived to accrue only to the bondholders. Indeed, Green and Shoven [13, p. 50] show that "the prospect of bankruptcy may make debt finance so expensive that it results in the premature termination of socially beneficial ventures." This underinvestment by the firm has nothing to do with the excessive cost of credit. The potential for stockholder-bondholder-banker conflicts of interest and the attendant agency costs will further increase the indirect costs of bankruptcy. Stone [31], in his critique of Warner's work, called for a more definitive accounting of indirect costs and suggested alternative bases of measurement.

An aspect of indirect costs that has received a good deal of publicity of late is the lost sales and profits resulting when potential buyers of a product or service perceive that default is likely. This no doubt occurred in the recent Chrysler Corporations's near bankruptcy, the Franklin National Bank receivership, and the Braniff International failure.[2] Indeed, Chrysler's management spent a great deal of time as well as expense in order to shore up the public's confidence in Chrysler as a continuing entity! Similar efforts have been observed regularly from the managements of Manville Corporation and Wickes Companies.

Indirect costs occur as well after the firm has declared bankruptcy and is attempting to operate and manage a return to financial health. A current example illustrates this clearly. In November, 1983, the President and Chief Executive Officer, Mr. Joe B. Freeman, of AM International, a manufacturer and supplier of duplicating equipment, was quoted as claiming that "The company is still feeling (since the petition date of April, 1982; *ed. note*) the stigma of Chapter 11 in the marketplace. For example, I suspect that the bankruptcy proceedings were a factor when the company recently lost out in bidding for a distribution contract with a foreign manufacturer" (Dow Jones, interview, November 15, 1983).

Indirect bankruptcy costs are not limited to firms which actually do fail. Firms which have high probabilities of bankruptcy, whether they eventually fail or not, still can incur these costs. For example, the current International Harvester case illustrates this clearly. Recent journalistic quotes infer significant costs attributable to customer wariness, dealer problems, and managerial opportunity costs.[3] In addition, suppliers of materials may be reluctant to continue to sell to the high risk candidates except under fairly significant restrictions and higher costs, e.g., cash on delivery.[4] Baxter [4], Jensen and Meckling [16], and Titman [33] also point to these conditions. The two latter references argue that agency costs, i.e., the costs of negotiations, security precautions and monitoring of debt covenants, and other debt-related agency costs that are incurred to protect the priority of creditors, may offset the tax advantage of debt and lead to a choice of an optimal capital structure.

The Chrysler near bankruptcy, the current International Harvester crisis, and the Braniff bankruptcy are examples of where the indirect costs of a potential bankruptcy

---

[2] A recent commentary in *Business Week* (Dubin [11]) documents passengers' "fear of flying" on potentially insolvent and bankrupt carriers.

[3] For example, "Harvester's Financial Problems Test Loyalty of Customers and Dealers." (*Wall Street Journal (WSJ)*, October 11, 1982, p. 23) and the costs due to management's preoccupation with staying alive; "the whole financial fiasco has drained a lot of company management time . . . its got to have an impact on their ability to tend the store" (*WSJ*, October 12, 1982, p. 2). With respect to Chrysler, its President was quoted as saying that "its share of new car sales dropped nearly two percentage points because potential buyers feared the company would go bankrupt," (*WSJ*, July 23, 1981).

[4] This is currently the case for several large bankruptcies, e.g., Wickes & Co. – a $2 billion failure in 1982. In a letter to Wickes' stockholders, Mr. Sanford Sigaloff, the new Chairman and President of the company stated on April 26, 1982: "Our company has been plagued by serious business problems, including mounting pressures from a reduction of trade credit, that have become increasingly debilitating to Wickes' future."

could be sizeable. Even if the perception by the market of eventual failure is imperfect, bankruptcy potential conveys information about the risks to firm perpetuity and its ability to provide service and replacement parts. In the case of Braniff, there was even the uncertainty as to whether discount coupons would be honored by competitors. Further, Warner [34] points out that, to the extent a bankruptcy trustee makes nonoptimal decisions from the standpoint of the firm's claimholders, the firm incurs an opportunity loss *vis-à-vis* management decisions under normal circumstances.

A controversial aspect of the indirect cost issue is the argument which attests to the ability of owners and claimants to diversify their investments and reap the gains that competitor firms realize when, for example, potential customers of Chrysler buy instead from Ford. This implies that there will be a perfect substitution of goods and services and that the loss from one firm is fully compensated for by the gain to others. Also, prices will reflect these shifts such that investors will be equally as well off. Costs to society, it is argued, are zero despite the bankruptcy possibility. Of course, this assumes that markets are perfect and information is available and unambiguous. And, it assumes that securities from firms that benefit are in fact available to the owners of those endangered firms.[5] But, markets are not perfect nor are investments always available in competitor firms – especially when the market is as internationally competitive as automobiles, tractors, and airlines, and alternative investments in foreign firms are not easily transacted, available, or deemed significant enough to alter international diversification strategies.

Despite all of these arguments for including indirect costs in the calculation of overall bankruptcy costs, no study has attempted to empirically measure them. The reason is fairly obvious, it is extremely difficult to do so. By its nature, indirect costs are illusive and difficult to specify, let alone measure. For sure, one needs to specify a proxy measure for the indirect costs discussed above. This is one of the major purposes of this study.

III   Measuring Bankruptcy Costs

Measurement of bankruptcy costs (BC) includes both direct (BCD) and indirect (BCI) costs. Direct costs are those explicit costs paid by the debtor in the reorganization/liquidation process. These costs are documented in the bankruptcy records of individual firms. Unfortunately, no aggregate records are kept and it is necessary to go through the files (usually voluminous and ill-kept) in the US District Bankruptcy Courts. This has been done for a sample of 12 retailers and seven other industrial firms (tables 25.1 and 25.2).

Measures of indirect bankruptcy costs are based on the foregone sales and profits concept. A methodology is specified for estimating expected profits for the period up to three years prior to bankruptcy and then expected profits with actual profits (losses) are compared to determine the amount of bankruptcy costs (unanticipated profits or losses). Profits are estimated in two ways: (1) a regression procedure and (2) security analyst forecasts.

---

[5]   A possible way to assess competitor gains from bankruptcies is to observe abnormal returns for competitors around the bankruptcy petition date. This has not been assessed here. I thank Walter Holman for pointing this out.

Table 25.1 Absolute and relative bankruptcy costs – retailing industry

Bankrupt company (Year)	BCD ($000)	BCI ($000)	R²	Value of firm (V) ($000,000)				(BCD + BCI)/Value				BCD/Value					
				t-3	t-2	t-1	t	t-3	t-2	t-1	t	t-5	t-4	t-3	t-2	t-1	t
Abercrombie & Fitch (76)	471	2,312	0.31	10.7	12.5	13.3	10.5	0.260	0.222	0.210	0.265	0.049	0.042	0.044	0.038	0.036	0.044
Ancorp Nat'l Service (75)	523	2,383	0.60	104.2	104.3	110.5	49.8	0.028	0.028	0.026	0.058	0.005	0.004	0.005	0.005	0.005	0.011
Beck Industries (70)	650	–	0.73	47.7	114.4	145.6	108.4	0.014	0.006	0.005	0.006	0.020	0.016	0.014	0.006	0.005	0.006
Fishman, M. H. (74)	703	1,267	0.98	41.2	36.5	40.6	8.6	0.048	0.054	0.048	0.051	0.016	0.009	0.017	0.019	0.017	0.018
Food Fair (78)	n.a.	6,058	0.94	376.2	387.7	466.8	416.9	n.a.	n.a.	n.a.	n.a.	n.a.	n.a.	n.a.	n.a.	n.a.	n.a.
Grant, W. T. (75)	2,000	2,703	0.98	1,393.0	1,269.7	1,076.0	917.0	0.003	0.004	0.004	0.005	0.002	0.001	0.002	0.002	0.003	0.003
Interstate Stores (74)	1,664	22,294	0.68	269.1	249.9	202.6	98.2	0.089	0.096	0.118	0.244	0.005	0.006	0.006	0.007	0.008	0.017
Kenton (74)	950	7,029	0.90	47.0	47.5	34.6	29.7	0.170	0.170	0.231	0.268	0.014	0.023	0.020	0.020	0.028	0.032
Mangel Stores (74)	9,019	587	0.83	47.5	52.3	60.0	38.6	0.202	0.184	0.161	0.249	0.155	0.206	0.190	0.173	0.151	0.234
National Bellas Hess (72)	255	2,269	0.59	42.7	41.0	45.5	40.0	0.069	0.072	0.065	0.074	0.004	0.005	0.006	0.006	0.006	0.006
Neisner Bros. (77)	1,630	415	0.89	86.9	99.1	94.2	91.0	0.024	0.021	0.022	0.023	0.017	0.020	0.019	0.016	0.017	0.018
United Merchants & Mfg. (77)	9,513	9,652	0.96	407.6	433.5	306.0	203.6	0.047	0.044	0.063	0.094	0.020	0.021	0.023	0.022	0.031	0.047
Average	2,489	4,747	0.78	239.5	237.4	216.3	167.7	0.087	0.082	0.087	0.122	0.028	0.032	0.031	0.030	0.027	0.040
Median	950	2,543	0.86	67.3	101.7	102.1	70.4	0.048	0.044	0.063	0.074	0.016	0.016	0.017	0.016	0.017	0.017

Note: n.a. = not available; V = Market value equity + Book value debt + Market value debt + Capitalized leases.

Table 25.2 Absolute and relative bankruptcy costs – industrial company sample

Bankrupt company (Year)	BCD ($000)	BCI ($000)	R^2	Value of firm (V) ($000,000)				(BCD + BCI)/Value				BCD/Value					
				t-3	t-2	t-1	t	t-3	t-2	t-1	t	t-5	t-4	t-3	t-2	t-1	t
Bowmar Instruments (75)	1,950	–	0.47	35.7	67.3	29.2	11.3	0.055	0.029	0.067	0.173	0.278	0.170	0.055	0.029	0.067	0.173
Drew National (75)	2,278	2,018	0.74	32.5	16.5	12.7	11.1	0.132	0.250	0.338	0.387	0.135	0.099	0.070	0.138	0.179	0.205
Frier Industries (78)	297	816	0.39	6.3	9.0	9.1	6.9	0.175	0.124	0.122	0.161	0.028	0.046	0.047	0.033	0.033	0.043
Precision Polymers (76)	468	117	0.88	13.9	8.1	6.1	3.6	0.042	0.073	0.096	0.161	0.123	0.121	0.034	0.058	0.077	0.129
Universal Container (78)	500	243	0.20	11.7	14.7	14.8	16.0	0.064	0.051	0.050	0.046	0.029	0.042	0.043	0.034	0.039	0.031
Valley Fair (77)	541	–	0.31	8.4	9.5	7.4	17.7	0.147	0.192	0.089	0.064	0.160	0.133	0.147	0.192	0.089	0.064
Winston Mills (78)	335	5,131	0.21	9.1	11.2	18.8	8.2	0.604	0.487	0.291	0.669	0.024	0.041	0.037	0.030	0.038	0.041
Average (N = 7)			0.46	16.8	19.5	14.0	10.7	0.174	0.172	0.150	0.237	0.111	0.093	0.062	0.073	0.075	0.098
Median			0.39	11.7	11.2	12.7	11.1	0.132	0.124	0.096	0.161	0.123	0.099	0.047	0.034	0.067	0.064

Regression Technique

First, the bankrupt firm's sales are regressed on the appropriate industry sales figure for the 10-year period prior to the forecasted year. For example, if one is estimating indirect costs for the third year prior to failure, sales of the firm are regressed on industry sales for the period t–13 to t–4. Industry sales are then inserted for the period t–3 and firm sales are estimated. Applying the average profit margin on sales over that 10-year period to the expected sales figure, one arrives at expected profits. Expected profits are then compared with actual profits to determine that year's indirect costs and those costs compared with the total value of the firm for up to three years prior to bankruptcy. The steps, again, are as follows:

1 Regress:
$$S_{i,t} = a + b \, S_{I,t}$$
$t = 10$ years, e.g., t–13 $\rightarrow$ t–4; t–12 $\rightarrow$ t–3, etc.
$S_{i,t}$ = Sales of firm i in period t
$S_{I,t}$ = Aggregate sales of industry I in period t

2 Insert $S_{I,t}$ and estimate:

$$\hat{S}_{i,t} = a + b \, S_{I,t} \quad t = -3, -2, -1, 0$$
$$\hat{P}_{i,t} = \hat{S}_{i,t} \cdot \overline{\text{PM}}$$

where

$\hat{S}_{i,t}$ = Estimated sales
$\hat{P}_{i,t}$ = Estimated profits
$\overline{\text{PM}}$ = Average historical profit margin

3 Observe:

$$\Delta P_{i,t} = P_{i,t} - \hat{P}_{i,t} \quad t = -3, -2, -1, 0$$
$$\Delta P_{i,t} = \text{Unexpected profits (losses)}$$

For the sample of 12 retailers, the appropriate (department store, food store, discount store) series were used to estimate industry sales. For the industrial firm sample, seven different industries are represented. An aggregated industry sales figure was utilized, comprised of the largest 10 firms in each sector. Also, a four-year as well as a 10-year average profit margin was applied with similar results.

A rather simple, linear association was specified between firm and industry sales over time. In most cases, however, the fit was a rather good one with the average R^2 of the entire 18-firm sample equal to $\bar{R}^2 = 0.78$ for the retailers and 0.46 for the industrial sample (tables 25.1 and 25.2). Note that some of the fits were excellent, i.e., $R^2 > 0.9$, with a small number of poorer fits ($R^2 < 0.5$). Perhaps the latter could have possibly been improved upon by using a different functional form, e.g., quadratic.

4 The total value of the firm was measured by adding the market value of equity (preferred and common) to the market value of debt (where available) plus the

book value of other debt plus the capitalized value of financial leases. Since financial leases are an alternative to debt financing and are estimated to have involved close to 20 percent of the value of total assets (Altman et al. [3]) during periods when leases were not capitalized, i.e., prior to 1980, it is important to include those values. This is especially relevant for retailers who lease a good deal of their premises. Capitalized leases comprised 35 percent of total value of our retailer sample and 25 percent of the industrials.

5 The indirect plus direct costs of bankruptcy were compared to the total value of the firm for up to three years prior to failure.

Note that this measure of firm total value is potentially considerably higher than Warner's which only considered the *market value* of securities. Of course, there is a higher percentage of marketable securities relative to total permanent capital for railroads than most other firms. Still, this measure of total value will certainly bias the cost/value ratio *downward* relative to Warner's method.

While my assumption is that the prospect of bankruptcy will often lead to lower than expected earnings, it should be pointed out that lower than expected earnings could cause the firm's management to declare bankruptcy. In my opinion, both series of events can and, in most cases, will be occurring at the same time. This does not impact the measure of indirect costs, although it could affect the timing of the direct bankruptcy costs which are petition-date determined. Still, the complexity of factors occurring at the same time makes it clear that it is extremely difficult to isolate completely the indirect bankruptcy costs with these current empirical methodological techniques.

IV RESULTS

A Direct Costs

Tables 25.1 and 25.2 present the findings for the retailer and industrial firm samples, respectively. The absolute direct bankruptcy costs (BCD) are listed in the second column and are compared with firm values for the five years prior to bankruptcy (in the last columns). The average BCD/Value percentages for the retailer sample are similar to those Warner reported in his earlier 1977 study. I find that five years prior this percentage averaged 2.8 percent (compared with 1.4 percent for Warner's railroads) and was 4.0 percent (compared with 5.3 percent for Warner) just prior to bankruptcy (table 25.1). Some of the difference is due to my somewhat higher measure of firm value. My percentages are slightly lower if median results instead of averages are used.

The results for the industrial sample (table 25.2) are somewhat higher. The average BCD/Value ratio was fairly stable for the entire five-year period prior to failure and varied between 6.2 percent and 11.1 percent. These are not trivial percentages. In some cases, e.g., Bowmar Instruments (17.3 percent), Drew National (20.5 percent), Precision Polymers (12.9 percent), and Mangel Stores (23.4 percent), the latter a retailer, the direct costs account for a very high percentage of the firm's value just prior to the bankruptcy. In Bowmar's case, as well as Valley Fair, the percentage is even greater when measured five years prior to the bankruptcy date.

The overall average of the BCD/Value was 6.0 percent measured just prior to bankruptcy and also 6.0 percent five years prior. These results are higher than Warner's and cannot, even without inclusion of indirect costs, be dismissed as trivial.

Note that the average value of the bankrupt retailers remained fairly steady from t–3 to t–1 and only fell noticeably in the year just prior to failure. The mean retailer's value was \$239.5 million in year t–3, fell slightly to \$237.4 and \$216.3 million at two and one years prior, and was \$167.7 million at the bankruptcy date. The industrial sample's average value actually increased between the third and second years prior and then proceeded to fall. I do not find, therefore, as Warner did, that bankrupt firm values fall consistently as failure approaches but the decrease is very moderate. Of course my samples are different, especially since Warner's bankrupt railroads had a significant amount of publicly traded debt, whereas my firms did not. Since market values reflect economic values more closely than do book values, my results are somewhat biased. Therefore, these BCD/Value percentages would have been even higher if only market values on the firms' outstanding debt were included.

B Indirect Costs

The indirect bankruptcy costs (BCI) are given in column 3 and the results for (BCD + BCI)/Value are listed in tables 25.1 and 25.2. Note that in many cases, e.g., Abercrombie & Fitch, Interstate Stores, Kenton, Drew National, Freir Industries, and Winston Mills, the indirect costs are a very high percentage of firm value. In two cases (Bowmar and Valley Fair) the indirect costs were negligible for the four periods prior to bankruptcy, indicating no unexpected losses. When I aggregate the direct and indirect costs, the average percentage relative to firm value is 8.7 percent at year t–3 and 12.2 percent at t for the retailer sample. The results for the industrial firms are considerably higher with as high as a 23.7 percent average (16.1 percent median) in period t and 17.4 percent in t–3 (13.2 percent median). Together, the two samples (18 firms) resulted in an average (BCD + BCI)/Value of 12.4 percent at t–3 and 16.7 percent at t (table 25.3). One cannot simply dismiss these costs as trivial. In fact, they are quite sizeable and, when combined with probability of bankruptcy estimates and presented in a present value context, the results could have considerable relevance for capital structure policy.

Table 25.3 Average bankruptcy costs relative to firm value for the combined corporate sample (N = 18 firms)

	Years prior to bankruptcy			
	3	2	1	0
Direct bankruptcy costs/Value	4.3%	4.6%	4.6%	6.2%
Indirect bankruptcy costs/Value	8.1%	7.1%	6.6%	10.5%
Total bankruptcy costs/Value	12.4%	11.7%	11.2%	16.7%

C Indirect Costs as Measured by Security Analyst Estimates

A second attempt to measure indirect costs of bankruptcy involves the use of experts' expectations of firm profits for the years prior to bankruptcy compared with actual results. Again, I identify indirect costs as *unexpected* or *abnormal* profits whereby

Indirect costs = Abnormal profits (losses)
             = Analyst earnings estimates – Actual earnings

The I/B/E/S data base, constructed and maintained by the firm of Lynch, Jones & Ryan, was utilized to determine security analyst earnings estimates of a sample of bankrupt firms.[6] Essentially, the data, also utilized by Elton et al. [12], lists consensus estimates of earnings per share made by professional security analysts for one- and two-year horizons. Average, median, number of analysts, and other sample data are presented for these estimates. The expected earnings for any given year are the consensus median earnings expectations based on the previous year's estimates. For example, analyst estimates utilized for December 1981 were made as close as possible to December 1980. The differences between these estimates and the actual earnings are unexpected earnings. These differences are the second proxy measure for indirect bankruptcy costs.

I am aware that there are other reasons, besides bankruptcy potential, which cause firms to realize earnings which are different from expectations. The estimates of earnings, however, are unbiased to the extent that analyst expectations are without bias. It is also assumed that analysts have considered industry characteristics in their expectations.

The data base consists of analyst estimates made since 1976 and includes only those firms followed by Wall Street professionals.[7] As such, it does not include the vast majority of bankrupt companies. The sample is made up of seven recent large bankruptcies listed in table 25.4.[8] Since most of these bankrupt companies are still involved in reorganization proceedings, direct bankrupt costs cannot be assessed. Hence, I restrict the analysis to the indirect costs element.

The indirect bankruptcy costs estimates encompass unexpected earnings (losses) for the period up to three financial statements prior to bankruptcy. Costs have not been included for the period between one statement prior and the bankruptcy date, nor during the reorganization, since earnings estimates and results are usually not available. I continued to track, however, the change in value of the firms and assess total value of the firms up to the month prior to bankruptcy. Hence, the designation of Indirect costs/Value at point t includes three years of indirect costs and the value just prior to bankruptcy.[9]

Table 25.4 lists the consensus median estimate for earnings per share (eps) for statement dates 3, 2, and 1 period prior to bankruptcy and the actual earnings and results for these periods. Note that in all but three cases (two in year $t–3$ and one in year $t–1$), estimates were for higher eps than what actually occurred.

Based on the second proxy for indirect bankruptcy costs, it is observed (table 25.5) that the BCI/Value ratio is quite high in five of the seven recent large bankruptcies. The average ratio is close to 20 percent for the three annual statement dates prior to petition

---

[6]   I would like to thank the firm of Lynch, Jones & Ryan for providing the data, and Mustafa Gultekin for assisting in the interpretation of this data base.

[7]   It is interesting to note that as a firm approaches bankruptcy, the number of analysts following the company tends to diminish. This phenomenon was observed in five of the seven cases.

[8]   A few other recent bankrupts, e.g., Saxon Industries, are not included since there is some doubt as to the validity of the reported earnings.

[9]   Actually, the value of the firm is based on the market value of debt and equity just prior to bankruptcy and the book value of other debt plus capitalized leases at the date of the last financial statement prior to petition.

Table 25.4 Security analyst consensus earnings *P/S* estimates vs. actual results of recent bankrupt firms (estimates made 1 year prior to result)

		3 Statements prior		2 Statements prior		1 Statement prior	
Firm	Date of bankruptcy	Estimate ($)	Actual ($)	Estimate ($)	Actual ($)	Estimate ($)	Actual ($)
Braniff Int'l	5/82	0.75	(2.21)[a]	(0.70)	(6.57)	(2.00)	(8.02)
Itel Corp.	1/81	2.93	1.46	(2.47)	(38.35)	(0.50)	(5.69)
Lionel Corp.	2/82	1.26	1.08	1.08	0.93	1.25	0.93
McLouth Steel	12/81	3.47	1.58	1.05	(10.08)	(9.50)	(10.22)
Sambo's Restaurants	6/81	2.24	0.59	0.67	(6.05)	(0.66)	1.50
White Motor Co.	9/80	1.50	2.26	1.50	(0.66)	1.50	1.43
Wickes Cos.	4/82	1.43	3.49	0.89	0.50	2.80	(17.91)

Source: I/B/E/S date base, Lynch, Jones & Ryan, New York, NY.
[a] Negative earnings per share in parentheses.

Table 25.5 Indirect costs of bankrupt firms as a percentage of total value (costs based on analyst estimates of earnings procedure)

	BCI	Firm total value (V)[a]			BCI/V (%)		
Firm	($ millions)	t−2	t−1 ($ millions)	t[b]	t−2	t−1	t[b]
Braniff Int'l	297.3	917.7	1095.6	1065.8	0.271	0.271	0.279
Itel Corp.	513.8	1279.3	1880.9	1761.3	0.408	0.291	0.319
Lionel Corp.	2.0	133.2	163.4	309.1	0.015	0.012	0.006
McLouth Steel	73.3	328.3	356.2	357.4	0.223	0.206	0.205
Sambo's Restaurants	112.6	485.1	502.2	489.0	0.232	0.224	0.230
White Motor Co.	12.2	475.9	418.2	714.0	0.026	0.027	0.017
Wickes Cos.	277.4	762.8	1489.3	1507.0	0.364	0.186	0.184
		Average (1) − Average of 7 firm ratios		= 0.220	0.175	0.177	
		Average (2) − Summation of IC/V		= 0.301	0.218	0.208	

[a] Total value = Market value equity + Market value debt (when available) + Book value other debt + Capitalized leases
[b] Period t = one month prior to petition date for Total value.

filing.[10] It was not possible, in most cases, to compare actual with forecasted estimates for the post-petition periods since estimates are not available. The total significance of bankruptcy costs is not assessed here since direct costs are not available. But, if the average direct bankruptcy costs are used from the prior sample (table 25.3), it is expected that the total bankruptcy cost to value ratio will be over 26 percent at three years prior and about 24 percent just prior to petition. The slightly lower percentage at the latter date is due to the increase in total value of debt as bankruptcy approaches.

[10] If the average is measured based on summation of the seven firms' costs and value, the result is even higher (ranging from 20 percent to 30 percent for the three periods).

Comparing the second proxy method with the first, bankruptcy costs are found to be even more significant (on average) for this sample of large, recently bankrupt firms, than the first method (regression) was for the retailer and industrial samples.

Measuring indirect bankruptcy costs is indeed a thorny problem. Ideally, I would like to capture a shift in the long-run demand and/or supply functions due to changes in a firm's risk attributes and bankruptcy probabilities. This is not possible to measure exactly since changes of this type are confounded with sales and earnings fluctuations which are possibly not associated with bankruptcy. In my specification of unexpected losses as a proxy for indirect costs, I am aware that these changes are likely to have other influences affecting their magnitude. Indeed, one could argue that a sample of bankrupt firms will usually have larger unexpected deterioration in earnings than other firms of similar ex ante risk characteristics but which do not declare bankruptcy.

To assess whether an ex post selection bias in the sampling of bankrupt firms only has been introduced, additional samples of observations are assessed. To be specific, the unexpected changes are analyzed in reported earnings for three additional groups, each group comprised of firms with very different bankruptcy probabilities. One group is comprised of very low (bad) ZETA® (Altman et al. [3]) scores without stratifying by their eventual fate, i.e., bankrupt or not. A second group is comprised of high ZETA (low bankruptcy risk) firms. A final group includes firms with fairly low ZETA scores, where the probability of bankruptcy is above average but not excessive, i.e., about 50 percent.

These tests will also help to assess another potential critique of the measurement of bankruptcy costs. While I am convinced that public awareness of a firm's financial difficulties and bankruptcy potential will negatively impact its subsequent performance, it could also be argued that the reverse takes place; namely, that poor and unexpected earnings will add to a firm's financial vulnerability and lead to bankruptcy. If high risk (low ZETA score) firms are found to realize significant *unexpected* losses, then I have more confidence that high bankruptcy potential firms, regardless if bankruptcy occurs or not, suffer abnormally when bankruptcy is thought to be a distinct possibility. This conclusion will be further confirmed if medium and low bankrupt potential firms do not suffer these unexpected losses.

Table 25.6 compares the average differential between actual earnings per share results and the estimates of earnings made one year earlier for three samples of firms. Again, the I/B/E/S data base is used. The first sample is firms with very low probabilities of bankruptcy in 1978–80, i.e., firms with ZETA scores greater than +10.0. Sample two is comprised of firms in the middle bankruptcy probability area, i.e., ZETAs around zero, and the final group is comprised of those firms with extremely high bankruptcy probabilities, i.e., ZETAs below –3.0. The latter group's probability of bankruptcy classification is greater than 90 percent. Indeed, five of the 61 firms actually went bankrupt from this group.

The average differential between actual and estimated eps for the high bankruptcy probability group is ($0.98) compared to a $0.08 differential for the low probability group. The difference between these two groups (Group 1 vs. Group 3) is significantly different from zero at the 0.01 level. The middle groups' average differential is (0.12) and the low probability of bankruptcy group's differential is 0.08. Both are not significantly different from zero but are significantly different from the high probability group's average differential.

These results are offered to indicate that extreme bankrupt probability firms tended to underperform what was expected from them. It is not possible to know with absolute

Table 25.6 Actual earnings per share vs. experts' estimates for different bankruptcy probability firms

Group number	Zeta interval of group	Number of firms	Average difference ($)[a]	Standard deviation
1	≥ 10.0	140	0.08	0.62
2	−0.05 < ZETA < +0.5	124	(0.12)	2.39
3	≤ −3.0	61	(0.98)	2.95

Tests of Significance:
  Difference of two means[b]
Group 1 vs. Group 3 = 2.78[c]
Group 1 vs. Group 2 = 0.93
Group 2 vs. Group 3 = 2.00[d]
  Difference from zero[e]
1.50 (Group 1)
0.55 (Group 2)
2.59 (Group 3)

[a] Average difference = Actual eps − estimated eps.

[b] $t = \dfrac{\overline{X}_1 - \overline{X}_2}{\sqrt{\dfrac{\sigma_1^2}{N_1} + \dfrac{\sigma_2^2}{N_2}}}$

[c] Significant at 0.01 level.
[d] Significant at 0.05 level.

[e] $t = \dfrac{\overline{x} - \mu}{\sigma} \sqrt{N}$

certainty if this less than expected earnings performance is caused by indirect bankruptcy costs. Suppose that low ZETA firms will do worse than expected due to the superior forecasting ability of the ZETA model over security analysts' estimates, then the bankruptcy costs might not be the sole element involved in these findings. If, however, analysts who assess the same public information as is used by ZETA can be expected to fully discount this information in their own estimates, then these firms should not demonstrate significant differences from estimated earnings unless indirect bankruptcy costs occur and these costs were not expected by professional security analysts.

The above evidence provides some confidence that the less than expected performance of firms with high bankruptcy probabilities is not restricted to those firms which actually do go bankrupt. This is consistent with the prior conclusion that indirect bankruptcy costs can be incurred by any firm, regardless of its eventual fate.

D Post-Bankruptcy Comparison

A variation in the method of analyzing the costs of bankruptcy is to investigate the direct and indirect costs only for the period after the company has filed for protection under Chapter 11. This would probably provide a *lower bound* estimate since data on unexpected post-petition earnings might be available for one or two years at most and do not consider pre-petition consequences of potential bankruptcy. A complication is that most large firms in bankruptcy-reorganization undergo substantial asset-size and sales reductions as they attempt to divest unprofitable activities. Therefore, absolute earnings comparisons based on substantially different asset-size structure could be distorted. In addition, there are very few professional analysts who attempt to forecast earnings of firms in distress and even fewer once bankruptcy is declared. Indeed, only five firms were found where security analyst estimates and post-petition results were available, and then only for approximately one year after the petition. In only one case (Braniff), was there more than one analyst involved once the petition was filed. The alternative, regression method does not estimate percentage return on assets or sales. Since all of these estimates are somewhat arbitrary with respect to the year to commence and terminate the analysis, these issues are mentioned for those interested in further empirical tests.

Table 25.7 compares the professional security analyst(s) estimates of earnings per share and net earnings with actual results for the subsequent fiscal year after the petition date. The average interval was slightly over eight months for the five firms. Note that in every case both the earnings per share and net earnings *estimates* were far better than actual performance. In terms of these *indirect* costs relative to total firm value, the average for this small sample was 17.3 percent. Note that this was for one year only and does *not* include *direct* costs.

While I hypothesize that the above method will indicate a lower bound estimate of indirect bankruptcy costs, note that the average of this five-firm sample is quite similar to the averages listed in table 25.5 for a slightly larger but overlapping sample. In both cases, the percentage costs are quite high.

It should be reemphasized that the interpretation of the difference between actual and estimated earnings cannot unambiguously be interpreted as a measure of indirect bankruptcy costs. It is likely that the realization of lower than expected earnings in the pre-bankruptcy petition period helps to contribute to the eventual filing. Further, the management's own expectation of earnings might differ from the professional analysts', i.e., lower management prospects, which could motivate the filing. On the other band, one could persuasively argue that management is often more optimistic than outsiders, and only when the results are unavoidable do they concede the reality of

Table 25.7 Post-bankruptcy comparison of actual vs. estimated earnings

Company	Bankruptcy date	Actual ($A)[a]	Estimate ($E)[b]	$A – $E	(A – E) Value
Braniff Int'l	May, 1982	(17.54)	(3.50)	(14.04)	–
		(341.9)	(60.01)	(281.0)	0.264
Lionel Corp.	February, 1982	(7.20)	(1.05)	(8.25)	–
		(51.1)	(7.5)	(58.61)	0.189
Sambo's Restaurants	June, 1981	(6.78)	(0.97)	(5.81)	–
		(84.5)	(12.5)	(72.0)	0.147
Saxon Industries	April, 1982	(6.69)	(0.65)	(7.34)	–
		(51.9)	(5.0)	(56.9)	0.114
Wickes Cos.	April, 1982	(17.12)	(0.75)	(16.37)	–
		(298.7)	(10.7)	(232.6)	0.154
				Average	0.173

[a] *Earnings per share on first line and net profit (loss) on second line ($ million).*
[b] *Median estimate from one month after bankruptcy date for next fiscal year (8-month average).*

their plight. In either scenario, however, I am convinced that the situation is significantly exacerbated by what is known as indirect bankruptcy cost conditions.

V EXPECTED BANKRUPTCY COSTS – TAX BENEFITS TRADEOFF

As indicated earlier, one way of specifying the relevant decision on capital structure issues is to compare the expected present value of bankruptcy costs to the expected present value of tax benefits derived from debt capital. In an absolute sense, this comparison can be specified as:[11]

$$\frac{P_{B,t}(\text{BCD}_t + \text{BCI}_t) \cdot (\text{PV})_t}{\text{MV}_t} \text{ vs. } \frac{T_c(iD)_t(\text{PV})_t \cdot (1 - P_{B,t})}{\text{MV}_t}$$

where

$P_{B,t}$ = Probability of bankruptcy estimated in period t
BCD_t = Direct bankruptcy costs estimated in t
BCI_t = Indirect bankruptcy costs estimated in t
MV_t = Market value of the firm in t
T_c = Marginal tax bracket of the corporation
iD = Interest expenses from period t to infinity (i is the interest rate, and D the level of debt)
PV_t = Present value adjustment back to period t

I suggest using one of the available bankruptcy prediction models to measure P_B at any point in time. The ZETA model has been utilized (first presented by Altman et al. [3] and identified by Scott [28] as being both conceptually and practically sound) to measure bankruptcy probabilities. These are given in table 25.8 for the two samples of firms.

Note that the complement of P_B, i.e., the probability of non-bankruptcy, is used to adjust the tax benefits and it too is specified on a present value basis. In essence, the firm can only enjoy the tax benefits from leverage if it continues as a going concern. In liquidation, these benefits are lost completely. The interest rate, the levels of debt, and the marginal corporate tax rate (i, D, T_c) are assumed to remain constant from period t to infinity and adjust for present value by the same rate i.

A Calculating Costs and Benefits

The tradeoff between the expected value of bankruptcy costs and the expected tax benefits from leverage has been measured for those firms in the sample where data on both direct and indirect bankruptcy costs exist for each of the periods prior to and after the bankruptcy petition. It is assumed that all of the direct costs take place during the

---

[11] I have not included an adjustment for personal taxes paid by investors on interest payments. Such an adjustment would, of course, reduce the after-tax benefits from the right-hand side of the equation. Corporate tax benefits from *direct* bankruptcy costs are also not included.

Table 25.8 Bankruptcy probabilities – ZETA® (1977) estimates[a]

Company	Year of bankruptcy	Probability of bankruptcy 1 year prior (%)	Probability of bankruptcy 2 years prior (%)
Industrials			
Bowmar Instruments	1975	99+	61
Drew National	1975	79	34
Freir Industries	1976	57	27
Precision Polymers	1975	89	48
Universal Container	1976	88	72
Valley Fair	1978	97	85
Winston Mills	1978	99+	97
Retailers			
Abercrombie & Fitch	1975	78	77
Ancorp Nat'l Services	1973	95	63
Beck Industries	1970	57	14
M. H. Fishman	1974	65	32
Food Fair Inc.	1978	57	62
W. T. Grant	1975	97	72
Interstate Stores	1974	99+	89
Kenton Corp.	1994	99+	90
Mangel Stores	1974	98	27
National Bellas Hess	1974	78	78
Neisner Bros.	1977	54	33
United Merchants & Mfg.	1977	73	48

[a] Based on Altman et al. [3].

12-month period after the petition.[12] In addition, the expected present value of tax benefits is calculated on interest bearing debt alone as well as on the combined total of interest bearing debt and capitalized leases. The latter are an important financial mechanism for many firms, especially for the retailer sample.

The comparison of expected present values of bankruptcy costs vs. tax benefits from leverage is listed in tables 25.9 and 25.10. Table 25.9 measures the tradeoff for the sample of bankrupt firms from two financial statements prior to petition. Table 25.10 repeats the process but the reference date is one financial statement date prior to petition. The indirect costs, therefore, are for the periods $t–2$, $t–1$, and t in table 25.9 and $t–1$ and t in table 25.10.

I am primarily interested in observing whether or not the expected present value of bankruptcy costs exceeds the expected present value of tax benefits from leverage.[13]

[12] I found (Altman [1]) that the average bankruptcy reorganization period for industrial firms is closer to two years. The *new* Bankruptcy Code (1978) requires that the debtor file a reorganization plan within 120 days. It is possible, however, to petition for extensions which are usually granted if the reorganization appears to be progressing toward a feasible plan. Recent evidence appears to indicate that even for large bankruptcies, two years is not an unreasonable time to expect a plan to be submitted and evaluated.

[13] Gordon and Malkiel [14] utilized statutory corporate tax rates to estimate expected bankruptcy costs when the firm balances the marginal tax advantage of debt with marginal expected bankruptcy costs. Cordes and Sheffrin [9] provide estimates of the marginal effective tax advantage to leverage. They find that the actual tax advantage to debt can be quite different from the statutory rate advantage and that there is considerable variation between firms.

Table 25.9 Comparison of the present value of bankruptcy costs vs. present value of tax benefits from interest on debt and capitalized leases (at period *t*–2 prior to bankruptcy)

(1)	(2)	(3)	(4)	(5)	(6)	(7)
	Probability of bankruptcy (*t*–2)	Expected present value of bankruptcy costs ($000)	Expected present value of tax benefit from debt ($000)	Expected present value of tax benefit from debt & capitalized leases ($000)	(3)/(4)	(3)/(5)
Company						
Abercrombie & Fitch	0.77	1,749	559	1,328	3.13	1.32
Ancorp Nat'l Services	0.63	1,618	1,769	32,120	0.91	0.05
Bowmar Instruments	0.61	1,628	673	1,073	2.42	1.52
Drew National	0.34	519	959	959	0.54	0.54
Fishman, M. H.	0.32	547	468	8,241	1.17	0.07
Freir Industries	0.27	262	1,577	1,577	0.17	0.17
Interstate Stores	0.89	19,179	3,104	11,495	6.18	1.67
Kenton Corp.	0.90	6,279	1,406	1,406	4.47	4.47
Mangel Stores	0.27	2,075	10,722	14,137	0.19	0.15
National Bellas Hess	0.63	1,360	428	3,865	3.18	0.35
Neisner Bros.	0.33	609	7,240	30,780	0.08	0.02
Precision Polymers	0.48	206	95	182	2.17	1.13
United Merchants & Mfg.	0.48	7,680	50,400	88,730	0.15	0.09
Winston Mills	0.97	818	84	179	9.73	4.57

Table 25.10 Comparison of the present value of bankruptcy costs vs. present value of tax benefits from interest on debt and capitalized leases (at period $t-1$ prior to bankruptcy)

(1)	(2)	(3)	(4)	(5)	(6)	(7)
Company	Probability of bankruptcy	Expected present value of bankruptcy costs	Expected present value of tax benefit from debt	Expected present value of tax benefit from debt & capitalized leases	(3)/(4)	(3)/(5)
Abercrombie & Fitch	0.78	1,673	88	1,345	19.01	1.24
Ancorp Nat'l Services	0.95	2,200	271	1,867	8.12	1.18
Bowmar Instruments	0.99	2,782	75	97	37.09	28.68
Drew National	0.79	1,111	439	439	2.53	2.53
Fishman, M. H.	0.65	1,023	240	5,919	4.26	0.17
Freir Industries	0.57	530	978	978	0.54	0.54
Interstate Stores	0.99	19,257	366	889	52.61	21.66
Kenton Corp.	0.99	7,400	140	140	52.85	52.85
Mangel Stores	0.98	8,180	427	521	19.16	15.20
National Bellas Hess	0.95	2,014	398	959	5.06	2.10
Neisner Bros.	0.54	1,029	3,888	19,720	0.26	0.05
Precision Polymers	0.89	581	12	30	48.42	19.36
United Merchants & Mfg.	0.73	11,910	7,450	28,940	1.60	0.41
Winston Mills	0.99	549	37	70	14.70	7.77

If bankruptcy costs exceed tax benefits, then I conclude that the firm had too much leverage in its capital structure and its optimum point, at least with respect to the bankruptcy-cost/tax benefit tradeoff, was at a lesser debt/equity ratio.

For ease of computation, the cost/benefit tradeoff has been specified in absolute terms rather than marginal analysis.[14] It should be noted, however, that the marginal increase in the present value of bankruptcy costs could exceed the marginal tax benefit from interest payments before the absolute tradeoff no longer favored increasing leverage. This is due to the fact that the probability of bankruptcy (P_B) rises at an increasing rate as debt increases beyond a certain point, while the expected tax benefit is linear or perhaps increases at a decreasing rate; e.g., if $(1 - P)$ falls at an increasing rate.

B *Empirical Results*

The results listed in table 25.9 show that eight of the 14 firms studied, as of period t–2, had the present value of expected bankruptcy costs (column 3) exceeding the present value of tax benefits from debt alone (column 4). This is shown clearly by the ratio of (3)/(4) listed in column 6. If this ratio exceeds 1.0, then leverage appears to have been excessive. If bankruptcy costs are compared with the tax benefits from debt *and* capitalized leases (column 7), i.e., (3)/(5), then six of 14 firms appear as overleveraged in period t–2.

In table 25.10, observe the bankruptcy-cost/tax benefit tradeoff as of t–1 prior to bankruptcy. As expected, the probability of bankruptcy increases (column 2) for most firms as bankruptcy approaches, i.e., P_B increases from t–2 to t–1. For most firms, this more than compensates for the no longer calculated indirect costs from period t–2. Hence, 12 of 14 firms had ratios in column 6 greater than 1.0 and 10 of 14 had ratios greater than 1.0 in column 7. It appears that most of the firms were overleveraged at one statement prior to their bankruptcy petition, regardless of how one measures the leverage factor. Since there are other factors, besides aggregate leverage amounts and ex ante bankruptcy factors which explain bankruptcy petitions, e.g., cash flow deficiencies, the statement about "overleveraged" conditions is most relevant to the bankruptcy cost vs. tax benefit tradeoff.

VI CONCLUSION

In this paper, I investigate the empirical evidence with respect to both the direct and indirect costs of bankruptcy. This should be of interest to most analysts for three related purposes. First, there is a need to provide further evidence as to whether or not bankruptcy costs are trivial. Second, for the first time a proxy methodology for measuring indirect costs of bankruptcy is specified *and* actually measured. Finally, a simple format is specified for measuring the present value of expected bankruptcy costs and this amount is compared to the present value of expected benefits from interest

---

[14] For marginal analysis, if the market value (MV) is factored out as the common denominator, then:

$$\frac{dp_R}{dD}(BC)PV + P\frac{dBC}{dD} PV > \frac{di}{dD} T_c \cdot D \cdot PV + iT_c \cdot PV \cdot (1 - P_B)$$

payments on leverage. This comparison has important implications for the continuing debate as to whether or not an optimum capital structure exists for corporations.

The samples include 19 industrial firms which went bankrupt over the period 1970–78 and a second sample of seven recent large bankrupt companies. The results are quite strong that bankruptcy costs are not trivial. In many cases they exceed 20 percent of the value of the firm measured just prior to bankruptcy and even in some cases measured several years prior. On average, bankruptcy costs ranged from 11 percent to 17 percent of firm value up to three years prior to bankruptcy. These results are based on a regression method for determining indirect bankruptcy costs. Indirect costs are essentially defined as unexpected losses. A second method for measuring indirect costs is based on security analyst's expectations of earnings vs. actual earnings, and these results show even more dramatically that bankruptcy costs are significant.

The expected present value of bankruptcy costs is measured by using a reliable bankruptcy estimator technique and the aforementioned measure of bankruptcy costs. The present value of expected bankruptcy costs for many of the bankrupt firms is found to exceed the present value of tax benefits from leverage. This implies that firms were overleveraged and that a potentially important ingredient in the discussion of optimum capital structure is indeed the bankruptcy-cost factor.

I am well aware of the arguments for and against using expectational variables to measure opportunity costs and the potential confounding flaws in my techniques. As such, the results and implications are not airtight and will be subject to debate and comment. If this paper will eventually generate more acceptable and better defined measures and estimation techniques of indirect costs of bankruptcy, this author will be most interested in them and the implications of the consequent empirical results. The potential impact of bankruptcy costs on firm valuation and capital structure issues is too important to speculate about on a conceptual basis only.

REFERENCES AND FURTHER READING

1. E. Altman. "Corporate Bankruptcy Potential, Stockholder Returns and Share Valuation." *Journal of Finance* 24 (December 1969), 887–900.
2. ———. "Predicting Railroad Bankruptcies in America." *Bell Journal of Economics and Management Science* (Spring 1973), 184–211.
3. ———, R. Haldeman, and P. Narayanan. "ZETA Analysis, A New Model to Identify Bankruptcy Risk of Corporations." *Journal of Banking and Finance* (June 1977), 29–54.
4. N. Baxter. "Leverage, Risk of Ruin and the Cost of Capital." *Journal of Finance* 22 (September 1967), 395–403.
5. R. Brealey and S. Myers. *Principles of Corporate Finance*, 2nd edn, New York: McGraw-Hill, 1984.
6. E. Brigham. *Financial Management: Theory and Practice*, 3rd edn, Hinsdale, Illinois: Dryden Press, 1982.
7. R. Castanias. "Bankruptcy Risk and Optimal Capital Structure." *Journal of Finance* 38 (December 1983), 1617–35.
8. T. Copeland and J. F. Weston. *Financial Theory and Corporate Policy*. Reading, Mass.: Addison Wesley, 1979.
9. J. Cordes and S. Sheffrin. "Estimating the Tax Advantage of Corporate Debt." *Journal of Finance* 38 (March 1983), 95–105.
10. H. DeAngelo and R. Masulis. "Optimal Capital Structure Under Corporate and Personal Taxation." *Journal of Financial Economics* 8 (1980), 3–29.

11. D. Dubin. "The Fear of Flying That Airlines Must Conquer." *Business Week* (November 29, 1982), 115.
12. E. Elton, M. Gruber, and M. Gultekin. "Expectations and Share Prices." *Management Science* 27 (September 1981), 975–87.
13. J. Green and J. Shoven. "The Effects of Financing Opportunities and Bankruptcy on Entrepreneurial Risk Bearing." In *Entrepreneurship*, J. Ronen (ed.), Lexington, Mass.: Lexington Books, 1983.
14. R. H. Gordon and B. Malkiel. "Corporation Finance." In *How Taxes Affect Economic Behavior*, H. Aaron and J. Peckman (eds.), Washington, D.C.: The Brookings Institutions, 1981.
15. R. Haugen and L. Senbet. "The Insignificance of Bankruptcy Costs to the Theory of Optimal Capital Structure." *Journal of Finance* 33 (May 1978), 383–93.
16. M. Jensen and W. Meckling. "Theory of the Firm: Managerial Behavior, Agency Costs and Ownership Structure." *Journal of Financial Economics* (October 1976), 305–60.
17. E. H. Kim. "A Mean-Variance Theory of Optimal Capital Structure and Corporate Debt Capacity." *Journal of Finance* 33 (March 1978), 45–63.
18. A. Kraus and R. Litzenberger. "A State-Preference Model of Optimal Financial Leverage." *Journal of Finance* 33 (September 1978), 911–22.
19. R. Litzenberger. "Debt, Taxes, and Incompleteness: A Survey." Paper presented at the Thirty-Ninth Annual Meeting of the American Finance Association, Denver, September, 1980.
20. M. Miller. "Debt and Taxes." Presidential Address, *Journal of Finance* 32 (May 1977), 261–75.
21. F. Modigliani and M. Miller. "The Cost of Capital, Corporation Finance, and the Theory of Investment." *American Economic Review* (June 1958), 261–97.
22. ———. "Corporate Income Taxes and the Cost of Capital: A Correction." *American Economic Review* (June 1963), 433–43.
23. J. Morris. "Taxes, Bankruptcy Costs and the Existence of an Optimal Capital Structure." *Journal of Financial Research* (December 1982).
24. S. Myers. "Determinants of Corporate Borrowing." *Journal of Financial Economics* 4 (December 1977), 147–75.
25. A. Robichek and S. Myers. "Problems in the Theory of Optimal Capital Structure." *Journal of Financial and Quantitative Analysis* (June 1966), 1–35.
26. J. Scott. "A Theory of Optimal Capital Structures." *The Bell Journal of Economics and Management Science* (Spring 1976), 33–54.
27. ———. "Bankruptcy, Secured Debt, and Optimal Capital Structure." *Journal of Finance* 32 (March 1977), 1–20.
28. ———. "The Probability of Bankruptcy: A Comparison of Empirical Predictions and Theoretical Models." *Journal of Banking and Finance* (September 1981), 317–44.
29. C. Smith and J. Warner. "On Financial Contracting: An Analysis of Bond Covenants." *Journal of Financial Economics* (June 1979), 117–61.
30. J. Stiglitz. "Some Aspects of the Pure Theory of Corporate Finance: Bankruptcies and Takeovers." *The Bell Journal of Economics and Management* (Autumn 1972), 458–82.
31. B. Stone. "Discussant Remarks" on J. Warner's "Bankruptcy Costs: Some Evidence." *Journal of Finance* 32 (May 1977), 366–7.
32. S. Titman. "Determinants of Capital Structure: An Empirical Analysis." UCLA Working Paper, #10–82, 1982.
33. ———. "The Effect of Capital Structure on a Firm's Liquidation Decision." UCLA Working Paper, revised, February 1983.
34. J. Warner. "Bankruptcy Costs: Some Evidence." *Journal of Finance* 32 (May 1977), 337–48.

26 | Firm Valuation and Corporate Leveraged Restructurings

with Roy C. Smith

INTRODUCTION

The concept of corporate value, and how to maximize it, will be one of the key elements in the dynamics of corporate activity in the next decade. While always central to the field of finance, corporate valuation issues have never been more relevant than today. This is so because of the massive organizational changes that took place in the USA in the 1980s and the almost certain explosion in corporate governance and capital structure issues in Europe in the 1990s. And new texts and articles are being written, extolling the virtues of value enhancing techniques, e.g., Copeland et al. (1990).

The purpose of this chapter is to examine valuation, not from the standpoint of specific techniques and procedures, but from the perspective of the firm's capital structure. We analyze capital structure issues within the context of massive changes brought about by leveraged restructurings, particularly leveraged buyouts. In doing so, we also address the venerable query in corporate finance – does debt matter and is there an optimal capital structure?

Our inquiry follows a decade of extraordinary activity in mergers and acquisitions in the USA. The transaction values of these restructurings rose as exceptionally high acquisition prices were offered due to the competitive interaction of numerous buyout funds and other sources. In turn, the debt amounts and proportions in the merged firms' capital structures also rose to levels never before seen in corporate America. Hence, both values and bankruptcy risks escalated.

We will show that these high values can, in most cases, be sustained only if the levels of debt and distress risk are reduced very quickly after the initial restructuring. If this is not achieved, similar transactions will not be successful in attracting capital from the markets. In the case of leveraged restructurings which prove to be unsuccessful, debt levels will still be reduced through distressed exchange arrangements or, failing that, through Chapter 11 bankruptcy reorganizations. If all of these fail, the firm's assets will need to be liquidated. In these latter distressed situations, corporate values will decline sharply to levels significantly lower than if the firm had been able to reduce its debt as planned within a short time after the restructuring.

We will first examine classical and modified financial theories dealing with corporate valuation in terms of debt policy. These theories can, in our opinion, help to explain not only why leveraged restructurings can change the valuation of firms, sometimes substantially, but also why these restructurings have met with the full spectrum of results, from great success to dismal failure, in the USA during the 1980s. In so doing, we hope to provide some insights into successful capital structure changes for future transactions.

CORPORATE RESTRUCTURINGS – DEFINITIONS, OBJECTIVES, AND EXAMPLES

A corporate restructuring is any substantial change in a firm's asset portfolio or capital structure. Its objectives are usually to increase value to the owners, both old and new, by improving operating efficiency, exploiting debt capacity, and/or redeploying assets. In some cases, the objective is less strategic, in an operating sense, and not necessarily value maximizing, being directed simply to effect a change in corporate control or to defend against a loss of control, i.e., to preserve "independence." Independence of operation has long been important to boards of directors or principal shareholders of some corporations, who have been accustomed to rule their firm's actions without full regard for the rights of public shareholders or in fear of being taken over against their will. In addition, senior management has often professed a goal to be independent of the influence that large lenders may exert on the operations of the firm.

Mergers and Acquisitions (M&A)

The USA has gone through at least four distinct cycles of M&A activity. The latest one, in the 1980s, involved large corporate financial restructurings, often resulting in acquisition of control by another industrial or a non-industrial firm. Though this cycle has been completed in the USA, the forces behind it have been manifest somewhat in Europe, which has recently seen its first major M&A movement. This movement is primarily a result of an overdue need for industrial restructurings and other influences. European merger and acquisition activity began after the 1985 EC Commission's announcement of a single European market objective to be achieved by 1992. Reduced barriers to cross-national firm mergers were the result of newly found confidence that deregulated, private sector markets could result in improved corporate performance compared to previous national income and protectionist policies. For more details on economic restructuring in Europe, see Smith and Walter (1990) and Altman and Smith (1991).

Leveraged Restructurings

Corporations have also tried to increase value to shareholders by massive changes in leverage. These restructurings are mainly in the form of leveraged recapitalizations or leveraged buyouts. The former involves some type of debt for equity swap and the latter involves management either acting alone or as a partner with a third-party investment firm, purchasing all of the outstanding common stock so that the firm effectively becomes a private entity. The vehicle to buy back the equity is leverage – hence the name leveraged buyout. We will explore this mechanism in much greater depth after discussing the evolution of financial theory in valuation analysis and its relationship with a firm's capital structure.

Before we try to reconcile the financial theories, discussed below, with current corporate financial practice, it will be beneficial to define and discuss what has come to be known as the leveraged restructuring movement of the 1980s, particularly the late 1980s. The objectives of corporate restructurings are usually to do one or more of the following in order to **increase the value of the firm** – however one chooses to define value:

- Redeploy assets to change the mix of the business
- Exploit leverage and other financial opportunities
- Improve operational efficiency

These objectives can be achieved by one or more of the following restructurings:

- Acquiring other companies or businesses
- Divesting businesses or assets owned
- Leveraged buyouts
- Recapitalizations – i.e., stock repurchases or swaps of debt for equity
- Major organizational, leadership, or corporate policy changes

Leveraged Management Buyouts

A number of new techniques for increasing the value of firms were developed in the USA in the 1980s, usually involving several of the steps outlined above. The most visible, in many aspects, was the LBO in which control of a company was acquired in the market through a takeover bid, usually at a substantial premium over the market price of the shares (estimated at about 46 percent by Kaplan (1989) for LBOs in the early and mid-1980s and growing to even a greater premium for the LBOs of the late 1980s). Often, the transaction was bitterly opposed by existing directors and managements if they were not part of the takeover team. As the premium grew, the new equity team had to rely more and more on borrowed capital from banks and the public. This resulted in a number of leverage excesses.

Management buyouts (MBOs) have been around for many years, both in the USA and Europe. The early transactions essentially involved the senior management of a publicly held company "buying out" all the outstanding shares and "taking the firm private." A significant amount of the financing for the buyout was provided primarily by commercial bank loans with the balance coming from the managers' equity investment. The transaction was a leveraged one but the size of the firm and the consequent amount of financing were relatively small. The resulting capital structure, while heavily leveraged, was quite simple with essentially one class of debt.

The type of firm most suitable to a management buyout was, and still is, one with a relatively stable and predictable cash flow sufficient to easily repay the fixed costs from the additional interest and principal on the debt. The major motivation behind the buyout is that management will now directly benefit from their own efforts and reap the firm's profits in the form of equity returns, instead of a fixed or semi-fixed salary earned as managers. Indeed, it is often argued that the manager-owner will work more efficiently due to the added incentives built into ownership and control.

The leveraged MBO differs from the MBO by the larger size and greater complexity of the transaction and the inclusion of a significant second ownership interest. Indeed, this second party, usually in the form of an investment company or partnership, provides and acquires the bulk of the equity capital, with at most 10–15 percent going to management. The greater complexity involves several layers of debtholders (some with deferred as well as current-pay interest payments as well as equity participation features) and also several types of equity capital (preferred and common stock, sometimes including equity warrants and options).

A typical capital structure of a large LMBO in the USA in the 1987–88 period is shown in figure 26.1. Note that the senior debt from banks and insurance companies provided a maximum of 60 percent of the transaction value and amounted to about two thirds of the total debt financing. These creditors were not willing to provide 100 percent of the debt financing, since the amounts came to be so large and the perceived risk greater. Indeed, many of these buyouts were greater than $1 billion with the largest, by far, being the $25 billion RJR Nabisco buyout in 1989.

Below the senior debt was the subordinated current-paying debt, i.e., when interest payments commenced immediately. The primary innovation here was that this debt was, in many instances, sold directly to the public markets as part of the growing "junk bond" issuance. This debt is also known as "mezzanine" financing since its priority is below the "balcony," i.e., senior debt, and above the "orchestra," i.e., equity financing. After 1986, the subordinated debt came mainly from publicly placed "junk" bonds. About 25–30 percent of the transaction price was provided by this source.

Figure 26.1 Selected capital structures: US LMBOs, 1987, 1988

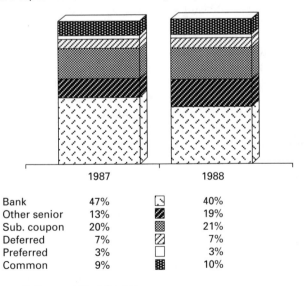

	1987		1988
Bank	47%		40%
Other senior	13%		19%
Sub. coupon	20%		21%
Deferred	7%		7%
Preferred	3%		3%
Common	9%		10%

Source: Author's compilation and First Boston

Several new variants of subordinated debt were introduced in the late 1980s in order to reduce the initial cash interest payment burden of the transaction. These involved deferred payment interest bonds (DIBs) and payment-in-kind (PIKs) bonds. The latter paid whatever the coupon stated, not in interest but in additional bonds, so the liability and future interest payments grew over time.[1]

The Role of Subordinated Debt and Equity

The subordinated debt in these restructurings played a pivotal role. Usually included as debt by those interested in total firm valuation, subordinate cash-pay and non-cash-pay debt nonetheless provided an important equity-like "cushion" from the standpoint of potential senior creditors. But, unlike the preferred stock financed mergers of the 1960s, subordinated debt provided important tax benefits, i.e., the "constructive equity" nature of low level debt.

Finally, below the multi-layered debt structure came the preferred and equity financing, over 85 percent owned by the investment company with the residual owned by management. Despite this small percentage ownership for management, the sheer magnitude of the transactions could lead to extremely high returns to all of the equity owners – if the restructuring was successful.

SUCCESSFUL AND UNSUCCESSFUL LBOS

A successful LBO from the standpoint of all parties concerned, including the old and new debt and equity holders, is one that:

- Results in relatively quick and successful repayments to the debt-holders
- "Cashes out" within 3–7 years so that the equity holders recoup their investment and earn substantial profits
- Does not cause any significant economic disruption of the acquired company, e.g., unemployment resulting in some political reaction

Operating efficiencies and asset sales (if necessary) can provide sufficient cash to the firm to repay a large portion of the senior debt, within two years. After this period, even the increasing debt burden from the deferred interest junk bonds can be met without difficulty. If, however, earnings and cash flows are disappointing and asset sales are unsuccessful, then distress can set in and the LBO will, in many cases, fail.[2]

To "cash out" means that the firm is sold or recapitalized, either in part or as a whole, or the LBO goes public again by selling shares in the open market. In the case of

---

[1]   Another innovation pioneered by US investment banks was "rest" notes which "guaranteed" that the interest rate would be reset periodically so as to cause the bonds to sell at par value. This innovation, like so many of the others, ultimately operated adversely to the interests of the issuers as the junk bond market became more concerned with credit quality. Such innovations can increase the likelihood of credit problems in the future.

[2]   This occurred in 1989–90 to several of the large LMBOs and other highly leveraged transactions that resulted in critical bankruptcies and other distressed situations. These include the Campeau (Allied and Federated Stores) fiasco, Hillsborough Holdings, Southland, National Gypsum, and several others. In the UK, the Isosceles PLC buyout of Gateway Corporation is a current distressed situation due mainly to disappointing asset sales and smaller than forecasted reductions in debt.

partial firm sales, proceeds were often paid out to the new owners and debt refinanced, usually over a longer maturity period. Table 26.1 lists statistics on the average large-firm LBOs that took place in the period 1980–86, and in 1988. The former period was prior to the leverage excesses of 1987–89 that resulted in many failures. Note that the average premium paid to the original selling shareholders was 46 percent in the earlier period, resulting in average incremental debt of $400 million on a $524 million transaction. The initial debt/equity ratio was about 6:1. Successful LBOs netted the new owner returns of about 250 percent over 3–5 years.

With respect to the leverage excesses and inflated prices paid in 1988, results in table 26.1 show how the average premium rose to about 74 percent from the earlier 46 percent and the average cash flow multiplier rose to almost 12 times from the 6–8 times of the earlier period. Finally, the average size of larger firm transactions grew from $500 million to $1.8 billion in a relatively short period. The use of subordinated debt as tax deductible "equity" helped to spark this dramatic increase.

The average post buyout sale of the 1980–86 deals resulted in a $750 million payment; or a $250 million (50 percent) post buyout gain from the sale. The actual gain to the equity holders was magnified, of course, as a result of the large amounts of leverage employed. Since their investment was only $100 million, the return on equity was 250 percent over an average period of 3–4 years. Clearly, these are examples of how value was increased via the LBO.

A very recent example of a successful LMBO was the sale of the budget motel company, Motel 6, to the French-based hotel giant Accor S.A. Motel 6 was bought by the largest LBO firm, Kohlberg, Kravis and Roberts, (KKR) in 1985 for $125 million. Its sale for $1.3 billion in 1990 gives KKR and its partners a return of more than five times their original equity investment. The original purchase involved a cost of $881 million, financed with the $125 million in equity and $756 million in debt – a debt/equity ratio of 6:1. One year after the buyout, KKR sold nearly half of its common

Table 26.1 Average historical LBO experience based on sample of 76 LBOs in 1980–86[a] and 64 LBOs in 1988[b] – ($ millions)

	1980–86	1988
Prebuyout value of equity	$360	$1,023
Average buyout purchase price	$524	$1,783
Average gain to prebuyout shareholders	46%	74%
Equity as a percentage of total capital	15%	12%
Debt as a percentage of total capital	85%	88%
Debt/Equity ratio	5.8:1	7.3:1
Incremental debt	$400	$1,570
Post buyout sale of firm	$750[c]	n.a.
Post buyout gain from sale (50%)	$250[c]	n.a.
Return to new equity owners (total)	250%[c]	n.a.
Cash flow multiplier (earnings after taxes before depreciation, amortization and deferred taxes)	6–8×[b]	12×

[a] From S. Kaplan, "Management Buyouts: Evidence on Taxes as a Source of Value," Journal of Finance (1989), p. 616.
[b] Compiled by the authors from data supplied by Merrill Lynch Capital Markets.
[c] Based on 46 completed LBOs.

equity units to the public and began repaying the debt. As will the shown next, value can be increased via the buyout-restructuring route, especially if the enormous debt incurred is reduced quickly.

LINKING CAPITAL STRUCTURE THEORY WITH LEVERAGED RESTRUCTURINGS

The relationship between a firm's capital structure and its true valuation has interested financial theorists for over forty years, but it was the works of Modigliani and Miller (M&M) in 1958 and 1963 that catapulted the subject to center stage in the finance literature. In their classic 1958 article, M&M argued that the relationship between a firm's debt and equity had absolutely no impact on its overall value; the only variables that determined firm value were its future earning power (encompassed in expected cash flows) and the business risk-return class of the firm. In other words, how the firm packaged its financing had no material impact on value or the firm's overall weighted average cost of capital (WACC). Value was determined by what businesses a company was in and how well its managers ran it – nothing else. Their conclusion is represented by the horizontal line V in figure 26.2. [Note that these representations, and those found in figures 26.3–26.5, are fairly standard, e.g., see Brigham and Gapenski (1991).]

Figure 26.2   Original M&M theory

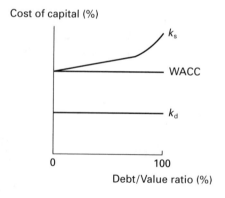

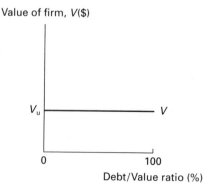

Figure 26.3 Effects of leverage: Traditional approach

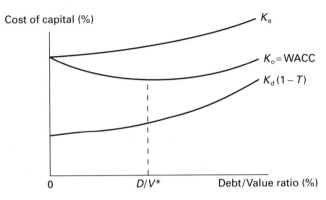

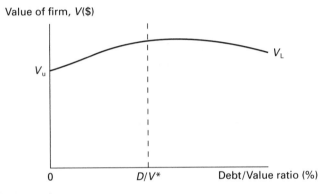

K_e = cost of equity capital
K_d = cost of debt capital
K_o = Weighted average cost of capital
T = Corporate tax rate
V_u = Value of unleveraged firm
V_L = Value of leveraged firm

Even though this theory rested upon a set of unrealistic assumptions, (many of which were addressed in footnotes to their original (1958) article), and some rather simplistic empirical tests, the theory caused an immediate and strong response from the academic community.[3] A number of "traditionalists" opposed M&M's ideas; for example, Durand (1959) argued that the amount of debt did matter and that therefore there was an optimal debt/equity ratio represented by the minimum point on the WACC schedule in figure 26.3. It was felt that a firm could lower its WACC, and at the same time increase

---

[3] Miller (1989) argued, however, that "the view that capital structure is literally irrelevant or that 'nothing matters' in corporate finance, though still sometimes attributed to us, is far from what we ever actually said about real-world applications of our theoretical propositions." One could infer that when M&M relax their restrictive assumptions – e.g., no taxes, perfect information about earnings prospects – they too agree as to the value-enhancing power of debt. Indeed, Miller's comment (1989) on the rise in junk bonds to help bring about leveraged restructurings was that he was puzzled why the use of such instruments took so long to develop.

Figure 26.4   Effects of leverage: MM with taxes

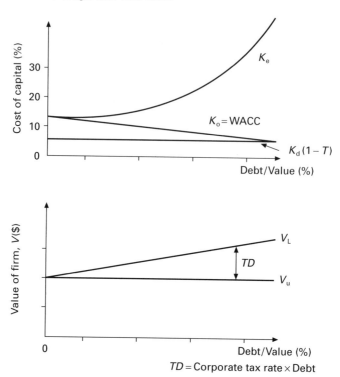

TD = Corporate tax rate × Debt

its value (V_L), by adding a judicious amount of debt. The relatively low after-tax cost of debt $[K_d(1 - T)]$ would bring down the overall cost despite the higher and rising cost of equity (K_e). At some point, however, the combination of increasing costs of debt and equity would begin to raise the overall cost (its capitalization rate) and lower the firm's value. And some empirical tests, notably by Weston (1963), showed that leverage did indeed impact the firm's overall cost of capital. Two and a half decades later, Weston (1989) reflected on the M&M capital structure controversy.

In 1963, M&M published a correction article which stated that they had underestimated the important contribution to firm value from the tax subsidy on debt interest payments. They reasoned that a firm could indeed lower its capitalization rate and increase its value by adding debt and receiving a "bonus" equal to TD (the tax rate times the amount of debt) (figure 26.4). And it appeared that this increasing value of the leveraged firm (V_L) was evident *regardless* of the amount of debt. Could this have been the seminal work that guided the leveraged buyout movement that emerged in the USA over 20 years later?[4] We will return to this question at a later point.

Finally, a combination of renewed traditional theory and some new concepts dealing with financial distress costs (or bankruptcy costs) and "agency" conflicts added both

---

[4]   Indeed, Dr. Modigliani was asked this very question soon after he had received the Nobel Prize in Economics and after the LBO boom had begun. He vehemently denied this, citing other factors that might lower a firm's value as leverage increased.

Figure 26.5 Net effects of leverage on the value of the firm

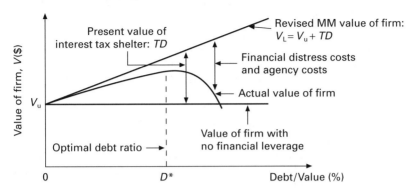

rigorous new theory and empirical tests to support the traditional view of an optimal capital structure which was not 100 percent debt. It was argued that as a firm's leverage increases, the probability of bankruptcy also increases and if the costs of bankruptcy are significant, then a firm's value will fall when the marginal increase in the expected value of financial distress costs is greater than the increase in the expected value of the tax benefits from debt. The overall cost of capital will rise beyond some optimum leverage proportion and the firm's value will fall.

Altman (1984) measured the costs of bankruptcy, not only in terms of the direct out-of-pocket costs to lawyers, accountants, etc. and the lost opportunities due to management's diversion from running the business, but the indirect costs as well. Indirect costs were defined as those lost sales and profits caused by customers choosing not to deal with a firm which was a high potential bankrupt as well as increased costs of doing business (e.g., higher debt costs and poorer terms with suppliers) while in a financially vulnerable condition. He found that while the direct costs were consistent with Warner's (1977) earlier results, the indirect costs were quite significant.

Agency effects, first articulated by Jensen and Meckling (1976), argued that due to conflicts between debt and equity stockholders, indeed also between holders of different classes of debt (Bulow and Shoven, 1978), a firm incurred real costs as the threat of bankruptcy grew. On the other hand, many have argued that the highly leveraged LBO, transforming the "manager-only" to a "manager–owner," has positive agency benefits by removing some manager–owner conflicts of interest.

Figure 26.5 shows that financial distress and agency costs are the major factors accounting for the difference between the so-called pure MM value of the firm with the tax subsidy and the revised traditionalist value of the firm. The net result is an optimum point on the debt/value axis (D^*), at which the firm's value is maximized.

DELEVERAGING – THE TREND FOR THE 1990s?

As we postulated, a successful highly leveraged restructured firm must reduce its debt substantially and usually within a short time after the restructuring transaction. The consequences of not achieving this deleveraging are apparent both in theory (figure 26.5) and in our observance of the substantial increase in highly leveraged, high priced,

LBO distressed situations of the 1980s and the consequent increase in defaults. Table 26.2 shows that through the first eleven months of 1990, junk bond defaults mounted to $16.5 billion, resulting in a default rate of 7.8 percent (the rate for the entire year was 8.74 percent). This default rate is substantially higher than the weighted average default rate of 3.2 percent for the period 1978–89. Losses from the recent defaults, most but not all of which were the result of restructurings, also increased due to the lower lender recovery rates, i.e., lower prices just after default. The average recovery in 1990 was about 26 percent, compared to about 35 percent for the five-year period 1985–89 and 40 percent for most of the history of defaults.

Deleveraging can be either voluntary or not – the latter can result from forced distressed exchange issues whereby the creditors of a distressed firm agree to accept a package of new securities in lieu of the existing debt. Invariably, this package contains equity in the troubled firm. The ability for firms to effect an equity for debt swap before distress becomes apparent was severely hampered by the malaise in the equity markets, starting in the second half of 1990. Conditions improved markedly in 1991 as new equity issues soared. Deleveraging can also be prompted by the fear of a crisis situation especially prior to some "trigger" date such as an interest rate reset or cash-pay commencement date.

Some voluntary debt reductions have occurred from debt repurchases by firms with sufficient cash to take advantage of the significant reduction in bond prices of virtually all highly leveraged firms starting in the summer 1989. Deleveraging will continue

Table 26.2 Historical default rate – low rated, straight debt only, 1978–90 ($ millions)

Year	Par value outstanding ($)	Par value default ($)	Default rate (%)
1990[a]	210,000	16,480.00	7.848
1989	201,000	8,110.30	4.035
1988	159,223	3,944.20	2.477
1987	136,952	7,485.50[b]	5.466[b]
1986	92,985	3,155.76	3.394
1985	59,078	992.10	1.679
1984	41,700	344.16	0.825
1983	28,233	301.08	1.066
1982	18,536	577.34	3.115
1981	17,362	27.00	0.156
1980	15,126	224.11	1.482
1979	10,675	20.00	0.187
1978	9,401	118.90	1.265

Arithmetic average default rate
   1970–1989   2.485%
   1978–1989   2.096%
   1983–1989   2.706%

Weighted average default rate
   1970–1989   3.179%
   1978–1989   3.201%
   1983–1989   3.383%

[a] *Through December 1, 1990.*
[b] *$1,841.7 million without Texaco, Inc., Texaco Capital, and Texaco Capital N.V. The default rate without these is 1.345%.*

from debt repurchasing and may expand even more rapidly when the equity markets rebound.

Two examples of major firm deleveraging efforts in the face of economic and financial uncertainties are the recent attempts by RJR Nabisco and Macy's – both large LBOs of the late 1980s. RJR Nabisco, bought by KKR in 1989, had already reduced debt by over $6.0 billion by mid-1990, but still found itself with about $20.0 billion of debt outstanding. RJR's recapitalization plan commenced in July 1990 with an additional $6.9 billion in debt reduction, featuring retirement of about $2.4 billion of publicly held "reset" notes, using a combination of cash and stock. While one might argue that the swap was prompted by the firm's perceived financial vulnerability, even so, its cash flow in 1990 was extremely positive permitting partial bond paybacks and other deleveraging actions. Indeed, debt repurchases continued into 1991, culminated by the upgrading of most of the RJR Nabisco debt to investment-grade status in December.

Macy's, an LBO with several large institutional stockholders, was attempting in 1990 to reduce its considerable debt burden. One strategic move was to reduce some of its $5.6 billion in debt through periodic repurchases financed by the sale of new convertible preferred stock to the public. The preferred stock sale was complemented by the sale of Macy's receivables and some real estate. These actions were precipitated primarily by the drastic reduction in market value of several of its outstanding debt issues and the perceived concern in the markets of the deterioration in credit quality of Macy's.

LEVERAGED RESTRUCTURING AND VALUE – THREE EXAMPLES

We will explore a number of scenarios whereby a restructuring of the permanent capital can be shown to increase firm value.

Case 1: Debt for Equity Swaps

The first scenario involves a classic debt for equity exchange, or "swap," which is a type of leveraged recapitalization. Table 26.3 illustrates a situation whereby a firm in a 40 percent tax bracket swaps $3,000 of its equity for new debt. Before the transaction, the firm had $2,000 in debt at a before-tax cost of 8.0 percent and $4,032 in equity – the latter based on a price/earnings ratio of 8 times after-tax earnings of $504. The total value of the firm's securities was therefore $6,032 and the weighted-average cost of capital (WACC) was about 10.0 percent.[5]

After the swap, the cost of debt rises to, say, 10 percent, as the debt/total value ratio increases from 33 percent to 67 percent and the equity multiplier falls to 7 times due to the higher financial risk. But, since debt is now a greater proportion of total capital, although its after-tax cost has increased from 4.8 percent to 6.0 percent, the WACC decreases to 8.7 percent. The new equity value is $2,268 (7 times earnings of $324), plus the $4,600 in debt raises the firm's total value by $836 to $6,868. This is a 14 percent increase.[6] Note that if the firm's increase in value was equal to the tax benefits from the

---

[5] The WACC is equal to the sum of the component after-tax costs of debt and equity, each multiplied by the amount of each as a proportion of total capital; i.e., 10.0 percent = .048(2000/6032) + .125(4032/6032).

[6] The breakeven firm value point, comparing the before situation to after recapitalization, would manifest if the equity multiplier fell to about 4.4 times instead of 7.

Table 26.3   Restructuring and value – Case 1: Leveraging up (Debt for equity swap = $3,000)

	Before	After	Change (Return %)
EBIT	$1,000	$1,000	–
Debt			
(BV)	$2,000	$5,000	$3,000
(MV)	$2,000	$4,600	$2,600
Cost of debt:			
Before tax	8.0%	10.0%	2.0%
After tax	4.8%	6.0%	1.2%
Tax rate	40%	40%	–
Interest	$160	$460	$300
EAT	$504	$324	–$180
Cost of equity	12.5%	14.3%	1.8%
Equity multiplier	8×	7×	–1×
Equity value	$4,032	$2,268 ($+3,000)	$1,236=31%
Total firm value	$6,032	$6,868	$836=14%
Cost of capital	10.0%	8.7%	–1.3%

additional debt, the increase would be $1,200 (.4 × 3,000) instead of $836. We are therefore implicitly assuming bankruptcy and agency costs of $364. This increase in value was depicted earlier in our theoretical discussion and shown in both figure 26.3 (M&M with taxes) and figure 26.4 (traditional approach). Indeed, the value to the old equity holder has increased 31 percent, even more than the 14 percent increase in firm value.[7]

In addition to the tax benefits inherent in a debt for equity swap, there is evidence that a company's exchange offer is interpreted by the market as a signal about future cash flows. Copeland and Lee (1990) examine data on exchanges covering the period 1962–84 and find evidence consistent with the signaling hypothesis. They also find that leverage-increasing exchange offers result in decreases in systematic risk, increases in adjusted earnings, sales, and assets. Opposite results are found for leverage-decreasing exchange offers. We postulate that the vast majority of the firms in the Copeland and Lee sample had excess debt capacity – not found in many of the over leveraged firms in today's environment.

Case 2: LBO Restructuring

The second scenario involves the same initial condition as in Case 1, except now the swap is an extreme one with all of the equity purchased through an LBO and the public firm becomes privately owned. The purchase or $4,032 in equity is accomplished by offering the old shareholders a 40 percent premium, or $5,645 (recall that 40 percent was about the average LBO premium in the period 1983–86). The cost is financed by 90 percent debt and 10 percent equity, increasing the total book value of debt from

[7]   Based on a 7 times P/E ratio, the new equity value is $2,268 (7 × $324) plus the $3,000 derived in the swap brings the total value of the old equity holder to $5.268 – a 31 percent increase over $4,032.

$2,000 to $8,048. The dollar equity investment is $565 (10 percent of the cost). Case 2 is illustrated in table 26.4.

After the buyout, the firm's cost of debt increases to, say, 11 percent (a 3 percent increase), which if publicly issued would no doubt be rated as a "junk" bond. The after-tax cost of debt rises from 4.8 percent to 6.6 percent and the old debt's value falls from $2,000 to $1,250. Due to the high debt amount and increased cost, the interest expense is now $719 ($160 on the old and $559 on the new debt) and net earnings drops to $169. Since this is now a highly leveraged private firm, the P/E approach cannot be used directly to value the equity or the entire firm, although an estimate of value can be made by using P/E ratios of comparable highly leveraged firms that are publicly traded. Instead, a commonly used firm valuation practice in highly leveraged companies is the cash flow multiplier approach.

A typical range of total firm value to cash flow during the 1983–86 period of LBOs was from 6–8 times.[8] The firm in Case 2 has earnings before interest and taxes plus depreciation – sometimes referred to as EBITD – of $1,500. Assuming the more con-servative multiplier of 6 times, the total firm value is $9,000. Subtracting the market value of debt ($6,330) from total firm value results in an equity value of $2,670. Since the equity investment was only $565, the rather immediate returns to the new equity holders are estimated at 373 percent. Of course, at this point these returns are merely hypothetical. Total value of the firm also increases dramatically by 49 percent over the initial $6,032, reflecting the future benefits of the restructuring.

Note, we have not indicated any increase in EBITD from before to after – both are at $1,500. Most LBO and financial restructuring advocates, however, argue that a firm

Table 26.4 Restructuring and value – Case 2: LBO financed by 90 percent debt and 10 percent equity

	Before	After	Change (Return %)
EBIT	$1,000	$1,000	–
Depreciation	$500	$500	–
Total debt			
(BV)	$2,000	$7,080[a]	–
(MV)	$2,000	$6,330	$5,080
Cost of debt:			
Before tax	8.0%	11.0%	3.0%
After tax	4.8%	6.6%	1.8%
Interest	$160	$719	$559
Tax rate	40%	40%	–
EAT	$504	$169	$335
Equity multiplier	8×	–	
EBITD based firm multiplier	6×		
Equity value	$4,032	$2,670	373%
(Investment = .10 × $5,645 = $565)			
Total firm value	$6,032	$9,000	$2,968 (49%)

[a] *LBO Purchased at a 40% Equity Premium = $5,645, New Debt = $5,080*

[8] Indeed, as the LBO movement in the USA heated up and exceptional profits were made, cash flow multi-pliers increased to 10–12 times and even higher.

will usually become more efficient in its cost containment and productivity increases after it goes private. Indeed, Jensen (1989) argues for the "discipline-of-debt" as a positive motivation for increasing firm values – not to mention the tax benefits that we have seen in Cases 1 and 2. Evidence of sizeable increases in cash flow can be observed in several articles from Amihud (1989), especially Bull.

On the other hand, opponents of LBO restructurings argue that the enormous debt burden stifles new investment and puts the highly leveraged firm at a distinct long-term disadvantage *vis-à-vis* its less leveraged competitors. Further, optimistic forecasts of higher earnings and cash flows and successful asset sales do not always materialize and the suffocating amounts of debt cause perfectly good companies to falter. In faltering situations, both the new debt and equity holders will lose a significant proportion of their investment.

Case 3: Asset Sales and Debt Paydown

Our last restructuring scenario picks up where we left Case 2 and assumes that within a few years the firm sells 50 percent of its assets and uses all, or in another case only part, of the proceeds to repay or repurchase debt (table 26.5).

Selling one half of its assets results in a 50 percent reduction in earnings and cash flow. We assume that these assets are sold for six times their cash flows (the same conservative multiplier as in our earlier assumption). This results in an asset sale cash generation of 50 percent of $9,000 or $4,500. These proceeds are used to pay down debt to a total of $2,580 from $7,080 (middle column of table 26.5).

Since debt is considerably reduced, we assume the cost of debt falls to 10 percent and earnings after interest and taxes rises to $194. The new interest cost is based on a blend

Table 26.5 Restructuring and value – Case 3: LBO financed by 90 percent debt with subsequent asset sale and debt paydown (50 percent of assets sold)

	Post LBO (From case #2)	Sell assets and 100% debt paydown	Sell assets and 50% debt paydown
EBIT	$1,000	$500	$500
Depreciation	$500	$250	$250
Total debt			
(BV)	$7,080	$2,580[a]	$4,830[b]
(MV)	$6,330	$2,815[a]	$5,050[b]
Cost of debt			
Before tax	11.0%	10.0%	10.5%
After tax	6.6%	6.0%	6.3%
Interest	$719	$324	$471
Tax rate	40%	40%	40%
EAT	$169	$194	$17
Firm Multiplier (EBITD Based)	6×	7×	5×
Equity Value Withdrawal	$2,670	$2,435	−$1,300+$2,250
Total Value	$9,000	$5,250	$3,750
Debt/Total Value	70%	54%	135%

[a] *$7,080 − .5 × $9,000 = $2,580; market value of debt increased by about 9%.*
[b] *$7,080 − .5 × $9,000 = $4,830; market value of debt increased by about 5%.*

of the original $2,000 in old debt of 8 percent and $580 of the debt issued by the LBO at 11 percent. The new cash flow of $750 is assigned a seven times multiplier since the financial markets are usually favorably impressed with successful asset sales and immediate debt paydown. The seven times multiple results in a new firm value of $5,250 (7 × $750) and an equity value of $2,435 ($5,250 − $2,815 debt). Hence, the new equity value is similar to the hypothetical equity value just after the LBO occurred. The LBO equity holder realizes a 331 percent return but the risk exposure is greatly reduced. This scenario of Case 3 shows a positive reaction to the chain of events surrounding the LBO.

A less positive scenario is depicted in the last column of table 26.5. Here the same asset sale takes place but only half of the proceeds are used to repurchase debt, i.e., .5($4,500) = $2,250. This reduces total debt to $4,830 and we assume the cost of debt decreases but only to 10.5 percent.

Since only one half of the proceeds are used for debt reduction and earnings after taxes drop to $17, the new EBITD cash flow multiplier on the remaining operations is assumed to be five. This results in total firm value of $3,750 (5 × 750) and a negative equity of −$1,300. The LBO equity holders, total value and return are still positive, however, since half of the asset sales ($2,250) is added to their wealth. But the result is not as positive as the first asset-sale scenario with the higher debt paydown, i.e., a return on equity investment of 68 percent as compared to 330 percent in the 100 percent debt paydown scenario. Note the negative book equity situation and the 135 percent debt/ value ratio in the lower paydown case.

In the scenarios we have illustrated, the result described is of course dependent on our assumptions – ones we think are fairly realistic. The end result, regardless of the multipliers selected, shows the impact that financial structure can have on firm valuation. And, with the exception of one case, all showed the positive effects of a leveraged restructuring on the value of the firm.

While positive results were common in the mid-1980s, the end result was not always so happy. In Appendix A, we chronicle the results of two leveraged buyouts that took place in 1986–87. One, Borg Warner Corporation, seems to have worked out very well for everyone involved. The other, Fruehauf Corporation, did not work out as well, although it was not the disaster that several large LBOs (e.g., Revco, Jim Walter, Southland, Integrated Resources, National Gypsum, became in the late 1980s and early 1990s).

LINKING BACK TO FINANCIAL THEORY

As we observed in figure 26.5, the value of an enterprise could be increased by an addition to debt and the present value of that increase in value was equal to TD (tax rate times the total amount of debt). Since an LBO is probably the extreme of a voluntary increase in debt, no doubt one of the motivations is to accrue these tax advantages. Hence, an ever-increasing debt/value ratio makes sense in a world of insignificant distress and agency costs. But these costs are not trivial, and the curve marked "Actual Value of Firm" falls after some optimum debt amount (D^*).

In an earlier paper (Altman, 1984), it was shown that a firm's optimum debt was where the expected bankruptcy (distress) costs were equal to the expected value of the tax benefits from debt; i.e.,

$$P_{B,t}(\text{BCD}_t + \text{BCI}_t) \cdot (\text{PV})_t = (\text{PV}_t)T_c(Id_t) \cdot (1 - P_{B,t})$$

where

$P_{B,t}$ = Probability of bankruptcy estimated in period t
BCD$_t$ = Direct bankruptcy costs estimated in t
BCI$_t$ = Indirect bankruptcy costs estimated in t
T_c = Marginal tax bracket of the corporation
Id = Interest expenses form period t to infinity
PV$_t$ = Present value adjustment to period t

Where the expected bankruptcy costs are lower than the expected tax benefits, increased leverage can be successfully undertaken. Altman reported (1984) that most firms in his sample of bankrupt companies had expected bankruptcy costs greater than expected tax benefits.

The Concept of Temporary Debt

The bankruptcy cost/tax benefit tradeoff analysis rests on the assumption of fairly permanent, or at least long-term, debt. If, however, the initial burst of debt in an LBO is planned to be temporary, then the objective could, and in our opinion should, be to move back along the $V_L = V_u + TD$ function, in figure 26.5, to an optimal amount of debt (approximately D^*). While the expected value of the tax benefits are probably lower at this point than further out on the line, the probability of bankruptcy is also considerably lower. In so doing, the owners of an LBO can reap the initial increase in value and sustain that increase until they cash out. The new debt holders will benefit either by having their debt repurchased within, say, two years (especially the senior debtholders) or continuing to receive the high yields on the subordinated debt (mezzanine or junk bonds) in highly leveraged restructurings.

If, however, the firm cannot move back successfully along the value line, then distress may grow to the point that the firm's value decreases sharply – perhaps to its liquidation value in extreme cases. This will occur when disappointing cash flows occur, lowering the unlevered value of the firm (V_u), and/or asset sales are disappointing or impossible (usually due to changed market conditions). Finally, another type of distress could occur when a seemingly healthy entity cannot refinance its existing debt. Theoretically, this should not occur as long as the intrinsic value of the assets exceed the debt burden. But difficult conditions in the debt and equity capital markets can prevent refinancings, even for reasonably healthy but highly leveraged firms. This was the case in 1990, as markets lost confidence in highly leveraged transactions, the new issue junk bond market in the USA dried up, banks were increasingly hesitant to refinance the highly leveraged transactions, and equity markets were performing poorly.

Empirical Evidence on Successful LBOs and Debt Paydown

We are beginning to amass some empirical evidence on successful and unsuccessful LBOs. In a study carried out in cooperation with the Controller of Currency, Moore

(1990) investigated a sample of 11 successful and 9 unsuccessful LBOs as to their three-year post-LBO experience on a number of performance variables. Unsuccessful LBOs are those which have failed, bonds have defaulted or a distressed exchange issue was completed. Successful LBOs are those which were still in operation without disturbance for at least three years after the LBO and were considered healthy by the Controller of Currency.

The average long-term debt/total assets (LTD/TA) ratio was 62.4 percent for the successful sample, just after the LBO. This ratio fell to 53.6 percent, 39.7 percent, 37.6 percent, and 49.4 percent in the four post-LBO years (table 26.6). The unsuccessful LBOs, on the other hand, had a lower (46.4 percent) LTD/TA at the time of LBO, but saw the ratio rise to 71.2 percent in the fourth year after. Hence, we observe evidence of the correlation between debt paydown and successful LBOs.

Admittedly, this is a small sample with a fair amount of variation, but the data seem quite compatible with our "temporary debt" thesis.

Table 26.6 Successful vs. unsuccessful LBOs and debt paydown experience (long-term debt/total assets ratio)

Observation #	LBO -3	LBO -2	LBO -1	LBO YEAR	LBO +1	LBO +2	LBO +3	LBO +4
Successful LBOs (%)								
1		25.8	23.8	60.6	52.7	35.8	20.3	4.2
2	8.3	1.3	3.7	76.0	72.7	38.7	42.7	44.6
3				54.0	44.7	31.6	18.0	40.6
4					36.7	36.7	63.7	69.6
5	0.6	0.3	2.9	36.0	60.5			
6						38.5	26.4	52.2
7			2.2	59.8	59.3	56.9		
8	2.8	2.9	2.2	83.8	61.4	43.5	34.0	
9	30.4	45.1	34.5	49.5	62.6	58.3	82.0	85.0
10			9.7	64.2	44.5	27.7	31.1	
11				77.6	40.9	29.3	20.2	
Average	10.5	15.0	11.2	62.4	53.6	39.7	37.6	49.4
Number	4	5	7	9	10	10	9	6
Standard deviation	11.8	17.7	11.8	14.2	10.9	10.0	20.6	25.2
Unsuccessful LBOs (%)								
1		12.6	41.1	33.7	36.1	36.6	33.6	41.7
2			37.3	33.0	35.8	28.1	36.9	75.2
3	8.4	5.1	4.2	61.9	62.8	64.4	67.7	129.6
4			32.4	24.9	36.4	38.0	38.1	
5	35.9	35.3	23.1	65.0				
6			21.3	41.1	34.2	46.1	64.1	
7			14.6	56.4	57.1	46.0	76.1	
8			19.5	43.9	49.6	57.0		
9	17.8	31.2	41.2	49.9	50.2			
Average	0.2	21.1	25.3	46.4	43.8	44.9	52.7	71.1
Number	3	4	8	9	8	7	6	4
Standard deviation	11.3	12.5	12.5	11.8	12.1	11.6	16.9	36.7

Source: H. Moore, "Trends and Characteristics of Recent LBO Experience," NYU working paper, November 1990.

Conclusion

We have noted the increased importance of financial restructurings in corporate securities valuation. To the extent that different forms of financing, including subordinated debt, are available to firms to complement the traditional role played by banks, firm valuation can be raised by increasing the leverage in the capital structure. In the case of overleveraged companies with significant risk of distress and/or default, the opposite tonic is called for, namely deleveraging to a less burdened capital structure. Thus, capital structure is shown to be one of the key variables in determining (and changing) corporate valuation.

Appendix A: Two Leveraged Management Buyouts

The following discussion illustrates a relatively successful venture (Borg Warner) and one less successful (Fruehauf).

Borg Warner

Borg Warner, primarily a manufacturer of automotive components and accessories, was a classic LBO candidate with fairly stable and positive cash flows, a low debt level, and strong management. Despite a substantial profit margin, however, the firm's return on equity was relatively low (under 4.0 percent). Borg Warner was taken private in an LBO transaction in March 1987. The purchaser was Merrill Lynch Capital Partners, Inc., one of the leading LBO firms. Table 26.7 illustrates the Borg Warner situation just before, just after, 14 months after, and 26 months after the leveraged buyout took place.

The LBO was financed by a large infusion of over $3.6 billion in long term debt and an equity infusion of just $200 million. Total debt rose to $4.66 billion resulting in a debt/asset ratio of 92 percent.

The cost of debt, measured by the yield-to-maturity, rose from 8.55 percent on the existing $5\frac{1}{2}$s of 1992 to 13.64 percent, an increase of over 5 percent, indicating its "fallen-angel" – junk bond status. A second issue of 8 percent bonds due in 1996 went from 8.11 percent to 14.69 percent over that same time span. The actual premium paid to the existing shareholders was a relatively low 24 percent, compared to the average of over 40 percent typical of LBOs in the mid-1980s and much below the premiums paid in the late 1980s. The cash flow, EBITDA (earnings before interest and taxes plus depreciation and amortization) multiplier was about 10 times. The company, therefore, was transferred from a conservatively financed company to a heavily leveraged one operating with an interest coverage ratio of 1.29 on continuing operations.

The buyout's progress was extremely positive with higher returns on a much smaller asset base, strong asset sales, and, most importantly, significant debt paydown. Long-term debt was reduced to $1.3 billion in 1988 and $926 million at the end of 1989 – a reduction of over $2.3 billion within the first 14 months after the buyout and a continuing reduction thereafter. As a result, the cost of debt on the first debt issue noted above dropped to 10.85 percent in December 1988 – a fall of about 2.8 percent. (The yield to maturity as of December 1989 was even lower at 9.46 percent). While its bond rating still reflected a junk bond, its yield was more consistent with an investment grade rating.

Table 26.7 Pre- and postbuyout experience – Borg Warner Corporation ($ millions)

	Before buyout (3/87)	Immediately after buyout (9/87)	14 months after buyout (12/88)	26 months after buyout (12/89)	
EBIT	$315	$336	(177)[a]$187	$196	
Depreciation and amortization	$143	$174	$111	$92	
EBITDA	$458	$510	$298	$314	
Cost of debt					
(YTM) ($5\frac{1}{2}$s, '92)	8.55%	13.64%	10.85%	9.46%	
(8s, '96)	8.11%	14.69%	12.48%	12.02%	
Cost of LBO/EBIT(M1)	–	14.16×	–	–	
Cost of LBO/EBITD(M2)	–	10.02×	–	–	
EBIT/Interest	5.80×	1.29×[b]	1.00×	1.46×	
EBITD/Interest	8.20×	2.38×	1.47×	2.44×	
% Premium paid per share	–	24%	–	–	
Total assets	–	$5,386	$2,668	$2,252	
EBIT/Total assets	–	6.2%	7.0%	8.7%	
Long-term debt	–	$3,642	$1,300	$926	
Total debt	$395	$4,655	$1,491	$1,229	
Total value (TV)	$3,987	$4,855	$2,385	$3,512	
			$2,980	$3,140	
			$3,576	$3,768	
Equity value	$3,592	$200	$893	$1,283	
(TV – Debt)			$1,481	$1,911	
			$2,085	$2,539	
			vs. $541	$632	(Book equity)

[a] $177 million from continuing operations and a 1.29 interest coverage.
[b] Equivalent to an EBITDA multiplier of six.

If the entire firm was liquidated or shares sold again to the public in December 1988, we estimate that its equity would have been worth from $893 million to $2,085 million depending upon the cash flow multiplier consistent with the value of the firm. For instance, an EBITDA multiple of 10 – the multiplier paid for the LBO of Borg Warner by Merrill Lynch Capital Partners, would result in a total firm value of $2.980 billion as of 12/88 (EBITDA = $298 million). Multiples of 8 or 12 give the lower and upper figures ($2,384 and $3,576) for the total value as indicated in table 26.7.

A total firm value of $2.980 billion as of December 1988 results in an equity value of $1.489 billion ($2.980 – total debt of $1.491 billion). The lower bound equity value of $893 million is somewhat above the value that the private owners estimated ($541 million).[9] This appeared at the time to have been a conservative estimate of the LBO's equity. One year later, a six-times multiplier would have resulted in an equity value consistent with its book value of $632 million. Cash flow multiples did certainly decline in 1989, although it is not clear what Borg Warner's would have been.

[9] Derived from 1988 Borg Warner Corporation Annual Report.

The Borg Warner LBO appears to be a success with an increase in profitability (from 6.2 percent return on assets to 7.0 percent and 8.7 percent), a reduction of the cost of debt capital and the amount of debt (discussed earlier), and an increase in equity value of at least 200 percent. This is an excellent example of the concept of "temporary debt," discussed earlier, as the key to a successful highly leveraged restructuring.

Of course, the final judgment on this LBO will not be known until either the firm is sold, new equity issued to the public, or, on a negative theme, a distressed situation develops. The outlook, however, is quite bright for just about everyone involved. An indicator of that is the fact that the Borg Warner Corporation 5 percent bonds, while Ba3/B+ rated, were selling at a relatively low yield (high price) of 11.5 percent in September 1990 – almost three years after the buyout. The 8 percent bonds were selling at a 12.75 percent yield at this time. The latter bond is perhaps a better indicator of yield since there were still $100 million outstanding compared to only $3 million for the 5s of 1992.

Fruehauf Corporation

While Borg Warner is an example of a successful LBO, Fruehauf was a type of qualified failure. Restructured in December 1986, the manufacturer of truck trailers and automotive parts was bought for almost $750 million based on a cash flow multiple of 7.6 times and resulting in a 56 percent premium paid to the old shareholders. The acquisition was financed by an increase in debt of about $1.0 billion, of which $579 million was long-term (table 26.8). The debt to asset ratio was 85 percent – fairly typical of LBOs in 1986. Immediately after the increase in debt, the yield-to-maturity on the existing $9\frac{3}{4}$s of 1996 increased from 9.8 percent to 13.1 percent – a sizeable rise of over 3 percent, although not as much as in the Borg Warner case.

The situation deteriorated within two years of the LBO due to a combination of factors including lower profitability, disappointing asset sales, and the consequent diminution in equity. EBIT dropped 74 percent to $18 million although fixed assets were reduced by just 9 percent. Return on assets also fell to just 1.10 percent from 2.88 percent. Interest coverage by earnings dropped to just 0.18 times while cash flow coverage barely exceeded 1.0. The anticipated asset sales reduced fixed assets by less than $100 million and long-term debt was reduced by $400 million (37 percent). The high interest burden and low cash flow resulted in a cost of debt increase to 14.25 percent – over 1 percent higher than just after the LBO. Clearly, the LBO was in trouble.

As a result of Fruehauf's deterioration, we estimated the value of equity to be between –$297 million to a positive $201 million. This is based on firm multipliers on cash flow ($124.6 million) of 3.6–7.6 times. The latter was the multiplier paid for by the new owners. The lower multipliers were more likely although the book value of equity as of 12/88 was very close to the higher estimate of $201 – i.e., $181 million.

As the situation developed, Fruehauf's problems resulted in a distressed exchange in 1989 of cash and securities to the debenture holders worth approximately 89¢ on the dollar. This was accomplished by a sale of the firm's assets and the assumption of its remaining liabilities by Varity Corporation. While sustaining a capital loss, this distressed LBO was spared the more dramatic loss typically found in a default or a severe distressed exchange, i.e., a recovery of only from 20–60 percent of par value after the default or exchange, depending upon the particular situation and the priority status of the debt. For a discussion of recoveries after default, see Altman (1990).

Table 26.8 Pre- and postbuyout experience – Fruehauf Corporation ($ millions)

	Before buyout (11/86)	Immediately after buyout (12/86)	2 years after buyout (12/88)	
EBIT	$68.9	$68.9	$18.1	
Depreciation	$96	$96	$106.6	
EBITD	$165	$165	$124.6	
Cost of debt				
(YTM) ($9\frac{3}{4}$s, '96)	9.79%	13.07%	14.25%	
Cost of LBO/EBIT (M1)	–	18.47×	–	
Cost of LBO/EBITD (M2)	–	7.61×	–	
EBIT/Interest	0.86×	0.65×	0.18×	
EBITD/Interest	2.05×	1.56×	1.23×	
% Premium paid per share	–	56%	–	
EBIT/Total assets	–	2.88%	1.10%	
Fixed assets	$582	$811	$736	
Long-term debt	$544	$1,123	$710	
Total debt	$566	$1,553	$747	
Total value	$1,001	$1,835	$450	
			$699	
			$948	
Equity value	$525	$283	–$297	
(Common + Preferred)		($25)[a]	–$48	
			$201	
			vs. $181	(Book)

[a] Common.

In the case of Fruehauf, it appears that the optimistic earnings forecast, not realized, was the prime reason for the problems that developed for the debtholders. Of secondary, but still considerable, importance was the relatively small reduction in debt.

REFERENCES

Altman, Edward, (1984), "A Further Empirical Investigation of the Bankruptcy Cost Question," *Journal of Finance*, (September).

Altman, Edward, (1990), "Investing in Distressed Securities: The Anatomy of Bankrupt Debt and Equities," *Altman Foothill Report*, (April) and *Distressed Securities: Analyzing and Evaluating Market Potential and Investment Risk*, Chicago: Probus Publishing, 1991.

Altman, Edward and Roy Smith, (1991), "Highly Leveraged Restructurings: A Valid Role for Europe," *Journal of International Securities Markets* (Fall).

Amihud, Yakov, (1989), *Leveraged Management Buyouts: Causes and Consequences*, Homewood, IL: Dow Jones-Irwin.

Brigham, Eugene and Luis Gapenski, (1991), *Financial Management: Theory and Practice* (6th ed.), Hinsdale, IL: Dryden, chapter 12.

Bulow, J. and J. Shoven, (1978), "The Bankruptcy Decision," *The Bell Journal of Economics* (Autumn).

Copeland, Thomas, T. Koller, and J. Murrin, (1990), *Valuation*, New York: John Wiley & Sons.

Copeland, Thomas and W. H. Lee, (1990), "Exchange Offers and Stock Swaps – New Evidence," UCLA working paper.

Durand, David, (1959), "The Cost of Capital in an Imperfect Market: A Reply to Modigliani and Miller," *The American Economic Review* (June).

Jensen, Michael, (1989), "Eclipse of the Public Corporation," *Harvard Business Review* (September–October).

Jensen, M. and W. Meckling, (1976), "Theory of the Firm: Managerial Behavior, Agency Costs and Ownership Structure," *Journal of Financial Economics* (October).

Kaplan, Steven, (1989), "Management Buyouts: Evidence on Taxes as a Source of Value," *Journal of Finance* (September).

Miller, Merton, (1989), "The Modigliani–Miller Propositions after Thirty Years," *Journal of Applied Corporate Finance* (Spring).

Modigliani, Franco and Merton Miller, (1958), "The Cost of Capital, Corporation Finance and the Theory of Investment," *American Economic Review* (June).

Modigliani, Franco and Merton Miller, (1963), "Corporate Income Taxes and the Cost of Capital; A Correction," *American Economic Review* (June).

Moore, Harvin, "Trends and Characteristics of Recent LBO Experience," NYU working paper (November 1990).

Smith, Roy and Ingo Walter, (1990), "Economic Restructuring in Europe and the Market for Corporate Control," presented at Conference on Economic Restructuring in Europe, INSEAD and Stern School of Business, NYU (May and Fall).

Warner, Jerald, (1977), "Bankruptcy Costs: Some Evidence," *Journal of Finance* (May).

Weston, J. Fred, (1963), "A Test of Cost of Capital Propositions," *Southern Economic Journal* (October).

Weston, J. Fred, (1989), "What MM Have Wrought," *Financial Management* (Summer).

27 | Evaluating the Chapter 11 Bankruptcy-Reorganization Process

I INTRODUCTION

After almost 15 years of experience under the new Bankruptcy Code of 1978, there is enough evidence to do an evaluation of how the new process is working.[1] Will we have to wait another 40 years (1898, 1938, 1978, 2018[?]) for the nation's bankruptcy laws to be revised or has the increasing importance and incidence of corporate distress and bankruptcy hastened the need to critically review the current state of affairs? I take the position that the new Code has made some improvements to the system but it also has been disappointing in other respects. Although the legislative process in the USA is oftentimes slow to react to complex and indirect evidence, the Bankruptcy Laws will, I believe, be revised again rather than completely "scuttled" – as some have proposed.[2] And, the revision will come before 2018!

II TIME IN BANKRUPTCY

One of the important objectives of the new Bankruptcy Code of 1978 was the attempt to make the reorganization process less time-consuming. It gives just 120 days after the bankruptcy petition's filing as the exclusive right period for the debtor-in-possession (the bankrupt firm's management) to file a reorganization plan.[3] After 120 days, theoretically, any interested party may propose a plan, unless the Bankruptcy Court specifically

---

[1] At least 50 firms with liabilities greater than $1 billion have filed for Chapter 11 under the new Code. See Edward I. Altman, *Corporate Financial Distress and Bankruptcy* 20–1 (1993).

[2] See Michael Bradley and Michael Rosenzweig, The Untenable Case for Chapter 11, 101 *Yale L.J.* 1043 (1992).

[3] US Bankruptcy Code, 11 U.S.C. § 1121 (1978).

lengthens the exclusivity period. Lengthening is based on the debtor demonstrating at a formal hearing sufficient reasons for so doing.[4] Under the old Act, only the debtor could propose and promulgate a reorganization plan and she had no time limitation.[5] Since time and out-of-pocket direct bankruptcy costs are obviously positively correlated, any shortening of the reorganization period under Chapter 11 versus the old Chapters X or XI would probably provide a net benefit by conserving assets.

What has been the result? Based on a careful and comprehensive analysis of the time in bankruptcy-reorganization under the old Act versus the new Code, my conclusion is that average time in reorganization has been shortened somewhat under the new Code but is still much too long. Some years ago, I analyzed 90 industrial firm (non-railroad) reorganizations under the old Act and, for this study, 284 cases under the new Code. I found that the average time between the petition date and the confirmation date, under the old Act, was two years and three months (27 months) and a median time of 20 months.[6] As can be seen in table 27.1, under the new Code, the comparable average period during reorganization was somewhat lower – at one year and nine months (21 months) with a median length of 17 months. The distribution of reorganization periods under the new Code is as shown in table 27.1. Note that 54.2 percent of the cases took less than 18 months but in 21.8 percent of the cases, the reorganization period was longer than two and one half years (5 percent longer than four years).

Hotchkiss examined 684 complete reorganizations and found the average time from filing to confirmation was 18 months with a median of 16.2 months.[7] LoPucki has compared a number of empirical studies with respect to the median time spent in reorganization and concludes that the sample of firms helps to explain the differing results;[8] that smaller firms tend to complete the process quicker than larger ones; and that the new

Table 27.1 Chapter 11 reorganization experience: From filing to confirmation (number of months – 1979–91 bankruptcies)

Months	Number of confirmations	Percentage of total
0 to 12	89	31.3
13 to 18	65	22.9
19 to 24	40	14.1
25 to 30	28	9.9
31 to 36	25	8.8
37 to 48	23	8.1
>48	14	4.9
Total	284	100.0

Mean: 21.0 months
Median: 17.1 months

[4] US Bankruptcy Code, 11 U.S.C. § 1121(d).

[5] Altman, *supra* n. 1, ch. 1.

[6] Edward I. Altman, Bankrupt Firms' Equity Securities As An Investment Alternative, *Fin. Analysts J.*, July–Aug. 1969, at 129.

[7] Edith Hotchkiss, Does Chapter 11 Lead To Efficient Investment Decisions? (1992) (unpublished Ph.D. dissertation, New York University, Stern School of Business).

[8] Lynn M. Lopucki, The Trouble With Chapter 11, *Wis. L. Rev.* (forthcoming June 1993).

Bankruptcy Code of 1978 had "little impact" on the largest Chapter 11 companies compared to the old Chapters X and XI filings, but that the change from Chapter XI to Chapter 11 for smaller firms "was a disaster" since the time it took to reorganize more than doubled.[9] Even if the average time under the new Code is statistically significantly shorter, an average of 18–21 months is still a long and costly period.[10]

The new Code has the potential to shorten the period more significantly, but sympathetic judges seem to routinely give extensions to the 120 day exclusivity.[11] Admittedly, the competing issues in a modern bankruptcy-reorganization are oftentimes quite complex and a quick settlement is difficult. For example, as we enter the first quarter of 1993, the LTV Corp. bankruptcy (1986) has been mired by complex pension liability responsibility for well over six years.

My recommendation is to establish a reasonable exclusivity period and to adhere to it unless the debtor makes a convincing case that the firm is worth more as a going concern than it is in liquidation. The burden of proof as to the going concern and the liquidation values should be put on the debtor and good cause shown as to why the firm should be *permitted* to reorganize. Reorganization under the protection of the Bankruptcy Code is a privilege, not a right. In actuality, this privilege is granted with little or no discussion at the time of the filing. Since the determination of a going concern value based on estimates of future flows to the firm usually will require a restructuring plan for assets and liabilities, the debtor will typically not be in a position to submit values at the time of filing. A period of four to six months is sufficient time to do the analysis.

Routine extensions to the exclusivity period should be avoided. In addition, the courts should ensure full disclosure of all relevant information so that if existing claimants, or another firm or a group of investors wants to make a bid to buy the debtor, there is ample time to study the situation. This full disclosure must be mandated by the Court at the time of filing or else the firm's managers will probably have little incentive to provide data. Under the Bankruptcy Code, the fiduciary responsibility of the Board of Directors of the Chapter 11 firm must be clearly defined – to maximize the value of the debtor's estate and not solely to act in the best interest of the old shareholders.

III CHAPTER 11 RESOLUTION: EMPIRICAL FINDINGS

Based on the findings by Hotchkiss[12] and an earlier study by Morse and Shaw,[13] some important information is revealed about the Chapter 11 process since the new Code was enacted. Hotchkiss analyzed 1,096 publicly held company Chapter 11 filings from October 1979 to September 1990 as to their fate under the bankruptcy-reorganization process (table 27.2). Of the 1,096 filings, 412 (37.6 percent) were either still in reorganization (138) as of 1 April 1992 or the resolution of their reorganization effort was not known (274). Of the remaining filings, the following resolutions were documented:

---

[9] *Ibid.* at 16.
[10] Unfortunately, I do not have the complete distribution data on the reorganization time for each of the cases under the old Bankruptcy Act, so no definitive statistical tests are possible at this time.
[11] For example, some recent Chapter 11 bankruptcies still are or were under the supervision of the courts for five to seven years, e.g., Wheeling-Pittsburgh Steel, LTV, and Manville Corporation.
[12] Hotchkiss, *supra* n. 7.
[13] Dale Morse and Wayne Shaw, Investing in Bankrupt Firms, 43 *J. Fin.* 1193 (1988).

Table 27.2[a]   Outcomes of bankruptcy filings for 1,096 public companies filing for Chapter 11 between October 1979 and September 1990

	Merged or acquired	Liquidated[b]	Emerged public	Emerged private[c]	Unknown or still in bankruptcy	Full sample
% Total firms	6.6	15.0	22.6	18.2	37.6	100.0
Years in Bankruptcy						
Mean	1.3	1.8	1.1	2.1	–	1.5
(Median)	(1.1)	(1.2)	(1.4)	(1.3)		(1.35)

[a] Edith Hotchkiss, *Investment Decisions Under Chapter 11 Bankruptcy* (unpublished work in progress, New York University, Stern School of Business).
[b] Time in bankruptcy uses date of conversion to Chapter 7 or date of confirmation of a liquidating Chapter 11 plan.
[c] Reorganized but did not continue to file financial statements with the SEC.

- 248 (22.6 percent) emerged as a public company.
- 199 (18.2 percent) emerged as a private company.
- 164 (15.0 percent) were liquidated.
- 72 (6.6 percent) were either merged or acquired.

Even if all of the 412 unknown resolutions were liquidations of some type, the proportion of those publicly owned companies that had a plan confirmed and emerged in some continuing form was quite high at 519/1,096 (47.4 percent). In actuality, that proportion will no doubt be higher. Indeed, assuming that all of the unknowns (274) were liquidated, and of those still in reorganization (138) the same proportion (74 percent) emerge as a continuing entity as was observed above, the total number of successful emergences would be about 621 of the 1,096, or 56.7 percent.

Morse and Shaw examined a sample of 162 large firm bankruptcies spanning the old Act and new Code periods (1973–82). They found that 60 percent of their large, publicly held firm sample emerged from bankruptcy, 7 percent were merged in reorganization, and only 15 percent liquidated.[14] While it is difficult to compare liquidation propensity in the pre- and post-Act periods, Morse and Shaw's liquidation proportions are the same as those found by Hotchkiss. The former covered primarily the pre-Act period while the latter was concerned solely with post-Act cases.

The above results show that over one-half of publicly owned Chapter 11 debtors emerge out of reorganization as a continuing entity. This is considerably higher than the 10–12 percent of all (public and private firms) Chapter 11 filings estimated by Flynn (1989)[15] and the 17 percent that reached a court confirmed plan. The high proportion of successfully confirmed Chapter 11 filings is perhaps greater than many had thought to be the case. At the same time, it is safe to assume that the incidence and probability of successful confirmation of large publicly held firms, e.g., greater than $100 million in liabilities, is considerably greater than those noted above for firms of all sizes. No doubt this is one of the reasons for the substantial growth in the buying and selling

---

[14]   Morse and Shaw, *supra* n. 13.
[15]   Edward Flynn, *Statistical Analysis of Chapter 11*, Administrative Office of the U.S. Courts (1989).

of defaulted debt securities and the emergence of over 60 institutional investors who specialize in this heretofore backwater investment asset class.[16]

Actually, the fact that a significant number of firms emerge from the Chapter 11 process as a continuing entity is good news only if they in fact "deserved" to emerge, i.e., their going concern value exceeded their liquidation value. Since we observe that 30 Chapter 11's had to refile, the reorganization process was probably not successful and possibly liquidation would have been the better decision.[17]

The not so good news is that a non-trivial number of emerged Chapter 11's file for bankruptcy again; and, in the case of Braniff Airlines, a third time. One can call these refilings Chapter 22s or Chapter 33s. Obviously, for most of these instances the firm did not emerge as a healthy going concern; either still too loaded down with debt or without sufficient earnings and cash flow prospects to remain solvent. Hotchkiss discusses post-emergence results of Chapter 11 companies as well as reasons for their performance.[18]

IV AUCTIONING OFF THE BANKRUPT FIRM

There has been a number of recent articles commenting on the problems with the Chapter 11 process and encouraging revisions or outright "scuttling" of the bankruptcy-reorganization process.[19] In general, these articles criticize the reorganization process in that it motivates inefficient and costly actions by managers of distressed firms and is a process which impedes the allocation of corporate resources to the highest valued user of those assets. The result is that the creditors of these corporations disproportionately bear the costs of these inefficient actions and of the process itself. Implicit in these notions is that there are sizeable bankruptcy costs and, in many cases, violations of the so-called absolute priority doctrine.

Absolute priority holds that senior creditors be paid in full before anything is allocated to junior creditors and that the stockholders receive nothing unless all creditors are paid in full. Eberhart, Moore and Roenfeldt find, however, that in corporate reorganization, violations of absolute priority are the rule rather than the exception and that, on average, these violations account for 7.6 percent of the total amount paid out to all claimants.[20] Others, e.g., Weiss[21] and LoPucki and Whitford,[22] also find numerous

---

[16] See Edward I. Altman, *Distressed Securities* (1991).

[17] Altman, *supra* n. 1, ch. 1.

[18] Hotchkiss, *supra* n. 7. She finds that, on average, reorganized firms do rather poorly in the post-emergence years.

[19] For critiques of the old Bankruptcy Act and the newer Chapter 11 system, see generally Joseph Stiglitz, Some Aspects of the Pure Theory of Corporate Finance: Bankruptcies and Takeovers, *Bell J. Econ. and Mgmt.* 458 (1972); Michelle J. White, Bankruptcy Costs and the New Bankruptcy Code, 38 *J. Fin.* 477, (1977); Mark J. Roe, Bankruptcy and Debt: A New Model for Corporate Reorganization, 83 *Colum. L. Rev.* 527 (1983); Thomas H. Jackson, *The Logic and Limits of Bankruptcy Law* (1986); Douglas G. Baird, The Uneasy Case for Corporate Reorganizations, 15 *J. Legal Stud.* 127 (1986); Lucien A. Bebchuck, A New Approach to Corporate Reorganization, 101 *Harv. L. Rev.* 775 (1988); Barry E. Adler, Bankruptcy and Risk Allocation, 77 *Cornell L. Rev.* 439 (1992); Bradley and Rosenzweig, *supra* n. 2.

[20] Allan C. Eberhart et al., Security Pricing and Deviations from the Absolute Priority Rule in Bankruptcy Proceedings, 45 *J. Fin.* 1457, 1458 (1990).

[21] Laurence A. Weiss, Bankruptcy Costs and Violation of Claims Priority, 27 *J. Fin. Econ.* 285, 286 (1990).

[22] Lynn M. LoPucki and William Whitford, Bargaining Over Equity's Share in the Bankruptcy Reorganization of Large, Publicly Held Companies, 139 *U. Pa. L. Rev.* 125, 186–90 (1990).

instances of absolute priority violations. Eberhart and Sweeney, however, find that the market has discounted these violations in the pricing of outstanding publicly held debt at the time of default or bankruptcy (whichever comes first).[23] In other words, "relative" rather than "absolute" priority is the current doctrine under reorganization, while liquidation is more likely to adhere to absolute priority.

The Bankruptcy Code does not state in explicit terms that absolute priority should always be followed in an expedient Chapter 11 solution. Therefore, the word "doctrine" is perhaps inappropriate except in liquidation where the assets are no longer preserved. I see nothing wrong with debtholders making investment decisions based on an expectation that their residual claim after a Chapter 11 petition will not adhere strictly to absolute priority. Rather, debtholders of different seniority can expect "recovery" rates after default equal to something like the observed experience found in table 27.3. I will return to these data shortly.

Table 27.3[a] Average recovery prices on defaulted debt by seniority per $100 face amount; 1985–91[b]

| Year | Secured ($) | Senior ($) | Senior subordinated ($) | Subordinated | |
				Cash pay ($)	Non-cash pay ($)
1991	54.50 (02)	58.15 (62)[c]	34.62 (21)	20.28 (35)	21.06 (04)
1990	35.04 (07)	32.02 (27)	24.04 (28)	17.93 (17)	18.99 (12)
1989	82.69 (09)	53.70 (16)	19.60 (21)	23.95 (30)	NONE
1988	67.96 (13)	41.99 (19)	30.70 (10)	35.27 (20)	NONE
1987	12.00 (01)	70.52 (29)[d]	53.50 (10)	40.54 (07)	NONE
1986	48.32 (07)	37.09 (08)	37.74 (10)	31.58 (34)	NONE
1985	74.25 (02)	34.81 (03)	36.18 (07)	41.45 (15)	NONE
Average 1985–91 all issues	60.51 (41) 39.24 (486)	52.28 (164)	30.70 (107)	27.96 (158)	19.51 (16)

Number of issues in parentheses.
[a] Altman, supra note 1, at 118.
[b] Prices at end of default month.
[c] Includes 23 issues of Columbia Gas; without these issues the recovery rate was $43.30.
[d] Without Texaco, 1987 recovery rate was $29.77.

V SHOULD WE SUBSTITUTE AN AUCTION PROCESS FOR CHAPTER 11?

Perhaps the most dramatic and revolutionary change in our bankruptcy system has been proposed by Bradley and Rosenzweig. They indicate that a number of scholars have advocated important changes to the existing system but all present their solutions based on the premise that business failure is essentially an exogenously determined

[23] Allan C. Eberhart and Richard J. Sweeney, Does the Market Predict Bankruptcy Settlements?, 47 *Journal of Finance*, 47 (1992) 943–7.

event.[24] Roe argues for a public auction of a new equity issue[25] and Bebchuk proposes that all claimants be given both stock and options based on a formula which preserves absolute priority through a type of excise tax.[26] Baird and Jackson[27] also suggest changes in the system.

As noted above, Bradley and Rosenzweig (B–R) claim that others assume that the distressed firm's problems are exogenously (e.g., competition, interest rates, the economy, etc.), determined. B–R assert, on the contrary, that corporate bankruptcy frequently is endogenous, chosen by corporate managers, rather than imposed upon them. They assert that managers have no real incentive to maintain an adequate liquid asset balance to meet current obligations as long as there is the possibility of a court supervised and protected reorganization whereby existing management will more than likely remain in control.[28]

B–R then assert that the new Bankruptcy Code of 1978 does not promote efficient asset allocations but is a mechanism that permits managers to abridge contractual agreements with creditors and other stakeholders in order to enhance their own welfare and therefore reduces social welfare.[29] In addition to their conceptual arguments, B–R present some interesting, but seriously flawed, empirical tests to show that returns to both stockholders and debtholders have been significantly worse under the new 1978 Code compared to the old Act.[30] I will return to those tests and their problems after reviewing the B–R proposal.[31]

B–R advocate repealing the existing Bankruptcy Code and substituting a process whereby successive classes of claimants, starting from the most junior stockholder interests and advancing through the seniority hierarchy to the most senior creditors, have the opportunity to pay off the company's unpaid debts or else be eliminated from the process. If the default, or possible default, is not cured at any level, then the most senior creditor class would be entitled to either run the firm and retain the firm's equity position, sell its equity to outside investors or liquidate the firm's assets for their exclusive use. In essence, the process involves a series of call options where the

---

[24]   Bradley and Rosenzweig, *supra* n. 2.

[25]   Roe, *supra* n. 19. Roe argues that the present system leaves Chapter 11 firms with too much debt threatening the future success of the emerging companies. The number of Chapter 22s (about 3 percent) seems to substantiate this claim, to some extent.

[26]   Bebchuck, *supra* n. 19.

[27]   Baird, *supra* n. 19; Jackson, *supra* n. 19.

[28]   Bradley & Rosenzweig, *supra* n. 2, at 1047.

[29]   *Ibid.* at 1043.

[30]   *Ibid.* at 1076.

[31]   For other critiques of the B–R article, see Lynn M. LoPucki, Strange Visions in a Strange World: A Reply to Bradley and Rosenzweig, 91 *Mich. L. Rev.* 79 (1992); Elizabeth Warren, The Untenable Case For Repeal of Chapter 11, 102 *Yale L.J.* 437 (1992); Martin J. Whitman, et. al., A Rejoinder to The Untenable Case for Chapter 11, 2:2 *J. Bank. L. & Prac.* 839 (1993). These articles contain numerous legal, conceptual, and financial market arguments which are too copious to review in this paper. They do not, except in passing, comment on the empirical flaws of the B–R piece. For example, LoPucki comments on the seniority distribution of the B–R bond sample – a crucial factor that I will analyze in depth at a later point. In a recent paper, Jagdeep A. Bhandari and Laurence A. Weiss, The Untenable Case for Chapter 11: A Review of the Evidence, *Am. Bankr. L.J.* (forthcoming June 1993) argue that B–R's conclusions "are not compelled by the evidence." These authors conduct their own empirical tests of the causes of the increase in bankruptcy filings under the new Chapter 11 Code. They find that the increase was primarily due to the change in corporate leverage and reduction in corporate profitability and not the consequence of the change in law. The latter was significant, however, but only in a marginal way.

exercise price is the outstanding interest and/or principal due. If the option is not exercised, that class passing on the option is totally eliminated thereby preserving absolute priority.[32]

VI EVALUATION OF THE BRADLEY AND ROSENZWEIG PROPOSAL

I am sympathetic to any proposal that involves the market mechanism and a clearing price to settle valuation issues. B–R have proposed a clever, hierarchical type of auction process, albeit not totally original, to settle the distressed corporate governance problem. Indeed, Haugen and Senbet use the arbitrage argument to show that firms could be auctioned off prior to bankruptcy thereby eliminating direct bankruptcy costs which take place during court supervised reorganization proceedings.[33] B–R's proposal provides a framework for the auction process.

As noted above, the market, if free to work in an efficient manner, should be the preferred mechanism for settling valuation issues – even for distressed firms. Unfortunately, the bidding process for a distressed firm's assets is not efficient and is potentially chaotic. First, a consensus opinion within the various classes of creditors is a heroic but an unrealistic assumption. Second, the ambiguity of disputed claims by the myriad of different creditors (real or perceived) would make the process uncertain as to its eventual disposition. Third, efficiency assumes equal information for all parties. While in theory this is always possible, it is not likely that, at the time of default, all claimants possess the same information. Some time is needed to assess a number of issues such as expected business conditions and financial structure alternatives, management succession, and in some cases, anti-trust issues. An immediate auction process would not provide that framework in a feasible manner.

Easterbrook directly addresses the auction process proposed and argues against its inception into the bankruptcy process. He suggests that despite the inevitable errors in the valuations of distressed companies, these mistakes are less costly than that of conducting an auction.[34]

What is needed in a complex distressed firm situation is a period of time to sort out all the relevant alternative plans, including the raising of new equity capital by the current owners. In a sense, a firm in Chapter 11 is immediately "in play" once the exclusivity period has expired. A formal buy-out offer can form one of the alternatives for the firm's creditors to consider. While the existing debtor and its management have the right to propose a plan in the exclusivity period, an outside bid can always be made known to existing creditors who can vote down the proposed plan and wait for the exclusivity period to expire. As long as the existing management feels that it can get extensions, they will not be motivated to come to grips with their own plan in an expeditious manner. They also may not be forthcoming with timely disclosure of the appropriate information for others to accurately value the enterprise. Any auction

[32] Bradley and Rosenzweig, *supra* n. 2, at 1084.
[33] Robert Haugen and Lemma Senbet, The Insignificance of Bankruptcy Costs to the Theory of Capital Structure, 33 *J. Fin.* 383 (1978); Robert Haugen and Lemma Senbet, Bankruptcy and Agency Costs: Their Significance to the Theory of Optimal Capital Structure, 23 *J. Fin. & Quant. Anal.* 27 (1988).
[34] Frank H. Easterbrook, Is Corporate Bankruptcy Efficient?, 27 *J. Fin. Econ.* 411 (1990).

process, whether immediately after the bankruptcy filing or at a later date, should involve adequate disclosure.

There are numerous recent cases where an outside bid either did form the eventual successful reorganization format or stimulated a higher offer from existing owners. For example, an external buy-out offer was the basis of the plan that determined the Coleco (1990) and Allegheny International (1990) bankruptcy emergence cases and is now being evaluated in the Circle K (1992) case. In the case of Revco, D.S. (1992), several outside bids fostered a more acceptable "inside" offer. In Revco, like the Southland (1990) reorganization plan, outside equity was infused, although the existing equity retained some ownership in the debtor. Additionally, creditors, through a new package of debt and new equity, voted favorably on the plans. The alternative could have conceivably been rejection and liquidation – especially if the bankruptcy judge had established a final date for all bids to be submitted and a vote taken. In the case of Revco, however, there were competing bids from Jack Eckerd Corp. and Rite-Aid, so liquidation was not likely.

My proposal is therefore to permit an orderly reorganization and/or auction process to take place under the supervision of the courts in order to ensure fairness to all stakeholders and a reasonable information gathering period. The initial choice for the firm to be put "in play" is, as always, at the option of the existing owners by their decision not to exercise their explicit call option to meet their contractual debt commitments as they come due. An alternative to putting a company "in play" is to propose and effect a distressed restructuring before a bankruptcy petition or to decide before to accept a restructuring but wait until after the petition to take a vote (prepackaged Chapter 11). In these cases, a long and costly formal bankruptcy period is avoided. Out of court settlements usually result in lower costs.[35]

If the various stakeholders, both insiders and potential outsiders, knew that bids must be filed within, say six months of the actual bankruptcy petition, then the bids will be forthcoming in that timeframe. Legitimate claims as to fairness must be handled expeditiously by the courts and important resources preserved. Admittedly, the size and scope of the Bankruptcy Court process would need to be assessed to provide a structure to ensure that the process has the chance to work.

VII EMPIRICAL TESTS COMPARING THE OLD ACT WITH THE NEW CODE

One of the important elements in the B–R (1992) criticism of the new Bankruptcy Code is their empirical comparison of how stockholders and bondholders fared under the old Act versus the new Code. They compare the abnormal return on a portfolio of bankrupt stocks versus the market portfolio for different holding periods from before filing to up to six months after filing.[36] A similar test is performed on public bondholders, again for up to six months following the bankruptcy petition date.[37] They also perform a number of other comparisons, including the size of the default premium on corporate

---

[35] See Stuart C. Gilson et al., Troubled Debt Restructuring, 27 *J. Fin. Econ.* 315 (1990).
[36] Bradley and Rosenzweig, *supra* n. 2, at 1068, 1093.
[37] *Ibid.* at 1071–2.

debt in the pre- and post-Act periods.[38] In most cases, they conclude that the security holders did significantly worse in the post-new-Code period compared to pre-Code security holders. Their conclusion is that the wealth position of stock and bond holders has been dramatically hurt by the 1978 bankruptcy legislation.[39]

I find some rather incomplete, biased and problematic aspects of their empirical tests which casts serious doubt about the veracity of the B–R findings and conclusions. I will concentrate on their tests of bondholder wealth comparisons. For these comparisons, B–R perform two tests:

1 on the experiences of bondholders of firms that have filed bankruptcy petitions, and
2 on the change in the default premium in the yields of defaulting bonds relative to the risk-free rate.[40]

A Bondholder Returns

B–R examine the experience of 175 publicly traded debt issues from 88 firms (not 326 as indicated in their *New York Times* article) from twelve months prior to filing to six months after.[41] They calculate the abnormal return by comparing the return on the bankrupt bonds to Moody's Corporate Bond Index – the latter is essentially an investment grade yield index.[42] Since abnormal returns from both before the 1978 Code and after are compared, the market index could not have included low grade bonds since returns on these more risky securities were not available until about 1978. B–R conclude that, while bondholders of bankrupt firms experience significant capital loss in both periods, as they found for stockholders, they also find that all security holders suffer significantly greater losses in the post-Code period than in the earlier period.[43] They conclude that, "like stockholders, bond-holders have not benefitted from the adoption of the 1978 Act."[44]

At least two problems are apparent in the B–R tests. First, and perhaps most important, the authors have not controlled for the seniority of the bond issues. This potential problem is apparent since they do find that at one year prior to bankruptcy, the average bond rating of the post-Act sample was significantly lower than the pre-Act sample.[45] Not only were the bonds in the post-Act sample of lower quality, they more than likely were of significantly *junior* seniority. The pre-Act period had few subordinate issues while defaults in the 1980s have been comprised of a large proportion of senior-subordinated or junior-subordinated issues.[46] Indeed, it is even possible that the B–R sample included secured bonds; they did not disclose their exact sample. Secured bonds usually trade on the value of the collateral and an accrued interest basis rather than based on

---

[38] *Ibid.* at 1070.
[39] *Ibid.* at 1072, 1076.
[40] *Ibid.* at 1070–1.
[41] Michael Bradley and Michael Rosenzweig, Time to Scuttle Chapter 11, *N.Y. Times*, Mar. 8, 1992, §3, at 8.
[42] *Ibid.* at 1071; and from discussion with the authors.
[43] *Ibid.* at 1076.
[44] *Ibid.* at 1076.
[45] *Ibid.* at 1072.
[46] Altman, *supra* n. 1, ch. 5.

the future expected income of the debtor. The latter basis, however, is the primary influence on more junior bonds and equities.

One of the important issues that was all but ignored by B–R is the far more complex and more heavily leveraged capital structures that typified US corporations in the 1980s. Indeed, original issue subordinated debt was issued far more frequently in the 1980s, particularly in corporate restructuring, e.g., LBOs. Multi-layered debt structures became more common, especially if there were some previously issued debt securities outstanding at the time of the restructuring.

The lower seniority issues, whatever the health of the company, are more equity-like than the more senior issues. B–R assert that bankrupt firms were financially stronger in the post-Act period and "therefore less likely to resort to junk bond financing".[47] This is a strange finding since junk bond financings almost did not exist in the B–R pre-Act sample period (1962–78) but were increasingly issued in the post-Act period.[48] And, junk bonds are issued by financially weaker companies than are investment grade bonds.

From table 27.3, we observe that debt prices just after default are directly related to the issue's seniority. Senior bonds averaged 52.3 percent of face value while senior-subordinated and junior-subordinated bonds averaged only 30.7 percent and 28.0 percent respectively. More importantly, the more junior the issue, the more "equity-like" is its valuation basis. Since we know from B–R and others, e.g., Morse and Shaw (1988)[49], that equity-holders do poorly in bankruptcy-reorganization, it is therefore not surprising that both the actual equity holders and the equity-like debt issues will also do poorly and certainly experience lower returns than the more senior issues. This probable seniority differential in the B–R sample could certainly explain their pre-filing period comparative results, i.e., from 11 months prior to bankruptcy to the filing date, which favored the pre-Act sample.

To illustrate the possible bias in the B–R study, we have examined a portfolio of 60 post-1978 Code *senior* corporate bonds over the same 18 month period, i.e., from 12 months prior to 6 months after default. B–R examined 105 post-Code bonds but presumably many were either senior-subordinated or subordinated issues. Our sample more than likely conforms closely, in terms of seniority, to their pre-Act sample. We also calculate mean percentage abnormal returns. We utilized, however, the updated Blume–Keim low-grade debt index as the comparison standard instead of the Moody's Corporate Bond Index.[50] The latter is not as appropriate when analyzing high risk defaulted bonds.[51] Of course, the low-grade or junk-bond index was not available in the pre-Act period so B–R could not have used it.

Our results [in table 27.4] show how important it is to control for seniority. While B–R find that the post-Act abnormal return was −70.66 percent from −11 to +6 months after bankruptcy, I find that for senior bonds only, the average abnormal return was −32.4 percent. And, this result is *better than* B–R's pre-Act average of −42.23 percent. For the period +1 to +6 months after bankruptcy, I find the average abnormal return

---

47   Bradley and Rosenzweig, *supra* n. 2, at 1072 n. 72.
48   Edward I. Altman, *Investing in Junk Bonds* 22 (1987).
49   Altman, *supra* n. 1, at 118.
50   Marshall E. Blume and Donald B. Keim, Lower Grade Bonds: Their Risks and Returns, *Fin. Analysts J.*, July–Aug. 1987, at 26.
51   There are several new indexes developed to analyze the performance of defaulted bonds, including one developed and maintained by the author called The Altman–Merrill Lynch & Co. Index of Defaulted Debt Securities. See Altman, *supra* n. 1, ch. 7.

Table 27.4 Holding period returns – pre and post Bankruptcy Act

Holding period	Pre-Act (B–R)	Post-Act (B–R)[52]	Post-Act (Altman)
−11 to +6	−42.23%	−70.66%	−32.4%
	[70]	[105]	[60]
+1 to +6	1.85%	−13.64%	+12.1%
	[48]	[78]	[60]

(Number of issues in brackets.)

was +12.1 percent vs. B–R's post-Act finding of −13.64 percent. Again, only the senior bonds sample did better in the post-Act period than did B–R's pre-Act result of 1.85 percent.

This is confirming empirical support to our hypothesis that the B–R bondholder results are suspect. And, our new comparative results are so obvious that no statistical tests are necessary.

B Some Additional Concerns

There is also little doubt that the bond rating breakdown in the B–R sample has influenced their results, despite their protestations to the contrary.[53] For example, they calculated the average bond rating for the pre- and post-Act samples and found, not surprisingly, that the post-Act sample had a significantly lower average rating one year prior to filing, i.e., below B for the post-Act and slightly above Ba for the pre-Act firms.[54] One can assume quite safely that the *original* ratings of the pre-Act sample were also higher than the post-Act issues. And, from table 27.5, we observe that the average price just after default is significantly greater for investment grade bonds in the three A categories than lower rated bonds. Since there were far more original issue lower rated bonds in the post-1978 period than prior to the new Code, one can conclude that unless B–R controlled for the original issue rating, their results are biased, perhaps seriously.

Finally, the B–R study examines only the first six months after filing in their calculation of abnormal returns.[55] It is certainly plausible that they find negative abnormal returns in this interval for the post-Act sample. But, B–R do not go beyond the six-month period and the results from Hradsky and Long show that defaulted bonds' abnormal returns in the post-Act period did quite well in the 18 month period following the initial six months after default.[56] While the pre-Act issues might also have done well in this more lengthened post-filing period, B–R's work is unfortunately incomplete in this assessment of how bondholders actually did in the reorganization period. An even more complete analysis would be to track the bond returns for the entire period from bankruptcy filing until the plan's confirmation date or liquidation date.

[52] Bradley and Rosenzweig, *supra* n. 2, at 1072.

[53] *Ibid.* at 1043 n. 72.

[54] *Ibid.* at 1072.

[55] *Ibid.* at 1072.

[56] Gregory Hradsky and Robert Long, High Yield Losses and the Return Performance of Bankrupt Debt Issues: 1978–1988, *Fin. Analysts J.*, July–Aug. 1989, at 38.

Table 27.5[a] Average price after default by original bond rating (per $100)

Original rating	1971–91			1971–87			1988–91		
	Average (weighted) price after default	Average (arithmetic) price after default	Number of observations	Average (weighted) price after default	Average (arithmetic) price after default	Number of observations	Average (weighted) price after default	Average (arithmetic) price after default	Number of observations
AAA	79.44	78.68	5	79.44	78.68	5	NA	NA	0
AA	82.11	69.24	20	87.19	79.30	13	52.69	50.57	7
A	60.63	60.84	49	71.55	46.40	19	50.11	69.98	30
BBB	45.52	44.07	51	39.82	43.27	21	46.85	44.64	30
BB	29.68	28.92	38	33.01	29.27	23	28.22	28.38	15
B	33.29	35.85	233	44.51	37.90	86	31.01	34.66	147
CCC	22.76	31.57	64	32.03	30.57	25	19.44	32.21	39
C	13.27	13.13	4	13.27	13.13	4	NA	NA	0
Average	45.84	45.29		50.10	44.81		38.05	43.40	
Total			464			196			268

[a] Edward I. Altman, Defaults and Returns on High Yield Bonds: Through 1991, Merrill Lynch & Co. High Yield Research, Special Report, March 6, 1992.

C *Default Risk Premiums*

B–R conclude that the risk premium required by bondholders in the post-Act period was significantly greater than in the pre-Act years, indicating that *expected* losses were greater in the later period. They attribute this result to the fact that bondholders did not expect to benefit from the new Act.[57] By implication, the higher default risk premium would burden all firms as the cost of credit increases. If B–R are correct in this assertion, then clearly the social costs to society as a whole will have been increased.

An alternative hypothesis, perhaps more plausible, is that the significantly higher risk premiums in the later period are dominated by higher *probabilities of bankruptcy* and not the higher costs of bankruptcy. It turns out that higher default risk was coincidental with the post-Act period. One only has to observe the incidence of corporate bond downgrades in the 1970s versus the 1980s to confirm this.[58] For example, newly issued AAA bonds rated by Standard & Poor's in the 1970s saw 8 percent of their issues downgraded after three years and 20 percent after five years. In the 1980s, 33.1 percent after three years and 50.7 percent after five years were downgraded. For single-A rated new issues in the 1970s, after three years, 7.9 percent were downgraded (4.3 percent upgraded) while in the 1980s, 21.4 percent were downgraded (10.7 percent upgraded).[59]

We can conclude, therefore, that in the post-Act period the credit worthiness of companies clearly deteriorated *vis-à-vis* that which took place in the pre-Act period. This is the primary reason default risk premiums increased in the post-Act period, not the costs of bankruptcy as B–R postulate. Further confirmation of this can be seen from the sizeable increase in actual bond defaults in the 1980s compared to the 1970s.[60] Credit costs are indeed higher in the last dozen years or so, but the B–R explanation appears to be spurious.

VIII SOME RELATED EMPIRICAL BANKRUPTCY ISSUES

Two other aspects of Chapter 11's evaluation are related to the bankruptcy announcement effect and the issue of managerial succession and compensation. The former is important to assess the impact of financial distress and bankruptcy on the society as a whole while the latter issue is often cited by detractors of the current system.[61]

It is well documented that the announcement of a bankruptcy petition has a significant negative impact on the share price.[62] This impact of at least an average 25 percent

---

[57] Bradley and Rosenzweig, *supra* n. 2, at 1071.

[58] See Edward I. Altman and D. L. Kao, *Corporate Bond Rating Drift: An Examination of Rating Agency Credit Quality Changes Over Time* (1991); Douglas J. Lucas and John C. Lonski, Changes in Credit Quality 1970–1990, *J. Fixed Income*, March 1992, at 2,7. These studies show the greater propensity for rating downgrades in the 1980s (post-Code) versus the 1970s (pre-Code years).

[59] Edward I. Altman and D. L. Kao, The Implications of Corporate Bond Trading Drift, *Fin. Analysts J.*, May–June 1992, at 64–75.

[60] Altman, *supra* n. 1, ch. 5.

[61] See Pat Wechsler, Rising Use of Chapter 11 Has Experts Rethinking Law, *Hous. Chron*, Mar. 29, 1992 (Business), at 6.

[62] See Edward I. Altman, Bankrupt Firms' Equity Securities As an Investment Alternative, *Fin. J.*, July–Aug. 1969, at 129; Thomas Clark and Mark Weinstein, The Behavior of Common Stock of Bankrupt Firms, 38 *J. Fin.* 489 (1983).

decline in price can be attributed primarily to a reduction in expected value of the equity as its call option value on the firm's assets is lowered and the added direct and possibly indirect costs of a formal Chapter 11 proceeding.[63]

The bankruptcy petition gives unambiguous evidence as to the gravity of the firm's problems. Before the filing, the market usually knows that problems exist but is not totally sure with a probability of 1.0 that the situation is so grave. Simultaneous with the impact on the filing debtor's equity, is the so-called contagion effect of the Chapter 11 announcement on the firm's competitors.[64] Lang and Stulz (1992) document this phenomenon and find that competitors' stock prices also fall on the bankruptcy news, indicating that the problems are common to other firms in the same business risk class. This loss to equity investors is more related to expected earnings deterioration than to the bankruptcy process.[65] And, this contagion effect has probably been quite apparent in the post-Act period as a number of industries have gone through difficult times due to chronic problems, international and domestic competitive effects, deregulation, and the oil industry crisis. Lang and Stulz conclude that the contagion effect is greater than the competitive gains to firms which witness the default of one of their competitors.[66] And, the contagion effect is an exogenous factor, contrary to the B–R thesis.

As for the assertion that managers gain from the Chapter 11 process, Gilson finds that managers and directors do not fare as well as many believe.[67] He found that the average CEO cash compensation of bankrupt companies fell by about 6 percent compared to an overall average 10 percent increase of CEO cash compensation in the 1980s. Further, many senior managers are replaced before and during the reorganization period with the new leaders' compensation about 35 percent higher than the deposed group.[68]

In his 1990 study, Gilson finds that both CEOs and Directors of bankrupt companies leave or are replaced quite frequently after the filing.[69] Indeed, only about 43 percent of the CEOs and 46 percent of the incumbent Directors remain following a bankruptcy or distressed debt restructuring.[70] Gilson's results certainly question the profound "management entrenchment" hypothesis of B–R and others.

Wruck presents evidence that financial distress has benefits as well as costs.[71] Benefits, she argues, accrue from the high turnover of inefficient managers and the ability in Chapter 11 to deal with diffuse creditors who may be combined into a single class.[72]

The above evidence mitigates the management entrenchment arguments of B–R, and others, who wish to eliminate the Chapter 11 process. There is little doubt that any

---

[63] See e.g., Jerome Warner, Bankruptcy Costs: Some Evidence, 32 *J. Fin.* 237, 237–48 (1977); Edward I. Altman, A Further Empirical Investigation of the Bankruptcy Cost Question, 39 *J. Fin.* 1067, 1067–89 (1984).

[64] Larry H. R. Lang and Rene M. Stulz, Contagion and Competitive IntraIndustry Effects of Bankruptcy Announcements: An Empirical Analysis, 32 *J. Fin. Econ.* 45 (1992).

[65] *Ibid.* at 48.

[66] *Ibid.* at 59.

[67] Stuart C. Gilson, Bankruptcy, Boards, Banks and Block-Holders, 30 *J. Fin. Econ.* 355 (1990); Stuart C. Gilson, Management Turnaround and Financial Distress, 25 *J. Fin. Econ.* 241 (1989).

[68] Gilson (1989), *supra* n. 67.

[69] Gilson (1990), *supra* n. 67.

[70] Gilson (1989), *supra* n. 67.

[71] Karen H. Wruck, Financial Distress, Reorganization and Organizational Efficiency, 27 *J. Fin. Econ.* 419 (1990).

[72] *Ibid.*

modifications in the current system which increase the frequency of ownership change or liquidation will also reduce the likelihood that existing management will remain in control of the firm – even as agents of owners. To the extent that these managers were the cause of the firms' problems, in part or in total, these changes will benefit our economic system.

IX CONCLUSION

Proposals for the elimination of the existing Chapter 11 system are helpful in that they provide a stimulus for re-evaluating the process and possibly to motivate important modifications. The above discussion presents a number of the relevant issues to consider and suggests one area for serious study, i.e., the time in bankruptcy reduction. Admittedly, I have not covered a number of other important aspects of our Bankruptcy system, e.g., the relative performance of firms after emerging from Chapter 11. This is beyond the scope of this paper.

As for the B–R proposal and its empirical foundation, I find their tests and conclusions seriously flawed, so much so that nothing can be concluded from them with respect to how the new Bankruptcy Code has or has not benefitted corporate security holders. In my opinion, to completely scuttle the Chapter 11 system based on the evidence to date, would be a mistake.

28 | Financial Distress and Restructuring Models

with Yehning Chen and J. Fred Weston

This paper provides a synthesis of the theoretical literature on financial distress. It employs a two-state framework, which more clearly captures the generalizations of the more complex models. The equation systems that are derived permit the development of a series of examples that convey the logic and intuitions behind the generalizations. The graphics illuminate aspects of financial distress not treated in the previous literature. The role of risk is treated explicitly. Alternative assumptions generate different predictions of the effects of financial distress on investment efficiency and restructuring strategy. Central to these strategies are the recontracting arrangements between owners, creditors, and other relevant stakeholders. The resulting framework permits an evaluation of some central provisions of the prevailing US bankruptcy laws.

The basic social motivation for the legal, bankruptcy-reorganization process is to preserve organization value. One of the primary purposes of bankruptcy law is to facilitate the restructuring of financially distressed firms. The laws seek to provide a recontracting process that enables firms to once again invest in value-creating opportunities. Or, where liquidation values are greater than the going-concern evaluation, firms should be forced to liquidate or be sold to some other entity where this inequality is reversed. Many issues in this recontracting process have been identified. Can the distress be removed and a positive going-concern value be re-established, or will liquidation result in a higher value? How can the interests of the central parties (owners, managers, creditors, employees, and consumers) be balanced? What are the effects on security prices and claims of owners, creditors, and other stakeholders?

In recent years, the legal rules for bankruptcy, reorganization, and other recontracting processes have been reassessed. Proposals have been made to change the 1978 Bankruptcy Code (or, indeed, to eliminate the Chapter 11 reorganization option entirely), which prevails in the USA, as well as to reform the bankruptcy laws of many other countries. Issues of legal reform have been analyzed by Adler (1992), Bebchuk (1988), Bradley and Rosenzweig (1992), and Roe (1983), among others.[1] These reform proposals have been criticized by Altman (1993a), Bhandari and Weiss (1993), LoPucki (1992), Warren (1992), and Whitman (1993).[2]

Some central analytical issues raised by the bankruptcy process include:

1 the time in bankruptcy
2 the effects on security prices preceding, during, and after the relevant "bankruptcy announcement" date
3 default losses
4 application of absolute priority versus relative priority rules
5 managerial incentives and the effects on managerial turnover and executive compensation
6 the role of exchange offers, and
7 the performance of the firm after emerging from bankruptcy proceedings.

Our understanding of the relationships among these elements has been advanced by the development of formal models of financial distress by Altman (1993b), Berkovitch

---

[1] In general, these articles criticize the bankruptcy-reorganization process in that it motivates inefficient and costly actions by managers and is a process that impedes the allocation of corporate resources to the highest-valued user of those assets. Bradley and Rosenzweig (B–R), in particular, claim that the distressed firm's problems are frequently endogenously determined, chosen by managers, rather than imposed upon them by such things as competition and interest rates. They assert that managers have no real incentive to maintain an adequate liquid asset balance to meet current obligations as long as there is the possibility of a court-supervised and protected reorganization mechanism whereby existing management will likely remain in control. In essence, creditor and other stockholder contractual agreements are abridged and violated in order to enhance manager welfare. Empirical tests are provided, albeit claimed to be seriously flawed by critics of B–R, which attempt to show that stockholders and debtholders have received significantly lower returns under the new 1978 Bankruptcy Code as compared to the prior bankruptcy code.

B–R advocate repealing the existing bankruptcy code (the Code) and substituting a process whereby successive classes of claimants, starting from the most junior stockholder interests and advancing through the seniority hierarchy to the most senior creditors, have the opportunity to pay off the company's unpaid debts or else be eliminated from the process. If the default is not cured at any level, then the most senior creditor class would be entitled to either run the firm and retain the firm's equity position, sell its equity to outside investors, or liquidate the firm's assets for their exclusive use. In essence, the process involves a series of call options where the exercise price is the outstanding interest and/or principal due. If the option is not exercised, that class passing on the option is totally eliminated thereby preserving absolute priority (B–R, 1992, p. 1047).

[2] Many of the articles that are critical of the B–R thesis contain legal, conceptual, and financial market arguments, which are too numerous to review here. Others emphasize the empirical flaws of their paper, including Altman (1993a and b) and LoPucki's (1993) concern with the seniority-biased nature of the sample of bonds in the pre-Code period (more senior) compared to the post-Code (more subordinated) period. Altman (1993a and b) and Bhandari and Weiss (1993) find contra evidence and conclude that the increase in filings in the post-1978 period was primarily due to the change in corporate leverage and reduced profitability and was not the consequence of the change in law and its abuses. Altman also conducts extensive tests on bondholder returns, controlling for both seniority and credit quality, and concludes that the B–R results are suspect. And for the assertion that managers gain from Chapter 11, Gilson (1989 and 1990) finds that they do not fare very well in terms of job retention and salary.

and Kim (1990), Brown et al. (1993), Bulow and Shoven (1978), Diamond and Dybvig (1983), Franks and Torous (1989), Gertner and Scharfstein (1991), Giammarino and Nosal (1994), Hart and Moore (1994), Heinkel and Zechner (1993), Jensen and Meckling (1976), John (1993), Myers (1977), and Scott (1981).[3] Empirical evidence has been gathered on the issues set forth.[4]

The theoretical literature on financial distress is couched in complex models. However, the underlying concepts are straightforward and can be conveyed by relatively simple models. Also, despite their apparent generality, the predictions of the theoretical models are dependent upon their underlying (explicit or implicit) assumptions or postulates. This will be clear from our analysis. Our discussion is organized into seven sections. Section I provides a general framework. Section II develops base case formulations. Section III examines how debt maturity can affect investment efficiency. Section IV allows the firm to alter the seniority of its claims holders. Section V analyzes the role of exchange offers. Section VI introduces financial intermediaries into the bankruptcy process. Section VII develops several important implications concerning how the bankruptcy process should operate. Section VIII furnishes concluding remarks.

I GENERAL FRAMEWORK

The literature depicts three major players in the financial distress game: the shareholders (equity holders), banks (more generally financial institutions), and public debtholders. The literature aligns the goals of managers with those of the shareholders, an underlying assumption that focuses the analysis and that we follow. Banks (financial institutions) are defined as debtholders with whom the shareholders can directly negotiate. Public debtholders are assumed to be dispersed so that negotiation is not feasible. These are obviously arbitrary but useful underlying assumptions. Other related assumptions are:

1 All parties are risk neutral.
2 Since management's goals are aligned with those of shareholders, management seeks to maximize the welfare of shareholders.
3 Managers and shareholders prefer more investment to less, other things being equal.

We adopt the definition of financial distress as the condition in which the liquidation value of the firm's assets, Y, is less than the total face value of creditor claims, D.

Reflecting the theoretical literature, our evaluation criteria emphasize the effects on investment efficiency. We endorse this emphasis because of its importance for the efficient allocation of resources and for economic performance. Equations (1), (2), and (3) provide a basis for analyzing the efficiency of investment actions or decisions:

---

[3] A number of these works are reviewed in detail in the body of this paper.
[4] Betker (1995a) calculates security return losses to bondholders (34 percent) and to shareholders (40 percent). Recent empirical studies on the post-reorganization performance of Chapter 11 firms consider both the average operating performance (Hotchkiss, 1995) and the restructured firms' ex-post leverage (Gilson, 1994). Both studies find that the reorganized firms perform relatively poorly and imply that the process can be improved.

$$\text{NPV} = P_b X_b + P_g X_g - I \tag{1}$$

$$
\begin{aligned}
\text{RSH} &= P_b \max[X_b - (1 - q)D, 0] + P_g \max[X_g - (1 - q)D, 0] - (I - Y) - qD \\
&= V_S
\end{aligned} \tag{2}
$$

$$
\begin{aligned}
\text{RDH} &= qD + P_b \min[X_b, (1 - q)D] + P_g \min[X_g, (1 - q)D] - Y \\
&\equiv (V_D - Y)
\end{aligned} \tag{3}
$$

where

> NPV = net present value
> P_b = probability of bad state
> P_g = probability of good state
> X_b = return in bad state
> X_g = return in good state
> I = investment outlay
> RSH = return to shareholders, if the investment is made
> q = ratio of short-term debt to total debt
> D = face value of debt outstanding
> Y = liquidation value of the firm's assets = L_D, also the value of debt if the investment is not made
> V_S = market value of equity
> V_D = market value of debt, if the investment is made
> RDH = return to debtholders, if the investment is made $\equiv (V_D - Y)$

The logic of this equation system follows basic finance concepts. Expected values are understood throughout, so the expectation operator is omitted. Our base case analysis is facilitated by assuming that all debt is long-term and publicly held so that in our equation system q drops out.[5] Since both NPV and the risk of a project affect the decision to invest, we also consider the role of risk.

II BASE CASE FORMULATIONS

With $q = 0$, the resulting system is shown in Equations (1a), (2a), and (3a).

$$\text{NPA} = P_b X_b + P_g X_g - I \tag{1a}$$

$$\text{RSH} = P_b \max[(X_b - D), 0] + P_g \max[(X_g - D), 0] - (I - Y) = V_S \tag{2a}$$

$$\text{RDH} = P_b \min[X_b, D] + P_g \min[X_g, D] - Y \tag{3a}$$

The NPV equation does not change because it is unaffected by financing. In the most general case, an infinite number of alternative future states of the world could be analyzed with continuous probability distributions. The results of the formal models

---

[5] Different values of q are reintroduced in section III, which analyzes the effect of debt maturity on the efficiency of investment decisions.

using continuous distributions are captured and can be conveyed more easily by assuming a two-state world characterized by either a good outcome or a bad outcome. Thus, P_b and P_g are the equal probabilities of the outcomes in the bad state and the good state, respectively. Similarly, X_b and X_g are the outcomes in the bad and good states. The balance sheet [in table 28.1] illustrates the situation facing a firm in financial distress.

The balance sheet shows that the firm has debt claims of $100 and assets with a liquidation value of $70. The book value of equity is negative $30.[6]

In addition, we postulate that the firm has an investment opportunity requiring an outlay of $80. The firm would have to raise $10 of additional funds since its liquid assets are only $70. In this specific example, the equation system becomes:

$$\text{NPV} = 0.5X_b + 0.5X_g - \$80 \tag{1b}$$

$$\text{RSH} = 0.5\max[X_b - \$100),0] + 0.5\max[(X_g - \$100),0] - (\$80 - \$70) \tag{2b}$$

$$\text{RDH} = 0.5\min[X_b,\$100] + 0.5\min[X_g,\$100] - Y \tag{3b}$$

For a range of values of X_b and X_g, we use the above equations and the criteria in table 28.2 to define four types of investment decisions. The operating performance can result in either a negative-NPV or positive-NPV project. The results of the operating performance of the firm will be reflected in the changes in the market value of financial claims, equivalent to returns to shareholders (RSH) and returns to debtholders (RDH).

Table 28.1 XYZ Company balance sheet

XYZ Company Balance Sheet

Liquid assets (Y)	$70	Debt (D)	$100
		Equity	(30)

Table 28.2 Criteria for investment decisions

Operating performance	Changes in market values		
NPV	Return to shareholders (RSH)	Return to debtholders (RDH)	Investment decision
+	+	+, −	Efficient investment
+	−	+	Underinvestment
−	+	−	Overinvestment
−	−	+, −	Efficient noninvestment

Combinations of positive and negative changes in NPV, RSH, and RDH define four types of investment actions (see figure 28.1).

[6] Its market value would be positive because, in some future states, the equity's call option to take over the firm has value.

Figure 28.1   Isolines for characterizing investment decisions

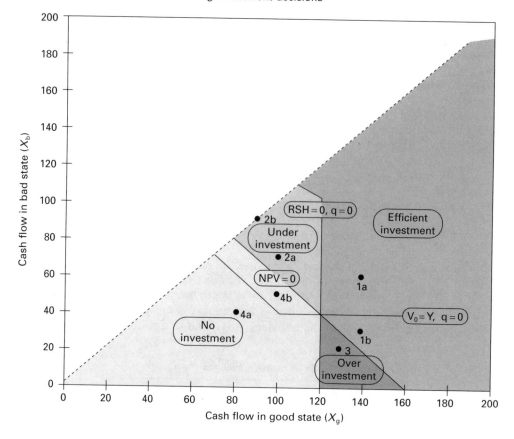

Combinations of positive and negative changes in NPV, RSH, and RDH define four types of investment actions, which are shown in table 28.2.

Set Equations (1b), (2b), and (3b) equal to zero. In Equation (3b), V_D is equal to Y. Since Y is the value of the debt if the investment is not made and the firm is liquidated, it is a critical benchmark for determining the return to debtholders. The isolines for NPV = 0, RSH = 0, and RDH = 0, ($V_D = Y$) are graphed in figure 28.1. Since the investment decision is made by the shareholders, the RSH = 0 and the NPV = 0 lines define the four types of investment action shown in figure 28.1.

Table 28.3 provides values of X_b and X_g to illustrate aspects of the four types of investment actions shown in figure 28.1. In Example 1a, NPV and RSH are both positive, so point 1a unambiguously falls in the efficient investment region. In Example 1b, RDH is negative. But since the shareholders make the decision, the investment is made because RSH is positive. Since NPV is also positive, the investment is efficient.

In Example 2a, RSH is negative. Even though NPV and RDH are both positive, the investment will not be made, which represents an underinvestment case. Example 2b illustrates the Myers (1977) model under certainty in which under both alternative states of the world $X_b = X_g = \$90$. Our framework enables us to convey the intuition of

Table 28.3   Illustrations of tests of investment efficiency

Example	X_b	X_g	NPV	RSH	RDH ($V_D - L_D$)	Investment decision
1a	60	140	20	10	10	Efficient investment
1b	30	140	5	10	-5	Efficient investment
2a	70	100	5	-10	15	Underinvestment
2b	90	90	10	-10	20	Underinvestment
3	20	130	-5	5	-10	Overinvestment
4a	40	80	-20	-10	-10	Efficient noninvestment
4b	50	100	-5	-10	5	Efficient noninvestment

Various examples illustrate how investment efficiency can vary. Values were calculated using selected values of X_b and X_g in the equations (1b), (2b), and (3b), and illustrated in figure 28.1.

this special case. The firm has an investment opportunity requiring an outlay of $80 with a gross present value of $90. Hence, the net present value (NPV) of the project is $10. The firm would have to raise $10 from new equity since the investment outlay required is $80, and there is only $70 of liquid assets available. Since the gross present value of cash inflows from the investment is $90, and the claim of the creditors is $100, with perfect "me-first" rules or absolute priority, debtholders would receive the entire $90 and the equity holders would receive nothing. Assuming no divergence of interests between equity holders, old or new, we can treat them as the same party.[7] Since the equity holders would be unwilling to make a $10 equity investment and receive no return, one form of underinvestment occurs.

Indeed, most firms that are insolvent and restructure, do so by attempting to sell assets rather than investing in new ones. The assumptions of certainty and risk neutrality are critical to Myers' case. With uncertain returns, the expected NPV could be negative, but some outcomes may be sufficiently high to yield positive returns to equity.

This suggests Example 3 in which overinvestment occurs. The return to shareholders is positive, but the NPV of the project is negative. In figure 28.1, the return to debtholders is negative as well. Nevertheless, investment takes place. Thus, the uncertainty of the future cash flows may give rise to overinvestment.

The intuition of this result is brought out by the illustrative numerical example within the framework of the more general figure 28.1. To make the investment, $10 has to be raised because I exceeds Y by that amount. In the bad state, when the cash flow is $20, shareholders receive nothing. If the cash flow is $130, they receive $130 - 100 = $30. The expected payoff for new shareholders is

$$0.5(\$0) + 0.5(\$130 - \$100) - \$10 = \$5$$

In this example, the expected value of the debt if the investment is made ($V_D = \$60$) is less than Y, the liquid assets of the firm ($70). Y represents the current liquidation

---

[7]   This assumption is not critical. An alternative assumption that provides identical results is that new shares are fairly priced in the market such that the expected return to new equity holders is 0. For simplicity, we assume there is no divergence of interests between old and new equity holders.

value of the firm and is also the value of the debt if the investment is *not* made. Hence the investment causes a loss (to creditors) of $10, reflecting the negative NPV of $5 from the investment and the $5 gain on the underpriced option that accrues to the equity investors (at the expense of the creditors).

The analytics behind this result are based on the agency problems related to the insight from the options literature that equity is a call option (Black and Scholes, 1973; Merton, 1973). By investing, shareholders receive an option to buy the firm at an exercise price of $100 (face value of the debt). Obviously, the option is exercised when the cash flow is $130, because the value of this option is positive: $0.5(\$130 - \$100) = \$15$. However, shareholders obtain this option by paying only $10. The difference, $5, is a loss to creditors.

RESULT 1

By investing, shareholders force creditors to sell a call option below cost, giving rise to an overinvestment problem. Moreover, from the properties of call options, we know that shareholders will prefer riskier projects, other things being equal.

Nevertheless, if the shareholders "rolled the dice," thereby jeopardizing the return to debtholders, there exist outcomes that will be in the region of efficient investments. For example, the upper section in the lower right quadrant of figure 28.1 represents efficient investment in which the return to debtholders is negative. It corresponds to Example 1b in table 28.3.

In areas 4a and 4b of figure 28.1, investment does not take place because both NPV and RSH are negative, which results from the low values of X_g and X_b. Nevertheless, there is a segment of this region in which the return to debtholders is positive. This illustrates a situation in which shareholders may efficiently forgo investment even though the returns to debtholders would be positive. Thus, efficient investment may occur when the return to debtholders is negative, and an efficient noninvestment may occur when there would have been a positive return to debtholders. The examples in table 28.3 illustrate the nature of the four regions in figure 28.1.

Gertner and Scharfstein (1991, p. 1195) state that for the pivotal lender to supply funds to restructure debt and to invest, NPV must be equal to or greater than $(V_D - L_D)$, the return to debtholders (RDH). This is somewhat misleading since the above examples show that the effect on RDH is irrelevant to the investment decision. Nevertheless, since NPV equals the sum of RSH and RDH, their inequality implies a positive RSH as well as a positive NPV, the two conditions required for efficient investment.

The Gertner–Scharfstein discussion is couched from the viewpoint of "the bank," which they argue to be the likely pivotal supplier of funds. In our view, it would be equally plausible to postulate other alternative pivotal fund suppliers. For example, trade creditors have a strong incentive to continue to ship goods to keep the debtor firm a going concern. This helps to preserve the value of their existing claims as well as provide profits and contributions to overhead on continuing sales. In addition, suppliers are likely to understand the business of their customers better than banks, which lend to a wide variety of businesses. Furthermore, their common interests lead to the creation of groups of creditors with common interests whose coalitions facilitate negotiation. But since the literature typically aligns the goals of the pivotal fund supplier with those of the existing shareholders, the analysis is performed more directly from the standpoint of the existing shareholders.

A *Relationship between* **Y** *and* **D**

Overinvestment or underinvestment may also occur depending upon the relationship between the value of liquid assets, Y, and the face value of debt, D.[8] The general expression for the return to shareholders' line (RSH) *when D may vary* is

$$\text{RSH} = P_b\max[(X_b - D),0] + P_g\max[(X_g - D),0]$$
$$- (I - Y) - \max[(Y - D),0] \geq 0 \qquad (2b')$$

Therefore, equity holders will make the investment if and only if the payoff from investing (RSH) exceeds the payoff from no investment, $\max[(Y - D),0]$.

For $D = \$70$, $Y = \$70$, and $I = \$80$, the required X_g is

$$0.5(X_g - \$70) - (\$80 - \$70) - (\$70 - \$70) = \$0$$
$$0.5X_g - \$35 - \$10 = \$0$$
$$0.5X_g = \$45$$
$$X_g = \$90$$

Thus, at a cash flow in the good state X_g of \$90, the return to shareholders would be zero (actually, a small positive amount) so that investment would take place even though NPV would be less than zero at an $X_g = \$90$. This amount determines the low point of the RSH = 0 curve in figure 28.2.

Figure 28.2 Relation between debt levels and efficient investment

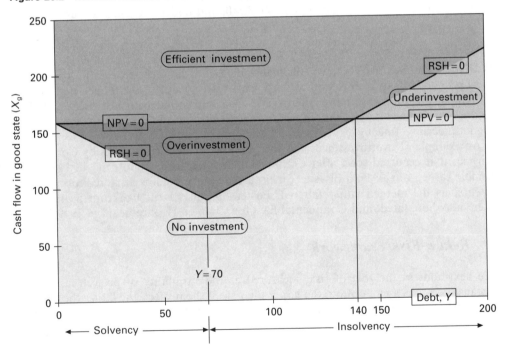

[8] Thanks to Jonathan Howe for this generalization.

More generally, for $X_b = \$0$, and $P_b = P_g = 0.5$, we seek a relation between X_g and D as depicted in figure 28.2. Equation (2b′) now becomes

$$RSH = 0.5(X_g - D) - (\$80 - \$70) - [\max(\$70 - D),0] \geq \$0$$

For $D < Y$, we have the declining left segment of the RSH = 0 line in figure 28.2. It is

$$0.5X_g - 0.5D - \$10 - \$70 + D = \$0$$
$$0.5X_g = \$80 - 0.5D$$
$$X_g = \$160 - D \quad \text{for } D < Y$$

For $D \geq Y$, we have the rising right segment of the RSH = \$0 line in figure 28.2. It is

$$RSH = 0.5(X_g - D) - \max[(Y - D),0] - \$10 = 0 \quad \text{for } D \geq Y$$

When $D \geq Y$, the $\max[(Y - D),0]$ term is always zero, so we have

$$0.5(X_g - D) - \$10 = 0$$
$$0.5X_g - 0.5D - \$10 = 0$$
$$X_g = \$20 + D$$

Thus, as shown in figure 28.2, for a debt level between zero and $140, the return to shareholders is positive, but NPV < 0 so overinvestment takes place. At a debt level greater than $140, in the area of the triangle formed by RSH = 0 and NPV = 0, the return to shareholders is negative, but NPV > 0, and underinvestment occurs.

RESULT 2

With uncertain future cash flows, the higher the (D/Y) ratio (when $D \geq Y$), the greater the likelihood of an overinvestment problem With an out-of-the-money call option, shareholders cannot lose more. Figure 28.2 also shows that with extremely high D/Y ratios, shareholders may feel it not worthwhile to even make the effort to invest, resulting in underinvestment.

An example of overinvestment was the purchase of Eastern Airlines by Continental Airlines that occurred soon after Continental emerged from Chapter 11 in 1986. This gamble turned out to be a disaster for both the equity holders and creditors of Continental as the merged entity faltered. Eastern Airlines went bankrupt in 1989 and eventually liquidated, and Continental filed for Chapter 11 once again in 1990.[9]

B   Return-Risk Framework

We next address the role of risk, measured as the variability of project cash flows. Because equity is a call option, the larger the risk of the project, the larger the value of the option, and therefore the more likely that shareholders will increase the riskiness of its project portfolio. That is, if the investment project is riskier, it is more likely that

---

[9]   For a discussion of multiple Chapter 11 filings (sometimes called Chapter 22s), see Altman (1993b).

the firm would invest (and therefore it is more likely the firm would have an overinvestment problem). We, therefore, analyze the expected return (expected NPV) in relation to risk.

We again employ the two-state formulation to show how the expected return to shareholders rises with increased risk, as illustrated in table 28.4. Columns (1) and (2) represent alternative combinations of cash flows in the bad and good states, respectively. When the outcomes in both states are 80, the special case of certainty results since the outcome is the same for either possible state. The (0,160) combination reflects the greatest uncertainty since the standard deviation of the difference between the two returns would be the largest for this combination. Columns (3) and (4) present calculations of the return to shareholders and the return to debtholders using Equations (2b) and (3b). Column (5) contains the standard deviation of the returns for each combination of outcomes.

These data are graphed in figure 28.3. The expected return to shareholders increases with the level of risk while the expected return to debtholders decreases with the level of risk. The intuition underlying figure 28.3 results from the recognition that low standard deviations are associated with relatively equal returns in both states of the world. Hence, debtholders receive a high percentage of their claims in the bad state when the standard deviation of returns is low. When the standard deviation of returns is high, debtholders experience low returns in the bad state relative to the good state. The returns to the shareholders increase as a consequence.

Also, table 28.4 illustrates that the sum of RSH and RDH equals NPV. NPV in this example is zero since $P_b = P_g = 0.5$ and gross present value and I are both always 80. With NPV = 0, RSH and RDH must be of equal absolute magnitude but of opposite signs.

Table 28.4 Calculation of the standard deviation of various pairs of possible outcomes (X_b, X_g) when NPV = 0

(1) X_b	(2) X_g	(3) RSH	(4) RDH	(5) Std dev. (X)
0	160	20.0	−20.0	80
5	155	17.5	−17.5	75
10	150	15.0	−15.0	70
15	145	12.5	−12.5	65
20	140	10.0	−10.0	60
25	135	7.5	−7.5	55
30	130	5.0	−5.0	50
35	125	2.5	−2.5	45
40	120	0	0	40
45	115	−2.5	2.5	35
50	110	−5.0	5.0	30
55	105	−7.5	7.5	25
60	100	−10.0	10.0	20
65	95	−10.0	10.0	15
70	90	−10.0	10.0	10
75	85	−10.0	10.0	5
80	80	−10.0	10.0	0

Figure 28.3 Expected returns in relation to risk when NPV = 0

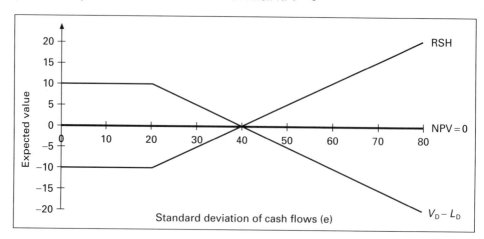

In the preceding example, NPV is held constant while RSH and RDH vary with the level of risk. Next, we hold RSH constant in order to investigate the influence of risk on the required NPV. We employ the following definitions:

$$X_g = V + e \quad X_b = V - e$$

where V and e are positive parameters. Under these assumptions, the gross present value ($P_g X_g + P_b X_b$) of the project is V (so NPV = $V - I$), and the standard error of the present value is e.

In table 28.5, we select combinations of X_g and X_b that satisfy the above definitions. We can also verify that the NPV values satisfy Equation (1a) where investment is equal to 80. For example, when X_b and X_g sum to 180, the expected GPV is 90 so NPV = 10. Using Equation (2a), RSH will be zero. RDH will decline as shown in table 28.5.

These results are displayed in figure 28.4. The intuition underlying the RSH = 0 line is that with increasing risk (the possibility of really high returns in the good state), the NPV required to induce equity holders to make the new investment is lower. Also, as

Table 28.5 Coordinates for RSH = 0 in risk, NPV space*

X_b	X_g	e = Std dev.	NPV	RDH
110	110	0	30	30
100	120	10	30	30
60	120	30	10	10
40	120	40	0	0
20	120	50	−10	−10
0	120	60	−20	−20

Various examples illustrate how NPV and RDH vary with the level of risk (e) while RSH is held constant.

Figure 28.4 Characterizing investment decisions in risk, NPV Space

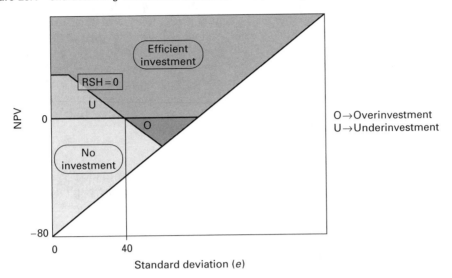

shown in table 28.6 for NPV = 30, for any constant level of NPV, RSH will rise with the level of risk and RDH will decline.

Four regions of investment action are defined by the NPV = 0 and RSH = 0 lines in figure 28.4. These four regions in risk, NPV space parallel the four regions defined in figure 28.1 in X_g, X_b space. Points in the underinvestment area have a positive NPV but a negative RSH. In the overinvestment area, RSH is positive, but the NPV is negative.

Thus, we have demonstrated the role of risk in relation to NPV and RSH. Next, we consider the role of debt maturity.

Table 28.6 Risk and returns*

X_b	X_g	e	NPV	RSH	RDH
110	110	0	30	−5	30
100	120	10	30	0	30
80	140	30	30	10	20
60	160	50	30	20	10
40	180	70	30	30	0
20	200	90	30	40	−10
0	220	110	30	50	−20

* Various examples illustrate how RSH and RDH vary with the level of risk (e) while NPV is held constant.

III INFLUENCE OF DEBT MATURITY

The role of debt maturity is analyzed assuming two periods, denoted 1 and 2. The financially distressed condition of the firm is still as depicted by the balance sheet in table 28.1. The firm has public debt totaling $100. Debt maturity is now introduced with the ratio of short-term debt to total debt defined as q, with $0 \leq q \leq 1$.[10] Short-term debt matures at date 1, before the investment is made; long-term debt matures at date 2, after the cash flows from the investment are realized. The outcome of the investment is uncertain. In the bad state of the world, the cash flow is $20; in the good state, the cash flow is X_g.[11]

We calculate the efficient investment criterion using Equation (1). The NPV of the project is

$$NPV = 0.5X_g + 0.5(\$20) - \$80$$
$$= 0.5X_g - \$70$$

If the investment decision is efficient, the investment should be made if NPV is greater than $0, or $X_g \geq \$140$. This will be our point of reference for the required level of an efficient investment. In the following analysis, we vary the value of q to illustrate the role of debt maturity.

A   All Debt is Long-Term

In Case IIIA, we assume that $q = 0$, so the entire $100 of debt is long-term. This is equivalent to our base case Equations (1b), (2b), and (3b) but with a different assumed X_b. The firm can use the liquid assets ($70) to finance part of the project. It still needs to raise an additional $10 (from the old shareholders). At date 2, the amount of public debt due is $100. If cash flow X_b is $20, shareholders receive nothing (and creditors receive $20). If the cash flow is X_g, shareholders receive $X_g - \$100$. Hence the gain to shareholders is

$$0.5(X_g - \$100) + 0.5(\$0) - \$10 = 0.5X_g - \$60$$

Shareholders will make the investment if $0.5X_g - \$60 \geq 0$, or $X_g \geq \$120$. Since the required X_g under the efficient investment criterion is $140, the firm has an overinvestment problem.

The reason for the overinvestment is clear. Shareholders can gamble using creditors' money. As before, if the investment is not made, creditors will receive all the liquid assets. By using the liquid assets to finance the project, shareholders receive an underpriced option. Therefore, the problem is an overinvestment one.

B   All Debt is Short-Term

In Case IIIB, all debt is short-term ($q = 1$), so that the entire $100 debt obligation has to be repaid before the investment is made. Therefore, to make the investment at date 1, the firm must raise: $100 + $80 - $0 = $110. In this example, we assume that the funds raised are equity, so that the firm becomes an all-equity firm. If the investment is made, then in the bad state the cash flow is $20, and the shareholders receive $20 since

---

[10]   This is the same symbol Gertner and Scharfstein (1991) chose; it has no relation to Tobin's q.
[11]   The cash flow assumptions are chosen to illustrate better the principles involved.

all debt was short-term and had to be repaid. In the good state, the cash flow is X_g. The expected payoff to the shareholders from making the investment, using Equation (2), is

$$0.5X_g + 0.5(\$20) - \$110 = 0.5X_g - \$100$$

Shareholders will make the investment if $0.5X_g - \$100 \geq 0$, or $X_g \geq \$200$. Compared to the efficient investment criterion of $X_g \geq \$140$, the firm has an underinvestment problem. The required X_g is much higher solely because of the debt's maturity.

The NPV equation for the efficient investment is NPV $= 0.5X_g - 70$. When the entire debt is short-term, NPV $= 0.5X_g - 100$, so the firm has to pay creditors a \$30 differential before it makes the investment. Since the good state occurs with probability 0.5, the additional amount of X_g required is \$60. Therefore, the firm has an underinvestment problem. If the firm must pay off a pre-existing debt before it can invest, the repayment obligation effectively serves as a "tax," which causes an underinvestment problem. Alternatively, when the owners can exercise their option to buy out the creditors at a cost below the value of the option, there is a subsidy that gives rise to an overinvestment problem.

RESULT 3

The maturity structure of debt influences investment efficiency. The shorter the maturity structure of debt, the more likely it is the firm will have an underinvestment problem. Since the equity is a call option, reducing debt maturity is equivalent to reducing "time" in the Black–Scholes option valuation model. The value of the option decreases, which reduces the incentive to invest unless even riskier prospects are available. The longer the maturity structure of the debt, the more likely it is the firm will have an overinvestment problem. The value of the equity call option in that case increases.

C   *Restructuring the Debt Maturity*

The underinvestment problem illustrated in the preceding example can be mitigated, or even eliminated, by adopting strategies for altering the liability term structure, known as distressed extensions or exchanges. Extension results in a lengthening of the maturity of all or a portion of the debt so as to enhance the probability of repayment and to enable the firm to avoid the higher cost of a Chapter 11 reorganization.[12] In our case, the additional funds needed to make the investment are reduced by the amount of the debt repayment that is deferred.[13]

Exchanges typically result in substituting equity for debt. Distressed exchanges have been widely used in recent years by firms that issued high-yield "junk" bonds and tried to work out what they felt was a short-term problem owing to overleveraging a basically sound operating company. Exchanges usually involve either a total exchange of

---

[12] A number of studies have compared the out-of-court restructuring arrangement with the more formal Chapter 11 procedure. All such studies, e.g., Franks and Torous (1989), Gilson et al. (1990), and Helwege (1995), conclude that out-of-court arrangements, usually exchanges, are less costly when they are successful. However, often the attempt to restructure is not successful, and Chapter 11 is merely postponed.

[13] Of course, if the short-term debt can be "rolled-over," the debt maturity is effectively extended. Healthy firms do this routinely, but it is much less common in situations of financial distress.

preferred and/or common equity for the old debt or a combination of some equity and some new, but extended, debt for the old debt.

The classic distressed exchange involves a firm whose operating and financial condition has deteriorated due to both chronic and cyclical problems. It attempts to restructure both its assets and its liabilities. For example, International Harvester Corporation, a large farm equipment, truck, and bus manufacturer, was on the verge of total collapse in 1980–82. The firm first exchanged preferred stock for its interest payment obligations to banks and extended both its interest payments to creditors and payables to suppliers. Next, it converted its short-term bank debt (1–3 years) to longer term "junk" bonds (10–12 years). Finally, it exchanged common equity in its newly named entity, Navistar International, for the "old" junk bonds. These distressed restructuring strategies helped the firm to recover; it eventually paid its short- and long-term creditors in full.[14]

D   Debt Maturity for Efficient Investment

The two previous examples illustrated the extreme cases of $q = 0$ and $q = 1$. Case IIIC calculates a value of q that eliminates both the overinvestment and underinvestment problems. For example, if $q = 0.2$, the amount of short-term public debt is $20, and the amount of long-term public debt is $80.

To finance the investment, the firm uses liquid assets plus $10 of new equity. It also has to raise $20 of additional equity to pay off the short-term debt. Since the $30 of new financing is equity, at date 2, the amount of debt due is $80. If the cash flow is $20, the shareholders receive nothing, and the public debtholders receive $20. If the cash flow is X_g, shareholders receive $$X_g$ – $80. Using Equation (2), the shareholders' return from investing is

$$0.5(\$0) + 0.5(X_g - \$80) - \$30 = 0.5X_g - \$70$$

Shareholders will invest if $0.5X_g - \$70 \geq \$0$, or $X_g \geq \$140$. The investment decision in this case is efficient. There is neither an overinvestment nor an underinvestment problem.

RESULT 4

Our demonstration that it is possible to choose a q (a maturity structure of the debt) that will enable the firm to make an efficient investment decision suggests another relationship. Recall the basic assumption that the cash or liquid assets of the firm, Y, are less than the face value of total debt. If X (cash flows from the investment) is subject to greater uncertainty (leading to an overinvestment problem), raising q (more short-term debt) creates an offsetting underinvestment tendency that results in efficient investment. If X is subject to lower uncertainty (leading to an underinvestment problem), lowering q (more long-term debt) creates an offsetting overinvestment tendency that results in efficient investment.

---

[14]   In addition, and perhaps most important, International Harvester sold its farm equipment division. The cash proceeds, when combined with the cash flow savings from the debt rescheduling, enabled it to invest in plant modernization and develop new models of trucks and buses.

E   Toward Generalizations

The examples convey the basic intuition concerning the influence of debt maturity on the investment decisions of distressed firms. The general relationships are conveyed by Equations (1), (2), and (3), which include the effect of debt maturity. Equation (3) makes explicit the requirement that the value of the debt, if the investment is made, must not fall below the liquidation value of the firm, Y, which the creditors could have realized.[15]

Figure 28.5 illustrates that the $V_D = Y$ line and the RSH = 0 line both shift as q changes. When q increases from 0 to 0.2 (short-term debt goes from 0 percent to 20 percent of total debt), the intersection of the three decision lines shifts. The $V_D = Y$ line

Figure 28.5   RSH and RDH under varying q

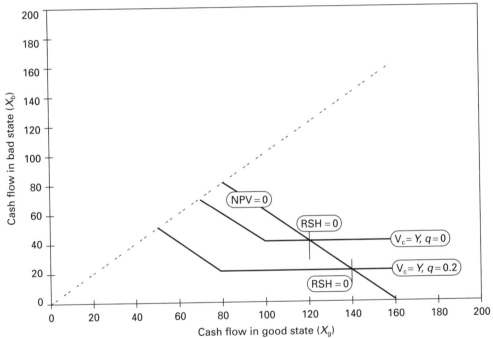

[15]   In a formal Chapter 11 proceeding, this relationship conforms with the concept of "adequate protection," which "guarantees" certain secured creditors compensation at least equal to the value of the collateral at the time of the claim confirmation – usually shortly after the bankruptcy petition is filed. If the reorganization is not successful and the liquidation value falls below the amount of adequate protection, then indeed these creditors would have been better off with liquidation at an earlier date. This conforms to the overinvestment sector in figure 28.1. Therefore, the $V_D = Y$ line in figure 28.1 illustrates whether equity holders can take advantage of debtholders. In most cases, adequate protection results in attractive returns to the debtholder. For example, the creditors who owned Youngstown Sheet & Tube's secured bonds in the parent company's (LTV Corp.) bankruptcy did extremely well despite a long and costly reorganization. Unlike the Eastern Airlines case, the extended Chapter 11 proceeding of LTV did not negatively impact those creditors who were adequately protected. In an out-of-court restructuring, it is possible under certain circumstances for this inequality to be justified, as demonstrated by Kahane and Tuckman (1993).

shifts downward as q increases. This results from the debtholders receiving more up front in the form of the short-term debt that has to be repaid before the investment is made. Hence they can accept a lower cash flow in the bad state and provide more for the shareholders in the good state. The RSH = 0 line shifts to the right as q increases. Shareholders must now receive a higher return in the good state to offset the tax that must be paid to retire the short-term debt as a condition for making the investment.

Another example will reinforce these general relations. Table 28.7 illustrates the effects of a high value of q. Table 28.7 uses a $q = 0.9$, implying that most of the debt is short-term and resulting in a large tax up front. The NPV is positive, but the RSH becomes negative. The market value of the debt rises from $70 to $100. The $30 increase in V_D represents what is taken from the shareholders.

The effects of debt maturity can also be illustrated within the framework of the risk-return example. Table 28.8 and figure 28.6 illustrate the sensitivity to q of the

Table 28.7   Illustration of the effect of high q*

Case IIIC

$X_b = \$20$
$X_g = \$150$
$q = 0.9$
NPV = 0.5($20) + 0.5($150) − 80 = $5
RSH = 0.5($20 − 10) + 0.5($150 − 10) − $80 + $70 − $90 = −$25
$V_D = \$90 + 0.5(\$10) + 0.5(\$10) = \$100$ ($30 from SH)

* A high value for q tends to create an underinvestment problem because of the large up-front "tax" the firm must pay when it retires short-term debt.

Table 28.8   Risk–return relationships for alternative maturity structures

X_b	X_g	NPV	RSH, q = 0	E(X)	Std dev. (X)	RDH, q = 0	RSH, q = 0.2	RDH, q = 0.2
0	160	0	20.0	80	80	−20.0	10.0	−10.0
5	155	0	17.5	80	75	−17.5	7.5	−7.5
10	150	0	15.0	80	70	−15.0	5.0	−5.0
15	145	0	12.5	80	65	−12.5	2.5	−2.5
20	140	0	10.0	80	60	−10.0	0	0
25	135	0	7.5	80	55	−7.5	−2.5	2.5
30	130	0	5.0	80	50	−5.0	−5.0	5.0
35	125	0	2.5	80	45	−2.5	−7.5	7.5
40	120	0	0	80	40	0	−10.0	10.0
45	115	0	−2.5	80	35	2.5	−12.5	12.5
50	110	0	−5.0	80	30	5.0	−15.0	15.0
55	105	0	−7.5	80	25	7.5	−17.5	17.5
60	100	0	−10.0	80	20	10	−20.0	20.0
65	95	0	−10.0	80	15	10	−22.5	22.5
70	90	0	−10.0	80	10	10	−25.0	25.0
75	85	0	−10.0	80	5	10	−27.5	27.5
80	80	0	−10.0	80	0	10	−30.0	30.0

The maturity structure of the firm's debt, as proxied by q, alters the relationship between risk and return for both debtholders and equity holders.

Figure 28.6 Returns under NPV = 0, and $q = 0$, $q = 0.2$

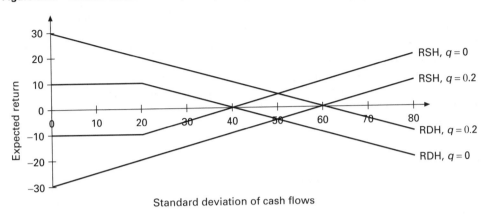

relationship between risk and return to the security holders. Figure 28.6 shows that raising q shifts the RSH line downward and shifts the RDH line upward.

IV SHIFTED PRIORITY POSITIONS

In the previous case, we assumed that the firm raises the required funds by issuing equity (to old shareholders). An implication of this assumption is that existing publicly held debt has a higher seniority than the new (equity) security issued.

In Case IV, we assume the firm issues new debt to obtain the required funds. We also assume that existing debt carries no covenants to protect its priority position, so that the firm is able to give the new debt a senior priority position. When the firm is able to grant seniority to the new debt, it is more likely to make the investment.

Case IV illustrates the effect of assigning senior priority to the new debt. It again assumes an efficient debt maturity structure in which q is equal to 0.2. As before, the firm has liquid assets of 470, and the required investment outlay is $80. To make the investment, the firm needs to raise an additional $10 for the investment and $20 to repay the maturing short-term debt. Therefore, at date 2, the firm has $30 of new debt and $80 of existing long-term debt. If the cash flow from the project is X, all debt is repaid in full, so that the old shareholders receive $X - 80 (the old shareholders hold the $30 new debt). Since the new debt is senior to the old debt, if the cash flow in the bad state is $20, the shareholders receive $20 when the new debt is repaid. The return to shareholders from investing is

$$\begin{aligned} RSH &= 0.5(\$20) + 0.5(X_g - \$80) - \$30 \\ &= 0.5X_g - \$60 \end{aligned}$$

Shareholders will invest if $0.5X_g - \$60 \geq 0$, or $X_g > \$120$ (versus $140 for efficient investment). Now the firm has an overinvestment problem. By manipulating the seniority of its debt (more long-term relative to short-term), shareholders gain at the expense of public debtholders. Therefore, they have more incentive to invest.

The creation of new debt with a seniority or super-priority status *vis-à-vis* old debt is the prime factor that has stimulated the growth and importance of debtor-in-possession (DIP) financing. DIP financing, supplied primarily by banks and finance companies, is used to provide needed investment and working capital funds to firms that have just filed for Chapter 11 protection. It has been critical to the success of many formal in-court restructurings.[16] The super-priority status of the new debt need only be sanctioned by the bankruptcy judge, which obviates the need for prior-creditor approval. An out-of-court restructuring that involves new debt being given priority over old debt, on the other hand, requires virtually 100 percent creditor approval and is very difficult to obtain.

RESULT 5

The greater the firm's ability to manipulate the position of its claimholders, the more the firm can take advantage of debtholders whose priority position is unprotected. This highlights the importance of bond covenants. Furthermore, when the firm has the power to manipulate seniority, the overinvestment problem is likely to be more severe.[17]

V   ANALYSIS OF EXCHANGE OFFERS

When the present value of the firm's assets is less than its liabilities, an out-of-court exchange offer is considered a "distressed" restructuring.[18] Case V analyzes exchange offers. It retains all of the previous assumptions except that it assumes that the firm has sufficient liquid assets ($80) to cover the cost of the investment project. Thus, one of the complicating elements of the cash flows is removed to simplify the analysis. To analyze the payoffs to a creditor to whom an exchange offer is made, we assume a 0.5 probability of a cash flow of $50 and a 0.5 probability of a cash flow of $130. The firm makes an unconditional exchange offer to the public creditors. Initially, we assume there is no short-term debt and that all debt matures in period 2.

The face value of the debt is $100. It is held equally by 10 creditors, and these creditors cannot coordinate their actions. All debt is long-term. It matures after the cash flow from the investment is realized. The firm makes an unconditional offer to the public debtholders to exchange $10 of old debt for $8 of new debt. The new debt will be senior to any remaining, nonexchanged old debt whereas it now ranks *pari passu* with all the other debt (a critical assumption). Two issues are posed. If each creditor believes that all the others will tender, will the exchange offer be successful? After the exchange offer, are creditors better off or not?

---

[16]   See Chapter 4 of Altman (1993b) for a discussion of DIP financing. These loans, in addition to their super-priority status, are usually also secured.

[17]   Although the guiding principle of distressed restructuring is the so-called absolute priority doctrine, it has been estimated by many researchers that as many as 75 percent of reorganizations result in violations of absolute priority. Still, these violations are not material, and seniority really does provide significant investor protection. See Altman and Eberhart (1994).

[18]   Public unsecured debt that is "distressed" typically sells in the range of 50–70 percent of par value. The exchange is treated as a default by market practitioners and other analysts (e.g., see Merrill Lynch (1994) for default statistics on high-yield debt where defaults include distressed restructurings).

Table 28.9 shows the payoff table for an individual debtholder under the above assumptions. We first consider the position of a creditor who decides to hold out.[19] For the nine others who tender, the face value of the new debt is $72. If the cash flow is $130, $58 is available to pay off the hold-out creditor in full, $10. If the unfavorable state occurs, the $50 is not sufficient to cover the senior claims of the nine creditors who tendered, and the payoff to the hold-out, now a junior creditor, would be zero.

We next consider the tender alternative for an individual creditor. The face value of the new debt would become $80. In the favorable state, when the cash flow is $130, all creditors are paid in full, and each receives $8. If the cash flow is $50, each creditor receives $5. As shown in table 28.9, the expected payoff for tendering is larger. Hence, all creditors tender, and the offer succeeds.

The creditors become worse off because of the exchange offer. Without the exchange offer, the expected payoff for a creditor is 0.5($10) + 0.5($5) = $7.5. On average, therefore, each creditor loses $1 because of the offer. If creditors can work as a group, they will reject the offer.[20] However, under the assumptions that creditors cannot coordinate and that they think that all others will tender, tendering dominates holding out. Gertner and Scharfstein (1991) call this phenomenon a "hold-in" problem.

Mooradian (1994) extends this analysis. He observes that with a single creditor there is no coordination problem of the type discussed above. He also analyzes the role of asymmetric information in a model of public debt restructurings. In the absence of Chapter 11, an inefficient firm always mimics an efficient firm. As a consequence, either inefficient firms overinvest or efficient firms underinvest. But Mooradian observes that Chapter 11 provides an incentive for an economically inefficient firm to reveal its condition because management bargains on behalf of equity holders to preserve a valuable claim on the firm for them.

Table 28.9   Payoff to a creditor

Action of the creditor	Cash flows (probability)		Expected payoff
	$130 (0.5)	$50 (0.5)	
Tender	$8	$5	0.5($8) + 0.5($5) = $6.5
Hold out	$10	$0	0.5($10) + 0.5($0) = $5.0

VI   EXTENSIONS WITH FINANCIAL INTERMEDIARIES

For the first set of cases, we assumed that no "banks" are formally involved. Banks and other financial institutions have several characteristics that distinguish them from atomistic creditors:

---

[19]   Bernardo (1995) presents a generalized treatment of exchange offers analyzed in terms of symmetric Nash equilibria. He specifies the conditions that support a symmetric tendering equilibrium as well as the conditions that support a symmetric holdout equilibrium.

[20]   See our discussion in section VI concerning the increasingly common development of organized creditor committees represented by sophisticated distressed restructuring specialists.

1 They are better informed about the debtor.
2 They write debt contracts of relatively short maturity to facilitate monitoring and recontracting.
3 They are smaller in number, facilitating communication and negotiation.
4 In practice, they generally seek a priority position.[21]

In Gertner and Scharfstein (1991), the bank, unlike public debtholders, can negotiate with old shareholders costlessly and maximize the joint payoff to itself and the shareholders. Moreover, bank debt is always short-term (maturing at date 1). Unless the bank agrees to make concessions, the bank debt needs to be repaid before the investment is made.[22]

If the firm can negotiate costlessly with "bank-type" lenders, there is no bargaining problem. The parties will function according to a Coase (1937) Theorem, which holds that they will work as one party seeking to maximize investment returns in their joint interest.

In a bank debt restructuring, the bank extends the maturity of the old debt to date 2 and provides the firm with the cash necessary to make the investment and pay off short-term public debt. The face value of the new bank debt will be equal to the face value of the old bank debt plus the new loan. Interest on new bank debt is allowed. If the bank refuses to refinance the firm, the firm may try to get financing from other sources.[23] If no other source is available to finance the project, the firm will be liquidated at date 1.

The basic assumptions made in the previous examples with only public debtholders are maintained. The balance sheet of table 28.1 applies with liquid assets of $70 and total debt claims of $100. The new project requires an investment of $80. The cash flow in the bad state is $20 and in the good state is X_g.

The assumptions about the debt structure, however, are altered.

1 The firm has two types of debt: bank debt and public debt. The sum of the bank debt and the public debt is $100 (face value).
2 All debt (old and new, bank and public) has the same priority. There is no interest payable on old debt. The interest on the new debt is *junior to the principal*.
3 There is still both long-term and short-term public debt. The variable q continues to be defined as the ratio of short-term public debt to total public debt.

In Case VI, we begin our analysis of the implications of the use of bank debt by considering the extreme case in which there is no public debt and the $100 debt is all bank debt. Case VI differs from Case IIIB where q was equal to one in that the bank can defer payment on its claims due at date 1, while in Case IIIB all of the short-term debt had to be repaid before the investment could be made. The same question arises:

---

[21] The rationale for this is set forth in Welch (1994).
[22] A recent working paper by James (1994) argues that bank debt forgiveness can mitigate holdout and information problems, and increase the chance of success of exchange offers. The bank, however, must be willing to go along with the restructuring plan.
[23] As noted above, new debt financing after the Chapter 11 filing is usually given a super-priority status over the old debt. The lender can be either the old bank or an entirely new financial institution. If the latter is the case, the interest rate on the new debt is usually higher than if the original bank was the lender.

What is the lowest X_g that will induce the bank to agree to restructure the bank debt and finance the new investment project? We also investigate whether the investment is efficient.

If the bank does not refinance the firm and liquidation occurs, the bank receives $70, the value of the liquid assets. On the other hand, if the bank lends the firm the additional $10 and defers the maturity of the old bank debt to date 2, the amount of the bank debt (principal) due at date 2 will be $110. (The bank was already owed $100 and loaned $10 more.) Since the bank debt is the only debt and the bank maximizes the joint welfare of itself and shareholders, we can treat the firm as an all-equity firm. Therefore, the bank's expected payoff from bank debt restructuring is

$$0.5(\$20) + 0.5X_g - \$10 \geq \$70$$

If $X_g \geq \$140$, the project will be financed.[24]

The investment decision is efficient in this case. Since the bank is the only source of debt financing, it seeks to maximize the joint welfare of itself and the shareholders. In order to meet maturing obligations and finance the new investment, the bank does not face an extra "tax," which would lead to underinvestment, and it does not receive a free option on the firm, which would lead to overinvestment.

RESULT 6

When the principal amounts of all forms of debt have the same seniority (and interest is junior to principal), the higher the ratio of bank debt to total debt, the more efficient is the investment decision. In the extreme case, when all debt is bank debt, the investment decision is efficient. The logic of these results follows from the previous analysis. Compared to most public debt, the bank debt is shorter term. The overinvestment problem is reduced since the underpriced option is not offered to the source of the new financing. With the bank as the source of new financing, the firm does not face the inflexible requirement of paying off the short-term public debt (it avoids that "tax"), thereby mitigating the underinvestment problem.

VII Some Implications for Bankruptcy Rules

The foregoing analysis has several important implications regarding how the bankruptcy process should operate.

We begin with the automatic stay provision of Chapter 11 of the US Bankruptcy Code. An automatic stay permits the firm to stop all principal and interest payments, and prevents secured creditors from taking possession of their collateral. These creditors must be compensated, however, with "adequate protection," which stipulates that, at the very least, they should receive the value of the collateral in any subsequent reorganization. This is equivalent to converting all debt to a longer-term maturity. Other things being equal, when a firm is in financial distress (liquid assets are less than debt

---

[24] If, however, there was $20 of public debt due in period 1 and it could not be deferred to period 2 without considerable costs, then the project will be financed only if $X_g \geq \$180$.

claims), the automatic stay will increase the firm's incentive to invest. The automatic stay strengthens the position of the existing control group – the debtor-in-possession (DIP). This makes it easier to obtain additional financing. The possibility of DIP financing with priority over existing debt facilitates new investment.

The 1978 Bankruptcy Code introduced new voting rules for approval by creditors of a reorganization plan. The new Chapter 11 specifies majority (in number) requirements for approval of the plan and provides that dissenters must accept the same terms as approved by the majority.[25] In this sense, each class of creditors behaves as one party in which minority creditors cannot hold out. The new voting rules facilitate renegotiation of the debt so that the potential for investment efficiency is improved by reducing bargaining costs.

The Code also provides for absolute priority rules in establishing the order of claims under reorganization. Frequent, but small (2.3–7.6 percent) deviations from absolute priority occur. Some possible explanations include:

1 One or more classes of claimants may provide new or future financing as a basis for improving their position over what it would have been under absolute priority.

2 Managers retain considerable power after a firm has filed for bankruptcy. Managers are able to continue to make operating decisions, and for 120 days after the Chapter 11 filing, managers have the exclusive right to propose a reorganization plan. The court often grants one or more extensions of this deadline. Management has 180 days from the filing date to obtain creditor and shareholder approval. If a firm fails to propose a plan or its plan is rejected, creditors can propose their own plan. To do so, they must provide proof of values for claims to be issued and assets to be retained or sold. This requires costly appraisals and hearings, as compared with a management plan that requires the bankruptcy judge to evaluate it as "fair and reasonable."

3 Estimated market values are used as a basis for establishing priority positions. But market values depend on the success of the restructuring and the future performance of the firm. The future cannot be known with certainty, so that the imputed values are subject to error and therefore subject to negotiation among the claimants. Thus, deviations from absolute priority may facilitate approval of a plan earlier than otherwise would be possible. Early emergence from the uncertainty of bankruptcy proceedings will also have a positive influence on investment.

---

[25] If the reorganization is proposed in an out-of-court distressed restructuring, i.e., not under Chapter 11, then a virtually unanimous acceptance by those creditors who are impaired must be received. This explains the relatively recent phenomenon known as a "prepackaged Chapter 11," whereby the required (but not necessarily unanimous) proportion of accepting creditor votes is assembled for a plan *prior to* the filing of the petition for relief (which initiates the bankruptcy process). In most cases, the formal Chapter 11 reorganization that follows the prepack agreement is a relatively simple procedure. The actual time spent in the bankruptcy process has been as little as one month, and it generally averages only a few months. The money spent in a prepackaged bankruptcy is also typically less. See Altman (1993b), Betker (1995b), McConnell and Servantes (1991), and Salerno and Hansen (1991) for discussions of prepackaged plans and their recent experience. Betker analyzes 49 cases and concludes that while direct costs of prepacks are comparable to those of traditional Chapter 11s, gains come from the binding of holdouts and from favorable tax treatment on tax loss carryforwards.

Two relatively recent developments strengthen the position of individual creditors. The first is the aggressive strategies of powerful, active investors who purchase a controlling interest in a key class of claims in order to block unpopular plans or to propose a plan that results either in dramatically better terms for the creditor or even control of the company when it emerges from Chapter 11. A well-known example of the latter is the role of Japonica Partners, creditors and equity infusers in the Allegheny International Corporation case, which achieved sole ownership of the entity (Sunbeam-Oster) that was formed after Chapter 11. Successful examples of the former are the negotiation strategy of M. J. Whitman & Company, significant holders of the third mortgage debt in the Chapter 11 reorganization of the Public Service of New Hampshire, and Oppenheimer & Company's accumulation of the unsecured debt of Wheeling Pittsburgh Steel in its contentious reorganization.[26]

The second phenomenon is not really new but involves the more organized and aggressive posture of well-informed and well-financed representatives of a group of creditors in the Chapter 11 or pre-Chapter 11 negotiations. Skillful investment bankers, with sufficient voting power, or even "nuisance-power," have gained far better terms in reorganization than atomistic creditors might have achieved.

VIII SUMMARY

In this paper, we have presented a synthesis of the literature on financial distress. Within a two-state framework, we have developed a system of equations that generalizes more complex models. We explored the effects of financial distress on investment efficiency and restructuring strategy under alternative assumptions.

In the base case formulation, Myers' (1977) underinvestment model is shown to be a special case under certainty. The intuition of his result is that if the present value of the firm's assets is less than the debt claims, the deficiency represents a tax that must be paid by the shareholders before they can receive any returns from additional investments. This gives rise to an underinvestment problem.

Under uncertainty, the equity holders generally receive an undervalued option. Shareholders have incentives to overinvest since in some states the favorable outcomes may re-establish some value for them. Overinvestment is more likely to occur when big differences between X_b and X_g are expected. In contrast, when expected returns in the alternative states are relatively equal, the value of the option to pay off the debt and retain control over the firm is diminished.

Underinvestment may occur even in the uncertainty case. For cash flow levels at which debtholders are paid off, but very little remains for the shareholders, the returns to shareholders may be negative. But NPV may be positive since no debt payoff is required. So the influence of debt as a "tax" that has to be paid can also result in an underinvestment problem in the more general framework.

The shorter the maturity structure of debt, the more likely it is the firm will have an underinvestment problem. The longer the maturity structure of the debt, the more likely it is the firm will have an overinvestment problem. A higher (lower) ratio of short-term debt to total debt can be used to create an offsetting underinvestment (overinvestment) tendency.

---

[26]   These cases are discussed in detail by Rosenberg (1992).

Extending the maturity of existing debt and creating new debt senior to existing debt increases investment incentives. However, it also increases the risks to the old debtholders. Similarly, exchange offers provide opportunities for managers acting on behalf of shareholders to behave strategically toward creditors.

Our findings help to evaluate key elements of the Bankruptcy Reform Act of 1978.

1 The automatic stay has the effect of extending debt maturity, thereby increasing the firm's ability to obtain new financing to make the investments required for its recovery.

2 The new voting rules require only a majority in number of a class of creditors (and at least two-thirds in principal amount) to approve a reorganization plan, thereby facilitating negotiations and approval of a plan for reorganization.

3 Debtor-in-possession (DIP) financing changes the seniority of claims, thereby stimulating new investment.

4 The law provides for absolute priority rules but has permitted frequent small departures, which facilitates obtaining agreements to achieve plan approval. In general, departures from absolute priority increase the riskiness of debt. However, they may increase the prospective returns by reducing the time required to obtain approval of a proposed reorganization plan.

REFERENCES

Adler, B., 1992, "Bankruptcy and Risk Allocation," *Cornell Law Review* (No. 3), 439–89.

Altman, E. I., 1993a, "Evaluating the Chapter 11 Bankruptcy-Reorganization Process," *Columbia Business Law Review* (No. 1), 1–25.

Altman, E. I., 1993b, *Corporate Financial Distress and Bankruptcy*, 2nd edn, New York, John Wiley & Sons.

Altman, E. I. and A. C. Eberhart, 1994, "Do Seniority Provisions Protect Bondholders' Investments?," *Journal of Portfolio Management*, (Summer), 67–75.

Bebchuk, L., 1988, "A New Approach to Corporate Reorganization," *Harvard Law Review* (February), 775–804.

Berkovitch, E. and E. H. Kim, 1990, "Financial Contracting and Leverage Induced Over- and Under-Investment Incentives," *Journal of Finance* (July), 765–94.

Bernardo, A., 1995, "Exchange Offers: A General Case," AGSM, UCLA, Unpublished manuscript.

Betker, B., 1995a, "Management's Incentives, Equity's Bargaining Power, and Deviations from Absolute Priority in Chapter 11 Bankruptcies," *Journal of Business* (April), 161–83.

Betker, B., 1995b, "An Empirical Examination of Prepackaged Bankruptcy," *Financial Management* (Spring), 3–18.

Bhandari, J. and L. Weiss, 1993, "The Untenable Case for Chapter 11: A Review of the Evidence," *American Bankruptcy Law Journal* (Spring), 131–50.

Black, F. and M. Scholes, 1973, "The Pricing of Options and Corporate Liabilities," *Journal of Political Economy* (May–June), 637–54.

Bradley, M. and M. Rosenzweig, 1992, "The Untenable Case for Chapter 11," *Yale Law Journal* (March), 1043–89.

Brown, D. T., C. M. James, and R. M. Mooradian, 1993, "The Information Content of Distressed Restructurings Involving Public and Private Debt Claims," *Journal of Financial Economics* (February), 93–118.

Bulow, J. I. and J. B. Shoven, 1978, "The Bankruptcy Decision," *Bell Journal of Economics* (Autumn), 437–56.

Coase, R. H., 1937, "The Nature of the Firm," *Economica* (New Series, November), 386–405.

Diamond, D. W. and P. H. Dybvig, 1983, "Bank Runs, Deposit Insurance and Liquidity," *Journal of Political Economy* (June), 401–19.

Franks, J. R. and W. N. Torous, 1989, "An Empirical Investigation of U. S. Firms in Reorganization," *Journal of Finance* (July), 747–69.

Gertner, R. and D. Scharfstein, 1991, "A Theory of Workouts and the Effects of Reorganization Law," *Journal of Finance* (September), 1189–222.

Giammarino, R. M. and E. Nosal, 1994, "The Efficiency of Judicial Discretion in Bankruptcy Law," Unpublished paper (November).

Gilson, S. C., 1989, "Management Turnaround and Financial Distress," *Journal of Financial Economics* (December), 241–62.

Gilson, S. C., 1990, "Bankruptcy, Boards, Banks, and Blockholders: Evidence on Changes in Corporate Ownership and Control When Firms Default," *Journal of Financial Economics* (October), 355–87.

Gilson, S. C., 1994, "Debt Reduction, Optimal Capital Structure, and Renegotiation of Claims During Financial Distress," Harvard Business School Working Paper (January).

Gilson, S., K. John, and L. Lang, 1990, "Troubled Debt Restructurings: An Empirical Study of Private Reorganization of Firms in Default," *Journal of Financial Economics* (October), 315–54.

Hart, O. and J. Moore, 1994, "Debt and Seniority: An Analysis of the Role of Hard Claims in Constraining Management," National Bureau of Economic Research Working Paper, No. 4886 (October).

Heinkel, R. and J. Zechner, 1993, "Financial Distress and Optimal Capital Structure Adjustments," *Journal of Economics and Management Strategy* (Winter), 531–65.

Helwege, J., 1995, "How Long Do Junk Bonds Spend in Default?" Federal Reserve Board Working Paper, Washington, DC, presented at the 24th Annual FMA Meeting, St. Louis, Missouri (October 14, 1994); revised New York Federal Reserve Bank (April).

Hotchkiss, E., 1995, "Post Bankruptcy Performance and Management Turnover," *Journal of Finance* (March), 3–22.

James, C., 1994, "The Mix of Private and Public Debt Claims and Capital Structure Flexibility in Financial Distress," University of Florida Working Paper (July 25).

Jensen, M. and W. Meckling, 1976, "Theory of the Firm: Managerial Behavior, Agency Costs, and Ownership Structure," *Journal of Financial Economics* (October), 305–60.

John, K., 1993, "Managing Financial Distress and Valuing Distressed Securities: A Survey and a Research Agenda," *Financial Management* (Financial Distress Special Issue, Autumn), 60–78.

Kahane, M. and B. Tuckman, 1993, "Do Bondholders Lose from Junk Bond Covenant Changes?," *Journal of Business* (October), 499–516.

LoPucki, L., 1992, "Strange Visions in a Strange World: A Reply to Bradley and Rosenzweig," *Michigan Law Review* (No. 1), 79–92.

LoPucki, L., 1993, "The Trouble with Chapter 11," *Wisconsin Law Review* (June), 729–60.

McConnell, J. and H. Servantes, 1991, "The Economics of Prepackaged Bankruptcy," *Journal of Applied Corporate Finance* (Summer), 93–7.

Merrill Lynch, 1994, "Defaults and Returns on High Yield Bonds," High Yield Debt Research Dept. (January 24).

Merton, R. C., 1973, "The Theory of Rational Option Pricing," *Bell Journal of Economics and Management Science* (Spring), 141–83.

Mooradian, R. M., 1994, "The Effect of Bankruptcy Protection on Investment: Chapter 11 as a Screening Device," *Journal of Finance* (September), 1403–30.

Myers, S. C., 1977, "Determinants of Corporate Borrowing," *Journal of Financial Economics* (November), 147–75.

Roe, M., 1983, "Bankruptcy and Debt: A New Model for Corporate Reorganization," *Columbia Law Review* (April), 527–602.

Rosenberg, H., 1992, *The Vulture Investors*, New York, Harper Business.

Salerno, T. and C. Hansen, 1991, "A Prepackaged Bankruptcy Strategy," *Journal of Business Strategy* (January/February), 36–41.

Scott, J., 1981, "The Probability of Bankruptcy: A Comparison of Empirical Predictions and Theoretical Models," *Journal of Banking and Finance* (September), 317–44.

Warren, E., 1992, "The Untenable Case For Repeal of Chapter 11," *Yale Law Journal* (November), 437–79.

Welch, I., 1994, "Why is Bank Debt Senior? A Theory of Priority among Creditors," AGSM, UCLA Working Paper, No. 18–94 (November).

Whitman, M., 1993, "A Rejoinder to the Untenable Case for Chapter 11," *Journal of Bankruptcy Law and Practice* (January–February), 839–48.

Index